**Learning English**

# *TOP LINE*

Teacher's Book

von Frank Michael Bülow, Werner Kundmüller,
Ernst Pöhler, Josef Schmid, K.E. Schuhmacher,
Helmut Slogsnat und Wolfgang Stütz

Ernst Klett Schulbuchverlag
Stuttgart Düsseldorf Berlin Leipzig

**Learning English**

**Top Line – Teacher's Book**

Handbuch für die Unterrichtsgestaltung von OStR Frank Michael Bülow M.A., Ottobrunn; OStR Werner Kundmüller, Ingolstadt; StR Ernst Pöhler, Ingolstadt; StD Josef Schmid, Ingolstadt; StD K.E. Schuhmacher, Römerberg; StD Dr. Helmut Slogsnat, Neckargemünd; StD Wolfgang Stütz, Stuttgart.

Schülerbuch: *Top Line* (Klettbuch 51034)

---

**Tonträger zu Top Line**

- **S**  *Compact-Cassette - Selected Texts:* ausgewählte Texte und Lieder für Schüler und Lehrer, Klettnummer 510342.

- **L**  *Compact-Cassette - Additional Texts for Listening Comprehension:* enthält je einen Hörverstehenstext pro Kapitel, für die Hand der Unterrichtenden, Klettnummer 510343.

Lieferung durch jede Buchhandlung

---

Recyclingpapier, hergestellt aus Altpapier mit einem geringen Anteil von chlorfrei gebleichtem Zellstoff.

1. Auflage     1  5  4  3  2  1  |  1996  95  94  93  92

Alle Drucke dieser Auflage können im Unterricht nebeneinander benutzt werden, sie sind untereinander unverändert. Die letzte Zahl bezeichnet das Jahr dieses Druckes.
© Ernst Klett Schulbuchverlag GmbH, Stuttgart 1992. Alle Rechte vorbehalten.

Redaktion: Glenine Hamlyn, M.A., Katherine Inglis-Meyer, M.A., Verlagsredakteurinnen, und Noreen O'Donovan, Pforzheim.

Umschlagentwurf: Manfred Muraro unter Verwendung eines Photos von Heinz Mack, © Bildarchiv Heinz Mack.
Druck: Röck, Weinsberg.

ISBN 3-12-510341-X

# Vorwort

*Top Line - Teacher's Book* will in mehrfacher Hinsicht Hilfen bei der Unterrichtsplanung geben:

**Strukturskizzen:** In einer graphischen Übersicht wird zunächst für jedes Kapitel dessen innere Struktur aufgezeigt. Diese einleitenden Strukturskizzen sollen den Stellenwert des Einzeltextes im Gesamtgefüge der Textsequenz deutlich machen und es so auch den Unterrichtenden erleichtern, zu kürzen oder alternative Textsequenzen zu erstellen, die den spezifischen Bedingungen der Lerngruppe angemessener sind als die im Schülerbuch selbst vorgezeichnete Abfolge.

**Kurzreferate:** Um eine rechtzeitige Planung zu ermöglichen, ist jedem Kapitel eine Liste mit Themen für Kurzreferate mit dem jeweiligen Einsatzort vorangestellt. Die Themen erscheinen wieder, dieses Mal ausführlicher formuliert und mit bibliographischen Hilfen versehen, als Teil der *post-reading activities* zu den einzelnen Texten.

**Wortschatzarbeit:** Durch Hinweise auf die relevanten Teile von *Words in Context* (Klettbuch 51961) und *Thematischer Grund- und Aufbauwortschatz Englisch* (Klettbuch 51955) am Anfang eines jeden Kapitels wird die Planung der Wortschatzarbeit erleichtert.

**Grundkurse:** Besonders grundkursadäquate Texte sind im Inhhaltsverzeichnis des Lehrerbuchs und nach der jeweiligen Textüberschrift gekennzeichnet. Die so gekennzeichneten Texte bilden in sich eine stimmige Sequenz. Wegen des oft sehr unterschiedlichen Leistungsstandes von Grundkursen sind diese Kennzeichnungen selbstverständlich nur als Vorschläge zu verstehen.

**Listening comprehension:** Der Hörverstehenstext zum jeweiligen Kapitel wird als Transkript dargeboten. Die Aufgaben *Listening for the gist* des Schülerbuchs werden durch die Rubrik *Listening for detail* ergänzt.

**Klausurtext:** Zu jedem Kapitel wird ein Klausurtext mit Aufgabenapparat angeboten. In Einzelfällen wird es notwendig sein, den Aufgabenapparat gemäß den Bedürfnissen der Lerngruppe zu modifizieren.

**Visuelles Material:** Die Funktionalität der Bebilderung des Schülerbuchs hat als logische Konsequenz, daß diejenigen Bilder, die sich besonders hierfür anbieten, ausführlich im *Teacher's Book* besprochen werden. Durch eine entsprechende Gestaltung der Überschrift erhalten sie den Rang eines normalen Textes. In den meisten anderen Fällen werden die Bilder in den *pre-* und *post-reading activities* gebührend berücksichtigt.

**Einzeltext:** Beim Einzeltext können folgende Rubriken im *Teacher's Book* erscheinen:
*Background information:* Zusätzliche Information über Autor bzw. Autorin; landeskundliche Hinweise; Kontext des Textausschnitts; Querverweise zu anderen Texten und zu Bildern; Hinweise auf die *fact files* am Ende des Schülerbuchs.
*Methodisch-didaktische Hinweise:* Verankerung des Textes im Kapitel; didaktische Begründung; Zugang zum Thema oder Text; Einsatz der Tonträger; Anregungen zu Partner- und Gruppenarbeit; methodische Alternativen.
*Pre-reading activities:* Aktivierung von Vorwissen; Einstimmung; Vorbereitung auf das Thema; Hinweise auf den Einsatz der Bilder.
*Suggested answers:* Diese haben grundsätzlich Vorschlagscharakter.
*Additional questions:* Diese Fragen beziehen sich noch direkt auf den Text. Schwerpunkte: Wortschatzarbeit und Grammatik; Sprachbetrachtung.
*Post-reading activities:* Über den Text hinausgehende Beschäftigung mit dem Thema; Üben verschiedener Fertigkeiten; Aufgaben zur Textproduktion.

# Alternative Sequenzbildungen

Auf Grund der mehrfachen Funktionen, die Texte je nach Erkenntnisinteresse erfüllen, sind über die vorgeschlagenen thematischen Gruppierungen hinaus andere Sequenzbildungen mit den in *Top Line* enthaltenen Texten möglich. So besteht zunächst die Möglichkeit, das vorhandene Textmaterial nach gattungs- und textsortenspezifischen Kriterien neu zu ordnen. Darüber hinaus lassen sich u.a. die folgenden themenorientierten "alternativen" Sequenzen aufführen (2/8 = Kapitel 2, Text 8):

**Language:** 2/1 (Rolle des Englischen in Indien); 3/4 (Soziolekt); 4/3 (Rolle des Englischen in Irland); A Welsh hymn, S. 167 (keltische Sprachen in Großbritannien); 7/9 (Sprache von Minderheiten in Großbritannien); 8/8 (Dialekt und soziale Stellung); 10/10 (Englisch als "offizielle Sprache" in den USA).

**Advertising:** Die Anzeigen auf den Seiten 73, 83, 113, 148, 163, 169, 252, 258, 263, 281 und Text 6/8 (Werbestrategien der Industrie).

**Ecology:** 6/Auftaktbild; 6/3 (Energieverbrauch); 6/4 (angemessene Technologien); 6/7 (Gentechnologie); 6/8 ("grüne" Werbestrategien der Industrie); Anzeige S. 148; 7/2 (Landwirtschaft bei den Amish); 11/2 (Landwirtschaft als Ausbeutung von Mensch und Natur); 11/9 (ökologisches Bewußtsein im Nordwesten der USA); Anzeige S. 258; *fact file* S. 296–297.

**Immigration, ethnicity and mutliculturalism:** 1/6 (Einwanderungsbeschränkungen); 1/7, 1/8 (Einwanderer in Großbritannien); 3/10 (Großbritannien als multikulturelle Gesellschaft?); Anzeige S. 83; 7/9 (Muslime in Großbritannien); 9/8, 9/9 (Rassenbeziehungen in den USA); 9/11 (Repräsentation in Geschworenengerichten); das gesamte Kapitel 10 "A Nation of Immigrants", insbesondere 10/4 (*ethnicity* in den USA); Übersicht S. 229 (Einwanderung in die USA); 10/11 (multikulturelle Zukunft der USA); 11/5 (Kings Plädoyer für die Gleichberechtigung); 11/6, 11/7, 11/8 (Rassenbeziehungen in den USA).

**Women's issues:** 2/8 (Frauen in Indien); 2/11 (Erbfolge im britischen Königshaus usw.); 3/4 (Frauen im Berufsleben); 5/6 (Frauen im Kunstbetrieb); 5/8 (Stereotypisierung in Filmen); 7/6, 7/7, Anzeige S. 163, Flugblatt S. 164 (Rolle in der anglikanischen Kirche); 7/9 (Rolle im Islam); 8/4 (Berufschancen); 8/9 (Klassenzugehörigkeit und Schulbildung); 9/4 (Suffragetten); 9/12 (Streben nach Gleichberechtigung: Seneca Falls Declaration); Tabellen S. 197 u. 211 (Wahlrecht); 9/13 (Equal Rights Amendment); 10/8 (Vater-Tochter Beziehung); 11/6 (Frauen und der *American Dream*).

**Town and country:** 2/10, 2/11 (Kontrast in Indien); 3/3 (Städter auf dem Land; UK); 3/9 (Wohnungslose in London); 5/1, Anzeige S. 113, 5/2, 5/3 (Architektur); 5/7 (Kontrast Edinburgh-Highlands; 6/3 (Einfluß einer Erfindung auf Leben auf dem Lande; USA); 7/2 (Landwirtschaft bei den Amish); 11/2 ("agribusiness" als Ausbeutung von Mensch und Land); 11/4 (von der Stadt aufs Land); 11/7 u. Anzeige S. 252 (sozial Benachteiligte in der Stadt); 11/9 (Zukunftsvision "Ecotopia").

**The U.S. Supreme Court – The Constitution:** 7/4 (Trennung von Staat und Kirche); 8/5 (Geist der Verfassung); 9/8 (die Verfassung im Bewußtsein der Amerikaner); 9/9 (Lincolns Reaktion auf eine S.C. Entscheidung); 9/11 (Verfassung und Geschworenensystem); 9/12 (Frauen und die Verfassung); 9/13 (Equal Rights Amendment); 9/14 u. Cartoons S. 214 (Entscheidung im Streit um die amerikanische Flagge); *fact file* S. 309–310.

**Young People:** 2/9 (junge Menschen und das Kastensystem in Indien); 2/10 (junge Menschen und Armut in Indien); 3/9 (Wohnungslose in London); 4/11 (eine konfessionell integrierte Schule in Nordirland); 7/1 (und Kirche in den USA); das gesamte Kapitel 8 "Values in British and American Education"; 7/9 (islamische Mädchen in Großbritannien); 10/2, 10/6 (junge Einwanderer in Amerika); 11/6 (Werte und Träume junger schwarzamerikanischer Frauen); 11/7 u. Anzeige S. 252 (junge Menschen in der Großstadt); 11/8 (Bedeutung der Schulbildung für schwarzamerikanische Jugendliche).

# Contents

## 1 From Empire to Europe

Structure of the chapter ............................................................................................. 10

    1. The spectacle of Empire ............................... Jan Morris ...................................................... 11
- S -   2. Envoy ............................................................ W.E. Henley ................................................... 14
    3. The path of progress? (GK) ......................... George Orwell ............................................... 18
    4. A dignified retreat ........................................ Keith Robbins ................................................ 20
- L -   5. Listening Comprehension:
       Home thoughts (GK) ................................... Germaine Greer ............................................. 23
    6. Colony of fear (GK) ..................................... *The Independent* ............................................ 25
    7. Immigrant autumn ....................................... Rick Ferreira .................................................. 27
    8. Finding a niche (GK) ................................... Timothy Mo ................................................... 30
- S -   9. A vision of Europe ....................................... Winston Churchill .......................................... 33
    10. 1973: Britain sleepwalks into Europe (GK) . *Newsweek* ..................................................... 36
    11. Autobahnmotorwayautoroute (GK) ............ Adrian Mitchell ............................................. 38

       Test: The future for Britain ......................... *The Sunday Times* ........................................ 40

## 2 India

Structure of the chapter ............................................................................................. 43

    1. The Raj through Indian eyes ....................... Zareer Masani ................................................ 44
    2. The poorest country in the world ................ V.S. Naipaul .................................................. 47
- S -   3. Gandhi's Salt March (GK) .......................... Gita Mehta ..................................................... 49
    4. Midnight, 14 August 1947 .......................... Larry Collins and Dominique Lapierre ........ 51
    5. The practical process of partitioning (GK) ... Shashi Tharoor .............................................. 53
    6. Souls crying out for God ............................. Ruth Prawer Jhabvala .................................... 55
- L -   7. Listening Comprehension:
       An intensely religious society ...................... Anita Desai .................................................... 58
    8. Freedom and suppression ............................ Anita Desai .................................................... 59
    9. The grim face of the caste system (GK) ....... Howard G. Chua-Eoan/Anita Pratap .......... 61
    10. Life in a Bombay shanty-town (GK) ........... Jeremy Seabrook ............................................ 63
    11. A country of extremes (GK) ........................................................................................ 66
       Peasants waiting for rain .............................. G.S. Sharat Chandra ..................................... 66
       Monsoon ....................................................... Ruskin Bond .................................................. 66
    12. Superpower rising ....................................... *Time* .............................................................. 68

       Test: Gandhi and the street-sweeper's son ... R.K. Narayan ................................................. 69

## 3 Modern Britain

Structure of the chapter ............................................................................................. 73

    1. Britain in decline? ........................................ John Osmond ................................................. 74
- L -   2. Listening Comprehension:
       Divided Britain (GK) ................................... Frank Field, MP / Anthony Gibbs ............... 76
    3. Rural England struggles to survive
       the urban blitz ............................................... Jimmy Burns .................................................. 79
    4. Lifestyles (GK) ............................................. David Lodge .................................................. 80
    5. The Archbishop and the wealth ethic (GK) . Carol Kennedy .............................................. 83

|  | 6. A great prime minister | *The Independent* | 84 |
| --- | --- | --- | --- |
| •S• | 7. In retrospect: a letter to the editor | Ken Livingstone, MP | 86 |
|  | 8. Monitoring the heart (GK) | Sue Townsend | 87 |
|  | 9. Filed away in a cardboard box city (GK) | Michelle Beauchamp | 88 |
|  | 10. A long way from basic decency | Michael Ignatieff | 89 |
|  | 11. Modernise the monarchy (GK) | *The Sunday Times* | 90 |
|  | Test: Thatcher's children | Janie Dettmer | 92 |

## 4 Britain and Ireland

Structure of the chapter .................................................................................. 95

|  | 1. The teddy bear's head (GK) | Brian Warfield / Wolfe Tones | 96 |
| --- | --- | --- | --- |
| •S• | 2. The Anglo-Irish heritage (GK) | Garret FitzGerald | 97 |
| •L• | 3. Listening Comprehension: The English language in Ireland | McCrum, Cran and MacNeil | 98 |
|  | 4. The Easter Proclamation 1916 | *document* | 101 |
|  | 5. The sniper (GK) | Liam O'Flaherty | 102 |
|  | 6. Carrickfergus | Louis MacNeice | 103 |
| •S• | 7. Civil rights in Derry (GK) | Bernadette Devlin | 104 |
|  | 8. The boat to Ulster | Paul Theroux | 106 |
|  | 9. The Anglo-Irish Agreement | Ken Williamson | 107 |
|  | 10. Bad, not mad (GK) | *The Spectator* | 108 |
|  | 11. Learning to live together (GK) | Robin Lustig | 109 |
|  | Test: A new radical approach is needed | R. Iwaskow | 110 |

## 5 Art, Culture and Society

Structure of the chapter .................................................................................. 112

|  | 1. What is American about America? | John A. Kouwenhoven | 113 |
| --- | --- | --- | --- |
|  | 2. "We have ended up with monsters" (GK) | HRH The Prince of Wales | 115 |
|  | 3. Why Prince Charles is wrong (GK) | Maxwell Hutchinson | 117 |
| •L• | 4. Listening Comprehension: Henry Moore - a sculptor speaks (GK) | Henry Moore | 119 |
|  | 5. A challenge to high art | Julia Markus | 121 |
|  | 6. "Why do you paint?" | Margaret Atwood | 123 |
| •S• | 7. At the Edinburgh Festival (GK) | Alasdair Maclean | 127 |
|  | 8. Hollywood's view of society | Carl H. Scheele | 130 |
|  | 9. They came, we saw, they conquered (GK) | Neil Postman | 132 |
|  | 10. The little room of literature | Salman Rushdie | 134 |
|  | Test: Film and the novel | James Monaco | 136 |

## 6 Science, Technology and the Environment

Structure of the chapter .................................................................................. 139

| 1. A late but fruitful marriage (GK) | *Great Decisions 79* | 141 |
| --- | --- | --- |
| 2. Technological innovation | R.A. Buchanan | 143 |
| 3. An artificial climate (GK) | Raymond Arsenault | 144 |

| • L • | 4. Listening Comprehension: Technology and culture | Thomas P. Hughes / Hal Bowser | 146 |
| | 5. The secret of the machines | Rudyard Kipling | 148 |
| • S • | 6. True love (GK) | Isaac Asimov | 149 |
| | 7. Tomorrow "rabbit" will have no meaning | Bill McKibben | 150 |
| | 8. Exhaust the subject (GK) | Benjamin Woolley | 152 |
| | Test: The promise of gene therapy | *Time Magazine* | 153 |

## 7 Religious Life

Structure of the chapter .................................................................................................. 155

### The U.S.A.

1. Shopping for a church ........................... *Newsweek* ........................... 156
2. The Amish answer (GK) ....................... Pat Stone ............................. 158
3. Religion on the screen (GK) ................. Neil Postman ....................... 160
4. Is "humanism" a religion? .................... Ted Gest .............................. 161

### Britain

| • S • | 5. Private conscience and public duty (GK) | Robert Bolt | 163 |
| | 6. Runcie: "Let the Pope lead all Christians" | Judith Judd | 165 |
| | 7. Women: second-class citizens of the Church (GK) | Joanna Moorhead | 166 |
| | 8. Hearing the cry of the poor (GK) | *pamphlet* | 167 |
| • S • | Cwm Rhondda: a Welsh hymn | William Williams | 168 |
| • L • | 9. Listening Comprehension: The Prophet's Birthday in Bradford | Mrs Wright/Anthony Gibbs | 169 |
| | Test: Anger of a female Church militant | Judith Judd | 171 |

## 8 Values in British and American Education

Structure of the chapter .................................................................................................. 174

### The U.S.A.

1. Not just doing it for kicks (GK) ............ Martin Walker ..................... 176
2. Americanize and equalize? ................... Edmund Fawcett and Tony Thomas ... 177
3. It's a tragedy we cannot afford (GK) ..... Mary Hatwood Futrell ........... 178
• S • 4. Fast car (GK) ........................................ Tracy Chapman ................... 180
5. Students, get mad! ............................... Lee Iacocca ......................... 182

### Britain

| | 6. Why abuse and scorn are the wrong treatment (GK) | Robert Chesshyre | 183 |
| | 7. Next term, we'll mash you (GK) | Penelope Lively | 184 |
| | 8. Accent and equality | John Honey | 186 |
| • L • | 9. Listening Comprehension: A working-class girl in a grammar school | Irene Payne | 188 |
| | 10. Education and economic prosperity | John Rae | 190 |
| | Test: The Pledge of Allegiance in public schools | Carol Seefeldt | 192 |

## 9 The Struggle for Democracy

Structure of the chapter .................................................................................................. 195

### Britain

| | | |
|---|---|---|
| 1. The call to Freedom ............................... | Percy Bysshe Shelley ............................... | 196 |
| 2. A working man's share ............................... | George Eliot ............................... | 198 |
| 3. Two great movement (GK) ............................... | John Randle ............................... | 198 |
| •L• 4. Listening Comprehension: Black Friday (GK) ............................... | Sylvia Pankhurst ............................... | 199 |
| •S• 5. Put the rules of the game in writing (GK) .... | Bernard Crick ............................... | 201 |
| 6. A Scottish parliament? ............................... | Neal Ascherson ............................... | 204 |
| 7. A way to rescue British freedoms ............... | Ronald Dworkin ............................... | 206 |

### The U.S.A.

| | | |
|---|---|---|
| •S• 8. Equality before the law (GK) ............... | Harper Lee ............................... | 207 |
| 9. A maxim for free society ............................... | Abraham Lincoln ............................... | 209 |
| 10. The jury system perverted (GK) ............... | Mark Twain ............................... | 211 |
| 11. Is jury selection unconstitutional? ............... | USA Today ............................... | 213 |
| 12. The Seneca Falls Declaration of Sentiments ............................... | document ............................... | 214 |
| •L• 13. Listening Comprehension: A claim to a share of America ............... | Mario Cuomo ............................... | 216 |
| 14. Congress should pass the flag amendment (GK) ............................... | Robert J. Dole ............................... | 218 |
| Test: The Bill of Rights that's ours for the taking ............................... | Lord Scarman ............................... | 220 |

## 10 A Nation of Immigrants

Structure of the chapter .................................................................................................. 222

| | | |
|---|---|---|
| 1. The epic of American immigration ............... | Leslie Allen ............................... | 223 |
| •L• 2. Listening Comprehension: Going to the Promised Land (GK) ............... | Mary Antin ............................... | 226 |
| 3. The Golden Land ............................... | Henry Roth ............................... | 229 |
| •S• 4. Ellis Island (GK) ............................... | Joseph Bruchac ............................... | 232 |
| 5. An abundance of jobs ............................... | Alan M. Kraut ............................... | 234 |
| 6. Where is America? (GK) ............................... | Anzia Yezierska ............................... | 236 |
| 7. The new sweatshops ............................... | Newsweek ............................... | 238 |
| 8. The oldest racket in the country (GK) ........ | Arthur Miller ............................... | 240 |
| 9. The Tortilla Curtain (GK) ............................... | Al Santoli ............................... | 242 |
| 10. The language of the country ............... | S.I. Hayakawa ............................... | 245 |
| 11. Birth of a new culture? ............................... | Henry Cisneros ............................... | 247 |
| Test 1: Rich-heard Road-ree-guess: Becoming an American ............................... | Richard Rodriguez ............................... | 249 |
| •L• Test 2: Listening Comprehension: The real Chinatown ............................... | Andy Lanset/Charlie Chin ............... | 251 |

## 11. The American Dream in a Changing Society

Structure of the chapter .................................................................................................. 255

| | | |
|---|---|---|
| 1. A richer and fuller life for all .................. | James Truslow Adams ............................... | 258 |
| 2. Bonanza farming ..................................... | William Godwin Moody ........................... | 259 |
| 3. Reflections of a self-made man (GK) .......... | Ronald Reagan ......................................... | 261 |
| •S• 4. Second chance - Fred Ringley, ex-salesman, farmer (GK) ....................... | Studs Terkel ............................................. | 262 |
| •L• 5. Listening Comprehension: I have a dream ............................................. | Martin Luther King .................................. | 264 |
| 6. The new believers (GK) ............................. | Ruth Sidel ................................................. | 266 |
| •S• 7. Subcity (GK) .............................................. | Tracy Chapman ........................................ | 269 |
| 8. The key to success (GK) ............................. | Bill Cosby ................................................. | 271 |
| 9. Ecotopia .................................................... | Joel Garreau ............................................. | 273 |
| Test: America II ......................................... | Richard Louv ............................................ | 275 |

## 12 America and the World

Structure of the chapter .................................................................................................. 278

| | | |
|---|---|---|
| 1. A Second American Century? (GK) ........... | Henry Grunwald ...................................... | 280 |
| 2. Two archetypes in U.S. foreign policy ........ | Robert N. Bellah ...................................... | 282 |
| 3. Let every nation know ............................... | historical quotations ................................. | 283 |
| 4. The conscience of a president (GK) ........... | John Heaton ............................................. | 284 |
| •S• 5. The Four Freedoms .................................... | Franklin D. Roosevelt .............................. | 285 |
| •S• 6. An investment in freedom and peace .......... | Harry S. Truman ...................................... | 287 |
| 7. Rice for Sarkhan (GK) ............................... | William J. Lederer and Eugene Burdick ... | 288 |
| •L• 8. Listening Comprehension: The expulsion from Vietnam (GK) .............. | *The Des Moines Register* ....................... | 289 |
| 9. Veteran (GK) ............................................. | Ron Kovic ................................................. | 291 |
| 10. The American liberal ideology .................... | Robert L. Wendzel .................................... | 293 |
| Test: A profound change in thinking .......... | Daniel J. Boorstin ..................................... | 294 |

Überrsicht über die Tonaufnahmen ................................................................................ 296

# 1 From Empire to Europe

## Structure of the chapter

| The Empire at its height | | |
|---|---|---|
| 1. The spectacle of Empire<br>1200 words<br>history book (excerpt) | 2. Envoy<br>124 words<br>sonnet | 3. The path of progress?<br>c. 1245 words<br>novel (excerpt) |

| The end of Empire |
|---|
| 4. A dignified retreat<br>877 words<br>expository text (excerpt) |

| The Commonwealth |
|---|
| 5. LC: Home thoughts<br>3 min. 32 sec.<br>essay |

| Emigration/Immigration | | |
|---|---|---|
| 6. Colony of fear<br>588 words<br>news report | 7. Immigrant autumn<br>247 words<br>poem | 8. Finding a niche<br>c. 1275 words<br>novel (excerpt) |

| Britain and Europe | |
|---|---|
| 9. A vision of Europe<br>1165 words<br>speech | 10. 1973: Britain sleepwalks into Europe<br>600 words<br>news story |

| A united Europe? |
|---|
| 11. Autobahnmotorwayautoroute<br>118 words<br>poem |

**Suggestions for reports/papers/talks**

Life in the British clubs – after text 1 or text 3.

Compare "Envoy" and the "Hunnenrede" of Kaiser Wilhelm – after text 2.

Book report: *Burmese Days* – after text 3.

Find out about Portuguese/French/Dutch/German colonialism – after text 4.

Choose one of the former colonies mentioned in the text and find out about how and when it achieved independence from Britain (SB, p. 19, question 8) – between text 4 and 5.

Trace the development of Australia from discovery by Europeans to the status of Pacific power – after text 5 (LC).

What do you know about other immigrant groups in Britain, the reasons for them being there and their problems? (SB, p. 22, question 8) – after text 7.

Sir Winston Churchill: his life and political career – after text 9.

Discuss your own country's role in the EC. What main aims do you think it has? (SB, p. 30, question 5) – after text 11.

**Vocabulary**

*Words in Context,* Klettbuch 51961, pp. 34–39 (The British Empire – The Commonwealth), pp. 40–45 (The European Community), pp. 62–65 (Racial Problems: Immigrants in Great Britain).

*Thematischer Grund– und Aufbauwortschatz Englisch,* Klettbuch 51955, pp. 124–146 (Staat, Politik, Gesellschaftsordnung).

# 1. The spectacle of Empire

### Background information

James Morris made himself a name with a trilogy, *Pax Britannica*, which tells of the rise and fall of the British Empire in a lively, almost novelistic manner, distinguished by the author's brilliant prose style: *Heaven's Command: An Imperial Progress*; *Pax Britannica*; *Farewell the Trumpets* – all available as Penguin paperbacks. During the writing of the trilogy James Morris underwent a sex change and now lives and writes as Jan [dʒæn] Morris. Her other publications include books on Spain, Wales (she is of Anglo-Welsh parentage), Venice, Oxford, and travel essays.

For useful books on the theme of the British Empire see the bibliography at the end of the chapter (p. 42).

### Didaktisch-methodische Hinweise

1. Der Aufgabenkatalog weist typographisch keine Hierarchisierung aus. Es sollte daher bedacht werden, daß die Aufgaben 2–5 eine detaillierte Aufbereitung der summarischen Aufgabe 1 bedeuten, also teilweise oder anfänglich Dubletten bei den Antworten/Ergebnissen unvermeidlich sind. Sinnvoll wäre es daher auch, zuerst die Aufgaben 2–5 zu bearbeiten und danach die Aufgabe 1.

2. Der Text ist sprachlich sehr anspruchsvoll. Jan Morris' Stil ist jedoch eine kongeniale sprachliche Spiegelung des grandiosen Themas. Die sprachliches Niveau stiftende Dialektik zwischen Stil und thematischem Gegenstand kann hier beispielhaft den S bewußt gemacht werden. Aufgaben 7 und 8 helfen, dieses Bewußtsein zu schärfen.

3. Der Betonung der visuellen Selbstdarstellung des Empire im Text kann man eine entsprechende akustische, musikalische Komponente hinzugesellen.

a) Man kann den S Stück Nr. 1, aus der Komposition "Pomp and Circumstance" von Edward Elgar (1857–1934) zu Gehör bringen (Dauer: 6'41 in der unten genannten Einspielung, cf. Lehrercassette, Klett 510343), sie einen Titel zu der Komposition finden lassen und fragen, was der Text von Morris und die Musik von Elgar miteinander zu tun haben ["pomp, solemnity, self-awareness"]. Zum Stück Nr. 1 aus dem Werk Elgars ein Auszug aus dem Begleittext zur CD aus der "Leonard Bernstein Edition", Deutsche Grammophon, Nr. 431033-2:

"Elgar composed five *Pomp and Circumstance* Marches between 1901 and 1930. Nos. 1 and 2 belong to 1901, in the midst of the Boer War. When they were given their first London performance, no.1 was encored twice. The audi-

ence, said Sir Henry Wood, 'rose and yelled' with delight over the melody in the trio. Some weeks later King Edward VII told Elgar that if words were fitted to the tune, it would 'go round the world'. He was right: as 'Land of Hope and Glory', it did."
(Text und Musik in Perspectives 8: *Empire, Commonwealth, Europe,* Klettbuch 51368, S. 24.)

b) Dasselbe Musikstück kann auch motivierend als Auftakt der Unterrichtseinheit vorgespielt werden. Allerdings bleibt es dann der Geschicklichkeit des L in dem gelenkten Unterricht überlassen, vom Sammeln der Impressionen über deren Auswertung den Bogen bis über die Themen "staatliches Selbstverständnis, bzw. Selbstdarstellung, Nationalgefühl, Größe, Imperialismus" zu spannen, der auf den Text hinführt.

4. Das Thema "Imperium, Imperialismus" ist den Schülern aus anderen Fächern (z.B. Latein, Französisch, Geschichte, Gemeinschaftskunde) bekannt. Man kann beim Einstieg daher an Vorwissen anknüpfen. Daher sind Schülerreferate zu prinzipiellen Imperialismustheorien bei diesem und den folgenden Texten nicht nötig, eine Überfrachtung der Unit sowie eine Überforderung der S. Je nach verfügbaren Schulbuchmaterialien an der jeweiligen Schule wäre es aber sinnvoll, wenn die S ihr historisches Wissen noch einmal auffrischen. Aber auch ohne diese Zusätze wird den S zusammen mit den Informationen aus dem Fact File eine Gesamtschau der imperialen Vergangenheit Großbritanniens möglich. Bei genügender Zeit und Motivation des Kurses wäre es denkbar, ein Kapitel aus Jan Morris' Buch referieren zu lassen, z.B. Chapter 8, "Life-Styles", das gleichzeitig eine Brücke schlägt zu der Institution des Clubs, der in George Orwells Roman *Burmese Days* eine große Rolle spielt (SB, S. 12–15): Jan Morris, *The Spectacle of Empire,* S. 198–205. Wegen des sprachlichen Niveaus sollte dieses Referat, das spätestens in Ergänzung zum Orwell-Text in den Unterricht einzubringen wäre, nur einem guten S zugemutet werden.

**Pictures**

The painting reproduced on p. 7 (SB) is dominated by the use of a central perspective. The viewer, therefore, focuses his attention on the barouche (cf. Text 1, l. 27) containing the Queen-Empress although it is very small. The exotic-looking troops in the foreground are obviously Indian, representatives of the faraway lands governed by the British. They provide too, of course, an element of splendour and pageantry, as do the beefeaters. White Horse Guards, footmen and other uniformed participants in the background. The dominant colour is red – cf. the colour "red" on maps (Text 1, ll. 160–163). The picture on p. 10 (SB) is also dominated by the colour "red". Here we have the "flags and the scarlet uniforms" of line 14, the exotic-looking soldiers, the pomp and spectacle described in the text. Here, too, it is quite clear who is in command – the white soldier.

The historical photograph of a durbar on p. 285 (SB) is an excellent example of the use of pageantry and spectacle in the British Empire. The sheer scale of this exotic show is emphasized by the perspective. It is clear why the British took over the custom of durbars: to show that they were now the rulers, to impress the ruled with their magnificence, the symbols of their power.

**Pre-reading activities**

*1. Which empires do you know that were Britain's rivals?*
France, Spain, Netherlands, Portugal

*2. What makes an empire?*
Trading system; "flag follows trade"; centralised political power; economic power; military power; a fully developed infrastructure; a mission; national pride

*3. Do you think it is possible that there will be new empires in the future?*
Empires are, in their social organisation, simply anti-democratic, and based on the principles of authoritarianism, exploitation, and the neglect of human rights. Wherever these conditions prevail, they could make an empire possible again, provided there are countries without an efficient system of self-defence.)

*4. Look at the pictures on p. 7, p. 10, p. 285 (SB). Answer the questions and say what the pictures have in common.*

**Suggested answers**

1. 
- the British Empire was an *odd phenomenon* (because a rather small nation governed the destinies of the world)
- the *theatre of empire* (uniforms, ships, railways, palaces, fortresses, cities, polo players, Queen Victoria)
- *spectacle as an instrument of imperialism*
- the imperial *style* of the British as a potent force (the result of the prevailing social structure in England: sense of superiority or inferiority, example of the public schools, influence of evangelical Christianity, legacy of the Industrial Revolution)
- the *lustre of British national history* (feeling of superiority, separateness, pound sterling as most powerful currency, Shakespeare, Nelson, Queen Victoria, the Sceptred Race)
- *Englishman abroad unmistakable* (acting out of imperialist attitudes)
- the *nobility* of both courage and sacrifice (doing the world a service)
- *with the admirable there came the rotten* (snobbery, racialism, *hubris*, conceit, gulf between rulers and ruled)
- *apogee as political force* and *fruition as theatre* (end of nineteenth century)
- a minority ruled a majority yet *hardly anyone thought this wicked*
- *Britain was not so powerful as it appeared*
- the *Boer War* signals the beginning of decline
- the British Empire had cast *its unmistakable effect around the world*

2. The British Empire is an odd phenomenon because it was established by a rather small nation which nevertheless dominated the world for a generation or two, surpassing even the ancient empires.

3. Power was maintained not only by making the best use of institutional instruments such as administration and military force. Power was also a matter of psychology: the outward representation of power (pomp) reinforced its real existence. "Spectacle" comprises all the material things that symbolized empire and could be used "theatrically": uniforms, architecture, colours, great cities, the empress herself. "Style" was the special way in which imperial grandeur was "acted out", a powerful force in history. It was something that lay between illusion and reality, half performance, half the real use of power.

4. 
- social (class) structure
- a glorious national history (and a resulting feeling of superiority)
- public school education
- evangelical Christianity
- material superiority (legacy of Industrial Revolution)
- the separateness of the British islands (sense of uniqueness)
- the powerful pound sterling (economic superiority)
- pride in one's own culture (Shakespeare)
- pride in national heroes (Nelson)
- monarchy

5. The anecdote illustrates that pride in being a representative of the most powerful nation of the world forbade "natural" social intercourse or conversation with a fellow countryman until one knew where he stood in the imperial hierarchy. It illustrates what Morris means by *over*-acting the imperialist style.

6. The author seems fascinated by the bygone grandeur and splendour of the empire. Using metaphors from the theatre he conjures up a lost world. He is interested in the phenomenon of spectacle in the empire, but at the same time he attempts an analysis of how such an empire was made possible. His admiration for the empire does not exclude a critical approach. The very use of theatrical metaphors takes away something of the seriousness and political weight from the historically outstanding epoch. He, especially at the end, clearly articulates the dark sides of imperial ascendancy.

7. a) "theatre, impresario, circus-mistress, performance, acted them out, *over*-acted them, charade, theatricals, theatre, act, top of the bill." The word "spectacle" is not a metaphor: life in the empire can be seen and admired in its diversity and grandness as a dramatic show, its policies and activities influencing the lives of millions of individuals. The theatrical terms, however, are metaphors. They are meant to introduce the illusion of unreality and entertainment and have only a temporary effect on the onlooker. The terms, therefore, are not to be taken literally. The aim of the metaphors is to belittle the real force of political power in the empire: the metaphor of the "circus-mistress", in particular, used in connection with Queen Victoria, makes this clear.

b) sprang from the loins (l. 2)
grave palaces (l. 16)
cities of Empire sleeping (l. 17)
forcing grounds...honed...tempered
facade of empire
confidence ...began to crack, pace...began to falter
splodges of red...like spilled claret, shed blood (simile!)
The metaphors insinuate that the empire was a living organism and a work of art. Metaphors are a characteristic of literary or imaginative writing. This text is more like a novel than a factual history book as the metaphors make the ideas more vivid.

8. Anaphora, a rhetorical device of repetition ("there was..." is used eleven times), underlines or stresses that the consciousness, the pride of the British before they went out to rule an empire, was deeply founded (see above the argumentative elements as such in question 4).

9. – frontier fortresses (l. 17)
– northern night (l. 18)
– southern sunshine (l. 18/19)
– panache of polo players (l. 19)
– complacency of colonial...(l. 19/20)
– swagger of subalterns (l. 20/21)
– proud but portly (l. 21)
– stately in statuary (l. 24/25)

### Additional questions

*Word formation:*
a) *Give the corresponding adjectives*
– history, l. 1
– to govern, l. 4
– surface, l. 7–8
– rival, l. 10
– empire, l. 11

– *justice, l. 16*
– *effectiveness, l. 51*
– *influence, l. 74*
b) *Give the corresponding nouns*
– *implicit, l. 32–33*
– *to envy, l. 49*
– *superior, l. 46*
– *constant, l. 63*
– *sub-conscious, l. 81–82*
– *opposite, l. 88–89*
– *to succeed, l. 125*
– *aesthetic, l. 126*
– *complete, l. 128*
– *serious, l. 141*

### Post-reading activities

*1. Discuss: An empire founded by war has to maintain itself by war* (Montesquieu, 1689–1755).

*2. Describe the spirit expressed in the following lines of a famous anthem still sung on national occasions (and at football matches!):*

When Britain first at Heaven's command
Arose from out of the azure main,
This was the charter of the land,
And guardian angels sang the strain:
'Rule Britannia, rule the waves;
Britons never will be slaves.'
(James Thomson, *Rule Britannia*, 1740)

*3. Listen to the tape of "Land of Hope and Glory" and comment on the text.*
See Bibliography 17, p. 24.

*4. Write a report on Chapter Eight ("Life-Styles") of* The Spectacle of Empire *by Jan Morris: Life in the British clubs.*
See Bibliography 14.

## 2. Envoy

### Background information

1. Envoy or envoi: "1. A brief dedicatory or explanatory stanza concluding certain forms of poetry, notably ballades. 2. A postscript in other forms of verse or prose." (Collins *Dictionary of the English Language,* Klettbuch 51716.)
2. W.E. Henley was a chauvinist writer, who stood in the shade of the more famous and slightly more subtle Rudyard Kipling. Henley's undifferentiated commitment to imperial greatness is often seen as a compensation for a severe handicap: from boyhood he suffered from tubercular arthritis and had a foot amputated. His best-known poem is the defiant and stoic 'Invictus', written in 1875. It would be wrong, however, to reduce Henley's poetical achievements to sheer jingoism which becomes domi-

nant only towards the end of his life. It should also be noted that the poem was written when the second Boer War (1899–1902) was in full swing: in June 1900.

3. The poem makes mention of the English Rose: this has been the national emblem of England since the time of the Wars of the Roses (1455–85), when the civil wars between the Houses of Lancaster (the red rose) and York (the white rose) for the possession of the English crown took place; leek and daffodil are the national emblems of Wales, the thistle being that of Scotland (and shamrock for the now independent Ireland).

4. For the discussion of the word "jingoism" in Question 6 (aggressive patriotism or chauvinism) it might be of interest to the pupils to know that the term derives from a popular music-hall song by G.W. Hunt which appeared at the time of the Russo-Turkish War (1877–1878) when anti-Russian feeling ran high and Disraeli ordered the Mediterranean fleet to Constantinople:

"We don't want to fight, but by Jingo if we do,
We've got the ships, we've got the men, and got the money too …".

**Didaktisch-methodische Hinweise**

1. In einem Leistungskurs läßt sich folgende Variante des im SB vorgeschlagenen Einstiegs (Aufgabe 1) praktizieren: Nach einer dem Kopftext des Schülerbuches entsprechenden Einführung durch L erhalten S – das Buch bleibt hierfür vorerst geschlossen – den Text als Lückentext und setzen, in Partnerarbeit, das ihrer Ansicht nach jeweils passende Wort ein, das sie aus einem Wortangebot auswählen können. Die auszulassenden sechs Wörter sind: bred (l. 2), stand (l. 3), blood (l. 6), God (l. 7), bounty (l. 8), governing (l. 14). Sie werden mit (in etwa) antonymischen Distraktoren gemischt und S als Gruppe von zwölf Wörtern zusammen mit dem Text ausgehändigt: z.B. "governing, blood, bred, stand, water, society, losses, recede, bounty, despairing, lost, God". Eine zweifache, dosierbare Erleichterung ist möglich: Richtiges Wort und Distraktor zusammen werden als Alternative in willkürlicher Reihenfolge angeboten; oder sie werden in der chronologisch korrekten Reihenfolge präsentiert: "bred/lost, stand/recede, blood/water, God/society, bounty/losses, governing/despairing". Die anschließende Diskussion über die richtige Wortauswahl sollte sich an einem Lückentextexemplar orientieren, das über OHP projiziert wird. Mit löslichem Folienschreiber in Farbe können die Vorschläge der S jeweils eingetragen und gegebenenfalls wieder gelöscht werden. Es ist klar, daß ein solches Vorgehen *in medias res* keine klare Chronologie des Interpretierens erlaubt, wie es die Aufgabenfolge im SB zuließe, daß aber das Unterrichtsgespräch sinnvoll strukturiert werden kann, wenn sich L an den einzelnen Aufgaben im SB als Leitlinien orientiert.

Zu (weiteren) Möglichkeiten des kreativen Umgangs mit Texten cf.: R.A. Carter, M.N. Long, *The Web of Words* (Cambridge, 1987) – CUP.

2. Das Gedicht ist auf Cassette aufgenommen *(Selected Texts* 510342). Also könnte man es als Hörtext präsentieren. Die Schüler bekommen den Lückentext zuerst und müssen versuchen, ihn während des Hörens auszufüllen. Ein zweimaliges Hören wäre ratsam.

3. S lassen sich ein solchermaßen chauvinistisches Gedicht einfach nicht gefallen. Daher tendieren sie dazu, die Aufgabe 1 *(paraphrase)* – teilweise unbewußt – zu kommentieren, die Aufgabe 2 *(title)* ironisch zu lösen. Hier ist es evtl. teilweise geboten, die S zur "Fertigkeiten-Disziplin" zu ermahnen und auf die diskussionsbezogenen Aufgaben/Phasen im Verlauf der Interpretation zu "vertrösten" (Aufgaben 5 und 6)

4. Aufgabe 3 läßt die für englische Sonette nicht untypische strukturelle Diskrepanz zwischen Form und Inhalt sichtbar werden. Aufgabe 3 läßt sich von Aufgabe 4 nur schwer trennen und es ist damit zu rechnen, daß die Diskussion sofort zu den in Aufgabe 4 genannten Stichwörtern führt. Doch ist es wichtig, mit der Aufgabe 3. das genannte grundlegende Interpretationsproblem (Form vs. Inhalt) zu isolieren.

Die Aufforderung, drei und nicht vier Teile finden zu lassen, ist für die S eine Herausforderung und so begründbar: Formal, vom Reimschema her, ist dieses Sonett als "Shakespearean" oder "English sonnet" vierteilig (abab cdcd efef gg). Jedoch überlappen sich Reimschema, Syntax und Inhalt in den Zeilen 9–14: Die Zeilen 9 und 10, die erste Hälfte des dritten Quartetts ("quatrain"), schließt sich syntaktisch – in rhetorischer Frage und Antwort – und inhaltlich ganz an das zweite Quartett an (ll. 5–8), obwohl sie vom Reimschema her zum dritten Quartett zählen. Die Zeilen 11 und 12, also die zweite Hälfte des dritten Quartetts, bilden syntaktisch und inhaltlich eine Einheit mit dem vom Reimschema her eigentlich selbständigen, auch durch Zeileneinrückung ("indentation") abgesetzten Schlußcouplet, das in vielen anderen (z.B. Shakespeares no. 116, 130) englischen Sonetten oft eine summarische Pointierung des in den Versen 1–12 Gesagten vornimmt. Hier hingegen leisten die Verse 11–14 die Bilanzierung. Syntax und Inhalt erlauben daher eine Unterteilung des Gedichtes in drei Teile:

ll. 1–4 : dedicatory address
ll. 5–10 : fictitious indictments and justifications of British rule
ll. 11–14: conclusion: missionary task for England remains

Man kann diesen Konflikt zwischen Reimschema und den syntaktischen/inhaltlichen Strukturen so deuten, daß die Bilanz der Zeilen 11–14 – die finstere Drohung, der eigenen nationalen Mission nicht auszuweichen – wuchtiger ausfällt, als sie das in zwei Schlußzeilen könnte.

4. Im Sinne eines fächerverbindenden Unterrichts könnte man ein diesem Gedicht in seinem nationalen Geist entsprechendes deutsches Gedicht (z.B. von Walter Flex – s. Bibliographie S. 42) an die Seite stellen. Der Geschichtsunterricht könnte mit einer Analyse der sogenannten "Hunnenrede" von Kaiser Wilhelm II am 27.7.1900 in Bremerhaven einen vergleichenden Beitrag zu "Sendungsbewußtsein und nationale Mission" leisten. "Zur Not" bindet der Englischlehrer selbst den einen oder anderen Text in die Sequenz ein, u.U. auch in Form eines Schülerreferats.

Die "Hunnenrede" Kaiser Wilhelms II ist zugänglich in: Ernst Johann, ed., *Reden des Kaisers. Ansprachen, Predigten und Trinksprüche Wilhelms II.* (München, 1966), 90–91 – dtv, Reihe "Dokumente"; in einer anderen Ausgabe wird durch einen Kommentar zur Geschichte dieser Rede deutlich, woher sie ihren Beinamen "Hunnenrede" erhalten hat: Michael Neher, *Der Imperialismus*. Ploetz Arbeitsmaterialien Schule (Würzburg, 1974), 35–37. – Verlag Ploetz.

**Pre-reading activities**

*1. Look at the picture on p. 11 and read the caption. What image of a soldier's life at the time of the Empire does it give? Compare it to the picture on the opposite page.*

Again it is a scarlet uniform that dominates the picture. Two soldiers on horseback form the centre. This strategic position contrasts with that of the Zulu warrior lying on the ground, thus symbolizing victory and defeat. The British soldiers are obviously seen as heroes in a difficult situation, the Africans as very black savages who are being crushed.

*2. Listen to the poem on tape and fill in the blanks.*

See "Didaktisch-methodische Hinweise".

**Suggested answers**

1. Paraphrase (see box p. 193, SB):
I write this poem in order to glorify and praise England, its women and its dead, and also to praise their descendants who are fighting for the Empire all over the world. I do not care about us being called proud – the English Rose as a symbol stands for itself. If people accuse us of shedding blood: we have shed our own. If people say we are only interested in commerce: God knows what we have paid and been paid. We are said to be mean, and yet we have shared our riches with half the world. I do not care about people's hate or people's envy. They can go to Hell. What we are doing is our fate, for a nation that ignores its fate is damned. We will let all our critics know this and England too, home of future mothers and men born to rule.

2. England forever/Let's be proud/England is the greatest/"Am englischen Wesen wird die Welt genesen"/Our mission/England's destiny/England, my England/ In praise of England/The glory that is England etc.

3. and 4.
(Sections, syntax, rhyme scheme/stanza form, content)
*First section: ll. 1–4:*
form: the rhyme scheme *abab* and the sentence pattern (one sentence only) form a stanza;
content: the address or dedication of the verses to the glory of England.

*Second section: ll. 5–10:*
form: the rhyme scheme *cdcd* plus *ef*, the fivefold question – answer pattern form a second section, not a stanza;
content: (defiant – "be it so!") justification of British imperial policy.
*Third section: ll. 11–14:*
form: the rhyme scheme *ef* plus *gg*, one sentence
content: final admonition – England's fate/mission/destiny is clear and should be accepted.
*Choice of words, imagery*
- "green land" (l. 1)/"green England" (l. 13): overall assessment of the country = healthy, vital, fertile country; the country is personified – it gives birth ("bred", l. 2); "her" (l. 3, 4); "mother"
- "my women" – "my dead" (l. 2): possessive pronoun indicates total identification and even (macho) ownership
- "broods" (l. 3): animal life, suggesting vitality
- rhetorically evoked fivefold series of contrasts (ll. 5–10): self-justification, no self-criticism or sense of guilt
- proud/rose: symbol of country and symbol of English womanhood
- "shedders of blood"/self-sacrifice
- "shopkeepers"/God knows the true account
- "close"/shared riches with half the world
- envy and hate/"Be it so!" (may they end up in hell!)
- "high God" (l. 7)/"Pit's edge" (l. 10)/"fate" (l. 11)/"God's good time" (l. 12)/religious/metaphysical frame of reference (God is on our side)
- a marked contrast between "they" (ll. 5, 9) on the one hand and "us"(ll. 5, 9) and "our" (ll. 5, 6, 7, 8) on the other evokes the sense of superiority and "difference" of the Empire-builders.

5. The role of men: they are seen as "strong broods" (l. 3), an image of animal-like virility (lions!); they are here to fight (l. 4), to govern (l. 14), and to sacrifice their lives for the Empire. The role of women is that of the "super-woman" England: to bear children for the Empire, beautiful girls who in turn become mothers of men-children who will fight and govern (women as the symbol of fertility).

6. All definitions from: Collins *Dictionary of the English Language* (Klettbuch 51716):
*patriotism* – devotion to one's own country and concern for its defence
*nationalism* – sentiment based on common cultural characteristics that binds a population and often produces a policy of national independence or separatism; loyalty or devotion to one's country; patriotism; exaggerated, passionate, or fanatical devotion to a national community
*jingoism* – the belligerent spirit or foreign policy of extreme patriots; chauvinism (see "Background information")
*chauvinism* (after Nicolas Chauvin, legendary French soldier under Napoleon, noted for his vociferous and unthinking patriotism) – aggressive or fanatical patriotism; jingoism; irrational belief in the superiority of one's own race
Henley would no doubt think of himself as a patriot or a nationalist as there was no criticism attached to such an attitude at that time. On the contrary, such patriotism was laudable. Seen from a foreign perspective and from a modern perspective his attitudes would now be called jingoist or chauvinist (they can be used synonymously) as nationalism has become a bad word since the experiences of two World Wars.

**Post-reading activities**

*1. Discuss what the words patriotism or nationalism mean to you as regards your own country.*

*2. Discuss the new nationalism of the post-cold War era and since the break-up of the Soviet Union.*

*3. Compare this poem with one by Walter Flex.* "Deutsche Schicksalsstunde" or "Dem Kaiser zum Geburtstag 1917" from *Im Felde zwischen Nacht;* or "Wir sanken hin ..." from *Der Wanderer zwischen beiden Welten.*
See Bibliography 4 and 5.

*4. Read a sonnet by Shakespeare and discuss the sonnet form.*

*5. Report/paper/talk: Compare the spirit of this poem with Kaiser Wilhelm II's "Hunnenrede".*
See Bibliography 9 and 16.

# 3. The path of progress? (GK)

**Methodisch-didaktische Hinweise**

1. Der Textausschnitt wirft – wie der gesamte Roman – drei Fragen auf:
a) Wieviel Imperialismuskritik – durch die Romanfigur Flory formuliert – enthält er? b) Wie weit mag Orwell selbst diese Kritik geteilt haben? c) Welche Position sollen die S beziehen: für den britischen Kolonialismus oder gegen ihn? Die ersten zwei Fragen lassen sich nicht eindeutig beantworten – auch nicht im Kontext des gesamten Romans.
a) Orwell läßt den Holzhändler Flory im gewählten Textausschnitt als "advocatus diaboli" oder "agent provocateur" auftreten. Von seiner Berufstätigkeit als Holzhändler her ist er nicht gerade als Intellektueller gedacht. Eigentlich gäbe es keinen Grund, ihn hier als den Ankläger der britischen imperialistischen Politik auftreten zu lassen, zumal auch die Intellektuellen in England sich nicht besonders als Kritiker des britischen Imperialismus hervorgetan haben. In seiner Kritik am Imperialismus scheint Flory die Sehweise, die man Orwell allgemein zuspricht, wiederzugeben. Flory ist also eine Art impliziter Autor ("implied author"). Allerdings findet man beim selbstzweiflerischen Flory an anderen Textstellen des Romans eine halb-überzeugte Apologie Anglo-Burmas. So wird denn auch in einer etwas überzogenen literarkritischen Bewertung Florys politische Dauerkritik an der englischen Herrschaft entschärft, indem sie zum Reflex seiner persönlichen Frustration umdefiniert wird: "...'Burmese Days' is really less a considered critique of imperialism than an exploration of private guilt, incommunicable loneliness and loss of identity for which Burma becomes at points little more than a setting. The pain which Flory suffers is 'the pain of exile'": Terry Eagleton, "Orwell and the Lower-Middle-Class Novel", in *George Orwell. A Collection of Critical Essays*, ed. Raymond Williams (London, repr.1986; Englewood Cliffs, 1974), p. 17. Im Aufgabenapparat macht die Aufgabe 4 auf dieses auch im Textausschnitt selbst sichtbare Problem aufmerksam.
b) Orwell selbst war während seiner fünf Dienstjahre in Burma wahrscheinlich kein Anti-Imperialist reinsten Wassers (Cf. Bernard Crick: *George Orwell. A Life*, London, 1980, pp.76–103). Es könnte also sein, daß mit Florys zumindest ambivalenter Kritik auch Orwells Hin- und Hergerissensein zwischen Anpassung an die in Burma gegebenen Lebensverhältnisse einerseits und grundsätzlicher moralischer Ablehnung imperialer Politik andererseits gespiegelt wird. Es ist aber genausogut möglich, daß Orwell sich die Apologie des Dr. Veraswami als eine grandiose Ironie britischen Selbstverständnisses ausgedacht hat: Das "Opfer" bedankt sich auch noch beim "Täter".
c) Daß einer der von der britischen Herrschaft Abhängigen, Dr. Veraswami, seine imperialen Herren überschwenglich lobt, ist ebenso Ausnahme wie Florys Position – und hat erzähltechnisch seinen guten Grund, da der Doktor von den Engländern Hilfe erwartet. Diese Umkehrung der üblichen Haltungen provoziert die S zur Stellungnahme; sie zweifeln die Plausibilität der Haltung beider an. Andererseits wäre die Wahl der alternativen Perspektive – ein systemkonformer Engländer, ein kritischer "Eingeborener" – weniger geeignet, den Widerspruch zu erregen, den Orwell in seiner Zeit sicher als vermeintlicher "Nestbeschmutzer" hat erregen wollen. Diese provokative Wirkungsabsicht zu erarbeiten ist möglich mit einer Anfangsfrage wie : "Why does the author not make Dr. Veraswami accuse and Flory defend British rule in Burma?"
Es kommt darauf an, mit den S die Schwierigkeit der eindeutigen moralischen Bewertung des Textes zu erarbeiten, ihnen aber gleichzeitig eine klare persönliche Gewichtung nach dem Motto "imperialism is oppression/exploitation/bad" einzuräumen.
Eine Einbeziehung der Verfilmung von E. M. Forsters Roman *A Passage to India* nach Behandlung dieses Textes bietet sich an.
2. Die Aufgaben 1–3 eignen sich gut für Partner- bzw. Gruppenarbeit. Die Resultate der Partner- oder Gruppenarbeit werden von je einem Sprecher präsentiert. In wenig leistungsfähigen Kursen oder Gks kann es sinnvoll sein, die Arbeitsschritte des Sammelns der Argumente und ihrer Gewichtung ("ranking") methodisch voneinander zu trennen. Die Argumente Florys und Dr. Veraswamis (Aufgaben 1 bis 3) werden zwar auch in Partner- bzw. Gruppenarbeit gesammelt, aber dann zunächst *kontrastiv* den

jeweiligen Themen zugeordnet und etwa nach folgendem Muster als Tafelanschrieb festgehalten:

| Issue | Flory | The doctor |
|---|---|---|
| Forests | British trade monopolies | forests saved from ruin |
| ... | ... | ... |
| The British | up-to-date, hygienic louse | torchbearers of progress |
| ... | ... | ... etc. |

Danach erst erfolgt eine Diskussion über ein "ranking" im Plenum.

3. Nach Lösung der Aufgaben 1 bis 4 können vor der Klasse zwei S als "Flory" und "the doctor" ein Streitgespräch in Anlehnung an den Text bzw. Tafelanschrieb und die "ranking"-Diskussion führen, wobei die Diskutanten auch die Kursteilnehmer mit einbeziehen können. ("What do you think?" etc.)

4. Man könnte den Text auch als Dialog vorlesen lassen, um den S die Lebendigkeit des Gesprächs deutlich zu machen.

5. Aufgabe 7 könnte als Hausaufgabe (Essay/Comment) gegeben werden als Grundlage für eine intensive Diskussion.

**Pre-reading activities**

*1. Look at the historical photo on p. 13 and read the caption.*
The formality of the picture underlines the formality of the relationship between master and servant/two businessmen or civil servants with four servants/exotic uniforms/grand style of life/tropical setting but very English tea things for tea-time/European clothes, complete with waistcoat, in spite of different climate

*2. Does the photo correspond to your image of life in the British Empire or do you have a different one?*

**Suggested answers**

1. Flory's arguments:
– purpose of the British is to steal, officials help businessmen, the British have trade monopolies (ll. 3–15)
– the British do not give the natives a good education, and do not teach manual trades for fear of competition (ll. 31–35)
– various Burmese industries destroyed by the British, e. g. muslins, ship-building etc. (ll. 37–50)
– Britain keeps the peace by means of banks (money lending) and prisons (ll. 62–68)
– Pax Britannica is really Pox Britannica (pun or play on words ll. 61–62)
– by modernising Burma the British are wrecking Burmese culture by replacing it by their own inferior culture (ll. 80–90)
– the British "build a prison and call it progress" (ll. 112–117)
– the British brought diseases with them (l. 125); cf. "Pox Britannica" (l. 61)
– the British are only interested in what they can get out of Burma, not in civilising it (ll. 137–140)

2. –

3. The doctor's arguments:
– the Burmese are unable to trade, are helpless (ll. 18–21)
– forests that otherwise would be ruined are improved by the British (ll. 21–26)
– British businessmen develop resources of the country (ll. 26–27)
– British officials civilise the Burmese, educate them in a totally disinterested way (ll. 27–30)
– Oriental character: apathy and superstition (ll. 56–57)
– law and order, British Justice and Pax Britannica a boon (ll. 59–61)
– prisons are necessary (l. 70)
– instead of dirt, torture, ignorance in the past, now hospital, school, police station: uprush of modern progress (ll. 72–77)
– civilisation at its worst is an advance compared to Oriental sloth (ll. 102–107)
– the British: "torchbearers upon the path of progress" (ll. 110–111)
– the British build infrastructure and bring hygiene (ll. 119–124)
– diseases: the Indians bring them, the British cure them (ll. 127–130)

4. The last lines suggest that Flory is wording his criticism not seriously, but with tongue in cheek in order to provoke his friend, or that he is merely motivated by personal reasons so that his arguments suddenly appear in a dubious light and in

turn make the doctor's views appear more trustworthy.

5. Dr Veraswami is more emotional; this shows in the following:
he is not able to control or check his accent ("iss" l. 16, 17, 29, 37, 102, 104); body language: "waved his hand excitedly" (l. 51); interrupts Flory, nervous repetition: "My friend, my friend" (l. 36), exclamation: "'What ...!' cried the doctor."; imperatives: "look": four times (ll. 73–76); "alas" (l. 100); "...eager to claim..."(l. 126)
Flory's choice of words, however, is not objective either, e. g. "gangs of Jews and Scotchmen" (ll. 14–15), Pox Britannica (l. 62), "our dirt" (l. 83) etc., but he is on top of his subject and in charge of the argument, guiding it where he wants it to go.

6.a) dear, friend, pathetic, bosh, dare, frightened, excitedly, apathy, cry, alas, pleasure, horrible, regretful, eager, disapprove, proclaim
b) – friend, (un)friendly, friendlily(!), (un)friendliness, to befriend s.o., to be friends (with), to make friends (with), to become friendly (with), friendless, friendlessness, friendship, boyfriend, girl-friend, friendly match, friendly society
– (un-)pleasant, pleasantness, pleasantry, please, to please, pleased, pleased with, pleasing, pleasure, pleasurable, pleasureful, pleasureless, pleasure-boat, pleasure-craft, pleasure-ground, pleasure-seeking, pleasure principle
– frightened, frightening, fright, to frighten, to take fright (at), frightful, to give s.o. a fright, to get a fright
– excitable, excitability, to excite, excited, excitedly, exciting, excitement
– horrible, horror, horrendous, horrid, horridness, horrific, to horrify, horrifying, horror-stricken/horror-struck

7. The discussion will focus on the question of whether the colonies (have) profited from imperialism (and in what way) rather than suffered from it and whether they (have) irretrievably lost their own identity and culture.

**Additional question**

*The map on p.14 covers a certain period. Why do you think this period was chosen? You may refer to the Fact File (pp. 284–285) for help.*
The Second Empire and the New Imperialism together mark the last and most impressive phase of extension. From 1914 onwards the Empire crumbled. See p. 284, SB. "In 1914 the British Empire reached a climax of power and influence."

**Post-reading activities**

*1. Read the short story "Shooting an Elephant" by Orwell as homework and discuss the image of Empire conveyed in it.*

*2. Write a book report on* Burmese Days *(or any other novel dealing with the Empire, e.g. by Somerset Maugham, E.M. Forster, George Lamming etc.).*

# 4. A dignified retreat

**Background information**

1. The different spelling of "Guyana" and "Guiana" in the comment on the picture on page 16 is not a misprint. Former British Guiana gained autonomy in 1966 and its name since then has been Guyana (cf. "The British Empire 1558-1983, table VII, 'Territories of the British Empire'" – Bibliography 10). Most other former colonies have totally changed their names on gaining their autonomy (e. g. Rhodesia/Zimbabwe).

2. Further reading:
a.) While the given text is preoccupied with sketching mainly the historical phases of imperial decline, the psychological, economic and political sides of the loss of empire are discussed in a worthwhile, short chapter, "Post-imperial Britain", in Ralf Dahrendorf's *On Britain*, (London, 1982), pp. 135–138, which the teacher can also well use for some aspects of Chapter 3 in this book, "Modern Britain".
b.) A chronological survey, densely packed with information and written for pupils, of Britain's

position in the world since World War II, is given in: John Randle, "Britain and the World", *British Life and Institutions* (Stuttgart, 1990), pp. 53–60, Klettbuch 51344.

## Methodisch-didaktische Hinweise

1. Absatz 1 (ll. 1–21) wird im Text selbst zusammengefaßt im *Schlußsatz* "In short ... guardians." (ll. 17–21)
2. Absatz 2 (ll. 22–58) wird im Text selbst zusammengefaßt im *Eingangssatz* "Territorially ... heard." (ll. 22–25)
3. In den *Fact Files* zu diesem Kapitel findet sich ein Schaubild (S. 284, SB), das die verschiedenen Phasen der Entwicklung des Empire bis zur Zeit vor dem Ersten Weltkrieg skizziert. Es ist aus Gründen der Chronologie didaktisch sinnvoll, erst diese Information im Unterricht zu vermitteln, und methodisch sinnvoll ist es, die S die Tabelle selbst versprachlichen zu lassen, weil das eine Vorübung zur Erstellung des Summary (Aufgaben 4 und 5) bedeutet.
4. Der Text "From Empire to Commonwealth" in den Fact Files (S. 284–285, SB) liefert weitere Detailinformationen zur Entwicklung des Empire in diesem Jahrhundert. In den Unterricht kann dieser Text nach Bearbeitung der Aufgabe 5 einbezogen werden: Nach kurzer Stillesephase stellt L einige Comprehension-Fragen.
5. Aufgabe 8 könnte unter den S aufgeteilt und für Kurzreferate genutzt werden.

## Pre-reading activities

1. *How and why do empires usually end?*
e.g. Rome, Third Reich, Russia

2. *Can you think of any British colonies that have become independent in your lifetime?* See map p. 18.

## Suggested answers

1. a) *from the context:* e.g.
at the turn of the century (l. 4)
groaned (l. 13)
extent (l. 23)
determined to withstand (l. 73)
British-descended (l. 84–85)
faded (l. 87)
impact (l. 124)
b) *from the word family/root word:* e. g.
half-disclosed (l. 20)
uncertainty (l. 20)
recognition (l. 41)
decolonization (l. 59)
c) *from similar German, French or Latin words and expressions:* e.g.
drastically (l. 2)
consolidation (l. 13)
territorially (l. 22)
confident (l. 25)
hegemony (l. 28)
voluntary (l. 37)
association (l. 37)
transfer (l. 54)
substantially (l. 57)
compatible (l. 82)
intimacy (l. 97).

2. –

3. It is an expository text (exposition), because it conveys a lot of information. Text 1 was descriptive, while Text 3 was narrative.

4. key words and phrases:
*First paragraph:* 1901–1975; Britain's international position drastically changed; turn of century Empire an extraordinary concoction; a "century of consolidation" or a burden; Empire could look solid; uncertainty amongst ...guardians.
*Second paragraph:* Empire to reach its greatest extent after the First World War; still confident voices; splendours of Empire exhibitions at Wembley and Glasgow; the British as an imperial race; Imperial Conference; tendency towards independence; empire morally unacceptable, incompatible with democracy; India and Pakistan set a pattern after World War II; process of transfer of power completed in mid-seventies.
*Third paragraph:* Decolonization as an indication of decline; loss of will to govern; British governments control timetable of independence; process of handover amicable; former colonies form Commonwealth of Nations; British influence fading; definition of the Commonwealth difficult.
*Fourth paragraph:* unusual dispossession of an empire; dignified retreat; partnership instead of domination in new Commonwealth; Commonwealth links developed and developing countries; gives Britain a mission in the world; expectations of Commonwealth not really fulfilled.
*Fifth paragraph:* Commonwealth cushioned loss of empire.

5. a) 1901
ll. 1–21: although a heterogeneous mixture, the empire gives a solid impression, especially when one looks at the map (with British possessions coloured red, cf. Text no 1, p. 10, l. 160), but there is already uncertainty about its guardians.
b) between the two World Wars
ll. 22–33 – positive aspects: the Empire reaches its greatest extent; splendours of the Empire Exhibitions at Wembley (20s) and Glasgow (1938); emotional identification with the Empire.
ll. 34–52 – negative aspects: voices warning of the end of empire could already be heard; the Imperial Conference testifies to a sense of independence of the white dominions; the left increasingly finds an empire morally unacceptable; incompatibility of democracy and imperial rule becomes more and more evident.
c) post-war years
ll. 52–58 – With India and Pakistan becoming independent shortly after the Second World War a pattern is set for the future development of the Empire; rebellions are put down in Malaya and Kenya as Britain insists on deciding when colonies become independent; the process of handover is normally amicable; republican constitutions allowed within the Commonwealth.

6. At the turn of the 20th century optimists expected a century of consolidation, pessimists suffered from the burden of running an empire. In this sense even the Boer war could be seen as either a shock or as a precedent. The British between the wars were emotionally involved in the Empire as portrayed in the Empire Exhibitions. They felt themselves an imperial race. But gradually people, especially the political left, found the Empire unacceptable. Victorians would have seen this loss of the will to govern as a decline. But the British governments suceeded in handing over the colonies smoothly, and the idea of a Commonwealth of Nations aroused high expectations. As a matter of fact the Commonwealth made the loss of the empire easier to bear.
What used to be the view of the political left in Britain between the wars, namely that empires are not compatible with democracy, has become an established moral attitude in the Western world.

7. Britain did not lose her Empire due to decisive military defeats but managed to hand over its former colonies peacefully, and change its Empire into a Commonwealth of nations some of whom had republican constitutions but nevertheless accepted the British Crown as the unifying force.

8. – India: became independent in 1947, became a Republic in 1950
– Pakistan: became independent in 1947 (separated from India), became a Republic in 1956, left the Commonwealth in 1972, but formally re-acceded on October 1, 1989
– Malaya: became independent in 1957; in 1963 formed Malaysia, together with Sabah and Sarawak
– Kenya: became independent in 1963, a Republic in 1964 etc.

**Additional questions**

*1. Compare this style of writing history with that of Jan Morris (Text 1).*

*2. Translation : "Decolonization ... chose."*(ll. 59–72)
Eine "Entkolonisierung" in dieser Größenordnung war nichts, was man sich zu Beginn des Jahrhunderts hätte vorstellen können. Die Viktorianer hätten einen solchen Wandel zweifellos als Zeichen des Niedergangs, ja sogar der Dekadenz angesehen. Der Wille zum Herrschen ging verloren, obwohl man andererseits wenig Eifer an den Tag legte, die Insignien der Macht loszuwerden. Aber es schien in der Tat so, daß ein in die Länge gezogener Widerstand gegen die Machtübergabe sinnlos war. Aber trotzdem waren die Briten in Malaya und Kenya willens wie auch in der Lage, aufständische Bewegungen niederzuschlagen, die ihnen die Möglichkeit nehmen konnten/genommen hätten, sich nach eigenem Belieben zurückzuziehen.
Lexikalische/idiomatische Schwierigkeiten: *on this scale; not something; envisaged; no doubt:* Ausdruck für Negation; *interpreted:* naheliegendes "interpretieren" stilistisch unangemessen; *indication:* "hard word"; *there was:* im D. ein Vollverb erforderlich ; *to shake off:* im D. schlecht genauso bildlich auszudrücken; *even so:* wie dem auch sei, gleichwohl, dennoch; Syntaxprobleme – *which would have been envisaged:* im D. unpersönl. "man" statt Passiv im E., Zeit und Modus im D.; *would no doubt have interpreted:* Zeit und Modus; *it did seem:* emphatisches "do"; *might:* Wahl der angemes-

senen Zeitstufe im D. ein Problem; *when they chose:* ein kombiniert lexikalisch-syntaktisches Problem: "wenn sie es für richtig hielten", "nach eigenem Belieben", Wahl zwischen Gliedsatz oder adverbialer Bestimmung.

**Post-reading activities**

1. *See question 8, p. 19, SB.*

2. *Report/paper/talk: Find out about Portuguese/French/Dutch/German colonialism.*

# 5. Listening Comprehension: Home thoughts (GK)

**Background information**

1. The poem by Robert Browning (1812–1889) referred to by Ms Greer is contained in *English and American Poetry*, Klettbuch 5064, p. 45. The first verse is especially well-known:

> Home Thoughts, from Abroad
>
> Oh, to be in England
> Now that April's there,
> And whoever wakes in England
> Sees, some morning, unaware,
> That the lowest boughs and the brush-wood sheaf
> Round the elm-tree bole are in tiny leaf,
> While the chaffinch sings on the orchard bough
> In England – now!

2. The Nationality Act of 1981 aimed at cutting down the number of immigrants into Britain. Commonwealth citizens were no longer regarded as British subjects and had no automatic right to settle in the UK as before. There were now 3 categories of citizenship with 3 different passports:
a) British Citizenship for those born in the UK or of British-born parents;
b) British Dependent Territories Citizenship;
c) British Overseas Citizenship.
For more details see *Abiturwissen Landeskunde Great Britain/USA*, Klettbuch 929509, pp. 40–46.
The Hong King Chinese with British passports were affected by this new law and have now the second category of citizenship and no right of abode in Britain (see Text 6).
As regards Greer's last paragraph, there is no legal difference between Commonwealth members who recognize the Queen as head of state and those who do not. They all have the same category of passport. She is no doubt referring to the racialist attitudes of many immigration officers.

**Methodisch-didaktischer Hinweis**

Eine Einleitung, Worterklärungen und Fragen zum Globalverständnis sind im SB, S. 19 abgedruckt.

**Text**

Thirty-five years ago in Australia I learnt by heart Browning's poem "Home Thoughts from Abroad". I had no doubt where abroad was. I was in it, born in it. I did not think of England as home, rather as the centre, while I lived some- 5
where on an outer edge of a geographical suburbia called the Commonwealth. My head was stuffed with Englishness. I knew more about hedgehogs and squirrels than I did about echidnas and possums. [...] 10
We were all meant to "go home" when we completed our studies, but we knew that if we were any good we would be allowed to stay at the centre, with its great libraries and museums with their heaped-up spoils of empire. We didn't 15
think of ourselves as having the best of both worlds, for we had been taught to think of England and our homelands as part of the same world, the British Commonwealth. Because we were treated as a homogeneous group, we may 20
be forgiven perhaps for not realising that the Commonwealth was already falling apart.
The crown was declared divisible by the Statute of Westminster in 1931; when I took up my scholarship in 1964, the two most populous 25
members of the Commonwealth, India and Pakistan, had ceased to recognise the Queen as head of state, and most of the others were

*From Empire to Europe*    23

unilaterally cancelling the British heritage. Now, 25 years later, only the Queen in her chameleon crowns is left trying to hold the tattered fabric together. My *Longman's New Generation Dictionary* (1981) informs me that the British Commonwealth is an "organisation of independent states formerly part of the British Empire, to encourage trade and friendly relations among its members". Britain's entry into the Common Market cannot be said to have encouraged trade between the ex-colonies and Britain. The trade links established by the Empire connected the colonies with each other. Intra-Commonwealth trade is still insignificant. After more than a century of divide and rule, friendly relations between the ex-colonies are not to be expected either.

While I was studying in Britain my homeland was turning away from Europe and towards the Pacific. Twenty years after bitter fighting, as Britain's ally, with Japan, Australia was forced to acknowledge Japan as its chief trading partner. The Commonwealth now comes together chiefly in the longest, slowest and most exhausted queues at British ports of entry. Australians, New Zealanders and Canadians, who still acknowledge the Queen as head of state and keep her picture on their money, have plenty of time for bitter reflection as they wait through the most suspicious and humiliating questioning which their fellow Commonwealth members, the Indians, the Pakistanis and the Bangladeshis, have to undergo.

By Germaine Greer, *The Independent Magazine*, 1 July 1989.

## Suggested answers (Listening for the gist)

In her childhood and during her studies she was England-orientated, but did not notice that the Commonwealth was already falling apart.
Now she is fully aware of the fact that Australia cannot rely on Britain or on intra-Commonwealth links but rightly has turned to Japan. What is left of the Commonwealth is a depressing sight.

## Listening for detail

*1. What immediate feelings did Browning's poem "Home Thoughts from Abroad" evoke in the young Germaine Greer? (l. 1-10)*
She was English-orientated. Knowing that Australia was a kind of abroad, she had a desire for England, not as her home, but as the centre of the Commonwealth.

*2. How did Greer differentiate between England as a home and as a centre? (ll.11-22)*
While studying in England, Australian or Commonwealth students were expected to regard their countries of origin as their "homes". But they felt "at home" in Britain and thought that Britain and their homelands were part of one group, while objectively the Commonwealth was already falling apart.

*3. What was the state of the Commonwealth when she started studying and what is it like now (ll. 23-45)?*
India and Pakistan had ceased to recognize the Queen as head of state, and many other colonies were fighting for independence. Since Britain joined the Common Market even trade relations with the Commonwealth countries have deteriorated. Intra-Commonwealth links were always weak and are even more so now.

*4. Explain the new constellation between Australia, Britain and the Pacific (ll. 46-50)*
Australia has turned away from Britain and Europe to the Pacific, and especially to Japan. It realizes now that its trade interests lie here, with its former enemy, and not with the old mother country.

*5. How does Greer experience the decline of the Commonwealth? (ll.51-61)*
Commonwealth people now meet in long queues waiting to get through customs in Britain. There is plenty of time there to reflect on how one once belonged and how one now is a foreigner. The differences in the treatment of races is visible too.

## Post-listening activities

*1. Browning's poem (see "Background information") is a beautiful piece of nature poetry and – if time should allow – is worth reading in class.*

*2. Report/paper: Trace the development of Australia from discovery by Europeans to the status of Pacific power.*
See Bibliography 18.

# 6. Colony of fear (GK)

**Background information**

On September 26, 1984, a declaration, known as the Joint Declaration, was formally signed in Beijing by representatives of the Chinese and British governments and sealed Hong Kong's fate: with effect from 1 July 1997 the last "jewel" of Britain's former Empire will be restored to the People's Republic of China. In this declaration Britain also renounced her rights to Hong Kong island and the Kowloon peninsula, which had originally been ceded to Britain 'in perpetuity'. Legally only the New Territories on the mainland, Kowloon's hinterland, leased in 1898 for ninety-nine years, were to be handed back. But publicly the British position has been that Hong Kong and Kowloon were unviable alone and their handover unavoidable. The formula for the handover was coined by the Chinese: one country, two systems. Hong Kong is to be a Special Autonomous Region under Chinese sovereignty and allowed to retain its own legislation, judiciary, and socio-economic system for fifty years. Under the threat of the Communist takeover it was part of the British insurance policy that at least a Basic Law for Hong Kong, if not a Bill of Rights, should be worked out for the fifty-year period of transition. As a colony, however, Hong Kong has never experienced free, direct, general elections. Admittedly, various representatives of the British government have promised Hong Kong direct elections, but the when and how have remained rather vague; and Beijing does not want direct elections to take place, "that Western stuff". According to the Basic Law, completed in early 1990 and drawn up by China in consultation with Hong Kong, less than half the legislature will be directly elected by as late as 1999. Although Beijing has made it clear that the Basic Law cannot be changed any more, London is still hoping for improvements.

Only a minority in Hong Kong, however, has committed itself to demanding direct elections like the well-known, highly successful barrister Martin Lee. In his view only a democratically elected local government could be protection against the future whims of Beijing's mandarins. Martin Lee's protest activities (he was a contestant for the Legislative Council election in September 1991, where he was the most popular candidate) have already been denounced in Beijing as 'counter-revolutionary' and he himself has been told that even if he were elected after 1997 he would not be allowed to be part of any government. The majority are rather seeking for ways out of a dilemma that reached its peak after the brutal massacre of hundreds or even thousands of peaceful pro-democracy demonstrators in Beijing's Tiananmen Square on 4 June 1989. Since then people have been frightened, they do not trust Beijing's promises any more, and have been waiting for political signs from Britain encouraging them to stay in Hong Kong. Most people feel that Britain is morally responsible for the fate of six million people being handed over to a harsh regime – approximately 90% of the population are expected to stay until the handover. Britain has offered the most distinguished fifty thousand and their families the right of abode in Britain, i.e. full British citizenship, and has thus created a new form of class system: what will be the criteria for selecting the privileged, not to mention those who have to remain behind? The British government, surprisingly enough supported by the Labour opposition, does not seem to intend to increase that number, although giving all the citizens of Hong Kong full British citizenship would not result in a mass exodus to Britain. Most young people would rather prefer to go to Taiwan, Singapore, Canada or the USA. Many, too, would still like to stay and, trusting in full British citizenship, would only leave if the situation after 1997 became totally unbearable. An opinion poll showed that only 6 per cent of people in Hong Kong would wish to live in Britain. But even a mass exodus to Britain would do Britain's economy more good than harm – says a nongovernmental scholarly study. The fact remains that the Nationality Act of 1981 took away the right of abode in Britain which the Hong Kong Chinese had had up to then (see p. 23). This change in the immigration laws is what the picture is referring to, too.

On his visit to Beijing in September 1991 Prime Minister Major warned Chinese officials that he intends to exert "unrelenting, unremitting pressure" for human rights in China. China's Prime Minister Li Peng countered by saying that for more than 100 years the human rights of the

Chinese people had been ignored by foreign powers. China's recent approval for the building of a new airport in Hong Kong – after months of sulking for not having been consulted – has brought on a new economic boom.

For further reading see Bibliography 1, 12, 20, 22 and 24.

## Didaktische Hinweise

Die Aufgabe 4 setzt voraus, daß den S klar ist, unter welchen Voraussetzungen sie in Hong Kong leben könnten: 1. als "Rot"chinese und ursprünglicher Flüchtling mit Verwandtschaft im z.B. kantonesischen Hinterland, der sich zufällig nach Hong Kong hat absetzen können; 2. als Chinese mit Verwandtschaft im Ausland; 3. als reicher oder durchschnittlicher gebürtiger Bewohner Hong Kongs; 4. als Chinese von Übersee; 5. als Chinese mit britischem Paß (Kategorie: British Dependent Territories); 6. als Brite

## Pre-reading activities

*1. What do you know about Hong Kong?*

*2. Did you see James Clavell's Hong Kong saga on TV? What impression did you get of the place?*

## Suggested answers

1. The offer is 50,000 British passports to select heads of households on a points system. This is meant to prevent panic, stop people emigrating and safeguard that important people will stay in Hong Kong during the time of transition. People are already emigrating very fast and now tens of thousands of people within one week have tried to apply for British dependent territory citizenship, a precondition for being given a full passport with right of abode in Britain.

2. Many members of the lower social classes see no chance to qualify for a British passport. There is a points system and certain jobs are excluded. So a social divide is being created causing anger and disillusionment.

Crime is rising fast, the use of fire-arms has increased. The police force cannot recruit enough staff. As nobody wants to be a police officer under a communist regime, many policemen are quitting.

The drain of nurses makes hospital services suffer while social workers are emigrating, too, as they have been told they probably won't get British passports. Yet they are needed as social problems are increasing.

Families are already planning to have their children educated abroad.

There is a tendency to rent property rather than buy it.

60,000 is the annual emigration rate, which is, however, not yet regarded as a mass exodus.

3. The atmosphere is generally one of fear: people are afraid they won't get a British passport; they are afraid they won't be able to leave when they want to; and they are afraid of what will happen under the communist regime.

The government in Beijing might:
– dispossess all private property owners, abolish free enterprise and oust all foreign businesses
– forbid direct and free elections
– imprison pro-democracy spokesmen
– react to political conflict with the brutality shown at the demonstration in Tiananmen Square on June 4, 1989
– make travelling abroad, let alone emigrating, impossible.

Citizens now voicing their criticism of Beijing's position might be registered on secret lists and persecuted after 1997.

The social and economic situation might become unbearable by the time of the changeover even for those who have no choice and must stay in Hong Kong.

4. As one of the Hong Kong-born "worthies" I would prepare for emigration and apply for a British passport, because under a Communist regime I can only lose. I could also possibly prepare for my survival in Hong Kong – should timely signals from Beijing encourage such behaviour – because I feel Chinese at heart, ethnically, and culturally.

As one of the Hong Kong-born members of the workforce I would try to emigrate – should financial means and immigration laws of a foreign country of my choice allow, and application for British citizenship be futile.

As an overseas Chinese I would go back home before the state of affairs worsens.

As a foreign entrepreneur I would leave rather today than tomorrow.

As an English official or civil servant I have nothing to fear, but it would be worthwhile reflecting on whether to leave Hong Kong or not etc.

5. Die Übersetzungsaufgabe ist äußerst anspruchsvoll. Bereits der 1. Satz führt Strategien und Grenzen des Übersetzens deutlich vor Augen: Wortkombinationen *(insurance policy)*, im Englischen (ungewöhnlich) kompakter Nominalstil *(major insurance policy on offer)* erfordern Flexibilität in deutscher Syntax und im Treffen einer durchgehend richtigen Stilebene. Wäre der Ausdruck "insurance policy" in diesem Kontext nicht allgemeiner politischer Sprachgebrauch, böte sich auch ein wertendes "Politik des Abwiegelns" an. Partizipialkonstruktionen *(snaking, queuing up, exacerbating)*, idiomatischer Gebrauch des Passivs *(are expected to be)*, nicht alltägliche Konjunktionen *(once)* und die Parenthese *(– which...full passport -)* erscheinen zusammen in einem einzigen langen ( dem Schluß-) Satz und erfordern große Konzentration.
(Translation)
Die wichtigste Rückversicherung/Versicherungspolice, die die Regierung anzubieten hat, sind die britischen Pässe für 50,000 Haushaltsvorstände. Sie (die Regierung) argumentiert, daß diese Maßnahme Panik verhindern wird, indem sie ausgesuchte, wichtige Leute bis zum Machtwechsel an die Kolonie bindet. Aber das sieht immer mehr wie ein riesiges und gefährliches Vabanquespiel aus. Man geht davon aus, daß die Auswanderungsquoten mit 60,000 dieses Jahr höher denn je sein werden. In Regierungskreisen ist man zuversichtlich, daß der Abzug/Exodus gestoppt werden wird, wenn einmal die britischen Pässe nächstes Jahr erhältlich sind. Aber der Anblick diese Woche von schätzungsweise 40.000 Leuten, die sich in riesigen Schlangen in den Straßen von Wanchai anstellen, um den Termin für den Antrag auf einen Paß der Kronkolonie nicht zu verpassen – sie müssen diesen Paß haben, um den Anspruch auf einen vollwertigen britischen Paß geltend zu machen – wirkte in der Kolonie nach und verstärkte die Ängste.

**Additional questions**

*1. Explain why the will-future is used in ll.63-65.*

*2. Explain the ing-forms: rising (l. 27), having (l. 38), judging (l. 71), devastating (l. 76).*

*3. Give synonyms for: escalate (l. 26), affected (l. 48), confused (l. 77), option (l. 81).*

*4. Explain the following words: divisive (l. 24), cohesion (l. 48), hostile (l. 80).*

**Post-reading activities**

*1. Discussion: Do you think it lies in Communist China's interest to bring Hong Kong's capitalist system to an end?*

*2. Martin Lee, a Hong Kong barrister who fights for more democracy and direct elections before the take-over, says of the British government: 'They kowtowed.' Do you agree?*

# 7. Immigrant autumn

## Background information

1. As some of his titles suggest (see SB, p. 22), Ferreira is preoccupied with the physically felt contrast of warmth and coldness in the two worlds he has known. Another aspect of his English experience is that of race. In an autobiographical essay, *The Lucky Londoner* (1963), he describes painfully how he was treated as a first-class citizen, thanks to his Portuguese parents and resulting almost-white skin, while his best friend, also Carribean, but black, was discriminated against. He relates, too, how he had a guilt or inferiority complex about his accent at the beginning: he was always ashamed when he heard the mere hint of a calypso lilt in a voice. He decided to "iron out" the West Indian lilt from his voice and try to pass for a (much more acceptable) South American. But after a while he became aware of the fact he would never succeed in gaining a new identity. He now considers himself extremely lucky that the colour of his skin spared him the humiliation and discrimination his fellow countrymen had to suffer in London.

2. For more information on immigration see *Abiturwissen Landeskunde* (Klettbuch 929509) pp. 40-48.

### Didaktische Hinweise

1. Der Herbst hat als Jahreszeit in unseren gemäßigten Breiten von jeher intensiv zum Schreiben gerade von Gedichten angeregt. Zu fächerverbindendem Unterrichten aus Sicht des Faches Deutsch sei auf die reizvolle, chronologische Anthologie aus der Serie Piper (Nr. 1200) verwiesen: Walter Flemmer, ed., *Dies ist ein Herbsttag, wie ich keinen sah* (München, 1990). Viele von diesen deutschen Gedichten können jedoch nur kontrastive Folie sein für das Besondere, das ein Mensch aus völlig anderem Kulturkreis und anderer Klimazone empfindet. In der Regel sind die deutschen Herbstgedichte "schön", wie auch z.B. Keats' *To Autumn*, oder meditativ, wie Shakespeares Sonett 73. Kälte und das Gefühl, einer "falschen" Rasse anzugehören, mit daraus resultierenden paranoiden Ängsten, bestimmen hingegen Ferreiras Gedicht atmosphärisch.

2. Beherrschendes Konstruktionsprinzip des Gedichtes ist, daß der Sprecher seine eigenen Gefühle und Sorgen auf die sinnliche Außenwelt, auf anonyme Menschen bzw. Naturphänomene projiziert, die ihrerseits zu aktiven Antagonisten und dem Sprecher bedrohlich werden. Das Verständnis dieser komplizierten Psychologie hängt sehr vom Nachdenken über die Bedeutung des "they" im Gedicht ab (cf. Aufgabe 4) sowie von einer genauen Analyse der "autumn leaves – old crones"-Metaphorik. Bei letzterem haben wir es mit einer Art *reverse simile* zu tun. Während der dichterische Prozeß üblicherweise darin besteht, das Reale, hier die Blätter, in einem Vergleich zu überhöhen – das Rascheln der Blätter wie die Stimmen alter, nur zu Blättern verzauberter, kleiner Weiber – geschieht nun das Umgekehrte: Die alten Weiber werden als physisch wahrnehmbare Realität eingeführt, die Blätter sind quasi nur ihre Tarnung. Der Dichter verstärkt mit dieser spiritistischen Umkehrung den Grad seiner subjektiven Bedrohung.

3. Wichtig ist, die S den Prozeßcharakter der Eingewöhnung in der Fremde beschreiben zu lassen: "...but never found me." (l. 39/40) ist zumindest teilweise geglückte Anpassung eines Einwanderers, der sich ab Strophe 3 gegen die Bedrohung zu wehren beginnt: "I kicked them savagely" (l. 21). (Es könnte aber auch heißen, daß er in seine Heimat zurückgekehrt ist.)

### Methodische Hinweise

Folgende Einstiegsmöglichkeiten sind denkbar:
1. Am ökonomischsten: *Pre-reading activities Nr. 1, 2,3;* dann Präsentation des Gedichtes durch den Lehrer; Klärung sprachlicher Schwierigkeiten; Aufgabenkatalog
2. Am motivierendsten: Präsentation des alten Schlagers "Island in the sun", von Harry Belafonte, dessen Eltern aus Jamaica stammten und der selber ein paar Jahre dort verbrachte. Fragen nach dem Lebensgefühl im Song und seinen Konstituenten; dann direkte Kontrastierung mit dem Gedicht wie bei Weg 1.
3. Am anspruchsvollsten und aufwendigsten: Nach Klärung der *Pre-reading activity Nr. 1* an oben genannten zwei englischen Gedichten (Keats und Shakespeare) Ausformungen zweier wichtiger Aspekte des Herbstes (Reife/Fülle – Vergänglichkeit/Tod), eventuell in zweisprachiger Fassung (z.B. dtv 9181, *English Poems – Englische Gedichte*), verifizieren; dann mit *activity Nr. 3* auf die Probleme des Einwanderers überleiten; dann Präsentation wie bei Weg 1.
4. Aufgabe 8 könnte als Thema eines Kurzreferats dienen oder für Gruppenarbeit benützt werden mit erst nachfolgender Diskussion.

### Pre-reading activities

*1. What do you usually associate with the word "autumn"?*

*2. How do you read the title?*
Autumn of an immigrant/autumn coming in like an immigrant
*What do you expect from the poem?*

*3. What do you think is hardest for immigrants to bear when they come to Europe? How does the climate add to their problems?*

### Suggested answers

1. *First stanza*: chill – sun – blood – Whitey – cold – sing-song – stone-cold – Blackie – island
*Second stanza*: accent – lilting – chilly – hauntings – whisper – laughter – calypso
*Third stanza*: savagely – withered...old crones – Autumn leaves – hooting

*Fourth stanza*: taunted – snowfall – chanting – freezing – stiffly dead – mutely buried – ice-cold – Omo-white – hearing
*Fifth stanza*: chortling – sadistic – scurried – scolded – but never found me.

2. The refrain is in the rhythm of a calypso and even quotes the well-known Belafonte song. This adds to the musical character of the poem as well as underlining the speaker's Caribbean identity. It reflects simultaneously both the speaker's anxieties (he feels haunted and not accepted – "run") and his homesickness, the repetition emphasizing both.

3. The "I" of the poem is a coloured person ("Blackie") as opposed to the "Whitey" in l. 5, has come from a warmer climate, obviously the Caribbean ("calypso", l. 18), and is now suffering from the coldness of a European autumn and the coldness of the city. He keeps hearing voices in his own lilting West Indian accent telling him to go home. He feels haunted all through the winter but by the autumn the following year (l. 37) he has learnt to cope with the new situation (or he has indeed gone home).

4. The first "they" in l. 12 seems to be anonymous persecutors: either English people who imitate and mock him, or other Caribbean immigrants to England who remind him of his origin when he accidentally hears them speak ("... wasn't anyone in sight." l. 14), or simply his alter ego because he cannot stand his own way of speaking and thinks it inappropriate in the new surrounding so that his own way of speaking turns to voices in his head. The second stanza leads over to a seeming solution to the riddle ("I knew", l. 16). "Them" (l. 21) and "they" (l. 25) refer to the autumn leaves ("rustling whispers", ll. 16–17) or old crones that haunt him with the refrain; so does "They" in l. 28. Parallel to the physical decay of the autumn leaves – they are covered by snow (and might then rot away) – the voices stop haunting him until "they" (l. 37), the leaves with their sounds, come back again the following year and
seem more frightening than ever ("sadistic glee", l. 38).

5. One year later the leaves, embodying the threat of the year before, have no might over their victim any more. They can no longer haunt or persecute the speaker any more. The "they" is in italics to emphasize a contrast with himself who is *not* there ("... and never found me"). He has either "run" back to his island in the sun, or the taunts don't worry him any more. He has got used to the situation and adapted. Therefore, the threatening refrain is missing.

6. The speaker is obviously a coloured immigrant from the West Indies. He suffers from the coldness of the climate, the coldness of the city, and the awareness that he does not belong to this place where he has just arrived. "Voices" with his own accent aim at discouraging him and making him return to his sunny, warm world in the Caribbean, or haunt him to remind him of his home and to make him homesick. He manages to get over this difficult phase, or he returns home (ambiguity).

7. The poetic diction/quality comprises:
– rather long sentences, which reflect the vividness and strength of the emotions
– irregular length of lines: also reflect the speaker's agitation
– numerous words relating to "sound" (cackling, sing-song, accent lilting, rustling whispers, cracked peals, tinny laughter, calypso singing, hooting, taunt, silence, chanting, mutely, hearing, chortling, scolded)
– numerous words relating to "temperature", especially "coldness" (chill, sun-heated, too cold, stone-cold, chilly, snowfall, freezing, stiffly dead, ice-cold, Omo-white)
– the reverse simile "...old crones, looking just like Autumn leaves"
– "Autumn" occurs three times and is always written with a capital emphasizing, perhaps, the importance of the season
– the refrain is repeated four times and each time marks the end of a stanza as in a calypso
– an element of the mysterious (voices, hauntings, whisper, witch-spell– small old crones)
– alliteration
– imaginative language/imagery (e.g. chilly hauntings, hooting shower etc.)

8. Traditionally, Commonwealth citizens were allowed to enter the UK freely. Between 1955 and 1960 almost 250,000 immigrants came to Britain to look for work at a time when the economy was expanding rapidly and more workers were needed, especially in the public services. The continuous influx from Asia and the

Caribbean led to a demand for limitations, which were introduced in 1962 with the first Immigration Act. Indians and Sikhs found jobs in the building industries as had many Irish workers before them; West Indians were often employed on London's buses and Underground. Pakistanis worked in the prosperous textile mills of Yorkshire and Lancashire. Greek Cypriots still run most of the Greek restaurants. The final wave of immigrants started in the 1970s with workers coming from countries such as the Philippines, Morocco and Latin America. They came to work for hospitals and hotels, filling positions in catering and domestic work.

1980 figures of the main immigrant group in Britain:
650,000 West Indians
460,000 Indians
200,000 African Asians
350,000 Pakistanis and Bangladeshis

Minor immigration groups are from Africa, the Mediterranean (Cyprus, Malta, Gibraltar) and Hong Kong. (See also *Abiturwissen Landeskunde,* pp. 40–48.)

In 1990 52,400 people were accepted for settlement in Britain. (See also text 6 and text 8.)

**Post-reading activities**

*1. Look at the picture on p. 22 and answer the question.*
Garbage disposal, waiters, cleaners, etc., usually the menial jobs Germans refuse to take

*2. Which immigrant groups do you have in your own country and why are they there?*

*3. Which problems do you think foreigners (political refugees, immigrants, guest workers, tourists, students) have in your country?*

## 8. Finding a niche (GK)

**Background information**

1. Timothy Mo is one of the many successful British writers of Commonwealth background. So far he has written four books. His first, *The Monkey King* (1978), won the Geoffrey Faber prize. The following three, *Sour Sweet* (1982), *An Insular Possession* (1986), and even his fourth and most recent novel, *The Redundancy of Courage* (1991), were all shortlisted for Britain's most prestigious literary award, the £_2020,000 Booker Prize. Timothy Mo came to England in 1960 and in an interview of April 1991 says of himself that it is wrong to see the offspring of mixed parents as being like 'café au lait', that he does not consider himself as a mixture of races but as someone who can switch 100 per cent from one to another. His parents have been divorced in the meantime. His father, a retired lawyer, now lives in Hong Kong again, while his mother has remarried and lives in England. He himself feels a desire at the moment to go back to the Far East again and marry an oriental rather than a western woman.

2. The novel has been made into a film, its screenplay being written by Ian McEwan, well-known novelist and short-story writer, the first and most famous protegé of Malcolm Bradbury's creative writing course at the University of East Anglia.

3. There is a tendency in London as well as in other big cities of the world where overseas Chinese from China, Taiwan and Hong Kong have tried to settle, to create "ghettos" as in San Francisco, Los Angeles and New York for example. The Chinese quarter in London is situated in Soho, in the heart of the West End, where tourists can still get meals that are good value. During the last few years architectural features have been added to the district to make it look more "Chinese": little pagodas giving shelter for customers in front of shops or restaurants, and equally stylized telephone booths with Chinese writing on them, street names in Chinese etc., imitating the famous San Francisco Chinatown in order to attract tourists. At the beginning of the Chinese New Year in February many Chinese from all over Britain come together in Soho, around Gerrard Street, to celebrate.

4. The "sign" mentioned in l. 9 refers to a board on which the restaurant's name is painted: Dah Ling Restaurant. It is named after Lily's home village near Hong Kong. It is a pun because its pronunciation suggests the English word "darling."

## Didaktisch-methodische Hinweise

Zu Aufgabe 8 können die S befragt werden, welcher Textteil sich am besten für eine Änderung des *point of view* eignet und warum.
Die Teile *(scenes)* zwei und drei des Romanauszuges eignen sich am besten für diese Übung, da sie viel Handlung beinhalten. Der "Handel" zwischen den beiden Männern ist die wirkungsvollste Szene. Die dramatischste Änderung wäre, wenn man einen Ich-Erzähler wählte, der seine Version des Abkommens erzählt, entweder aus der Sicht von Constantinides oder Chen. Man könnte auch die Erzählung in der 3. Person beibehalten, aber die Technik der *selective omniscience* (cf. SB, S.222) benutzen. Das würde heißen, daß man alles erzählt, was im Kopf von *einem* der beiden Geschäftsleute vorgeht. Man könnte auch die Erzählung in der 3. Person bei der zweiten Szene (Muis Umgang mit den Lastwagenfahrern) modifizieren, indem man die Technik der *omniscience* anwendet und von Muis Gedanken und Gefühlen erzählt. Die Wahl der Ich-Erzählung ist bei beiden Szenen die einfachere Aufgabe.
Will man gleichzeitig die Regeln der indirekten Rede üben, so könnte man den S die Benutzung direkter Rede untersagen.
Der Text könnte aus Gründen der Zeitersparnis als häusliche Lektüre aufgegeben werden zusammen mit der Aufgabe 1, die eine konzentrierte Lektüre sicherstellt.
Alternative: alternierendes Lautlesen und Stillesen im Unterricht, wobei L durch die entsprechende Auswahl der Leseabschnitte bereits die "Szenen" vorgeben und Überschriften finden lassen oder aber die Aufgabe 1 in Gänze nach der Lektüre von den Schülern in Partnerarbeit bearbeiten lassen kann.

## Pre-reading activities

*1. Look at the picture on p. 23 and answer the question in the caption.*
Italian, Greek, Chinese, Yugoslavian

*2. Why do you think restaurants run by foreigners and offering foreign food are so popular in Germany?*

*3. Which do you like and why?*

## Suggested answers

1. Introduction, ll. 1–18: The Chens' business gets off to a good start
– Scene 1, ll. 19–97: The deal with Mr Constantinides
– Scene 2, ll. 98–140: The new co-operation with the garage
– The menu, ll. 141–177: The food the Chens sell

2. The Chens were lucky. Although drawing prospective customers' attention to their takeaway had been attempted only half-heartedly, they soon had a sound base for their business: the garage beside their takeaway provided customers from the beginning; word of mouth recommendation did the rest.

3. The garage owner, Mr Constantinides, complained about the fact that lorry drivers who were Chen's customers blocked his forecourt with their lorries while parking there. Mr Constantinides suggested a deal, a compromise: in order to attract more customers to both businesses he would encourage his customers to order meals from Chen, who, in turn, would have to pay a five per cent commission to Constantinides.

4. Meals at any hour of the day or night without customers having to leave their lorry or car; quick service; cheap, wholesome, nutritious food; "Chinese" food of the type the British are now used to. Mui or Lily take the order from Mr Constantinides; Chen cooks the simplified version of Chinese cuisine the customers want; and Mui and Lily carry the food to the garage in containers. Chen allows them to keep their tips, treating them as colleagues for the first time.

5. Greek or Greek Cypriot (Mr Constantinides, the garage-owner) and West Indian (customers at the garage).
To the reader it is clear from the name that Mr Constantinides belongs to another ethnic group, but to the new Chinese immigrants he is a "flesh and blood Englishman" (l. 57). As a former, now successful, immigrant he reacts in the familiar way of looking down on newer, poorer immigrants and those of other ethnic groups (cf. cartoon on p. 225, SB). He obviously dislikes the manners and style of the young West Indians who hang around his garage and has a more favourable image of the Chinese (Chen, after all,

has just agreed to something that is mainly to Mr Constantinides' advantage).

6. The role of women in this excerpt:
a) *traditional*
– official deals like that between Chen and Mr Constantinides are men's business; Mui and Lily leave the house and go into the garden (ll. 71–73)
– in order to calm down Mr Constantinides, Chen plays down Mui's possibly irritating titter by treating her as a "stupid girl" (l. 66).
– Mui serves the tea while Chen is talking business (ll. 71–72)
– Chen cooks while Mui and Lily serve
b) *modern*
– Mui and Lily seem to be the driving force behind all business activities (suggest advertising, insist on a sign under their bedroom window, ll. 7–10; save and are careful with money, l. 164)
– Mui tries to adapt quickly to English customs (answering the telephone, ll. 70–73)
– Mui is very clever at dealing with the lorry drivers ("Mui isn't as stupid as she looks, Lily used to think.", ll. 126–127), playing on their pity to get good tips
– Mui and Lily are given "the status of colleagues" (ll. 138–139) and allowed to keep their own tips as Chen realizes they are now working as a team, as equals

7. – "...lest a splinter should lodge in an English behind." ll. 32–33; "(Careful, Mr Big Man)", l. 69 -70: humourous, because showing exaggerated respect for the English.
– "a flesh and blood Englishman" etc. (irony of situation)
– Lily's and Mui's ways of answering the telephone, ll. 100–107: humourous due to the contrast between serious endeavour and resulting inefficiency, causes sympathy for "the girls" in the reader.
– Mui's way with the drivers, ll. 110–131: situational irony, because she manages to profit from her calculated pitiable outward appearance without the drivers knowing about this "strategy".
– "drab English money", l. 131: satire, criticizes the uninteresting design of English banknotes.
– "it has no resemblance at all to the Chinese cuisine" (satire)

– "English tastebuds must be as degraded as their care of their parents;", ll. 148–149: a satirical view of English cooking and attitudes to food as well as of something more important, although treated in an aside: the different social structure in England where family ties do not count as much as in China and the extended family has almost disappeared, which means that parents are often put into homes in their old age.
– ll. 155–159: humorous, alluding to Lily's sexual appetite, not his own.
– "whatever they were" (ll. 161–162), satirical again, the food the British want.
– "food coffins", l.166: satire, because if the food is so un-Chinese and dull, then "coffins" are the right containers for it.
– "The only authentic dish they served was rice...", ll. 167–168: verbal irony, only the very basic, simplest part of a Chinese meal has anything to do with China.

8. It is mainly the unlimited point of view of an omniscient, third-person narrator (cf. SB, p. 222): e.g. in contrast to Chen the narrator knows about Mr Constantinides' secret, selfish motives in finding a "compromise" that is identical with his initial plan. At the same time he is able to look into Chen's mind and explain why he is so polite and receptive and that his defensive approach is also calculated. He also lets us know what Lily thinks about Mui's cleverness. The point of view is selective in relating Mui's actions. As a *persona* the narrator expresses his own thoughts about some English habits or customs (food and family ties) that go beyond the text. The choice of perspective here, then, gives the writer more possibilities than, for example, a perspective limited to a first-person view of the whole affair.
scene 1, ll. 19–97: the deal
– 1. first-person narrator
a. Mr Constantinides relates the deal
b. Chen relates the deal
– 2. third-person narrator, but *selective omniscience*, applied only to
a. Mr Constantinides or
b. Chen
scene 2, ll. 98–140: the new arrangement with the garage
– 1. first-person narrator: Mui relates her dealings with the lorry drivers
– 2. third-person narrator, but *omniscience* about Mui's thoughts and feelings

### Additional questions

1. *Explain the use of "would" in ll. 110, 112, 113, 118.*
Regular activity in the past

2. *Translate into English:*
a. *Chen berichtete seiner Frau, daß Mr Constantinides Kunden zu ihnen schicken würde, wenn er, Chen, nur bereit wäre, ihm fünf Prozent Provision zu zahlen.*
Chen told his wife that Mr Constantinides would send them customers if only he, Chen, was/were prepared to give him five per cent commission.
b. *Mui wußte, daß Chen sie nur als "dummes Mädchen" abqualifiziert hatte, um Mr Constantinides nicht noch weiter zu verärgern.*
Mui knew that Chen had dismissed her as a "stupid girl" only in order not to/so as not to further annoy/irritate Mr Constantinides.
c. *Mr Constantinides hatte nicht darüber nachgedacht, was er tun würde/getan hätte, wenn Chen sein Angebot ablehnte/abgelehnt hätte.*
Mr Constantinides had not thought about what he would do/would have done if Chen rejected/had rejected his offer – should Chen reject/have rejected his offer.
d. *Chen erklärte, es sei nicht seine Schuld, wenn die Lastwagen die Zufahrt zur Tankstelle blockierten.*
Chen declared/explained it was not his fault if the lorries blocked the forecourt of the garage.

3. *How do you think the novel will continue? Happy ending? sad ending? success? setbacks? change in relationships?*
The novel is available in paperback should the teacher wish to inform the students of the actual ending.

### Post-reading activities

1. *Discuss the role of women among the ethnic minorities in your own country and compare it to that in your own culture, past and present.*

2. *If you had to start from scratch (like the Chens) as an immigrant in an Asian country, what would you do? Write a short essay.*
Work as a waiter? start a sausage business? teach? etc.

## 9. A vision of Europe

### Background information

In an *Observer* series in the 1960s the Zurich speech is called "one of the most influential speeches of his career." Churchill's "dream" of something like a United States of Europe is still a challenge for the European nations, which have been struggling towards this goal since World War II. Churchill's conciliatory attitude towards Germany probably did not represent the feelings of the majority of his fellow countrymen in the late 1940s after the ravages of war, and his suggestion for a partnership between France and Germany can truly be called visionary.

### Pre-reading activities

1. *Look at the World War II picture on p. 26 and comment on it.*
Coventry, Glasgow and, of course, London

2. *How would you have expected the former enemies to have behaved towards Germany after World War II? How did they in fact react?*

### Didaktisch-methodische Hinweise

Es wird in der Diskussion mit den S darauf ankommen, drei Aspekte dieser Rede herauszuschälen: 1. Diese (gekürzte) Rede besticht durch ihre Humanität und staatsmännische Weitsicht. 2. Churchills Vision ist faszinierend, da sie doch in Teilen schon verwirklicht wurde und als Herausforderung immer noch besteht, seit dem Verschwinden des "Iron Curtain" in neuer Nuancierung. 3. Die historische Ferne der Vision ist gleichwohl nicht zu übersehen: Großbritannien hat sich nicht als selbständige, von Europa gelöste Weltmacht behaupten können. Diese historische Rede sollte wegen ihrer Authentizität und ihrer Rhetorik wegen unbedingt und als Ganzes von der Cassette präsentiert werden. Erste Fragen sollten ausschließlich dem rhetorischen Gesamteindruck auf die Schüler gelten. Es könnte dann sofort der Teil der Aufgabe 6 zur genaueren Verifikation der rhetorischen Wirkung erarbeitet werden, der die Definition *rhetoric* betrifft; *register* kann erst nach der Textbehandlung treffend beschrieben werden. Eine schrittweise Erarbeitung der Rede anhand der Aufgaben 1 bis 5 schließt sich dann an.

Bei Erarbeitung des Textes ohne akustische Präsentation empfiehlt sich die abschnittsweise Texterarbeitung, in der Aufgabenreihenfolge 1 ff. Die vorgeschlagene Diskussion über drei Zitate aus englischen Zeitungen wäre aus erzieherischer Sicht besonders wichtig: Die Zitate problematisieren den Umgang mit Klischees wie "die Engländer, Franzosen, Deutschen" und zeigen ansatzweise die Meinungsvielfalt zum Thema "Europa" auf.

**Suggested answers**

1. While some smaller states have already recovered from the war, the greater part of Europe lies in ruins with its population suffering starvation, confusion and despair. Fear of the future is dominant. This is all the result of Germanic aggression in the Second World War, but fortunately the U.S. has already signalled its willingness to provide help and guidance (ll. 20–41).

2. Europe could be as happy and free as Switzerland if one re-created the European Family by building a kind of United States of Europe which would provide a structure under which Europeans could live in peace, safety and freedom (ll. 42–60). The first step in this process must be a partnership between France and Germany, in Churchill's opinion, and the former states of Germany united in a federal system (ll. 110–125).

3. Germany caused two world wars and spread havoc in Europe in order to win a leading position in the world. The last war was especially barbaric and without parallel since the invasion of the Mongols in the fourteenth century. Therefore Germany ought not to be rearmed and be able to wage another war. But retribution should not be endless, past crimes should now be forgotten, and one should look to the future. All in all Churchill's attitude towards Germany is surprisingly conciliatory considering the date of his speech. The use of "Teutonic" and "Germanic" is to be noted (ll. 13–19; ll. 30–34; ll. 85–108; ll. 113–116).

4. Churchill sees no conflict between a "United States of Europe" and the United Nations. While the British have their Commonwealth of Nations, which is seen to strengthen the UN rather than weaken it, a newly-formed European group of nations, too, could create a sense of common citizenship and extended patriotism and work with other groupings for a better future (ll. 64–84).

5. Churchill's vision has not yet been fulfilled but still remains a challenge. Although Europe has grown together, especially since 1957, when different European countries formed the EC (European Community), and although there will be one single internal European Market by the end of 1992, we are still far from anything that could be called a United States of Europe. (See box p. 31.) Some countries, especially Great Britain and to a lesser degree France, find the thought of having to give up their national sovereignty unbearable, while the discussion of a common currency has escalated in several countries since the signing of the Treaty of Maastricht (1992). The whole idea of a United States of Europe has changed in character and scale since the former USSR has disintegrated and satellite states gained independence. The idea of political union has thus become much more complex. Astonishingly enough, Churchill's vision of an axis between France and Germany has come true.

What Churchill could not envisage is the fact that Great Britain was not able to maintain its position as a world power, that today it is no longer outside Europe but part of the European Community, and that the Commonwealth has lost almost all its political importance. The triangle: US – Britain and the Commonwealth – Europe has changed into a partnership US – Europe, in spite of the "special relationship" between the US and Great Britain so fondly invoked by the British and the special links between GB and the Commonwealth countries.

6. As regards the rhetorical structure of the speech it should be noted that only a very short first sentence has been left out of the original in the first paragraph. It becomes immediately clear that the first half of the first paragraph is what in the Latin technical term is called *captatio benevolentiae*, i.e making the audience well-disposed to what the speaker is going to say. This is the reason for a great deal of hyperbole (noble continent, fairest, most cultivated, enjoying..., great parent races of the world, fountain of faith, origin of most..., no limit to the happiness...)

*Alliteration:* e.g. fountain of...faith, ll. 5–6
- some of the smaller States, l. 21
- tyranny or terror, l. 27
- victors ... voices, l. 28
- sullen silence, l. 29
- "f"- and "v"-sounds in ll. 104–108
- strength of a single state less..., l. 119
- contribution to the common cause, ll. 121–22
- four freedoms, ll. 129–30

*Anaphora:* e.g. that is all, ll. 30, 31; there must, l. 97; We..., l. 99–101, 142, 143; if this is, ll. 132–133

*Direct address:* gentlemen, l. 41; we all, l. 85; we, l. 99, 100, 101; you, l. 110, l. 137

*Allusions:* e.g. babel of voices, l. 28; Dark Ages, l. 39; invasion of the Mongols, ll. 90–91; President Truman, l. 62; Mr Gladstone, l. 98; four freedoms...Mr Roosevelt, ll. 130–31; Atlantic Charter, l. 132.

*Antithesis:* e.g. yet, l. 13, leads over to the description of Europe's present state;
- yet, l. 42, announces the remedy for the plight.
- on the contrary..., l. 67, a United States of Europe will not conflict with a world organization;
- on the contrary..., ll. 72–73, the Commonwealth of Nations supports the UN;
- but, l. 95, retribution is understandable only to a certain limit.

*Rhetorical questions:* e.g. ll. 20–21, ll. 48–49, ll. 74–81

*Inversion:* In this way only will/can...", l. 54, ll. 112–13

*Parallelism:* without...Germany, ll. 115–16

*Register:* the vocabulary is formal and flowery. There are very long complicated sentences, e.g. ll. 42-49, and also short ones, e. g. ll. 138–144. Thus monotony is avoided, which is very important to keep the audience's attention. The tone is very committed and full of pathos: this is a speech intended to rouse emotions and enthusiasm. These were the days of the radio when the sound of the language and a wide scope of vocabulary could impress more than in the days of the visual image and "soundbites".

7. Lexikalisch schwierig: all the while, spontaneous, adopted, as if by a miracle, sovereign remedy, under...dwell in peace, toilers, process, to do right...wrong, gain as their reward blessing instead of cursing

Syntaktisch schwierig: der ganze erste "Bandwurmsatz", der am besten geteilt wird. (Translation)
Es gibt jedoch seit langem ein Heilmittel, das – würde es nur allgemein und spontan von einer großen Mehrheit der Menschen in vielen Ländern angewendet – wie durch ein Wunder die gesamte politische Landschaft verwandeln würde. Und in nur wenigen Jahren würde dieses Heilmittel ganz Europa, oder wenigstens den größeren Teil davon, so frei und glücklich machen, wie die Schweiz es heute ist. Was ist nur dieses Allheilmittel? Es besteht darin, die europäische Familie wieder neu zu schaffen, oder so viel von ihr wie wir können, und sie mit einer Struktur zu versehen, innerhalb derer sie in Frieden, in Sicherheit und in Freiheit leben kann. Wir müssen eine Art von "Vereinigten Staaten von Europa" aufbauen. Nur so werden Hunderte von Millionen hart arbeitender Menschen in der Lage sein, wieder die einfachen Freuden und Hoffnungen zu erlangen, die das Leben lebenswert machen. Das Vorgehen ist einfach. Alles was nötig ist, ist der feste Wille von Hundertmillionen Männern und Frauen, das Richtige statt das Falsche zu tun und als Lohn dafür Segen statt Fluch zu ernten.

**Additional questions**

*1. You are to deal with the following words within the given context.*
*a) Explain; you may change the sentence structure.*
- *noble, l. 1*
- *prosperity, l. 11*
- *care-worn, l. 24*
- *synthesis, l. 68*
- *Western Hemisphere, l. 70–71*
- *turn our backs upon, l. 99–100*

*b) Find suitable substitutes; keep to the sentence structure.*
- *realised, l. 36*
- *destinies, l. 81*
- *accomplished, l. 82*
- *infinite, l. 105*
- *recover, l. 113*
- *embodied, l. 132*

*c) Find antonyms (which occur in the text).*
- *modern (ancient, l. 8)*
- *decline (prosperity, l. 11)*
- *to loathe (enjoy, l. 13)*

– *disappearance (approach, ll. 26–27)*
– *to exclude (to involve, l. 37)*
– *hatred (sympathy, l. 63)*

2. What is the difference between rhetorical language like Churchill's and everyday prose?

**Post-reading activities**

1. Discuss the following three quotations from national papers:
a) *"Many, perhaps most, Britons would rather be stranded on a desert island with a German than with a Frenchman. Despite enmity in the two world wars, the British and Germans believe they have certain values in common, like dependability, straightforwardness, pragmatism and a businesslike approach to life."*
*(from a leader in* The Independent, *31 March 1990)*

b) *"The Germans today are certainly more economically nationalistic than ever. They are convinced that such is the productive power of German industry that a new Eurostate would have a German body."*
*(from a column by Peregrine Worsthorne in* The Sunday Telegraph, *November 25, 1990)*

c) *"Our interests suggest that our natural partner and ally in the new European world will more and more be France."*
*(from a leader in* The Independent, *1 April, 1990)*

2. How do you see the future of Europe? Which problems have still to be dealt with before political or monetary union is achieved? Write a short essay.

3. Report/paper/talk: Sir Winston Churchill: his life and political career.
See Bibliography 6.

# 10. 1973: Britain sleepwalks into Europe (GK)

**Background information**

1. The beginnings of the European Community date from the proposal of Robert Schuman, the French Foreign Minister, that France and Germany should pool their coal and steel industries under an independent, supranational high authority, in a Community open to the membership of any other European wishing to join. (See table p. 31, SB.)
2. The European Community originated in three different Communities: the Coal and Steel Community; the European Economic Community (EEC), and Euratom. Up to July 1967, each Community had its own executive body. They were merged into one in 1967. Since then the name EC has been used officially, rather than the Common Market.
3. The Maastricht EC summit in December 1991, which was seen as a "giant stride toward the creation of authentic political union" (Newsweek), brought, among others, the following results that are of special interest to Britain and that are laid down in the Treaty of Maastricht:
– a European Central Bank will be established

– a single currency will be adopted, which will eventually replace the national currencies of those members prepared to accept it
– in the case of monetary union Britain is allowed an opt-out clause
– the Community will bring social policy, including labour laws (workers' rights), into closer harmony throughout the EC except in Britain
– there will be no federal state, but "an ever closer union among the peoples of Europe" (preamble to the treaty)

**Photograph and cartoons**

1. The woman in the historical photograph on p. 29, SB, who incidentally wore a Union Jack as an apron in the full picture, is holding a placard with the text: Queen's Speech Xmas Day: "It will *never* be the same without our Commonwealth." *Too true.* Would we be here today without their help? *No.* That is *one* of the reasons why *patriots do not* want to join *Europe.*
At the moment, the British do not want to give up the sovereignty of their Parliament in favour of political union in a federal system where a European Parliament would be sovereign. The

present Conservative government is also against certain elements in the European social charter which comes into force in 1993. Many British people would prefer the proposed Central Bank to be in Britain as it has played such a great role as a banking centre for much longer than Germany, for example. There are also still some anti-German feelings from the two world wars, but also anti-French ones resulting from a historical rivalry. Being an island does make people feel separate and different (cf. Japan).

2. The cartoon on p. 30, SB, alludes to Britain's imperial past (the tiger-skin rug), the wealth resulting from it (huge fireplace, Tudor hall style) and a feeling for tradition (coat-of-arms above a very English fireplace).

3. The register of *The Sun* is vulgar slang (go to hell .../Du kannst mich mal ...) and shows the level of the newspaper and the type of people who read it. Many ordinary people resent having Europe deciding things for them (e. g. types of apples or potatoes allowed) and are conservative about hanging on to British things and British ways of doing things, but a British supermarket today is full of European foods as are pubs full of European drinks. The cartoon is a satire on this contradiction. There is a fashion for German beer or for beer with a Germanic-sounding name.

## Didaktisch-methodische Hinweise

Es empfiehlt sich eine (stille) Lektüre in vier Abschnitten: ll. 1–22, ll. 23–44, ll. 45–58, ll. 59–82

## Pre-reading activities

*1. What do you know about Britain's entry into Europe?*
De Gaulle, Edward Heath, referendum etc./see table p. 31, SB

*2. What have you heard or read about Britain's present attitude to Europe?*
Thatcher/Major/Maastricht etc.

*3. Look at the picture on p. 29, SB, and answer the question in the caption.*

## Suggested answers

1. *Headings:*
– To celebrate or not to celebrate?/Mixed feelings
– Half the British still "anti"
– Europeanization well on the way
– Changes in European power structure

*Argumentative structure:*
Mixed feelings about entry – unwillingness of many "to turn European" – in fact European influence in Britain well-advanced – British entry will change balance of power in Europe

2. and 3. The European Economic Community was established without Britain because in the late 40s and 50s the latter was still concerned with colonial questions. Only Britain's Liberal Party favoured Britain's entry when the Treaties of Rome were signed in 1957. In the 1960s both major parties in Britain wanted Britain to join the EEC. A fierce debate between the people of Britain and its politicians began over the advantages and disadvantages of joining. Twice, however, Britain's entry was blocked by President de Gaulle of France because of Britain's insularity and its links with so many other countries in the world, as well as because of its special relationship with the US. Britain's initial motives for entry were economic. Soon after its accession Britain found fault with Brussels' Common Agricultural Policy (CAP). With the advent of a Labour Government in the UK in 1974, there followed a period of renegotiation of the terms of entry, culminating in a referendum in 1975 about whether or not Britain should remain a member of the EC. The result of the referendum showed two to one in favour of staying in. Even so, there remain important differences between Britain and its EC partners. The main issues are sovereignty, the question of political union (shall there be a federal state or just cooperation between independent national states?) and monetary union (with the ecu as common currency).

Psychologically the British were still world-oriented but now had to adapt to the European dimension in all fields of life and policy-making. They also wanted to introduce into the EC political principles they thought worth preserving (e. g. the British parliamentary system, which is based on confrontation rather than consensus; free trade etc.)

*From Empire to Europe*

4. The agricultural policy has been kept better under control, fewer subsidies; Britain has introduced more EC legislation than other member countries with a better EC image; freer trade; freer flow of capital. Without Britain CAP would still be chaotic; more trade restrictions, perhaps no Channel tunnel; perhaps more intensive attempts to keep the Commonwealth together and strengthen its political weight. Without the EC Britain might have become isolated on the edge of Europe, away from the centre stage, merely an ex-great power.

5. Germany is interested in European union, a federal body. It wants to give the European Parliament in Strasbourg a greater say. A European currency must be strong and is to be controlled by an independent Central Bank, comparable to the Bundesbank in Frankfurt. Germany would like to have the Central Bank in Frankfurt as the German mark is the strongest European currency.

### Additional questions

1. a) *Explain the use of "will" in ll. 5, 39, 44.*
An event in the future that cannot be influenced by the persons involved, but will inevitably take place.

b) *Explain the use of the infinitive: "to be attended", l. 14.*
Attributiver Gebrauch des passiven Infinitivs anstelle eines *defining relative clause*: "that will be attended".

c) *Explain the use of the ing-forms: "ringing out", l. 1 (gerund); "prompting", l. 20 (pres. part.); "sleepwalking", l. 22 (pres. progr.); "menacing", l. 31 (pres. part. as adj.); "trading", l. 35 (pres. part. as adj.); "becoming", ll. 45-46 (pres. progr.); "giving", l. 51 (pres. progr.); "eating", l. 56 (gerund).*

d) *Replace by an alternative construction: "prompting", l. 20; "given", l. 48.*
"which prompted"; "that are given"

### Post-reading activities

1. *Britain has got the reputation of being the chief complainer in the EC. Should it leave the EC if it is so dissatisfied with being a member of it?*

2. *What does Europe mean to you personally? Do you feel European or German? What role do you think Germany should play in the EC?*
Group work with concluding discussion

# 11. Autobahnmotorwayautoroute (GK)

### Background information

It is important to note the date of publication of this poem to place it in a historical text (1971). Britain was not then a member of the EC and this satirical, surrealistic text embodies much of the contemporary criticism expressed especially by the Left: i.e. that the EC is only about markets and material goods, that no real unification is possible and that the aims of "Europeanization" are totally unclear. The object chosen in the poem to epitomize this criticism is the car, the consumer good par excellence.

It is interesting to see how topical the poem has remained, as the traffic problems and "unification" or standardization of consumer commodities have proceeded apace. Mitchell's vision of a never-ending line of cars does not seem very unrealistic now when one sees the traffic jams on motorways at every holiday season, summer and winter.

### Didaktischer Hinweis

Die Diskussion über die Erklärung der Anspielungen und Assoziationen bei den Wortschöpfungen (z.B. Zeile 17) sollte den S demonstrieren, daß es selten eine eindeutige Gedichtinterpretation gibt, da sehr viel von dem Sprachschatz und der Spracherfahrung der Leser/-innen abhängt, sowie von ihrer Assoziationsfähigkeit.

### Pre-reading activity

*What was Britain's relationship to the EC when this poem was published?* (See table p. 31, SB.)

### Suggested answers

1. The title makes it clear, in three European languages, that there is an "uninterrupted" flow

of traffic on Europe's main roads: three words for the road one can travel fastest on are made into one. This prepares the reader for something to do with traffic, cars, Europe and inseparable connections.

2. The perspective chosen is that of a bird's eye, which makes it possible to look at Europe as if it were a "map" (l. 1). The length of the lines is irregular, suggesting changing speed; similarly the length of the stanzas suggests the process of slowing down, culminating also semantically in l. 9, (the first three stanzas with 5, 3 and 1 lines each), speeding up (the fourth and fifth stanzas with 6 and 7 lines each) and slowing down again (one final 3-line stanza). Within the stanzas long sentences suggest movement.

The idea of the process of "welding together" (unification, standardization) is introduced in the title; to the same effect place names ("Londonoslowestberlin Athensromemadridparis", ll. 3 – 4), and makes of cars ("Citroenjaguarbugattivolkswagenporschedaf", l. 15), are drawn together. All the capitals are unified in one conglomerated name, which is no longer individual, as are all cars in one "make", not separate or national like Citroën (French) or Daf (Dutch). The unexpected linkings or juxtapositions in l. 17 and ll. 21–22 are in a different, more imaginative category. All the objects are consumer goods and/or status symbols (like the car, the Golden Calf of our society), and the interpretation of these newly coined words depends on the reader's associations. For example l. 17 hints at colour TVs and pianos, frozen goods (freezers), magazines, hi-fi sets, dogs or hot dogs or His Master's Voice records' mascot dog, whereas ll. 22–23 have frightening associations with lampshades made of human skin in Nazi concentration camps, genetic engineering ("instant children") and destructive technology ("exploding clocks"). There are, therefore, elements of surprise, amusement and shock in the reader's reaction to these word formations. The effect of ll. 12–13 is quite clearly to suggest a never-ending stream of traffic in a circular movement, using the double meaning of "roundabout" (a merry-go-round at the fun fair or a circular island in the road to slow down traffic). Finally the repetitive use of the negation "no" in ll. 24–25, with punctuation missing, rounds off the impression of a never-ending circular ("circle", l.23) movement. The car has become a circle, like the wedding ring, without driver or direction.

3. The increasing numbers of cars throughout Europe has tied all the countries closer together blurring cultural distinctions. Europe is, in a way, united, but it is a type of unification that is rejected or at least criticised by the poet. The occupants and their cars are not seen as individuals but as anonymous parts of traffic moving all over Europe in an endless circle from which there is no escape. Cars (and consumer goods) have taken over people's lives in Europe.

4. – gleaming map, l. 1: in fact it is the cars that gleam, so now the map does too
– wedding ring: a symbol taken from the sphere of human relationships for union, linking, unification (usually a positive symbol); symbolizes visually the circular movement of the traffic/cars
– ring, circle, circular movement (cf. ll. 2, 3, 5, 8, 9, 12, 13, 23): regular monotony
– traffic is seen as a car ("Great European Limousine, Famous Goldenwhite Circular Car"), written with capital letters hinting at the position of an idol, a Golden Calf ("Goldenwhite")
– car as a symbol of European unity (part for the whole) etc.

**Post-reading activities**

*1. Is the car a blessing or a curse?*
Group work/debate/discussion

*2. Try to write a similar poem about another Euro-product or some other aspect of Europeanization/European unification.*

# Test: The future for Britain

At the start of the new millennium [...] an 80 m-strong united Germany will be the dominant power in Europe, set to grow even more dominant as the people of East Germany rapidly raise their living standards to the level of those in West Germany; and German capital, skills and resources are deployed to rebuild the economies of Eastern Europe as they emerge from marxism to market economies. Even just joining the two Germanys together creates a country twice as big economically as the next biggest European power. And by winning the lion's share of the business to be won from dragging its eastern neighbours into the modern world, Germany will enjoy an economic supremacy over Eastern Europe that Hitler aimed to secure through invasion and occupation.

What will be Britain's role in a world dominated by the three power blocs of America, Japan and Germany? The options are hard to discern, and those that can be made out are not particularly palatable for they all involve a second-class status. In a Europe that is being increasingly pulled east by a dominant and eastward-looking Germany, Britain could easily become peripheral to the main event. That is all the more likely given that Britain will no longer be able to count on its special relationship with the United States to give it European clout. For, by the end of the 1990s, we are likely to have seen the withdrawal of America from Europe as the price Moscow will demand for sanctioning the reunification of Germany. So our major ally will no longer be an active force in shaping Europe's future.

Playing second, or third, fiddle to the Germans will not come easily to Britain. Even if the country were to play a less grudging and more wholehearted role in European affairs than the Thatcher government has been prepared to encourage, it might give Britain more influence in shaping the new Europe, but it would essentially be no more than the negative influence of trying to keep a booming and united Germany within the constraints of the European Community. The rest of the EC, led by France, is already attempting to do that, and it is not clear whether adding Britain's voice would make much difference. In any case, if the EC tries to shackle the Fourth Reich too tightly, it will simply break free and face even more resolutely eastwards.

It would be a mistake, however, for Britain to leave the rebuilding of Eastern Europe entirely to the Germans. The Thatcher government has yet to capitalise on the fact that its prime minister is the inspiration for many of those who are seeking to build market economies in Eastern Europe. And, as the oldest major democracy in Europe, the British parliamentary system is also a source of inspiration for people shaking off totalitarian rule (which is why delegations from Eastern Europe are already arriving in London to study the British system). So Britain has plenty to offer Eastern Europe, and it has the prestige to play a bigger role than it thinks in the rebuilding. But it is hard to see how it can match the Germans – unless, that is, it grows into ever closer alliance with France.

A new Anglo-French *entente cordiale* has a lot going for it. With a combined might of 115 m people it would be potentially more powerful than a united Germany. Both Britain and France are nuclear powers and, as the American nuclear umbrella over Western Europe is folded up in the 1990s, it will make sense for Britain and France to combine their nuclear defences, perhaps even to offer Europe the protection of an Anglo-French nuclear shield. And, of course, the two countries are going to be physically linked for the first time ever in the early 1990s by the Channel tunnel. Perhaps that would be a good time to revive Winston Churchill's wartime scheme for joint Anglo-French citizenship. [...]

If Britain is not content with a diminished role in the world, but will not consider throwing its lot in with France, then what? All that would be left is unsplendid isolation or an application to become the 51st state of the United States of America and Britain. An unlikely event, perhaps, but the reshaping of the world in the 1990s is going to present Britain with some pretty unpleasant, and unusual choices.

From *The Sunday Times*, 19 November 1989.

**Annotations**

7 **to deploy**   to use effectively
22 **palatable**   pleasant or acceptable to the mind
29 **clout**   power or influence
32 **to sanction**   to authorize or approve

44 **constraint** limit, restriction
48 **to shackle** Fesseln anlegen
54 **to capitalise on s.th.** to use s.th. to one's own advantage

Das folgende Aufgabenangebot ist als Rahmen gedacht, aus dem sich L eine dem Niveau seines Kurses und seinem Zeitrahmen entsprechende Klausur "maßschneidern" kann. Auch die Gewichtung sollte den Gepflogenheiten der einzelnen Bundesländer entsprechend individuell erfolgen.

## I. Language

1. *Vocabulary* (ohne – einsprachiges – Wörterbuch zu bearbeiten)
In the following you are to deal with the words/expressions in italics within the given context.
a) 14-15: "...Germany will *enjoy...supremacy*..."
Explain; you may change the sentence structure.
b) 25-26: "Britain could easily *become peripheral* to the main event."
Explain; you may change the sentence structure.
c) 26-27: "That is all the more likely *given* that Britain will..."
Find a suitable substitute; keep to the sentence structure.
d) 37-38: "...a...more *wholehearted* role..."
Find a suitable substitute; keep to the sentence structure.
e) 52-53: "...to leave the rebuilding of Eastern Europe *entirely* to the Germans."
Find a suitable substitute; keep to the sentence structure.
f) 65-66: "...how it can *match* the Germans..."
Explain; you may change the sentence structure.
g) 68-69: " A new Anglo-French entente cordiale *has a lot going for it.*"
Explain; you may change the sentence structure.
h) 70: "...it would be *potentially* more powerful..."
Find a suitable substitute; keep to the sentence structure.
i) 83: "If Britain is not content with a *diminished* role ..."
Explain; you may change the sentence structure.
j) Find the corresponding adjective:
6: skill
20: option
42: influence
59: inspiration
64: prestige
75: defence
k) Find the corresponding abstract nouns (not the -ing-forms):
8: emerge
9: join
16: secure
28: special
40: encourage
81: revive

2. *Grammar and style* (ohne – einsprachiges – Wörterbuch zu bearbeiten)
a) 12-13: "And by winning the *lion's share* of the business..."
Explain the stylistic device and its function within the given context.
b) 13: "...the business *to be won* from dragging..."
Replace the infinitive construction by a subordinate clause.
c) 23-24: "...is *being* increasingly pulled..."
35: "*Playing* second, or third, fiddle..."
42-43: "influence of *trying* to keep a *booming* and united Germany..."
Explain the -ing-forms.
d) 36-38: "Even if the country *were* to play a less grudging...role..."
Explain the use of "were" in this sentence.
e) 46-48: "...and it is not clear *whether adding Britain's voice would make much difference.*"
Identify the subject in the underlined clause.
f) 1-3: "...an 80m-strong united Germany *will* be the dominant power in Europe..."
77-78: "...the two countries *are going to* be physically linked..."
Explain the two different forms of futurity.

## II. Comprehension

Answer the following questions in complete sentences. Keep to the information given in the text, but do not quote.

1. How does the author see Germany's position at the start of the new millenium?

2. Explain the potential roles within a future Europe which the author can imagine for Britain.

3. Where might Britain's strength lie, according to the author?

4. How does the author justify a new Anglo-French *entente cordiale*?

### III. Comment

Choose *one* of the following topics:

1. Why do you think the author uses the term "Fourth Reich" for Germany? Is the use of the term helpful in shaping a new Europe?

2. Discuss the pros and cons of an *entente cordiale* against the background of recent political changes in Europe.

3. Write a letter to the editor and argue your case for European Union.

4. "Playing second, or third, fiddle to the Germans will not come easily to Britain." (ll. 35–36) Explain this statement against the background of both Britain's and Germany's history.

5. "With the European borders disappearing old animosities and a new hostility towards strangers are coming up in Europe." Do you agree?

### IV. Translation

Translate lines 1–17 ("At the start...occupation.") into German. Do not give alternatives in brackets.

# Bibliography

1. Branegan, Jay. "Perils of 1997", *Time*, May 13, 1991, No. 19.
2. Crick, Bernard. *George Orwell. A Life.* London, 1980.
3. Dahrendorf, Ralf. *On Britain.* London: BBC Publications, 1982.
4. Flex, Walter. *Im Felde zwischen Nacht.* München.
5. Flex, Walter. *Der Wanderer zwischen beiden Welten.* München.
6. Gilbert, Martin. *Churchill: A Life.* London: Heinemann, 1991.
7. *Great Commonwealth Stories*, Klettbuch 57944.
8. Haigh, Christopher, ed. *The Cambridge Historical Encyclopedia of Great Britain and Ireland.* Cambridge: CUP, 1985.
9. Johann, Ernst, ed. *Reden des Kaisers.* Ansprachen, Predigten und Trinksprüche Wilhelms II. München: dtv, Reihe "Dokumente", 1966, S. 90–91.
10. Lloyd, T.O.. "The British Empire 1558–1983", *The Short Oxford History of the Modern World.* Oxford: OUP, 1984.
11. Lloyd, T.O.. "Empire to Welfare State", *English History 1906–1985. The Short Oxford History of the Modern World.* Oxford: OUP 1986.
12. Mo, Timothy. *An Insular Possession* (novel). London: Picador, 1986.
13. Mommsen, Wolfgang J.. "Der Fieberwahn des Imperialismus 1885–1906", *Das Zeitalter des Imperialismus*, Fischer Weltgeschichte, Bd. 28, S. 152–177. Frankfurt/M.: Fischer, 1969.
14. Morris, Jan. *The Spectacle of Empire.* London: Faber & Faber, 1982.
15. Morris, James (Jan). *Pax Britannica.* London: Penguin, 1979.
16. Neher, Johann, ed. *Der Imperialismus.* Ploetz Arbeitsmaterialien Schule. Würzburg: Verlag Plötz, 1974, S. 35–37.
17. Perspectives 8: *Empire, Commonwealth, Europe*, Klettbuch 51368.
18. Perspectives 14: *Australia*, Klettbuch 51374.
19. Porter, Bernhard. "The Lion's Share", *A Short History of British Imperialism 1850–1983.* London: Longman, 1984.
20. Rafferty, Kevin. *City on the Rocks.* Hong Kong's Uncertain Future. London: Penguin, 1989.
21. Randle, John. "Britain and the World", *British Life and Institutions*, pp. 53–60, Klettbuch 51344.
22. Shawcross, William. *Kowtow*, Chatto Counterblasts No. 6. London: Chatto & Windus, 1989.
23. Spann, Ekkehard, *Abiturwissen Landeskunde* Great Britain/United States of America, Klettbuch 929509 (Chapters 2 and 9).
24. Terrill, Ross. "Hong Kong. Countdown to 1997", *National Geographic*, vol. 179, no. 2, February 1991, pp. 103–131.
25. Williams, Raymond, ed. *George Orwell. A Collection of Critical Essays.* Englewood Cliffs, 1974.

# 2 India
## Structure of the chapter

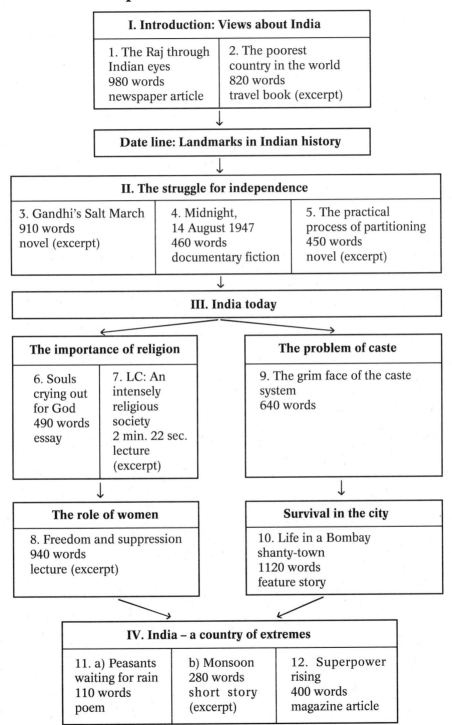

*India* 43

**Suggestions for reports/papers/talks**

The British in India/India during the Raj – after text 1.

The role of English in India today – after text 1.

The main reasons for Third World poverty – after text 2.

V.S. Naipaul's books on India (with excerpts) or one of his novels/short stories – after text 2.

Mahatma Gandhi: His life and his philosophy – after text 3.

The movement for independence – between texts 3 and 4.

Jwaharlal Nehru and his role in the new India – after text 4.

Hinduism – India's dominant religion – after text 6.

Other religions in India (Jainism, Buddhism, Sikhism) – between texts 6 and 7.

The life and work of Salman Rusdhie – after text 7.

The role of women in the Third World – after text 8.

The caste system – before text 9.

Urban problems in the Third World – after text 10.

Rural India – after text 11.

The geography of India – before or after text 11.

Recent events in India – before or after text 12.

**Vocabulary**

*Thematischer Grund– und Aufbauwortschatz*, Klettbuch 51955, pp. 132–138 (Politik, politische Systeme).

*Words in Context*, Klettbuch 51961, pp. 34–40 (The British Empire – The Commonwealth), and pp. 106–116 (The Third World).


# 1. The Raj through Indian eyes

**Background information**

The role of English in India:
One of the longstanding social issues that have resurfaced with new bitterness over the last years is the controversy about the retention of the English language in India. In a country where 3,300 dialects are spoken, where 15 main languages are used in regional governments and 67 in the schools, debates and campaigns between the pro- and anti-English lobbies have, periodically, exploded into demonstrations and riots. In 1950, three years after Independence, Hindi was made the national language, on condition that English would continue to be used for another 15 years. When it came to that deadline, violent resistance to Hindi in some southern states (Tamil Nadu) forced the government to keep English as a common official language. Thus English has remained the lingua franca up this day.
The anti-English lobby's main arguments are

– that a kind of linguistic caste system is being perpetuated because the best education and the best jobs are open only to the English-speaking elite, which puts 90% of all Indians at a disadvantage.

The pro-English lobby's most powerful arguments are
– that people of different regions can communicate with one another only in English
– that India would break up into linguistic nation-states, if English was banned
– that the 40% of Indians who speak Hindi want to force their language on the rest of the country ("English imperialism would be replaced by Hindi imperialism")
– that the abolition of English would widen the gulf between north and south Indians and could provoke communal tensions.

Reality is that in the South and Northeast, where animosity to Hindi is strongest, state governments have already switched to local languages (like Kannada and Bengali) and want English – not Hindi – to be the national language. Finally, more Indians want to learn English today than ever before: Teach-yourself-English books in local languages are sold in great numbers, and thousands of Indians attend conversation classes.

## Methodisch-didaktische Hinweise

Dieser Text soll zum Thema Indien unter verschiedenen Aspekten hinführen, über die der Autor, aus indischer Sicht, Grundeinsichten und Grundinformationen vermittelt, insbesondere über
1. die historische Rolle der Briten
2. die gesellschaftlichen Verhältnisse in Indien
3. die besondere Bedeutung der englischen Sprache für das Land.

Je nach Anknüpfungspunkt bzw. Zielrichtung lassen sich dann auch leicht 4 mögliche Einstiegsvarianten finden:
1. Anknüpfung an Ausdehnung, Macht und Einfluß des Empire (vgl. Fotos S. 7, 10, 13, 34 oder 285 im SB, evtl. auch Text 1 oder 3, Kapitel 1).
2. Kommentierung der Fotos S. 33, die die unterschiedliche soziale Rolle von Mann und Frau in der indischen Gesellschaft exemplarisch darstellen (diese Thematik wird dann im Text 8 genauer analysiert) wie auch das alte und das neue Indien.
3. Einstieg mit der Abb. S. 36, wo auf der 10-Rupien Banknote die herausragende Bedeutung des Englischen für Indien sichtbar wird. Damit werden die S auf einen der zentralen Inhaltspunkte von Text 1 hingeführt.
4. Einstieg durch einen Film, der in der Raj-Zeit spielt: z.B. *Passage to India* (E.M. Forster), *Heat and Dust* (Ruth Prawer Jhabvala) or *The Jewel in the Crown* (Paul Scott).

## Pre-reading activities

See "Methodisch-didaktische Hinweise"
*1. What image do you have of India?/What do you know about India?*

*2. What image of India do you get from the photographs on p. 33?*
Women are the backbone of the rural community: they have to fetch water, collect firewood, grow vegetables, work in fields etc. Cf. Text 8 "Background information".
Men in front of big industrial plant, working with new technology, repairing railways, building roads etc.
Contrast of old and new lifestyles and clothes, but women do hard physical work too.

*3. Look at the illustration at the top of p. 36 and answer the question. Why do you think English is so widely used in India?*
See "Background information".

## Suggested answers

1. Both his families had served the Empire and were proud of it (the grandfather had got three orders of knighthood); had associated socially with the British rulers during the Raj (dined, danced and golfed); and yet had also had links with the anti-British underground movement in the 1940s. His mother had, moreover, taken a Master's degree in English literature. After Independence a British life-style still continued in the writer's home as he grew up (English was spoken in the family/British etiquette governed behaviour and table manners/servants used the titles previously used for the British masters, etc.) The writer was educated at an Anglican school (morning assembly with British hymns, the Lord's Prayer, prefects and British or Anglo-Indian teachers). He was proud to learn English literature and history, scorned Indian languages and learned little about his own culture. At his Indian university the language of instruction was English and he looked down on Indians who only spoke Indian languages (cf. class consciousness and attitudes of old imperialists). The aim was to get to Oxbridge as it was in upper-class Britain, and the writer made it.

2. English is the language of the upper classes at home, in education and at work. This gives them a great advantage in life (admission to British and American universities, superiority at Indian university, jobs etc.). Since Independence English has become more and more important. It is the language of the universities, the main professions, central government, the higher law courts, the ever increasing English-language newspapers and magazines, i.e. the lingua franca of India's ruling classes, a necessity for social and international mobility.
On the other hand, the great majority of students and lecturers who use "Indian English" as their

*India* 45

second language are put at a permanent disadvantage. Thus for the majority of Indians English is an acquired foreign language, in which they are never really at home.

3. The writer classifies himself as a member of a minority, "a few thousand among several hundred millions" (ll. 43–44). He belonged to that privileged English-speaking elite of Indians who could afford the best education and who were given the best jobs. Since he never felt that they were "the odd ones out" (l. 46) it is clear that Indian society was/is a class society in which everybody's position was/is well-defined (cf. caste system, Hinduism). Fashions and lifestyles of this upper class hardly differed from those in Western societies, making a sharp division between that powerful class and the mass of the 'lower' classes. The text shows that class was not just defined by wealth, but by language: the upper classes were English-speaking; the masses or majority used Indian languages or acquired English painfully later. The attitudes of this elite also reflect the old class attitudes of the former imperial rulers.

4. Possible reasons:
– nostalgia for the good old days of the past which is idealised in the memories of it
– life in India was indeed colourful, exotic and exciting compared with dull, drab present-day Britain; images of the period heightened by memory, films and romantic bestsellers (e.g. Paul Scott's *The Jewel in the Crown* from the *Raj Quartet*)
– the period of the Raj was the height of the power of the British Empire: it is not surprising if British people regret those glorious days and compare them unfavourably with Britain's position of comparative powerlessness in the world today
– Indians wish to forget that they were ruled by the British so long, that so many of them collaborated with and kowtowed to them.

5. The article shows a high level of journalistic writing. (As it was published in *The Listener*, the BBC journal, it was probably given as a talk on the radio first.) One could not tell the writer was foreign or Indian, as his command of English is excellent with a very wide vocabulary and varied sentence structure showing his level of education and culture. The style is quite natural, but the writer doesn't use a specific register, relying on a balance between factual reporting and personal narrative.

The tone is neither too emotional nor too critical, but quite factual and thus shows an objective attitude towards the problem (cf. quotations). The writer has nevertheless a rather personal approach towards the subject matter and includes many details of his own family background.

**Additional questions**

1. Comment on the following statements:
a) Only in English can people of different regions communicate with one another.
b) Being fluent in English remains essential for upward mobility.
c) *If English was banned, united India would break up into linguistic nation states.*

2. *Which other developments are mentioned in the text that have influenced India since Independence?*
The arrival of American film and television culture/Americanization/a technological revolution/the rapid expansion of education/unprecedented demand for English-language newspapers and magazines

3. *Look at the picture on p. 34 and answer the question.*
Background information: Jaipur, about 150 miles southwest of Delhi, is one of the prominent old 'princely states' (like Jodpur, Bikaner and Jaisalmer) in Rajasthan (see photo p. 55), a large desert region which is well-known in Indian history as the cradle of Hindu chivalry and culture. The Rajput clans, whose principles were founded upon the heroes of the ancient Hindu epics, resisted the early Muslim invaders (see "Landmarks" p. 38). Today their social structure is rather conservative.

In colonial times these states were isolated, remaining under Indian rulers, deprived of any opportunity of cooperation. The subjection of a whole continent was made possible by the innate divisiveness of Hindu society, its class and caste divisions, which often called in unwelcome outsiders to defeat the still more unwelcome neighbour; for defeating a rival the British were in the last resort accepted as masters in preference to dominance by a rival. The Rajput clans, for example, accepted British suzerainty (*Oberhoheit*) c. 1818.

Historical photograph: exotic splendour of the Maharajah's clothes and those of his entourage/class divisions – the Maharajah seated with highest white official, the rest standing, with the station master or porter even more separate/formality of the scene with luxurious carpet and chairs/newness and importance of railway emphasized by this reception – the railway as one of the main contributions by the British to the development and unification of India.

**Post-reading activities**

1. Report/paper/talk:
a) *The British in India or India during the Raj.*
See Bibliography 7, 19, 28.
b) *The role of English in India today.*

2. *Collect articles from newspapers or magazines dealing with developments/problems/events in India and report on them in class.*
See Bibliography 25, 26, 27.

## 2. The poorest country in the world

**Background information**

V.S. Naipaul (born 1932) is one of the major writers to emerge from Trinidad where he grew up in the Indian community, moving later to Britain to study at Oxford and settle there in 1950. His ancestors had emigrated from India to Trinidad to work on the colonial sugar estates, and the world of this ethnic minority is satirically portrayed in Naipaul's early work: *The Mystic Masseur* (1957), *The Suffrage of Elvira* (1958) and *Migmel Street* (1959), all available in Penguin. He visited India for the first time in 1962, and out of his complex reactions and impressions as a "foreign" Indian grew the book *An Area of Darkness* from which our text is taken. In two later books on India (*India: A Wounded Civilisation*, London: Penguin 1979; and *India – A Million Mutinies Now*, London: Heinemann 1990) he discusses his experiences on that first visit, and excerpts from these works (e.g. pp. 7–8 in *A Million Mutinies Now*) would provide interesting additional material for our topic as well as for reports or papers.

**Methodisch-didaktische Hinweise**

Mit diesem Text lassen sich 3 Zielgebiete abdecken, die – je nach Interessenlage – besonders vertieft werden können:
a) Landeskundliche Informationen und Einführung in die Dritte-Welt-Problematik (vgl. Aufgabe 1 und 6)
b) Textverständnis bzw. *Reading Comprehension* (vgl. Aufgaben 1–4)

c) Analyse des besonderen Stils von V.S. Naipaul (5)

Bei der Bearbeitung der Aufgaben sollten die Nr. 1–4 (Kontext), 5 (Stil und Form) und 6 (Diskussion, Materialsammlung) klar voneinander getrennt angegangen werden.

Naipaul ist besonders als Schriftsteller bekannt. Man könnte daher auch seine Romane oder Kurzgeschichten für Bücherreferate empfehlen. Die meisten sind bei Penguin verlegt.

**Pre-reading activities**

1. *Many Indians like Naipaul's ancestors emigrated to other countries. Can you imagine why?*
Poverty/more opportunities: South Africa, Kenya, Uganda, Caribbean, Great Britain

2. *Look at the pictures on page 36 and page 37 and answer the questions.*
Some reasons for poverty: natural catastrophes/bad harvests/uneven distribution of wealth/rich minority of landowners/low productivity/primitive technology etc.

**Suggested answers**

1. Poverty is the main theme of this text: the notorious poverty of India. The author deals with this subject in a personal/semi-autobiographical and direct way, i.e. how he as a visitor was affected by it/experienced it/was changed by it.

2. A Sikh returning weeps/newcomers are all shocked, outraged, angry and contemptuous/ sons and daughters of Indians returning from abroad feel the same – yet this observation is obvious and superficial and therefore of no value. Most people, too, are so shocked by the poverty that they do not see the positive aspects of what they are looking at (ll. 33–38; ll. 41–50) although they claim to be sensitive.

3. When Naipaul first arrived in India, he felt the same anger and sense of outrage experienced as most newcomers, but was obviously already aware of positive impressions too (SB p. 37). After a ten-month tour of India he had learned to see things differently, to find his first reaction hysterical and to gain a certain distance to the horrors of poverty that he had seen and that had exhausted him emotionally. In order to bear all the negative experiences he had learned to separate the pleasant from the unpleasant, things from people, i.e. to ignore the poverty and see the beauty included in it.

4. He realised that he had to separate himself from what he saw in order to survive emotionally and psychologically, that otherwise the horrors of poverty were too much to bear. In order to regain his self-respect he had to escape the poverty, to ignore it if necessary, and concentrate on the beautiful and pleasant things connected with his experiences. He found, too, that such an escape was possible and that there were periods of calm or places he could then enjoy.

5. *Vocabulary:* the author uses many formal or literary words, e.g. preoccupation, sensitivity, remission, compassion; he employs a rather elevated or even poetic diction.
*Sentence structure:* the author makes use of well structured, varied sentences, e.g. different beginnings, short and simple as well as long and complex sentences, imperatives (l. 51) to address the reader personally etc.
*Repetition:* poverty (ll. 4, 7, 10, 16, 20, 25, etc.)/ beggars (ll.16, 18), beggary (l. 18), begging (l. 33)/empty-handed (ll. 16, 19) etc. – to emphasize the points he is making.
*Anaphora:* I had seen ... (ll. 64, 70, 72)
*Parallelism:* It is an Indian story ... (ll. 4–5) ...It is Indian (ll. 6–7)
That ... is our poverty (l. 17) ... This is our poverty (l. 20)
It is your gaze (ll. 43–44) ... It is your surprise (l. 50)
I had seen (ll. 64, 70, 72) ... I had learned (l. 91)
Parallelism occurs in many ways. Thus the author manages to present and emphasize the different stages/levels or ways of seeing/experiencing Indian life.
*Personification:* the winter will bring .. (l. 52)/ Nature mocking herself (ll. 75–76)/compassion ... did not answer (ll. 76–77)/in a trinity of love (l. 36)
*Alliteration:* filth and food (l. 67)/baby .. swollen-bellied, black with flies (ll. 69–70)/corner of comparative order (ll. 93–94)/pretty girl to prostitution (l. 22), etc.
*Inversion/parallelism:* fear was what I felt. Contempt was what I had .. (ll. 78–79) – a literary inversion in order to emphasize the parallel or contrasting emotions.
Naipaul uses such varied structures, language and stylistic devices in order to express as closely as possible his varied and complex reactions to India. They are too complicated to be described in merely factual language or in a superficial, realistic style. The text is non-fiction – it is obviously autobiographical – but it is highly literary in style, written by someone with an impressive command of language who is obviously used to reflecting on and articulating very complex subjects. The mingling of the personal and the reflective captures the reader's interest and convinces him/her of the authenticity of Naipaul's report of his Indian experience. Here is a writer who, while looking for his own identity, is confronted with the identity of India in a way he had not expected.

6. – overpopulation, demographic explosion
– natural catastrophes: drought, floods etc. leading to poor harvests and loss of income as well as food in rural areas
– lack of education/illiteracy leading to lack of job prospects and chronic unemployment
– lack of infrastructure and industry in many areas which could provide work
– uneven distribution of wealth (caste system and continuing colonial structures)
– fall in world prices for raw materials (dependence on First World markets and prices)
– poverty as a consequence of decades of colonial exploitation

– government spending on prestige projects (e.g. computer industry in Bangalore) and armaments.
(Cf. *Words in Context*, Klettbuch 51961, pp. 106–115.)

### Additional questions

1. Collect all the words and phrases connected with poverty, e.g. empty-handed (l. 17), undernourishment (l. 42/43), etc. and build up word families (e.g. poor, poverty, impoverishment, poverty line).

2. Read an excerpt from India – A Million Mutinies Now *(1990) and try to explain Naipaul's ideas on India and Indian poverty.*

3. *After you have read Text 10* (Life in a Bombay shanty-town), *compare it with Naipaul's text.* Style, author's position as regards his subject, language, etc.

### Post-reading activities

1. *Report/paper/talk: The main reasons for Third World poverty.*

2. *Book report: V.S. Naipaul's books on India (with excerpts), or one of his novels/short stories.*
See Bibliography 16, 17.

## 3. Gandhi's Salt March (GK)

### Background information

See "Landmarks in Indian history" (SB pp. 38 – 39) and the fact file on pages 286–287.
Gandhi's campaign against the salt tax in 1930 was one of the most spectacular displays of non-violent resistance *(satyagraha)* to the British Raj. In 1931 he was invited to attend the Round Table Conference in London as the only representative of the Indian National Congress. When the British continued to attempt to suppress his movement and break his influence, he initiated a vigorous campaign for the rights of the "untouchables" (or *harijans*, "the children of god", as he called them). In 1934 he resigned as the leader of the Congress Party because he felt its members had not adopted non-violence as the fundamental creed it was for him. He went to live at Sevagram, a village in central India, from where he worked on his "constructive programme":
– to build the nation "from the bottom up"
– to uplift the rural masses of India (about 85 per cent of the population lived in the country's villages) and to revive village India
– to continue his fight against untouchability
– to promote handspinning, weaving, and other cottage industries to give the underemployed some additional income
– to develop a system of education suited to the needs of these people
– to foster economic self-sufficiency in small centres rather than the expansion of industrial centres or big cities.

Gandhi, however, did not leave politics for good, organizing, for example, the "Quit India" campaign during the Second World War and refusing to cooperate with the Allies, to Churchill's fury. After the war he was one of the Congress leaders, along with Nehru, to negotiate Independence with the British Government, represented by Lord Mountbatten, and to try to prevent Partition. It is a bitter irony that Gandhi died a violent death at the hands of a Hindu fanatic (1948).
*Raj* (1989), the first novel of Gita Mehta [meɪta], is set in the Indian states ruled not by the Viceroy but by Indian royalty (Native India) and it covers the period from Victoria's Diamond Jubilee (see p. 7) to Independence (see p. 43). Mehta has known some of the royal matriarchy since childhood, one of whom, an 80-year-old Himalayan queen mother, first unveiled her face in public when she stood as a candidate in the first Indian elections (cf. Princess Jaya). Mehta's family, too, was directly involved in the struggle for Independence: one uncle was shot in 1930 as he led an insurrection by the nationalist Indian Republican Army, while her politician father was imprisoned by the British just after her birth.

### Methodisch-didaktische Hinweise

1. Vor der Textbesprechung empfiehlt es sich, den Text auf Kassette im Ganzen zu hören *(Selected Texts,* 510342), die Annotationen zu bearbeiten, und dann den Text nochmals zu hören oder zu lesen. Die Leseart des indischen Sprechers ist sehr lebhaft, besonders bei den

*India* 49

Dialogen, und die Schüler gewinnen dadurch einen guten ersten Eindruck vom indischen Englisch (Intonation, Vokale, Konsonanten), wie auch vom tadellosen Englisch eines gebildeten Inders. Anschließend können die Fragen 1–3 beantwortet werden, nach intensivem Lesen (u.a. mit Hilfe der Texteinführung) können die Aufgaben 4 und 5 gelöst werden.

2. Eine Einstiegsvariante bzw. auch visuelle Ergänzung wäre sehr gut geeignet: Die Szene aus Attenboroughs Film *Gandhi* (1982), die genau mit dem Salzmarsch zu tun hat. Die englische Filmversion läßt sich relativ leicht besorgen.

3. Fächerübergreifend, für Schüler mit Leistungskurs Musik, wäre eine Besprechung der Gandhi-Oper von Philip Glass, *Satyagraha*, oder wenigstens die Szene um den Salzmarsch, zu empfehlen.

4. Das Bild sollte lieber am Ende besprochen werden.

**Pre-reading activities**

See "Methodisch-didaktische Hinweise".

**Suggested answers**

1. The physical image of Gandhi is of a thin, elderly ascetic (toothless, knobby knees, bony shoulders) dressed in simple Indian style (cotton *dhoti* and shawl). He seems to have a sense of fun (ll. 16–19) in spite of his awareness of injustice (ll. 73–79), his determination to fight against it and his critical attitude towards certain aspects of Indian society (caste discrimination, arranged marriages, drunkenness etc. – ll. 91–102). Gandhi appears to be the beloved hero of the Indian masses, an energetic and wise old man full of mystique and charisma who is able to attract people and influence their minds, somebody like a saint who inspires devotion and enthusiasm and who brings people of different classes together.

2. They seem to be quite fanatical, revering him like a saint, trying to touch him etc. They have travelled for miles to see him; scatter flowers in his path to welcome him; carry and use spinning-wheels to show they follow his ideals; wear his style of clothing (even Lady Modi); are excited, passionate, angry and enthusiastic when he talks to them; and the ashram workers have to protect him from the frantic crowd.

3. An emotional mood surrounds the actions of Gandhi, and great expectations are set up as to the course of events. There is an overall atmosphere of excitement, optimism and hope for the future.

The author creates this atmosphere by her mode of presentation: In the first paragraph she employs a panoramic mode of presentation (see p. 96 SB), summing up Gandhi's campaign so far, then she changes to the scenic mode of presentation, presenting the characters and action in great detail and using direct speech (exclamations, questions, cries, Gandhi's speech etc.).

4. Gandhi first of all aims at winning affection and solidarity ("Brothers and sisters ... I greet you.") among his followers so that he can rely on them in his fight for independence later on. His message is simple: The British imperial system is wicked and should be destroyed, but it is not just British power but the behaviour of Indians themselves that keeps their country oppressed – that's why he points out their own imperfections (problems of untouchability, child marriage and prostitution, preference for cheap imported British cloth and goods, etc.), and recommends a simple, pure life.

On the one hand he wants to make the British aware that they are cruelly oppressing India by putting a tax on salt, which especially affects the poorest people; on the other hand he tries to create a spirit of community and national feeling. He preaches love not hate, and resistance to the British only in a non-violent form.

One could summarize with the quotation: "Gandhi had given India a new idea of itself, and also given the world a new idea of India." (Naipaul, *India: A Wounded Civilization*, p. 46)

5. *Fact:*
Gandhi/his appearance/his march from his ashram (on the river bank at Ahmedabad, where he lived after his return from South Africa) to Dandi/people and events around the Salt March: supporters, sweepers, ashram workers, etc./the atmosphere of his campaign/his ideas as expressed in his speech

*Fiction:*
Jaya, who is the author's central character in the novel, and her story/Lady Modi's actions and thoughts/Jaya's son, Tiny Dungra/this scene is probably based on many similar historical incidents

6. See fact file (pp. 286–287), encyclopedias, biographies etc. See also Bibliography p.72.
The following points should not be missed:
a) Gandhi was a major figure in three of the major revolutions in the 20th century: against colonialism, racism and violence.
b) Religion (without formalism, dogma, ritual or sectarianism) was the mainspring of his life.
c) He believed in reconciliation and non-violence, or "soul-force", not in violent resistance.
d) He identified himself with the peasant masses and wanted to improve their lot.
e) He was a fervent nationalist who worked tirelessly for India's independence.

**Additional questions**

*1. Look at the picture on p. 40 and comment on the woman on the right.*
She's wearing a fine sari with embroidered edging and jewellery, but is carrying a skein of handspun wool or cotton symbolizing the life of rural simplicity and industry that Gandhi recommended – cf. the spinning wheels of l. 10. She is, therefore, probably a middle– or upper-class supporter of Gandhi like the women mentioned in the text.

*2. Try to describe the tone of the text (see box p. 124). Where do you think the sympathies of the writer lie?*

*3. Translate the following excerpt from Clement Attlee's tribute on the death of Gandhi:*
"Mahatma Gandhi, as he was known in India, was one of the outstanding figures in the world today, but he seemed to belong to a different period of history. Living a life of extreme asceticism he was revered as a divinely inspired saint by millions of his fellow countrymen. His influence extended beyond the range of his co-religionists, and in a country deeply riven by communal dissension he had an appeal for the Indians. For a quarter of a century this one man has been the major factor in every consideration of the Indian problem. He had become the expression of the aspirations of the Indian people for independence."

Mahatma Gandhi, wie er in Indien genannt wird, war eine der hervorragendsten Persönlichkeiten der heutigen Welt, aber er schien einer anderen Epoche der Geschichte anzugehören. Da er ein Leben äußerster Askese führte, wurde er von Millionen seiner Landsleute als ein von Gott erleuchteter Heiliger verehrt. Sein Einfluß reichte weiter über den Kreis seiner Glaubensgenossen, und in einem Lande, das tief von innerer Zwietracht gespalten war, hatte er eine Anziehungskraft für alle Inder/sprach alle Inder an. Ein Vierteljahrhundert lang ist dieser eine Mann bei jeder Erörterung/Betrachtung des Indienproblems/der Indienfrage der entscheidende/ausschlaggebende Faktor gewesen. Er war zur Verkörperung der Sehnsucht des indischen Volkes nach Unabhängigkeit/zum Ausdruck des Unabhängigkeitsstrebens geworden.

**Post-reading activities**

*1. Discussion: Why do you think Gandhi is still a role model or hero for many people?*

*2. Compare Gandhi's campaigns of non-violent resistance with the Civil Rights Movement in America (Martin Luther King) and the movements against nuclear power and nuclear weapons in Europe.*
Wackersdorf, Greenham Common, Greenpeace, Pershing blockades etc.

*3. Report/paper/talk:*
Mahatma Gandhi: his life and his philosophy.
See fact file, encyclopedia, Bibliography 4, 6, 8, 9.

# 4. Midnight, 14 August 1947

**Background information**

See fact file "Independence and Partition" (SB p. 286) and "Landmarks in Indian history" (SB pp. 38–39).
The Round Table Conference in London in 1931 (which Gandhi could attend as the only representative of National Congress because he had called off a campaign of civil disobedience) was a great disappointment to the Indian nationalists as they were only granted limited powers but not full independence, but by 1937 provincial autonomy was introduced with the Indian National Congress controlling seven out of eleven provinces. The Second World War ended this

experiment in partial autonomy with the Congress refusing to co-operate except on terms of political advance. Gandhi's "Quit India" campaign enraged Churchill and, as the war against Japan was in a critical phase (the Japanese had invaded Burma), all the leaders of the Congress Party were imprisoned. It is said that the British encouraged discord between the Hindus and Muslims, but it is a fact that Jinnah, the leader of the Muslim League, feared Hindu domination in an independent India when he saw the hold Gandhi had over the masses and began to campaign for a separate Muslim State in 1940, taking till 1946 to win the support of Muslims as a whole. The new Labour government after the war under Clement Attlee was determined to push through Indian independence, sending Lord Mountbatten as the last Viceroy to negotiate with all parties which lead to the Mountbatten Plan of June 3, 1947 for independence with partition.

N.B. The people born on or around the day of Independence are often called "midnight's children" (cf. Salman Rushdie's novel *Midnight's Children*, 1981).

## Methodischer Hinweis

Da der Wortschatz verhältnismäßig schwierig ist, empfiehlt sich die Vorbereitung des Textes zu Hause anhand eines Wörterbuchs. Alternativ könnte das Vokabular gemeinsam erarbeitet werden, bevor man an die Aufgaben herangeht. Den historischen Hintergrund könnten die S auch vorher zu Hause/in der Bibliothek aufarbeiten und ihre Ergebnisse vergleichen und diskutieren (s. "Pre-reading activities").

## Pre-reading activities

1. *Collect information about the movement for independence in India. Compare and discuss your findings in class, or give a paper on the subject.*

2. *When did most other colonies become independent?*
After World War II, in the 1950s and '60s

3. *Name the latest country to become independent and discuss the reasons for this.*

## Suggested answers

1. A man wearing a robe of handwoven Indian cotton and holding a big conch shell in his arm is waiting at the edge of a gallery to announce India's independence in New Delhi's Constituent Assembly at midnight, 14 August 1947. Nehru, the Congress leader, waits in the speaker's stand surrounded by the flags of the new India which have replaced the portraits of British Viceroys, while opposite him are seated the very varied representatives of this new nation – a country more diverse in race, culture, religion and language and faced with more contrasting problems than any other nation in the world. When the clock strikes twelve, the ancient cry of the shell marks both the passing of an age and the birth of a nation.

2. The authors do not use commonplace phrases, their extensive vocabulary is well-chosen, literary (see annotations) and formal words are widely used: clamouring for (l. 14), ranged (l. 27), calamities (l. 39), protruding (l. 46).
The excerpt is full of imagery and metaphors: vast reaches of time (l. 1), transposed from legend to stone (l. 2), the herald of the dawn (ll. 4–5), ghosts hacking down the pillars of an empire (ll. 15–16), etc.
– personification: the hands of the clock ... crept (l. 49)
– repetition: a land (ll. 34, 35, 38, 40)
– parallelism: To those ... (l. 57) ... To the world (l. 59)/unmatched (l. 33) ... unsurpassed (l. 39)
– antithesis: supreme spiritual attainment/the most debasing misery (ll. 34–35) etc.

3. This elevated style is used to express the uniqueness and solemnity of this famous moment in history. The specific register, expressed by formal and literary language, is appropriate to such an occasion. The detailed language and imagery, too, is necessary to convey the atmosphere of the scene exactly and vividly. The tone of the passage is serious and ceremonial, reflecting the authors' attitude towards this historic day, whose importance they want to emphasize or even glorify for future generations.

4. Translation: Schwierige Ausdrücke sind kursiv gedruckt!
Nehru gegenüber saßen *dicht gedrängt* und aneinandergereiht auf den *Abgeordnetenbänken* im Sari und Khadi, im Prinzengewand

und Smoking die Vertreter der Nation, die in dieser Nacht geboren werden sollte. Das Volk, das sie vertraten, war eine *Mischung* von Rassen und Religionen, Sprachen und Kulturen, von einer *Vielfalt und Gegensätzlichkeit ohnegleichen* auf der Welt. Ihr Land war *gekennzeichnet* durch die überragendste geistige *Leistung* und das erniedrigendste Elend auf der Erde, ein Land, dessen *größter Reichtum in seinen Widersprüchen bestand*, und dessen Menschen fruchtbarer waren als seine Felder; ein Land, das von Gott besessen war und von Naturkatastrophen heimgesucht wurde, die an Grausamkeit und in ihren Ausmaßen unübertroffen waren; ein Land der vergangenen *Leistungen* und der gegenwärtigen *Sorgen*, dessen Zukunft durch Probleme *gefährdet* wurde, die *höhere Anforderungen* an diese Versammlung von Menschen stellten als an irgendeine andere *auf der Welt*. Und dennoch, trotz allem, trotz all seiner *Mißstände* war ihr Indien gleichzeitig eines der *höchsten* und *bleibenden* Symbole, das über den Kulturhorizont der Menschheit hinausragte.

5. *Freedom at Midnight:*
– documentary fiction
– built around a particular event in history, which is in the centre of interest
– no fictional characters
– everything is based on truth
– precise and extensive reporting about people, places, events etc. is the dominant objective
– the reader's interest is caught by factual documenting and vivid description
– documents history in order to make it come alive

*Raj:*
– historical fiction

– a narrative form attempting to recreate past events rooted in history
– history and fiction are interwoven: both nonfictional/historical/biographical material and fictional/imaginary characters are presented in a mixed form
– the story element, i.e. an interesting plot, is most important for the reader's interest, reviving history is less important
– story-telling within a historical context

6. A chapter in a history book would be an expository text. This is descriptive. (See forms of discourse, SB p. 195.) The tone and register of a history book would be factual and objective, using clear and concise language and sticking to historical, documented facts. There would be no imaginative language as here, no vivid description, no personal, literary style.

### Additional questions

*1. Comment on the photograph on p. 43 SB (atmosphere, clothes, setting etc.).*

*2. Examine the -ing forms in the first paragraph, describe them and explain their different functions.*

*3. Rewrite the third paragraph (ll. 27–47) in less formal/colloquial English.*

### Post-reading activity

*Report/paper/talk: Collect information for a paper on Jawaharlal Nehru, his role in the independence movement and in the new India.*
This can be a group effort with results pooled in class as in the pre-reading activity. See also Bibliography 28, 24.

# 5. The practical process of partitioning (GK)

### Background information

See fact file SB p. 286.
Jinnah, the leader of the Muslim League, having gradually gained the support of the majority of Muslims for his campaign for a separate Muslim state, demanded partition of India at a conference under Lord Wavell at Simla in 1946. The rousing of religious passions caused riots and massacres, and the Congress were faced in the negotiations preceeding Independence with two opponents, the British and the Muslims. Gandhi called the partition of India "a spiritual tragedy", and when the mutual massacres of Sikhs, Hindus and Muslims in the Punjab caused great migrations on either side of the new border bringing waves of refugees to Delhi (see picture

p. 44) and threatening new massacres, he intervened and threatened to fast to death if the Muslims were not given security. This outraged militant Hindus and cost him his life.

*Note on map p. 45:* Sikhs are members of a reformed Hindu sect, founded in the 16th century, that teaches monotheism and that has the Granth as its chief religious document, rejecting the authority of the Vedas. Sikhs can be recognized by their turbans as they must not cut their hair.

### Methodischer Hinweis

Um diesen fiktionalen Text lebendig, vor allem aber um die Erzählperspektive klarer werden zu lassen, sollte man ihn 3 Schülern zur Vorbereitung aufgeben und ihn dann mit verteilten Rollen (1. narrator or reader 2. Mr Nichols, a political geographer 3. Mr Basham, an old administrator) lesen lassen. Der Text würde sich auch sehr gut zum Nach– bzw. Vorspielen eignen (Mimik, Gestik, Vortragsweise!).

### Pre-reading activities

*1. Do you know any other partitioned countries?*
Ireland, Korea, Germany till 1990

*2. What were the reasons for partition there and how were the countries divided?*

*3. Look at the map on p. 45, or at any map of British India. Suggest ideas or develop criteria as to how to divide the territory into two independent parts.*

### Suggested answers

1. The actual partition of India seems to have been done too quickly without considering the human aspect of divided towns and areas of mixed Hindu and Muslim population. It seems to have been done by academic geographers like Mr. Nichols with no experience of the areas in question and no time or opportunity to visit the places they were dividing. As old hands like Mr. Basham foresaw, this led to mass migrations of people who were now afraid to stay in areas where one religious group dominated. These migrations were accompanied by massacres and raping and looting of the desperate refugees.

2. The writer uses satire in order to show how absurd the criteria were for dividing India, and in order to criticize the hasty and amateurish way it was done. He fictionalizes one example (one scene) with one geographer in one area to make the whole problem personal, vivid and understandable. He also chooses a narrator who is telling a story to someone else (Ganapathi), a story from his own experience ("We"), which makes it direct and credible.
In a history book that process could be summed up in one or two sentences, or just be neglected, or even distorted ("the creation of two independent states"). The style would be factual (statistics of changes of population etc.) and the tone would remain impersonal. In general, the presentation of this period of history in a novel has more effect on the reader than a factual report as it deals with the human consequences and human suffering.

3. Part 1 (ll. 1–13)
*content:*
narrator's introductory remarks before the main story, looking back on history
*function:*
to set the historical context, provide a framework for the story
Part 2 (ll. 14–64)
*content:*
scene with geographer who divides up India
*function:*
to show the listener/reader how absurd the project is through satire and humour, to criticize and to entertain
Part 3 (ll. 65–91)
*content:*
the consequences of such scenes
*function:*
to present the consequences in an unforgettable way
The best way of analyzing the three parts of this excerpt is to study the *mode of presentation:*
Part 1
*mode of presentation:*
telling/summary/panorama, narrator's comments help the reader
*function:*
to give a generalized report/a comprehensive view of that event (cf. "carnage ... a political geographer") and some background to the reader

Part 2
*mode of presentation:*
showing/scene, characters and action presented directly through dialogue
*function:*
to offer an intensive view, like a film scene (the geographer is in the centre of attention and speaks for himself!) and achieve an effect of immediacy ("living" dialogue)

Part 3
*mode of presentation:*
reporting/telling and description in one long, unbroken sentence
*function:*
to give a summary and an interpretation ("lines ... lives.") of the consequences of such geographers' actions, and to convey the endlessness of the streams of refugees and the endlessness of their suffering by piling up descriptive verbs

4. Narrative perspective
*The Great Indian Novel:* first-person narrator telling the story to his counterpart Ganapathi so that he can write it down (see ll. 1, 7, 65, 81). The story he is dictating is told from a rather omniscient point of view, giving details and a lively picture of the historical facts. Although not a character in the story, the narrator seems to be, as an observer-narrator, both an eye-witness and a commentator who finds out by talking to other people (Ganapathi, the reader) and succeeds in throwing light on the complex facts, bringing to life historical incidents.

*The Raj:* third-person narrator, who stands outside the story and is partly omniscient, partly restricted to the point of view of one character. He has a good knowledge of the historical background but

– doesn't reveal it directly to the reader
– doesn't comment for or against social and historical developments
– allows his characters to state their opinions, because the story (plot, characters and their views) is important and not the narrator's comments, although the ironical tone does at times reveal his or the author's attitudes to people and events.

**Additional questions**

*1. Examine the use of the word "lines" in the text.*

*2. Collect nouns and verbs connected with "line" and check their meaning and usage.*
Nouns: airline, lifeline, poverty line, line-up, party line, breadline, skyline, linesman, picket line etc.
Verbs: to cross the line, to reach the end of the line, to read between the lines, to drop s.o. a line, to toe the line, to hold the line, to line the road etc.

**Post-reading activities**

*1. Compare the partition of India with the partition of Germany after the Second World War. Discuss the reasons for the latter and the human consequences.*

*2. Compare the partition of India with the partition of Ireland.*
See Chapter 4.

*3. Choose one period or event in history that you would like to write a historical novel or documentary fiction about. Give your reasons for choosing this particular period, and, if possible, sketch a rough draft of a plot.*

# 6. Souls crying out for God (GK)

**Background information**

India is the most socially heterogeneous nation-state of modern times and every major religion in the world is represented there: 83% Hindus (700 million), 11% Muslims (about 100 million), 2.5% Christians, 2% Sikhs, 0.8% Buddhists, 0.5% Jains and uncounted millions of small sects and sub-groups. The uniqueness of India lies in the variety of differences: castes within religion, language within class, class within religion, class within language, class within caste, etc. In this ethnic variety (of 15 major languages and 844 dialects) one has only a 11 percent chance of randomly selecting two people from the same ethnic-linguistic group (in the USA there is a 50 percent chance).
Religious allegiance implies choice of name, costume, diet, role of the sexes, and a vast range of patterns of group behaviour, which are very complex.

*Hinduism:* the complex of beliefs, values and customs comprising the dominant religion of India, characterized by the worship of many gods, including Brahma as supreme being, a caste system, belief in reincarnation etc. The Hindu religion had its origin in the concepts of the early Aryans who came to India more than 4,000 years ago. It is not merely a religion but also a philosophy and a way of life. It does not originate in the teachings of any one prophet or holy book. The most ancient sacred writings of Hinduism are the Vedas, while the Upanishads, Sanskrit sacred books written between 400 and 200 B.C., embody the mystical and esoteric doctrines of Hindu philosophy. Hinduism respects other religions and does not attempt to seek converts. It teaches the immortality of the human soul and three principal paths to ultimate union of the individual soul with the all pervasive spirit. Hinduism has been a great unifying force in India, but its association with the caste system has also been a divisive factor in Indian history.

*Islam:* In the 7th century Arab traders brought Islam to South India. 712, however, marks the first Arabic-Islamic conquests in the Indus area, while the period 1200-1800 was a time of Muslim hegemony in northern India. This included the era of the famed Mogul Empire established by Babur in 1526, which left such priceless architectural monuments as the Taj Mahal. With about 100 million Muslims India has the second largest Muslim population in the world. Muslim citizens have occupied some of the highest positions in the country since 1947.

*Christianity:* With the arrival of the apostle St. Thomas Christianity reached India very early. Most of the 21 million Christians live in Kerala in South India.

*Sikhism:* see "Background information" to Text 5.

*Buddhism* (see also map SB p. 45): Gautama Buddha, a prince, renounced the world and gained enlightenment (c. 560–c. 480 B.C.). He preached that "Nirvana" was to be attained through the conquest of self. In the 3rd century B.C. it became the state religion under Emperor Ashoka. The Lion Capital, erected by Ashoka to mark the spot where Buddha first proclaimed his gospel of peace and emancipation to the four quarters of the universe, is the national emblem of India today, reminding of India's ancient commitment to world peace and good will (see banknote SB p. 36).

*Jainism:* Jains believe that they should not hurt or kill any living thing; so they are vegetarians. In the 6th century B.C. Mahavira propagated his message of asceticism, austerity and non-violence. Jainist principles of non-violence and asceticism strongly influenced Hindu thought and also Gandhi.

**Didaktischer Hinweis**

Dieser Text bietet allgemeine, aber grundlegende Aussagen über die Bedeutung der Religion in Indien. Interessant ist dabei, vor dem Hintergrund der Biographie und Person der Autorin, der vergleichende Standpunkt, nämlich eine indische und eine europäische Sicht der Dinge. Gerade deswegen sollte dieser Text als Einleitung zum Thema Religion und Gesellschaft nicht übergangen werden.

Text 7 stellt (als Hörtext) die zentrale Rolle und die Auswirkung der Religion auf die indische Gesellschaft dar und kann als Kontrast bzw. Ergänzung zu Text 6 gelesen werden, während Text 8 das Thema Religion in Zusammenhang bringt mit der gesellschaftlichen Rolle der Frau, einer für die Zukunft Indiens entscheidenden Frage.

Diese Religionseinheit bietet sich natürlich für den fächerübergreifenden Unterricht mit den Religions- und Ethikkollegen an, da der Vergleich zwischen Religionen im Lehrplan vorgesehen ist.

Für weitere Texte zum Thema Religion s. Kapitel 7.

**Pre-reading activities**

*1. Does religion play an important part in your life?*
Note: In a study done by Gallup International in 1986 58 percent of Americans felt that religion was very important in their own lives, in (West) Germany the percentage was 17, in the UK 23.

*2. What do you know about religious life in India?*
Holy men, ashrams, yoga, etc.

*3. Look at the pictures on p. 48. Describe and compare them, commenting on the atmosphere of both.*

## Suggested answers

1. Indians have to seek refuge from an environment that is often unbearable, and they seek it in religion, for life in India is so terrible at times that is is hard to believe that this is all there is to it. Many people, therefore, seek a more satisfying spiritual dimension to their life. This brings up the question whether religion is so important in India because living conditions are so terrible – or whether life is so terrible because there is no drive to improve these conditions as people's interest is turned to spiritual things.

2. The writer conveys a picture of Indian religious life that shows how religion permeates everyday life so that "God seems more present in India than in other places". She evokes the religious atmosphere of an Indian day in a very personal and vivid way by enumerating many details such as early morning devotional song, conch shells blowing, temple bells ringing, the flowers at the feet of gods' statues, stories of the rebirth of Krishna, the widows who live in ashrams and play at being Krishna's milkmaids etc.

3. The Indian sky, unearthly blue by day and starry at night, makes one believe easily in a metaphysical dimension; and Indian devotional songs use such human imagery ("yearning for the lover") that they are easy to understand. The writer feels soothed and calmed by them, and she feels too that the world itself is a good place. (There is the hint that this is a momentary mood, not something lasting.)

4. The forms/practices/rites/ceremonies may be different, but there is religious life in Christian countries too. In India it seems that religion (first of all Hinduism) pervades all areas of life, whereas in a Christian country everyday religious practices more or less differ from person to person depending on whether one is Protestant or Catholic, on which area one lives in (e.g. Ireland or North Germany), on the school one attends (e.g. school prayers in England), on the customs of the family (e.g. grace at table) etc. Christian practices are especially concentrated on Sundays or certain holy days such as Christmas, Easter Sunday etc. Nowadays Christianity is more private and personal, not public as it is in India (or as it was in the Middle Ages, for example).
(Note: India was founded as a secular state, not as a Hindu state.)

5. Ceremonies/rites that could possibly be written about are:
christening – holy mass – wedding – religious processions – funeral – Protestant Confirmation – Catholic First Communion etc.

## Additional questions

*Paraphrase the following words and explain their function:*
– *the* slightly *overblown flowers (l. 22)* (adverb)
– *so* incredibly *beautiful (l. 38)* (intensifying adverb)
– *an ... unearthly blue (ll. 38–39)* (adjective)
– *in an* easily *recognizable way (l. 49)* (adverb of manner)

## Post-reading activities

*1. Collect information for a short paper on Hinduism.*
See fact file p. 286, encyclopedias, Bibliography 12, 28, 23.

*2. Collect information on other religions of India and report your findings.*
This could be done in groups, with each group reporting on one religion. Most encyclopedias contain enough information for the students.

*3. Why do you think the hippie generation of the '60s and '70s was attracted to India?*

# 7. Listening Comprehension: An intensely religious society

## Background information

See SB p. 49 for biographical note on Desai.
See SB pp. 131–132 for Rushdie text and picture (Chapter Five, "Art, Culture and Society").
See TB, p.134 for more information on Rushdie.
Herbert Read, born 1893, was an English poet, critic and professor for fine art whose most famous work was *The Meaning of Art* (1931).

## Methodisch-didaktische Hinweise

Eine Einleitung, Worterklärungen und Fragen zum Globalverständnis sind im SB, S. 47–48 abgedruckt. Vor Einsatz der Cassette empfiehlt sich ein genaues Studium der Annotationen. Da der Text ziemlich schnell vorgelesen wird, könnte man ihn in drei Abschnitten anbieten (eventuell zweimal vorspielen), da es ja eine Frage pro Abschnitt gibt.

## Text

We are brought up in India to think of religion as containing the highest truth, the greatest good, of the religious life as being the finest life, the one to which all Indians aspire, no matter what their
5 beginnings. To question this would be to question our whole society – an intensely religious society, a country where religion is not reserved for one place or one day of the week but is everywhere, at all times, a way of life, dictating
10 the way we eat, the way we dress, the way we bathe and marry and bring up our children, speak and live. To separate religion from such a society would be to tear out its heart or remove its limbs. People would not know how to live
15 with godlessness and unbelief. Who has the strength to face not God but – himself? Not the distant future – but the here and now? And so religion is not questioned. If it were, it would be the beginning of the end.
20 One writer who did question it was Salman Rushdie because he believed, as he stated in his Herbert Read lecture, that "To respect the sacred is to be paralysed by it. The idea tends to turn other ideas – Uncertainty, Progress,
25 Change – into crime." Crime is what he was accused of when he wrote *The Satanic Verses* and as you know, he has been in hiding ever since, in fear of his life.
His case is an extreme and exceptional one, of
30 course, but if there are not more such cases it is not because other iconoclasts have been luckier but because – in India and in the East generally – there are no iconoclasts, they would not be tolerated. If there are rationalists, those who like
35 him believe in inquiry, dialogue and deconstruction, they have chosen not to speak, not to take such risks as he has taken. And that is a form of suppression, of imprisonment. Imprisoned inside a hidebound religious structure, whether
40 Muslim or Hindu, too brainwashed or too browbeaten by religious leaders and the gullibility and naiveté of those they lead, too weak and fearful to try and turn the tide – the writer is silenced, paralysed.

By Anita Desai, *Times Literary Supplement*, September 14-20, 1990.

## Pre-listening activities

*1. How would you characterize religious life in India so far?*

*2. What do you expect to be different from our own society?*

## Suggested answers (Listening for the gist)

1. Religion is an inherent part of Indian society, a way of life, and cannot be separated from it. And it is not to be questioned either, since that would mean the end of this society.

2. She mentions Salman Rushdie to illustrate what can happen to someone who does question religion.

3. According to Anita Desai, iconoclasts would not be tolerated in India (nobody could dare to criticize in the way Rushdie did). As for rationalists, if there are any, they have decided not to criticize in public, and this is a form of suppression. Writers are silenced or paralysed by religion.

*India*

### Listening for detail

*1. Listen to the tape again and fill in the blanks in the first paragaph.*

"We are brought up in India to think of ____ as containing the ____ ____, the greatest ____, of the religious life as being the ____ life, the one to which all Indians ____, no matter what their beginnings. To question this would be to question our ____ ____ – an intensely religious society, a ____ where religion is not ____ for one place or one day fo the week but is everywhere, ____, a way of life, ____ the way we eat, the way we dress, the way we ____ and marry and bring up our children, speak and live. To ____ religion from such a society would be to ____ or remove its ____. People would not know how to live with ____ and ____. Who has the strength to face not God but – himself? Not the ____ future – but the here and now? And so religion is not ____. If it were, it would be the ____ of the ____."

religion/highest truth/good/finest/aspire/whole society/country/reserved/at all times/dictating/bathe/separate/tear out its heart/limbs/godlessness/unbelief/distant/questioned/beginning/end

*2. Which idea of Rushdie's does Desai quote? Explain it in your own words.*
Respect for religion paralyses people's thinking and makes new ideas/doubts seem criminal.

*3. What form of suppression does the writer discuss in the last part of the text?*
Suppression of writers by themselves/self-imprisonment/do not dare criticize religion or raise questions or doubts/power of religious leaders/writers brain-washed and afraid/no possibility of dialogue in a conservative religious society

### Additional questions

*1. Collect all the words and phrases in the text connected with religion.*

*2. Make up a semantic field around "religion", consulting other texts in the chapter, as well as Chapter Four ("Britain and Ireland") and Chapter Seven ("Religious Life").*

### Post-listening activities

*1. Discuss the role of the writer in a free/in an oppressive society.*

*2. Find out more about the life and work of Salman Rushdie and report to the class.*
See, for example, *British Life and Institutions*, p. 85, Klettbuch 51344.
This report could be a joint effort leading on to a further point of discussion.

*3. Where, for you, are the limits to freedom of religion and/or freedom of speech? Refer also to the Rushdie case.*

## 8. Freedom and suppression

### Background information

Although women played an important role in the struggle for independence, and Gandhi and Nehru laid the foundations for complete equality of the sexes in the Indian Constitution (1950), the traditionally subordinate role of women is still the norm for the mass of the people in India, especially for the 75% who live in rural areas. Women, of course, now have the vote, more possibilities in education and employment in the cities, but the literacy rate for women only rose from 29.7% in 1981 to 39.4% in 1991 (for the population as a whole it went up from 43.5% to 52.1%). An upper class education as described in Text 1 is the exception, not the rule. Women in rural areas, for example, have to work very hard physically as well as cope with the problems of frequent childbirth and insufficient health care, and it is in the country that the traditional way of life has a great hold (see Text 9). Although "suttee" (from Sanskrit "sati" = virtuous woman), the Hindu practice of self-immolation by a widow on the funeral pyre of her husband, has long since been banished, widows and single women have a very low status in society. Sons are preferred to daughters as dowries have to be provided when the daughters marry, in the form of cash and gifts, in instalments if necessary. Most marriages are still arranged (and at a very early age) and the size of the dowry depends on the social standing of the groom. Families with daughters get into debt as the dowries demanded become bigger and bigger, and although it was made illegal in 1961 the practice continues. The phenomenon of "dowry deaths" has caused great concern, and the latest statistics show that between 1988 and 1991 more people in India died because of the dowry system than in riots in the state of Punjab: 15,891 brides were killed or committed suicide in quarrels about dowries. Many deaths were in the form of kitchen accidents (burning) in the new husband's family, or starvation when payments were late or not forthcoming. The husband was then, of course, free to look for another bride and another dowry.

Current government programmes focus on measures to promote female literacy through poverty alleviation programmes, to encourage talented girls to pursue higher education by providing special scholarships and by setting up women's polytechnics and other institutions of learning. Note: PEN – abbreviation for International Association of *P*oets, *P*laywrights, *E*ditors and *N*ovelists.

## Pre-reading activities

*1. Look at Persian-style miniatures of the Moghul period/modern photographs/slides/pictures of Hindu art/cartoons etc. and discuss the image of Indian women you get from them.*

The geography and art departments at school could help provide visual material, as well as local libraries, etc.

*2. Study the picture on p. 49, and compare it to statues of Mary in Christian countries.*

## Suggested answers

1. *Summary:*
– There is a subtle form of suppression in India, which is rooted in its society and tradition and which many people consent to.
– One form of imprisonment is the image of woman as the humble, obedient loyal wife handed down from mythology.
– From infancy, women are influenced by these legends and myths, which are the cornerstone of Indian society and which they must live up to.
– This situation is not just created by men, but sustained and kept alive by women themselves.
– Illiteracy and conditioning cause a woman to accept her role because questioning it would make her life senseless.
– The suppressed state of women in Indian society can be explained in many ways, but it is mainly the lasting influence of the myth of Indian womanhood that hinders her emancipation.

*Structure:*
The speaker starts off by pointing at the main issue, then logically puts forward her arguments, paragraph by paragraph, without digressing from the main topic. She always puts forward arguments which are based on her logic, psychology and rhetorical competence and thus manages to present her ideas in an efficient and effective way.

When analyzing the structure you should look at the end of each paragraph:
– she quotes from Saul Bellow, a famous contemporary novelist
– she even quotes Sita to support her argument
– her own central statement/result of her analysis: The myth of womanhood is the cornerstone on which ... Indian society is built (ll. 62–64)
– she uses the rhetorical question "why" to link with paragraph 5
– she presents her key question ("her meaning?")
– final statement: by asking more questions she confronts her audience directly with the problems and hints at some possibilities of change

*Possible reasons for this structure:*
– she wants to pursue a convincing line of reasoning (this is a lecture)
– she tries to deepen the understanding of her audience
– she intends to cause the listeners/audience/reader to accept her view or at least seriously think about the problem
– thus she is able to give some idea of the complex situation of women in India to her audience and the reasons for it.

2. Formal language, here determined by the audience at a conference on "Freedom and Suppression" in Milan, 1989. The audience is not known to the speaker, therefore she uses precise and often difficult vocabulary in order to address that (well-educated) audience. Her wide range of vocabulary and command of complex sentences (e.g. ll. 3–9), as well as the tight, logical structure of her speech/text show a high level of

intelligence and linguistic competence which she expects of her listeners, too.
Formal words:
connivance (l. 4), indict (l. 9), adjoining (l. 14), deify (l. 18), consort (l. 28), recourse (l. 90) etc.
literary words:
fecund (l. 23), loins (l. 25), enticing (l. 26) etc.

3. Possibilities of change:
– change of attitudes in family/politics/society
– way of bringing up Indian girls (modern role models not myth)
– education of parents/husbands in different possibilities for women
– consciousness-raising among the women themselves
– education of women (literacy campaigns, school and higher education, vocational training)
– education of women in their legal rights (Constitution)
– better health care and education (nutrition programmes, family-planning, hygiene training etc.)
– creation of more possibilities of employment (at home, cooperatives, cottage industry etc.).

4. Suffrage/class differences/working women/women as slaves/financial dependence/education for all/medieval ladies in Europe/Victorian wives/women and literature/family-planning/birth control etc.

### Additional questions

1. Rewrite the third paragraph (ll. 47–64) in less formal or colloquial English, using shorter sentences and simpler vocabulary.

2. Find out more about the current situation of women in India from other sources (e.g. magazines, encyclopedias, Third World literature etc.) and discuss your findings in class.

### Post-reading activities

1. Report/paper/talk: The role of women in the Third World. Compare this with the situation in Europe.

2. Discuss the myths/traditions/images/expectations that determine the role and self-image of women in your own country.

## 9. The grim face of the caste system (GK)

### Background information

1. *Caste and Hinduism:*
The caste [kɑːst] system applies only to the Hindu part of Indian society (i.e. to over 80% of Indians). Caste is related to the Hindu belief in cosmological unity, and to attain this oneness with the eternal Hindus must follow the dictates of their *karma* (destiny or fate, the principle of justice which determines a person's state of life and the state of his reincarnations as the effect of his past deeds) by strictly observing *dharma* (laws of right living). In Hindu philosophy each caste has its appropriate status, rights, duties, and *dharma*. Thus caste is a matter of accepting the consequences of the birth and rebirth circle, and a Hindu believer cannot break that circle of rebirth which makes him part of the universal order (cf. ll. 56–59 of this text).
Today the caste system in its traditional sense has been outlawed (see Fact File "The problem of caste", SB p. 287), but it continues to manifest itself in the form of *jatis* or subcastes, which refer rather to an Indian's job and occupation than his religious beliefs. Political power has now shifted from the highest caste, the Brahmins, to the major cultivating and artisan castes, but the Brahmins, thanks to their tradition of education, have moved into the key positions of economic and technological power.

2. *Harijans/Untouchables:*
With the social classification and differentiation of Hindu society into four main castes, in the course of time a fifth group developed that was so low as to be considered 'outside' and 'beneath' the caste itself. The members of this 'casteless' group are referred to as "untouchables", "outcastes", "scheduled castes" or (by Gandhi) *harijan* – "children of god". These people inherited the kinds of work that were considered least desirable, such as slaughtering animals, sweeping the streets, leather tanning and scavenging. Under Nehru the government initi-

*India*

ated an affirmative action programme that guaranteed the untouchables 22.5 percent of all government jobs and provided them with free education.

This plan succeeded in uplifting a small part of the untouchable population, but at the same time angered members of the lower castes (the Shudras), who did not receive such benefits. In 1990 Prime Minister V.P. Sing's proposal to reserve 27 percent of all government jobs and university seats for the members of 3,000 lower caste groups caused violent protests, especially by upper-caste students (who felt they would be disadvantaged) and finally led to his resignation.
*Note:* Jats are members of an Indo-European people widely scattered throughout the Punjab, Rajputana and Uttar Pradesh – not to be confused with *jati* (=sub-caste).

## Methodisch-didaktische Hinweise

Dieser Bericht über das tragische Schicksal von zwei verliebten jungen Leuten stammt aus *Time* (April 15, 1991, S. 61), wobei die genaue Beschreibung der Hinrichtung im SB nicht abgedruckt wurde, da die Grausamkeit des Geschehens für manche Schüler/Klassen zu schockierend sein könnte. Die Herausgeber überlassen es daher den Lehrern/Lehrerinnen, ob dieser Zusatztext behandelt wird oder nicht. Der vollständige Textauszug läßt sich aber, abhängig von Unterrichtssituation und individueller Methode, jederzeit in den Unterricht einbauen, z.B. bei der Bearbeitung von Aufgabe 2: Hier kann die Präsentierung des vollständigen Texts (z.B. auf Folie) eine erneute Kommentierung dieser Hinrichtungsaktion sowie eine umfassende Diskussion auslösen.
Im SB nicht abgedruckter Abschnitt:

"Brijendra and his friend Ram Kishen – another untouchable, who had helped the couple in their getaway – as well as their brothers and fathers were thrashed with sticks. The two young men were hung upside down, and their lips and genitals scorched with burning cloth. At dawn, Roshni was dragged out of her house and, along with the young men, taken to a huge banyan tree that spreads over a temple to the god Siva. Ropes were thrown around their necks, and then the fathers, including Roshni's, were forced to hoist their children up. The parents could not summon the strength to complete the task, and bystanders rushed to take their places. When the young people were taken down, Ram Kishen was dead; Roshni and Brijendra may still have been alive. All three were then placed on a pyre and burned beyond recognition."

Die Aufgabe 5 kann entweder als Hausaufgabe nach der Erarbeitung des Textes oder als Referat aufgegeben werden.

## Pre-reading activity

*Imagine you have fallen in love with someone and want to marry, but the family of the person you love is totally against the marriage.*
*– How would you react?*
*– Can anybody/any institution forbid you to marry whoever you want?*
e.g. Catholic/Protestant; Black American/White European; Turkish boy/German girl; upper-class girl/working-class boy; Chinese/Irish etc.
This could also be done as a post-reading activity: class discussion.

## Suggested answers

1. *Romeo and Juliet (ca. 1595):*
The Montague and Capulet families are enemies to the death
Romeo and Juliet fall in love in the Capulets' house
They get married with the help of a monk
As he kills an enemy in a quarrel, Romeo must flee
Due to tragic complications both Romeo and Juliet die
Shocked by the death of their children, both families are reconciled
*A village in India (1991):*
Hostilities between castes and discrimination of certain castes are widespread in India, especially in rural areas
The two lovers are not allowed to socialize with each other
They elope/run away
(Thus they break the Hindu ban on intercaste marriages)
The village council decides to punish the two lovers:
They are brutally executed (by parents, too)
The tragic fate of the young couple brings no reconciliation between families or castes/the problems caused by caste remain unresolved

2. Elders as guardians of tradition and honour/offence against tradition/tradition as opposed to law/extreme punishment/cruelty and brutality of punishment/an example for other young people etc.
Arguments of high-caste villagers: endangering marriages of other daughters/reputation of village/disgrace must be punished/social structure of village threatened.

3. – executions
– acts of lawlessness (l. 40)
– declaring roads etc. "off-limits" (l. 44)
– murder, rape, injury, arson (l. 47)
– forcefeeding excrement to untouchables (l. 53)
– stripping Harijan women and making them dance to their husbands' drums (ll. 53–56)

4. See ll. 31–37, ll. 60–66 and ll. 73–76 – Constitution, affirmative action, literacy programmes, education, Parliament, etc.

5. Use fact file SB, p. 287, encyclopedias etc.

6. See "Background information".
The advantages for the "untouchables" are clear – education/training; more possibilities of employment; more independence from landowners; more social mobility etc. Disadvantages: affirmative action, in a way, is another form of discrimination and usually leads to protests of the other groups, social tensions, bitterness and rivalry (e.g. for jobs, places at university etc.).

7. Cf. Asians at American universities/Afro-Americans applying for jobs/equal opportunities employers in Britain/women in political office in Germany etc. Some people find affirmative action and/or jobs quotas unfair, a new form of inequality.

### Additional questions

*1. Discuss the picture on p. 52, SB.*
Solid, clean house/tents on dry waste ground; colourful saris and men in European dress/dark, poor-looking clothes and bare feet; separation, too, of men and women in upper-caste scene

*2. Choose one of the following words and construct a word family around it: forgive/socialize/touch/furious/punishment.*

### Post-reading activities

*1. Report/paper/talk: The caste system.*
Cf. Question 5, fact file p. 287 etc. See Bibliography 29.

*2. The pre-reading activity in this case could also be done after the text in order to provoke a lively, personal discussion.*

## 10. Life in a Bombay shanty-town (GK)

### Background information

With 12.6 million inhabitants (1991) Bombay is now the largest city in India (Calcutta 10.9, New Delhi 8.4, Madras 5.3 million).
Cf. Anita Desai's novel, *Baumgartner's Bombay* (Penguin) and *Such a Long Journey* by Rohinton Mistry, a young writer from Bombay who was a finalist for the 1991 Booker Prize.
*Dr. B.R. Ambedkar* (1891-1956) fought all his life for securing justice for the *harijans*. Born the fourteenth child of a poor Harijan, A. knew from his own experience what it meant to be born an untouchable in India. In 1912 he was the first Harijan to graduate in India and – through scholarships – studied in the USA, Germany and England. His struggle for the betterment of the deprived classes took the form of non-violent campaigns to establish the right of the untouchables to use the water in the village tank, for example, and to enter the temples. He objected to violence and had great faith in education and law as instruments of change. After India's independence he was appointed as chairman of the Drafting Committee of the Constituent Assembly and thus he helped to draft the constitution for the new nation. In 1951 cooperation with the nationalist leaders ended when in frustration he resigned from the cabinet. In his opinion the cultivated elitism of the majority of caste Hindus, who were obsessed with pollution and the material advantages of a hierarchical order, had not really changed.
In the last years of his life he broke with Hinduism and embraced Buddhism, which he considered as a religion preaching brotherhood and humanitarianism, and in it he saw the ultimate

emancipation of the untouchables. This religious conversion on a mass scale – with him over 3 million untouchables converted to so-called neo-Buddhism – was an unprecedented event in the history of India. (See SB p. 54, ll. 83–88.)

Only recently were the neo-Buddhists included in the Scheduled Castes, who – due to a political action programme – are guaranteed 22.5 percent of all government jobs and provided with free education. Practically, however, only a small percentage of the untouchable population has been uplifted in society.

## Methodische Hinweise

1. Als Einstieg in diesen Themenkomplex könnte man Bilder oder Dias verwenden, die die Lebensbedingungen in einem Slum der Dritten Welt zeigen (z. B. aus der Erdkundesammlung).
2. Die Aufgabe 5 könnte als Hausaufgabe aufgegeben, die Schülertexte verglichen und in der Klasse diskutiert werden, um das ganze soziale Problem Armut auf einem persönlichen Niveau zu besprechen und in Relation zu den indischen Problemen zu bringen.

## Pre-reading activities

1. *Look at the picture on p. 53 and describe it.*

2. *Why do you think so many live like this?*
Looking for work/hope of better material life/no land etc.

3. *How/where do poor people live in your country? What kind of housing problems are there here and what are the reasons for this?*

## Suggested answers

1. Mohan's life:
– left his home village with his mother, his sister and his two brothers 20 years ago to live in the streets of Bombay because his father was mentally ill and couldn't work
– left school to work, first rag-picking, then helping in a tea-stall
– from the age of seven was left to guard the pavement dwelling while his mother was at work
– with the money he now earns he supports his whole family (mother's operation/brothers' education/sister and her baby/his father back in the village)
– he is now catching up with his education (college in the afternoon)
– he tells his family he works in a hotel but he is in fact a male prostitute

2.
| line: | problems: | causes: |
|---|---|---|
| 11 | people can't afford an operation | poverty, no medical insurance, inefficient health system |
| 16-18 | lowering of the water table, soil erosion, loss of land | intensive cultivation, e.g. sugar cane, destruction of ecosystems, e.g. forests |
| 20-22 | migration to the big cities | loss of land, few employment opportunities in most rural areas |
| 25 | begging | poverty, welfare system cannot cope |
| 35 | young people leave school to work | inadequate social welfare, poverty, large families |
| 38 | pavement dwellings | not enough houses for large population |
| 42-45 | growth of slums/shanties made of cardboard | rapid migration of millions of people to urban areas, poverty, lack of proper housing |
| 46 | high land prices in big cities | booming/expanding big cities, the centres of administration and industry |
| 47-54 | poor hygienic conditions, lack of water/sanitation | inadequate infrastructure which can't cope with urban explosion |
| 73-75 | whole family needs to work | low wages, few social benefits |
| 77-79 | sweat shops/exploitation | low wages, people desperate for work |
| 132-3 | young people forced into prostitution | poverty, lack of education, few opportunities of employment |

3. He presents a personal/an eye-witness report of an individual case which appeals to the emotions and yet provides enough objective information to let the reader form his own opinion. So he not only gives a very detailed and vivid account of Mohan's life, but also provides background and supplementary information about life in an Indian shanty-town and the social and economic problems of Indian cities. This is typical of a feature story (see p. 54, SB). The intention is to evoke interest, to inform and to move.

4. See *Words in Context*, pp. 106–116, Klettbuch 51961.
– encourage labour-intensive industry in rural areas/to stop rural exodus
– support an ecological beneficial agriculture/spend more on improved methods of irrigation etc.
– slowly build up an adequate infrastructure both in the cities and in the country
– encourage work-study projects for young people so that they can both have an education and earn money
– abolish discrimination (caste system of land ownership) so that fewer people are forced to leave the villages
– limit the (excessive) population growth (of 2.1 percent per year in India in the last decade)
– increase the literacy rate (in 1991 it was 52 percent nationwide, but only 40 percent among women, and there are big differences between the regions)
– give housing priority
– give project-linked aid to small ventures in rural areas (cottage industry, cooperatives) etc.

5. Homelessness/unemployment/take to drink/vicious circle/on the streets/sleeping rough/slip through social net/loss of job = loss of flat/new guest-workers/refugees/tramps

**Additional questions**

*1. Give synonyms for the following:*
– *peer (l. 1)*/look closely
– *remove (l. 5)*/take off
– *allow (l. 30)*/permit
– *cease (l. 32)*/end, stop
– *dwelling (l. 38)*/home, house
– *noisy (l. 45)*/loud

*2. Give antonyms for the following:*
– *privacy (l. 51)*/public
– *reduce (l. 54)*/increase
– *construct (l. 56)*/destroy
– *insert (l. 69)*/remove, take out
– *flexible (l. 69)*/inflexible, rigid
– *cramped (l. 78)*/spacious

*3. Write a short but creative essay about Mohan's/his family's future. What do you think will happen to them?*

**Post-reading activities**

*1. Discussion: What can the rich First World do for the Third World?*
Group work leading on to class discussion.

*2. Give a talk on Bombay/Calcutta/Delhi – portrait of an Indian city.*
Past and present/problems of urban growth/slides from geography department
Cf. Roland Joffé's film *City of Joy* from Dominique Lapierre's bestseller. See Bibliography 13.

*3. Report/paper: Urban problems in the Third World.*

# 11. A country of extremes (GK)

## Background information

India's climate is governed by periodic rains or monsoons. There are three main seasons:
- the cold season from about November to the end of February (the north-west monsoon brings light, irregular showers)
- the hot season from March to June (temperatures in central and northern India can be very high then)
- the rainy season from June till October (southwest monsoon)

India, however, is a large country with many topographical variations: mountains which include the highest mountain system of the world, plateaus and fertile plains as well as deserts. Therefore there is great climatic diversity: India has the wettest place on earth with about 20,000 mm rainfall in Meghalaya, southwest of Assam, as well as the Thar desert in Rajasthan (see photo p. 55), which receives only 12 mms of rain annually. Temperature varies as much as rainfall in different regions in India: Hill stations in the Himalayan region have the lowest annual averages of about 13° C (Germany: only 7–10° C), the Indo-Gangetic Plain registers an average of 26° C, and Tamil Nadu in the south has the highest average with 29.5° C.

This diversity, not only of people, languages, lifestyles and religion, but first of all of landscape and climate is the most striking aspect of this subcontinent. Because of these extremes of climate the land can be hit by the following disasters:

1. Floodings, especially along the big rivers like the Ganges where most of the population live, but also in drier regions after heavy monsoon rains.
2. Droughts, not only in naturally dry regions, but often across the whole land.
3. Destruction of fertile land/soil erosion due to heavy rains, intensive cultivation, deforestation etc. in all parts of India.

Even when such natural hazards threaten only single areas, the lives of millions of Indians are affected. The consequences can be loss of homes and crops, bad harvests, epidemics etc.

## Didaktischer Hinweis

Die unterschiedliche fiktive Umsetzung einer analogen Situation (nämlich der Zeit vor und während des Monsunregens) in einem Gedicht bzw. einem Prosatext zu erkennen und in ihrer Wirkung auf den (möglichen) Leser zu bewerten, bleibt vorrangiges Lernziel. Gleichzeitig soll dem Leser die fundamentale Bedeutung des Monsuns für Indien vor Augen geführt werden. Fächerübergreifende Kooperation mit den Erdkunde-Kollegen wäre hier sehr zu empfehlen.

## Pre-reading activities

*1. Look at the pictures on pp. 55–56, describe and compare them.*

*2. Why do you think millions of Indians long for the monsoon period every year?*

*3. Is there any aspect of climate in Europe that plays an important role in people's lives?*

## Suggested answers

1. *Poem:* drought – peasants waiting for rain
*Prose excerpt:* the coming of the monsoon in a small town

2. *Poem:*
- free verse (unrhymed)
- imaginative language (metaphors, similes etc.)
- timeless scene (a typical village)
- poet/speaker not personally involved (description from outside)
- many details to create a full picture

*Prose text:*
- narrative prose
- popular mythological references
- exact names of people
- one particular place
- first-person narrator observes and reports the scene, but also involved (his own experience)
- many details which make it vivid

3. Possible points:
- both texts are products of a writer's imagination, which may influence the reader's imagination
- the reader gets a vivid picture of both scenes
- the writers offer an intense view, like a close-up photo or film shot

- the language of the poem is more imaginative
- the poem appeals more to the imagination
- the poem is more timeless
- the prose text is livelier and more realistic
- the prose text is more personal
- the prose text is more direct/immediate
- the poem is more difficult/less accessible than the prose excerpt

4. *Poem:*
- l. 2: parched fields
- l. 3: ancient plow
- l. 4: untethered oxen
- ll. 6 and 14: banyan (tree)
- l. 9: mud wall
- l. 10: turbaned shadows

*Prose excerpt:*
- ll. 1, 3, 7, 10: Lord Krishna
- l. 8: King Kamsa's elephant
- l. 17: temple tank
- l. 21: naked young man with dancing bear
- l. 23: rickshaw
- l. 30: Deep Chand/Ramu (names)

5. *Simile:* lean like the helmets of knights (l. 11), i.e. the shadows of the heads with turbans are distorted and therefore thin.
*metaphor:* – a mirror of water (l. 5), i.e. the surface of the water is so smooth that it acts like a mirror (they are perhaps just dreaming of water)
- the sudden charge of wild horses (l. 21), i.e. the noise of pouring rain (wild horses is a common metaphor for a rough sea)
- whittled cumulus (l. 18), as if carved, or cut up

*personification:*
- oxen dreaming (l. 4), as if they were human
- the twilight swallows their stillness (l. 13), i.e. absorbs
- the evening throws their turbaned shadows (l. 10) ... slithering their heads (l. 12)

*alliteration:*
- lean like the helmets (l. 11)
- swallows their stillness (l. 13)
- sound of a stone skimming (l.15)

The poet's careful choice of words and images, which is much more subtle than in the prose excerpt, contributes to evoke a scene full of stillness and suspense. The atmosphere is like the calm before a storm, with little hints of a possible change in the weather ("leaves ... ripple", "whittled cumulus"), very little movement ("a hawk dives ... flutters") and only the light sound of a stone skimming.

6. *Scenario 1:*
little rain/periodic lack of water/droughts result in bad harvests/crop failure/malnutrition/famine/hunger

*Scenario 2:*
too much rain/floods (like other natural catastrophes or hazards) can destroy houses, fields, barriers, water-tanks etc., take human lives and affect the whole economic and political system. In a populous country where 75 percent of the people live in rural areas and depend largely on agriculture, the monsoons are a matter of life and death, and essential for the survival of the people.

**Additional questions**

*1. Describe and compare the two pictures on p. 287 (fact file).*
Dry, dusty place/wet area – rice-planting; women's work fetching and carrying water/men working in fields; women in long saris/men almost naked; both traditional lifestyles with no technical aids in sight

*2. Make a list of the different "-ing" forms in the last paragraph of the prose text (ll. 25–36, p. 56) and explain their function.*
Wading/salvaging/using/flooding/sailing

**Post-reading activities**

*1. Report/paper talk: Rural India.*
See Bibliography 10, 14, 15.

*2. Give a talk on the geography of India, using maps and slides from the geography department.*
This could be done before or after the comparison of poem and prose excerpt.

# 12. Superpower rising

## Background information

Facts that support India's claim to "superpowership":
- India is the dominant military power in the subcontinent
- India is the world's largest arms importer (but spends less than 5 percent of its GNP on defence)
- India has quadrupled its military research and development budget since 1982
- in 1974 India exploded what it called a "peaceful nuclear device"
- India possesses the world's third largest pool of scientists, engineers and technicians, next only to the USA and Russia
- Indian scientists and engineers have developed nuclear weapons (which they could produce "overnight") and ballistic missile programmes; on May 20, 1992 they succeeded in launching India's first satellite, and on May 29, 1992 they successfully tested a 1,500-mile-range missile that can carry a nuclear warhead, thus changing the strategic balance
- Indian armed forces are the fourth largest in the world (after Russia, China and the USA)
- according to India's strategic thinkers, this build-up will help persuade the world to give India its rightful place in international diplomacy; many Indians cannot understand why the second largest country (and the largest democracy) is not even a permanent member of the U.N. Security Council
- India is self-sufficient in food, textiles and a number of industrial products
- rich in natural resources, India has built up a strong industrial base and widespread infrastructure
- soon India could become a major world trade and economic power; it is the 'economic giant in the making' and plans to export high-technology products (research reactors, radioisotopes, radiation technology, computer software, etc.)

Critics say that this build-up is mainly responsible for India's huge debts and could seriously affect the economy in a country where 65 percent of the population still depend on agriculture for their livelihood and where more than a quarter of the population earn only about $20 a month.

## Pre-reading activity

*Look at the picture on p. 57. How does it contrast with the image of India you have so far?*
Modern, militaristic, western

## Suggested answers

1. a) India the military power/India of Gandhi's pacifism
b) *Modern India:*
- highly developed, self-confident and capable (ll. 28–30)
- technicians have mastered modern welding techniques to assemble expensive weapons (ll. 35–36)
- fighter pilots zip overhead at supersonic speed (ll. 45–46)
- engineers call up colour video displays of design cross-sections for combat planes (ll. 50–53)

*Traditional/old India:*
- backward and mired in superstition and squalor (ll. 25–26)
- a slum where poor families live in cardoard shacks beside rubbish dumps (ll. 40–41)
- bullock carts creep past the perimeter (ll. 43–44)
- women collect fallen tree branches for firewood (ll. 48–49)

2. – traditional enmity between India and Pakistan (at war three times since independence)
- it is part of India's ambition to gain international respect as a modern industrial power (see third paragraph)
- India wants to be taken seriously and viewed as a world power (last paragraph)

3. Some points to be made: border problems with neighbours Pakistan and China/problem of other Asian countries having the bomb, e.g. China/prestige of advanced technology/aid from West often linked to armaments/desire for modern image/money spent on arms out of proportion to money spent on basic problems of food, housing etc./contradiction with pacifism preached by Gandhi and emphasis on religious, spiritual matters etc.

4. "Western" India/advanced technology/militaristic nation/skilled workers/computers/army etc.
Cf. Gandhi's pacifism/emphasis on spiritual matters/traditional society with rigid roles/caste system/poverty/Third World problems etc.

### Additional questions

1. Explain the use of "breakup" (l. 9) and "buildup" (l. 15). Find more phrasal verbs that are often changed into nouns.
To break down, to break through, to hold up, to take away etc.

2. Comment on this quote from Anita Desai: "The West has two fixed notions about India. One is that it is a romantic land, full of holy men, maharajas, palaces and elephants. The other is of India as a land of horrors – a place of intolerable poverty and squalor, hunger and disease."

### Post-reading activities

1. Report/paper/talk: Give a short report on recent events in India.
See Bibliography 25, 26, 27 and other recent newspapers.

2. How has your image of India changed since you started reading this chapter?
Group work followed by classroom discussion

3. If you were to visit India, what would you like to see/look for/study?

## Test: Gandhi and the street-sweeper's son

### Biographical note

Rasipuram K. Narayan was born in Madras in 1906. He worked as a teacher and in journalism before publishing his forst novel *Swami and Friends* in 1935 which enabled him to become a full-time writer. His 'Malgudi' novels are set in an enchanting fictitious South Indian town. He has also written four collections of short stories and two travel books. His characters, who represent all possible aspects of Indian life, struggle to carve out a future for themselves in a society which is torn between old-established Indian traditions and Western attitudes and influences. Narayan has been awarded many literary prizes and is often considered India's foremost storyteller. His most recent novel, *The World of Nagaraj*, was published by Heinemann in 1990.

### Introduction to the text

Gandhi is visiting the fictitious district of Malgudi. The whole town is celebrating this important event and the Chairman, an important political leader and wealthy head of the district, has invited Gandhi to his house. Gandhi makes no show of being impressed as he is guided around this "palace", although the Chairman had gone to great pains to do so. He had spent weeks preparing everything; he had placed a huge Bentley at Gandhi's disposal; he had positioned a few spinning wheels in different parts of the house; he had bought a white Gandhi cap for himself and an appropriate plain white sari for his wife etc. In the lines preceding this excerpt the Chairman has tried at least three times to offer Gandhi a glass of orange juice (made from oranges grown in his own gardens, of course). But this only acts as a signal for Gandhi to invite all the children around and offer them lots of fruit from the Chairman's garden.

Gandhi had completely relaxed. His secretary was telling him: 'In fifteen minutes the deputation from ... will be here, and after that –.' He was reading from an engagement pad.
The Chairman regretted that both the District  5
Superintendent of Police and the Collector had turned away at his Buckingham Palace gate after escorting the procession that far as an act of official courtesy: if they had been here now, they would have managed the crowd. For a moment  10
he wondered with real anxiety whether the crowd proposed to stay all night. But his problem was unexpectedly solved for him. Mahatmaji saw one child standing apart from the rest – a small dark fellow with a protruding belly and  15
wearing nothing over his body except a cast-off knitted vest, adult size, full of holes, which reached down to his ankles. The boy stood aloof

from the rest, on the very edge of the crowd. His face was covered with mud, his feet were dirty, he had stuck his fingers into his mouth and was watching the proceedings on the veranda keenly, his eyes bulging with wonder and desire. He had not dared to come up the steps, though attracted by the oranges. He was trying to edge his way through.

Mahatma's eyes travelled over the crowd and rested on this boy – following his gaze the Chairman was bewildered. He had a feeling of uneasiness. Mahatmaji beckoned to the young fellow. One of his men went and fetched him. The Chairman's blood boiled. Of course people must like poor people and so on, but why bring in such a dirty boy, an untouchable, up the steps and make him so important? For a moment he felt a little annoyance with Mahatmaji himself, but soon suppressed it as a sinful emotion. He felt the need to detach himself sufficiently from his surroundings to watch without perturbation the happenings around him. Mahatmaji had the young urchin hoisted beside him on the divan. 'Oh, Lord, all the world's gutters are on this boy, and he is going to leave a permanent stain on that Kashmir counterpane.' The boy was making himself comfortable on the divan, having accepted the hospitality offered him by the Mahatma. He nestled close to the Mahatma, who was smoothing out his matted hair with his fingers, and was engaged in an earnest conversation with him.

The Chairman was unable to catch the trend of their talk. He stepped nearer, trying to listen with all reverence. The reward he got for it was a smile from the Mahatma himself. The boy was saying: 'My father sweeps the streets.'

'With a long broom or a short broom?' the Mahatma asked.

The boy explained, 'He has both a long broom and a short broom.' He was spitting out the seeds of an orange.

The Mahatma turned to someone and explained: 'It means that he is both a municipal sweeper and that he has scavenging work to do in private houses also. The long broom ought to be the municipal emblem.'

'Where is your father at the moment?'

'He is working at the market. He will take me home when he has finished his work.'

'And how have you managed to come here?'

'I was sitting on the road waiting for my father and I came along with the crowd. No one stopped me when I entered the gates.'

'That's a very clever boy,' Mahatmaji said. 'I'm very happy to see you. But you must not spit those pips all over the place, in fact you must never spit at all. It's very unclean to do so, and may cause others a lot of trouble. When you eat an orange, others must not notice it at all. The place must be absolutely tidy even if you have polished off six at a time.'

He laughed happily at his own quip, and then taught the boy what to do with the pips, how to hide the skin, and what to do with all the superfluous bits packed within an orange. The boy laughed with joy. All the men around watched the proceedings with respectful attention. And then Gandhi asked:

'Where do you live?'

The boy threw up his arm to indicate a far distance: 'There at the end of the river ... .'

'Will you let me come to your house?'

The boy hesitated and said, 'Not now – because, because it's so far away.'

'Don't bother about that. I've a motor-car here given to me, you see, by this very rich man. I can be there in a moment. I'll take you along in the motor-car too if you will show me your house.'

'It is not a house like this,' said the boy, 'but made of bamboo or something.'

'Is that so!' said the Mahatma. 'Then I'll like it all the more. I'll be very happy there.'

He had a brief session with a delegation which had come to see him by appointment; when it left, he dictated some notes, wrote something, and then, picking up his staff, said to the Chairman, 'Let us go to this young man's house. I'm sure you will also like it.'

'Now?' asked the Chairman in great consternation. He mumbled, 'Shall we not go there tomorrow?'

'No, I've offered to take this child home. I must not disappoint him. I'd like to see his father too, if he can be met anywhere on the way.'

Mahatmaji gave his forefinger to the young boy to clutch and allowed himself to be led down the veranda steps.

From *Waiting for the Mahatma* by R.K. Narayan, Lansing: Michigan State University Press, 1981, pp. 47–50. Reprinted by permission.

## Annotations

29 **bewildered**   confused, puzzled
39 **perturbation**   anxiety and worry
41 **urchin**   a very poor child
42 **gutter**   *Straßenrinne, Gosse*
44 **counterpane**   a decorative cover for a bed or couch
47 **to nestle**   to move into a comfortable position, to snuggle
63 **to scavenge**   to collect things by searching among waste and unwanted objects
75 **pip**   *(Obst -)Kern*
81 **quip**   an amusing or clever remark
84 **superfluous**   *überflüssig*

## I. Language

1. Find a suitable substitute; keep to the sentence structure.

a) l. 8: ... after *escorting* the procession
b) l. 12: ... the crowd *proposed* to stay ...
c) l. 18: The boy stood *aloof* from the rest
d) l. 25: He was trying *to edge* his way through
e) l. 105: ... *picking* up his staff
f) l. 108: ... asked the Chairman in *great consternation*.

2. Explain; you may change the sentence structure.

a) l. 29–30: *he had a feeling of uneasiness*.
b) l. 42: ... *all the world's gutters* are on this boy
c) ll. 51–52: ... was unable to *catch the trend* of their talk.
d) l. 91: Will you *let* me come to your house?
e) l. 115: ... gave his forefinger to the young boy to *clutch*.

3. Find the corresponding abstract nouns (not the -ing-forms):
a) l. 12: propose
b) l. 45: accept
c) l. 49: engage
d) l. 89: indicate
e) l. 112: disappoint

4. Name the stylistic devices used here and explain their function:
a) l. 32: The Chairman's blood boiled.
b) ll. 74–76: But you must not spit ..., in fact you must never spit ...

## II. Questions

1. Give a brief summary of what happens at the Chairman's house.

2. Characterize Gandhi as he is presented in this excerpt from the novel.

3. How does Narayan characterize the Chairman and in what tone?

4. Which other devices does Narayan use to make his narrative lively and interesting for the reader?

## III. Comment/composition

Choose one of the topics and write about 200 words.

1. The writer of this narrative, R.K. Narayan, writes in English although he is Indian. Can you imagine why contemporary Indian writers such as Anita Desai, Salman Rushdie and Gita Mehta do this?

2. The practice of untouchability is an offence against human rights.

3. Social discrimination is a problem in Europe as well as in India.

# Bibliography

1. Alter, Dissanayake, eds. *Penguin Book of Modern Indian Short Stories*. Harmondsworth: Penguin, 1990.
2. *British Life and Institutions*. Klettbuch 51344.
3. Centre for Science and Environment. *India's Environment*. New Delhi, 1984-85.
4. Copley A. *Gandhi – against the tide*. Kent, UK: Basil Blackwell, 1987.
5. Desai, Anita. *Baumgartner's Bombay*. Harmondsworth: Penguin, 1989.
6. Fischer, L. *The Life of Mahatma Gandhi*. London: Jonathan Cape, 1951 (Grafton, 1982).
7. Forster, E.M. *Passage to India*. Harmondsworth: Penguin, 1936.
8. Gandhi M.K. *The Words of Gandhi* (selected by Richard Attenborough). New York: Newmarket Press, 1982.
9. Gold & Attenborough. *Gandhi; a pictorial biography*. New York: Newmarket Press, 1983.
10. Government of India Tourist Office (Indisches Fremdenverkehrsamt, Kaiserstr. 77 III, 6 Frankfurt/Main 1). *India – A democracy on the move*.
11. Hutchins, Francis G. *India's revolution. Gandhi and the Quit India Movement*. Cambridge, Mass: 1973.
12. Jhabvala, Ruth Prawer. *How I Became a Holy Mother and Other Stories*. Harmondsworth: Penguin.
13. Lapierre, Dominique. *The City of Joy – An Epic of Love, Heroism and Hope in the India of Mother Theresa*. New York: Warner Books, 1992.
14. Ministry of External Affairs. *India Perspectives*. Published monthly.
15. Ministry of Information and Broadcasting, Government of India. *India 1987* (1988....) – *A reference annual*.
16. Naipaul, V.S. *India: A Wounded Civilization*. London: Penguin, 1979.
17. Naipaul, V.S. *India – A Million Mutinies Now*. London: Heinemann, 1990.
18. Narayan, R.K. *Malgudi Days*. London: Heinemann, 1982.
19. Perspectives 8, *Empire, Commonwealth, Europe*. Klettbuch 51368, pp. 11–24.
20. Rushdie, Salman. *Midnight's Children*. 1981.
21. Scott, Paul. *The Raj Quartet*. London: Granada, 1985 (Panther Books).
22. Sharp, Gene. *Gandhi as a political strategist: with essays on ethics and politics*. Boston: 1979.
23. Singh, Khushwant. "The Mark of Vishnu" from *Great Commonwealth Short Stories*, Klettbuch 57944.
24. Spear, Percival. *India, a Modern History*. Ann Arbor: University of Michigan Press, 1961.
25. *Time*, "Superpower Rising", April 3, 1989.
26. *Time*, "Unity or Chaos", November 12, 1990.
27. *Time*, "Moment of Truth", May 20, 1991.
28. Wint, Guy, ed. *Asia Handbook*. Harmondsworth: Penguin, 1969.
29. Zinkin, Taya. *Caste Today*. Oxford: Oxford University Press, 1965.

Other novels by Desai, Narayan, Naipaul, Jhabvala etc. are available in Penguin paperbacks.

# 3 Modern Britain

## The structure of the chapter

| Changing Britain (overall views) |
|---|
| 1. Britain in decline<br>724 words<br>book excerpt (current affairs) |
| cartoon (map) p. 60 |
| 2. Listening Comprehension: Divided Britain<br>6 min. 3 sec.<br>interview |

| Lifestyles: urban, rural, academic, business, class |
|---|
| 3. Rural England struggles to survive urban blitz<br>834 words<br>newspaper article (feature) |
| 4. Lifestyles<br>c. 1460 words<br>novel excerpt |
| comic strip p. 68 |

| The Thatcher era |
|---|
| 5. The Archbishop and the wealth ethic<br>1002 words<br>feature story based on interview |
| 6. A great prime minister<br>898 words<br>editorial |
| 7. In retrospect<br>418 words<br>letter to the editor |
| advertisement p. 73 |

| Particular issues: health, race, poverty, the monarchy |
|---|
| 8. Monitoring the heart<br>1274 words<br>pamphlet excerpt (personal account) |
| 9. Filed away in a cardboard box city<br>903 words<br>newspaper article (feature) |
| 10. A long way from basic decency<br>846 words<br>newspaper article (column) |
| advertisement p. 83 |
| 11. Modernise the monarchy<br>753 words<br>newspaper article (editorial) |

## Suggestions for reports/papers/talks

The nations/regions of Great Britain: England (north and south); Scotland; Wales (three or four reports) – before/after text 1

Ethnic minorities in other European countries: a comparison with the situation in Britain – after text 1

Church and State in England – before text 5

Margaret Thatcher – before/after text 6 or 7

Britain's National Health Service – before text 8

Racial violence in Britain today – after text 10

The historical origins of the exclusion of Catholics from the monarchy – after text 11

### Vocabulary

*Thematischer Grund- und Aufbauwortschatz Englisch*, Klettbuch 51955, pp. 108–123, 132–138, 152–177

*Words in Context – Thematischer Oberstufenwortschatz*, Klettbuch 51961, pp. 46–57, 62–65

# 1. Britain in decline?

### Methodisch-didaktische Hinweise

Am motivierendsten ist der Einstieg über eine Beschreibung des *Punch cover* "Disunited Kingdom" von 1987, SB S. 60. Dieser Cartoon ist als *unit-opener* gemeint, konnte aber in diesem Fall aus drucktechnischen Gründen nicht weiter vorne plaziert werden. Ohne Hilfe werden die Schüler nur einige Elemente des "Vexierbildes" auf Anhieb erschließen können – was jedoch als "Appetitanreger" ausreichend wäre. Hilfreich wäre es, die Schülerreferate zu den Landesteilen (s.u.) vorauszuschicken. Ansonsten informiert der Lehrer; die Schülerreferate können dann später die landeskundlichen Kenntnisse über "Modern Britain" vertiefen helfen.

### Picture p. 60: Punch cover

The three constitutive parts of Great Britain – Scotland, Wales, and England, are seen drifting apart in the sea. Wales and Scotland show their national flags, England shows the royal English flag, with Margaret Thatcher's portrait instead of the lion's head.
Scotland is laden with bottles, especially on the western islands. Together with the placard "Loch Malt" (in a lake suggesting Loch Ness complete with Nessie) this hints at the high number of (malt) whisky distilleries in the country. "Ben Porage", standing for Ben Nevis, Scotland's and Britain's highest mountain (Gaelic *Ben* = mountain peak), makes fun of "porridge" (old spelling: porage), the dish traditionally popular in Scotland. The round brown objects are haggis, another Scottish speciality (a kind of sausage-meat contained in pig's bladder). "Ben Chippy" stands for the present-day deterioration of Scottish cuisine (chips = French fries = pommes frites). "Gers" and "Celts" stand for the devoted fans of the two rival Glasgow soccer teams "Glasgow Celtic" and "Glasgow Rangers". (This rivalry has a strong element of the religious animosity familiar from Northern Ireland: Rangers = Protestants; Celtic = Catholics.) The Scots seem to be extremely belligerent among themselves – a common cliché about the Celtic people. The placard "free Scotland" unmistakably points at Scotland's strong wish for autonomy, or devolution of power from London to a Scottish parliament. The oil barrels at the east coast underscore Aberdeen's recently won importance for the oil coming from the Northsea oilfields, on which the Scots would like to base their economic independance from England. The Duke of Edinburgh, Prince Philip, is thrown into the North Sea, an event commented with the cry, "Awa(y) ye go" and malicious glee on the faces of the Scots. This action also seems to be supported by deer, deer-hunter and folk-singer. The "devilish" English part of Great Britain is kept at a distance by Presbyterian ministers holding out the holy bible, supported by a band of bagpipers, who "blow" against possible English invaders. But native Scottish culture is still not safe from foreign infiltration – as shown by the tartan-clad Arab. The Welsh are considered to be very musical and poetic. Thus we see a choir singing, a woman playing the harp, and a Celtic bard reciting poetry on the islands of Anglesea. Rugby players – rugby is Wales' national sport – proudly present themselves to their "weedy" English opponents. Col-

lieries, miners and coal mark the traditional industrial centres. Welsh culture seems to thrive in the coalfields, as exemplified by the leeks (the national emblem) and the harpist in the traditional Welsh costume. Daffodils are another Welsh symbol. HRM Prince Charles, Prince of Wales, and his wife, Lady Diana, Princess of Wales, seem to be highly esteemed by the Welsh and, crowned and inthroned, incorporated into the Welsh nation. Half-kneeling, praying people seem to be thanking God for the dissolution of Great Britain. As in the case of Scotland, opposition seems to have a religious element: the nonconformist Methodist Church (particularly strong in Wales) also wants to keep the English "devil" out of the country by holding up a bible.

The most conspicuous features of England, which has obviously been deserted by its ethnic "partners", are the masses of vandalized telephone booths and, in block capitals, catchwords obviously signalling the moral and cultural decline of England: ROCK, DISCO, SEX, ORGY, PORN, STRIP. Disharmonious punk rock seems to be the English answer to the Welsh choir. At second sight one notices dogs, everywhere leaving their excrement or, unmistakably, lifting their hind legs: an attack on the animal-loving English. A computer monitor proclaims what the British might still wishfully think: "England rules – OK?" A cornucopia of money is emptied where one rightly assumes the position of London: the City of London, standing for the wealthy South, is where money can be made, whereas in the traditional industrial areas of the Northwest (Liverpool, Manchester) placards draw our attention to the high rates of unemployment there: "Out of work". Further items: cigar-smoking pig-faced bosses, bowler-hatted city bankers, working-class women with their hair in curlers, fashion freaks, yuppies, lazy people lying in their beds, cricketers, football hooligans, scandalous tabloids (in London) spreading gossip and "lies". While the Scotts have their whisky, the English have their gin: bottles mark the site of the Isle of Wight in the Channel. Waste decorates the Southern coastline.

Note that the drawing only shows Great Britain proper. Though Northern Ireland (referred to briefly in text 1) is still officially part of the United (or Disunited?) Kingdom, the cartoonist seems to have given it up for lost!

## Pre-reading activities

*1. Look at the picture on page 59 and answer the question.*
Other areas of Britain suffering from industrial decline: the North; the Midlands; Clydeside, i.e. the area around Glasgow; these are all areas dependent on the heavy industries which rely on coal and steel. They developed with the Industrial Revolution and are now generally in decline.

*2. Discuss the picture on page 60.*
– What are the three "islands"?
– What seems to be their attitude to each other?
– What details referring to "national character" can you recognize in each?
– Which details refer to present social problems?
– What can you say about the cartoonist's sympathies and antipathies?
See background above.

## Suggested answers

1. While the people themselves had become wealthier compared to former times, the economic state of the nation had declined in comparison with other countries.

2. Drop in the ranking list of industrial countries; mass redundancies; absolute economic decline in certain regions; inner city riots.

3. Consequences of the economic decline:
– loss of consensus on a mixed economy;
– undermining of the authority of the State and public institutions;
– polarization between Labour and Tories;
– civil service, media, universities, business, trade unions, church have all come under attack.

4. High defence spending is seen by the author as a reason for low investment. But high defence is itself a historical heritage, dating back to the growth of British world power in the Tudor and Stuart periods. It still expresses a sense of national importance, but one with which only the English can fully identify. There has never been such a thing as British national identity.

5. Possible aspects:
– cf. ch. 1, text 1: effect of the Boer War;
– exaggerated defence spending/low industrial investment (though recent experience of de-

fence cuts in both east and west suggest economic dependence on investment);
– nationalism;
– cf. ch. 1, text 10: Britain's entry into the EC;
– cf. ch. 8, texts 6–10: inefficiency of a class-ridden educational system.

6. Semantic field "the economy" (words in italics are not to be found in the text):
decline, wealthy, wealthier, *wealth*, poor, *poverty*, to be well off/better off, economic, economic superiority/*inferiority*,*economical*, (low) industrial investment, *to invest*, manufacturing output, gross domestic product, *gross national product*, recession, *boom, trade/business cycle*, the economy, (mass) redundancies, *to be made redundant*, manufacturing industry, *heavy industry*, unemployment, *employment, employer, employee/employed person*, mixed economy, *nationalization, privatization*, defence spending, defence expenditure, cuts, purchase, trading country

**Post-reading activity**

*1. Classroom report: The nations/regions of Great Britian: England (north and south); Scotland; Wales.*
Three or four separate reports.
See Bibliography 3, 5, 13, 14, 16.

*2. Classroom report: Ethnic minorities in other European countries – how are they treated politically?*

 ## 2. Listening Comprehension: Divided Britain (GK)

**Background information**

Since Benjamin Disraeli, brilliant Tory Prime Minister of Scottish descent, wrote his novel *Sybil, or The Two Nations* (1845), the awareness of the British nation being divided into two has always been present. In Disraeli's novel, the two nations are the rich and the poor; the country is shown to be governed by the rich in the interests of the rich. Only ten years later (1855) Elizabeth Gaskell published her novel *North and South*, a study of industrial relations centering on a southern English heroine who comes to the North as to a foreign country. Today the so-called "North-South Divide" refers to the contrast between the impoverished North and the prospering South (cf. Fact Files, p. 288), while the border lines are ever shifting, as remarked by Michael Prestage in *The Observer* of 22 July 1990: "Britain is more deeply divided than ever, although the boundary between the affluent South and impoverished North has changed from the Severn/Wash to the Mersey/Humber."

During the election campaign in April 1992 the main parties presented the following policies in dealing with the question of "devolution" and local government reform:
*Wales:*
– Conservative: No independence or devolution. Remains firmly within UK with a new Welsh Economic Council. Abolition of one tier of local government.
– Labour: Elected Welsh Assembly responsible for domestic issues within lifetime of Parliament. Abolition of one tier of local government.
– Liberal Democrat: Immediate creation of Welsh *Senedd* responsible for domestic issues, to be elected by proportional representation. Abolition of one tier of local government.
– Plaid Cymru: Independence for Wales within the European Community.
*Scotland:*
– Conservative: "We will fight to preserve the union". No independence or devolution. Regional tier of local government to be abolished.
– Labour: Scottish Parliament, elected by proportional representation, responsible for domestic issues. Abolition of one tier of local government.
– Scottish Nationalists: Independence for Scotland within the European Community.
*England:*
– Conservative: Abolition of one tier of local government. No regional authorities. Cabinet Committee for London.
– Labour: New regional tier of government leading to elected assemblies. Abolition of one tier of local government, restoration of a Greater London Authority.
– Liberal Democrat: Regional assemblies elected by proportional representation, including Stra-

tegic Authority for London. Abolition of one tier of local government.

*Northern Ireland:*
- Conservative: Return of powers from Northern Ireland department to locally elected politicians.
- Ulster Unionists: Stormont restored with devolved powers.
- Democratic Unionists: Stormont restored with wide-ranging devolved powers.
- Social Democratic and Labour Party: Power sharing restored at Stormont within the framework of the Anglo-Irish agreement.
- Sinn Fein: British withdrawal, re-unification of Ireland as an independent Republic.

Moderate Kinnockite Labour MP Frank Field had to get over some inner-party trouble concerning the mandatory reselection process for the general election in April 1992. He was challenged by a rival of the Merseyside hard Left, Paul Davies, whom he clearly defeated. The result is certain to spark a fresh row over Labour's mandatory reselection process, under which party members and trade union affiliates choose whether to retain their sitting MP. Mr. Field called it "a system designed to destabilize MPs".

**Methodisch-didaktische Hinweise**

Eine Einleitung, Worterklärungen und Fragen zum Globalverständnis sind im SB S. 62 abgedruckt. Nachfolgend werden zusätzliche Hörverständnisfragen angeboten.

**Transcript**

*Anthony Gibbs: Mr Field, you are Member of Parliament for Birkenhead up in the North, and also Chairman of the Social Services Committee – the House of Commons Social Services Committee. How far do you think Britain is in fact divided? Is it a simple divide, North – South, rich – poor, or is it much more subtle?*
Frank Field: It always has been divided on (a) class basis and there's always been (a) North-South divide. At one time as the Industrial Revolution got underway people moved to the North where there was the new prosperity. And what we are now seeing with another stage in that same Industrial Revolution – many of the newer jobs are being created in the South and there's a population move now from the North back to the South. So there is a divide geographically, but it would be wrong to somehow imagine that once you come south of the Wash everybody is rich and when you pass going north everyone's poor.
*I was going to say – because I am thinking of near your constituency, the Cheshire belt ...*
Well, actually, in the constituency itself parts of the area are considerably wealthy. You go beyond that, three miles from the poorest centres in Birkenhead, you're in the forms of wealth which make Hampstead, which is a very rich area of London, look positively downmarket. So although it's generally true, there are more unemployed, more people on lower incomes in the North than in the South, one mustn't have the image that everybody up there's poor and everybody in the South is rich.
*Now, Mr Field, in 1981 you wrote a book on inequality in Britain and in 1989 you published a book on the emergence of the under-class in Britain. Have you seen changes, therefore, over the ten years in this divide?*
Yes, very big ones. Britain has always had these big divisions, although it's had governments committed to lessening them. But the divisions have either remained the same or in some areas actually grown. Since 1979 we've had a government committed to widening those divisions and it's done that very successfully. And it's been elected three times on that programme, on the belief that if Britain became more unequal, if the rewards were spread less fairly, as I would claim, then that would unlock an entrepreneurial spirit in the country. Our growth-rate would be like the German growth-rate, our wealth would be like the German wealth and that everybody, including the poor, would be better off as a result. Now that has not happened. Certainly there's been greater inequalities. Certainly there has been a very, very substantial increase in wealth but the crumbs have yet to drop off the rich man's table into the laps of the poor beneath the table. And what we've seen, in fact, is the opposite's been occurring. Actually wealth has been pushed up and the people at the bottom have become relatively worse off.
*In what areas do you think this has made itself apparent?*
Well, first of all the government has redistributed through the budget. Practically every budget since 1979 – that's our annual big statement to parliament – and we have had a redistribution of wealth in this country on a scale unknown since the

dissolution of the monasteries. I mean, there have been new fortunes made which are certainly ... (would) have been unthinkable in postwar Britain.

*Are you thinking of the yuppies making their money on the stock exchange, simply those people?*

There has been that, but it has been generally that made by hard work, that made by speculation, the bringing forth of a whole new job, of career structure of people, who seem to be selling nothing but people's opinions and getting large sums of money for it. So there's been that happening. But there have also been at the same time other forces at work. The economy was squeezed at the beginning of the '79 period, so we had a very big increase in unemployment, and that separated a lot of people off from mainstream Britain. We've had the widening of class divisions. There has always been a difference, for example, whether you survive birth in this country, between rich families and poor families. That has remained and in some instances it can be argued that it's actually been widened. So class divisions, on a historical basis, have widened. We've also had, sadly, the poor excluded from this record economic growth. The government at one time claimed that their living standards had jumped twice the rate of anybody else's and then they had to admit they'd somehow got the figures wrong. And far from going up twice the rate, they've only gone up at half the rate of everybody else. So it's not difficult to imagine, is it, if you're on a very low income and you're only seeing that income rise half the pace of everybody else you are a lot worse off relatively speaking at the end of the period than at the beginning.

*And certain benefits have been reduced, especially perhaps for young people.*

Some benefits have just been abolished. And partly on the basis that we want to try and encourage young people into work (which is a very good thing if jobs are available), one's made claiming benefit that much more difficult. And the last and maybe perhaps the most significant change that's contributed to a different Britain today than it was in 1979 was a big change in public attitudes. Up to then there was much more of the feeling that we were all in the same boat and that it was the job of making sure the whole crew arrived safely. The crew has now been divided up and all acting on its own behalf, scrambling away. And the feeling has been that once individuals have made it they've got no responsibilities to those who don't make it. And I would call it – that was the introduction of a drawbridge mentality. People get past, get into riches and want the drawbridge pulled up behind them rather than letting other people follow them.

From *English Feature*. Eine Aufnahme des Süddeutschen Rundfunks Stuttgart. Used by permission of Anthony R. Gibbs and SDR.

## Suggested answers (Listening for the gist)

Since 1979 the government, which was twice re-elected, has caused a widening of the traditional divisions in order to foster an enterpreneurial spirit from which the whole country should profit – this, however, did not happen. (Teacher's note: cf. Ch. 11, text 3, "Reflections of a self-made man")

## Listening for detail

*1. What was the influence of the early Industrial Revolution on the population movement?*
In the early Industrial Revolution people moved from the South to the prospering North.

*2. What is the influence of today's industrial revolution?*
Today's industrial revolution is causing a movement back from the North to the prospering South.

*3. Why is it wrong to generally say that people in the North are poor?*
Because the poor and rich areas cannot be strictly kept apart, although poor areas clearly dominate in the North.

*4. What are the special qualifications of Mr Field?*
He is not only an MP – he has also written books on social problems.

*5. What have been the government's plans since 1979 for bringing wealth to the whole country?*
It let the degree of inequality increase in order to encourage enterpreneurial activities.

*6. What were the actual effects of those policies?*
The desired effects were not produced.

*7. What has especially happened to the poor?*
The poor have become even poorer.

8. What makes it difficult for the young to start a career?
Benefits have just been abolished so that young people will find it more difficult to get a job.

9. In what sense have public attitudes changed since 1979?
There is no sense of belonging together any more among the population. People follow their individual interests and just care about getting to the safe side.

10. Explain the meaning of the phrase "drawbridge mentality".
The term "drawbridge" refers to the architecture of medieval castles: as fortresses they were surrounded by thick walls and ditches or "moats". For defence purposes one could draw up the bridge over the moat from inside, leaving those outside to fend for themselves. A "drawbridge mentality" is therefore one of ensuring one's personal security and well-being by cutting oneself off from those less well off.

# 3. Rural England struggles to survive the urban blitz

### Methodisch-didaktische Hinweise

Es empfiehlt sich ein schrittweises Erarbeiten (alternierendes Stillesen, lautes Lesen) des Textes mit sich anschließenden *comprehension*-Fragen, da die Schüler sonst wegen der Textlänge und der vielen Namen und Detailinformationen leicht die Orientierung verlieren können.

### Pre-reading activities

1. *The article you are going to read was part of a series called "Images of Britain". Look at the drawing accompanying this article of the series, and comment on the "image" it suggests.*
The old cliché of the city businessman with his umbrella and bowler hat; probably used ironically, as everybody knows it's an image from the past.

2. *Discuss the title of the article. What problem(s) does it suggest?*

### Suggested answers

1. (ll. 1–24)
A previous group of townies that had moved to the village had behaved badly: left rubbish dumps, caused boundary disputes.

2. (ll. 25–41)
Fry's father had to work hard and needed luck in order to acquire his own piece of land; Burns had no difficulty in buying a weekend cottage to relax from his work in the city. Old Mr Fry had lived in the village all his life; Burns is a recent arrival, and had previously worked abroad.

3. (ll. 42–81)
– The economic framework is negatively affected: redevelopment and renovation have pushed up property prices; the locals cannot afford to buy houses any more.
– The social structure is broken up: few people work in the agricultural sector; the village has turned into a community of commuters, weekenders, the wealthy retired.

4. (ll. 68–135)
Still hedgerows and grassland; more communication among neighbours. Due to the Figes' initiative: village shop and post-office saved; bridleways and footpaths re-opened.

5. (ll. 136–175)
They turned the former village shop into a communication centre. They founded the first community paper, the *Tytherton Tatler*. Clare was involved in saving the state primary school which survived through an innovative job share. She fears that the only future for rural England may lie in tourism.

6. Example of summary:
In his article, Jimmy Burns describes the experiences he and his wife had when they moved from the city to live in a cottage in a village. Two years after their arrival they are still there, contrary to all expectations. The initial scepticism of their neighbour, farmer David Fry, is attributed to the villagers' previous bad experience with some other townies who had settled there. Now they have become more or less accepted. The author ex-

plains the reasons for any lingering resentment on the part of the villagers: their different experience of scraping a living on the land, and the fact that newcomers from the city tend to push up property prices beyond their reach. He explains that the social structure of the village has already changed radically, but that enough of the rural idyll remains to make it a very pleasant place to live. One particular couple from the city are described as good examples: Clare and John Figes, who run the local shop. We are told that they were also initially greeted with suspicion, but have since done a lot to improve life in the village – reinstating old footpaths, making their shop a meeting place, starting a local newspaper, and saving the village school. For themselves they gain a more neighbourly and communicative life-style than they would have had in the city. The article ends, however, with a note of scepticism. Clare is quoted as fearing that tourism may be the only future for rural England.

7. Bald nachdem wir 1987 unser neues Häuschen, das tief im ländlichen Wiltshire liegt, bezogen hatten, kam der im Ort wohnende Bauer David Fry vorbei. "Ich wette, Sie verkaufen wieder, bevor das Jahr um ist," sagte er voraus.
Zwei Jahre sind vergangen, und wir sind immer noch da. Im Gemüsegarten, der mit dem Viehmist des Bauern gedüngt wird, gedeiht das Gemüse prächtig, und anstatt der kalten Begrüßung gibt es nachbarschaftliche Ratschläge.
Seinerseits gesteht David Fry ein, daß wir gegenüber den bisherigen Städtern, die er als Nachbarn hatte, einen wohltuenden Wandel darstellen. Aus einem der Felder haben sie eine Müllhalde gemacht, und wegen einer erbitterten Grenzstreitigkeit sind sie vor Gericht gegangen.

Aber selbst heute noch sind unsere Gespräche durch ein tiefes Unbehagen geprägt.
Herr Fry lebt seit seiner Geburt in East Tytherton, genauso wie sein Vater. Dieser war früher Pächter. Er kam in Besitz seines eigenen Grundes, als der ortsansässige Lord durch Erbschaftssteuern dazu gezwungen wurde, einige seiner Besitztümer zu verkaufen und sein herrschaftliches Anwesen dem Tourismus zugänglich zu machen.

8. Some aspects:
– urbanization of the country;
– overpopulation;
– agricultural aspects (jobs, food production, EC policy);
– environmental issues (over-fertilization of fields, wildlife, biotopes, hedgerows);
– tourism, recreational activities (skiing, golf-courses, etc.).

**Additional questions**

1. *Explain the* ing-*forms in ll. 1, 64, 78, 84 und 112.*
L. 112: verbale *ing*-Fügung nach *have* – als Objektergänzung; vgl. Lamprecht, *Grammatik der englischen Sprache,* Berlin, 1986, § 966.

2. *Explain the use of the tenses in ll. 77, 86–87 and 129–130.*

3. *Explain the use of the infinitive in ll. 168–169.*

4. *Find antonyms of the following:*
– *l. 16: to admit* (to deny)
– *l. 17: previous* (subsequent, later, following)
– *l. 64: fading* (increasing, growing)
– *l. 135: to ensure* (to endanger)
– *l. 171: gradual* (sudden)

## 4. Lifestyles (GK)

**Background information**

The novel *Nice Work* is set in the fictional city of Rummidge, which, the author admits, shares the geographical location of the real city of Birmingham. The main story concerns the relationship between university lecturer Robyn Penrose and a man of a totally different type, someone normally outside her social circle, namely Vic Wilcox, manager of a local engineering works. In our excerpt she is confronted with another unfamiliar aspect of modern British society – that represented by her brother Basil and his girl-friend Debbie. This sub-plot is elaborated later in the novel when Robyn's boy friend Charles takes up with Debbie, abandons academic life and goes to work in the City.
Robyn is an expert on the Victorian "Condition of England" novel, a genre to which she applies the most advanced and abstruse critical theories, especially Derrida's "deconstruction". An ardent

feminist, she also teaches a class in Women's Studies.

Philip Swallow – he appears in l. 194 – is an unsophisticated Rummidge lecturer in English, who, in Lodge's earlier work *Changing Places*, had gone to a university in California as an exchange professor and has come back in the meantime.

For information on the author, see Bernard Bergonzi, *David Lodge*, in the series *Contemporary Writers*, British Council 1988.

**Suggested answers**

1. Some possible impressions:
– Britain is still a very class-conscious society: Cockney accent almost inexcusable in some circles, at least mocked at; hunt balls in the country something aspired to even by otherwise classless yuppies; "Debbie was decidedly lower-class" (ll. 65–66), she comes from poor Whitechapel in the East End.
– But the unfettered capitalism of the Thatcher era is having some strange effects on the class system. In the City, the ability to make money is now more important than class and accent, and Debbie's Cockney heritage (cf. ll. 108, 117–118) perversely enables her to break into upper-class society (e.g. hunt balls, cf. ll. 44–45) – something normally beyond the reach of even upper-middle-class people like Robyn and Basil.
– While the City is flourishing, those areas dependent on government subsidies (e.g. education, ll. 195–196) are in trouble.
– Marriage seems to have declined in importance for most young people.

2. Basil and Debbie are yuppies (young urban/upwardly-mobile professionals), who prefer to show off their affluence: drive posh cars (preferably BMWs), wear Sloaney, expensive clothes, drink wine, visit snobbish social gatherings, spend holidays at expensive places, e.g. St. Moritz; they tend to be "metropolitan snobs" (l. 159), but are relatively free of the old-fashioned snobbery based on social class, accent, the "right" schools, etc.
Robyn and Charles are theory-oriented academic people, and somewhat divorced from everyday economic reality; have their own kind of snobbery, both intellectual and social; are against Thatcher's educational policy. They have a more moderate lifestyle than Basil and Debbie, do not spend much money (because they do not have it!) on prestigious things, are left-wing intellectuals. However, they tend to look down on lower-class people, especially those who want to climb socially without the benefit of education.

3. Most of the following emerges from indirect characterization, which includes evidence from the way people talk about themselves; – exceptions are noted.
– Robyn is a left-wing, feminist (ll. 137–139) intellectual, a temporary university lecturer, slightly frustrated over her present job situation, because she faces unemployment. Once she is *directly* characterized by Charles (ll. 191–196) as being very good at her job. She is somewhat alienated from her brother since he left the academic world to make money. For all her progressive, left-wing views, she is the most class-conscious and even snobbish of the four (ll. 62–71, 101, 170–177), and her assumption that Debbie must be a secretary or typist is not what one would expect from a feminist! Being the central character, Robyn's personality comes across most clearly, with all its contradictions.
– Charles plays a minor role in this scene. An intellectual like Robyn, he mildly resents having to stop reading a book on critical theory. Otherwise he politely expresses interest in what Debbie is telling him about her "gadget". Charles is fond of Robyn and praises her intellectual abilities. He deplores the government's budget cutting in the educational field. (But see "Background information" for later developments in the story.)
– Debbie is a pretty, though almost anorexic Cockney girl from Whitechapel. Her accent betrays her lower-class origins. She has not had a university education. She is a hard worker. She seems to be quite happy with the new social status and material wealth which she has achieved through her own abilities. Debbie is perfectly self-confident, and sees no reason to disguise her social origin by acquiring a "classier" accent. She is partly *directly* characterized during Basil's talk with Robyn in the kitchen (lines 70ff).
– Although Basil, Robyn's brother, has had an excellent university education at Oxford he shocks his family with his plan to go into the City. (This is something we are told directly in lines 13–22.) Like Debbie, he does not really care about anything other than material values, and is prepared to work hard to finance his typical yuppie lifestyle. He is quick to counter his sister's implicit criticism of his new lifestyle.

4. The episode is almost totally told from Robyn's limited point of view (with ll. 7–12 being the one exception). This is indicated by the frequency of such phrases as: "... Robyn repeated, with a raised eyebrow." (ll. 48–49); "At first Robyn thought ... but soon realised ..." (ll. 62–63); "Robyn assumed" (l. 68); "The word reminded her of ..." (l. 83); "... thinking to herself ..." (ll. 171–172).
We have to do with a third-person narrative in which the selectively omniscient narrator "presents things as they are seen through the eyes of one or several ... characters in the story" (cf. the box on p. 222).

5. Academic job: do s.th. that interests you, intellectual freedom, research, working with young people, etc.
Finance: good wages, feeling that one is one of "the movers and shakers" (cf. the advertisement on page 169), etc.

*Question on picture, p. 66:* The technology seems to be a strange mixture between hi-tech and lo-tech: the former represented by the cordless phone and the computers; the latter by the now old-fashioned monitors and the simple electric fan.

**Additional questions**

*1. Discuss the significance of the various consumer goods trade names and designers mentioned in the excerpt.*
The "sheepskin coats" are obviously very high quality and expensive; similarly the cashmere jacket by Aquascutum, an old-established, prestigious English brand; Katherine Hamnett is a very trendy designer. Together with the new BMW, they are examples of conspicuous consumption. The "four-year-old Golf" is probably the best Charles can afford – though he might claim to be uninterested in material goods. Robyn, for her part, betrays her own kind of conspicuous consumption, namely in her choice of a particular kind of tea: she is obviously aware of the class connotations of choosing Lapsang Suchong instead of the cheaper, more popular commercial blends she thinks more appropriate for a working-class girl like Debbie.

*2. Construct a semantic field around the phrase "the materialistic society."*

**Comic strip, p. 68**

1. The interviewee is seated opposite the two interviewers and, at the beginning, appears to be self-confident. But from the second frame on he is obviously getting more and more nervous, as he does not know what to answer to a question about correct social behaviour in a bus. The interviewers perfunctorily assure him that they will be in touch with him. But after he has left, they tear the notes they have taken about him: he will definitely not be given the job. The interviewers are not mocking his "old-fashioned" behaviour or even his obvious insecurity and confusion. The interviewee has failed because he does not know that taking the bus is, by the standards of the new job, out of the question – he ought to drive a car appropriate to his new status – preferably a BMW (cf. Basil's car in the novel excerpt).
The cartoonist obviously wants to make a point about status-consciousness in the business world. One could discuss whether such attitudes are really typical, to what extent status symbols (the right car, the right style of dress, etc.) can affect one's career and take precedence not only over personal character, but also over one's ability to do the job.
In any case, the point is made quite effectively and economically.

2. He probably realized he was not going to get the job, since this is what "we'll be in touch" usually means. But most likely he will have attributed his failure to his hesitation and insecurity in not being able to work out whether "yes" or "no" is the right (i.e. approved) answer.

3. The cartoon seems to suggest that a certain lifestyle is not just the consequence of high earnings (as might be the case for Debbie and Basil in the novel excerpt) but practically a prerequisite – that a kind of materialistic snobbery has crept in to replace the old status symbols of class, accent, the right education, etc. The Archbishop (text 5) would no doubt reject the morals and aspirations of all three characters.

# 5. The Archbishop and the wealth ethic (GK)

## Background information

The King or Queen, as the head of the Church of England, appoints bishops and archbishops on the recommendation of the Prime Minister, who, in turn, usually seeks the views of others. According to his biographer, Adrian Hastings, Dr Robert Runcie (Archbishop of Canterbury from 1980–1991) was "more profoundly affected by a single prime minister than any before him". Runcie's personality and attitudes were in many ways in conflict with those of Mrs Thatcher. Though he had served in the Second World War, and had been decorated with the Military Cross, he was a pacifist at heart. In 1982, at the service of remembrance for the Falklands War, he infuriated Mrs Thatcher by asking the congregation to pray for Argentinian as well as British dead. In 1985, the Church again seemed to oppose the Government with a report, *Faith in the City*, which urged for more welfare spending.

## Methodisch-didaktische Hinweise

Falls Ch. 7, "Religious Life (Britain)", noch nicht im Unterricht behandelt wurde, so ist es wichtig, an die Informationen im dazugehörigen *Fact File* (S. 299–300) anzuknüpfen. Besonders die Stellung der *Church of England* im politischen System in England gehört geklärt (siehe *Post-reading activities* zum 6. und *Background information* zum 8. Text des Kapitels 7).

## Pre-reading activities

*1. Discuss the cartoon on page 70. What do you think the Christian churches would have to say about the situation described?*
See the advertisement, "Hearing the cry of the poor", SB p. 166.

*2. Classroom report: Church and State in England.*
See fact file pp. 299–300 and Bibliography 3, 13, 16.

## Suggested answers

1. Archbishop believes wealth creation is necessary – but may not create a happy society – differences between the Church's and the Thatcher administration's views of society – polarization between south and north – Church sensitive to the needs of the population – Christian ethics at variance with government's individualistic approach – Church supports community life throughout the country – the successful look down upon the unsuccessful like Pharisees – success in business is not success in life – profit and self-interest not the sole dynamics of society
(For example of summary see suggested answers to text 3.)

2. In the Archbishop's opinion:
– A happy society does not solely depend on wealth creation.
– Conflicts between the Church and the Government exist, but have been exaggerated in the media.
– The Church puts much of its energies and resources into building community life; it rejects pure individualism.
– Self-interest may be the necessary dynamic of a capitalist society, but it does not contribute to the community life of a given society.

3. Er hat gelernt, vorsichtig mit den Schlagzeilen der Boulevardpresse umzugehen, die einem den Eindruck vermitteln, daß Kirche und Regierung sich ständig uneins sind, aber er leugnet nicht, daß es Divergenzen gibt mit der Thatcher-Regierung, was deren Vorstellungen über die Gesellschaft betrifft. Dies ist zum Teil das Ergebnis, so merkt er an, der politischen Polarisierung zwischen dem weitgehend konservativen, reichen Süd- und Mittelengland und den ärmeren nördlichen Regionen und Wales, wo die Regierung nur geringe Unterstützung findet.
"Dieses ist ein gravierender Wandel in der letzten Generation", merkt er an. "Im Gegensatz dazu erhält die *Church of England* ihre Präsenz und Gemeindearbeit in jeder Gemeinde im ganzen Land aufrecht. Sie bleibt weiterhin in täglichem Kontakt mit den Gebieten, in denen die konservative Partei wenig Gefolgschaft hat. Das sensibilisiert die Kirche für die Bedürfnisse der Gegenden und den Teil der Bevölkerung, die nicht von den letzten zehn Jahren einer konservativen Regierung profitiert haben."

4. Runcie does not agree with many politicians and business people on the role of the Church. He rejects the idea that the Church alone has to care

for the people's goodness on the basis of material wealth brought about by the politicians. A "healthy society" (l. 134) should also be a concern of business people and political leaders. The Church does not aim at people's goodness but their godliness. Although Runcie stresses the Church's task of making people godly he does not insinuate that the Church should totally refrain from political issues, because politics is often closely linked with general aspects of morality and ethics.

5. He criticizes
– the political polarization between largely Conservative, prosperous centre and south and the poorer areas in the north and in Wales (ll. 23–27);
– too great an individualism as encouraged by the government (ll. 46–67);
– a Pharisaical attitude towards the unsuccessful (ll. 68–88);
– profit and self-interest seen as the sole dynamics of society (ll. 121–130)

6. –

# 6. A great prime minister

**Background information**

For better or worse, Margaret Thatcher has certainly left her mark on Britain. Originally seen as a compromise candidate for the Conservative leadership, she confounded her critics by winning three consecutive elections for the party (1979, 1983 and 1987). But during her third term in office, doubts were growing whether she could possibly win a fourth election.

One particularly unpopular measure was the poll tax, a "per head" (poll = head) local tax which Mrs Thatcher insisted on introducing to replace property-based rates as a means of financing local government. It was introduced in Scotland in 1988 against massive protests and later extended to the rest of Britain.

Another controversial issue was Margaret Thatcher's attitude to the European Community, and in particular her rejection of any further steps towards political and monetary union. In the summer of 1990 the Trade and Industry Secretary, Nicholas Ridley, was censured severely by members of all British parties over unfavourable remarks about re-unified Germany's future role in Europe. His remarks, published in an interview by the weekly magazine *The Spectator*, seemed to have been made with full consent of Prime Minister Margaret Thatcher. On July 14 Mr. Ridley had to resign from the Cabinet. This affair, together with the struggle over the introduction of the poll tax, ushered in Margaret Thatcher's fall from power.

In November Sir Geoffrey Howe, Leader of the House of Commons, resigned from the Cabinet in protest at Mrs Thatcher's attitude to the European Community. Michael Heseltine (nicknamed "Tarzan" because of his outward appearance) challenged Mrs Thatcher for the leadership of the Conservative Party. In the ballot for the leadership she won by 204 to 152 votes. But Mrs Thatcher, on November 22, declared she would not be standing in the second round of the contest. Douglas Hurd, the Foreign Secretary, and John Major, the Chancellor of the Exchequer, put their names forward for the second ballot, from which Major (Thatcher's favourite) surprisingly emerged victorious. A third ballot did not take place. On November 28 Mrs Thatcher resigned as Prime Minister.

The positive evaluation of Margaret Thatcher's leadership is most striking in that it comes from *The Independent*, which is by no means a Conservative mouthpiece like *The Telegraph*, or even inclined to the right, like *The Times*, but in general lives up to its name.

**Methodisch-didaktische Hinweise**

Manche Schüler meinen, diese Eloge (*eulogy*) könne nicht ernst gemeint sein. Es entgeht den Schülern beim ersten Lesen der durchaus stattliche Katalog von Mißerfolgen von Mrs Thatcher im zweiten Teil des *leader*. Es sind allein der hyperbolische Anfang und Schluß, die den Schülern einen Eindruck blinder Bewunderung vermitteln. Aufgaben 2 und 3 dienen dazu, diesem Eindruck entgegenzuwirken.

Aufgabe 4 sollte nur pauschal behandelt werden, da sonst Aufgabe 5 vorweggenommen würde. Generell könnte man die Reihenfolge der Aufgaben 4 und 5 auch umkehren.

## Pre-reading activities

*1. What do you know about Margaret Thatcher's eleven years as Prime Minister? For what policies and achievements will she be remembered?*

*2. Look at the photo on page 72 and answer the question.*
The logo is that of the Conservative party. It is a stylized burning torch (actually in blue, this being the Conservatives' colour). It symbolizes "carrying the torch" of true conservative policies from generation to generation.

*3. Look at the cartoon on page 70 and the photo on page 75 and discuss the criticisms of Mrs Thatcher's rule that they refer to.*
See background information.

*4. Classroom report: Margaret Thatcher.*
See Bibliography 9, 15, 20.

## Suggested answers

1. She deserves praise because she
– leaves her country much stronger than it was;
– arrested Britain's ... decline;
– improved and revolutionized economic management (monetarism, "enterprise culture", cut taxes;)
– curbed unions leaders' power;
– fought and won the Falklands war.

2. She failed because she
– later ran out of intellectual steam/lacked coherent ideas;
– neglected the battle against inflation;
– invested her personal authority in an ill-advised poll tax;
– failed to improve educational standards;
– had no realistic vision for Europe.

3. The overall impression is that of a balanced account of Thatcher's achievements and failures, in which the author concludes that the achievements dominate.
There are elements of eulogy (ll. 1–76; 115–122) especially at the beginning (which parodies a famous quote: "Let us now praise famous men ..." from the biblical *Apocrypha*, Wisdom of Solomon 40:1) and the end. Positive words of praise and even hyperbole abound (ll. 5, 7, 8–9, 12, 15, 38, 40, 42, 48, 57, 65–66, 75, 116–117, 121).
– anaphora: again...again ...again (ll. 73, 74, 75)
– inversion: Never was her staunchness more necessary...(l. 35)
The critical passages (ll. 77–122) are marked by a more sober style, making do with fewer subordinate clauses than the eulogy. Sentence structure is standard, with the exception of the emphatic inversion (Nor did she have ...) in line 106.

4. The answers to this question will depend on which elements of the Thatcher image have got across to the students (e.g. the cliché of the "Iron Lady", her regal style of government, her economic dogmatism, etc.) and to what extent she continues to exert an influence on British politics even after entering the House of Lords.

5. –

## Additional questions

1. Find substitutes for the following which do not change the sentence structure:
to master (l. 4); restored (l. 21); reckoned (l. 32); undermined (l. 54); ballot (l. 65); neglected (l. 87); apparent (l. 92); admitted (l. 100).

2. a) Explain the ing-forms in lines 44 and 71.
b) L. 53: "forces we could blame": Name the construction and explain why it can be used; give an alternative construction.

3. Name at least two examples of metaphor from lines 77–91.
fall from power, intellectual steam, appetite for reform, battle against

## Advertisement, p. 73

The drawing alludes to the opening scene of Shakespeare's tragedy *Macbeth*. In that scene, three witches mix some gruesome and disgusting ingredients together in a cauldron for a "magic spell" which enables them to foretell that Macbeth shall be king of Scotland. In the text of the advertisement, potentially profitable shares are offered in what was previously a state-run public service. The three witches of the drawing make it clear that a deadline has to be observed if one does not want to miss one's chance. The pun is based on the two meanings of "spell": a short time/a magic spell. Another idea conveyed by the drawing is the Scottish background of the two companies offering the shares.

## 7. In retrospect: a letter to the editor

### Methodisch-didaktische Hinweise

Optimal ist die Präsentation von der Cassette, da der Brief vom Verfasser selbst gelesen wird. Je nach Leistungsstärke des jeweiligen Kurses kann sie bei geschlossenen (= *Listening Comprehension*) oder geöffneten Büchern erfolgen – das Vokabular der Annotationen unbedingt vorher semantisieren bzw. vorher lesen lassen; ansonsten Stillesen des gesamten Textes.

Aufgaben 1 und 3 eignen sich besonders für Partnerarbeit, Aufgabe 4 ist besonders gut für eine längere Stillarbeitsphase (im Lk) oder als Hausaufgabe (Lk, Gk) geeignet. Hierbei ist dann eine (wiederholende) Anleitung zum effektiven Gebrauch des einsprachigen Wörterbuches zu empfehlen.

### Pre-reading activitiy

*You are going to hear a letter written by Ken Livingstone, and read by him for this recording. Read about him on page 75, then say how he is likely to react to* The Independent's *praise of Mrs Thatcher.*

### Suggested answers

1. Overall impression: Ken Livingstone not only totally contradicts the views formulated in the leader, he also expresses his astonishment at the fact that the leader could at all dare to praise Mrs Thatcher.
The view of the premiership:
   - leader: great prime minister, firm will, determination, halted the decline by means of monetarism and fighting the unions, especially important the Falklands war, had her shortcomings, though.
   - letter: she wrongly tried to maintain Britain's (bygone) imperial greatness, stopped the process of decline only temporarily and by pure luck, maintained a kind of Byzantine empire (collapse after periods of seeming recovery), wrecked the economy.

Reason for Thatcher's fall from power:
   - leader: record deteriorated (lack of intellectual steam, no coherent political vision, ignored inflation, introduced poll tax, failed in the educational field, wrong vision of Europe);
   - letter: she placed too much of a strain on the economy and on the people, a typical example being the poll tax.

2. The leader-writer's aim is to summarize a political epoque (in which *The Independent* itself was established) as objectively as possible, since it represents the view of a newspaper that tries to live up to its name.
   - Ken Livingstone has great reason to hold a grudge against Mrs Thatcher for her policy towards the Greater London Council, of which he was in charge several years ago (see the note on p. 75). As a Labour MP he finds it unbearable that Mrs Thatcher is praised exactly for measures that run counter to traditional convictions of the Labour Party. At the end he broadens the scope of his letter to make an attack on the Conservative Party in general.

3. For a comment on the style and language of the leader, see previous question 3. By comparison, Livingstone's letter is much sharper in tone, and wholly negative. The letter begins and ends with the claim that the leader is totally wrong and concentrates on one principal reproach: that Thatcher's attempt to maintain Britain's imperial greatness was totally mistaken. All the other critical points he makes are variations of this theme. He does not have a good word to say about Mrs Thatcher.
The language is marked by contradiction (On the contrary, ll. 5–6, the exact opposite, ll. 55–56) and negative expressions. Very conspicuous is the repeated use of "attempt" and "try" in order to describe Thatcher's vain activities (ll. 4, 7, 13, 16, 25, 33, 35, 36, 42).

4. –

### Additional questions

*Explain the different use of "should" in lines 3 and 35.*
L. 3: In *that*-clauses the subjunctive "should" can be used to express something that is seen as in some way unreal, or, as in this case, surprising.
L. 35: It expresses the speaker's own feeling that there is an obligation to do s.th.

# 8. Monitoring the heart (GK)

## Background information

Sue Townsend, creator of the fictitious adolescent Adrian Mole and his diaries, is, in a very literal sense, a child of the Welfare State and a vociferous defender of it. In her *Counterblast* pamphlet *Mr Bevan's Dream* she has written a powerful series of vignettes describing her own experiences of it, in bad times and good. Her motive for writing as expressed in the introduction, p. 10: "I am [...] writing this pamphlet because without the Welfare State and its progeny, the National Health Service, I wouldn't be here. I would have died of pneumonia in my infancy." Proud of her working class background, Sue Townsend has chosen a kind of writing which she herself calls "the traditional working class method of expressing ideas" – the form of the anecdote. The pamphlet's title, *Mr Bevan's Dream*, refers to the social commitment of Aneurin (Nye) Bevan, a Labour MP who, in the early Forties, against the leading figures in the party rallied the Labour backbenchers to vote for the so-called Beveridge Report and demand its speedy implementation, and thus made the Welfare State become a reality.

## Methodisch-didaktische Hinweise

Es empfiehlt sich, den Text in Sinneinheiten bzw. angemessenen Textquantitäten zu erarbeiten und dabei zwischen Still- bzw. Lautleseverfahren zu wechseln. Dabei sollten sich jeweils 1–2 Comprehension-Fragen anschließen. Es könnte bereits als Leitauftrag Task no. 2 ("tone") integriert werden. Vorschlag zur Textaufteilung: ll. 1–16; 17–32; 33–61; 62–85; 86–102; 103–116; 117–138; 139–159.

Es empfiehlt sich ebenfalls gezielte Wortschatzarbeit zu den Sachfeldern (*semantic fields*) "Gesundheit/Krankheit, "Gesundheitswesen" (cf. *Words in Context*, "The Welfare State and Social Security").

## Pre-reading activities

1. *Have you ever been to hospital? What were your fears and hopes?*

2. *Look at the cartoon on page 78. Explain its "black humour", and the political point the cartoonist is making.*

3. *Classroom report: Britain's National Health Service.*

See Fact File p. 290; also Bibliography 3, 10, 11, 12, 13, 14, 19.

## Suggested answers

1. Sue Townsend begins telling her "anecdote" (see above) *in medias res*, i.e. going "into the middle of things"; *ab ovo* – "from the egg" – would be the alternative) and only afterwards explains what has led up to the situation she is in. Only towards the end does she make an explicit political point – for the most part she lets her personal experience speak for itself.

2. The tone is, almost throughout the whole text, one of forced casualness, characterized by many examples of (black) humour (ll. 5, 21–22, 34–35, 37, 39, 63, 81–82, 95, 99–101, 106, 112 ff). Only twice does the tone change: into a serious immediacy in one or two sentences where she refers to her fear of death (ll. 48 ff), and at the end into a seriously intended list of deficiencies of the NHS system around her (ll. 126–159).

3. The image of the NHS: people (wardens, nurses, doctors) OK; a tinge of heroism around them because they are doing their jobs against all odds; the material equipment: lamentable, a shame.

4. The humorous tone suggests that she – seemingly – does not take her own health problem too seriously. What makes her sad is the deterioration the Welfare State, especially in the case of the NHS, has undergone since its noble beginnings. Critics of the NHS often claim that a fully privatized system would work better; they resent the amount of public money it takes to keep the NHS going.

5. Central point: conflict between aspect of social justice and what society can afford to pay for.

6. In Germany, health insurance is compulsory for the greater part of the population. A monthly premium, depending on age and family status, has to be paid to the insurance company. Because the revenue does not cover all the costs (and because the system practically encourages people to exploit it), the insured have recently been obliged to pay parts of the costs themselves in order to make them use the medical facilities more sensibly or moderately.

*Modern Britain*

# 9. Filed away in a cardboard box city (GK)

## Background information

Housing statistics released by the Department of Environment in Great Britain in June, 1992, revealed that 62,000 households were living in temporary accommodation such as bed-and-breakfast hotels. The figures do not include single homeless people on the streets. In the Thatcher era, emphasis was placed on home ownership. Those who could not afford to buy suffered most. Rural homelessness has risen sharply – in Scotland it has trebled over the last six years.

## Methodisch-didaktische Hinweise

Das Thema "homelessness" hat in Großbritannien eine lange Tradition. Es lohnt sich, diese historische Perspektive andeutungsweise in den Unterricht einzubringen. Am anschaulichsten schildert George Orwell, in seinem autobiographischen *Down and Out in Paris and London*, was Obdachlosigkeit in London im ersten Viertel dieses Jahrhunderts bedeutete (cf. Textausschnitt in Meller/Slogsnat, *London. The Urban Experience in Poetry and Prose*, Paderborn, 1987, 101–105. Dieser Textausschnitt kann auch als Basis für ein Schülerreferat gewählt werden.) Ein Popsong von Ralph McTell, "The Streets of London" ist eine weitere Möglichkeit, eine Mini-Unterrichtseinheit zum Thema zu erstellen (auf der in Schweden hergestellten CD: *Ralph McTell, Greatest Hits*; Butterfly, Nr. BF 401-4, copyright Paradiso Records). Tracy Chapman's Lied *Subcity* (Text im Schülerbuch S. 253) behandelt das Thema Armut/Obdachlosigkeit im amerikanischen Kontext.

## Pre-reading activities

*1. What do you feel when you see homeless people in your town? Is it pity or anger? Why?*

*2. Picture p. 80: Read the caption and discuss the question posed in it.*
In Germany: people unable to pay rent when unemployed; people homeless after a marriage break-up or death in the family; some addicted to drugs or alcohol (often as a result of other problems); people who cannot find a flat; ex-prisoners and former patients in psychiatric hospitals etc.

## Suggested answers

1. Cold and hunger (l. 1), i.e. the need for food (ll. 8–9; l. 25: next cup of tea or meal) and shelter (l. 12, l. 25); other conveniences (l. 13: a shower)

2. The vicious circle: "You can't find a job because you haven't got a home. You can't get a home because you haven't got a job." (ll. 55–58)

3. This phrase refers to a myth rather than reliable facts. The homeless may reject help because they still possess self-respect and want to master their lives alone. However, most of them have simply slipped through the social net. The main cause of homelessness is joblessness. Those who come to town looking for work are refused any help from the local councils, who reject responsibility for them.

4. That the homeless still possess a well-developed sense of self-respect/self-esteem (ll. 20–22); that few are drug addicts or drunks (ll. 23–24); that there is a strong code of ethics in the homeless community (ll. 69, 98–106).

5. Few figures given: it is a personal feature story, full of understanding and empathy ("...I know because I've been there", ll. 3–4), taking sides with the homeless (cf. use of "you").

6. City/town councils offer small sums of money or food to be collected daily; special shelters supervised by social workers; police take action against them – transport them into different regions; charity organizations look after them; training programmes

## Additional questions

*1. Find the corresponding nouns (no ing-forms):*
l. 18: *to appear* appearance, apparition
l. 19: *to perceive* perception
l. 39: *to discover* discovery, discoverer
l. 51: *to refuse* refusal
l. 59: *to urge* urge
l. 91: *to enjoy* enjoyment
l. 105: *to laugh* laughter

*2. Find the corresponding verbs:*
l. 5: *desperation* to despair
l. 70: *inhabitant* to inhabit
l. 71: *suspicious* to suspect
l. 94: *resident* to reside

*3. Explain the use of "would" in l. 80.*
repeated action in the past

*4. Translate ll. 39–53 into German.*
Schwierigkeiten:
Lexik: to crack up "vorgaukeln, -machen, -geben"; local council: "Stadtverwaltung"; intentionally: "absichtlich"
Syntax: may: konzessiv: "mögen ..., wenn auch ..."; looking: als Rel.satz: "mehr Leute, die ..." oder als Nominalsatz; in trying to find: Nominalstil hier möglich "auf/bei der Suche nach; doing "mit Gelegenheitsarbeit"; to take...to house: zweiter Infinitiv hängt vom ersten ab: "lehnen die Verantwortung ab sie unterzubringen" oder: zweiter Inf. kann substantiviert werden: "... weigern sich, die Verantwortung für ihre Unterbringung zu übernehmen."

Bald wurde ihnen klar, daß London nicht die Utopie darstellt, die ihnen vorgegaukelt wird. Mag sein, daß es dort mehr Stellen gibt, aber die Anzahl der Arbeitssuchenden ist auch höher. Und es mangelt deutlich an Wohnraum. Eines der größten Hindernisse bei der Wohnungssuche ist die Forderung der meisten Vermieter nach einer saftigen Kaution – in den meisten Fällen sind es zwei Monatsmieten. Wenn du keine Arbeit hast oder mit Gelegenheitsarbeiten im Restaurant £2,00 pro Stunde verdienst, ist es nahezu unmöglich, so viel Geld auf einmal zusammenzubekommen. Weil diese Menschen nicht aus der Stadt sind, weigern sich die Stadtverwaltungen, die Verantwortung für ihre Unterbringung zu übernehmen. Sie sind diejenigen, die die Regierung als die "absichtlich Obdachlosen" bezeichnet.

## 10. A long way from basic decency

### Methodisch-didaktische Hinweise

Ein Einstieg in den Text empfiehlt sich über die Anzeige auf S. 83 (s. *pre-reading activities*).
Falls vor diesem Text Kapitel 1 bereits behandelt worden sein sollte, könnten bei der Besprechung des *advertisement* auch noch Wissen und Ansichten der Schüler über die imperiale Vergangenheit Großbritanniens integriert/wiederholt werden.
Zur Entstehung der CRE siehe Schülerbuch S. 309 (Fact File, Ch. 9) und *Britain 1992. An official handbook*. HMSO: London, 1992, p. 25.
Der erste Teil des Textes läßt sich in Abschnitten erarbeiten, die in etwa so den einzelnen Aufgaben zugeordnet werden können:
Task no.1: ll. 1–19, no.2: ll. 19–34, no.3: ll. 35–70.

### Pre-reading activities

*Questions on advertisement, p. 83:*
*1. Identify the ethnic origins of the children in the picture.*

*2. What do you think the picture is meant to convey?*

*3. What kind of help would you find most important for ethnic groups subject to racial discrimination?*

*4. Do you find the logo (shaking hands) convincing?*

*5. What people do you think the advertisement is aimed at?*

*6. Why do you think such an advertisement might be necessary?*

### Suggested answers

1. Hate mail sent to ethnic minorities; violence against ethnic minorities: stabbings, fire-bombings, tyre-slashings, threatening phone calls; 8 to 9 "racial incidents" reported in London every day. The tabloid press strengthens prejudice by reporting violence against whites but not against Asians.

2. A statistical increase in racial incidents from one year to the next may indicate simply that more people have the courage to come forward and not that there is a factual increase, the police say. The popular press reports more assaults and muggings by blacks against whites, but police statistics show that there are incomparably more attacks on Asians than on whites.

3. In Great Britain Nelson Mandela is celebrated as a victim of racism in South Africa and promoter of harmony between the races. Mandela's release was the motivating force behind the author's inquiry. It revealed that the "pious clamour" accompanying Mandela's release was far removed from the reality of London.

4. The *hate mail* that arrives in the letter-boxes of ethnic minorities shows that in Britain there is strong antipathy against them. *Statistics* reveal a rapid increase in reported racial incidents and contradict the impression created by the tabloid press that whites are more often the victims. In *South Africa*, racism is overt, in Britain less open. Nelson Mandela's vision of racial harmony can no more be fulfilled in Britain than it can in South Africa. *Dialogue* concerning multi-culturalism in Britain is difficult, since it is based on the mutual distrust of the groups involved (liberals, conservatives, blacks) and hampered by political rhetoric that reinforces prejudice. Showing "a little basic *decency*" is the prerequisite for the success of multi-culturalism.

5. Decency implies respect for others, tolerance, politeness and a rational approach to problems. Relevant points with respect to Germany (own impressions required): upsurge of racial violence in the east of Germany since unification; recent wave of violence against political refugees in all parts of Germany; increase in numbers of refugees, e.g. due to war in Yugoslavia; increase in settlers of German origin from eastern Europe since fall of the Iron Curtain; increasing unemployment and housing shortage cause many to blame incoming settlers and refugees; role played by political rhetoric (e.g. election campaigns); increasing acceptance of blatantly racist political parties.

6. Relevant aspects: The British have profited enormously from their empire (cf. Chapter 1, SB, text 3, "The path of progress?", for arguments against British colonialism and imperialism). But can the society and economy of Britain today cope with unlimited immigration? Might this not ruin the country for everybody, for the sake of a moral imperative?

7. –

**Post-reading activities**

1. *What should an advertisement for racial equality in a German paper take into account (cf. advertisement p. 83)? What ought to be designed similarly, what differently? Discuss.*

2. *Classroom talk: Racial violence in Britain today.*
See Bibliography 17.

# 11. Modernise the monarchy (GK)

### Background information

In his pamphlet *The Monarchy*, Counterblasts No. 10 (London, 1990), Christopher Hitchens refers to the monarchy as "Britain's favourite fetish". He accuses the monarchy of cementing encrusted political structures and upholding an "unlovely system of social distinction and hierarchy" (p. 19). Hitchens lists the following arguments used in favour of the monarchy before proceeding to refute them:
"1. The Royal Family provides continuity and stability.
2. The Royal Family provides glamour and pageantry.
3. The Royal Family does not interfere in politics, but lends tone to it.
4. The Royal Family is preferable to the caprices of presidential government.
5. The Royal Family is a guarantee of the national 'identity'."

### Suggested answers

1. Australia, an independent state, has a British monarch as its head of state. Sons of the sovereign take precedence over daughters in the succession to the throne. The succession rights of a prince over a princess go back to distant historical times and are no longer justifiable. The consort of a queen should be given proper recognition. The wife of a king is a queen, but oddly enough the husband of a queen cannot be king. The monarchs must be Protestant. This goes back to 1701 and is now devoid of relevance.

2. It is religious discrimination never to allow a monarch to be Roman Catholic. If this limitation were removed, the Church of England would be relieved from its burden of being the established church. The Prime Minister would no longer be responsible for choosing its leaders. English Anglicans would benefit from democratic structures within their church.

3. Some relevant aspects:
Role of monarchy in politics – necessary or not? Royalty a money-spinner for tourism and the media – Would the royals be boring without media coverage of their private lives? Pomp and pageantry incongruous in a democratic country – financial privileges of royals inacceptable – crass contrast to social problems after Thatcher era – royal patronage of social causes. Could the "very special place" in society be filled by anything else?

4. "...some of the monarchy's historical anachronisms... increasingly unacceptable." (ll. 13–15); "...the outdated notion that..." (l. 16); "the present arrangements are sexism, against women *and* men, gone mad."(ll. 47–48); "the law...should be thrown on the historical scrapheap."(ll. 53–55); "...Britain is unlikely to want religious as well as sexual discrimination enshrined at the apex of its national life." (ll. 65–67); "Protestant monopoly of the throne..."(ll. 68–69); oddities of the monarchy ...offensive..." (ll. 92)

5. Monarchy – pros and cons: see above, "Background information".
Pros:
– the societal system gains stability and continuity;
– glamour, pageantry; history made felt to reach into the present:
– does not interfere in politics, but atmospherically influences them;
– a presidency is mostly too powerful, too secretive, too complicated; danger of an 'imperial' or 'monarchical' presidency;
– royal family conveys a sense of national 'identity'.

Cons:
– too much pomp;
– hereditary principle: "bad eggs" likely to become kings or queens; no election of the fittest for the job;
– too expensive (tax policy, apanage);
– only seemingly exerting political power.

6. Translation
Ein weiteres Prinzip der Monarchie, das wahrscheinlich zunehmend in einem modernen und fortschrittlichen Land im 21. Jahrhundert Anstoß erregen wird, ist die Vorschrift, daß der König oder die Königin immer Protestanten sein müssen, und nicht römisch-katholisch sein dürfen. Diese Bestimmung, die dazu führt, daß Nichtprotestanten im Rennen um die Thronnachfolge keine Chance haben, gehört auf den Müllhaufen der Geschichte (geworfen). Sie geht auf die *Act of Settlement* von 1701 zurück, die die Thronnachfolge den protestantischen Nachkommen der Kurfürstin Sophie von Hannover, einer Nichte Charles I., vorbehielt. Es war seinerzeit ein kluger Schachzug, um die katholischen Nachkommen von Jakob II, Charles' Bruder – einem üblen Typ – von der Thronfolge auszuschließen. Aber außerhalb von Nordirland, wo der historische Konfessionskonflikt täglich neu ausgelebt wird, finden Erinnerungen hieran keinen Widerhall. Wenn erst einmal die Zeit eines Charles III gekommen ist, wird Großbritannien wohl keine religiöse und sexuelle Diskriminierung haben wollen, die man wie in einem Schrein an der Spitze seines öffentlichen Lebens aufbewahrt.

Machte man mit dem protestantischen Monopol der Thronnachfolge Schluß, so wäre das nicht nur gerecht, sondern man würde die Church of England auch von der drückenden Last befreien, Staatskirche zu sein. Der Erzbischof von Canterbury oder seine Bischofskollegen müßten nicht mehr so auf der Hut sein, wenn sie ihre Meinung frei äußern. Downing Street müßte nicht mehr darüber nachsinnen, welchen Prälaten man in der kirchlichen Hierarchie befördern soll. Die englischen Anglikaner würden endlich, wie die gesamte anglikanische Gemeinde in der übrigen Welt, die Freiheit haben, ihre eigenen Bischöfe zu wählen, ihre eigenen Statuten zu verfassen, ihren eigenen Weg zu gehen, befreit vom Verfassungsgerümpel eines anderen Zeitalters.

7. The words in italics occur in the text in order of appearance.
*royal* – royalty, the royals, royalism, royalist, royal speech
*duke* – duchess; earl, countess; viscount, viscountess; baron, baroness
head of state
*monarchy* – monarch, monarchical, monarchist
*sovereign* – sovereignty
to have precedence over
*succession (to the throne)* to succeed
throne
to take precedence over
the Princess Royal
succession rights over
prince
princess
monarch

*Modern Britain*

*queen* – queenhood, queenlike, queenly, queen mother, queen regent
*king* – kingdom, kingliness, kingly, kingship, the King's speech; regal
the queen's consort
Prince Consort
*descendant* – to descend from
*electress* – elector
royalty
the royals

**Post-reading activities**

1. a) When Prince Charles turned 40, Guardian commentator John Sweeney wrote the following remark in reply to public criticism of the heir to the throne:
"It might be thought that a Royal who recognised that, say, Wittgenstein was not an unspoilt Swiss ski resort should be the topic of national celebration, rather than scorn." (*The Guardian*, November 20, 1988).
*Explain this statement and comment on Sweeney's attitude to royalty.*

b) What sort of person do you think an heir to the throne should be?

2. *Classroom talk: The historical origins of the exclusion of Catholics from the monarchy.* ("Glorious Revolution" 1688 – Act of Settlement 1701; students should consult any British history book or encyclopedia.)

Pictures
– p. 84: The privileges and rights of the German aristocracy were abolished by an article in the Constitution of Weimar in 1919 and an Act of Parliament in 1920. The titles were allowed to remain part of the family name (e.g. Otto Graf Lambsdorff, leader of the German liberal party FDP; Marion Gräfin Dönhoff, editor of the German weekly *Die Zeit*).
– p. 85, cartoon: The workers are laying out an extremely long red carpet for the Queen – as is often done at airports, etc. The joke lies in the rather grotesque idea of the Queen jogging in the park while at the same time maintaining (through use of the red carpet) an air of regal dignity.

# Test: Thatcher's children

Each generation believes itself to be unique. The beatniks and hippies of the swinging Sixties had a particularly strong sense of breaking away from their parents and seemed ill at ease with Thatcher's children, that group of adults who reached voting age after Mrs Thatcher came to power in 1979 and have known no other prime minister. Thatcher's children were accused of being hard-nosed, greedy, uncaring, amoral yuppies who brayed loudly in the wine bars that sprouted up in virtually every town centre in the country. Their symbol was the Filofax, their preferred car, the brutish-looking Porsche.

Even supporters of Mrs Thatcher worried about the behaviour being spawned by the accumulation and spread of wealth. Peregrine Worsthorne in the *Sunday Telegraph* cautioned Conservatives after the 1987 general election against "bourgeois triumphalism". He wrote: "Vulgarity rules OK and the yuppies feel confident enough to shed all inhibitions about enjoying the spoils of the class war which they think Mrs Thatcher has fought on their behalf."

The Thatcher children who had not achieved the level of affluence of their peers in the City or in the estate agencies in the High Streets were portrayed by other commentators as equally marked by selfishness. They were the lager louts who disturbed the peace and quiet of rural England or the football hooligans who brought mayhem to the Continent. They were the new poor who felt dispossessed by Britain's political institutions, uncared for and alienated to the extent that they turned to violence.

The Labour party and liberal critics in the Church of England played on these perceptions, using them as a stick with which to beat Mrs. Thatcher. She, after all, they argued, had set herself up as a revolutionary in values, the prime minister who wanted to engineer a change in social attitudes. Social surveys throughout Mrs Thatcher's time in office suggested, however, that the picture was far more complex.

A survey conducted by Mintel in 1988 cast doubt on the free-wheeling, wine-bar image. "Thatcher's children have little time for frivolity," the report said. They wanted to be model citizens and desired a responsible place in the world of work. The respondents in the survey rejected non-conformity. They wanted money, consumer goods and designer clothes but placed an even higher value on family relationships. This survey did not satisfy some critics, and it sparked a series of articles on how boring Thatcher's children were and how a new, dull conformism was being established.

A series of group discussions with the young, and in-depth polling by *The Times* in 1986 provided a remarkable insight into Thatcher's children and showed their most characteristic political attitude was one of apathy. "This political apathy is surely something more than a listless unconcern for the issues of the day: rather a positive opting-out of the whole process."

The good news for the prime minister was that Thatcher's children were sceptical of the power of government to improve their lives. Generally, they did not blame government for unemployment. They were prepared to get on their bikes. But any high hopes Mrs Thatcher had of having encouraged the rise of a thrusting, confident generation seemed in one way to be dashed by the results of the polling by Mori in *The Times*. Thatcher's children were sceptical of their own powers to improve their lives.

More than 60 per cent of the respondents thought the prime minister was out of touch with young people. In group discussions she was highly criticised, but she also clearly had the strongest image of any party leader. The ambivalance of the young to the woman who had dominated their adult political lives was striking. The young displayed a perverse fascination with Mrs Thatcher. "I don't like her, I admire her," said one young woman. Another remarked: "I can't stand the sight of her, but her politics are quite good. I think it is good how she's kept things steady."

By Janie Dettmer, *The Times*, 24 November 1990. © Times Newspapers Ltd. 1990. Reprinted by permission.

## Annotations

2 **beatnik** (in the 1950s and 60s) person behaving and dressing unconventionally as a sign of protest
2 **hippie** (in the late 60s) person who rejected organized society and led an unconventional life
10 **to bray** to sound like a donkey
10 **to sprout up** to begin to grow or appear
12 **Filofax** elaborate kind of notebook popular with yuppies
13 **brutish** like a brutal and insensitive person
15 **to spawn** to appear or to produce in great numbers
21 **inhibition** inability to act naturally
21 **spoils** profit, benefits
28 **lager lout** young person who gets violent after drinking too much beer
30 **mayhem** violent disorder
36 **perception** *here:* the way s.th. is seen
44 **Mintel** polling institute
45 **free-wheeling** moving or acting freely or irresponsibly
62 **listless** having no energy
63 **to opt out** to choose not to take part
71 **thrusting** forcing oneself forward
72 **to dash** to strike forcefully
73 **Mori** polling institute
80 **ambivalence** state of having or showing mixed feelings about s.th.

## I Language

1. Name and explain the *-ing* forms in lines 6, 9, 36 and 55:

2. Explain the use or omission of the definite article in lines 8 (Thatcher's children), 24 (The Thatcher children), 31 (the new poor), 39 (values) and 49 (the respondents).

3. a) Find synonyms (or near synonyms) for the following words and expressions (keep to the sentence structure):
particularly (l. 3)
ill at ease (l. 4)
virtually (l. 11)
cautioned (l. 17)
dispossessed (l. 32)
the respondents (l. 49)
sparked (l. 53)
b) Explain the term "bourgeois triumphalism", (l. 19).

4. Give the corresponding nouns of: to accuse (l. 8), to prefer (l. 12), confident (l. 20), to enjoy (l. 21), to achieve (l. 24), to portray (l. 26), to disturb (l. 28), to alienate (l. 33).

5. Translate into German: "The good news...kept things steady." (ll. 65–87).

## II Comprehension

1. What was the standard picture people had of those of "Thatcher's children" who were successful?

*Modern Britain* 93

2. In what respect did even lager louts conform to this standard view?

3. Explain why the outlook of "Thatcher's children" can be said to be complex.

4. How did "Thatcher's children" themselves judge Mrs Thatcher?

**III Comment**

1. Do you think the political leader of a country is entitled to set new standards in values and morals?

2. It has been argued that the society we all live in is too egoistic. Give examples. Do you see any way out

# Bibliography

1. Ball, M./Gray, F./McDowell, L. *The Transformation of Britain*. London: Fontana Paperbacks, 1989.
2. Barnett/Corelli. *The Audit of War – The Illusion and Reality of Britain as a Great Nation*. London: Macmillan 1986.
3. *Britain 1992, An Official Handbook*, London: HMSO 1992.
4. Calvocoressi, Peter. *The British Experience 1945–1975*. Harmondsworth: Penguin 1979.
5. Critchfield, Richard. *Among the British*, London: Hamish Hamilton.
6. Dahrendorf, Ralf. *On Britain*. London: BBC 1982, pp. 18–39.
7. Dunn, Douglas. *Poll Tax: The Fiscal Fake*. Counterblasts No. 12. London: Chatto & Windus 1990.
8. Hitchens, Christopher. *The Monarchy*. Counterblasts No. 10. London: Chatto & Windus 1990.
9. Jenkins, Peter. *Mrs Thatcher's Revolution*. London 1987; Pan paperback edition available
10. Marwick, Arthur. *British Society Since 1945* (esp. Part 4). London 1982; Penguin paperback edition available.
11. Owen, David. *Our NHS*. London: Pan Book 1988.
12. Perspectives 12: *The Caring Society?* Klettbuch 51372.
13. Randle, John. *British Life and Institutions*, Klettbuch 51344.
14. Randle, John. *Understanding Britain*. London: Longman.
15. Ross, John. *Thatcher and Friends*. London: Pluto Press 1983.
16. Spann, Ekkehard. *Abiturwissen Landeskunde, Great Britain/USA*, Klettbuch 929509.
17. Tompson, Keith. *Under Siege – Racial Violence in Britain Today*. London: Penguin 1988.
18. Townsend, Sue. *Mr Bevan's Dream*. Counterblasts. London: Chatto & Windus 1989.
19. Widgery, David. *The National Health – A Radical Perspective*. London: Hogarth Press 1988.
20. Young, Hugo. *One of Us – A Biography of Margaret Thatcher*. London 1989; Pan paperback edition available.

# 4 Britain and Ireland

## Structure of the chapter

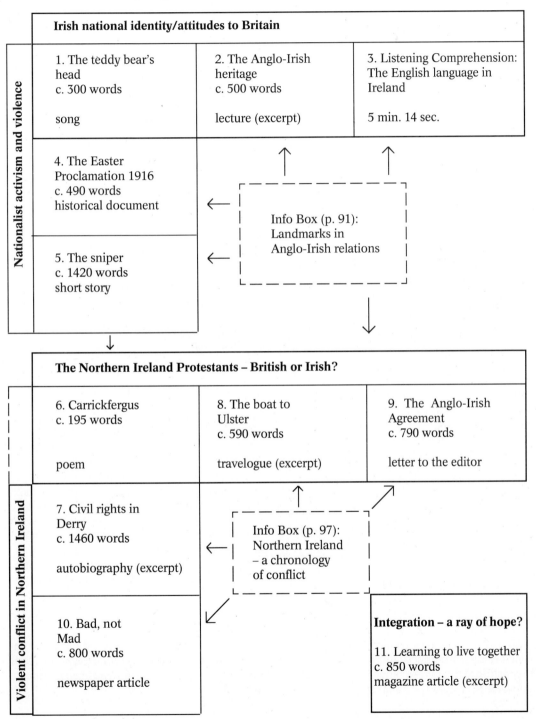

**Suggestions for reports/papers/talks**

The colonization of Ireland: a survey – after text 1

Irish rebel songs – after text 1

Jonathan Swift: his life and work – after text 2

Easter 1916 by W.B.Yeats – after text 4

The Anglo-Irish War – after text 4

Troubles in the South: from the Treaty to the declaration of the Republic – after text 4

The Northern Ireland Civil Rights Movement – after text 4

The IRA – after text 10

Loyalist paramilitary groups – after text 10

*Wednesday's Child* by Tony Higgins – before/after text 11

Handshakes and hope: a survey of attempts to break the vicious circle of violence in N.I. – after text 11

**Vocabulary**

*Thematischer Grund– und Aufbauwortschatz*, Klettbuch 51955, pp. 115–117, 132–151

*Words in Context – Thematischer Oberstufenwortschatz*, Klettbuch 51961, pp. 26–33

 **1. The teddy bear's head**

**Background information**

Whereas most Irish "rebel songs" refer to past situations and events – usually claiming a continuity of struggle through the past 800 years – this is one of the smaller number of such songs that relate directly to the present situation, namely to the fact of Partition (see "Landmarks" p. 91, 1921). In this context, the "rebels" referred to can be none other than the IRA as we know them today.

The message of the verses is clear, and simply (or even simplistically) expressed: The whole island of Ireland belongs to the Irish nation, and the foreign (i.e. British) domination of part of it is to be deplored. This nationalist view is, in fact, shared by a large proportion of the Irish people, and it is enshrined in the Constitution of the Irish Republic ("Article 2: The national territory consists of the whole island of Ireland, its islands and the territorial seas.") Few, however, go so far on to support the IRA's campaign of violence as a way of achieving territorial integrity. Most Irish people recognize that the problem is rendered much more complex by the existence on the island of Ireland of a group of people whose traditions are in conflict with Irish Nationalism – namely the Ulster Protestants. Such facts are not allowed to disturb the simplicity of this song's message.

The song was written by Brian Warfield, leading member of the "Wolfe Tones" (Brian and Derek Warfield, Timmy Byrne, Noel Nagle). This popular group has been performing now for well over 25 years (founded 1964). Their style resembles that of "The Dubliners" (better known on the continent), i.e. they play a straightforward, unsophisticated kind of Irish folk, but with less emphasis on instrumental virtuosity and more emphasis on politics. Their use of the name of the historical figure of Theobald Wolfe Tone (1763–1798) suggests that they see themselves as carrying on the Republican tradition established by Tone. But though Tone's Republicanism once united liberal Catholics and liberal Protestants in a movement for national independence, the Protestants have long since abandoned the movement, and what remains tends to be more narrowly nationalist and Catholic, excluding the other tradition.

Note that in the Irish context, the terms "nationalist" and "republican" have become almost interchangeable.

**Pre-listening activity**

*Look at the map on page 87. What does the shape of the island of Ireland resemble? Does its position in relation to Britain suggest anything to you?*

*Britain and Ireland*

**Suggested answers**

1. –

2. Ireland, unnaturally divided into two parts with Britain dominating the northern part – or even Irish politics in general (since the "brains" affect the whole). Suggested solution: reunification of Ireland, presumably to be brought about by "the rebels".

3. – four verses sung to a simple, folk-style 16-bar melody ;
– each verse consists of 4 lines, with a rhyming scheme aabb;
– chorus similar in form to the second half of a verse;
– verses sung by one member of the group, with banjo backing (other instruments added after first verse);
– rousing chorus sung by whole group in unison at beginning of song and after each verse (suitable for the audience to sing along with in pubs and at concerts);
– tin whistle sequences (e.g. after first chorus) give the song an Irish flavour.

4. The obvious intention of the song is to drum up support for the IRA ("the rebels"). (Plus personal reactions.)

**Additional question**

*Discuss the implication of the phrase: "We're facing towards America/With her ass to England." (ll. 27–28).*

**Post-reading activities**

*1. Classroom report: The colonization of Ireland: a survey.*
See Bibliography 4, 5, 10, 15.

*2. Classroom presentation: Irish rebel songs.*
See Bibliography 1, 9, 15. Two such songs are included in 15. Other suitable examples: "The Rising of the Moon"; "The Croppy Boy"; "A Nation Once Again"; "Off to Dublin in the Green"; "Kevin Barry"; "The Four Green Fields". Most of these have been recorded by well-known groups such as The Wolfe Tones and The Dubliners.

## 2. The Anglo-Irish heritage (GK)

**Background information**

Dr Garret FitzGerald was born in Dublin in 1926. His father was Minister of External Affairs in the Irish Free State's first government. His mother was an Ulster Protestant – but far from opposing Irish independence, (as most Ulster Protestants do today), she was so dedicated to the nationalist/republican cause that she opposed the Treaty setting up the Free State government as not going far enough. This family background no doubt contributed to Dr FitzGerald's awareness of the complications of Irish identity. He was educated at a Jesuit school and University College, Dublin. His first job was as an executive of Aer Lingus (Ireland's national airline). He joined Fine Gael (the party his father had belonged to) and was appointed Foreign Minister in 1973. He became leader of the party in 1977 and served two periods as Taoiseach up to his resignation from politics in 1987. His British colleague, Roy Jenkins, summed up FitzGerald's political achievements as follows (*The Observer,* November 3, 1991):

"In the higher office, he tried to lay to rest more of the ghosts of Irish history than anyone for 300 years, showed imaginative cross-border sympathy, moved the South away from the limitations of a confessional state, and, after infinite patience, got the limited achievement of the Anglo-Irish Agreement of 1985. But as Foreign Minister he made Ireland not merely an official but an integral part of the European Community, an honorary member of the somewhat exclusive club of the original Six. His conduct of the Irish Presidency, which came within two years of joining, was a model of triumphing over the limitations of small-power resources to exercise skilled and authoritative diplomacy."

**Pre-reading activity**

*Try to describe your own sense of national identity. With what group(s) of people do you identify? In what way(s)?*

## Suggested answers

1. In most parts of Ireland the British settlers have been largely assimilated, whereas in the northeast of Ireland, the numerical balance has helped to keep alive the British as well as the Irish sense of identity.

2. The conflict in Northern Ireland can be seen as one of inherited identities.

3. – economic gains: cheap goods and food, extraction of resources
– cultural enrichment by Irish writers

4. – parliamentary democratic system
– common law, judicial and administrative systems
– architectural heritage

5. While the view expressed in the song – biased and one-sided – represents a very simplistic nationalist standpoint, FitzGerald tries to do justice to both sides and to prepare the ground for a conciliatory solution.

6. ...Das Problem, dem wir gegenüberstehen, ist folglich ein Problem unterschiedlicher Zugehörigkeitsgefühle (hier gilt es Verwechslung mit "Identitätsproblem" einer einzelnen Person zu vermeiden), zum großen Teil geprägt durch den Geburtsort und die Erziehung der Menschen. Das Bewußtsein der Zugehörigkeit zu einer bestimmten Gemeinschaft mag vom Zufall bestimmt sein – man kann sich jedoch nicht mit Absicht (Antithese zu "Zufall") einfach darüber hinwegsetzen. Wir Menschen fühlen alle, daß wir nicht nur zu einer Kernfamilie gehören müssen, sondern auch zu einer größeren Gemeinschaft, die Treue verlangt, als Gegenleistung jedoch das beruhigende Gefühl verleiht, einem größeren Ganzen anzugehören, einer umfassenderen Familie von Millionen von Menschen. Diese Gegebenheit in der Politik nicht zu berücksichtigen, würde von mangelhafter Beherrschung ("mangelhafte Kunst" im Deutschen widersprüchlich) der Staatskunst zeugen..../Eine Staatskunst, die diese Gegebenheit nicht berücksichtigt, wäre als mangelhaft zu bezeichnen.

### Post-reading activity

*Introduce one of those Irish writers who have enriched Britain's cultural heritage, e.g. Jonathan Swift: his life and work.*
See Bibliography 9. In order to keep to the theme of Anglo-Irish relations, it is recommended that the student(s) should pay particular attention to Swift's "A Modest Proposal" (1729). An excerpt is included in *Life, Language, Literature* (Klettbuch 5098).

## 3. Listening Comprehension: The English language in Ireland

### Background information

Irish Gaelic is an Indo-European language. As a member of the Celtic group of languages it is very closely related to Scottish Gaelic (they are mutually comprehensible) and more distantly to Welsh and Breton.
In the course of this chapter the students will (have) come across a number of Irish Gaelic words:
– *Éire* ['eɪrə] Ireland (text 9);
– *poblacht/an phoblach*t (the) republic (text 4/picture p. 102);
– *Poblacht na hÉireann* [nə'heɪrən] the Republic of Ireland (text 4: a good example of the "cupla focal!");
– *sinn féin* [ʃɪn'feɪn] ourselves (in "Landmarks": name of political party);
– *loch* [lɔx] lake (text 4: the original form is identical in Irish and Scottish Gaelic; "Lough" is an anglicized form);
– *taoiseach* ['tiːʃɒx] 1. old meaning: chief, chieftain; 2. modern meaning: Prime Minister (text 2);
– *Fiche blian ag streacailt: Bua do mhuintir na hÉireann* Twenty years struggling: Victory to the people of Ireland! (picture p. 102).
These "cupla focal" reveal a number of the typical features of the language: frequent gutteral sounds [x] as in German *ach*; the quality of a consonant influenced by adjoining vowel ("s" adjoining "e" or "i" = [ʃ]); declined forms of nouns/articles

(Nominative: Éire; Genitive: Éireann/na hÉireann); aspiration or obliteration of initial sound in certain cases/declinations/with or without article (poblacht/phoblacht).
In addition, all the Irish place names and most of the personal names come from the Gaelic. Éamonn and Liam, for example, are Gaelic originals; Garrett comes from Gearoid, the Irish Gaelic form of Gerald. The *mac* in MacNiece means "son (of)". FitzGerald, however, is not a Gaelic, but a Norman name, *fitz* being the Norman version of *mac*. Some words of Gaelic origin commonly used in English:
*brogue* 1. heavy walking shoe; 2. Irish accent (from *bróg* = shoe)
*clan* large extended family (from *clann* = family)
*crag* large rock on a hillside (from: *carraig* = rock; cf. "Carrickfergus")
*galore* a lot, plenty (from *go leor* = enough, plenty)
*glen* valley (from *gleann*)
*lough* lake (from *loch*)
*(in) smithereens* (broken into) little pieces (from *smidirín* = fragment)

## Methodisch-didaktischer Hinweis

Eine Einleitung, Worterklärung und Fragen zum Text sind im SB, S. 90 abgedruckt. Neben den Fragen im Schülerbuch (*Listening for the gist*) werden nachfolgend zusätzliche Hörverständnisfragen sowie ein Multiple Choice Test angeboten.

## Text

In 1800, out of a total population in Ireland of about five million, Irish was the mother tongue of perhaps two million; one-and-a-half million spoke only English, while further one-and-a-half million were bilingual. Irish Gaelic, "the pagan speech", was still the language of the majority, though not, perhaps, the most influential. In the next one hundred years, this supremacy was to be dramatically overthrown. The English language in Ireland became so naturalized that it appeared to be indigenous. The figures tell the story. By 1901, English was the sole language of 85 per cent, and the Irish Gaelic culture had become almost totally submerged. Only a mere 21,000, living in the poorest and remotest parts of the country, especially the West coast, spoke Irish and were ignorant of English [...].

After the Act of Union in 1803, without official backing, Irish Gaelic went into decline, owing its survival mainly to the traditional support of the Roman Catholic church. Education, now in the hands of English administrators, meant learning English. Even the leaders of the independence movements, men like Daniel O'Connell, believed that in order to advance the campaign for an independent Ireland, the rank and file had to learn the language of the enemy. O'Connell was said to have delivered a speech in Irish on only two occasions – when he thought there were police spies present.
The slow erosion of Irish was matched by the great social crises of the nineteenth century which annihilated the Gaelic-speaking communities. One million died in the terrible famine; millions more fled abroad. Almost more important than the famine itself was the fear of another one. Irish parents encouraged their children to learn English and to leave in ever larger numbers for England, Australia and, above all, the United States. The land was seen as cursed, and there was a tragic and almost universal rejection of things Irish. During the darkest moments of the Victorian age, the reality of everyday life in Ireland was so intolerable the Irish felt that only an escape into the English way of life and language would solve their problems. What has been called "the mass flight from the Irish language" was enforced in the national schools by a series of frightening educational measures. Gaelic-speaking children were punished with wooden gags, and subjected to mockery and humiliation. Brothers were encouraged to spy on sisters. Under the regime of the tally-sticks, the child would wear a stick on a string round its neck. Every time the child used an Irish Gaelic word, the parents would cut a notch in the wood. At the end of the week, the village schoolmaster would tally up the notches and administer punishment accordingly. There was only one end in view: the eradication of Irish. The schools became the instrument of suppression, just as, ironically, they are today the chief promoters of Gaelic.
The new railway network spreading out from Dublin and Belfast extended the influence of the English-speaking towns. By mid-century the damage had been done. The census figures of 1861 tell a chilling tale. Of the Irish population aged between two and ten years, less than 2 per cent were monoglot Irish speakers. There were now more

Irish abroad than at home. The future was an English-speaking one, and for many it was to lie overseas: in America, the English "mainland", and throughout the British Empire.

For the leaders of the movement for Irish independence the replacement of the language of the oppressor by a return to Gaelic was a symbolic aim. In 1921, with the emergence of Irish Free State, Gaelic was acclaimed a national language, and promoted within the educational system. Today it is taught in schools as a second language and, though the majority know it about as well as most English know French, Gealic has become a focus of cultural and ethnic loyalty, a symbol for Ireland. In the Dail, the Irish have a phrase for the customary not at the Celtic past, the *cupla focal*, "the couple of words". Politicians are advised to start their speeches with the *cupla focal*.

From *The Story of English* by Robert McCrum, William Cran and Robert MacNeil, London: BBC Publications, 1986. Used by permission.

### Suggested answers (Listening for the gist)

1. Irish Gaelic.

2. It was almost eradicated.

3. It is taught in schools as a second language. It has become a focus of cultural and ethnic loyalty, a symbol of Ireland.

### Listening for detail

*1. What happened to the English language in Ireland between 1800 and 1900?*
It became naturalized.

*2. In what way did the Great Famine contribute to the eradication of Irish?*
Mass emigration to USA, England & Australia; escape into English way of life and language.

*3. What educational measures were taken to suppress the speaking of Irish?*
Wooden gags, encouragement to spy on family members; tally sticks.

*4. What did the future look like for the Irish population in 1860?*
An English-speaking future; for many their future would be overseas.

*5. What was the symbolic aim for the leaders of the movement for Irish independence?*
Replacement of English by a return to Gaelic, because English was seen as the language of the oppressor.

### Discussion

*1. How important is a person's language? What is the connection between language and national identity?*

*2. Explain the custom of the "cupla focal". Say what you think of it.*

### Multiple choice test

*Choose the correct sentences:*

1. In 1800 Irish was the mother tongue of
a) about one and a half million.
b) about two million.
c) about five million.

2. After the Act of Union
a) Irish Gaelic went into decline.
b) Irish English was refined.
c) education was newly defined.

3. Gaelic-speaking children were
a) punished with a wooden stick.
b) encouraged to beat their sisters.
c) subjected to mockery.

4. Daniel O'Connell believed that
a) Irish should be the national language.
b) Irish people should learn Irish.
c) Irish people should learn English.

5. In 1861 there were
a) more Irish monoglot speakers than before.
b) more Irish people abroad than at home.
c) Irish lessons in the schools.

6. When the Irish Free State was founded
a) Irish became an official language.
b) English was replaced by Gaelic.
c) Gaelic was declared dead.

7. Today Gaelic has become
a) a symbol of Irish culture and national pride.
b) a second foreign language in schools.
c) a language of the ethnic minorities.

# 4. The Easter Proclamation   1916

## Background information

Though the 1916 Easter Rising has become an integral part of the political folklore of the independent Irish state which finally did emerge from the conflict, it is still the subject of much controversy. On the one hand, many admirers of the idealism of the 1916 rebels question whether the Irish Free State (and later the Republic) came anywhere near to fulfilling the promise of paragraph four of the Proclamation (civil rights). On the other hand, their critics question their wisdom and judgement, or even their arrogance in claiming to speak for a population that up to that point had not supported violent action. At the time most Irish people were willing to wait and see whether Britain would "keep faith" (as Yeats put it in his famous poem) and grant Home Rule (to the whole of Ireland) after the War. The rebels obviously thought differently, i.e. that the British Government would inevitably give in to the threats of Sir Edward Carson and his Ulster Volunteers (see "Landmarks"), and that "England's difficulty is Ireland's opportunity" (Wolfe Tone).

The Rising itself was a dismal failure. Conflicting orders had caused confusion, and outside of Dublin the Irish Volunteers remained inactive. The promised shipload of arms from Germany (their "gallant allies in Europe", paragraph two) arrived late and out of reach on the west coast. The public remained apathetic – until the executions started. The resulting wave of sympathy and outrage finally led to the overwhelming victory of Sinn Fein in the 1918 General Election.

## Methodisch-didaktischer Hinweis

Bei der Besprechung dieses Textes geht es nicht nur um die Analyse eines historischen Dokumentes (cf. Lehrplan), sondern es bietet sich auch die Gelegenheit für die Schüler, bei der Erarbeitung des historischen Hintergrundes im Umgang mit Nachschlagewerken größere Vertrautheit zu gewinnen, sowie u.U. einen Vergleich unterschiedlicher Quellen vorzunehmen.

## Pre-reading activity

a) Look up the following words in your dictionary: civil war; insurgency; insurrection; rebellion; revolt; uprising.
b) What do these words have in common?
c) Find out their differences in usage.

## Suggested answers

1. – What does Ireland do through the "Provisional Government"?
– What preparations have been made?
– By what right does the Provisional Government proclaim an Irish Republic?
– What does this Republic claim, and what does it guarantee?
– How long does the Provisional Government want to administer the civil and military affairs of the Republic?
– What does the Provisional Government expect from the Irish Nation?

2. – 1567/79/95 rebellions in the names of Catholicism and Irish nationalism
– 1641 Catholic rebellion in Ulster
– up to 1691 Jacobite Wars
– 1798 rebellion of the "United Irishmen" (Wolfe Tone)
– 1803 rebellion of Robert Emmet
– 1848 rebellion of the "Young Ireland" movement
– 1867 Fenian insurrection

3. Yes: force only language Britain understands/ Britain not serious about granting Home Rule/ Britain would always side with the Protestant settlers/World War I: "Britain's difficulty is Ireland's opportunity" (Wolfe Tone)/Irish people need to be shaken out of their indifference.
No: rebels only a small minority/no right to speak or act for the people of Ireland/unfair to attack Britain in the middle of World War I/Home Rule promised for after the war.

4. Style: formal, literary; tone: exalted. Individual reactions to be described.

## Additional questions

1. Find less formal synonyms for the following words and phrases used in the Proclamation: summons (calls); manhood (men); pledge our lives (commit ourselves); opportune (suitable, convenient).

2. What foreign support were the rebels hoping for? Try to explain what their hopes were based on, and find out if any such hopes were realized.

Britain and Ireland

3. What civil rights were promised in the new "Republic"? Compare with the situation in the United Kingdom at the time.

### Post-reading activities

1. Classroom report: The Anglo-Irish War.
See Bibliography 1, 5, 6, 13, 15, 18.

2. Classroom presentation: "Easter 1916", poem by W.B. Yeats.
See Bibliography 9, 15. Since the literary qualities of a poem can hardly be conveyed by means of a short presentation, the student can be instructed to concentrate on its political content, i.e. the poets – and the Irish public's – change of attitude towards the rebels after their failed Rising.

## 5. The sniper

### Methodisch-didaktischer Hinweis

Die Kurzgeschichte kann ohne jegliche Einstimmung oder einführende Vorbemerkungen im Unterricht gelesen, oder besser noch mittels Cassette präsentiert werden, um die unmittelbare Wirkung nicht zu beeinträchtigen. Es empfieht sich jedoch, die Termini "Republicans" und "Free Staters" (l. 10) vorweg zu erklären, durch einen Hinweis auf die Situation direkt nach dem "Treaty".
– "Free Staters" were satisfied with the new Irish Free State, and thought it was the best that could be achieved at the time.
– "Republicans" rejected the compromise, and wanted to go on fighting for a Republic (outside the Commonwealth) which should include the whole of Ireland.

### Suggested answers

1. Although the story is told in the third person, the perspective is that of the Republican sniper. We are clearly told what he sees, feels, and we experience his thinking.
Reasons for this choice: The sniper is the protagonist; this perspective heightens the suspense; the reader shall identify with the Republican sniper and so experience the surprise ending to its full effect.

2. (l. 1–11) general setting; creating gloomy atmosphere;
– (l. 12–29) focusing on the Republican sniper's situation
– (l. 30–40) 1st event; introduction of a new character; Republican sniper threatened by an enemy;
– (l. 41–60) 2nd event; armoured car episode;
– (l. 61–142) situation develops into a duel, fight between the two snipers with the climax of the external action;
– (l. 143–184) Republican sniper's reaction to the killing of his enemy as preparation of the internal climax,
– (l. 185–186) surprise ending.

Suspense is created by the introductory paragraph and its atmosphere as well as by the fact that the narration concentrates entirely on the protagonist; all events take place in relation to the main character; apart from that there is a life-and death struggle at the centre of this story. Suspense is maintained by various devices: the chosen perspective forces the reader to take sides and to witness how the sniper tries to manage this precarious situation; the narrator introduces a number of exciting events, strategically placed to lead up to a climax; the reader is uncertain of the outcome as the narrator withholds information, and the reader only knows as much as the protagonist does; and finally the external climax is followed by an internal climax at the very ending of the story.

3. Direct: young, thin and ascetic face (l. 16); fanatic (l. 17); deep, thoughtful eyes (l. 17–18).
Indirect: reckless, likes to take a risk (ll. 2 7–29; 53–157); has good reactions (ll. 30–34); calm and controlled (ll. 35–37; 46–48); is strong-willed (l. 80); imaginative, inventive (ll. 103–108); enthusiastic about fighting (ll. 17, 22, 127); sensitive (ll. 145).

4. "Must" here denotes the necessity to fight, to kill the enemy, otherwise he would be killed, and thus points to driving force behind the sniper's actions, namely the struggle for survival.

5. Personal reactions required.
e.g. At first glance the ending seems to be exaggerated, (kitschy, trite); but it intensifies the central theme of this story, i.e. the tragedy of civil war.

6. It shows most of the commonly accepted characteristics of the traditional pattern:
– short narrative written in prose;
– one main event;
– concentrated on one protagonist;
– a conflict at its centre;
– open beginning and open ending, etc.

7. This task should best be assigned after the classroom talk given below has been presented and discussed.

### Additional questions

*1. In the first paragraph the scenery is described as dimly lit. What connotations does this description evoke?*

*2. Find further adjectives to describe the atmosphere which is created here.*

*3. Describe the sniper's reaction after he had hit his enemy. What do you personally think of his reaction?*

### Post-reading activity

*Classroom talk: Troubles in the South: from the Treaty to the declaration of the Republic.*
See Bibliography 1, 11, 15.

## 6. Carrickfergus

### Background information

A constant and recurring theme among poets from Northern Ireland's Protestant community is the feeling of separation, of being different from the other community. Whereas a poet like Seames Heaney, who grew up in a Catholic community, is able to express his sense of belonging to an age-old indigenous culture, Protestant poets like John Hewitt and Louis MacNeice often express a feeling of not belonging. This comes across clearly in these five verses of his poem "Carrickfergus" (the full poem has 11 verses). As expressed by Frank Ormsby in his introduction to his *Poets from the North of Ireland* (Belfast Blackstaff Press 1979, p. 4):
"Louis MacNeice is (...) conscious of the factors in his background and upbringing which cut him off from "the candles of the Irish poor" and is, too, caught in endless cycles of fascination and repulsion in his attitudes to Ireland. Poems about Ireland represent a small fraction of his output as he spent most of his school, university and working life in England, but much of his work is coloured by the experiences of his childhood years in Carrickfergus."
Carrickfergus is situated on the Antrim coast about 10 miles north-east of Belfast. As a Norman town it was much more important than Belfast (which only began to expand in the 18th century). This area of Antrim is strongly Protestant (only about 20% Catholics). Today Carrickfergus is best known for its imposing Norman castle. Since its industry has declined (and cleaned up), it is no longer "smoky" but quite a pleasant place. It is also known as the subject of a quite beautiful folksong expressing the feelings of a home-sick emigrant: "I wish I were in Carrickfergus". The Gaelic name means "Fergus's Rock".
The background of this story is the Civil War which followed the Anglo-Irish Treaty of 1921 (cf. "Landmarks" p. 21: 1921, 1922–23). Many of those who had fought side by side in the War of Independence now found themselves on opposite sides.

### Pre-reading activities

*1. What can you recall of the place where you spent your childhood? Are your impressions predominantly positive, negative, or mixed?*

*2. What do you think has influenced the way you see the place of your childhood? Discuss whether distance is a factor (i.e. whether you still live there, or near it).*

*3. What does the area where you spent your childhood mean to you today?*

### Suggested answers

1. For location, see background information.

*Britain and Ireland* 103

2. Positive: e.g. mountain, castle, residential houses, lights, peacock aura, church, candles, marble, ...
Negative: lost sirens, the mud, which jams the little boats, slum for the blind and halt, yellow brook stinking of chlorine, funeral cry, drowning moon, yelping of his slave, banned for ever, Irish poor, ...

The predominance of negative images may seem to suggest that he has unpleasant memories of the place of his birth. But even these "negative" elements are listed quite neutrally, and mixed with the positive ones, which suggests that he sees them differently, even sentimentally.

3. Mountain/gantries; little boats/Norman castle; Scotch Quarter/Irish Quarter, town/country; Norman/slave; anglican order/candles of the Irish poor.

These contrasts are used to express both the dual nature of that place and its history, and the ambivalence of the speaker's feelings towards the place.

4. All images here appeal to the senses of hearing or of sight, and they communicate the mood of the speaker's recollection of his childhood years in Carrickfergus:
– lost sirens: evoke a feeling of loneliness;
– funeral cry: signals "petrification", the end of life;
– drowning moon: "ominous" in contrast to rising moon (hope);
– yelping: life in the shadow of history, points to the Anglo-Norman oppression of the Irish
– candles of the Irish poor: symbolizes Catholicism as source of hope for the Irish;

5. Since this is only part of a longer poem, one can only comment here on the form of the verses:
– regular number of lines (4) per verse;
– fairly conventional rhyming scheme (lines 2 and 4 rhyme);
– irregular metre (4 to 4 stresses per line, 10 to 15 syllables) gives the lines a conversational tone.

6. Some examples:
– Norman castle, etc. : Anglo-Norman invasion 1169
– Anglican order: the legacy of the English Reformation (established church);
– Scotch Quarter: refers to Scottish colonists, planters in 17th century, who became a prosperous middle class;
– Irish Quarters, etc.: refers to natives, who became the lower class in this part of Ireland;
– the Chichesters: Anglo-Irish family, members of the (Anglican) ruling class.

## 7. Civil rights in Derry (GK)

**Background information**

"Derry", the original and still commonly-used name of the city, comes from the Gaelic *Doire*, meaning "Oak grove". The "London" prefix was added in the 17th century as a sign of its close political connections with the capital of the Kingdom – after the native (Catholic) population had been forced to live in the boglands overlooked by the city walls. In the Jacobite Wars the city was besieged by the Catholic armies of King James II, forcing the Protestants to eat rats as they awaited their deliverance by William III. The "apprentice boys" of the city are said to have played a great part in its defence. This event has become part of Ulster Protestant folklore. Each year up to the sixties, the ruling Protestant minority would commemorate King Billy's victory over the invaders by marching around Derry's city walls and throwing pennies at the unemployed and disenfranchised Catholics below. Politically, the Protestants perpetuated their power in the city by means of gerrymandering, i.e. the manipulation of constituency boundaries so as to ensure that most of the Catholic majority in the greater urban area could only control a minority of the seats in the Council.

It is therefore not surprising that Derry was chosen as the location for the second important Civil Rights march in 1969 (the first having been a march of 2,500 demonstrators from Coalisland to Dungannon, on Saturday, 24 August 1968). This second march was planned for 5 October. A traditional Protestant group called the "Apprentice Boys of Derry", planned a rival march for the same day. The Minister of Home Affairs, William Craig, then banned both marches. The Civil Rights leaders decided to go on with their march and

2,000 demonstrators turned up. When the marchers tried to cross the Craigavon Bridge, the police charged, using batons and riot equipment. Stones were thrown in retaliation and there were 88 injured – 77 civilians and 11 police.

The Cameron Commission was set up to inquire into the affair, and their report concluded that the intentions of the organizers were peaceful; but it blamed them for bad organization and for allowing IRA members and sympathizers to take part. In fact, nobody had been excluded. The movement had created a broad alliance from traditional Catholic nationalists to the far left (Betty Sinclair, referred to in ll. 81–83, was a prominent member of the Communist Party).

After the "troubles" broke out, Derry was the scene of several demonstrations, many of which turned violent. For a time, the Catholic area called Bogside was defended by barricades against any incursions of the police and (later) the British Army.

**Methodisch-didaktische Hinweise**

Für die sich anschließende Präsentation des Textes eignet sich das Vorspielen von der Cassette (*Selected Texts*) besonders gut, da diese Form die für einen autobiographischen Text charakteristische Kommunikationssituation (Ich-Erlebnisbericht, Schüler als Zuhörer) beibehält.

**Pre-reading activities**

1. What do you regard as your "civil rights"?

2. What measures would you take if your civil rights were endangered? Discuss in class.

**Suggested answers**

1. To Bernadette Devlin the problems were based on the fact that basic needs of the people are not satisfied, i.e. she saw it in socialist terms. The politicians she refers to regarded the conflict as being religious discrimination.

2. It was chosen, because of its historical significance (cf. background information), but also because the housing problems and unemployment were extremely bad there.

3. Though banned, more people turned up than to any march before; march stopped by masses of police; a few scuffles; organizers tried to hold a meeting; Eamon McCann spoke to the marchers; police charges. (Cf. background information.)

4. It shows the strong resentment felt by many Protestants Unionists in Northern Ireland against the Civil Rights marchers.

5. Reasons for religious split:
– Henry VIII's unsuccessful attempt to impose Reformation on the Irish in 1536;
– policy of "plantation", encouraging English and Scottish Protestants to settle in Ireland, giving them land confiscated from Catholics (1603);
– Jacobite Wars (1691) which led to Protestant supremacy;
– "Penal Laws" oppressing Catholics.

Sources of Civil Rights movement:
– the inequities of the local government franchise (introduced by the Protestants);
– discrimination against Catholics in housing and employment.

6. –

**Additional questions**

1. Explain "Londonderry ... is the flash-point of N.I." (l. 40).

2. "Such was the impartial attitude of those ministering to the sick." (ll. 179–181). Name the stylistic device used here and explain its function.

3. Bernadette Devlin plays down the role of religious affiliation. Looking back now after 20 years of open conflict, do you think she was right?

**Post-reading activity**

*Classroom report: The Northern Ireland Civil Rights Movement.*
See Bibliography 5, 8, 10, 12, 15.

# 8. The boat to Ulster

## Background information

Lines 1–10, 26–49: Segregation is the norm in most areas of life in Northern Ireland: schools (see text 11), sports clubs, social life. Even pubs tend to be frequented mainly by one or other community. The only real contact between the two communities is in the work place – and even this may be segregated as well, as when an employer deliberately favours members of one community. Since the larger industries (e.g. textiles, shipbuilding) are mostly in Protestant hands, such discrimination has mostly been against the employment of Catholics.

Line 55–70: Partition has meant that the population of the Republic is overwhelmingly Catholic (ca. 95%), making it easy for the Catholic clergy to exert considerable influence on the state. The 1937 Constitution (turning the "Free State" into a "Republic") contained a number of Catholic-influenced Articles. The Article recognizing the "special position" of the Catholic Church was removed by referendum in 1972. But the constitutional ban on divorce remains, and a ban on abortion was added after a referendum in 1982. In addition, homosexuality is still illegal in the Republic. Up to the seventies no contraceptives could be sold or brought into the country legally – the "pill" only being available because of its other medical functions. At the time Theroux's book was published, contraceptive devices (including condoms) were only available on prescription in the Republic. In the age of AIDS, and after considerable controversy and protest, the latter restriction has been somewhat liberalized, but there remains enough to seemingly confirm Protestant fears that – in the words of the 19th century slogan – "Home Rule is Rome Rule". The question remains whether such a situation could have developed in an all-Ireland Republic, with a sizeable Protestant minority.

Pictures: The title of the newspaper (An Phoblacht) means "The Republic" (cf. text 4). The Irish tricolour on the left has the symbolic meaning of peace (the white) between the Irish nationalist tradition (green) and the Ulster Protestants (orange). Connolly's "Plough and Stars" flag had more socialist connotations. The slogan on the second wall painting refers (in Gaelic) to the "twenty years struggle" and calls for victory for "the people of Ireland".
As well as the Union Jack, the Orangemen carry banners showing a victorious King William of Orange at the Battle of the Boyne 1690.

## Methodisch-didaktische Hinweise

Obwohl thematisch fest in die Sequenz eingebunden (Identitätskonflikt), kann dieser Text eine Art Entspannungsfunktion für die Schüler haben. Denn bei der Textrezeption werden weder inhaltlich noch formal erhöhte Anforderungen an die Schüler gestellt. Außerdem ist die Perspektive (Autor sieht als amerikanischer Reisender Konflikt von außen) vom Schüler leichter nachvollziehbar, als die Perspektive der bisherigen Texte.

## Pre-reading activity

*If you met someone from Northern Ireland, what would you like to ask them? Make a list of the things you would like to know, and then try to formulate tactful questions.*

## Suggested answers

1. Some things mentioned or hinted at:
– religious conflict;
– cautious in conversation before revealing one's opinion;
– segregation is the rule in most areas of life (even football clubs and boy scouts);
– there are Protestants who are on friendly terms with Catholics;
– Protestants can no longer imagine a united Ireland;
– Protestants afraid of Catholic influence on state (as in Republic);
– during summer there are events showing "tribalism";
– Protestant = Loyalist;
– there is a lot of irrational prejudice (cf. ll. 79–81).

2. –

3. Mehaffy: Ulsterman of British descent, Protestant; responsible position (cf. l. 35) in the tailoring industry; grew up in County Down in quite miserable circumstances, often helped by Catholics; still on friendly terms with some Catholic

families; had been a scoutmaster, accepted Catholic boys in his troop; feels Irish, for being born there, as well as British (culturally).
Surprising: although he is Protestant, "it was the Catholics who helped..., not the Loyalists" (ll. 39–40); as a scoutmaster "he always had Catholic boys in his troop" (ll. 44–45). (But beware: This could be comparable to a "some of my best friends are Jews" attitude!)

4. Form: due to the author main purpose (travelogue: report of his impressions on his journey) he blends narration, dialogue and comment.
Style: rather simple sentence structure; ordinary vocabulary; coloquialisms; chatty tone.

5. They all touch on conflicts of identity. Jack Mehaffy: "I'm British. But I'm also Irish." (l. 55)

**Additional questions**

*Discuss Jack Mehaffy's attitude to the Republic:*
- *What could have changed his mind about a united Ireland?*
- *What does his reference to contraceptives (ll. 67–70) mean?*
- *How do you think the Republic would have developed if it had included all of Ireland, as was originally intended?*

## 9. The Anglo-Irish Agreement

### Background information

There is a long history of Ulster Protestants rejecting any changes in the status quo, especially anything which tends to loosen their ties to Britain or diminish their privileges. It has come to be known as the "Loyalist Veto". It was first used by Sir Edward Carson in 1912 when he threatened violent action by his "Ulster Volunteers" if the Home Rule Bill went through. Carson was also instrumental in insisting on Partition in 1921 rather than independence for the whole country. More recently, the 1973 Sunningdale Agreement set up a "power-sharing" executive for Northern Ireland which included Catholics in proportion to the population – but it was brought down by a Loyalist strike. Their efforts to stop the Anglo-Irish Agreement failed, but fears of Royalist violence have hampered its implementation. The 1990 Brooke initiative to organize talks between all parties (except the IRA and Sinn Fein) ran into similar trouble, and though "talks about talks" are to be resumed, it is not known at time of publication whether they will be productive.

### Methodisch-didaktische Hinweise

Nachdem die Schüler an diesem Punkt der Unterrichtseinheit bereits über ein beträchtliches Maß an Hintergrundswissen zum Nordirlandkonflikt verfügen dürften, können sie sich nun mit einer meinungsäußernden und meinungsbildenden Textsorte auseinandersetzen, in der klar Position bezogen wird. Dabei wird von den Schülern nicht nur gefordert, Argumentation inhaltlich und strukturell zu analysieren, sondern er soll seine erworbenen Kenntnisse und Fertigkeiten auch im Rahmen einer argumentativen Textproduktion ("reply to the letter") anwenden. Da die Erschließung des Textes die grundsätzliche Kenntnis des "Anglo-Irish Agreement" voraussetzt, ist es notwendig vor dem Text die Einführung im Schülerbuch zu lesen und zu besprechen.

### Pre-reading activity

*Look at the picture on pages 97 and 104 and give your impressions.*
Both show Unionist/Loyalist anger at the Anglo-Irish Agreement. The "traitor" referred to is Margaret Thatcher.

### Suggested answers

1. – He expresses his feelings in terms of great urgency ("I must..", l. 4).
– He claims to speak on behalf of thousands (l. 5) or even "almost a million" (l. 12).

2. He is worried about the Anglo-Irish Agreement; he fears that it will give the Republic of Ireland a say in Northern Ireland.

3. – it gives a foreign country a say in internal affairs;
– it means joint control – something previously rejected by Margaret Thatcher;

*Britain and Ireland*

– it means discussion with terrorists, which no decent democrat should do.

4. His favorite device is based on contrast; tries to prove contradictions thus accusing the government of making a policy of double standards.
– task force to Falklands/ but not to Ulster;
– Argentina no say in Falklands/ Ireland say in Ulster;
– reject joint authority/ accept agreement (= joint control);
– agreement shall improve security/ but supports terrorism;
– writer's family served their country/ but kicked in the teeth by their own Government.

5. "The 'crime' of being loyal" (ll. 64–65), "the audacity to try to serve his country" (ll. 73–74). The writer here employs "verbal irony" to point to the perversion of values which, in his opinion, is manifested in the A.I. Agreement.

6. Possible arguments:
– Catholics, Nationalists/Republicans are also dissatisfied with the Agreement.
– It recognizes the N. I. state, even though it was created to ensure Protestants (Unionists/Loyalists) had a guaranteed majority (artificial boundaries, etc.).
– It practically accepts the "Loyalist Veto" on any change, regardless of what the majority in Britain or in Ireland want.
– Co-operation on security is controversial, because of lack of trust in impartiality of N. I. police or in British justice ("shoot-to-kill" policy, Birmingham Six, etc.).
– Hesitation about security co-operation does not mean support of terrorism (ll. 38–44); the police and courts in the Republic have been quite tough on the IRA.
– In spite of all the above reservations, most Northern Irish Catholics are willing to accept the Agreement as a necessary compromise.
– Protestants must also compromise if there is to be any progress towards peace.
– Acceptance of consultation with the Irish Government is not too much to ask.

### Additional activity

*Translate the passage from l. 77 ("Do you...") to l. 90 ("...of double standards") into good German.*
Können Sie und die Bürger in Großbritannien (eigentlich "Festland", um seine Vorstellung zum Ausdruck zu bringen, auf einer "offshore island" von Großbritannien zu wohnen; aber für deutsche Leser vielleicht mißverständlich) sich überhaupt vorstellen, was es bedeutet, so zu leben, wie wir es nun schon seit 17 Jahren tun, um dann festzustellen, daß man von der eigenen Regierung einen Schlag ins Gesicht erhält? Die vielleicht gröbste (eig. "äußerste") Beleidigung ist die Tatsache, daß anscheinend Hinz und Kunz wissen, was gespielt wird, während unsere gewählten Vertreter nicht einmal anstandshalber vor dem Gipfeltreffen informiert wurden. Und auch dem Volk war es nicht gestattet, seine Ansichten demokratisch in einem Referendum kundzutun; und das, obwohl Sie während des Bergarbeiterstreiks der nationalen Bergarbeitergewerkschaft (oder "NUM" unübersetzt lassen) mit Nachdruck vorwarfen (wörtlich: "trotz Ihrer beharrlichen Behauptung"), diese habe völlig unrecht gehandelt, als sie ihre Mitglieder nicht abstimmen ließ (ein weiteres Beispiel doppelter Moral).

## 10. Bad, not mad (GK)

### Background information

The IRA (Irish Republican Army) is a paramilitary organization which evolved from militant remnants of the Irish Volunteers, who planned and fought the Easter Rising (1916). It remained active after 1921, refusing to accept the separation of Northern Ireland. In the early 70's, after the collapse of the Civil Rights Movement, the IRA split into two wings (both illegal) the "Officials" and the terrorist "Provisionals" ("Provos"). The Provisionals then launched a campaign of bombings and assassinations in Northern Ireland and in Britain.

### Methodisch-didaktische Hinweise

Bei der einführenden Beschäftigung mit der IRA sollte das SB noch nicht herangezogen werden. Die Antworten auf die erste Einstiegsfrage (siehe *pre-reading activities*) können auf unterschiedliche Weise erarbeitet werden: a) als vorbereitende Hausaufgabe; b) in einer Stillarbeitsphase, in der die Schüler ihr Wissen bzw. ihre Assoziationen schriftlich sammeln; c) im Rahmen eines Unterrichtsgesprächs in Form eines "brainstormings", bei dem die Antworten in einem Tafelbild festgehalten werden.

Im Anschluß an das gemeinsam erstellte Bild von der IRA sollte die zweite Einführungsfrage zu einer Diskussion darüber führen, inwieweit die Vorstellungen von der IRA auf Fakten bzw. Annahmen und subjektiven Assoziationen beruhen.

**Pre-reading activities**

1. What do you know about the IRA?

2. Where did you get your knowledge about the IRA from?

**Suggested answers**

1. With their reactions, which according to the writer are not correct, the British unintentionally join in a deception that encourages the IRA. (ll. 101–103).

2. He tries to show that the British leaders are wrong when regarding the IRA as "common murderers" and their deeds as "cowardice", "senseless" and "pointless" by which they will "achieve nothing". According to the author these attributes do not apply to the IRA. Their activities are certainly not pointless: they have clear aims in mind. Having a political goal, they are more dangerous than common murderers. And as they take great risks when carrying out their attacks, their deeds cannot be called cowardly either. Finally, the list of their achievements is "formidable" (cf. ll. 64–81).

3. For the last 20 years the IRA have tried to persuade ordinary people as well as civil authorities of "the reality of their power". This they have achieved partly by terrifying ordinary people, but mainly by terrorizing the civil authority, as the list of their achievements (ll. 64–81) clearly illustrates.

4. By that atrocity in Deal the IRA proved that neither their military power nor their determination had declined.

5. –

**Post-reading activities**

*Classroom talks:*
– *The IRA.*
  See Bibliography 3, 15, 17, 18.
– *Loyalist paramilitary groups.*
  See Bibliography 12, 14, 15.
– *Book report on Brian Moore's novel* Lies of Silence, *Klettbuch 57744.*

# 11. Learning to live together (GK)

**Background information**

The segregated educational system of Northern Ireland has historical roots. Ever since the "Penal Laws" and the efforts to suppress Irish Catholicism in the 18th century, the Catholic clergy in Ireland have been suspicious of state influence in schools. After Catholic Emancipation (1829) they fought for control of their own schools, effectively dividing the National School system. After Partition (1921) an officially non-denominational state system was set up, but the issue of religious education soon caused conflicts. Neither side wanted a completely secular system, but neither could the Protestant clergy tolerate the possibility of Catholic influence on "their" schools in areas with a Catholic majority. The end result was that the Catholics opted out of the system, feeling that it had been hi-jacked by the Protestants. Today most Catholics attend "maintained" schools (i.e. Church-controlled schools which are partly state-financed). Most Protestant children attend "controlled/state" schools – which are now de facto Protestant establishments.

A movement for integrated education started in the 1980s, and since 1988 some state funds have been made available to cover their costs. The numbers attending such schools still remain low – not quite 1% of Northern Ireland's schoolchildren.

**Methodisch-didaktische Hinweise**

Die Behandlung des Nordirlandkonflikts im Unterricht kann sich nicht mit dem Einblick in die historische Entwicklung und in die Hintergründe des Konflikts begnügen, sondern muß auch die vielen Bemühungen auf unterschiedlichsten Ebenen, den Konflikt zu beenden bzw. zu überwinden, sehen. Auch wenn im Augenblick keine realisierbare Lösung in Sicht ist, soll das Kapitel mit diesem Aspekt schließen. Es wäre jedoch völlig vermessen, bei der Vorbereitung auf den Text (siehe *Pre-reading activities*) hier von den Schülern auch nur Ansätze von praktikablen Lösungsvorschlägen zu erwarten. Vielmehr geht es darum, die Schüler gedanklich auf das Thema des nachfolgenden Textes einzustimmen.

**Pre-reading activities**

*1. The main obstacle to peace in Ulster is lack of trust between the two communities. What do you think could be done to try to surmount this obstacle?*

*2. Classroom report:* Wednesday's Child *by Tony Higgins – a story of young people growing up in the "troubles".*
See Bibliography 8.

**Suggested answers**

1. They want to overcome intolerance and hatred by bringing together Catholic and Protestant children and letting them learn about each other.

2. ll. 1–8: His article starts with a typical scene of the school which points to the spirit at that school and already contains the message the writer wants to bring home to the reader;
– ll. 9–20: puts this scene in a wider context;
– ll. 21–28: sets it in contrast to its surroundings (place scarred by the IRA bomb attack);
– ll. 29–46: leads up to the question of "Integrated education in NI" in general;
– ll. 47–104: informs the reader about this project going into details;
– ll. 105–116: personal judgement of this project.

3. She means children should get to know different views of history, tradition and culture, but keep their identity, i.e. should still feel they belong to a cultural group.

4. A very positive view: "lone beacon of hope" (l. 30), "Another little blossom on the tree of hope" (ll. 115–116); but not too optimistic (cf. ll. 105–111).

5. Cf. background information.

**Additional questions**

*1. Give a precise definition of the following words:*
initiative (ll. 25–26); to portray (l. 29).

*2. Find the corresponding abstract nouns (not the "ing-forms"):*
bleak (l. 72); to ignore (l. 85); sectarian (l. 94).

*3. "Another little blossom on the tree of hope" (ll. 115–116):*
Name the stylistic device used here and explain its function.

**Post-reading activities**

*Classroom reports:*
– *Handshakes and hope: a survey of attempts to break the vicious circle of violence in Northern Ireland.*
See Bibliography 2, 7, 15.
– Wednesday's Child *by Tony Higgins (if not presented as pre-reading activity).*

## Test: A new radical approach is needed

I remember just a couple of years ago the present government making gloating pronouncements about how they had finally dealt a crushing blow to the IRA organisation.
5 The events of the last year have clearly shown how premature those self-congratulatory statements were.
It is obvious that the policies pursued over the last twenty years, in particular, have been a total
10 failure. Military operations against the IRA have had minimal success – the killings still go on.

The government portrays the IRA as cold-blooded killers who take sadistic pleasure in murdering people. The IRA, on the other hand, see themselves as champions of the Catholic cause, freedom fighters 15 struggling to overthrow an occupying power. Both sides have blood on their hands. There are no winners in this mindless conflict, only losers.
Is Northern Ireland such a hopeless situation?
An answer must surely be possible, but first a 20 suitable climate must be created to encourage dialogue.

The main cause of the violence centres on the presence of British troops in Northern Ireland.
25 The government should admit its inability to solve the Northern Ireland issue and submit the problem to the forum of the European Community. The EC could then organise a multi-European force (excluding Britain) to replace the British
30 troops probably in a gradual phase-out.
This would not be the final solution to the problem, but it could go a long way to creating the necessary climate to finding that solution. It would, above all else, deprive the IRA of its main reason
35 for mounting the terror campaign.
A new radical approach is needed. Why not a European one?

R. Iwaskow, Nogoya, Japan Letter from The *Guardian Weekly*, October 14, 1991

## I. Language

1. Explain the following words and phrases (you may change the sentence structure):
– the gloating pronouncement (l. 2)
– had finally dealt a crushing blow to the IRA (ll. 3–4)
– in a gradual phase-out (l. 30)
2. Find suitable synonyms for the following words (do not change the sentence structure):
– portrays (l. 12)
– climate (l. 21)
– champions (l. 15)
– to replace (l. 29).
3. Explain the *-ing* forms in the first and fourth paragraphs: making, gloating, crushing, murdering, struggling.
4. "Both sides have blood on their hands" (ll. 16–17). Explain the stylistic device and its function in the context.

## II. Comprehension

1. What two views of the IRA are presented in this letter? What does the writer think of them?
2. What new suggestion does he or she make?
3. How is the letter structured? Give the writer's train of thought.

## III. Comment

1. Give your views on "the presence of British troops in Northern Ireland".
2. Write a letter to the editor endorsing or rejecting R. Iwaskow's proposal.

## IV. Translation

Translate lines 5–11 ("The events of ... still go on").

# Bibliography

1. Beckett, J.C. *The Making of Modern Ireland.* London: Faber 1966.
2. Collins, M., ed. *Ireland after Britain.* London: Pluto Press 1985.
3. Coogan, Tim Pat. *The IRA.* New York 1970.
4. Edwards, Owen D. *The Sins of our Fathers: The roots of conflict in N.I.* Dublin 1970.
5. Edwards, Ruth D. *An Atlas of Irish History.* London 1973.
6. Fitzpatrick, D. *Politics and Irish Life, 1913 – 21.* Dublin 1977.
7. Foot, Paul. Ireland: *Why Britain Must Get Out.* London: Chatto & Windus 1989.
8. Higgins, Tony. *Wednesday's Child.* London 1986; Stuttgart: Klett 1991, Klettbuch 57724.
9. Hyde, Douglas. *A Literary History of Ireland.* Dublin 1967.
10. Johnson, Paul. Ireland: *Land of Troubles.* London: Methuen 1980.
11. Larkin, Emmet. *The Roman Catholic Church and the Creation of the Modern Irish State.* London 1975.
12. Nelson, Sarah. *Ulster's Uncertain Defenders.* Belfast: Appletree Press 1984.
13. O'Connor, Frank. "Guests of the Nation" in *Great Irish Short Stories.* Klettbuch 5791.
14. de Paor, Liam. *Divided Ulster.* Harmondsworth: Pelican Books 1971.
15. Perspectives 11: *Divided Ireland.* Klettbuch 51371.
16. Spann, Ekkehard. *Abiturwisssen Landeskunde, Great Britain/USA* (Ch. 12). Stuttgart: Klett 1990; Klettbuch 929509.
17. Taylor, Peter. *Families at War: Voices from the Troubles.* London: BBC Books 1989.
18. Uris, Jill & Leon. *Ireland: A Terrible Beauty.* London 1976.

# 5 Art, Culture and Society

## Structure of the chapter

| Architecture ||
|---|---|
| **The American skyscraper** | **The architectural debate in Britain** |
| 1. What is American about America?<br>558 words<br>essay<br><br>Chicago ad, p. 113 | 2. "We have ended up with monsters"<br>416 words<br>essay<br><br>3. Why Prince Charles is wrong<br>672 words<br>argumentative text |

| Visual arts ||
|---|---|
| **Sculpture** | **Painting** |
| 4. LC: Henry Moore – a sculptor speaks<br>4 min. 3 sec.<br>interview (excerpt) | 5. A challenge to high art<br>407 words<br>magazine article |

| Art and public relations ||
|---|---|
| 6. "Why do you paint?"<br>c. 2100 words<br>novel (excerpt) | 7. At the Edinburgh Festival<br>160 words<br>poem |

| American film and TV ||
|---|---|
| 8. Hollywood's view of society<br>915 words<br>expository text | 9. They came, we saw, they conquered<br>875 words<br>newspaper article |

| Literature and society |
|---|
| 10. The little room of literature<br>722 words<br>lecture (excerpt) |

Das Kapitel bietet ein breit gefächertes Angebot an Themen. Sie präsentieren durch Gegenstand oder Autor signifikante kulturelle Aspekte. Die thematische Geschlossenheit des Kapitels ist vorwiegend durch den Bezug von Kunst auf Gesellschaft gegeben. Aus diesem Zusammenhang heraus legitimiert sich auch die schwerpunktartige Berücksichtigung von *popular art* und Erzeugnissen der elektronischen Medien. Eine besondere didaktische Funktion des Kapitels besteht in der Begegnung mit spezifischen lexikalischen Feldern, die für eine fortgeschrittene Kommunikationsfähigkeit unabdingbar sind. Es wird empfohlen, einen Schwerpunkt auf die Erschließung und Verarbeitung des Wortschatzes zu legen.

**Suggestions for reports/papers/talks**

The significance of the Land Ordinances of 1785 and 1787 – after text 1.

The Great Fire and the rise of Chicago architecture – after text 1.

The American skyscraper – origin and development – after text 1.

Mies van der Rohe: a German-American architect – after text 1.

The ideal city – after text 2 or text 3.

The architecture of your own town – after text 3.

Urban regeneration in Britain – between text 2 and 3.

Henry Moore and his art – after text 4.

Pop art – after text 5.

Women in art – after text 6.

Movies and novels – after text 8.

The Vietnam War in films – after text 8.

Television in the USA – after text 9.

Book report: "Fighting for Books" from Ray Bradbury's *Fahrenheit 451* – after text 10.

**Vocabulary**

*Thematischer Grund- und Aufbauwortschatz Englisch*, Klettbuch 51955, pp. 213–215 ("Theater, Fernsehen, Film") and pp. 219–222 ("Literatur, Bildende Kunst, Musik").

*Words in Context*, Klettbuch 51961, pp. 130–134 (Mass Media: Radio and TV), pp. 176–180 (Film), pp. 184–197 (Art, Literature).

# 1. What is American about America?

**Background information**

*The author:* John A. Kouwenhoven (born 1909) is a former editor of *Harper's Magazine* and taught literature in its relation to allied arts at Barnard College. He is, however, better known as a cultural historian and author of *Made in America: The Arts in Modern Civilization* (1948) which brought to a single perspective such different aspects of American culture as technology, architecture, fine arts, films, literature and jazz.

*The skyscraper:* The skyscraper did not originate in Manhattan but in Chicago. The Chicago of the mid-19th century was a booming city built almost entirely of timber. In the Great Fire of 1871 (see ad on page 113, SB) the city was largely destroyed. This allowed architectural innovation making use of technical advance. The development of metal skeletons and the invention of safe elevators enabled architects and builders to build bigger by building higher. The first skeleton-frame skyscraper was finished in 1885 and was just ten storeys high. Within three decades in Chicago, Manhattan and other American cities higher and higher buildings went up, so high that they seemed to scrape the sky.

As an architectural art form the skyscraper tried to incorporate artistic elements. The Manhattan Chrysler building (built in 1930) is memorable for its art deco styling making use both of geometrical and asymmetric patterns. As a distinctive architectural achievement it had a strong influence on skyscraper design. The Philadelphia skyscraper (see p. 110, SB) clearly 'quotes' the Chrysler building in a more modern fashion. The "Chippendale skyscraper", the AT&T Building in Manhattan, combines the basically geometrical pattern with a Chippendale top in a striking contrast (built in 1979 in 'postmodern' fashion). The epithet "Chippendale" comes from the style of furniture designed by the eighteenth-century English cabinet-maker, Thomas Chippendale.

*Louis Henry Sullivan (1856–1924)* – famous and influential Chicago architect; is considered as one of the "inventors" of the skyscraper; Sullivan objected to the close agglomeration of skyscrapers on the ground and felt it should stand alone and soar up to make an aesthetic impression.

*Frank Lloyd Wright (1869–1959)* – famous American architect, a student of Sullivan, who specialized in domestic architecture; he developed a type of simple, relatively bare house suitable to American conditions; he is considered to be one of the founders of modernism in architecture.

*Ludwig Mies van der Rohe (1886–1969)* – born in Aachen, worked in Berlin as an architect, became director of the Bauhaus in 1930, emigrated to the USA in 1937 and settled in Chicago; became one of the most significant American architects and teachers of architecture.

*The Ordinance of 1785* (see p. 111, SB): With more settlers going west, one of the most important issues for Congress after the War of Independence was the organization of the territory beyond the Appalachian Mountains. The first of the two basic laws called the Land Ordinance of 1785 established a method of selling the land. Unsettled regions were to be surveyed into squares 6 miles on each side. This township was subdivided into 36 sections, each having 1 square mile (256 hectares) which could be further subdivided. The townships and sections were to be sold at public auctions at one dollar an acre.

The Northwest Ordinance of 1787 laid down rules for the creation of states and their governments in the West.

## Pre-reading activities

*1. What do you consider as being typical of America or American culture?*

*2. Collective brain storming: what do you think of when "New York" or "Manhattan" is mentioned?*

*3. Look at the pictures on page 110 and read the caption.*
See "Background information".

*4. What do skyscrapers symbolize for you?*
Economic power, upward mobility, technological progress, a specific American achievement and aesthetic form

## Suggested answers

1. Looked at closely Manhattan is an accumulation of negative traits. It is the result of political mismanagement, capitalist egotism, exhibitionism of companies and individuals. This kind of haphazard town-planning has created a congested and polluted metropolitan centre that poses many problems to the people living and working there. Yet if Manhattan however is seen as a "skyline", as a cityscape observed from afar, it is one of the most beautiful things man has ever created. In spite of its chaotic development Manhattan leaves an intensely aesthetic effect of unity.

2. Although the innumerable Manhattan buildings rival for uniqueness and do not follow any preconceived pattern of any kind, they all unconsciously obey one fundamental, essentially American principle: both the horizontal pattern on the ground (street pattern, sections) and the vertical pattern of the steel-framed skyscrapers to back to the geometric grid once and still imposed upon American land.

3. Pockets of land – limited by natural or traditional boundaries (forests, rivers, streams, old lanes, roads, hills, etc) – are usually developed in a varied way in Europe so that any kind of geometrical pattern is avoided. Towns which originated in medieval walled cities, for example, have a circular centre with a network of small streets or lanes. Streets forming circles, long-drawn bends, cul-de-sacs, buildings ranging from bungalow to terraced houses and blocks of flats all stress the impression of irregularity and natural growth. There are of course historic and modern exceptions that rely on geometrical patterns and a strict zoning of building styles, for example eighteenth-century Mannheim, Karlsruhe and Ludwigsburg or Georgian Bath in Britain; and new planned towns such as Welwyn Garden City, Cumbernauld or Milton Keynes.

4. Although the basic pattern is geometric (numbered avenues and streets) there are striking deviances due to the peninsular form and old historic developments: Broadway; the 'Lower Broadway' area, Wall Street. South of 14th street the geometric principle is only loosely followed and more varied patterns prevail. The reason for this is that the tip of Manhattan was settled first and "European" patterns were used.

*Art, Culture and Society*

5. – advantages: e.g. easy orientation, clear regulation of traffic, expansion and further development of new areas is integrated from the beginning;
– disadvantages: e.g. faceless agglomeration of buildings, neglect and destruction of natural conditions (rivers, hills etc.), too many street crossings.

6. Chicago wants to be seen as the city that created modern architecture, revolutionized construction methods, employed architects of world fame. It is the "architecturally richest cultural center in America". As this PR ad appeared in the international editions of various magazines one may see it as part of the old competition for excellence between Chicago and New York which is generally better known abroad than Chicago.

### Additional questions

*1. Analyse the form and the language of the Chicago advertisement on p. 113.*
There are three elements: the title – in large capital letters – referring to a historic date in Chicago's development; a painting of the Great Fire; and a text inviting people to visit Chicago and its outstanding architecture. The ad's effect relies mainly on the paradox that destruction created something great, that the Great Fire was Chicago's 'brightest' day, as it gave rise to modern architecture.
The text is loosely arranged; it imitates oral language – short elliptic sentences – and makes use of superlatives to indicate Chicago's uniqeness. It finishes with a final word play ('burning') to close the metaphorical circle opened up in the title. (For a definition of "pun" see box p. 148, SB).

It is interesting to know that in certain magazines that address a narrower, more academic readership the text of this ad was more comprehensive, less oral in style, but much more informative in content.

*2. Can you explain why the USA in its national period (1770–1800) turned to the rational traditions of classical Rome, and, in a way, Greece?*
American rationalism was part of the conscious attempt to leave the still feudal European traditions behind and to look for Republican models in Ancient Rome and elsewhere. The new national government was to meet in the 'Capitol' (study its classical architecture!), one house was called the 'Senate', and a little stream running past through the Washington area was called 'Tiber'.

### Post-reading activities

*Reports/papers/talks:*
*1. The significance of the Land Ordinance of 1785 and 1787.*
See Bibliography 10 (pp. 168–169) and 8 (pp. 106–108).

*2. The Great Fire and the rise of Chicago architecture.*
See Bibliography 23 (pp. 15–38).

*3. The American skyscraper – origin and development.*
See Bibliography 13 (pp. 45–50), 1 and 9.

*4. Mies van der Rohe: a German-American architect.*
See Bibliography 13 (pp. 239–243) and 22.

## 2. "We have ended up with monsters" (GK)

### Didaktisch-methodische Hinweise

Die Texte 2 und 3 nehmen mit zwei repräsentativen Stimmen die heftige, gegenwärtig immer noch andauernde *architecture debate* auf, die Prince Charles mit seinen Attacken gegen die zeitgenössische britische Architektur und Stadtplanung ausgelöst hat. 1988 faßte Prince Charles seine Ansichten zusammen und präsentierte sie selbst in einem BBC *feature*, das dann auch in Buchform erschien (Text 2 und Bild S. 116, SB sind daraus entnommen).
Maxwell Hutchinson, Präsident des Royal Institute of British Architects (RIBA) und einer der angegriffenen Architekten, stellte seine professionelle Gegenansicht in Buchform und mehreren Zeitungsartikeln dar, um seinerseits die populistische negative Stimmung gegen moderne Architektur anzugreifen (Auszug in Text 3).

Die Photos, der Cartoon und die beiden Texte sollten als Einheit gesehen werden und methodisch entsprechend angelegt werden.

Es wird hier als *pre-reading activity* die Bearbeitung des visuellen Materials vor der Lektüre beider Texte vorgeschlagen.

Als Einstieg kann zunächst die Photoreihe für die Stadtentwicklung Londons in der St. Paul's Cathedral Area dienen, die von vielen als Zerstörung der traditionellen Silhouette Londons gesehen wird (siehe auch Frage 4). Ein Vergleich mit Manhattan (Text 1, Photo S. 112) müßte genügend Material für eine kontroverse Diskussion um *high-rise buildings* in gewachsenen Städten mit historischen Stadtbildern ergeben. Auch könnte der Bezug zu deutschen Großstädten hergestellt werden (Mainhattan = Frankfurt), wo allerdings die Kriegszerstörungen für besondere Situationen sorgten.

Zumindest als Variante könnte nun gleich in freier Diskussion der historisierende Zugang zur Stadtentwicklung (z. B. die Gestaltung des Römers in Frankfurt) und zur Architektur anhand des Photos des Craven Court in Skipton (S. 116, SB) angegangen werden. Die bissige Kritik von Maxwell Hutchinson an diesem Projekt (Text 3, ll. 70–94) sollte hier nicht vorweggenommen werden, sondern als Abschluß dieser Einheit dienen, um nach erweitertem Informationsstand zur Eingangsdiskussion zurückkommen zu können.

Als dritter einleitender Schritt kann dann das Cartoon bearbeitet werden, in dem der historisierende Stadtplaner bei umgebendem Modernismus sehr sorgenvoll im Hinblick auf seine *professional sanity* beobachtet wird.

**Pre-reading activities**

See "Didaktisch-methodische Hinweise".

**Suggested answers**

1. Prince Charles is dissatisfied with the urban environment, the architectural styles and urban planning since World War II. Above all he attacks the deliberate destruction of old buildings to make room for new, in his opinion heartless, modernistic developments. The result of this development is ugliness, mediocrity and monstrosity. He accuses the architects of having abandoned all traditional architectural principles and of having slavishly followed the fashionable modernistic theories of the 50s and 60s which are exclusively based on technological progress.

2. To fend off professional criticism Prince Charles explicitly stresses his views as personal ones (l. 1, l. 48). He nevertheless claims popular support (ll. 30 ff.) and he increasingly makes use of the collective 'we', implying that more or less everybody suffers from the dictates of modern technology. The choice of words reveals his extremely critical view of the development, his emotional involvement in the issue and the polemical aims of his writing. There is an accumulation of strong, negative adjectives and nouns in the first paragraph. Two metaphors graphically express Prince Charles' view: in adhering to modern architectural theories architects are said to have thrown "the baby out with the bathwater" (l. 12) and they have finally "spawned monsters" (l. 19). This last metaphor is extended in detail, referring to Frankenstein and professors concocting horrors in laboratories (ll. 25 ff).

3. Modern architecture is seen to have been occupied with an experiment based on modern science and technology. In Prince Charles' opinion the experiment has got out of hand and led to a deformed product that haunts town and village, as Frankenstein's man-made man turned out to be a monster, not the perfect man he had planned. This metaphor stresses the failure of modern architecture in a very graphic, but hyperbolic way. One may concede that there are many "deformed" or ugly modern buildings that are architectural eyesores, but there are, however, also aesthetically and functionally convincing modern developments in many towns.

4. Disappearance of trees, small parks, gradual increase of high-rise office buildings rob St Paul's Cathedral of its commanding position over this part of London. As this has been a much loved, often painted sight – it constitutes a part of London's identity – its loss is felt deeply by many. In addition the new skyline does not create an aesthetically convincing arrangement or pattern and to many people it reveals the blatant failure of urban planning. Economic expansion, the laws of the free market economy, the price of land, the accumulation of services in the city of London may be seen as some causes for this development.

5. Size, style, function, setting, evaluation by public opinion etc.

**Additional questions**

1. Find antonyms for the following nouns:
– ugliness (l. 4)
– mediocrity (l. 4)
– dominance (l. 42)
– triumph (l. 44)
– civilisation (l. 54)
– progress (l. 6)

2. Find synonyms for the following adjectives:
– crazy (l. 10)
– deformed (l. 19)
– revolutionary (l. 22)
– alien (l. 26)
– contemporary (L. 56)
– uneasy (l. 59)

3. Choose three words from the text, e.g. destruction (l. 2), heartlessness (l. 7), values (l. 14), and make up word families around them.
e.g. destruction, destructive, destructiveness, to destroy, a destroyer, to destruct (military, A.E.), destructible etc.

**Post-reading activities**

1. Group work and class discussion: planning the ideal city. What would you want in the centre, what on the outskirts? What style of architecture would you favour?
This topic could also be given as a report or talk for single students, followed by a class discussion of their ideas.

2. Collect and compare old and contemporary photos/aerial views of Munich/Stuttgart/Frankfurt/Hamburg etc. Describe the changes. Group work

3. Report/paper/talk: Urban regeneration in Britain.
See Bibliography 6, pp. 208–215.

## 3. Why Prince Charles is wrong (GK)

**Background information**

See "Didaktisch-methodische Hinweise" for text 2.

**Pre-reading activity**

*How do you think people in Britain – the general public and the professional architects – reacted to Prince Charles' attack?*
Many people agreed with him, but he was bitterly rebuked by others. Some said he had abused his position and should not have spoken out on a matter he is not an expert in. His views were even ridiculed as unprofessional and irrelevant as well as traditionalist and conservative. Prince Charles has, however, had a long standing interest in the subject and had found support in a school of British architects called 'community architects' whose aim it is to integrate the people who will use the new buildings in the whole planning process.

**Suggested answers**

1. Although the text is serious and informative in substance, it is enlivened by a mocking tone aiming irony and sarcasm at Prince Charles as well as his sycophantic supporters. There are only 'two cheers' for his specific achievment ("Halbhoch soll er leben!"); he has done very much to popularize the architectural debate, but he has transformed it into a kind of civil war; the prince is described as a "people's tribune" who prevents proper reflection on the side of architects but receives devout genuflection. Hutchinson ironically plays on the meaning of the word 'do' (ll. 32–33). 'Leading lights' of the Conservative Party are said to be using the Prince's attack to discredit professional bodies as they discredited trade unions (to do for s. o.). The rhetorical questions in ll. 41–43 and ll. 66–69, which are written in direct, colloquial English, contribute to the liveliness of the tone.

2. This phrase refers to the way the BBC telecast was presented. Much of the Prince's commentary on the towns he visited was televised on the train that took him from town to town and many shots were taken of the beautiful and pastoral English countryside rolling by. Hutchinson argues that Prince Charles with his exclusive, secluded, aristocratic upbringing cannot help but taking the dated perspective of Blake's time and Blake's rural England as a desirable ideal (compare Blake's famous poem/hymn "The New Jerusalem"). To Hutchinson, however, this is not present-day reality. This is nostalgia, as is the old-fashioned train (instead of using a modern one in the film)

*Art, Culture and Society*

and as is repro architecture à la Skipton. The Prince's aloneness in the train, without any companions, underline that he is separate from the people and from reality.

3. The Prince's tour through architectural England, which is compared to an odyssey, first takes him to Skipton. By a skilful use of language Hutchinson makes it clear that the Skipton projects are based on dated and false theories and do not fulfil the demands of our time ("What on earth has it got to do with the 1980s? Do we really want to keep our housing the way it was 100 years ago?", ll. 66 ff.). There is a "phoney" philosophy (l. 70) behind such projects, one project is "a fantasy Victorian repro affair" (l. 72), it is "Hovis-commercial architecture", the doors are "fake Georgian" (ll. 79–80), it is a "deceitful Disneyland" (l. 81). Instead of "repro" architecture Hutchinson suggests that "real architecture is real history" (l. 84).

Hutchinson tries to ridicule the false, nostalgic traditionalism in architecture (see ll. 61–62, 87–88) and wants the reader to see that Prince Charles supports a wrong cause. A final ironic twist is contained in Hutchinson's criticism of Charles' views when he says that we cannot build modern places to work in which look like classical "Temples of Diana" (l. 90).

4. On the one hand Hutchinson seems to welcome the fact that with Prince Charles in the ring architectural matters have acquired great publicity. He also appreciates that Prince Charles has shown great courage to speak out on a difficult and controversial subject. On the other hand Hutchinson seems to think that this royal initiative has been a disservice to architectural professionalism and Prince Charles has been misguided by his advisers. He feels the prince's intervention is not quite fair in that it has distorted the debate because of the weight of his position as royalty.

5. Whereas Prince Charles wants a stricter adherence to traditional principles, elements, styles of architecture as well as the use of traditional building materials Hutchinson clearly puts the demands of our post-industrial age first and concludes that for adequate solutions the best of modern technology must be used. The low-rise terraced housing built from local material and the historistic shopping arcade consequently got praise from Prince Charles, whereas Hutchinson saw the functional drawbacks of the old housing schemes (poor daylighting, back-to-back building) and the stylistic falseness of the shopping centre.

6. The teacher may ask the students if they have changed their views and evaluation of historicist buildings like the shopping arcade in Skipton after reading Hutchinson's answer or if they feel confirmed in their opinions.

**Additional questions**

*1. Study the use of participle and gerund constructions in the text:*
– ll. 25–27 (a)
– ll. 34–35 (d)
– ll. 43–46 (a)
– ll. 47–48 (b)
– l. 45 (a)
– l. 65 (b)
– ll. 74–74 (a)

a: present participle replacing a relative clause
b: past participle replacing a relative clause (passive voice meaning)
c: verb ("Sinneswahrnehmung") + present participle
d: noun + preposition + gerund

*2. Make up a semantic field around "architecture".*
Words and phrases about architecture could be gathered from texts 1 to 3 as a starting point. For further vocabulary in this field see the fact file pp. 293–295, SB.

*3. What are the political and constitutional implications of Prince Charles' active participation in public matters such as the debate on architecture?*
In his text Hutchinson maintains that Prince Charles embarrassed both the Queen and the Prime Minister. As a royal he is supposed to exercise political impartiality and even abstinence. So many critics saw Charles' intervention as unconstitutional; they thought that he exercised illegitimate influence because of his specific role as heir to the throne. Many contradicted and asked what role a longstanding king-in-waiting was supposed to play at all, Charles' social and cultural commitment being the only thing that could give his position a meaningful purpose. (See also text 11, Chapter 3.)

## Post-reading activities

1. Write a polemical letter to your local paper about a new building, sculpture or public work of art, in the style of the Prince Charles text; or answer such a letter defending the same against criticism, in the style of the Hutchinson text.

2. Report/paper/talk: The architecture of your own town.
This topic could also be given as the subject of an essay.

3. Conduct a debate or discussion on the subject of traditionalism versus modernism in contemporary city architecture and town planning. Prepare your statements with the help of texts 2 and 3 and considering another quotation by Maxwell Hutchinson: "Now we need a new architecture, a neo-modernism, for the new producers."

## 4. Listening Comprehension: Henry Moore – A sculptor speaks (GK)

### Background information

Henry Moore (1898–1986) was born in Yorkshire as the seventh child of a coalmining engineer. Encouraged by his grammar school teachers Moore was determined to become a sculptor. He was educated at the Leeds School of Art and the Royal College of Art in London. As a maker of monumental art and public sculpture many of his famous pieces are displayed in front of museums, public buildings (Bundeskanzleramt Bonn!), in parks and meadows worldwide. His treatment of the reclining female figure made him known to a wide public. The soft rounded forms, the large size of the body, the little heads, the holes are typical of this treatment. His preoccupation with form – forms he was confronted with in Yorkshire and in his immediate surroundings – and his approach to sculpture that relied on touch becomes apparent in this interview, that was conducted by Warren Forma in 1965 at Moore's home, Hoglands, in Hertfordshire, where he lived and worked for 46 years till his death in 1986.

Moore rarely sculpted male figures and when he did so they appeared in "social units", e.g. *Family group* (1948/49) and *King and Queen* (1952/53) – see photo, p. 118, SB.

Moore defined 'truth to material' as the first of his aims. He found a key to its realization in the art of 'primitive' cultures. He perceived African and Pre-Columbian art as belonging to the 'main world tradition of sculpture'. For him European Romanesque and Gothic belonged equally to this tradition, whereas 'the realistic ideal of physical beauty in art which sprang from fifth-century Greece was only a digression' (see Dawn Ades, *Henry Moore, Sculpture and Drawings, British Art in the 20th Century*, p. 276).

Moore's work is characterized by a close interrelationship with nature and landscape. His reclining females invite an analogy with mountains, hills and valleys of the natural landscape, and many of his sculptures were created for wide, open places in nature, as was his *King and Queen* series. This was in order to encourage people to look at sculpture in a three-dimensional way. He wanted them, too, to feel sculpture, and to make them feel the principles of form and rhythm which he himself had found in the study of natural objects such as pebbles, rocks, bones, trees and plants.

*Note:* The language of the transcript is not always grammatically correct as it follows the rhythms of spontaneous, spoken speech.

### Methodisch-didaktische Hinweise

Eine Einleitung, Worterklärungen und Fragen zum Globalverständnis sind im SB, S. 118 abgedruckt. Das Thema eignet sich im besonderen Maße zum fächerübergreifenden Unterricht, d. h. in diesem Falle zur Zusammenarbeit mit den Kunstkollegen, die viel mehr an visuellem Material bieten können, als ein Englischbuch das kann. Eine Besprechung von anderen Moore-Werken sollte natürlich erst nach der Hörverständnisübung stattfinden.

### Transcript

A sculptor has to be a practical person, he can't be just a dreamer. If you are going to shape a piece of stone into a sculpture you must handle a hammer and chisel, you must be able to do it without knocking your hand; you must be a workman; 5
you must be somebody with his feet on the

ground. I don't know whether it's true or not, but in England North-country people are looked upon as being very matter-of-fact and practical, hard-headed people. This may have something to do – I don't know, it's just a fanciful idea probably – that this may have something to do with the fact that if in England now, as there are, some twenty or thirty young sculptors who have cropped up since the war, four or five of them are certainly Yorkshire. There's me, there's Barbara Hepworth, there's Armitage, there's Ralph Brown, Thornton – well, I mean, I've thought of five immediately who come from Yorkshire. And perhaps there is something about Yorkshire itself. Though, of course, Yorkshire being a very big county has a lot of variety in it. The Yorkshire mining towns, the slag heaps which for me as a boy, as a young child, were like mountains; they had the scale of the pyramids, this triangular, bare, stark quality that was just as though one was in the Alps, so that perhaps those impressions when you are young are what count, I'm sure. You see, I think a sculptor is a person who is interested in the shape of things, a poet is somebody who is interested in words, a musician is somebody who is interested in or obsessed by sounds, but a sculptor is a person obsessed with form, with the shape of things. And it is not just the shape of any one thing, but the shape of anything, every thing. The growth in a flower, the hard, tense strength although delicate form of a bone, the strong, solid fleshiness of a beech tree trunk: all these things had just as much a lesson to a sculptor as a pretty girl, as a young girl's figure and so on. They're all part of experience of form. And therefore, in my opinion, everything, every shape, every bit of natural form, animals, people, pebbles, shells, anything you like, are all things that can help you to make sculpture. And for me, I collect odd bits of driftwood, anything I find (that) whose shape interests me, and I keep them around in that little studio, so that if any day I go in there – or evening – within five or ten minutes of being in that little room, there will be something that I can pick up or look at, that would give me a start for a new idea. And this is why I like leaving all these odds and ends around in this small studio – to start one off with an idea. (440 words)

From *5 British Sculptors talk*, produced by Warren Forma, Caedmon.

**Pre-listening activity**

*What is characteristic of sculpture as an art form? What problems do sculptors have to deal with?*
Creating objects by working in solid materials and in three dimensions to represent real or imaginary forms; like an engineer, architect or builder who create bridges and buildings the sculptor has to create a definite form or structure and in doing so has to solve the problems of shaping the material, the organization of balance, weight and space; in addition, however, the onlooker or viewer wants to find the appeal of an inner life, of a powerful creative idea and its aesthetic expression.

**Suggested answers (Listening for the gist)**

1. A practical person, not a dreamer, a skilful workman, a realistic, matter-of-fact person.

2. He must be interested in the *shape* of things; the poet – words; musician – sounds; the sculptor must be interested in form, in the shape of every single thing.

3. The Yorkshire landscape displays a lot of variety as it is a very big county, but in the part Moore grew up in (Castleford, near Leeds) the huge artificial slag heaps of the mining towns dominated like mountains or the pyramids.

4. They help to start him off with a new idea when he picks them up or looks at them.

**Listening for detail**

*1. Why must a sculptor be a very skilful, practical person?*
A sculptor must be able to handle a hammer and chisel properly; like a workman he must avoid hurting his hands with them. Here Moore emphasizes the practical side of sculpture.

*2. Why, according to Moore, do many of the leading British sculptors come from Yorkshire?*
According to Moore Yorkshiremen have the reputation of being matter-of-fact, hard-headed, practical people, all character traits essential to sculptors. The specific shapes of Yorkshire may also have contributed to this. (The roundness, bareness and stoniness of the Dales, as well as the slag heaps of the mining towns.)

*3. What role did the slag heaps of the mining towns play for Moore?*

For Moore as a boy they were like mountains, with the same triangular, bare stark quality of the Alps or the Egyptian pyramids. He feels that the impressions in childhood influence an artist greatly.

*4. What objects does Moore mention when he illustrates that all kinds of shapes are important to a sculptor?*
The growth in a flower, the form of a bone, a tree trunk, a pretty girl's face and figure, animals, pebbles, shells, driftwood.

**Additional question**

*Collect words of the word families of 'sculpture', 'shape', and 'form', and give collocations.*
Sculpture is the art of fashioning objects from solid materials such as stone, wood, metal, etc.;
an exhibition of twentieth-century sculpture;
there are few modern/classical sculptures in our town;
an iron sculpture;
to sculpture a statue out of stone;
sculptural art is the most practical of all arts;
Moore is one of the most famous modern sculptors;
Barbara Hepworth is a well-known British sculptress;
to take classes in sculpture at art school.
Without shape or form; it begins to take shape; the statue has a well-proportioned form;
all shapes and sizes;
it is a formless/shapeless mass;
to shape clay;
he shaped/formed his style by studying primitive art;
Moore spent his most formative years in Yorkshire;
to form a circle;

to give shape to a stone sculpture you use a hammer and chisel;
to take the form of s.th.;
to take form etc.

**Post-listening activities**

*1. Look at the photograph on p. 118, and answer the questions.*
See "Background information".
The *King and Queen* series of bronzes are set up in different landscapes of Britain, one being the lonely, bare hills of Dumfries in southern Scotland. This time the figures do not blend in with nature, as is often the case with the reclining figures, but rather watch the surrounding landscape from their seat. The king's head is more abstract that the queen's, with associations of coxcomb or helmet. The queen seems younger than her husband with her small breasts and straighter back – an ancient, archetypal couple ruling the world they survey. These skeletal figures remind one of "primitive" (or primeval) art, especially that of Black Africa.

*2. Report/paper/talk: Henry Moore and his art.*
See encyclopedias; Bibliography 7 (pp. 31–35 and 276–277), 15 and 3.

*3. Describe and comment on examples of traditional, realistic or abstract sculpture in your town/school. What function do they play within their specific surroundings?*
– Ornament, eye-catcher, to conceal or avoid the monotony of modern buildings, moral or national edification or warning, to honour a famous person, to fill empty spaces, to create a centre in a square or place;
– Aesthetic, architectural function or function within urban planning.

# 5. A challenge to high art

**Background information**

Andy Warhol (1930–1987) was born in Pittsburgh as the son of Slovak immigrants. From 1945–1949 he studied Pictoral Design and History of Art at the Carnegie Institute of Technology there. In 1949 he went to New York, worked as a decorator and designed advertisements for various companies. In the 1950s Warhol had his first exhibitions and he soon became one of the main representatives of American Pop Art. He acquired worldwide fame with his pictures and screen prints, in which he enlarged photos of film stars, dollar notes, soup cans, etc., reproduced them in variations and arranged them in rectangular patterns. Warhol tried to depict mass products and symbols of modern mass culture in his art, which itself again became a mass product and was 'consumed' by the masses. In this he followed the main idea of the 'pop art' of the 1960s which tried to present reality as art. Everyday objects of mass consumption were reproduced fairly realistically; the artistic perspective was created by isolation, enlargement, detail, serialization; the artistic aim was to alienate, to parody or to make fetishes out of the objects.

## Pictures

1. Page 119, SB: The variations on Campbell's Soup Cans were produced in 1962 – pictures with multiple motifs of the same can, enlargements beside small-size cans, cans with all kinds of labels indicating the various soups and the 'Torn Campbell's Soup Cans' of which we have one example (but unfortunately only in black and white).

As a symbol of fast-food production and consumption the canned soup stands for the ambivalent progress of modern industrial societies. We can speculate on the significance of the torn label. In spite of some missing letters we can still understand what it says without any difficulty; we subconsciously supply the missing parts; Americans at that time probably had no difficulty in remembering the complete version of the label because they had constantly been confronted with it. Campbell's Soup as a mass product becomes even more of a dime-a-dozen article when it is stripped of its label and well-known trade mark.

The main difference between this and a traditional painting may be seen in the fact that an everyday object of only trivial importance is represented – as it seems – without any special artistic perspective. The soup can, especially as it is torn and damaged, is not conventionally beautiful as are the flowers, fruit etc. of a traditional still-life. It is also flat, without much depth, like a poster or an ad rather than a painting.

2. Page 120, SB: Warhol's view of art and creativity was a very comprehensive one, and it included the ways objects were created and made known to the public. The staging of his exhibitions was an integral part of his art. For him real objects, production, and artistic reproduction overlapped: "die Grenzen zwischen Bild, Abbild und Abgebildeten sind fließend" (Tilmann Osterwold, *Pop Art*, p. 167). In this picture the three levels of reality are works of art (screen-prints) by Warhol representing living people (Sophia Loren and a "Red Jackie" Kennedy); Warhol as part of his exhibition reading a newspaper article on himself and his art.

## Didaktisch-methodischer Hinweis

Die Bearbeitung der beiden Bilder sollte als *pre-reading activities* den S die Möglichkeit zu spontanen Kommentaren und Bewertungen geben, die dann vor allem hinsichtlich der *Soup Cans* anhand des Textes, der hier speziell weitergehende Einordnungen gibt, überprüft werden können. Es wird dann sicherlich engagierte Diskussionen geben über die abschließende Wertung des Textes, daß man die *Soup Cans* sehen kann als "important and exciting examples of 20th-century art" (ll. 53–54).

Wie bei Text 4 wäre hier eine Zusammenarbeit mit den Kunstkollegen eine Bereicherung des Unterrichts.

## Pre-reading activity

*Describe and comment on the Warhol picture (p. 119) and the photo (p. 120). Do you consider the* Soup Can *a great work of art?*
See "Pictures" above.

## Suggested answers

1. Main characteristics: Warhol was fascinated by the everyday products (comics, Hershey's chocolate, Campbell's soup cans etc.) and the publicity aspects (ads, window displays, cards of film stars etc.) of the American culture of his time, a profoundly commercialized culture. He loved and depicted the things and the people that normal Americans were in touch with, directly or through the media; he thus recorded the American way of life of a whole generation. He saw America as the Woolworth's department store of the Western world, i.e. a collection of cheap, mass-produced consumer goods, and accepted it as such.

Formal elements: repetition, monotony, 'realistic' reproduction.

2. The function of Warhol's art is, on the one hand, to make us look anew at everyday objects, to teach us to see. Here he is following the ideas of (low) Pop Art. But his pictures can also be seen as abstract art, as conscious abstractions of reality, especially in his serialized and slightly alientated prints. And so Warhol's art "bridges the high art/low art schism" (ll. 37–38).

3. Warhol loved all aspects of American popular culture and felt very much a part of American consumer and media society. (There was no critical distance, not even to more negative forms of commercialization and star cult.) His attitude is contrasted with the traditional image of the artist (19th-century bohemian) who rebels against society and is torn within himself, too: art seen like this assumes a fundamentally critical function. There is an ongoing controversy as to what extent pop art did assume critical overtones in spite of its celebration of the objects of our consumer society.

4. America stands for the invention of modern mass production and the production of the widest range of commodities. Because of this consumer goods became cheap and available to virtually everybody in American society: the availability was guaranteed by department stores like Woolworth's that sold cheaply. The comparison of America and a cheap department store is apt both for commerce and for culture. The whole of the western world (and the eastern now, too!) buys modern American or American-style products (e.g. jeans, coke, cigarettes etc.) as well as "shopping" in the self-service store of American pop culture (film, music, fast food etc.).

5. Modern realism may be seen as a reaction to abstract art. It tries to regain objects and objectivity and turns to the world as it is. Realistic artists might try to create unbiassed, 'open' mirrors of modern society and the modern world, showing them as they are without any subjective interpretation or emotion. When they turn to everyday objects, which is of course a subjective act, they might pursue certain aims ranging from creating idylls to social criticism. They might want us to look at them from a different angle to make us see them anew.

**Additional questions**

*1. Study the use of adjectives in the first paragraph. What is their function?*
The enumeration of adjectives illustrates Warhol's extraordinary significance as an American artist. They express his enormous influence on the development of art and they characterize him as an extremely creative and productive artist.

*2. Collect further collocations of these adjectives with the help of your dictionary.*
*pivotal* – this scene is the pivotal point of the whole book;
1941 was the pivotal year of World War II;
*driven* – to be driven by greed, envy, ambition;
*prolific* – Simmel is a very prolific writer, Picasso remained prolific;
*inventive* – he is inventive when dealing with problems, an inventive child;
*ambitious* – ambitious plans, the president's ambitious wife;
*canny* – a canny smile, a canny Scot, a canny bargain;
*artistic* – artistic freedom, artistic expression, artistic people, an artistic arrangement (e.g. of flowers) etc.

**Post-reading activity**

*Report/paper/talk:* Look up the entry of "pop art" in an encyclopedia (Schülerduden Kunst *or others), and find out the names of other British and American pop artists. Try to find books showing their works. Select one artist and present some of his pictures in class.*
USA: R. Rauschenberg, Jasper Johns, Roy Lichtenstein, Claes Oldenburg;
GB: Peter Blake, Richard Hamilton, David Hockney.
See Bibliography 16.

# 6. "Why do you paint?" (GK)

## Background information

*The author:* Margaret Atwood, Canada's most eminent writer, was born in Ottawa in 1939. She grew up in the Northern Ontario and Quebec bush country, but also spent part of her early life in Toronto. A graduate of the University of Toronto (1961), she has taught English literature in America and Australia as well as in different Canadian universities, being, for example, Writer-in-Residence at her own university from 1972–73. Atwood first made her name as a poet (*Circle Game* 1966, *Selected Poems* 1976, *True Stories* 1981 etc.), but she is now especially well-known for her novels. *The Edible Woman* (1969) was her first success in this field, while her satirical novel *The Handmaid's Tale* (1985) has been recently made into a film. *Cat's Eye* (1989) is her seventh novel. She also has a reputation as a literary critic, and her study of Canadian literature, entitled *Survival* (1972), caused considerable controversy.

Atwood now lives in Toronto with novelist Graeme Gibson and their daughter Jess.

*Introduction to the novel:* Painter Elaine Risley, about fifty years old and in her second marriage, returns from Vancouver to Toronto for a retrospective of her work, which has been much celebrated by the women's movement. Toronto is the city she fled many years before, hoping to leave behind the memories of the negative experiences of her childhood, her years as an art student and of her first marriage. These disturbing memories, told in the form of flashbacks, constitute the main events of the novel. They centre around Elaine's relationship to her despotic schoolmate Cordelia. The two levels of the novel are very skilfully presented in alternating episodes. Our excerpt represents a complete episode and chapter.

**Methodischer Hinweis**

Da mit diesem ungekürzten Romankapitel ein ungewöhnlich langer Text vorliegt, wird empfohlen, ihn in der Form des *extensiven Lesens* zu erschließen. Die Episode sollte von den S nach Möglichkeit in einem Durchgang gelesen werden, um ein natürliches Leseverhalten zu fördern. Gleichzeitig kann so die Fertigkeit, unbekannte lexikalische Elemente selbständig aus dem Kontext, der Wortfamilie und anderen Sprachen zu erschließen, vertieft werden. Bei der weiteren Bearbeitung des Textes sollten einzelne Passagen, die von den S für wichtig erachtet werden, intensiv mit Hilfe von Wörterbüchern erschlossen werden.

Siehe auch Peter Brucks Einführung zu *The Wave*, Klettbuch 57728: "How to Read an English Book without a Dictionary".

**Pre-reading activities**

*1. Brainstorming: Give the names of any artists (painters or sculptors) you can think of. How many female artists are on your list? Why do you think there are so few famous women painters?*

*2. If you had to interview a successful woman painter from your town in order to present her and her work in your school magazine, which questions would you ask her?*

**Suggested answers**

1. ll. 1–28: *setting and background to the episode*
Elaine felt obliged to go to Toronto in spite of slight misgivings. When walking through Toronto she remembers her time here as an art student with her first husband Jon.
ll. 29–88: *thoughts on entering the gallery*
Elaine enters the gallery that exhibits her paintings. Confronted with her own works she comments on some of them, their owners, their price. She describes one painting in detail.
ll. 89–187: *Elaine meets Charna, the organizer of the exhibition*
Elaine is welcomed by Charna; they discuss the arrangement of the pictures. After that she is introduced to Andrea who is going to conduct an interview with Elaine which comes as a surprise to her. Most of this passage, however consists of 'inner action' with Elaine reflecting on Charna's appearance, her own, and the difference between herself and such women. In her thoughts she looks forward to meeting her ex-husband.
ll. 168–311: *the interview*
Andrea asks Elaine questions about how she handles fame, how she sees the women artists of her generation, about her relationship to men as a woman painter, if she paints for women, and why she paints. In most cases Elaine gives flippant, evasive or cryptic answers, not giving the information the interviewer is interested in.

2. For a woman painter it is an extraordinary event to have a retrospective exhibition of her own. She is grateful to the organizers and so as a polite and well-behaved person she feels obliged to accept the invitation to be present at the opening.

3. The narrator dislikes the atmosphere of galleries that present art almost like sacred objects. She also objects to the sterility of most galleries which robs the paintings of their real quality, which lies in the 'blood' and toil of the creative process. Therefore she enters this gallery with "that sinking feeling she always has in galleries" (ll. 33, 34). But this one is not completely smooth and polished; some things prevent the usual sterility (a

black wall, a heating pipe showing). There are other paintings still hanging on the walls which she hardly looks at but reacts very negatively to before seeing her own paintings leaning against the wall.

4. When she looks at her paintings she wonders about their owners and the great importance that is attached in the art world to ownership. It is as if it were better to own a painting than to paint one. She also thinks about the market value of art as her own pictures are worth a lot more now that she is famous than when she first sold them, and about how the image of the artist as an unusual, crazy individual can affect the prices paid for his/her paintings. She describes one of her own paintings for the reader in detail (ll. 68–79), commenting on the reactions of people at the time. But she does not want to look too closely at her pictures as she is sure she will find fault with them and want to destroy them and start all over again.

5. Wearing a powder-blue jogging outfit and unobtrusive make-up Elaine gets deeply unsettled as soon as she sees the women that organize her exhibition. They are considerably younger than she is, and their appearance is spectacular, flashy, loud which makes the narrator feel old, old-fashioned and unartistic. In her feelings of inferiority she images how these women classify her as a dowdy, middle-aged frump. She resorts to sarcasm when she considers the porcupine haircut, the leather boots, the handcrushing silver rings, the abstract-art earrings and the artistic hair arrangement of the two other women. Only "Dracula black" or "nun black" and "vampire lipstick" would have been suitable to compete with this new Toronto chic. Elaine realizes that times have changed dramatically, that she is fairly old and does not belong to the new generation of trendsetters in the art circles of Toronto. She gradually realizes that her being a painter has nothing to do with following fashions, and so she gains self-control by asserting her differentness, and takes her stand defiantly in the interview with Andrea, challenging the questions rather than obediently fulfilling the expectations of the interviewer.

6. Although these women are carrying out a project for her, she feels that they are fundamentally different from her in character and in their approach towards her art, as well as in their confident manner and fashionable appearance. She resents the self-assured talk about how her paintings should be arranged to achieve artistic effects, and she considers the interest in her work as it is presented in the interviewer's questions as irrelevant or misplaced. There is almost no common ground between her and these women who belong to a new age in a town that has changed considerably. Although the women seem to compartmentalize female art with this exhibition that is run by women and obviously for women, the female artist feels disturbed by this all too fashionable presentation and the one-sidedness of their attitudes.

7. The first question about handling fame might have been a trap. Andrea seems to agree with Elaine's evaluation that in her case one cannot speak of fame.
With the classifying mind of a critic Andrea obviously wants to get an encouraging description of female and feminist artists of the seventies. Elaine circumvents this question by referring to her formative years in the forties, thus confusing her interviewer.
As a third point Andrea wants to hear something about Elaine's position and career as female artist. We feel that she would have liked to get critical views referring to specific hardships and discrimination. But Elaine gives unhelpful replies, refusing to take up this anti-male line. With a sarcastic retort she exposes the ideological viewpoint of Andrea when the latter employs the masculine word ("mentor") for a woman's job. And defiantly Elaine informs Andrea that her teacher was a man whom she appreciated very much. Elaine conceals her ambivalent attitude towards Hrbik and Hrbik's sexist approaches to his female students, including herself.
Andrea obviously had hoped to get a useful definition of feminist art, but must put up with an almost furious and insulting Elaine who brushes aside this topic with one remark. Elaine hates this classification and compartmentalization. The fact that she is a woman has, according to Elaine, not much to do with the subjects of her art and whether her paintings are appreciated by men or women. Andrea obviously wanted to have a feminist explanation of the unusual depiction of women (e.g. witch-and-succubus pieces) in some of Elaine's paintings, which the narrator refuses to give her, retreating into the weak argument that famous painters had always painted women. The

way Elaine answers Andrea's final question with another question can be seen as flippant, as a sign of helplessness, or as a total refusal to talk any more on this level.

8. Atwood's style here is fairly informal and often has the rhythm of colloquial speech (e.g. l. 177, "she's out to get me"; l. 82 "I caught some shit for that piece"; l. 80 "a nifty thing to do"; l. 57 "worse luck"; l. 145 "the year zot"; l. 99 "Haggis McBaggis"; l. 176 "middle-aged frump"; l. 307 "crap" etc.). The tone is often ironical (e.g. ll. 191–3) and even sharply sarcastic (e.g. ll. 183–6). She frequently uses short sentences for emphasis (e.g. ll. 177–178; 194; 228; 269 etc.) and strong graphic verbs (e.g. l. 87 "knife", "torch", "clear"; Charna "strides" and "stalks"; "the giant slugs munch away", l. 6, "the coffee seethes within me", l. 288, etc.) The adjectives, too, are very vivid ("dirty greens and putrid oranges" l. 49; "sulky black clothing"; "Dracula black", "clotted-neck vampire lipstick", ll. 94–96, etc.) emphasizing Elaine's strong feelings in this tense situation. With these stylistic devices Atwood creates a very lively scene, showing Elaine's irritation at the feminist approach in a very graphic way. Elaine's bitter humour is strikingly expressed in drastic similes: "She looks a bit scared, as if I've resurrected from death, and incompletely at that. She did not know I was that old." (ll. 221–223); "I feel as if I'm at the dentist, mouth gracelessly open while some stranger with a light and mirror gazes down my throat at something I can't see." (ll. 229–232); "In a minute my teeth will be chattering like those of cornered mice." (ll. 300–301). These three similes illustrate ironically how Elaine feels at the mercy of a younger woman at this strange interview.

9. Whereas Andy Warhol looked for publicity and maintained that staging his art was part of his art, Elaine seems to be an artist that is not so involved in the selling, publicising or exhibiting of her own work. On the one hand she is grateful and acknowledges that a major retrospective exhibition of her work reaffirms her position as an artist, but on the other hand she is greatly irritated by the world of galleries, exhibitions, and art critics. Elaine also feels slighted: although she is the creator of the paintings, the owners are regarded as equally important, and the organizers of the exhibition have decided all important questions beforehand without consulting her. In a similar fashion she is caught unawares when she is suddenly forced to give an interview. The women at the gallery obviously find the publicity and presentation of art more important that the feelings of the artist. The question of the market value of art and what influences it also plays a part in this excerpt (see answer to question 4).

**Additional questions**

*1. What is the function and effect of the use of a first-person narrator (see box p. 222) and the present tense?*
The reader is completely drawn into the mind of the protagonist. Together with Elaine we are directly confronted with what is going on at this very moment. In this way the scene gains great immediacy. The reader tends, too, to take sides with the narrator as he/she knows more about her fears, motives and feelings than about the other characters.

*2. What do you think Andrea's article on Elaine will look like? Try to write a critical piece on Elaine Risley, the 50-year-old painter, based on the impressions Andrea might have had.*
– a female painter who rejects feminism
– a representative of an older generation of women artists
– matter-of-fact, unimaginative, evasive, cryptic behaviour
– a female painter who praises men
etc.

*3. Collect all the words connected with "paint" and "draw" in the text and enlarge your list into word fields.*
To put paint on a brush/wet paint!/he painted the living-room/he only painted abstract pictures/white paint/to paint s. th. green/painted furniture/the paint is peeling/paintbox/paintbrush/Elaine painted her lips with Rose Perfection/to paint one's nails/oil paintings by William Turner/a landscape painter/he's a painter and decorator/to paint a gloomy picture of the future etc.
To draw naked women, female nudes/I draw geometrical patterns when I feel bored/he drew a rough sketch on his pad/Henry Moore made famous drawings of the Underground shelters/a drawing board/pad/to draw a map/to draw funny pictures etc.

**Post-reading activities**

*1. Try to find information on Georgia O'Keefe, Frida Kahlo or other women painters. Select some pictures and present them in class.*
See Bibliography 19.

*2. Report/paper/talk: Women in art.*
As this is a very topical subject the local library should provide enough book or magazine material.

*3. Choose a short story by Margaret Atwood, from* Dancing Girls *(1977) or* Bluebeard's Egg *(1983), and write an essay about it.*
Margaret Atwood's novels are all available in Virago paperbacks.

## 7. At the Edinburgh Festival (GK)

**Background information**

Alasdair Maclean ['æləsdə mə'kleɪn] was born in Glasgow in 1926 of Highland parents but he was brought up at Sanna in the remote West Highland area of Ardnamurchan. After a variety of jobs and positions – in his late thirties he studied English literature at Edinburgh University – he returned to his family croft to write poetry. His only piece of non-fiction, *Night falls on Ardnamurchan*, (Penguin 1986) tells of the hard life of his family, farming a small plot of land that barely provided them with the bare necessities, using his father's diaries and his own. "At the Edinburgh Festival" is taken from the collection *Waking the Dead* (1976), which was written in the aftermath of the death of Maclean's mother. The second part of it, which contains our poem, is explicitly dedicated to the memory of Elizabeth Maclean.

Maclean writes of *Waking the Dead*: "These, then are poems about death, in some of its many moods and manifestations. I should like once again to insist, with however little success, that they are also fictions. I am not, in any direct sense, a reporter or a confession-monger. If I document reality at any time it is always first and foremost the reality of poetry." The death in the family "confirmed me, too, in my belief that death was the noblest and most profound of the great themes of poetry, or what the love poets turn to when they put away childish things."

The Edinburgh International Festival of Music and Drama is held every year for three weeks in August and September, and is one of the main cultural events in Scotland. It was founded in 1947 and has now won a reputation for its inclusion of experimental or 'avantgarde' events in the so-called Edinburgh 'Fringe'. It is accompanied by major art exhibitions, a Poetry Conference, literature readings etc.

**Methodischer Hinweis**

Da das Gedicht ganz deutlich aus zwei kontrastierenden Teilen besteht (ll. 1–12; ll. 13–20), kann dies im Sinne "schüleraktivierender" Verfahren methodisch aufgenommen werden.
Einmal könnte man die beiden Teile des Gedichts getrennt in Gruppen erarbeiten, bevor man das ganze Gedicht gemeinsam bespricht. Zum anderen eignet sich der Einschnitt und die Vorverweisung in Zeile 12 zur kreativen Gestaltung eines zweiten Teiles durch die Schüler (siehe die 2. Aufgabe der "Pre-reading activities").
In jedem Falle sollte man bei der Präsentation des ganzen Gedichts die Cassette einsetzen, damit man einen Eindruck von einem schottischen Akzent bekommt, der vielleicht zur Atmosphäre des Gedichts beiträgt.

**Pre-reading activities**

*1. Have a look at the two photos (p. 125) and discuss your impressions. What kind of life might the people that live there lead?*
– refined urban world, warmth, elegant Georgian architecture, Edinburgh (culture, parties, friends), comfortable living, civilisation, solid buildings, work inside;
– bare, open countryside, bleak Highlands, isolation, hardship, stony ground, exposed to the elements, poverty
= contrast of place and life-style

*2. Presentation of the poem in two stages.*
*– Read the first three stanzas only.*

a) What do you learn about the setting? What do you learn about the poets, the patrons and their women?
b) What does line 12 and the word "true" imply about the speaker's view of this social event?
c) What might "truth" mean to the speaker? Make use of the second photo and try to imagine which fundamental human experiences or basic human conditions can be seen as "truth" in life and poetry.
d) Write your own ending to the poem (after l. 12).
– Now listen to the whole poem on cassette.
e) What is your general impression?
f) Before studying the last two stanzas in detail say who and what they are about.
g) Does Maclean mention any of the ideas you suggested in the first part?

**Suggested answers**

1. The speaker is a member of a group of poets that are invited to discuss poetry at a party at the Edinburgh Festival. The gathering is organized by the wealthy patrons (publishers) of the poets who have also brought their wives or girlfriends along to indulge in literary small talk. When feeling drowned by the discussions of literary history the poet-speaker in his imagination turns to what to him is truth in order to survive: the death of his mother a year ago who had lived in the bare Scottish Highlands, struggling against the winter and death.

*The poets* appear, as on a stage, wearing designer jeans, a compromise between casual and formal dress. They have prepared quotations from literature for the evening as they are expectd to "perform". They are accompanied by their patrons (wealthy publishers probably) to give them support, but it is not clear who is the victim and who is the victimized (rabbit and stoat metaphor). The speaker feels lost in the theoretical discussion of literature he has to take part in.

*The patrons* are wealthy men, staying close to their poets (to help or to dominate). They use their cigars as if they were swords (metaphor), have hard eyes and are formally dressed ("hard shirts"). They are on the watch for weaknesses in the other patrons which they could attack quickly. "Knife" and "squirt" are concrete words standing for the fierceness of the attack and the "blood" drawn by it, and so used symbolically.

*The women* mentioned are wives or girlfriends, prowling like cats or tigers on the hunt from poet to poet, perhaps trying to catch or seduce one (they are "unleashed", i.e. they have been let loose or free) by involving them in theoretical discussions of literature.

*The mother* had been dying exactly a year ago in her cottage, struggling against winter and death, watching the approach of autumn (geese, leaves), ill with cancer ("the marrow falling in her bones"), and with only thin milk from "half-starved cows" and the harvest from a "field of stones". Winter and sickle are symbols of death, the field of stones her poor farm and her hard life.

2. Like Elaine, the artist in Text 6, the speaker assumes a critical view of the literary gathering and his own participation in it. He is ironical about the way the poets dress up and prepare themselves for their 'performance', and he obviously dislikes the atmosphere of aggressive competitiveness among the patrons/publishers. He is negative, too, about the women who engage him in useless theoretical discussions about literature. The poets seem to rely on their wealthy patrons and are probably obliged to make an appearance at such parties in order to stay in the market and in the public eye.

3. The artificial and irrelevant world of the literary gathering in which poetry degenerates to literary history is contrasted with the speaker's and poet's memory of his dying mother. Dying and death are central experiences in life and poetry and preclude all the sophisticated small talk and literary competition of such festival parties. The truth lies in the specific event. The speaker's mother died almost a year ago. Maclean makes use of the seasons and of images connected with animals and nature in their symbolic implications: the Edinburgh Festival is in early September, which is early autumn in the Scottish Highlands; the fight against the winter symbolizes the fight against death; the open door lets the autumn leaves come in; the geese flying south to escape the hardship and winter of the north; the marrow falling in the bones is a sign of fading life, and this is also symbolized by the cows that give little milk; the sickle as a symbol of death is used here to indicate that the speaker's mother tries in vain to reap a harvest where it cannot be reaped, that she fights a futile fight in a poor, bare, inhospitable environment.

4. Whereas in the first part the writer employs metaphorical language to graphically illustrate the literary gathering, he turns to concrete observations about the speaker's mother and her actions which all assume a highly symbolical value. The party is going on at present, the present tense is used to give an immediate report on what is going on; the past tense is used for the events that seem 'a long way off', but happened only a year ago and that provided the speaker with a basic, personal experience and an insight into a universal truth.

In the first part the writer presents groups of people mainly by plural words (we, poets, wealthy men, patrons, women). The turning point of the poem (l. 11) is emphasized by the prominent position of the 'I' for the speaker's mental escape. In the second part only the actions of the mother (my mother, she) as she fights her lonely struggle are related (we, they —> I —> she).

5. See answers to the questions 1 and 3.
Most of the images (metaphors and symbols) are taken from nature (rabbits/stoats; "unleashed women"; "awash — I cling" as to a lifebelt in stormy seas; geese; autumn leaves; cows; fields of stone etc.), apart from those from the field of weapons and fighting ("wielding a cigar" like a sword, the knife and squirt of blood). The use of a traditional symbol of death, the sickle, in the image of the old woman harvesting the little hay that grows in a stony Highland field is very moving, as it is usually Death that swings the sickle and reaps the life, not the dying person her-/himself.

## Additional questions

*1. What use does the writer make of repetition, anaphora, parallelism?*
The last two stanzas are closely knit together to form a separate part by the use of anaphora in the first lines ("last year"). They contain parallelistic structures followed by an indication of time and a simple sentence denoting an action. To stress the aggressive and competitive mood of the patrons repetition and parallelism are employed in the second stanza: "each wielding a cigar, each staring with hard eyes above hard shirt, each noting on the others where ...". With the main emphasis on the word "each" and the run-on line (lines 7 and 8) the second stanza acquires a powerful, fairly natural rhythm in spite of the use of a regular metre (iambic pentameter) and rhyme (lines 6 and 8).

*2. Explain in your own words:*
– *we poets ... ready with our quotes* (ll. 1–2)
– *with wealthy men on hand* (l. 3)
– *each noting on the others where he'd stick the knife* (ll. 7–8)
– *my mother lingered* (l. 14)
– *this same heart-stopping time* (l. 13)
– we poets have memorized passages from literature so that we can make use of them at any moment;
– rich men are present beside us (to support or help us);
– each noticing in the other people where the weak points are which he can attack
– my mother stood for a while/my mother was slowly dying
– the time when my mother's heart stopped/this time last year when I got a shock, a bad surprise

## Post-reading activities

*1. Compare the treatment of death in this poem with Emily Dickinson's "Because I could not stop" and/or Dylan Thomas's "Do not Go Gentle into that Good Night".*
See Hüllen/Künne, *English and American Poetry*, Klettbuch 5064.

*2. Discuss the quotation from Keats' "Ode on a Grecian Urn":*
"Beauty is truth, truth beauty, –
That is all
Ye know on earth, and all ye need to know."

*3. Write a poem about death or about your relationship with your father/mother.*
e.g. death of a friend in a motorbike accident; death of a relation from cancer; death of a beloved grandparent; suicide of a school friend/love-hate relationship with mother or father; expectations and demands of parents; desire for freedom; rejection of a certain lifestyle; lack of understanding; coldness etc.
A poem can be short and it need not rhyme!
Cf. box p. 57, SB.

*4. Compare a song you know about death with the poem by Maclean.*

# 8. Hollywood's view of society

## Methodischer Hinweis

Da dieser Sachbuchauszug verhältnismäßig lang und schwierig ist, empfiehlt es sich, die sprachliche Vorbereitung (eventuell zusätzlich anhand eines Wörterbuchs) von den S zu Hause machen zu lassen. Der nächste Schritt wäre dann die Aufgabe 1, um zu kontrollieren, ob die Hauptgedanken klar verstanden worden sind, bevor man tiefer in die Diskussion des Inhalts einsteigt. Die lexikalische und inhaltliche Erschließung kann auch in zwei Schritten (ll. 1–41 und ll. 41–133) vorgenommen werden.

## Pre-reading activities

*1. Do you think that movies create dream worlds to allow people to escape from reality? Or do you think that all films refer to reality in one form or another and confront the viewer with it?*
*Discuss with reference to films you have seen recently.*

*2. What kind of films do you like going to see?*

*3. Look at the photo on p. 128. What does the novel and the film* Gone with the Wind *deal with? In what way can it be said to be "typical" of Hollywood films? What other film would you put in this category?*
Novel by Margaret Mitchell (1936)/famous motion picture (1939): Against the backdrop of the American Civil War and the Reconstruction Period the story follows the life and loves of Scarlett O'Hara, a Southern belle.
Hollywood features: lavish decor, special effects, colourful costumes, mass scenes, romance with happy endings, emphasis on either love or war (here both), star cult (here Clark Gable and Vivian Leigh), traditionally upper or upper middle class as main characters etc.

## Suggested answers

1. *Paragraph one (ll. 1–22):*
Hollywood's movies shaped the perceptions of Americans about themselves and their society;
Hollywood images and visions were spread all over the world;
Hollywood movies reflected the state of and the changes in American society.
*Paragraph two (ll. 23–41):*
American movies are preoccupied with portraying life in America, therefore the movies represent a relevant field of cultural investigation.
*Paragraph three (ll. 42–76):*
Social issues as central themes are to be found in many film genres;
Social commentary through ethnic prejudices: the Indians, the Hispanics, the Chinese, the Japanese, the Italians.
*Paragraph four (ll. 77–108):*
Social stereotypes: the changing view of the role of women in society,
*Paragraph five (ll. 109–133):*
Crime as a social and political phenomenon in films.

2. The writer maintains that Hollywood movies refer to a variety of social issues and in this way helped to shape the image the Americans formed of themselves and their society.

3. Hollywood movies made broad use of national stereotypes, an old tradition of the popular theatre and vaudeville (even Shakespeare employed national stereotypes to poke fun at people). The Indians were depicted either as bloodthirsty and savage or noble and courageous. As to the Hispanics, the sympathetic and helpful shop girl or waiter were contrasted with the dubious and snobbish wealthy man. Orientals were seen as inscrutable, Italians as untrustworthy criminals. These stereotypes all showed an America sharply divided by class (ll. 69–71).

4. Hollywood very early gave up the image of the weak, innocent, and defenceless female typical of pre-World War I to turn to individually reflected characters and more "advanced" stereotypes, although the vamps and `dumb blondes' of the 20s stayed in fashion for a long time. Independent women feeling free to live independent lives of their own reflected the changing status of women in middle-class American society which, according to the text, became less male-dominated.

5. Beyond the various kinds of crime American films are basically concerned with corruption, juvenile delinquency, justice, social inequality, social discrimination, the role of the social environment as a cause of crime, the press as a weapon against injustice.

There are certainly some serious films that explicitly or implicitly are concerned with these basic questions of crime and punishment. On the whole, however, one gets the impression that most movies are only superficially interested in social criticism, and make use of crime to create suspense, to have powerful visual effects and shock the viewers with violent scenes.

It is doubtful whether mass audiences realize that, as the writer says to conclude this text, society's problems are "aired under the guise of entertainment".

6. One could discuss
   – in what way Spielberg's movies are related to aspects of American society (See *American Studies Newsletter* 20, January 1990)
   – how Kostner's movie (*Dances with Wolves*) portrays Indians
   – how women are portrayed in recent American films
   – what kind of violence is shown in movies etc.

**Additional questions**

*1. Collect collocations from the first two paragraphs that are linked to the word 'movie'.*
   – movies reach millions of people
   – movies are a popular art form
   – movies reflect the tensions in American society
   – the cultural implications of American movies
   – movies provide a better understanding of popular entertainment and a better understanding of society
   – they are a special form of the visual and dramatic arts
   – they contribute greatly to the ongoing dialogue about life
   – (this) is a distinguishing characteristic of American movies

*2. Paraphrase the following:*
   – *evidence of prejudice against ... is ample* (ll. 50–52)
     many examples/proofs of prejudice against ... can be found
   – *they eventually won the right to vote* (ll. 104, 105)
     they finally succeeded in getting the right to vote
   – *they questioned sexist and marriage-oriented attitudes* (ll. 106, 107)
     they challenged/fought against traditional attitudes that were based on male dominance and that saw women's social role solely in terms of marriage
   – *problems were aired under the guise of entertainment* (ll. 132, 133)
     problems were dealt with in the shape of entertainment

*3. The text lists some movie genres. What are they? Do you know other kinds of films? Which ones do you like best? Which ones do you dislike? Say why.*
e.g. Some people hate swashbucklers as they find the long scenes depicting improbable sword fights extremely boring.
Westerns are an interesting genre as they present beautiful American scenery, often make skilful use of visual metaphors and contain a dry kind of humour. The myth of the West in its manifold aspects has been mainly created by the Western and is kept alive by it. In spite of the obvious glorification there are some realistic, historical details to be found in Westerns. The clichés of good and evil as represented in Westerns are, moreover, reassuring.

**Post-reading activities**

*1. How do you explain Hollywood's longstanding tradition of concluding movies with happy endings (in some cases scripts based on famous novels changed the endings)?*
The desire of a mass audience for harmony and happiness is fulfilled by this convention. It is said that in a life full of unsolved conflicts and personal problems people need and expect something positive and uplifting.

*2. How do you explain and evaluate the worldwide spread of American movies?*
In spite of great efforts to encourage national film production in European countries it is often the American movie that wins the highest acclaim, the most renowned awards and attracts the biggest audiences all over the world. The Americans' advantages seem to lie in the rich resources – financial and others – , the technical perfection and the perfect publicity. As the text says, the world-wide spread of American movies is also due to American economic and political influence. American films play a great role in the 'Americanization' of other cultures in spite of the fact that in many countries the sound tracks of the movies are dubbed. One may regret this influence, but in our

small world with world-wide communication it would be futile to prevent it. It should be a challenge to other cultures to try to contribute more to the international give-and-take in the cultural field.

3. *Report/paper/talk: Collect information about films dealing with the Vietnam War. What does the American preoccupation with this period of history in popular art and literature for over a decade tell us about America's self-image at this time?*
See also Chapter 12, Text 9.

4. *Report/paper/talk: Movies and novels.*
See Bibliography 20.

## 9. They came, we saw, they conquered (GK)

### Background information

Neil Postman, born in 1931, is a well-known cultural critic. He is professor of communication arts and sciences at New York University. He has written widely discussed books on the effects of the electronic media *(The Disappearance of Childhood,* 1983; *Amusing Ourselves to Death,* 1985).

### Pre-reading activities

*1. Compare the cartoon (p. 129) with the photo: describe similarities and distinctive differences. What message does the cartoonist try to convey?*
The cartoon is in content and composition almost a perfect imitation of the photo, in which victorious American soldiers plant their flag to claim the island they have conquered in battle. The cartoonist replaces the flag pole by a TV aerial and broadcasting companies (ABC, NBC, CBS). The cartoonist thus compares the spread of American TV to the military campaigns or battles of World War II, stressing the aggressive nature of this 'cultural imperialism'.

*2. Go through the German TV programme for one week and single out American serials and films: Discuss their format and contents.*

### Suggested answers

1. The title alludes to the saying attributed to Julius Caesar: *veni, vidi, vici* – I came, I saw, I conquered. This saying hints at the effortlessness and swiftness of the victories Caesar won during his conquest. Thus as 'we' watch American TV that 'they' have brought to us 'they' conquer our culture, effortlessly and swiftly.

2. Neil Postman first turns to British imperialism in ironically defining their methods of military and cultural conquest. This he contrasts with the American method in which according to Postman troops are replaced by TV shows. Postman gives evidence for this surprising thesis by describing how the American TV companies operate world-wide and how the idea of American TV penetrates other countries. At the core of American TV is the idea of entertainment that permeates all programmes. The final aim of the world-wide spread of American TV and commercialized TV is to Americanize the world and make the world buy American goods. In this way cultural and capitalist imperialism go hand in hand. Speaking to a British audience he tells them that Britain is ready to surrender (continuing the military metaphor). At the end of the text Postman ironically identifies with the invaders and therefore ends his essay written for a British paper in the style of an American cultural imperialist.

3. As American TV viewers are primarily seen as consumers, programmes are devised to hand them over to advertisers. Watching TV takes the form of mass consumption: there are two or more TV sets in every home that are on almost all day and night. Americans watch an average of eight hours TV a day, according to Postman. This and commercialization have the effect that programmes lack depth and complexity and stress visual effects to the detriment of language and context. To allow mindless consumption almost all kinds of programmes must follow the rules of light entertainment, i.e. be amusing and leave no room for thought or criticism.

4. TV ratings clearly prove that in Germany, too, TV shows, entertainment and serials are most popular. Sports programmes and especially live broadcasting of international soccer and tennis matches often draw the largest audiences.
From polls it is known, however, that for many people TV has become the main source of political and general information. Newscasts and news magazines achieve astonishingly high ratings.

Another point is that, at least in public TV, programmes are not constantly interrupted by commercials as in the USA (and on commercial TV in Britain). So "consumer propaganda" does not reach such a wide audience.

5. Postman links the all-pervasive influence of TV to the decrease of the print media. He maintains that New York has only got one newspaper of quality left, and that many papers imitate TV in presenting more and more pictures instead of text. He also mentions the high rate of illiteracy in America, implying that this is due to the effect of too much TV. This argument may also be valid for the growing number of a-literate people who can read, but don't. TV has created a nation of consumers instead of critical citizens.

6. Informal language, word play and the use of slightly altered sayings (title; the Gang of Four – the Gang of Three; "the sun never sets on an American television show", referring to Charles V's description on his Empire in Europe and America; "there's the rub", quoting Hamlet etc.) is more typical of journalism than of scholarly writing. Much is said in the form of irony. As in his final address to the British, Postman often really means the opposite (the American method of imperialism has many advantages: "it is pleasurable and quick", ll. 10, 11; "we hope to entice the infidels to give up their native culture, diversity, point of view, heroes and values", ll. 85–87).

Postman's love for pointed and often exaggerated statements can be observed all through the text. In many cases they express sarcasm and bitter criticism (see the definition of a 'good' audience; "people must direct their energies and thoughts to the one thing that counts: the existential pleasures of buying things." – ll. 75–78; "Given a few years they will turn Peking into Omaha, Nebraska without a shot being fired", ll. 21–23).

His treatment of the material shows great selectiveness, generalization, and monocausal argumentation which all too clearly serves the purpose of establishing a daring thesis, namely that the world-wide spread of American TV and culture is a form of cultural, and finally commercial and economic imperialism, and of convincing his readers that this is true.

7. Dear Sir,
I was almost amused to death by Postman running down his own country. I think it is wishful thinking to assume that American TV dominates in my/our country ...

The evidence he gives is selective and shaky. With almost 250 million inhabitants 60 million illiterates (which in itself is a very dubious figure) hardly constitute the said one-third of the American population. The high immigration rate, bilingual education, the breakdown of the family definitely contribute more to illiteracy than too much TV consumption ...

Dear Sir,
As I deeply resent the Americanization of our language and our culture, I can only praise Postman for his outspoken criticism of American cultural imperialism ... etc.

### Additional questions

1. Do you remember Postman's statements and sarcastic remarks?

*An audience .........is useless.*
– not paying enough attention

*An audience .........is dangerous.*
– paying too much attention

*What is required is an audience ............*
– conditioned to minimal mental activity when watching television.

*In short, everything shown must ........*
– be entertaining.

*Educational shows for children emphasize that ........ are inseparable.*
– learning and entertainment

*All authentic ideological issues are made to appear ...........*
– trivial, evanescent, or merely amusing.

*During his lifetime, an American will see approximately ..........*
– two million amusing commercials, a thousand a week.

2. Carl Bernstein (of Watergate fame) recently called present-day America "a talk-show nation, in which public discourse is reduced to ranting and raving and posturing." Discuss this idea in relationship to the Postman article.

### Post-reading activities

1. Report/paper/talk: Television in the USA. See Bibliography 17, 21 and 11.

2. Compare an American and a German TV serial.

# 10. The little room of literature

## Background information

Salman Rushdie was born in Bombay (1947) and was first educated there. He then attended a famous public school in England (Rugby) and graduated in history from Cambridge University. Before starting his career as an Anglo-Indian writer he worked for the theatre and for advertising agencies. For his novel *Midnight's Children* (1981) Rushdie was awarded the Booker Prize. The *Satanic Verses* (1988), told partly in realistic, partly in surrealistic style, attacks the cultures both of the West and of India. He tries to expose religious and cultural taboos and false beliefs. The passages on Muhammad and Islam were looked upon as severe blasphemy by the Ayatollah Khomeini in Iran and Islamic fundamentalists, and British Muslims wanted the book banned. In 1989 Khomeini reacted by pronouncing a death sentence *(fatwa)* on Rushdie, making his murder a duty to the followers of Islam world-wide. Since 1989 Rushdie has lived in hiding, appearing unexpectedly from time to time on public occasions. All his appeals for reconciliation have not had any effect so far.

Rushdie, who was invited to give the annual Herbert Read Memorial Lecture in 1990, wrote the text *Is Nothing Sacred?* for this occasion but did not dare to appear publicly. It was read out by Harold Pinter, the dramatist.

In his lecture Rushdie reappraises the state and the function of literature in it after the Islamic attack on his books and his person have endangered the freedom of expression and his freedom as a writer as well as an individual.

Our excerpt constitutes the final passage of the lecture which is concluded by a parable to illustrate that literature and the freedom of literature is absolutely necessary for human life and any society.

(Herbert Read, born 1893, was an English poet, critic and professor of fine art whose most famous work was *The Meaning of Art*, 1931.)

Cf. Chapter 2, text 7 (transcript p. 58 TB).

## Methodische Hinweise

Da die Parabel im Zentrum unseres Textauszuges (ll. 26–74) nicht allzu stark verschlüsselt und vom Stil her sehr appellativ ist, empfiehlt es sich, diese Passage vor der Präsentation des ganzen Textes durch ein- oder zweimaliges Lehrerlesen bei geschlossenen Büchern darzubieten. Als Erschliessungshilfen können im Unterrichtsgespräch die Fragen der 2. und 3. Aufgabe Verwendung finden. Danach kann anhand des Bildes und der Bildaufgabe (p. 132) auf den Autor eingegangen werden (siehe "Background information").

Schließlich können dann die argumentativen Thesen Rushdie's zur Rolle der Literatur, die er um die Fabel herum formulierte, erschlossen (Aufgabe 1), auf die Parabel bezogen und textübergreifend diskutiert werden (Aufgabe 2). Nach der Diskussion könnten die S den Aufsatz (Aufgabe 4) als *post-reading activity* zu Hause schreiben.

## Pre-reading activities

See above ("Methodische Hinweise").

## Suggested answers

1. Rushdie rejects the idea that books and literary works could be considered sacred or sacrosanct, i.e. beyond criticism, as is the case with religion. They are the work of men/women and not prophets and are therefore imperfect, incomplete. They are only interim reports on how artists see reality or truth. But what has to be defended as one of the greatest goods is the privilege of literature to be the arena of free discourse, a privilege which is necessary for literature in order to exist and prosper.

2. (Die Bezugspunkte sollten durchaus offen, über das hier vorgeschlagene hinausgehend und nicht etikettenhaft angegangen werden. Auch die Textsortenfrage sollte offen und eher heuristisch gestellt werden.)
   – *large house without exits:* human life, our society, our culture
   – *bad condition:* our environment, state of the world
   – *people:* family, friends, in public life you meet hostile people and strangers, bullies and people you love
   – one has to be content with what one has got, with what is there
   – the *little empty rooms* full of *various voices:* literature with the great abundance and variety of books and writers: books you know well and not at all; books referring to life and society; books reporting on everything that is going on; pornographic, funny, loving ... books; the most interesting books contain all this at the same time; books do not seem so important but everybody makes use of them and seems to need them

- *disappearance of little rooms:* destruction of books and literature
- *the house becomes a prison:* life becomes unbearable

3. Without literature, if people have no opportunity to read all kinds of books, life will become unbearable, society a prison, and the foundations of society will begin to shake and threaten to collapse. The political implications of this general observation is given at the end of the text in which Rushdie obviously hints at the 'tumbling walls' in middle and east Europe in the late eighties and early nineties. Wherever literary freedom was destroyed (as part of dictatorial systems) walls came tumbling down because of the pressure from within, from people longing for freedom of all kinds.

The meaning of the last sentences of the fable ("You do not wake up. You are already awake", ll. 73–74) is a bit enigmatic. Rushdie may want to express that the consequences of lost freedom are not just a nightmare but already reality. On the other hand, you have woken up to this nightmare (l. 55). So unfortunately one cannot escape it by pretending it is a dream.

4. Possible points:
– personal enrichment, experiencing other worlds and other people
– substitute for personal experiences
– a way of escaping reality
– a form of entertainment/amusement
– reading for relaxation/fun/thrill
– a means of gaining in-depth information and learning
– a means of storing the common knowledge or heritage of a culture/society
– an important economic factor
– a superficial, artificial world of irrelevant ideals and slightly eccentric people who do not live in the real world etc.

## Additional questions

*1. Explain: "There is no fineness or accuracy of suppression. If you hold down one thing, you hold down the adjoining." (ll. 89–90)*
If one part of society – one group, one religion or one idea – is supressed it will lead to general oppression as all parts of society and culture are interlinked: freedom is indivisible. Rushdie might be alluding to his personal fate and with this quotation be warning the British and the whole of the Western world that with the Iranian threats against his life and his freedom, the foundations of culture are in danger.
Cf. Chapter 2, text 7 (transcript p. 58 TB).

*2. Collect collocations of the following words that help you discuss Rushdie's fate and text: sacred, sacrosanct, sacralization, sacrilegious, sacrilege,*
*to blaspheme, blasphemy, blasphemous, a blasphemer.*
e.g. sacred area of a church, a sacred mosque
the sacredness of the shrine has been violated
in their search for a good news story nothing was sacred
the sacredness of private property/literature
a sacred cow
many dictators think that their powers are sacrosanct
he seems to think that his actions are sacrosanct
the sacralization of secular matters
to attack people in a church is a sacrilege
it would have been sacrilegious to speak in the middle of communion
he turned away from religion and even no longer felt afraid of blaspheming
a blasphemous poem, thought, novel
any attempt to violate the reputation of Muhammad is blasphemous
Khomeini plays the role of an avenger of blasphemy who annihilates any blasphemer
laws of blasphemy etc.

*3. Do you know any writers or books who are/were the object of almost religious reverence or part of cults?*
e.g. Goethe, Shakespeare

*4. Why do some states try to restrict the freedom of writers? Discuss with reference to the Third Reich, Russia etc.*

## Post-reading activities

*1. Report/paper/talk: "Fighting For Books"* from Ray Bradbury's *Fahrenheit 451.*

*2. Is there any case for censorship of books or films which might offend the religious sensibilities of one group in society? How would you have felt if Rushdie had made fun of Christianity in his novel?*
Compare the reactions to certain films by Buñuel, Pasolini or Scorsese. Mention the Roman Catholic Index.

# Test: Film and the novel

Der Klausurtext und die Aufgaben beziehen sich vorwiegend auf die Arbeit mit Text 8. Aber auch die Texte 9 und 10 können gedanklich und lexikalisch Anknüpfungspunkte bieten.

The narrative potential of film is so marked that it has developed its strongest bond with the novel, not with painting, not even with drama. Both films and novels tell long stories with a wealth of detail and they do it from the perspective of a narrator, who often interposes a resonant level of irony between the story and the observer. Whatever can be told in print in a novel can be roughly pictured or told in film (although the wildest fantasies of a Jorge Luis Borges or a Lewis Carroll might require "special effects" work). The differences between the two arts, besides the obvious and powerful difference between pictorial narration and linguistic narration, are quickly apparent.

First, because film operates in real time, it is more limited. Novels end only when they feel like it. Film is, in general, restricted to what Shakespeare called "the short two hours' traffic of our stage." Popular novels have been a vast reservoir of material for commercial films over the years. In fact, the economics of the popular novel is such now that the possibility of recycling the material as a film is a prime consideration for most publishers. It almost seems, at times, as if the popular novel (as opposed to elite prose art) exists only as a first draft trial for the film. But commercial film still can't reproduce the range of the novel in time. An average-length screenplay, for example, is 125 to 150 pages in length; the average novel twice that. Almost invariably, details of incident are lost in the transition from book to film. Only the television serial can overcome this deficiency. It carries with it some of the same sense of duration necessary to the large novel. Of all the screen versions of *War and Peace*, for example, the most successful by far seems to me to have been the BBC's twenty-part serialization of the early seventies; not necessarily because the acting or direction was better than the two- or six-hour film versions (although that is arguable), but because only the serial could reproduce the essential quality of the saga – duration.

At the same time as film is limited to a shorter narration, however, it naturally has pictorial possibilities the novel doesn't have. What can't be transferred by incident might be translated into image. And here we come to the most essential difference between the two forms of narration. Novels are told by the author. We see and hear only what he wants us to see and hear. Films are, in a sense, told by their authors too, but we see and hear a great deal more than a director necessarily intends. It would be an absurd task for a novelist to try to describe a scene in as much detail as it is conveyed in cinema. [...]

More important, whatever the novelist describes is filtered through his language, his prejudices, and his point of view. With film we have a certain amount of freedom to choose, to select one detail rather than another.

The driving tension of the novel is the relationship between the materials of the story (plot, character, setting, theme, and so forth) and the narration of it in language; between the tale and the teller, in other words. The driving tension of film, on the other hand, is between the materials of the story and the objective nature of the image. It's as if the author/director of a film were in continual conflict with the scene he is shooting. Chance plays a much larger part, and the end result is that the observer is free to participate in the experience much more actively. The words on the page are always the same, but the image on the screen changes continually as we redirect our attention. Film is, in this way, a much richer experience.

But it is poorer, as well, since the persona of the narrator is so much weaker. There has only been one major film, for example, that tried to duplicate the first-person narration so useful to the novel, Robert Montgomery's *Lady in the Lake* (1964). The result was a cramped, claustrophobic experience: we saw only what the hero saw. In order to show us the hero, Montgomery had to resort to a battery of mirror tricks. Film can approximate the ironies that the novel develops in narration, but it can never duplicate them. (733 words)

From *How to read a film* by James Monaco, New York: OUP 1977. Reprinted by permission.

## Annotations

2 **bond**   close connection, link
10–11 **Jorge Luis Borges**   Argentinian poet, short-story writer and literary scholar, born 1899
11 **Lewis Carroll**   English writer (1832–98), author of *Alice's Adventures in Wonderland*
32 **incident**   *here:* a minor, subsidiary or related action or event
33 **transition**   change or passage from one state or stage to another
34 **deficiency**   weakness, imperfection
37 ***War and Peace***   novel by Tolstoy
85–86 ***Lady in the Lake***   from the novel by Raymond Chandler
89 **to resort to s.th.**   to turn to s.th. because there is no alternative
90 **to approximate s.th.**   to come close to s.th.
92 **to duplicate s.th.**   to copy s.th. exactly

## I. Language and vocabulary

1. – the narrator *often interposes a resonant level of irony* between the story and observer ... (ll. 6–7)
Paraphrase.

2. – "the short two hours' traffic of our stage" (Shakespeare), ll. 19–20.
Explain.

3. – the possibility of recycling the material as a film is of prime consideration for the publishers ... (ll. 23–25)
Paraphrase.

4. – to *participate* in the experience ... (l. 76)
Find a synonym.

5. Find the corresponding adjectives:
l. 7 irony
l. 10 fantasy
l. 33 transition
l. 50 image
l. 65 tension
l. 79 attention

6. Find the corresponding nouns:
l. 2 strong
l. 18 restrict
l. 20 popular
l. 56 necessarily
l. 57 describe
l. 82 weak

## II. Grammar and style

1. Study the use of words like 'film', 'drama', 'novel', 'cinema' and give reasons why in some cases the article is used and in others it is not.

2. Find some abstract nouns that are used without an article in the text.

3. "What can't be transferred by incident might be translated into image." (ll. 48–50)
Explain why the passive is used.

## III. Comprehension and analysis

1. In what way is film similar to the novel?

2. What differences result from the time factor?

3. What advantages has film got over the novel, what disadvantage?

4. The main structural principle of the text is comparison. Study the text to find out how this is expressed.

## IV. Comment

Choose *one* of the following topics:

1. Film as a popular art form can 'recycle' popular novels for films, but should never try to put serious literary works of art on the screen.
Give your opinion.

2. "Whatever the novelist describes is filtered through his language, his prejudices, and his point of view." (ll. 60–62)
Comment on this quotation referring to novels you have read.

3. Films provide a better understanding of the society in which they are made.

# Bibliography

1. Allen, Elisabeth Jones. "Ascent of the Skyscraper-Past, Present and Future", *American Studies Newsletter* 6, May 1985.
2. Argan, Giulio Carlo. *Henry Moore*. Stuttgart: Klett-Cotta, 1987.
3. Atwood, Margaret. *Dancing Girls*. London: Virago, 1977.
4. Atwood, Margaret. *Bluebeard's Egg*. London: Virago, 1983.
5. Bradbury, Ray. *Fahrenheit 451*. (Various editions).
6. *Britain 1991. An Official Handbook*. London: HMSO.
7. Compton, Susan. *British Art in the 20th Century*. Munich: Prestel, 1986.
8. DiBacco/Mason/Appy. *History of the United States*. Klettbuch 516153.
9. Ellis, W. S. "Skyscrapers", *National Geographic*, February 1989.
10. Garraty, J. A. *American History*. Orlando, Florida: Harcourt Brace Jovanovich, 1982.
11. Gunther, Max. "Television in the USA", *American Studies Newsletter* 3, May 1984.
12. Händel/Friebel. *Britain – USA Now*. Frankfurt: Diesterweg, 1974.
13. Handlin, David P. *American Architecture*. London: Thames and Hudson, 1985.
14. Hüllen/Künne. *English and American Poetry*, Klettbuch 5064.
15. Mitchinson, David. *Henry Moore*. Stuttgart: Klett-Cotta, 1981.
16. Osterwald, Tilman. *Pop Art*. Köln: Benedikt Taschen Verlag, 1989.
17. Paulu, B. "Public Television in the USA", *American Studies Newsletter* 8, 1986.
18. Postman, Neil. *Amusing Ourselves to Death*. London: Penguin 1986.
19. Prignitz-Poda, Helga et al. (Hrsg.). *Frida Kahlo, Das Gesamtwerk*. Frankfurt: Verlag Neue Kritik, 1988.
20. Sarris, Andrew. "Making Movies by the Book", *American Studies Newsletter* 20, January 1990.
21. Stevenson D. K. *American Life and Institutions*, Klettbuch 5136, Chapter VII.
22. Wust/Moos. *Three Hundred Years of German Immigrants in North America*. Munich 1983.
23. Zukowsky, J. *Chicago Architecture 1872–1922*. München: Prestel, 1987.

# 6 Science, Technology and the Environment

## Structure of the chapter

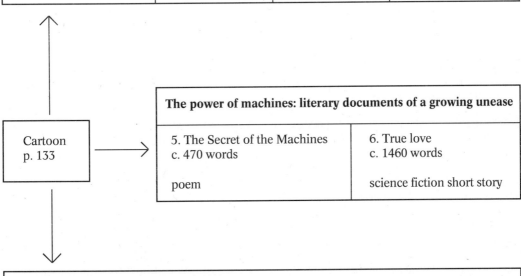

## Suggestions for reports/papers/talks

Archimedes/Aristotle/Thomas A. Edison/the Wright Brothers/ Marie Curie/Albert Einstein/ .../ and his/her/their contributions to the development of science and technology – after text 1

The Nobel Prize/Nobel Prize Winners (free choice) – after text 1

Women in Science – after cartoon or text 1

Life in the Old South – before/after text 3

Energy consumption and the limits to growth – after text 3

From the Mauretania to the Titanic – a lesson for mankind? – after text 5

Artificial Intelligence (AI) – achievements and failures – after text 6

*Frankenstein:* the novel and/or the film – before text 7

The discovery of the "double helix" (genetic code) – after text 7

Any SF novel/short story/film on the subject of genetic engineering – after text 7

Any environmental organization or influential book mentioned in fact file p. 296 – after text 8

### Vokabulary

*Thematischer Grund- und Aufbauwortschatz,* Klettbuch 51955, pp. 1–25, 161–167, 197–198

*Words in Context – Thematischer Oberstufenwortschatz* (Klettbuch 51961), pp. 134–161

# Cartoon (GK)

### Methodisch-didaktische Hinweise

Beim Einstieg vor allem in dieses Thema gilt es, zunächst die Kluft zwischen dem Vorwissen der Schüler und deren sprachlicher Kompetenz zu überbrücken. Das Hauptziel soll bei der Behandlung des Themas zunächst sein, das Sprachmaterial zur Formulierung grundsätzlicher Sachverhalte zu erarbeiten. Die Diskussion des vorliegenden Cartoons (oder irgendeines anderen bildhaften Stimulus) ist als *pre-reading activity* zu den ersten Texten, bzw. zum gesamten Kapitel zu sehen, wobei es darauf ankommt, sowohl früher erworbenes Sprachmaterial wieder aufzufrischen, als auch die folgenden Texte durch gezielte Einführung einiger *key terms* sprachlich etwas vorzuentlasten.

Die Präsentation des Cartoons läßt sich spannender gestalten, wenn man die zwei Bildelemente (die Kraftwerksruine und das feuermachende Pärchen) getrennt über OH-Folie oder Kopie anbietet und beschreiben läßt um anschließend den Bezug der beiden "Bilder" zueinander zu diskutieren, zu erschließen. Die Präsentation des Cartoons und die Formulierung einer Gesamtaussage erfolgt dann als Höhepunkt.

### Suggested answers

1. The power station:
 – ruins of (nuclear) power plant (... in ruins)
 – cracks in the cooling towers
 – result of a nuclear accident?
 – destruction caused by war/bombing/earthquake/ ...?
 – radioactive contamination/release of radioactivity?

 The two people:
 – (stark) naked couple
 – making fire with the help of a stone-age technology, (see text 1, ll. 9-10: "rapid friction on dry wood")
 – man active, woman looking on

 Implication: The energy supply has broken down for some reason, throwing people back on primitive technologies for survival.

2. It says nothing whatsoever about science as such. About technology it expresses a rather pessimistic message: that we may well lose control of our advanced technologies, bringing about the self-destruction of modern civilization. We may be forced to start all over again with primitive stone age technology. All in all a bleak prospect.

3. Our lifestyle/standard of living is highly dependent on the functioning of modern technologies (esp. on the energy supply). We should not take them for granted, as such technologies are easily vulnerable and often bear the danger of self-destruction.

4. – to explore our physical environment
– to satisfy our intellectual curiosity
– to make life easier (cf. text 1 l. 6: "... to make nature work for us"; also ll. 63–65; also cf. God's instruction, in Genesis 1.28, to "subdue" the earth and "have dominion over every living thing that moveth upon the earth")

The cartoon makes no statement about the ultimate purpose of science. It does, however, imply that if its ultimate goal is control and manipulation of nature for our benefit, then man has tried and failed miserably.

5. The active male/passive female in the cartoon may be coincidental. It may be a reflection of the cartoonist's own prejudices – just as most cartoons drawn by men tend to show a male figure doing the talking, etc.

It can, however, be taken as a comment on the male domination of the fields of science and technology. It would be difficult to deny the fact of such dominance, though one could argue over the reasons (to what extent genetic/natural differences between the sexes? – to what extent social pressures?).

If such a comment is intended, then the cartoonist could be criticized for assuming that fire-making was a man's job in stone-age societies – it may well have been the other way round, and we certainly don't know who first mastered the fire-making technique in question.

It might be useful to consider what the students' reactions would have been if the roles had been reversed in the cartoon. Would they have seen the woman as an active person applying a technology to solve a problem? Or would they have then interpreted the scene as the woman slaving over the "stove" to prepare a meal for her lord and master? The point being that whatever women do tends to get devalued.

# 1. A late but fruitful marriage (GK)

### Background information

Lines 30–45 contain some slight inaccuracies:
– Archimedes discovered the law of specific gravity. The Principle of Archimedes may be enunciated like this: When a body is immersed in a specifically lighter fluid, the weight lost by the body is equal to the weight of the quantity of fluid displaced. In our text the reference is to a solid body which is immersed in a specifically heavier fluid, say a piece of wood in water. The piece of wood floats on the surface. The weight of the water it displaces is equal to its own weight.
– Strictly speaking, it is not the "observation" (l. 38) which is subject to verification, but any hypothesis developed to explain it. The correct sequence is:
1. observation/collection of data;
2. classification and induction;
3. formulation of hypotheses;
4. verification/falsification of hypotheses.

Experimentation is used both at the beginning and the end of this procedure, i.e. both to collect further and more precise data, and to check a hypothesis. As regards the latter, it is more accurate to speak of falsification than verification. No hypothesis (or more general theory) is ever 100% verified, even if it does achieve a high degree of acceptance.

### Methodisch-didaktischer Hinweis

Zusätzlich zu den unten vorgeschlagenen *pre-reading activities* lassen sich über die Interpretation des Titels Mutmaßungen über den Inhalt des Texts anstellen.

Als erste *post-reading activity* bietet es sich an, ohne auf den Fragenapparat Bezug zu nehmen, den inhaltlichen Aufbau des Textes in kürzester Form skizzieren zu lassen, was praktisch sowohl zu den *headings* von Frage 1 führt, als auch zu den Stichworten in Frage 2 und 3. Danach folgt die Bearbeitung des Fragenapparats.

Das Ziel der Fragen 1–5 ist es, den thematischen Wortschatz des Textes zu aktivieren. Die Schüler sollten also dazu angehalten werden, das Vokabular des Textes so weit wie nur möglich zu übernehmen. Keinesfalls sofort nach eigenen Formulierungen sollte man suchen lassen.

**Pre-reading activities**

*1. How would you describe the difference between science and technology?*

*2. Which do you think came first – science or technology?*

*3. Name what you think are the most important fields of science and technology.*

**Suggested answers**

1. a) The historical development up to Bacon:
– learning through trial and error (l. 10);
– scattered, superficial discoveries (ll. 19–20);
– (pure) science pursued only by the leisure class (ll. 32–34);
– early scientific discoveries in ancient Greece: not all observations could be verified by demonstrations (ll. 35–45).
b) The 17th century:
– wider intellectual freedom (l. 52);
– inventions (printing, telescope, microscope, etc.) (ll. 53–54);
– discoveries of the explorers (ll. 54–55);
– rise of powerful nation-states (ll. 55–56);
– rise of business corporations (money to apply technical advances) (ll. 56–58);
– quickening of the development of science and technology (l. 51);
– the scientific method: disciplined collection of data (ll. 46, 66–67), controlled, repeatable experiments (l. 47);
– scientific associations (ll. 70–71);
– marriage between science and technology (l. 60).
c) The 18th and 19th centuries:
– industrial revolution (ll. 73–76)
– a relatively peaceful time in Europe (l. 79);
– opportunities of the American frontier (l. 81);
– (in the U.S.) land-grant colleges dedicated to technology (ll. 82–84);
– powerful stimuli to technology (ll. 78, 80);
d) The role of research
– basic research necessary for technological advances (ll. 100–104);
– research laboratories established by industrial firms and universities (ll. 85–86);
– promotion by the government for both military and economic purposes (ll. 89–91).

2. Basic research:
– main goal: extending the boundaries of the known;
– indifference to practical issues;
– provides the basic knowledge for the development of new technologies;
– discoveries are quickly published.
Applied research:
– main goal: developing new technologies;
– only interested in the practical issues;
– depends on the discoveries of basic research;
– findings often protected through patents or commercial and military secrets.

3. (Diese Aufgabe in jedem Falle schriftlich machen lassen. Dann vergleichen mit Definitionen aus gängigen Wörterbüchern und evtl. Diskussion.)
Science:
– the study of the nature and behaviour of natural things and the knowledge that we obtain about them through observation and experiments (COBUILD)
– organized knowledge, esp. when obtained by observation and testing of facts, about the physical world, natural laws and society; study leading to such knowledge (ALD)
Technology:
– the activity or study of using scientific knowledge for practical purposes in industry, farming, medicine, business, etc. (COBUILD)
– scientific study and use of mechanical arts and applied sciences, e.g. engineering; application of this to practical tasks in industry, etc.

4. –

5. –

*Picture p. 135:* The aim of such societies was, as the name of this one suggests, to promote the development of natural science. They provided funding for scientific projects and arranged for the publication of scientific findings.

**Additional questions**

*1. Find examples of inversion and explain their functions.*
See lines 6, 20–21, 25–26, 31, 101–102.

*2. What is "the scientific method"? List all of its elements, including those not mentioned in the text.*
Cf. question 1b) and background information.

## Post-reading activities

*1. Topics for classroom reports:*
– Archimedes/Aristotle/Thomas A. Edison/The Wright Brothers/Marie Curie/Albert Einstein/Werner von Braun/... and his/her/their contributions to the development of science and technology.
See Bibliography 5,13.
– Women in science.
   Students could be instructed to concentrate on the careers of the few prominent exceptions, e.g. Marie Curie, Lise Meitner. See also bibliography 14 for the contribution of Rosalind Franklin to the discovery of the genetic code.
– *The Nobel Prize/Nobel Prize winners* (free choice).
See Bibliography 5, 13, 14.

*2. Topic for composition writing:*
*There's no science without technology, no technology without science. Comment.*

# 2. Technological innovation

### Methodisch-didaktischer Hinweis

Soll der Schwerpunkt der Arbeit mit Text 2 und 3 auf dem Begriff "innovation" liegen, so ist es auch denkbar, Text 3 vor 2 zu besprechen. Der in Text 4 (LC) behandelte Aspekt schließt außerdem unmittelbar an diesen Aspekt an.

### Pre-reading activities

*1. You have made two inventions:*
*a) a "lawn watcher", i.e. an appliance that measures the growth of your lawn electronically, signalling the next lawn-cut automatically;*
*b) a small and simple appliance that helps to bring down gasoline consumption of cars to less than 50%.*
*Which of the two inventions is more likely to be a commercial success? Why?*

*2. Do you know any of the inventions that made the Industrial Revolution possible?*

### Suggested answers

1. (Mit dieser Aufgabe sollte das schnelle Auffinden wichtiger key words und deren Anwendung in einer mündlichen oder schriftlichen Teilzusammenfassung geschult werden. Bei der mündlichen Bearbeitung empfiehlt es sich in jedem Fall, die *pre-reading activities* vorzuschalten.)
First there was the new industrial middle class, a social group that was prepared to consider innovative ideas seriously. Second there were important social needs that had to be resolved. The third factor necessary for the coming of the Industrial Revolution was the existence of social resources, i.e. capital and raw materials, and skilled personnel, and technical know-how.

2. The main objective of the diagram should be to show that commercial success is not possible if only one condition is not fulfilled:

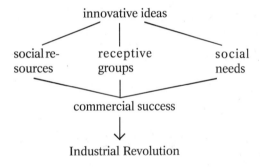

3. The examples show that the absence of only one of the factors mentioned will make inventions fail.
The author's strategy of argumentation is to give some striking examples of situations where almost all of the conditions for success were present; their failure shows how important the missing factor was.

4. Traffic: the need for fuel efficiency, for noise-reduction, for speed, for safety, for traffic reduction, ...
Energy: the need for clean forms of energy, for saving energy resources, ...
Materials: the need for materials that are light, strong, fully recyclable, ...

Computers: the need for better memory capacity, higher speed, more comfortable handling/programming, ...

Nutrition: cheap, plentiful food; more resistant breeds of plant; more efficient preservation and transportation; tastier and healthier foods, ...

Most of these needs stem from the wish to improve people's standard of living, whether by saving time, curtailing pollution, improving the situation of our environment, etc. But they have unavoidably been manipulated by social pressure and the media. People may naturally want a higher standard of living. But (to take nutrition as an example) should this take the form of better-tasting local produce – or a variety of (preserved/ irradiated/picked unripe) fruits and vegetables from all over the world?

Only the most imaginative students will think of needs which have not already been talked about, i.e. which have not been made explicit to some extent.

5. Developing countries always lack what Buchanan calls social resources. Besides, they are caught in the vicious circle of poverty. To be effective, foreign aid must begin in many problem areas simultaneously.

6. The function of salesmanship and advertising is to generate needs artificially. Dangers: manipulation; the race for status symbols; no sense for real needs, real values; increasing debt.

**Additional questions**

*1. What role did the new industrial middle class play during the Industrial Revolution?*

*2. Explain in your own words: "... needs must be explicit ..., they must be felt to be needs." (ll. 32–33)*

*3. What was – and still is – the role of advertising?*

*4. Why couldn't an industrial revolution take place at Leonardo da Vinci's time?*

*5. Why did the Industrial Revolution take hold in Britain, not in France, during the 18th century?*

*6. Collect all expressions from the text that make up the semantic field "innovation".*

*7. Discussion: Say what "needs" (if any) accounted for the commercial success of the following: TV remote control; the walkman; quartz watches; fax; micro-wave ovens.*

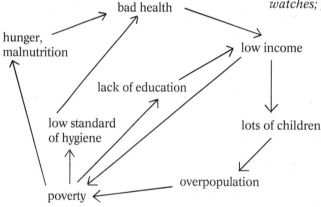

# 3. An artificial climate (GK)

**Background information**

All the background information on the Southern States the teacher will need at the "pre-reading activities" stage can be found in Perspectives 2: *The American South* (Klettbuch 51362). This should also be made available to any student directed to do a classroom report on the theme.

Ll. 21–23: John Egerton is the author of a book called *The Americanization of Dixie* (1974).

Ll. 88–92: David M. Potter is a historian specializing in the Civil War era. He is author of *The South and the Sectional Conflict* (1968) and *The Impending Crisis 1848–1861* (1976).

## Pre-reading activities

*1. Look at the map on page 259, and say what the area called "Dixie" makes you think of.*
As an alternative (or in addition) to this "free association" method, the following guiding questions can be asked:
- *By what other names is it known?*
- *What States does it include?*
- *What do you know about its history?*
- *What makes it different from the rest of the USA?*
- *What was life like there in the past (for blacks/whites/the rich/the poor)?*
- *What information have you got about life there today?*

In dealing with the last two questions, the students can be encouraged to list the impressions they have gleaned from literature, songs, movies, TV, etc. – e.g. (for the past) *Gone With the Wind* (cf. p. 128), *To Kill a Mockingbird* (cf. pp. 203-204) ; (for the present) the TV series *Dallas, Miami Vice, Golden Girls*.

*2. Now look at the picture on page 138 and try to answer the question asked about it.*

### Methodisch-didaktischer Hinweis

Die Frage 1 des Fragenapparates soll nicht vor oder nach dem ersten Lesen bearbeitet werden, sondern tatsächlich während der Text zum ersten Mal durchgelesen wird. Nur so kann das Erschließen von Wortbedeutungen mit Hilfe des Kontexts geübt werden.

### Suggested answers

1. Migrant: a person who moves from one place to another, esp. in order to find work;
distinctiveness: the special quality which makes s.th. easily recognizable and different from other things of the same type;
to accelerate: to speed s.th. up, to give it more speed;
advent: arrival, appearance, coming.

2. See lines 1–23: Air-conditioning has influenced all spheres of life in the South. Since the author allows for other factors, it would be difficult to dispute his claim that this technology has played a part in bringing about social change. One can argue only about how much, and why. The discussion might revolve around the questions raised by text 2:

- What developments/events brought forth the need for the invention/introduction of air-conditioning?
- Who was willing to introduce the new technology?
- For whom was it a basic need, who could articulate a need for this technology?
- To what degree can the need for air-conditioning be called artificial?

3. The South before air-conditioning:
- cultural isolation
- agrarianism
- romanticism, slow pace of life
- poverty
- neighborliness, strong sense of place
- front porch society (l. 99)

The South after the advent of air-conditioning:
- immigration from the North in the 60s; new ideas, life styles (ll. 30–48)
- industrialization, high tech, tourism (ll. 54–64)
- urbanization, urban forms of architecture, power and activity (ll. 66–85)
- migration makes population more heterogeneous (ll. 41–51)
- less human interaction/changes in architecture (ll. 98–101)

Other factors:
- equal rights for the Blacks, brought about by the Civil Rights Movement in the sixties
- the decentralization of traditional industries in the manufacturing belt
- the search of high-tech industries for new (cheaper) locations

4. – enumeration (ll. 5–6, 13–15, 66–81)
- parallelisms in the sentence structure (ll. 55–81), repetition
  The effect might be described as follows:
  The use of ...
- helps to intensify the author's main points
- stresses the author's competence on the subject matter
- makes it easy to follow the author's argumentation/ideas
- makes it easy to memorize the facts.

The overall tone of the text can be described as reasonable or even persuasive.

5. Semantic field "change/bringing about change":
- to influence everything from ... to (ll. 9–10)
- to accelerate the development of ... (ll. 21–69)
- to reverse a tradition ... (l. 25)

- to migrate to ..., to move to, to leave a region (ll. 42, 84, 43)
- to disrupt a region's isolation ... (l. 47)
- to foster a development ... (l. 66)
- to increase productivity ... (l. 58)
- to alter attitudes toward ... (l. 86)
- to become heterogeneous (l. 50)
- to fade from view (l. 53)
- to spread out (l. 79)
- to take one's toll (l. 88)
- to succumb to (l. 91)

(Diese angedeutete Liste läßt sich problemlos erweitern durch die Bildung der jeweiligen Wortfamilien, durch Suchen der *antonyms*, durch Ergänzen während der weiteren Textarbeit.)

6. Possible arguments to express
a) fascination:
- interesting point of view
- amazing facts
- good to mention both the positive and negative effects of technology
- it makes one think of other inventions and their effects

b) disapproval:
- exaggerated point of view/way of seeing things
- rather one-sided perspective

- description of direct impact of air-conditioning rather vague
- facts do not really support the assertions
- no answer to the question what came first: the developments described giving rise to the need for air-conditioning or vice versa

**Additional questions**

1. Analyse the use of the past tense and the present perfect in the text.

2. a) Explain the tense used in lines 75–81.
b) Rewrite the first part of the sentence ("Without air-conditioning, ...") as an if-clause.

3. Discuss the probable costs (in economic and environmental terms) of all this air-conditioning.

**Post-reading activities**

*Topics for classroom reports:*
- *Life in the Old South.*
  See Perspectives 2: *The American South*, Klettbuch 51362.
- *Energy consumption and the limits to growth.*
  See Bibliography 4, 5, 6, 7, 11.

## 4. Listening Comprehension: Technology and culture

### Methodisch-didaktische Hinweise

NB: Es handelt sich hier um eine Neuaufnahme des Interviewtextes.
Das Thema des Interviewausschnittes nimmt Bezug auf Text 2 "technological innovation", und zwar auf den im zweiten Absatz erwähnten "second factor" des "matching social needs". (ll. 29–64)
Eine Einleitung, Worterklärungen und Fragen zum Globalverständnis sind im SB, S. 140 abgedruckt.

Der Hörtext läßt sich auch abschnittsweise präsentieren. Zuerst "Listening for the gist" bis Zeile 28, dann sofort "Listening for detail" zu Teil 1. Der restliche Text dann als Ganzes. Dies empfiehlt sich vor allem in Klassen/Kursen mit wenig Erfahrung im Lernzielbereich "Listening Comprehension".

### Transcript of the interview

*One point that your book* Networks of Power *makes is that it isn't always easy to transfer technology from one country to another. Why is that?*
You remember the book *The Ugly American*? Part of its argument is that Americans assumed then – it 5 was written in the late 1950s – that they knew the best way and were generously bringing culture and technology to other peoples. Americans were, that is, imposing their solutions on non-American problems. I think there is something to that. Engineers, for 10 instance, often assume there is one best way. Certainly in the 1950s and '60s it was widely believed that the "one best way" was American technology. But in fact, technology must fit in with the culture, values, job skills and aspirations of the nation receiving the 15 "transplant." And if people differ, as they do, in their skills, aspirations and general objectives, then the

general technology needs to be modified to fit into that culture and fulfill its needs.

I remember stories about Americans insisting that a certain kind of insulation be used on electrical lines in India. The Indians said, "Well, we have various insects and natural forces that would destroy the kind of insulation you are using." And the Americans replied, "Oh, no, we've got the best insulation." So they used it, and sure enough, what with the Indian environment and its particular animal life, they found that the insulation failed to work. In other cases, we exported labor-saving technology to areas in which there was an abundance of cheap labor. The local population would point out that they needed a technology that would allow large-scale employment, even though it might not be as "efficient." So Americans in time readjusted and began to recommend more labor-intensive technology. What I'm saying is that technology is culturally shaped. When you move technology from one culture to another, the technology must be adjusted to fit the new culture.

I use the concept of style to cover the subject that I'm now discussing. Various cultures exhibit various technological styles. A case in point is the small European automobile of the 1950s, a time when Americans were still driving large cars. The small automobile suited the European culture, in which there was a horsepower tax – the consumer was charged according to the size of the car's engine. Therefore, it made sense for Europeans to drive a small car with a small engine. Americans didn't have such a tax, and gas was inexpensive, while for Europeans gasoline was expensive. For Americans to impose large automobiles on Europeans in the 1950s would have been imperialistic. To have imposed the small European automobile on the Americans would have been inappropriate.

In Networks of Power you show that electric-power networks, which should have spread like wildfire in Victorian England, actually encountered great resistance. That to me was one of the most startling aspects of your book.

One reason large-scale electric light and power systems did not initially spread into England was that the British highly value their local governments. Patchwork local governments and large, integrated technological systems do not suit one another well. For many years the British protected their local governments by rejecting large, interregional technological systems. So there you have a nice example of a culture defending itself against change brought on by the imposition of a technology that is not harmonious with preexisting values.

From "We Get the Technology We Deserve", An Interview with Thomas P. Hughes by Hal Bowser, *American Heritage* October/November 1985, pp. 66–67.

## Suggested answers (Listening for the gist)

1. a) Technology is "culturally shaped".
b) If a technology is to be transferred to/imposed on another country, it must fit into that culture and fulfill its needs.

2. Examples:
– Insulation to be used on electrical lines in India;
– the introduction of labor-saving technologies into areas of abundant cheap labor;
– small cars in Europe, large cars in the U.S.;
– electric power systems in Victorian England.

3. They didn't catch on because the British valued their local government systems, and large-scale power systems did not fit in.

## Listening for detail

*1. Complete the following sentences (you may use Hughes' words):*
– Technologies that are transferred from one country to another must ... (cf. ll. 19-23)
– A certain kind of insulation couldn't be used on electrical lines in India, because ... (cf. ll. 25-28)
– The export of labor-saving technologies is often inappropriate, because ... (cf. ll. 35-38)
– Imposing large American cars on Europe in the 1950s would have been inappropriate, because ... (cf. ll. 56-58)
– Large-scale electric power systems didn't spread quickly in Victorian England, because ... (cf. ll. 66-71)

*2. Are all his examples equally good?*
The "cars" example seems to suggest that the conditions mentioned were God-given, natural, or culturally ingrained. This is certainly not the case for cheap fuel/low taxes in the U.S. And far from it being "inappropriate" to "impose" small cars on the Americans, the introduction of smaller cars there has proved both necessary and successful. So this is a weak example by comparison with the others, which have to do with natural and social conditions it is either impossible or undesirable to change.

# 5. The Secret of the Machines

## Background information

Kipling's poem "The Secret of the Machines" was first published in 1911. It was one of the poems he wrote for inclusion in C.R.L. Fletcher's *A History of England*. By that time Kipling had already reached the height of fame, for works such as the story collection *Life's Handicap* (1891), the two *Jungle Books* (1894, 1895), the verse collection *The Seven Seas* (1896), the novel in praise of India, *Kim* (1901), and his children's book *Just So Stories* (1902). He had come to be regarded as the Bard of Empire, praising the empire-builders, the pioneers and technocrats as the leading spirits of their age, and extolling the virtues of self-reliance and undemanding service. The poem "The Secret of the Machines" belongs to a period of increasing maturity in his writing. It both expresses and subtly questions the optimism of his age.

Kiplings reputation as the Bard of Empire provides a connection to Chapter 1.

Lines 19–20: This is already a reference to the Cunard liner *Mauretania* (l. 22), which, with 70,000 horsepower distributed between four screws (propellers), was the largest and strongest ship yet built.

## Methodisch-didaktischer Hinweis

Bei Präsentation des Gedichts ohne Hinführung zunächst Fragen 1 und 2 vorgeben, dann das Gedicht zeilenweise darbieten (evtl. über OH-Folie) bis etwa Zeile 12 und Antwort zu Frage 1 finden lassen. Die Antwort zu Frage 2 bis zuletzt offen lassen, um den Schülern genügend Raum zur Diskussion zu geben.

## Suggested answers

1. The machines are speaking to the humans.

2. (Eine reizvolle Aufgabe, die sich mit einem Bibliotheksgang des ganzen Kurses verbinden läßt.)
Some clues from the poem:
- "we can fly and dive (l. 11): aviation, submarines (c. 1900)
- "Would you call a friend ..." (ll. 13–16). telephone, telegraphy, transatlantic cables (late 19th c.)
- "Mauretania" (l. 22): a ship of the Cunard line, built 1907
- no mention of World War I (1914)
- no mention of the Titanic (1912)
All this suggests it was written between 1907 and 1912. The poem was actually written in 1911.

3. At least two alternatives: a) Lines 1–36: enthusiastic depiction of the power of modern machines
37–44: warning of not to become arrogant
45–48: prophecy
b) Lines 1–12: statement of machines' potential
13–36: invitation to use their potential
37–48: warning not to be too arrogant

4. He is deeply impressed, full of awe and respect of the power of modern machines, but also deeply concerned about the dangers. The optimistic view of the future expressed in the last four lines could refer to the overcoming of all problems concerning machines – or their final disappearance, with the human race that created them.

5. (Da es den Schülern gewöhnlich schwerfällt, geeignete Attribute zu finden, bietet es sich an, ihnen eine Liste von möglichen Adjektiven vorzulegen und die zutreffenden gemeinsam erarbeiten zu lassen.)
The tone is serious at the beginning of the poem (ll. 1–8) and again at the end (ll. 37–48), where it could even be described as earnest or grave. In between, the tone is enthusiastic – with a possible touch of irony.

6. They help to express/emphasize enthusiasm for the potential of modern machinery.
- The vocabulary produces kind of an imitation of the sound of machines working, it brings their performance to life; an onomatopoeic effect is achieved (e.g. "wrought and hammered", "cut and filed", "crackling questions".
- The syntax in the first two lines creates a rhythmic pattern that reminds us of the working rhythm of machines. Here it is more like: - - + - - - + - - - + than the more conventional iambic metre reverted to later: (-) - + - + - + - + - +, etc. The "machine-like" variation of the iambic metre keeps recurring throughout the poem: e.g. ll. 17–18, l. 33, 36.
- The rhythmic enumerations (ll. 9–12) suggest the seemingly endless possibilities of the machines' performance.

– The regular rhyme scheme (ababcdcd...) underlines the rhythmical pattern, and this helps to stress dynamic aspects of the technological achievements described.

The use of imagery (personification of the machines; metaphors like "the question hurled across the arch of heaven", "the monstrous nine-decked city", "the iron-shouldered rocks", "the never failing cisterns of the snow"; symbols like "seventy thousand horses and some screws") clearly shows the speakers feelings of admiration and wonder.

### Additional questions

1. Find the rhetorical questions. What do they express?

2. Which machines can perform the activities listed in ll. 9–12?

3. What kinds of machinery impress you most? Say why. Have you any particular concerns?

### Post-reading activities

1. Try to write a poem of your own on the same or a similar subject. It needn't be longer than 8 or 10 lines.

2. Theme for classroom report: The age of the great ocean liners.
Or: From the Mauretania to the Titanic – a lesson for mankind? (See Richard Musman, *Titanic*, Klettbuch 5424.)

## 6. True Love (GK)

### Background information

Isaac Asimov died in 1992.
The basic capabilities of the computers that are on the market today are summed up in the following extract from an article by Thomas Levenson in *The Atlantic* (March 1990): "Computers in general are now omnipresent, and indispensable, because they can perform their arithmetic on anything, as long as the symbols the computer is asked to work with obey the strict rules of logic. Thus a computer can manipulate an alphabet for word processing, and shapes for graphics, and so on. It does so by following a list of instructions, a program, that can be whatever the user chooses – as long, again, as the rules of logic are obeyed. This means that any problem that can be stated rigorously can be studied with a computer, from the weather to financial markets, from baseball statistics (which don't require a very sophisticated computer) to quantum physics (which does).

However, the need to work within the strict rules of logic has proved to be a serious limitation on the use of computers in spheres previously thought promising – e.g. understanding or translating human language. One option is to concentrate on applications which exploit the machines' superior memory and logical skills, leaving those calling for intuitive common sense to humans. The other is further research in the area of 'Artificial Intelligence' (AI), in the hope of developing programs that will be closer approximations to the way humans actually think". A useful summary of the state of the art at the time of publication is given in *The Economist* (March 14, 1992) under the heading "Artificial Intelligence: Cogito, ergo something". Since research is progressing rapidly, it would be advisable to also consult more recent publications (especially computer magazines) on the subject.

### Methodisch-didaktische Hinweise

Selbstverständlich bietet es sich an, vor der Kurzgeschichte eine mehrstündige Unterrichtssequenz zum Thema Computer durchzuführen. Hierzu sei auf das Heft Special Perspectives: *Science and Technology in Modern Society* hingewiesen, insbesondere auf Kapitel I "Computers yesterday and today" und Kapitel II "The use and abuse of computers" (Klett 1990, Nr. 51382). Will man sich auf nur 1–2 Texte beschränken, so empfiehlt sich das Gedicht "Ten Good Reasons Why Computers Can ..."

### Pre-reading activities

1. Discuss what computers can do and can't do. Are there limits? Consider the following: calculate/draw logical conclusion from given facts/make decisions/guess/learn by trial and error/be conscious/have feelings.

2. Computers can be misused. What are the most common forms of computer abuse? What's your opinion about computer crime?

## Suggested answers

1. Place: a computer centre in an English-speaking country (l. 54), probably the U.S.A. (l. 168)
Time: any time in the future
Social circumstances: There seems to be something like a world government; data on all human beings are centrally controlled.

2. The story deals with computer technology as it might develop within the next century. The author clearly projects both the possibilities of today's computer technology and the problems of data control and misuse into the future. His extrapolation is optimistic with regard to the purely technological aspects, but pessimistic in warning us of a development when machines become smarter than their human masters.

3. The first-person narrator is Milton Davidson's computer; to a certain degree, especially at the end of the story, it is also Milton himself, because the computer's intelligence, his way of speaking and thinking as well as his emotions are the creation of Milton Davidson. The most unusual thing about it is that it credits a computer with consciousness.

4. Compare the following passages from the story:
– ll. 61–63 "Milton had arranged me to do things I wasn't designed to do."
– ll. 77–79 "... manipulation. I could do it now because Milton had arranged it. I wasn't supposed to do it for anyone but him, though."
– ll. 114–115 "another thing that is against my original instructions."
– ll. 148–149 "We always agreed; we thought so like each other."
– ll. 159–164 "Talking to you, Joe, is like ... the woman we choose."
– ll. 173–176 "Milton had coordinated .. It fit me."

5. What do looks matter? The computer is in for a surprise if he thinks his own looks won't matter to the girl! From the point of view of the programmer (Davidson), it may be seen as a case of computer error (programming error); but from the point of view of the computer it is no error, but a new form of computer crime.

6. –

### Additional question

*In what way is this computer more advanced than most present-day computers? What extra abilities must it have to be able to do what it did – and to tell the tale?*

### Post-reading activities

*1. Theme for classroom report: Artificial Intelligence – achievements and failures.*
See background information; also bibliography 1, 3, 15.
*2. Choose some lines/passages from "The Secret of the Machines" (p. 140) or "True Love" that might serve as alternative captions for the two cartoons on page 144. Give reasons for your choice.*

### Cartoons, p. 144

Both cartoons have to do with our fear that the machines we make to serve us may become our masters. This danger is touched on in the final two stanzas of Kipling's poem, and is the central theme of the Asimov story.
The cartoon on the left is more modern. It suggests that some employees on the job have already become machines, and that this is a necessary consequence of working with them.
The one on the right presents a rather old-fashioned view of the robot (who here stands for "Technology" in general). In fact, he looks a bit like Frankenstein's monster – probably a deliberate evocation of Mary Shelley's novel (and the films based on it), since the cartoon's message is much the same.

## 7. Tomorrow "rabbit" will have no meaning

### Pre-reading questions

*1. The novel Frankenstein by Mary Wollstonecraft-Shelley (1818) is one of the most famous literary works dealing with the responsibilities of scientists. What do you know about the novel (or any film version)? Report to your class.* (The question can be made to link with the second cartoon on p. 144.)

*2. What fields of science and technology were used by the fictional Dr Frankenstein? What more promising fields would be open to him today?*

## Methodisch-didaktischer Hinweis

Auf Grund des recht sachlichen Charakters des Textes und des nur mäßigen Schwierigkeitsgrades ist die häusliche Vorbereitung und Erschließung sinnvoll.

## Suggested answers

1. Genetic engineering:
– is a way to create new life (l. 2)
– is a new method of domination (ll. 5–6)
– genetically alters plants/animals (ll. 53)
– can make blends between unrelated species (ll. 33–34, 125)
Genes are:
– inserted in other animals (ll. 40–41)
– transferred to ... (l. 27)
– passed on from ... to ... (l. 43)
Pieces of DNA are cut out of two unrelated organisms and knit together (ll. 21–22)
Genetic engineering promises:
– "improved" crops. (ll. 11, 80)
– cures for new and old ailments (l. 11)
– a way to survive in almost any environment (l. 15)
– a way to continue our way of life, our economic growth (l. 10)
Compare the definition from COBUILD:
"Genetic engineering is the science of changing the genetic structure of a living organism in order to make it stronger or more suitable for a particular purpose."

2. By the term "the second end of nature" the author means that all forms of life could be genetically changed to a degree that traditional forms of life would no longer exist, that nature as we know it would be turned into some kind of artificial world. Nature would not be destroyed physically, it would be altered genetically.

3. See ll. 120–130 and 150–157.
The author's main concern is to make us aware of the difference between traditional practices of manipulating life forms (like selective breeding) and the new methods of genetic engineering. He tries to warn us of the dangers that lie in man's struggle to dominate the world. He wants to make us aware of the fact that "nature ... cannot coexist with our numbers and our habits" (i.e. with an overpopulated world), that we are going to create "an artificial world – a space station" if we don't "change our habits".

4. ll. 1–81: General remarks on genetic engineering and factual information about what genetic engineering is and about its development; a critical undertone by putting the word "improved" (l. 80) in inverted commas.
ll. 82–102: realistic speculations about some future developments.
ll. 103–157: indirect warning through some extreme speculations; direct warning of the dangers of this new technology (119–157).

5. Positive aspects:
– It can alter all living substances and give them a particular (desirable) quality;
– it can produce artificial living substances, i.e. new kinds of food;
– it can realize new kinds of medical treatment and cure.
Negative aspects:
– It can wipe out/change the traditional genetic plans of life;
– the whole range of side-effects can't be foreseen;
– it can get out of control;
– there is a wide range of misuse;
– the genetic manipulations of man raises numerous moral and ethical questions.
A more detailed list of arguments can be found in *Words in Context* (Klettbuch 51962), page 144.

## Additional questions

*1. The text contains numerous sentences in the passive. Find them and explain the use of the passive voice.*

*2. Quite few active sentences can be transferred into the passive voice. Find some examples where this procedure might make sense (i.e. find examples where the active voice subject seems to be of less importance to you.)*

## Post-reading activities

*1. Write an essay about the responsibilities of scientists. Choose a suitable title.*

*2. Translate a short German text passage on genetic engineering (for example from your biology book) into English.*

*3. Themes for classroom reports:*
*– The discovery of the "double helix".*
  See Bibliography: 14.
*– Any science fiction novel, short story or film dealing with the problems of genetic engineering.*

*Science, Technology and the Environment*

# 8. Exhaust the subject (GK)

**Methodisch-didaktischer Hinweis**

Der Einstieg könnte über die Analyse eines "green advertisements" der Automobil- oder der chemischen Industrie geschehen – z. B. die auf Seite 148.

**Pre-reading activities**

*1. First impressions:*
– *What strikes you first about this ad?*
– *What do you think is being advertised?*
– *What do you already know about the advertiser (Du Pont)?*
– *What does the picture convey?*
– *How effective are the slogans?*

*2. Read the text and sum up its message.*

*3. Discuss Du Pont's advertising strategy: What do they hope to achieve? Do you think their strategy is effective? Is it fair?*

*4. What other industries might need to improve their image in a similar way?*

**Suggested answers**

1. The pun is based on the ambiguity (double meaning) of the word "exhaust". The phrase "to exhaust a subject" means "to discuss a subject thoroughly". The second meaning of the word gives the topic that is being discussed (exhausted), i.e. the exhaust fumes escaping from a car.

2. Cars are amongst the worst polluters we know, a fact that has created a social climate increasingly hostile to cars. The car industry's problem is how to improve their bad image. The only real way to reduce pollution would be to reduce the number, size, performance, use of cars, which would be extremely damaging for the car industry.

3. They started to promote technical innovations like lead-free operation, lean burn and catalysis as environmental benefits. Thus they have managed to persuade people that driving their cars is not only less harmful to our environment but that it actively helps to protect it. Besides, these "green" technologies are promoted as new status symbols.

4. The car industry's strategy of distorting people's perception of things, and blurring the real problem, was very successful. It's a classic example of shaping and manipulating public opinion.

5. The most obvious points are:
– design/build smaller cars, esp. for city traffic;
– build electric cars;
– reduce the energy consumption to a technically feasible minimum;
– develop new kinds of fuel and engines;
– build/promote less powerful cars;
– abandon all forms of aggressive advertising, i.e. advertising cars as symbols of sportsmanship, social status, manliness, superiority, freedom;
– provide reliable information to customers on the exhaust levels of their various models.

**Additional questions**

*1. Analyse all the ing-forms of the verbs in the text. Group them as to whether they are gerunds, participles or progressive forms.*

*2. Translate the last paragraph.*
Die europäischen Grenzwertbestimmungen der 90er Jahre werden zur Folge haben, daß Katalysatoren langfristig wohl zur Normalausstattung gehören werden. Zur Zeit jedoch werden sie noch als statusfördernde Extras, wie z. B. die elektronische Bezineinspritzung, angeboten, was den Wert einer Ausstattungsvariante soweit erhöht, daß sie die Aufschrift /den Schriftzug/ "Kat" auf dem Kofferraumdeckel verdient, unmittelbar neben "GTI" oder "deluxe".

**Post-reading activities**

*1. What, in your opinion, should the government do to control or influence the motor industry?*

*2. Report on any of the environmental organizations or influential books mentioned in the fact file (page 296).*
See Bibliography 1, 6, 12.

*3. Collect car advertisements from English-language newspapers and magazines, and examine them in the same way as you did on page 148.*

# Test: The promise of gene therapy

She weighed around 16 kg, came down with an occasional cold or ear infection, and appeared to be a healthy four-year-old. But a dark cloud hung over her future. She suffered from ADA deficiency, the rare, incurable and deadly genetic disease that shuts down the immune system. [...] Last week, on the 10th floor of the massive Clinical Center of the U.S. National Institutes of Health (NIH) in Bethesda, Md., the still unidentified child assumed a historic role. In the first federally approved use of gene therapy, a team of doctors introduced into her bloodstream some 1 billion cells, each containing a copy of a foreign gene. If all goes well, these cells will begin producing ADA, the essential enzyme she requires, and her devastated immune system will slowly begin to recover.

The procedure lacked the drama of an epochal event. For 28 minutes, a grayish liquid in a suspended plastic bag dripped intravenously into the left hand of the child, who sat upright in a bed in the Clinical Center's pediatric intensive-care unit. That was it. But if the technique works as the doctors hope it will, the results could be little short of miraculous. Their patient may eventually begin to lead a normal life, without need for the costly and only partly effective drug now used to extend the lives of young victims of the disease. [...]

After all the controversy that has long surrounded genetic engineering and gene therapy, reaction to last week's pioneering effort has been generally favorable. Abbey Meyers, executive director of the U.S. National Organization for Rare Disorders, was ecstatic, noting that people with the genetic diseases have been waiting nearly 15 years for the first round of gene therapy experiments. "If we could find a cure for a disease with a genetic component such as diabetes," she says, "that would probably be the most important medical advance of the century, if not of all time."

Arthur Caplan, director of the Center for Biomedical Ethics at the University of Minnesota, who has kept a close eye on genetic advances over the years, is convinced that any ethical concerns "have been adequately met. The risks are similar to those involved when you are trying any innovative, invasive procedure. I don't think there's anything special about it because it's genetic."

Still, the gene therapy currently being practised affects only the patients. Opposition is bound to swell again if scientists turn toward a goal that is still far off: the genetic engineering of sperm and egg cells. Such Brave New World-style manipulations would affect the genetic endowment of future generations, raise new ethical issues and pose unknown risks.

For now, however, the promise of gene therapy appears to outweigh any potential pitfalls.

FUTURE TARGETS?
*Hemophilia*
Affecting only males, hemophilia results from a genetic mutation that impairs the production of one or more factors involved in blood clotting. Hemophiliacs can inject themselves with concentrated preparations of clotting factor at the first signs of bleeding, but taking doses of cells containing normal clotting-factor genes could be an easier way of controlling the disease.

*Diabetes*
Patients are incapable of producing sufficient amounts of insulin, the hormone responsible for regulating glucose levels in the blood. Thought to be at least partially hereditary, the disease arises when insulin-secreting cells in the pancreas mysteriously begin to die. Although daily injections of insulin or, in some cases, a strict diet can control diabetes, it may be possible to treat the disease by replacing the genes involved in insulin production.

*Time*, September 24, 1990. Copyright 1990 The Time Inc. Magazine Company. Reprinted by permission.

**Annotations:**

38 **diabetes** Zuckerkrankheit
53 **Brave New World** A famous science fiction novel by Aldous Huxley (1932) about the use of scientific methods like artificial insemination to create a totalitarian state.
60 **hemophilia** Bluterkrankheit
74 **pancreas** Bauchspeicheldrüse

**I. Language**

1. Find suitable substitutes for the following words, as used in the context:
epochal (l. 18); to extend (l. 27); component (l. 38); adequately (l. 45); goal (l. 51); pitfalls (l. 59).

2. Paraphrase the following two sentences:
- "The procedure ... event." (ll. 18-19)
- "... the results ... miraculous." (ll. 24-25).

3. Sum up the main advantages of gene therapy when applied to patients suffering from ADA deficiency, hemophilia and diabetes.

## II. Comprehension

1. Why is the treatment of the four-year-old girl called an "epochal event"?

2. Describe the controversy over gene therapy.

## III. Comment

"I don't think there's anything special about it because it's genetic" (ll. 47-48). Do you agree? Explain why.

# Bibliography

1. Asimov, Isaac. *Asimov's New Guide to Science*. Irvine, California 1972; Penguin edition available.
2. Carson, Rachel. *Silent Spring*. Boston: Riverside Press 1962; Penguin edition available.
3. Chandor, Anthony. *Dictionary of Computers*, Harmondsworth: Penguin 1981.
4. Hardy, John. *Science, Technology and the Environment*. New York: Holt, Rinehart & Winston 1975.
5. *Information Please Almanac* (pp. 529–577). Boston: Houghton Mifflin 1992; Klettbuch 516152.
6. Meadows, Denis and Donella et al. *The Limits to Growth*. New York: Universe Books 1972.
7. – *Beyond the Limits: Confronting Global Collapse, Envisioning a Sustainable Future*. Post Mills, Vermont: Chelsea Green Publishing Company 1992.
8. Parsell, Carrol W., Jr. (ed). *Technology in America: A History of Individuals and Ideas*. Cambridge, Mass. 1981.
9. Spann, Ekkehard. *Abiturwissen Landeskunde Great Britain/U.S.A.* (Chs. 3 and 5). Stuttgart, Klett 1990; Klettbuch 929509.
10. Special Perspectives: *Science and Technology in Modern Society*. Stuttgart: Klett 1990; Klettbuch 51382.
11. Topical Texts 24: *Civilization at the Crossroads*. Klettbuch 50863.
12. Schumacher, E. F. *Small is Beautiful*. London: Bond and Briggs 1973; Penguin edition available.
13. Uvarov, E. B. *Dictionary of Science*. Harmondsworth: Penguin 1960.
14. Watson, James D. *The Double Helix. A Personal Account of the Discovery of the Structure of DNA*. New York: Atheneum 1968; Penguin edition available.
15. Weizenbaum, Joseph. *Computer Power and Human Reasoning*. San Francisco: W. H. Freeman 1976; Penguin edition available.

# 7 Religious Life

## Structure of the chapter

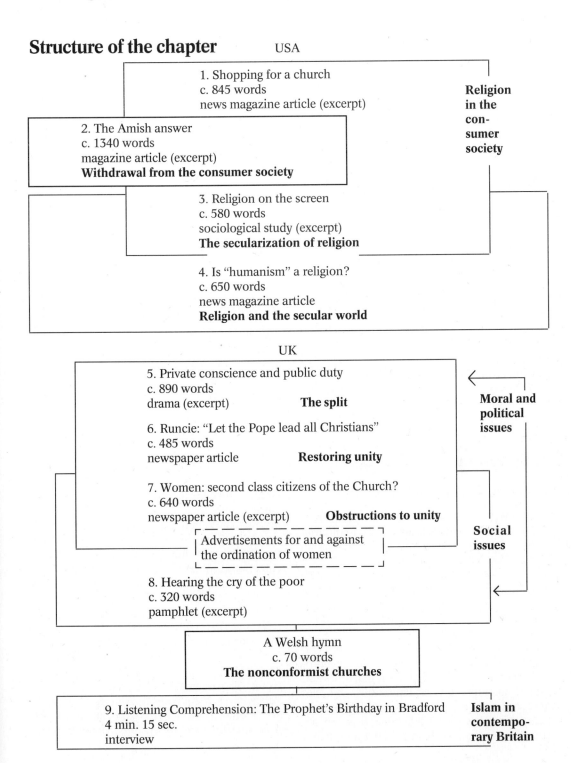

Religious Life 155

## Suggestions for reports/papers/talks

Religious diversity in the USA – after text 1

Religious customs among African-Americans – after text 2 (or elsewhere)

Essay: Television as the "opiate of the people" and its effects when combined with religion – after text 3

The wall of separation: church and state in the USA – before text 4

Book report: Neil Postman, *Amusing Ourselves to Death* – after text 4

One Supreme Court decision regarding the freedom of religion – after text 4

Comparison of the Reformation in England and in Germany – after text 5

The origins and development of the Church of England – after text 5

The introduction of Christianity to Anglo-Saxon England – after text 6

Time line: the spread of Christianity in Britain – after text 6

Personal comment on one of following:
a) "Our church is crying out for a woman's touch."
b) Would you take communion from a woman?
c) "The ordination of women priests would violate the intentions of God, who has given different roles to men and women."
– after text 7

Interview with advocate and opponent of women's ordination – after text 7

a) The free (Nonconformist) churches in Great Britain
or b) The Kirk of Scotland – after Welsh hymn

Letter to the Editor concerning cuts in public spending on a housing project – after text 8

The Welsh Methodist Revival of the eighteenth century and its place in Welsh society – before or after Welsh hymn

Comparison of Christian and Muslim religious practice – after text 9 (Listening Comprehension)

## Vocabulary

*Thematischer Grund- und Aufbauwortschatz, Englisch,* Klettbuch 51955, pp. 147–151

*Words in Context,* Klettbuch 51961, pp. 84–91

# 1. Shopping for a church

### Background information

Using the language of consumerism and a racy journalistic style, the author paints a colourful picture of the church landscape and church growth in the USA. According to a recent survey, over 80% of US-Americans claim to be affiliated with a major Christian denomination (Roman Catholic or a form of Protestant), the main Protestant denominations being Baptist, Methodist and Lutheran. The most successful congregations are those which fit in with the lifestyle of their members, utilizing advanced media technology, providing car parks, childcare, sporting facilities and other community services. Financially, churches are dependent on the contributions of their members. This fundamental difference between the structure of religious life in the USA and that of Germany (where members of the major churches automatically pay tax to support the church) means that churches in the US are market-oriented. They are characterized by the mobility of their members, who may move from church to church and to other non-Christian religious groups, of which there are also a large number in the USA (see ll. 33–36 of the text). For a survey of the range of Christian and non-Christian groups in the USA, see *The 1992 Information Please Almanac,* Boston: Houghton Mifflin Co. (Klettbuch 516152), 1992, pp. 392–393. The fact file (SB p. 299) contains a simplified breakdown of the main groups in percentages. See also Chapter 2 of Perspectives 7: *Religion in America and Britain,* Klettbuch 51367, especially pp. 18–19, and *American Life and Institutions,* Klettbuch 5136, pp. 22–24.

## Methodisch-didaktische Hinweise

Die Behandlung des Themas "Religiöses Leben" im Englischunterricht der gymnasialen Oberstufe stellt eine schwierige, aber auch reizvolle Aufgabe dar. Zum einen stellt sich das Problem der Stoffauswahl, da es nahezu unmöglich ist, in dem begrenzten Zeitraum einer Unterrichtseinheit ein ausgewogenes Bild der vielfältigen Landschaft des religiösen Lebens in den USA und in Großbritannien zu geben. Hier ist die Lehrkraft daher in besonderem Maße gefordert, im Unterricht den gezwungenermaßen ausschnitthaften Charakter der vorliegenden Textauswahl wiederholt deutlich zu machen und gegebenenfalls durch aktuelle Beispiele zu ergänzen.

Besonders ist darauf zu achten, daß keine bereits vorhandenen Vorurteile bestätigt oder neue gebildet werden.

Zum anderen besteht die Herausforderung, deutsche Schüler, die einer Behandlung des Themas Religion häufig zurückhaltend gegenüberstehen, dazu zu motivieren, sich offen und unvoreingenommen mit den Erscheinungsformen des religiösen Lebens auseinanderzusetzen, die vor allem in den USA, wo Religion einen völlig anderen Stellenwert einnimmt, die Gesellschaft prägen. Daher wurde bewußt das Mittel des Kontrasts als Einführung in dieses Kapitel gewählt: unmittelbare Konfrontation mit einem ungewohnten Ausschnitt aus dem religiösen Leben, einer völlig neuen Sehensweise von der Rolle, die Religion im Leben spielen kann.

Um die Wirkung dieses Kontrasts nicht zu beeinträchtigen, sollte auf eine allgemeine Einführung zum Thema Religion (historisch o.ä.) durch die Lehrkraft verzichtet werden. Vielmehr sollten sich die Schüler ihre persönlichen Vorstellungen und Erwartungen von Religion bewußt machen und dann direkt mit der Präsentation des Textes konfrontiert werden. In einer darauffolgenden Diskussion könnte anhand des Textes "Two archetypes in US foreign policy" (Schülerbuch S. 264–265) auf die Rolle von Religion in der Geschichte der USA eingegangen werden.

## Pre-reading activities

*1. What do you see as being the function of religion? Discuss.*

*2. Look at the picture on p. 149 (SB) and answer the questions below it.*

## Suggested answers

1. A time when religious beliefs are chosen and mixed according to one's personal needs and taste ("They don't convert – they choose", l. 66).

2. The desire to impart values to one's children and find other children with the same values as playmates; experiences in the counter-culture; the search for meaning and for answers to life's questions.

3. By adopting market strategies, adapting to needs of "consumers"; advertising, running the churches like businesses; setting up one-stop church complexes like shopping malls.

4. Church depicted as a shopping centre; "the customer is king" (ll. 13–14); "if ... church ... is to attract its share of the baby-boom market" (ll. 15–17); "inspect congregations as if they were restaurants and leave if they find nothing to their taste" (ll. 61–62); "businesslike approach for clergy" (l. 72); "polling, marketing, and advertising" (ll. 76–77); "that most resemble a suburban shopping mall" (ll. 91–92).

5. A large church complex offering all kinds of services and activities in order to meet both the spiritual and the physical needs of its members. The idea behind this concept is to make people come to this centre and above all to make them stay there, because all their needs can be met at this one place.

## Additional questions

*1. Find antonyms for the following words:*
l. 4: *rare* common
l. 12: *loyalty* disloyalty, betrayal
l. 71: *advocating* opposing, rejecting, deprecating
l. 99: *sacred* profane, secular

*2. Which tenses are used in ll. 42–54? Explain why each is used.*

## Post-reading activities

*1. Discuss the needs, spiritual and physical, you would like to be met by a church and design a "megachurch".*

*2. Write a paper or give a talk on the following topic:*
*Religious diversity in the USA: a survey.*
See Bibliography 3, 5, 6, 9, 10, 13, 22.

3. Compare the last sentence of the text with the following statement:
"(India is) an intensely religious society, a country where religion is not reserved for one place or one day of the week but is everywhere, at all times, a way of life, dictating the way we eat, the way we dress, the way we bathe and marry and bring up our children, speak and live." (from: Anita Desai, "A secret connivance", Times Literary Supplement, September 14–20, 1990; quoted in the listening comprehension on pp. 47–48 of the SB). Keep this statement in mind – not forgetting the cultural differences, however – when you read Text 2, "The Amish answer".

## 2. The Amish answer (GK)

### Background information

History: The first Amish people, followers of Jacob Amman, the Anabaptist from Alsace, came to America in the early 1700s to take part in William Penn's "Holy Experiment" of religious freedom.

In 1525, after the Reformation, students of the Swiss Protestant pastor Ulrich Zwingli became impatient with the slow pace of the Protestant Reformation and founded their own movement. Because they believed infants were incapable of making a conscious decision to accept God, they decided that only adults should be baptized. So adult baptism became the public symbol of their movement, and they were called Anabaptists ("rebaptizers"), because they had already been baptized as infants in the Catholic Church.

Eventually, the different Anabaptist groups joined under the Dutch priest Menno Simons and became known as Mennonites. In the late 1600s Amman, also a Dutch Mennonite, decided to form his own group.

The differences between the seven Amish, twenty-one Mennonite and nine Brethren groups in the USA are based on their interpretations of the Bible.

Worship: Amish worship services are held every second Sunday in a different home of the Amish community. As there are thirty families in one community, every family has to host a worship service once a year. The service is held in High German.

Schooling: Early in this century Amish children went to public schools, but many now attend the church-founded and church-operated schools that very much resemble the old one-room schoolhouses. Apart from English and German they are taught reading, writing, arithmetic, geography, history, and music. Some schools teach agriculture instead of history, others even science and art. Since the most important thing for an Amish child to learn is how to run a home and farm, Amish children do not go to high school after having completed eight grades. For background on a Supreme Court ruling concerning Amish attendance of high school see Perspectives 3: *The Supreme Court*, Klettbuch 51363, pp. 33–35.

Clothing: The clothing of the Amish today is similar to that of their ancestors in the 17th century. It is not only the most obvious sign of Amish lifestyle but also symbolizes the role one has in Amish society. There are, for example, different styles of hats denoting different ages, status in the community and the group of Amish a man belongs to. Outer garments are fastened with hooks, since buttons might be considered decoration, a forbidden feature for Amish clothing. Once an Amish man is married he must grow a beard, a custom that was practised upon baptism in former times.

Courting and marriage: When a young man is sixteen, he is given an open buggy which he can use for courting. This is a secretive affair among the Amish, so a young man often visits his girlfriend late at night after the girl's parents have gone to bed. Weddings are the most important Amish celebrations, and they are traditionally held on a Tuesday or Thursday in November. A newly married Amish couple have no honeymoon but spend several weeks visiting relatives before finally settling down in their own home.

### Pre-reading activities

1. Collect information on the Amish and pool it in class. Does the type of information vary according to the source?

*2. Can you think of a group of people in your country who live together as a community with a unified lifestyle and ideology? Give a talk on such a group, noting especially their attitudes towards technology, dress and social customs (e.g. various kinds of religious orders, both Christian and other).*
Teacher's note: The talk could be a post-reading activity, but the question should be discussed in advance.

**Suggested answers**

1. –

2. Dress; rejection of most modern conveniences and technology, community life, worship.

3. They refused to baptize infants, maintaining that baptism should accompany a conscious decision to accept God, which only an adult can make.

4. Submission to "God's will"; rejection of "worldliness" because it prevents closeness to God; abandonment of self in deference to the collective order ("Ordnung").

5. Apparent inconsistencies: not driving cars (ll. 6–7) but being able to hire a car and driver in emergencies (ll. 29–30, 84–85); rejecting electricity (l. 7) but using engines driven by other forms of power (ll. 15–20), in order to avoid contact with unbelievers over power lines and resist consumer culture (ll. 91–94); no personal telephones (ll. 7–8) but a shared phone for business (ll. 78–84); tractors used for stationary power but not field work, with two different kinds of tyres, so as to keep the farm small (ll. 95–102) and the tractor unsuitable for transport: practices differ from family to family due to differing congregations (ll. 104–106). Reluctance to forfeit identity and principles, but some compromises necessary for economic and social survival.

6. The Amish know how to handle technology selectively, making use of it without letting it take over their lives. In mainstream society, new inventions are used without a thought as to their effects.

**Additional questions**

*Characterize the style of ll. 6–11 and say why such a style might be used here.*
Very simple style: simple sentences, always "They" as subject; one fact per sentence (or an incomplete sentence, ll. 8–9). Repetition lends emphasis; "They" singles out the group being described, at the same time suggesting anonymity (parallel to lack of individual expression in the community?). The shortness of the sentences and the repeated negatives reflect the austerity of Amish life.

**Post-reading activities**

*1. Compare Amish agriculture with attitudes expressed in the texts "Technological innovation" (SB pp. 136–137) and "Bonanza farming" (SB pp. 243–245). Look particularly at the point of view of each text. Try to sum up your findings in two or three sentences.*

*2. Compare the attitude to community outlined in ll. 60–77 with the values underlying the text of the advertisement on p. 169.*

*3. a) Find out what you can about religious customs of Protestant African-Americans (e.g. the role of music in worship). Prepare a talk or paper.*
See excerpt from Maya Angelou, *I Know Why The Caged Bird Sings*, in Perspectives 7: *Religion in America and Britain*, Klettbuch 51367, pp. 24–27, and the teacher's book pp. 33–37. See also pp. 13–14 of Perspectives 7 ("Slave Religion") and pp. 19–21 of the accompanying teacher's book (Bibliography 7, 11, 13).

*b) Imagine you are a member of an African-American congregation in the southern United States. You are now visiting Germany for the first time on a scholarship to study here and have just attended a church service. Write a personal account of your experiences – what surprised you, what shocked you, what you liked and disliked – in a letter to a friend in the USA.*

# 3. Religion on the screen (GK)

## Background information

The so-called "Electronic Church" – an evangelical movement via religious radio and TV programmes - has gained enormous impact in the USA over the past two decades.

There are about 250 local TV stations and more than 1000 radio stations with predominantly religious programmes that attract some 80 million viewers and listeners. The roots of this evangelical ardour go back as far as the religious Great Awakenings of the 1730s and 1800s. The enormous growth of the Electronic Church over the last few years has been due to the fact that its programmes meet the spiritual and emotional needs of millions of viewers and listeners.

Religious broadcasting, however, is also big business. According to estimates, "the gospel broadcasters' total receipts probably approach $2 billion a year" (*Time*, April 6, 1987).

*Oral Roberts*, now in his seventies, began as an itinerant revivalist preacher and later set up a TV-based healing ministry supported by donations. He established a university and medical centre. Roberts is notorious for his outlandish fundraising schemes.

Pentecostal preacher-performer *Jimmy Swaggart* set up a 270-acre complex in Louisiana with a bible college, printing and media centre, television production centre and recording studios. In the late eighties Swaggart was involved in scandals that largely cost him his reputation.

*Robert Schuller*, now in his mid-sixties, built the huge "Crystal Palace" in California as a setting for his weekly show, "Hour of Power". Schuller is linked to the mainline Reformed Church in America.

*Jerry Falwell* is the founder of "Moral Majority" (now "Liberty Federation"), a fundamentalist organization propagating conservative moral and political views. Falwell owns a broadcasting network and has set up a fundamentalist college. He is known for his TV sermons on 350 TV stations.

"Heritage USA" is a luxurious pleasure complex founded by Assemblies of God (Pentecostal) minister *Jim Bakker*. He later established his own television network (PTL Network), broadcasting "The PTL Show" via satellite to 178 stations. Recent years have seen Bakker's involvement in various scandals.

The most successful TV entrepreneur, and once contender for the presidential candidacy, is *Pat Robertson*. His success is due to innovative strategies of broadcasting and fundraising. Robertson now runs a large cable TV operation.

## Methodisch-didaktische Hinweise

Im Mittelpunkt des Textes und seiner Bearbeitung stehen nicht die "TV preachers", sondern das Medium Fernsehen und seine Eigentümlichkeiten im Dienst der Evangelisierung. Sollten die Schülerinnen und Schüler noch keine Vorkenntnisse über "Televangelism" aus dem Unterricht der 11. Jahrgangsstufe mitbringen, empfiehlt es sich, Hintergrundwissen zu diesem Thema in Form eines Kurzreferats oder durch entsprechende Arbeitsaufträge in den Unterricht einbringen zu lassen. Auch die Präsentation von Ausschnitten religiöser Sendungen auf Video mit anschließender freier Diskussion wäre als Vorbereitung zur Textarbeit denkbar. Wichtig ist es, die Rolle des Fernsehens in der amerikanischen Gesellschaft zu untersuchen, um die Anziehungskraft von "Televangelism" verstehen zu können. Eben um dieses Phänomen geht es in einem anderen Text von Neil Postman, "They came, we saw, they conquered", im Schülerbuch auf S. 128–129.

Weiteres Material zum Thema "Electronic Church": Siehe Perspectives 7: *Religion in America and Britain*, Klettbuch 51367, S. 37–47.

## Pre-reading activities

1. Examine the range of religious radio and television programmes offered in your country. What kind of programmes are they? How much time do they occupy? What kind of listeners and viewers would you expect them to attract?

2. Do you think church services should be broadcast on television as well as on radio? Discuss.

3. List the differences between attending a church service and viewing one on television. (e.g. degree of participation, unity or disunity of your own surroundings and those of the service; atmosphere; freedom to look wherever one wishes; distractions from other people; ability to leave if desired).

**Suggested answers**

1. Religion is presented as entertainment, and all attention is focused on the preacher. The medium, not the preachers themselves, is to blame for this.

2. The TV set and the space around it are contaminated by being used otherwise for non-sacred purposes. They cannot provide the framework for a "nontrivial religious experience" (ll. 74–75).

3. The communal dimension (affinity groups), including attention to physical needs ("... where my wife can play and teach music and where I can play and coach basketball", Text 1, ll. 115–117).

4. –

5. –

**Post-reading activities**

1. Religion was once considered the opiate of the people, just as television is nowadays. Can you think of any long-term consequences that might arise out of the combination of the two? Write a short essay on this subject. Note: you may write an informal essay – conversational in style, humorous and personal in tone – or a formal essay, i.e. a well-organized, impersonal analysis, serious in tone.
See Bibliography 4, 6, 14, 15, 18.

2. *Look at the cartoon on p. 155 and answer the questions.*
Setting: an English church parish, probably in the country. The cartoon suggests a) that the vicar is none too successful in his efforts to "spread the word", a reflection of low church-attendance in England, and b) that the "electronic church" is not a feature of English ecclesiastical life.

3. *Write a book report on Neil Postman's* Amusing Ourselves to Death.

4. *Preparation for the next text. Write a paper or give a talk on the following topic: The wall of separation: church and state in the USA.*
See Bibliography 1, 3, 6, 8, 12, 13, 18, 22.

# 4. Is "humanism" a religion?

**Background information**

The US District Court's decisions in both cases mentioned in the text were later reversed in courts of appeal. The Supreme Court refused to hear the cases, which means that the decisions of the courts of appeal were upheld.
Further controversial issues concerning the freedom of religion:
– school prayer
– salute to the flag/pledge of allegiance
– public display of religious symbols
– evolutionism (Darwin) versus creationism (Bible)
See also Perspectives 3: *The Supreme Court*, Klettbuch 51363, pp. 33–36; Perspectives 7: *Religion in America and Britain*, Klettbuch 51367, pp. 48–55; *Skyline B*, Klettbuch 51032, pp. 137–139. For a note on Pat Robertson see "Background information" on Text 3, "Religion on the screen".

**Methodisch-didaktische Hinweise**

Die Diskussion über die Trennung von Kirche und Staat ist seit Gründung der USA ein fester Bestandteil des religiösen Lebens in Amerika, und ihre Komplexität findet immer wieder in zahlreichen Rechtsfällen vor Gericht seinen Ausdruck. Es ist unmöglich, deutschen Schülern, die mit dieser Problematik wenig vertraut sein dürften, auch nur einen einigermaßen umfassenden und ausgewogenen Einblick in diese Diskussion zu vermitteln. Ziel der Behandlung des vorliegenden Textes im Unterricht ist es daher vielmehr, den Einfluß der Verfassung als lebendiges Dokument auf das religiöse Leben in den USA deutlich zu machen. Folglich sollten die Schüler über grundsätzliche Kenntnisse von der verfassungsmäßigen Regelung des Verhältnisses zwischen Staat und Kirche in den USA verfügen.
Hier könnte ein Schülerreferat über "The Wall of Separation" (siehe *post-reading activities* zu Text

3) der Besprechung des Textes vorausgehen. Denkbar wäre auch, daß die Schüler sich im Rahmen eines häuslichen Arbeitsauftrags anhand des entsprechenden Textes im *fact file* (pp. 298–301) auf das Thema vorbereiten.

**Pre-reading activities**

*1. What do you know about the relationship between church and state in your own country? Discuss.*

*2. In which way is this relationship different from that in the USA? Discuss.*

**Suggested answers**

1. Religions and denominations from left to right: the German church (presumably Protestant – the cartoonist is German and is obviously poking fun at the German church's fusion with monarchist rule and incorporation of social customs such as beer drinking); the "heathen Chinese"; an Eastern church; Presbyterian; Roman Catholic; Jewish (to the right of the Catholic figure); Methodist (background); Mormon (M. Tabernacle in background); "Scotch"; "Holy Trinity" (Episcopalian); a representative of a Black church; an American Indian; "Quaker Meeting" (foreground). Many more denominations and religions are depicted in the background. All are attempting to gain entry to the state, i.e. to become a state religion, and all are being turned back by Lady Liberty (as the personification of religious freedom).
Possible title: "No entry"; "And never the twain shall meet"; "Turned away"; Nast's original title: "Church and state – no union, now and forever".

2. Use of the First Amendment for purposes which are the opposite of those intended – "secular humanism" is regarded as a religion. The effect of this movement on a) book publications and textbooks and b) classroom time devoted to creationism and evolution.

3. a) Fundamentalists: conservative Protestants. Stress morality, are rigidly conservative on social issues (abortion, school prayer, etc.), fight "liberal/secular humanism", which they identify with immorality and heresy.
b) Civil libertarians: believe in free will and in freedom of action and thought, stress individual rights, regard the state as the greatest threat to liberty and privacy.

4. The fundamentalists reversed the situation completely, placing "secular humanism" in the category of religion, so that those normally upholding the First Amendment appeared to be its opponents. Before that, the fundamentalists had been seen as the opponents of the First Amendment.

5. See box "Writing a summary", SB p. 181. Main ideas:
Fundamentalists use First Amendment in legal battle to ban textbooks promoting "religion of secular humanism" from public schools (para. 1, 2).
Examples of complaints lodged by fundamentalists (para. 3, 4).
Pressure already being placed on publishers to focus more on religion (para. 5, 6).
Civil libertarians: banning books is wrong tactic – means giving in to sectarian groups. Humanism a philosophy, not a religion (para. 7).
This controversy will go on. Soon to be decided in Louisiana, amount of classroom time spent on evolution and creation (para. 8).

6. The author does not explicitly take sides; refrains from any personal comment but presents all arguments by quoting directly the persons or groups involved in the conflict. Nevertheless his or her personal attitude towards the subject may have influenced the choice and presentation of the arguments. One may conclude that the author's attitude towards religion is positive, due to the number of arguments in favour of religion and the wording of the introductory sentence ("to squelch school-sponsored prayers ..."). Yet the title calls this position into question, and the quote in ll. 55–59 constitutes a strong warning.

7. Possible arguments:
– pro: Humanism provides a system of ethics and a world view that supply a stable context within which each person can relate him/herself to others and to the world; makes one understand his/her significance.
– con: Humanism does not believe in a superhuman power recognized as creator and ruler of the universe: no supernatural object of awe, worship and service.

**Additional questions**

*1. Find the corresponding abstract nouns (not the "ing–forms"):*

*l. 12: secular* secularism
*l. 17: divine* divinity
*l. 48: ridiculous* ridiculousness, ridicule
*l. 59: to settle* settlement

2. *l. 6: "ironically wielding the First Amendment as a club ..."* Name the "ing–form" here and explain its grammatical function.

3. *Define "humanism".*
Way of thinking in which human interests, values and dignity predominate. Humanism does not promote belief in a transcendent being.

**Post–reading activities**

*Report to your class on one previous Supreme Court decision on the "freedom of religion".*
See Bibliography 3, 12, 13.

## 5. Private conscience and public duty (GK)

### Background information

Born and educated in Manchester, Robert Bolt worked as a teacher before his first West End success, *Flowering Cherry* (1957). The film version of his best-known work, *A Man For All Seasons* (1960), won three Oscars. Other works include the screenplay *Lawrence of Arabia* (1962).
See "Fact file" and Perspectives 7: *Religion in America and Britain*, Klettbuch 51367 (student's book) pp. 4–7; Klettbuch 513671 (teacher's book) pp. 9–12.
Sir Thomas More (1478–1535), a man of brilliance, subtlety and wit, was much favoured by the King. He was made Lord Chancellor in 1529 but resigned only three years later, probably because of Henry's intention to divorce Catherine of Aragon in defiance of the Pope. Nevertheless he was still considered dangerously influential after his resignation, and as a consequence he was found guilty of high treason and beheaded. The Catholic Church acknowledged him as a martyr, and in 1935 he was canonized.

### Methodisch-didaktische Hinweise

Nachdem in den ersten vier Texten des Kapitels die Vielfalt der kirchlichen Gruppierungen in den USA vorgestellt wurde, führt dieser Ausschnitt aus *A Man for all Seasons* in die Geschichte der Kirche in Großbritannien ein – eine Geschichte, die unmittelbar mit den religiös motivierten Einwanderungen in die USA verbunden ist. Eine Betrachtung der Entwicklung in Großbritannien sollte diese Verbindung berücksichtigen.

Der Ausschnitt eignet sich gut zu einer fachübergreifenden Behandlung, bei der verschiedene Schwerpunkte gesetzt werden. Einmal könnte man die historischen Ereignisse um die Reformation und die Gründung der "Church of England" in den Mittelpunkt des Unterrichtsgeschehens stellen. In diesem Falle böte es sich zur Einstimmung auf das Thema an, von der bildlichen Präsentation Heinrichs VIII auszugehen (Bild Nr. 9, *Dias zur Landeskunde*, Klett-Nr. 51342). Unter politischen Gesichtspunkten bietet sich eine Diskussion über das Verhältnis von Kirche und Staat – die im Kontext der Vereinigten Staaten schon geführt worden sein dürfte – an. Der Text enthält aber auch viele Ansätze zur literarischen Analyse und läßt die Besonderheiten des Theaters gut hervorheben. Von der Thematik her (Spannung zwischen Gewissen und öffentlichen Verpflichtungen) lassen sich Vergleiche mit anderen literarischen Werken und Filmen ziehen.
Obwohl er einen anderen Stoff behandelt, weist der Text auf S. 267 des SB, "The conscience of a president" gewisse Parallelen zu unserem Text auf.
Das Nachdenken über die Besonderheiten des dramatischen Dialogs in den *pre-reading activities* bildet einen sinnvollen Einstieg in den Ausschnitt. Es empfiehlt sich, vor dem Hören des Dialogs auf der Cassette den Text mit den Regieanweisungen durchzulesen. Es könnten auch geeignete Stellen nachgespielt werden. Dabei bietet die *post-reading activity*, in der der Dialog näher untersucht wird, eine Hilfe.

**Pre-reading activities**

*1. What do you know about Henry VIII?*

*2. List the main elements of drama.*
Characters, plot, setting, stage directions, dialogue, theme.

*3. Not every dialogue would be suitable for presentation on stage. Thinking of plays you have seen, list the features of dialogue (and the way it was presented) that made it dramatic and interesting.*
a) Creation of suspense, usually involving a conflict (protagonist – antagonist):
– The audience often knows more about the situation than one character or both characters.
– Gestures; some aimed at audience, perhaps missed by other character. Facial expression.
– Symbolic actions illustrate what is being said.

b) Dialogue provides scope for emotional contrast:
– variation in tone and volume of voices
– interruptions
– exclamations, questions
– pauses
*Note the importance of stage directions!*

c) The dialogue paves the way for further action.

**Suggested answers**

1. Wolsey appeals to common sense; presses for a pragmatic approach; reminds More of his responsibilities as a statesman; tries to trick More into admitting necessity of divorce (ll. 73–79); cites historical events to illustrate possible consequences if divorce not granted (ll. 112–117); uses threatening gestures (ll. 67–68).

2. Humble and polite at first (ll. 23–26), then wary (ll. 58–66); horrified at Wolsey's suggestion (ll. 76–77); stubborn (ll. 85–89); answers Wolsey's question with a question (ll. 94–98); openly admits standpoint at end (ll. 127–130), though not directly mentioning the divorce.

3. His principles; his "private conscience", i.e. his ability to act according to what he believes is right; his integrity.

4. Regards both the King's behaviour and Ann Boleyn with disrespect (ll. 56–57, ll. 83–84 "That thing out there ..."). Henry's behaviour obviously makes him nervous (ll. 60–61 "visibly relaxes"), but his approach to the alliance with Ann Boleyn is pragmatic – she is "at least fertile" (l. 83).

5. Directly: generous (ll. 1–2 ); "plodder" (l. 46); scholar (l. 47); experienced (ll. 47–48); statesman (ll. 111–112). Indirectly: formal, polite (ll. 25–26); stubborn (ll. 108–109); capable of dry humour (ll. 64–66); devout (ll. 80, 133–136)); of high principles (ll. 127–130).

6. More: principle of acting according to conscience: honesty, uprightness. Chaos results if one acts otherwise.
Wolsey: principle of expediency: pragmatism, forsaking moral code in certain situations to avoid chaos.

**Additional questions**

*1. a) l. 9 "That's only Common Sense". Give a broad definition of "common sense".*
A person's natural ability to make sound judgements without specialized knowledge or training, and to behave in a sensible way.

*b) Compare the use of "common sense" in ll. 9 and 39. Is there a difference?*
l. 9: The steward assumes the audience will agree. It is "common sense" that More will want to keep something he is asked to forsake, i.e. his principles.
l. 39: Irony: "common sense" is the ability to forsake one's principles and compromise. If More has "common sense", he will give up his principles.

*c) Find other expressions with "common" as a component and explain them.*
The common cold *(Erkältung)*; common ground (an area of shared interest or understanding); common knowledge (something everyone knows)

**Post-reading activities**

*1. Answer the questions on the scene illustrated on p. 159 (SB).*
Henry VIII: skeptical; carefully scrutinizes More. Perhaps annoyed, dissatisfied.
More: thinking deeply; tense (note his hand); uncertain.

*2. Go back to the third pre-reading activity. Now analyse the dialogue in the extract you have read and heard, finding examples of the features you noted.*

*Something known by audience, not by both characters:* the steward knows something will be required of More.

*Suspense in visual presentation:* gestures for emphasis (Wolsey grasps More's shoulder, ll. 67–68; More starts up, l. 76); gestures meant specifically for audience (Wolsey signs More to sit at table where they can be overheard; More obeys "unsuspectingly", ll. 71–73); symbolic actions (extinguishing and lighting candle, l. 117, ll. 130–132).

*Emotional contrast:* tone and volume (ll. 64–77); interruptions (ll. 104–110); exclamations, questions (ll. 110–112); pauses (ll. 41–46).

*Paves way for further action:* The conflict between "private conscience" and "public duty" is exposed in the dialogue. The audience awaits More's course of action.

*3. Compare basic historical facts of the Reformation in England with those of the Reformation in Germany. Prepare a paper or talk, outlining similarities and differences.*
See Bibliography 2, 13, 16, 17.

*4. Prepare a talk or paper on the origins and development of the Church of England.*
See Bibliography 2, 13, 16, 17, 19, 20.

## 6. Runcie: "Let the Pope lead all Christians"

**Background information**

Robert Runcie was Archbishop of Canterbury from 1980 until he stepped down in January, 1991. During the Pope's visit to Canterbury in 1982 (ll. 43–45 of our text), the leaders of the two churches opened a round of negotiations aimed at enabling them to recognize each other's priests and bishops. A compromise has since been reached on central theological issues such as the relationship between "faith" and "works" in determining a person's standing before God (the theological issue behind the Reformation). Yet one issue still remains unsolved, one that prevents the mutual recognition of priests and bishops: the ordination of women (see article in *Time* magazine, May 8, 1989).

Runcie's successor as Archbishop is George Carey, Bishop of Bath and Wells, a moderate evangelical and a product of the working class. Carey is strongly in favour of the ordination of women. At the same time he encourages attempts to bring Anglicans and Roman Catholics closer together (see articles in *Time*, August 6, 1990, and in *The Observer*, May 25, 1992: "When in Rome Dr Carey will not do as the Romans.").

For background information on Rev. Ian Paisley, see Ch. 4 "Britain and Ireland", especially SB p. 97. The same chapter contains a text on attempts to encourage tolerance among Catholic and Protestant Irish children: "Learning to live together", SB pp. 108–109.

Pope Gregory I sent Augustine, a Roman monk, to christianize England in the late sixth century. Augustine was the first Archbishop of Canterbury from 597 till his death in 604. He was later canonized.

**Pre-reading activities**

*1. Note down what you know about ecumenical efforts (between Protestants and Roman Catholics) in your own country. If you have ever attended a church service or other event held by both denominations, tell your class about it.*

*2. What do you think of the idea that the Pope should be head of all churches? Discuss.*

**Suggested answers**

1. The Archbishop of Canterbury, Robert Runcie, presses for the unity of the Anglican and the Roman Catholic churches and for recognition of the Pope as head of both.

2. Theological justification: C of E never stopped seeing itself as part of the universal church, nor denied that that church is centred in Rome; need to uphold tradition in order to confirm the unity and continuity of the faith of Peter, Gregory and Augustine.

3. The ordination of women, now accepted in at least parts of the Anglican Communion (see picture p. 161). Additionally: the jurisdiction the Pope would exercise over a reunited church; authoritarian methods used by Vatican to silence progressive theologians; the ban on contracep-

tives; celibacy etc. (see *British Life and Institutions*, Klettbuch 51344, pp. 82–84).

4. Possible reasons: people in all churches are looking for more freedom to worship as they wish; some want to interpret scriptures in more modern and rational ways and question old prohibitions; others want to return to the authority of the scriptures; women and men are now seen to be equal, hence women should also be church leaders.

### Additional questions

"The idea of a primacy for the sake of unity was beginning to find a place in Anglican thinking, he said." (ll. 16–18).
Name the "-ing-forms" and explain their grammatical functions.

### Post-reading activities

*1. Examine the picture and answer the question on p. 161 (SB).*
Ordination of women; a crucial issue for those seeking unity of Anglican and Roman Catholic churches.

*2. Give a talk on the introduction of Christianity to Anglo-Saxon England, starting with the episode mentioned in ll. 45–49 of the text.*
See Bibliography 11.

*3. Draw a time-line depicting the main stages of the spread of Christianity in Britain.*
See Bibliography 2, 5, 13, 17, 21.

## 7. Women: second-class citizens of the Church? (GK)

### Background information

1975: The Anglican Church admits women as deaconesses (i.e. members of the lay ministry), but not as full members of the clergy.
1987: In March the governing body of the Church of England, the General Synod, passes legislation allowing women to be ordained as deacons (entitled to fulfill many of a priest's functions but still banned from pronouncing blessing, granting absolution and celebrating communion). As a result most of the 700 deaconesses in the Church of England are admitted to the office of deacon in the same year.
1992: The new General Synod has to decide whether or not to pass a bill which would admit women to the priesthood.

### Methodisch-didaktische Hinweise

Im vorhergehenden Text wird die Frage der Ordination von Frauen in der anglikanischen Kirche nur als Hindernis zur Einheit der Kirche erwähnt. Im Bericht der Rev. Anne Jennings findet dann die persönliche Betroffenheit ihren Ausdruck. Die zwei Beispiele von Öffentlichkeitsmaterialien auf den Seiten 163 und 164 können entweder vor oder nach dem Lesen dieses Berichts behandelt werden. Unterschiede nicht nur im Inhalt, sondern auch in Sprache und Gestaltung der zwei Anzeigen lassen sich leicht herausarbeiten. Auf Fragen wie die nach dem beabsichtigten Leserkreis, der Logik der Argumente und der möglichen Wirkung soll eingegangen werden. Diese Ausarbeitung findet dann ihre aktive Umsetzung in der zweiten *post-reading activity*. Dabei bieten die Boxen auf S. 165 eine Hilfe.
Eine Verknüpfung mit dem Text "Freedom and suppression" von Anita Desai, auf S. 48–49 des Schülerbuchs abgedruckt, läßt sich auf zweierlei Weise herstellen. Zum einen liegt beiden Texten die Frage der Unterdrückung von Frauen zugrunde. Zum anderen wird in beiden Fällen versucht, diese Unterdrückung unter Berufung auf die Religion zu rechtfertigen.

### Pre-reading activities:

*1. List areas of society in which, in your opinion, women are still disadvantaged. Discuss.*

*2. What role do women play in your church, or in a church you know of in your country? Discuss in small groups or as a class.*

### Suggested answers

1. Felt drawn to priesthood at 14 or even earlier; was made a deaconess at 30, after doing a degree,

166  *Religious Life*

teaching for two years, going to theological college and working in a parish for three years; assisted vicars for twelve years, then was the first woman in Britain to be put in charge of a church: became Cathedral Deacon at Wakefield in 1987.

2. Ll. 35–37: Anne Jennings wants "to exercise a fuller and deeper ministry" than she can as a deacon, e.g. speaking words of absolution (ll. 42–43). She wants to play her "full part in the Church" (ll. 68–69).

3. –

4. e.g. armed forces (esp. navy), banking, engineering, etc.

**Additional questions**

1. "*I* put a new slant on *things.*" (*ll. 61–62*). Find a suitable substitute; keep to the sentence structure.

2. Put the last paragraph into indirect speech. Begin with: "She said ...".

**Post-reading activities**

1. Write a personal comment (150–200 words). Choose one of the following topics:
a) "Our church is crying out for a woman's touch."
b) "Would you take communion from a woman?"
c) "The ordination of women priests would violate the intentions of God, who has given different roles to men and women."

2. Work in groups of three. One person is a supporter of women's ordination, one an opponent, and one a neutral television moderator. The latter has to interview the other two for a television programme. Using the advertisements on pp. 163–164, the excerpt from The Observer and other sources (e.g. biblical references, books, newspaper articles), prepare the interview. Gather arguments for and against. Work out a good beginning (e.g. the moderator might start by quoting a relevant article or citing a recent event). Set a time limit (10 minutes?). Try not to interrupt each other or talk for too long. Keep to a logical sequence of thought (the boxes on p. 165 will help you). The moderator should summarize or steer the discussion at appropriate points. Groups should then present their interviews to the rest of the class.
See Bibliography 13, especially pp. 66–69.

3. Write a paper or give a talk on one of the following topics:
a) The free (Nonconformist) churches in Great Britain.
b) The Kirk of Scotland.
See Bibliography 2, 5, 13, 16, 17, 19, 20, 21.

## 8. Hearing the cry of the poor (GK)

**Background information**

During the late eighties and early nineties, church representatives in Great Britain became increasingly vocal about the social effects of government policies ("We have seen with our own eyes society being driven in a direction that contradicts the Gospel", ll. 3–4). In an interview published in *Director* in October 1989, the then Archibishop of Canterbury, Robert Runcie, pointed to the widening gap between the wealthier, Conservative-dominated south of England and the poorer north. He said he would like to see "more awareness that we are using [...] wealth more responsibly to deal with the left-behinds, [...] the casualties of success, to deal with issues [...] like housing, homelessness and the mentally handicapped." (For further excerpts from this interview see SB pp. 68–71, "The Archbishop and the wealth ethic.")

See also Ch. 11 "Religion and morality" in *British Life and Institutions*, Klettbuch 51344, especially pp. 81 and 86.
From a different angle, Louis MacNeice's poem "Carrickfergus" (SB p. 98) sheds light on the attitude of the Anglican Church to the Irish (Catholic) poor.

**Methodisch-didaktische Hinweise**

Das abgebildete Pamphlet der *Church Action on Poverty* unterstreicht die Rolle der Kirche als Mahnerin überall dort, wo soziale Mißstände herrschen. Die erste *pre-reading activity* will auf die sozialen Fragen aufmerksam machen, mit denen sich die Kirche beschäftigt. Wie diese Beschäftigung konkret aussehen mag, soll die zweite *pre-reading activity* – am Beispiel Deutschlands – zeigen.

Das Pamphlet spricht die vom Leser selbst gewonnenen Einsichten an (l. 2 "We have seen ..."). Zur Veranschaulichung dieser Situation eignet sich der Text auf S. 79–80 (SB), "Filed away in a cardboard box city". Natürlich kann auch hier an die eigenen Beobachtungen in Deutschland angeknüpft werden.
Nach der Lektüre des Textes und der Beantwortung der Fragen bietet die *post-reading activity* den Schülerinnen und Schülern die Gelegenheit, selbst einen für die Öffentlichkeit bestimmten Text zu dieser Thematik zu verfassen.

### Pre-reading activities

*1. If you wanted to judge the moral fibre of a society, what would you examine? List relevant points.*
The way children, women, the elderly, minorities, the poor, the unemployed, the sick are treated.

*2. Find out about the kinds of social services offered by institutions of the major churches in your country (e.g. in Germany: Diakonisches Werk, Caritas ...). Pool your information in class.*

### Suggested answers

1. The poor are suffering (l. 2); society is "being driven in a direction that contradicts the Gospel" (l. 3); many people are being "hurt ... damaged and discounted" (ll. 7–8); "social divisions have widened and community life has been gravely eroded" (ll. 10–11).

2. Those who shape "public policy" (l. 8), i.e. politicians, and those responsible for the economic and environmental effects of "changing technology" (l. 13).

3. To urge people to "seek a new social order" (l. 4) enabling people to live to the fullest of their possibilities ("human wholeness", l. 5). No specific course of action is named, but the term "political challenge" (l. 20) hints at political action (e.g. how people vote). The call for change, however, is more universal than the choice of one political party.

4. –

5. Suggestions: narrowing social divisions, rebuilding community life, housing ...

### Additional questions

*Explain the grammatical function of "that" in each of the following quotes:*
*l. 3: "... in a direction that contradicts the Gospel."*
*l. 5: "... founded upon that vision ..."*
*l. 7: "... our inescapable conclusion is that many are being hurt ..."*

l. 3: relative pronoun introducing a defining relative clause.

l. 5: demonstrative determiner

l. 7: conjunction introducing a clause which complements the subject.

### Post-reading activities

*Imagine you are living in a British city. The council's budget for the coming financial year has just been made public. In it, funds for a housing project for low-income families have been cut drastically; at the same time a large amount has been set aside for the construction of a new sports complex, although the city already has sporting facilities.*
*Write a letter to the editor of your local paper, expressing concern at the situation.*

## A Welsh hymn (SB p. 167)

### Background information

When English Methodism spread to Wales in the eighteenth century, it gained a distinctive profile. Not unlike those who began the Reformation in Germany in the sixteenth century, the leaders of Welsh Methodism initially envisaged reform within the established church. However, the enthusiasm which marked the revival took it further. Wales became dotted with chapels and Methodist communities, so that by the beginning of the nineteenth century a Nonconformist church had emerged.
Religious life, the life of the mining communities and choral traditions are inseparably linked in the history of Wales. One of the outstanding figures in Welsh Methodism was the poet, travelling preacher

and hymn-writer William Williams of Pantycelyn, whose famous hymns capture the fervent emotions and aspirations of the Welsh revival.

In the two verses of the hymn on p. 167 (SB), the Old Testament story of the Israelites' wanderings in the desert on their way to the Promised Land becomes a metaphor for the journey of the Christian through life. The word "Jehovah" is an English version of the name for God used often in this story (in the ancient Hebrew manuscripts it is actually unpronounceable). "Jehovah" provides the Israelites with "bread from heaven" (manna) and water from a hidden spring in a rock, guiding them night and day by means of a "pillar" of fire and a cloud, and later protecting them from the attacks by the peoples whose lands they pass through.

The architecture of the chapel pictured on p. 167 is reminiscent of Gothic (arched windows – see *Fact file* on "Art, Culture and Society", SB p. 293) but decidedly simpler. It is interesting to compare it with the example of neo-Gothic industrial architecture pictured on p. 137 (SB). The chapel is made of brick.

**Methodisch-didaktische Hinweise**

Trotz seiner Knappheit führt dieser Einschub in einen wichtigen Teil der kirchlichen Welt Großbritanniens ein und läßt sich leicht zu einer kleinen thematischen Einheit ausbauen (siehe *Fact file*, SB pp. 300–301). Besonders interessant ist die Verbindung zwischen Religion, Musik, Gesellschaft (den Bergbausiedlungen) und Politik (dem Sozialismus), die die methodistische Erweckungsbewegung in Wales darstellt. Das Lied wird auf der Kassette von einem der traditionsreichen Männerchöre auf Walisisch gesungen. In jeder Strophe werden die letzten zwei Zeilen wiederholt. Es sollte darauf hingewiesen werden, daß die Umschrift nicht phonetisch ist: der gesungene Text (es werden alle drei Strophen gesungen) hört sich ganz anders an, als wir es vom geschriebenen Text erwarten.

Wales und die keltischen Sprachen sind Themen, die in der Mittelstufe kurz behandelt werden (siehe *Green Line 3*, Klettbuch 5833, S. 21). Auf diese Vorkenntnisse soll hier aufgebaut werden. Das Bild auf S. 300 verdeutlicht, daß auch in anderen Teilen Großbritanniens die keltischen Sprachen im religiösen Leben eine Rolle spielen.

**Pre-reading activities**

*1. Recall what you have learnt about Wales and the Welsh language.*

*2. Examine some famous German hymns (e.g. by Martin Luther, Paul Gerhardt and Jochen Klepper) and list – in English – the images used in them. Are there any from the Old Testament? If you have done the Listening Comprehension in Ch. 10 (SB p. 217), try to recall the metaphor from the Old Testament which was used in that personal account.*

*3. Discuss the influence of the Reformation on musical traditions in Germany.*
The hymns of Luther; Bach ...

**Post-reading activities**

*1. Paper or talk: Find out about the Methodist Revival of the eighteenth century in Wales and its place in the society of the time.*
See Bibliography 2, 13, 21.

*2. Compare the information on Religious Life in Scotland (Fact file, SB pp. 300–301) with what you have learnt about religious life in Wales.*
See Bibliography 2, 13, 17, 19, 20, 21.

## 9. Listening Comprehension: The Prophet's Birthday in Bradford

**Background information**

Since the 1950s Britain has not only developed into a nation with many races, but also with many religions. Due to immigration from Asian and African countries there is a variety of non-Christian beliefs. Although the followers of these non-Christian religions form only about five per cent of the British population, they have a great impact on British life, especially the largest group, the Muslims. There are now more than 1.5 million Muslims and about 1,000 mosques in Britain.

The religion of Islam was founded by Mohammed in the 7th century and is a monotheistic faith with elements of Christian and Judaic beliefs. Its holy book is the Koran, which sets forth the fundamental doctrines as well as rituals and a complete moral code. The legal system, the Shari'a, is also based on the Koran (the sacred text of Islam, believed to have been dictated to Mohammed by the angel Gabriel) and the Sunna (the traditional portion of Islamic law).

Islam has no priests, but worship is led by the Imam, a lay leader, in a mosque. Orthodox Muslims pray five times a day, facing towards Mecca. See *British Life and Institutions*, Klettbuch 51344, pp. 84–85.

## Methodisch-didaktische Hinweise

Eine Einleitung, Worterklärungen und Fragen zum Globalverständnis sind im SB auf S. 168 abgedruckt.

## Transcript

*The Council for Mosques in Bradford is an umbrella organization established in 1981, covering not only the 25 mosques in the city, but also some 15 other schools and evening organi-*
5 *zations, small privately funded schools, where amongst other activities instruction is given in the Koran and languages like the literary Urdu, languages often perforce neglected by the state educational services in the city due to govern-*
10 *mental financial cuts.*

*Middle schools with children from 9 to 13 are hardest hit, but even upper schools like Bellevue Girls despite its 90 % Muslim population is struggling to keep up its reputation for teaching com-*
15 *munity languages. Other aspects, however, of Muslim life are well catered for.*

*The headmistress Mrs Wright:*
We have available every day a private area for prayer with washing facilities. We have discussion
20 groups which are led by sixth form girls, which are connected to their faith. We also celebrate all the major Islamic festivals. One of the most important ones for the women is Mawlid of course, ...
*Which is what?*
25 Celebration of the birth of the prophet Mohammed, which is very important for women, and our girls and our Muslim staff organize that and, I would say, we have approximately 500 women – parents – every year come to school to partici-
30 pate in that.
*Why is it important for women, and what exactly happens?*

It is where they are given the opportunity to celebrate themselves the birth of the Prophet, to look at his life, to look at his teachings, to look at 35 the relevance that it has for them today and to corporately celebrate that, and because it is ... an all female affair, it's a very joyous affair as well, and it is – it is literally celebration.
*What in fact happens? Lots of dancing in the* 40 *playground, or what?*
No, it is quite formal in its production. There are usually a team of girls – ten, twelve ... with set pieces in both English and ... in Urdu, where the details of the Prophet's life are explained. Some of 45 his teachings are laid out to the listener. There are community prayers and community songs. There is a lot of singing without music, which is very, very difficult and very intricate, and the girls take great pride in their skill in that. It is also beautifully 50 laid out as far as presentation is concerned, the setting ... with the flowers and the decorations, and there is also a giving over of presents, usually sweets, ... which are provided for everyone who attends. It's a lovely, lovely day. 55
(singing)
*Let's go back to the conduct of Islam faith in the school. You say that there are rooms set aside for prayer and washing facilities, but suddenly five times a day or perhaps three times during* 60 *the school time... suddenly breaking into classroom routine, what happens?*
No, that doesn't happen in school. The girls on the whole use lunchtime for prayer. They pray before they come to school. They pray at school, and 65 usually they pray as soon as they get home, but ... there's an understanding on the community's part of the need to have continuity in the day, and they help and support us in that. So it is lunchtimes that the girls use for prayer. 70

From *English Feature*. Eine Aufnahme des Süddeutschen Rundfunks Stuttgart. Used by permission of Anthony Gibbs and SDR.

## Pre-listening activities

*Look at the picture on p. 168 (SB). Read the caption and answer the questions.*
Countries of origin: mainly the Indian sub-continent. See Bibliography 11, pp. 69–71.

**Suggested answers (Listening for the gist)**

1. Instruction in the Koran and languages like the literary Urdu; other activities related to Muslim life and culture.
2. Retaining their reputation in the teaching of community languages despite government cuts.
3. It gives them the opportunity to look at Mohammed's life and teachings and to see the relevance these have for the students.
4. It is a formal affair. A number of girls recite set pieces in English and Urdu explaining details of the Prophet's life and teachings. As well as community prayers and songs there is skilful unaccompanied singing. The venue is richly decorated, and gifts are distributed.
5. No. The girls use lunchtime, not class time, for prayer at school. Apart from that, they pray before they leave home and when they get home from school.

**Listening for detail**

*List three ways in which the girls actively practise their faith at school.*
Prayer and ritual washing, discussion groups, celebration of religious festivals

**Post-listening activities**

*1. In pairs or small groups, discuss reasons for the suspicion with which religious minorities are often regarded by other people.*

*2. List the main features of Christian religious practice in your country, e.g. frequency of worship, style of worship, practices at home, religous holidays and ways of celebrating. This is a good way of finding out the English terms for Christian practices. Find out about the main features of Muslim religious practice and compare the two.*
Perhaps the Muslim community where you live publishes information that may help.
See Bibliography 2, 13, 16, 17, 19, 20, 21.
Note for the teacher: There may be students of the Muslim faith in your class. They might like to answer questions – though this may be difficult in English and especially difficult for girls. We trust in the teacher's discretion on this point.
Should Salman Rushdie be mentioned, teachers can refer to the excerpts from a lecture by Rushdie on pp. 131–132 of the SB. The text deals with freedom of expression in literature.
A further discription of religious celebrations – this time in the Hindu religion – is provided in the text "Souls crying out for God" on pp. 46–47.

## Test: Anger of a female Church militant

**Einsatzort**

Die Verknüpfung zwischen Fragen der Ökumene und der Weihe von Frauen zu Priesterinnen geht aus den Texten 6 und 7 und dem auf den Seiten 163 und 164 abgebildeten Öffentlichkeitsmaterial deutlich hervor. Um diese Verknüpfung und um die Frage, ob sie rechtens ist, geht es im Klausurtext. Er stammt von der gleichen Autorin wie Text 6 und erschien nur eine Woche später in einer englischen Zeitung. Die Pfarrerin ("deacon"), mit der die Autorin spricht, ist Vorsitzende der *Movement for the Ordination of Women* (s. ihre Stellungnahme auf S. 163 des Schülerbuchs).
Es empfiehlt sich also, die Klausur erst nach der Behandlung dieses Abschnittes schreiben zu lassen. Somit bietet sie nicht nur einen Prüfstein dessen, wieviel die Schülerinnen und Schüler verstanden haben, sondern rundet das Thema auch inhaltlich ab.

**Text**

According to the Pope and the Archbishop of Canterbury, Rev. Cathy Milford is one of the main reasons why negotiations between the Anglican and Roman Catholic churches are in such trouble. As a woman deacon and moderator of the Movement for the Ordination of Women, she is a living symbol of the Church of England's faltering progress towards the admission of women to the priesthood.
That progress now appears to be in doubt. Last week the two leaders issued a joint statement saying that the question of women priests is preventing a reconciliation even in those areas where ecumenical progress is being made. The Archbishop also suggested that the issue of women's ordination might fall outside the legitimate bounds of diversity in a unified church.

Mrs Milford and her 1,000 fellow women deacons feel angry and betrayed. Sitting in the house of a friend in Cambridge last week, she said: "We feel we have been sold down the River Tiber. The archbishop hasn't taken us into his confidence and he didn't consult us before he went."

Dr. Runcie said in Rome that he could understand why women priests were unacceptable to the Roman Church but the message people are receiving, whatever his intentions, says Mrs Milford, is that he is against women's ordination in the Church of England. "As usual he is being too subtle by half. The opponents of women priests have seized on his words with glee."

Every sign that hostility to women priests is reviving brings the 4,000-strong movement new members. Last week there were dozens of calls to its London headquarters. The Archbishop, a recent convert to the idea that women should become priests "when the time is ripe", has made his statement at a particularly sensitive time. Legislation which would allow women priests in the Church of England is due to come before the general synod for the first time next month.

Mrs Milford says: "Our opponents think they can polarise things. You choose Rome or you choose women. I am quite clear that is a false position. Ecumenism is about wholeness and the search for unity in God, between black and white, between classes, between man and woman, between churches. They are all essential. You have to go with them all. You can't leave one behind."

She believes both the Pope and the Archbishop are out of touch with what goes on at the grass roots. "There are many Roman Catholics who already support women's ordination and for whom the Pope no longer speaks. Any Anglican parish which has women deacons working in it is wholeheartedly converted to the idea of women priests. I don't think Dr Runcie knows what goes on in ordinary parishes."

Women, she says, are simply being made scapegoats for the failure to make progress along the long and difficult road to unity. "The Roman Church has not yet recognised the orders of Anglican male clergy. If it really wanted to get on with unity it would do that instead of blaming women."

By Judith Judd, *The Observer*, 8 October 1989. © 1989 *The Observer*.

**Annotations**

7 **faltering**   unsteady, slow, hesitant
13 **reconciliation**   act of settling a disagreement, becoming friends again
21 **sold down the river**   to be betrayed by someone who was supposed to support you
21 **River Tiber**   Rome is on the River Tiber
31 **glee**   pleasure, excitement, especially when s.th. unpleasant happens to s.o. you do not like (Schadenfreude)
32 **hostility**   unfriendliness, opposition to a person or idea
59 **scapegoat**   s.o. who is blamed for s.th. he or she did not do (Sündenbock)
62 **orders**   *here:* status of being a priest (to take the orders: die Weihe empfangen, als Pfarrer eingesetzt werden)

**I. Language**

1. Vocabulary

Each of the following exercises refers to the word or phrase in italics in its context:
a) 45: *Ecumenism* is about wholeness ...
b) 51–52: ... out of touch with what goes on *at the grass roots*.
c) 22: The archbishop hasn't *taken us into his confidence* ... .
Find a substitute word or phrase. Keep to the sentence structure.
d) 29–30: As usual he *is being too subtle by half*.
Explain. You may change the sentence structure.
e) 31: The opponents of women priests *have seized on his words with glee*.
Explain. You may change the sentence structure.
f) 37: ... women should become priests *"when the time is ripe"*.
Explain. Keep to the sentence structure.
Make nouns from the following:
g) 19: betrayed
h) 16: legitimate
i) 30: subtle
j) 48: essential.

2. Grammar and Style

a) ... "the long and difficult road to unity."
Name the stylistic device used here.
b) "The archbishop hasn't taken us into his confidence and he didn't consult us before he went."
Which tenses are used in this sentence? List the verbs and explain why each tense is used.

c) Tell someone else (reported speech) what Mrs Milford said in ll. 52–65 ("There" to "women").

## II. Comprehension

Answer the following questions in complete sentences. Keep to the information given in the text, but do not quote.
1. What is the purpose of negotiations between the Archbishop of Canterbury and the Pope?
2. The author differentiates between what Dr Runcie actually says in Rome and how the opponents of women priests interpret his words. Express this difference in your own words.
3. What accusation against the Roman Catholic Church is implied in the last sentence of the text?

## III. Comment

Do you think the issue of women priests should be ignored until the churches are united, or do you think, like Mrs Milford, that the two issues are inseparable? Write a letter to the editor.

# Bibliography

1. Ahlstrom, S. *A Religious History of the American People.* New York: Doubleday, 1973.
2. *Britain 1992. An Official Handbook.* London: HMSO, 1992, pp. 203–208.
3. DiBacco/Mason/Appy. *History of the United States.* Boston: Houghton Mifflin Company, 1992 (Klettbuch 516153).
4. Elvy, P. *Buying Time. The Foundations of the Electronic Church.* Essex: McCrimmons, 1986.
5. Friebel/Händel. *Britain – USA Now: a Survey in Keywords.* Frankfurt: Diesterweg, 1979.
6. Hudson, Winthrop S. *Religion in America.* 3rd ed., New York, 1981.
7. Levine, Lawrence L. *Black Culture and Black Consciousness.* New York, 1977.
8. Marty, Martin E. *Religion in America: 1950 to the Present.* New York, 1979.
9. Moore, R. Lawrence. *Religious Outsiders and the Making of Americans.* New York, 1986.
10. *The 1992 Information Please Almanac.* Boston: Houghton Mifflin Company, 1992 (Klettbuch 516152).
11. Perspectives 2: *The American South.* Klettbuch 51362.
12. Perspectives 3: *The Supreme Court.* Klettbuch 51363.
13. Perspectives 7: *Religion in America and Britain.* Klettbuch 51367.
14. Perspectives 13: *Media and Messages,* Klettbuch 51373.
15. Postman, Neil. *Amusing Ourselves to Death.* London: William Heinemann, 1989.
16. Randle, John. *British Life and Institutions.* Klettbuch 51344.
17. Randle, John. *Understanding Britain. A History of the British People and their Culture.* London: Longman.
18. Reichley, James A. *Religion in American Public Life.* Washington, 1985.
19. Sampson, A. *The New Anatomy of Britain.* London: Hodder & Stoughton, 1971.
20. Sieper, R. *The Student's Companion to Great Britain.* 5th ed. München: Hueber, 1986.
21. Spann, Ekkehard. *Abiturwissen Englisch – Landeskunde Großbritannien/USA.* Klettbuch 929509.
22. Stevenson, D. K. *American Life and Institutions.* Klettbuch 5136.

# 8 Values in British and American Education

## Structure of the chapter

### USA

**The pursuit of success – from cradle to college**

*Fortune*, How to succeed
c. 200 words
advertisement

1. Not just doing it for kicks
c. 800 words
magazine article

**Public schools and private schools**

2. Americanize and equalize?
c. 850 words
book excerpt (socio-economic study)

**The dropout problem**

3. It's a tragedy we cannot afford
c. 350 words
newspaper article (column)

4. Fast car
5 min. 3 sec.
song

5. Students, get mad!
c. 1060 words
book excerpt (personal comment)

### GB

**Class divisions – can they be overcome?**

6. Why abuse and scorn are the wrong treatment
c. 820 words
newspaper article

7. Next term, we'll mash you
c. 2000 words
short story

**Language and class**

8. Accent and equality
c. 700 words
book excerpt (socio-economic study)

9. Listening Comprehension: A working-class girl in a grammar school
5 min. 35 sec.
autobiographical report

**Anti-utilitarian bias in British education**

10. Education and economic prosperity
c. 920 words
book excerpt (socio-economic study)

## Suggestions for reports/papers/talks

Sports in the USA – after text 1

The American Dream – after text 1

The American educational system – before text 2

Tracy Chapman: her life and her songs – after text 4

Short biographies of: Leonardo da Vinci, Joe di Maggio, Benjamin Franklin, Harry Truman, Winston Churchill – before text 5

The importance of Britain's "public schools" – after text 6

Language and class in Shaw's *Pygmalion/My Fair Lady*. – before/after text 8

### Vocabulary

*Thematischer Grund- und Aufbauwortschatz Englisch*, Klettbuch 51955, pp. 228–241

*Words in Context, Thematischer Oberstufenwortschatz*, Klettbuch 51961, pp. 78–83

# Advertisement, p. 169

### Methodisch-didaktische Hinweise

Die *Fortune*-Anzeige "How to succeed" kann entweder als selbständiger Text oder als *pre-reading activity* zu Text 1 eingesetzt werden. Im letzteren Fall empfiehlt es sich, maximal 1–4 der folgenden Fragen zu behandeln.

### Questions and answers

*1. Look at the picture. What feelings does it arouse in you?*
Baby conveys the impression of being full of life, happy, and optimistic though in need of protection; reader's maternal/paternal instincts are aroused.

*2. What idea is expressed in the headline and how does this idea relate to the picture?*
First line an explicit allusion to the key statement of the Declaration of Independence; second line: the idea expressed in this statement is confronted with harsh reality: all people are equal when they are born, but then they have to look after themselves, nobody helps you to get on in life.

*3. How does the text take up and develop the idea presented in the headline?*
Idea that you are "on your own" is repeated several times in different variations, all of them underlining the notion of success; success as the highest value in life; *Fortune* presented as the means to help people to be successful.

*4. Assuming the impression given by the advertisement is correct, do you think children in the USA are better off or worse off than those in other countries?*

– Better off: plenty of opportunity, no limits to what one can achieve, all talents recognized regardless of one's origin/class/colour/sex.
– Worse off: under considerable pressure to succeed, to live up to society's expectations; can't count on the state to help; must lead to great fear of failure.

*5. What arguments are put forward in favour of Fortune?*
*Fortune* as the "natural" reading matter of successful people; long tradition that has made it an "authority" in the business world; it is for those in the forefront of the race for economic success; therefore also attractive for people who want to advertise their products.

*6. What is the function of the final lines within the context of the ad as a whole?*
Slogan-like concentration on the name of the product that is being advertised and on the main idea that is to be associated with this product: *Fortune* is a synonym of success; those who read *Fortune* – or advertise in it – will make it.

*7. Analyse the language used in this advert (choice of words, sentence structure, stylistic devices).*
Vocabulary: modern, fast, colloquial (After that, baby, ..., guts, to make it, fast track, movers and shakers, the works, now it's OK to be upfront).
Syntax:
– elliptic sentences (Your own drive, your own guts, your own energy, your own ambition);
– short, emphatic sentences (It's the authority ...).

*Values in British and American Education*

Stylistic devices:
- repetition/parallelism (If you want to make it, you'll have to make it on your own. ... it's the one that ... And it's the one to ...);
- anaphora (Your own drive, your own guts, your own energy, your own ambition);
- rhetorical question (Isn't that what the fast track is all about?);
- pun (It helps the movers and shakers decide how to move and what to shake. ... help you make it – and keep it.);
- quotation from/allusion to a famous historic document (Declaration of Independence: We're all created equal.).

8. Write a short appreciation (about 60 words) of this advert with the help of the so-called AIDA model (Attention, Interest, Desire, Action).

The picture of the smiling, content baby draws the reader's attention to the ad. Interest is aroused by the unusual combination of two statements in the headline. The text of the ad stimulates the reader's desire to get to know this fabulous road to success, i.e. *Fortune*. This leads to action: he or she will buy the magazine or advertise in it.

**Post-reading activity**

*In groups of 3 or 4 design an advert for a computer, compact-disc player, video-recorder or any other commodity of modern society.*

# 1. Not just doing it for kicks (GK)

**Pre-reading activity**

Advertisement p. 169 – see above.

**Suggested answers**

1. The reader's interest is aroused by
- the ambiguous title: "it" is unclear; "kicks" can be understood in more than one way (die Schüler sollten ihr einsprachiges Wörterbuch benutzen und die verschiedenen Bedeutungen von "kick" herausfinden, s. dazu auch die Antwort zu Frage 6);
- the first three paragraphs: personal experiences always make us curious; the fact that Kate is a girl and only eight years old renders the whole affair particularly intriguing.

The reader's interest is maintained by
- the detailed description of the unexpected amount of requirements/equipment (satirical, hyperbolic comparison in lines 29–30 intensifies this impression);
- the gradual revelation that the author is an Englishman living in America;
- the first mention of Eric (the reader wants to know who Eric is and then what kind of a coach he is);
- the statement that the "results are impressive" (l. 57) (now the reader is keen to hear about the "results");
- the assessment of Americans by an Englishman (ll. 92–101);
- the personal story (ll. 102–109) of "the couple who kept score";
- the final opinion of the Walkers and their daughter on "the American way".

2. Eric is an amateur who is almost obsessed with coaching the Spearmints in his spare time. He is a charismatic personality who can really motivate and inspire his kids. If necessary he can also exert physical, psychological and moral pressure. (He seems to employ a kind of "carrot and stick" strategy). All these qualities make him a "born" coach (l. 53) who is respected and loved by his team.

3. The American values Eric stands for are summed up in lines 98–101:
- competitiveness;
- profound faith in coaching;
- conviction that you can redesign your life and become anything you want to be ("land of unlimited possibilities", "from dishwasher to millionaire", etc.).

Points for discussion:
- optimistic values originating from the Age of Enlightenment; enable great achievements in all walks of life; positive thinking still necessary today;

– too optimistic, many American dreams have turned into nightmares; potentially dangerous values: may lead to social Darwinism ("survival of the fittest") and political arrogance.

4. Martin Walker's memories of kids' soccer in England provide a negative contrast: a lot of boys running after the ball without aim or organization. In comparison, the girls' game under Eric's tuition looks quite professional. They obviously "know what they are doing".

5. Martin Walker and his wife (the author often says "we") have somewhat mixed feelings/are in two minds about Eric's professional approach: On the one hand, they complain a little about the amount of effort expected of the whole family (ll. 29–48) and feel it would be better if at least the children could be allowed to stay amateurs. On the other hand, they respect and even admire Eric (ll. 52–53, 53–54, 57–58, 87–88); and they come to appreciate the positive effect of American values (cf. ll. 99–101).

6. The title "Not just doing it for kicks" has a double implication. To "get a kick out of s.th." means to get a feeling of intense pleasure or excitement from it. So the title implies that there is a lot more to sport than a) just kicking a ball, and b) just doing it for pleasure. Being an active member of a team, practising hard and competing with others are activities that are likely to lead to social integration, success and recognition.
Kate obviously appreciates these results of her efforts – so in a sense she actually is doing it for kicks.

*Questions on picture:* Americans might be more inclined to consider soccer a girls' game since it is much less rough than American football. Martin Walker's article describes another manifestation of American competitiveness. It suggests that the ad's image of the baby who has to make it on its own is not at all unrealistic.

**Additional question**

*Look at the -ing- forms in lines 7, 17, 18, 37, 44, 46, 63–4, 78 and 102. Define them and explain their use.*

**Post-reading activities**

*1. Topics for classroom reports:*
– *Sports in the USA.*
See Bibliography 9, 10; also *Football/Baseball Rules Illustrated*, Klettbuch 53816/538159.
– *The American Dream.*
See Bibliography 6, 10, 11, 12; also Ch. 11 of this book, if not to be studied in class.

## 2. Americanize and equalize?

### Methodisch-didaktischer Hinweis

Da dieser Text eine Abweichung von der amerikanischen Norm behandelt, wäre es ratsam, vor dem ersten Lesen eine gewisse Vertrautheit mit dieser Norm zu sichern. Daher empfiehlt sich ein Schülerreferat als *pre-reading activity*.

### Pre-reading activities

*1. Classroom report: The educational system of the USA.*
See Bibliography 7, 9, 10; fact file pp. 302–303.)
*2. Why do all American teenagers attend the same type of school (High School)?*
*3. What differences might still exist between schools of this type?*

### Suggested answers

1. Besides the "three Rs" (reading, writing, arithmetic) the traditional aim of public education in the U.S. has always been the social integration of all Americans as equal members of society.

2. A certain measure of failure was unavoidable because the actual achievement was bound to be insufficient in comparison with the high ideal.

3. Dangers:
– gap between ideal and achievement, between good and bad public schools, between the public and private sectors in education is widening;
– the Americans' support for the public schools has been decreasing, more and more influential the most powerful people are sending their children to private schools for racial, religious, academic and elitist reasons.

*Values in British and American Education*

4. Since the vast majority of young Americans still receive their education in public schools, the statement quoted in the last line is obviously exaggerated. The original author probably meant it as a warning of possible future developments. Fawcett and Thomas, however, try to make it seem an imminent danger (cf. l. 44), even though the examples they give merely show a rise in the still very small percentage of children attending private schools. Other examples also show an intention to exaggerate (cf. ll. 44–46: we are not told how many adults in ten have any children of school age!).

The authors' reasons for such exaggeration can only be speculated about: possibly they wish to shake people out of their complacency and do something to save the public schools; possibly mere sensationalism.

5. The fact that a high proportion of America's "overachievers" are from Asian immigrant families, and (like the vast majority of the population) attend the public school system shows that this school system cannot be as bad as the authors of the book *The American Condition* seem to think. At the very least it does not prevent natural talent and competitiveness from emerging (regardless of race and culture), and most probably such schools actually promote the development of such talent and competitiveness.

(If any students should imagine – possibly influenced by the so-called *Ausländerproblem* in German schools – that high marks for immigrant students can only be explained by low standards, it should be pointed out that this is a racist assumption. In fact, the Asian immigrants seem to produce a higher number of excellent students than any other group in American society, regardless of what schools they attend. Their performance at college bears this out. The reasons may be cultural or genetic or a mixture of both.)

### Additional questions

*1. Sum up the reasons why some Americans send their children to private schools.*

*2. What schools would such parents favour if they were living in your country?*

### Post-reading activity

*Discuss the "Seven Cardinal Principles of Education" mentioned in ll. 5–11. Then make up your personal list of cardinal principles of education and justify any differences.*

## 3. It's a tragedy we cannot afford (GK)

### Pre-reading activity

*Look at the cartoon on page 175.*
*– What seems to be happening?*
*– What do the words written on the blackboard really mean?*

Kurze Verbalisierung des cartoon auf S. 175, hier nur als brainstorming gedacht; nach der Behandlung des Textes erfolgt die genauere Analyse.

### Suggested answers

1. Someone who drops out of school before graduation. (Anyone who successfully finishes high school is given a diploma. Those who don't get such a diploma are known as "dropouts", no matter if they have left school before they have finished their studies or if they stay in school until they can legally leave.)

2. Ll. 1–10 present the current situation in some big-city school districts; for the overall situation, cf. ll. 13–14.
Consequences: dropouts drift towards despair, drugs, suicide and crime (ll. 14–18; 32–34); doomed to constitute a new permanent underclass (ll. 18–25); cost the taxpayer billions of dollars every year (ll. 35–45).

3. Society's response should be rational as well as moral. Reason demands that unnecessary costs be cut (ll. 46–49); "morality", i.e. our feeling of what is right and wrong, "demands the same" (ll. 49–50).
Two forces must cooperate to attack the problem. At the federal level, the Washington Department of Education must "make the issue a top priority" (ll. 50–54), i.e. must provide financial aid and

public-relations skills to rouse the nation's consciousness. At the local level every single citizen must be activated and involved in anti-dropout initiatives (ll. 59–73); the age-old, pioneer spirit of voluntarism, of "neighbors helping neighbors ... must once again [be] put to work" (ll. 69–73).

4. First paragraph: shocking statistics for 8 big cities.
Second paragraph: national statistics (the problem is not restricted to big cities); fate of individual dropouts (drugs, suicide, crime, etc.) and of dropouts as a group (underclass, the deprived).
Third paragraph: first appeal to readers (don't be heartless and apathetic); "a tragedy that the USA cannot afford".
Fourth and fifth paragraphs: develop the "cannot afford" idea in economic terms.
Sixth paragraph: sums up the economic argument and adds that the U.S. cannot afford this tragedy morally either ("Morality demands the same"); reminds readers of national ideals.
Final paragraph: points out what has already been done and ends with the strongest appeal to the readers.

5. In addition to what answers 3 and 4 have already revealed, the following should be pointed out:
– emotional language, most of the connotations being characterized by fear, anger and pity (struggling, ll. 8–9; crisis, l. 11; lose, l.l. 14; suicide, l. 15; quiet desperation, l. 18; heartless, l. 29; tragedy, l. 30; etc.)
– pronouns involving the writer and reader ("we", ll. 14, 50, 54, 56, 63, 72; "us", ll. 19, 63; "our", 44, 46, 73)
– phrases equating the individual and the nation ("we as a nation", 28; the John Adams quote in ll. 59–61; "For our children's sake. For the USA's sake", ll. 73–74)

6. Argumentation and at times persuasion; ample evidence contained in answers 3–5.

**Cartoon, p. 175**

1. This cartoon shows a scene in an American classroom with the usual American flag and a clock (the time indicated on it is five past twelve). The teacher is writing the percentage of high school dropouts on the board, again and again correcting it upwards as two students literally "drop out" through trap doors. The teacher and one of the students look worried, whereas the other students don't seem to notice. The cartoonist focuses the reader's attention on a dropout problem that is national in scope (cf. the American flag) and must be tackled at once, because it is almost too late already, as the clock tells us. Furthermore, he clearly illustrates the split reaction to this issue: concern, even horror on the one side, apathy (or gratification at the elimination of potential rivals?) on the other.

2. Rising dropout rate; national in its implications; very urgent; some remain untroubled. Preference for article or cartoon a personal matter. Some arguments:
– Article best: It is true that the cartoon is an excellent visual summary of the message of the article, but evidently limited in its possibilities of expression. The article is more detailed and more persuasive (background information, causes of the problem, suggestion of measures, verbal appeals).
– Cartoon best: It makes the reader think about what the cartoonist probably intends to express. This experience is usually more intense and lasting than reading an article in which everything is put forward explicitly.

**Post-reading activity**

*Write a short column on a topic that deeply concerns you personally. Try to imitate the argumentative and persuasive style or Mary Futrell's article.*

## 4. Fast car (GK)

### Background information

A good summary of Tracy Chapman's career to date is given in "Singing for Herself" in *Time*, March 19, 1990; an abridged version of this article is included in Perspectives 15: Rock, *Pop and All That Jazz*, Klettbuch 51375.
Tracy Chapman's song touches on a whole complex of problems, not all of which are directly relevant to this chapter, but which may call for some discussion in class. For an explicit discussion of these problems (black students dropping out of school, the particular problems of black females, the abdication of responsibility of black males, single-parent families, unemployment, etc.) see the *Time* interview with the writer Toni Morrison, "The Pain of Being Black" (May 22, 1989), included in Perspectives 12: *The Caring Society*, Klettbuch 51372.

### Methodisch-didaktische Hinweise

Das Lied soll unbedingt akustisch präsentiert werden. Dabei kann entweder die Begleitkassette oder die Originalplatte (bzw. Cassette/CD) gebraucht werden. Originalalbum: *Tracy Chapman*, Elektra/Asylum Records; LP: 960 774–2.
Anstatt die Fragen im Schülerbuch an die ganze Klasse zu richten, könnte man hier einem Team von drei Schülern die Möglichkeit bieten, etwa zwei Unterrichtsstunden weitgehend selbst zu gestalten.
A. Ein(e) Schüler(in) kümmert sich um die technisch-formale Seite.
(Musik, Cassettenrecorder bzw. Sprachlabor, Vervielfältigung eines eventuellen Lückentextes)
B: Ein(e) Schüler(in) bereitet die Vokabeln im Schülerbuch vor und leitet anschließend die Diskussion über den Text.
C: Ein(e) Schüler(in) bereitet ein Kurzreferat über Tracy Chapman vor (siehe *post-reading activities*).

Unterrichtsdisposition:
1. Stunde unter Leitung der Schüler A und B:
– Präsentation des Liedes auf Cassette (Platte/CD) im Klassenzimmer oder noch günstiger im Sprachlabor (bessere Akustik, Möglichkeit des mehrmaligen, selbständigen, individuellen Hörens gewisser Passagen), wobei die Schüler einen Lückentext (Vorschlag s. weiter unten!) ausfüllen.
– Besprechung des Wortschatzes;
– Jeder Schüler formuliert bis zu fünf sinnvolle Fragen zum Text, Festhalten einiger wichtiger Fragen (evtl. auch als Hausaufgabe).
2. Stunde:
– Diskussion der Titelvorschläge und Analyse des Songs unter Einbeziehung der Schülerfragen (Leitung Schüler B);
– nochmaliges Hören, um Frage 3 zu diskutieren (Leitung Schüler A und B);
– Referat von Schüler C und anschließende Diskussion;
– evtl. Spielen von anderen Liedern auf der Originalplatte (bzw. Cassette/CD).

**Lückentext:**

You got a fast car,
I want a ticket to _____
Maybe we can make a deal,
Maybe _____ we can get somewhere.
Any place is better
Starting from zero we got _____
Maybe we'll make something,
Me myself I got _____

You got a fast car
I got a plan to get us out of here
I been working at the convenience store
Managed to save just a _____
We won't have to drive to far
Just' cross the border and _____
You and I can both get _____
And finally see what it means _____

You see my old man's got a problem
He lives with the _____ that's the way it is
He says his body's too old for working
I say his body's too young to look like his
My mama went off and left him
She wanted more from life than _____
I said somebody's got to take care of him
So I _____ and that's what I did

You got a fast car
Is it fast enough so we can _____
We gotta make a decision
Leave tonight or live and _____

*Chorus:* So remember when we were driving, driving in your car
The speed so fast I felt like I was drunk

City lights lay out before us
And your arm felt nice wrapped round my shoulder
And I had a feeling that I _____
And I had a feeling I could _____

You got a fast car
And we go cruising to entertain ourselves
You still ain't got a job
Now I work in a market as a checkout girl
I know things will get better
You'll find work and I'll get _____
We'll move out of the shelter
Buy a big house and live _____

*Chorus*: So remember we were driving, etc.

You got a fast car
I got a job that _____
You stay out drinking late at the bars
See more of your friends than you do of your kids
I'd always hoped for better
Thought maybe together you and me would find it
I got no plans I ain't going nowhere
So take your fast car and _____

*Chorus*:
I Remember we were driving, etc.

You got a fast car
But is it fast enough so you can _____
You gotta make a decision:
Leave tonight or live and _____

## Suggested answers

1. Possible titles: Dropout/I had a dream/A feeling I could be someone/You gotta make a decision/I wanted more from life/...

2. Summary of content:
The song "Fast Car" is about a girl or young woman who has grown up in a broken home: her father is an unemployed alcoholic, her mother left him, the girl quit school to take care of her father. Together with her young man (who has got a fast car) she has hopes of self-fulfillment. She dreams that by working hard, she will one day be able to buy a big house and live in the suburbs. But her dreams come to nothing. Her job enables them to make ends meet, but her partner is unemployed, stays out drinking and doesn't look after his children. The young woman is completely disillusioned and frustrated. Realizing that the young man with his "fast car" – far from helping her to realize her dreams – has actually dragged her down, she finally asks her partner to take his fast car and go away. Note that unlike her mother, she does not choose to leave her family herself.

The story is told indirectly. In each verse the girl addresses her young man at a different stage in her life, expressing some modest hopes for social betterment. The three refrains hark back to happier times when the "fast car" stood for such hopes. But in the final short 4-line verse (almost, but not quite identical with the one in lines 25-28) a significant change in the pronoun shows she no longer expects anything of her partner.

3. The simple, quiet melody of the verses matches the matter-of-fact way the story is told. The verses are underlined by a rather monotonous guitar riff which makes no harmonic concessions to the melody (no chord changes). This may suggest hopelessness, frustration, a feeling of being trapped. In the refrain, however, the girl re-lives a time when she was happier and more hopeful, and here the harmonic changes give the song a lift, allowing us to share her (momentary) optimism.

## Additional questions

*1. Discuss the various reasons for the failure of the girl in the song to achieve her dreams.*

*2. Try to explain why she had such dreams, and held on to them for so long.*

*3. Relate her story to the message of the advertisement on page 169.*

*4. The girl's mother left her husband and family (ll. 21–22). Discuss the rights and wrongs of such a decision, especially in the light of the girl's own experience.*

## Post-reading activities

*1. Classroom talk: Tracy Chapman: her life and her songs.*
See "Methodisch-didaktische Hinweise" and background information.

*2. Listen to and talk about another song by Tracy Chapman.*

*Values in British and American Education*

# 5. Students, get mad!

## Pre-reading activity

*Classroom reports: short biographies of Iacocca's five heroes (see introduction).*

## Background information

Here are some quotations from *Talking Straight* by Lee Iacocca explaining what he sees in his five personal heroes.

Leonardo da Vinci:
"Leonardo was a genius, the authentic Renaissance man. He was artistic (the "Mona Lisa"); he was a scientist (flying machines, jet propulsion, and parachutes); and he was a leading expert on anatomy. ... it was the versatility of this man that first made me think a person can be as great as he wants to be. His mind and his hands literally let him reach for the stars." (pp. 313–314)

Joe DiMaggio (born 1914 in California, American baseball player, he played with the New York Yankees (1936–1951), and set a record of hitting safely in 56 games running; he was Marilyn Monroe's second husband):
"He ... gave me hope. He helped me shed a feeling I had when I was young that an immigrant kid – an Italian at that – would have trouble making it or ever earning respect. I can still remember pinning on my bedroom wall a newspaper sketch of Joe titled 'The Walloping Wop'. My reaction was a curious mixture of hurt and pride, but I promised myself I was going to grow up and be like Joe. I didn't know him in his glory days, but today he is still the quiet and gracious gentleman who excelled in his job and lived his life the same way." (p. 314)

Benjamin Franklin:
"Like Leonardo, he was a thinker, a tinkerer, a doer. When you think of Ben, you probably think of him flying a kite in a storm to prove his theory of electricity, or of him and the printing press. But in the *Encyclopaedia Britannica* he shows up in no less than eighty-one places. ... of all the men who sat in that room and hammered out the Constitution, he'd probably be the least surprised by the amazing things that have happened since then. I don't think he'd fall off his chair when I told him we'd been to the moon. He was a philosopher and yet a practical scientist, always looking ahead. But above all, he understood what people can do when they pull together." (pp. 314–315).

Harry Truman:
"He was the greatest of our Presidents, and I've always tried to emulate him. He talked to the masses openly and in their own language. ... He was feisty, blunt, and very, very decisive. Most of all, he was a man of the people, who stood for basic American values." (p. 315)

Winston Churchill:
"My all-time favorite hero, though, is Winston Churchill. As you know, I'm big on communications, and to me the great communicator is not Ronald Reagan but old Sir Winston. He was eloquent and he was a leader, if only he had such a command of the English language. ... His keen mind and quick wit separated him from all other leaders of his day. ... Churchill was also one of the funniest and bawdiest guys who ever lived. ... he was more than just quick. He gave life to the phrases 'British pluck' and 'true grit', and he even made smoking long Havana cigars in public fashionable – God love him." (pp. 315–316)

## Suggested answers

1. Students (he says) should get angry about
   – bad economic policies;
   – the national debt;
   – ideological trade principles;
   – packaged solutions.
   Reasons why they should get angry:
   – only angry people change things;
   – Americans have always brought about progress by not putting up with certain situations, by being practical and putting common sense ahead of ideology.

2. American values mentioned by Iacocca:
   – practical approach, common sense;
   – tolerance;
   – freedom of speech, of religion, of assembly;
   – self-reliance;
   – optimistic response to challenges.

3. According to Iacocca, the American Constitution is not a "blueprint" (l. 44), i.e. a detailed plan with concrete instructions or a fundamental ideology (l. 37). He characterizes it as a general outline, a "framework to work in" (ll. 42/43).

Given this assessment it is clear that the American Constitution has survived for so long and because the basic principles need not be changed to adapt to new circumstances.

4. According to Iacocca, American students of today want to live on the safe side. As they are afraid of failure, many of them are not prepared to take risks.
But in the future, they will have to shape "their" America themselves, they will have to take risks and respond to a "whole new set of challenges" (l. 121), in order to live up to the American tradition of every generation leaving the following one a "little better off" (l. 119). And Iacocca is basically optimistic that they will manage to do so.

5. Iacocca uses everyday, straight forward language. It has the rhythm of spoken speech – and was probably dictated rather than written. Despite some formal words (to emulate l. 5, espousal l. 39) he uses predominantly informal vocabulary, slang, and colloquial phrases.
Informal vocabulary/slang:
– a fair shot (l. 25)
– hang-up (l. 81)
– to screw s.th. up (l. 82)
– it sure felt that way (l. 99)
– And we are leaving you a couple of dandies! (ll. 121–122)
Colloquial quotations: ll. 9–12, 21, 25, 28–29, 32, 81–82.
Sentence structure: fairly simple and clearly structured.
Tone: emotionally involved, concerned, again and again addresses the students directly.

6. Examples of anaphora:
– Get mad ... (ll. 19, 22, 26)
– Tell them: ... (ll. 20, 21, 24, 27)
– ... how to ... or what to ... or how to ... or how to ... (ll. 57–60)
– ... the fear ... the fear ... (ll. 82–83)
– We didn't duck them; we faced them. (ll. 103–104)
Examples of tautology (no true tautologies in the sense of words which add nothing, but some overlapping meanings):
– ... managing and moderating (ll. 13–14)
– ... invent or devise them (l. 72)
– ... a nice safe, secure, prosperous future ... (l. 78)
Possible reasons for their use:
– He uses them deliberately for the purpose of intensification.
– He has got a natural feeling for syntactical rhythm; he is a talkative person who likes to express himself with a certain degree of redundancy.

7. Typical self-made man; pragmatic doer; pioneer; practical-minded; self-assured; optimistic; willing to take risks; energetic; spontaneous; ambitious; proud of his achievements and his popularity; personally committed; conceited (?); megalomaniac (?); talkative.

**Additional questions**

1. Find the phrases with which Iacocca echoes the message of the advertisement on page 169.

2. "We've often done a lousy job of figuring out just where we should be heading but we've usually done a brilliant job of getting there" (ll. 62–64). Discuss Iacocca's statement. Can you find examples?

## 6. Why abuse and scorn are the wrong treatment (GK)

**Pre-reading activities**

1. Look at the advertisement on page 186. What is its purpose? Who is it aimed at?

2. Where is Marlborough College, and what kind of a school is it?

3. How does one become a pupil there?

4. What reasons might parents have for sending their children there?

**Suggested answers**

1. Tone: personally concerned; critical; ironic, sarcastic (in part).
The critical and sarcastic tone is set from the very beginning, i.e. in the first paragraph ("nasty surprises" revealing the irony of the first sentence.). After that the article abounds in reproachful, even contemptuous or satirical passages, all of which show that the author is personally concerned about the situation described.

2. Differences:
a) GB: ... ruthless assault on the [state] comprehensive schools by both the Government and the media (ll. 35–37);
US: ... public schools are the backbone of both community and society, from both of which they derive sustained support (ll. 38–40).
b) GB: ...self-selected elite (ll. 110-111); I believe that no nation ... in an exclusive system. (ll. 14–17);
US: ... get the best out of all children, not just from a self-selected elite (ll. 109–111).
The author's observations about Britain seem to be justified. But the situation in the U.S. may not be as positive as he presents it, if text 3 ("Americanize and equalize?") is to be believed. The latter, however, shows some signs of exaggeration (see questions/answers), and the overall impression of American education as more egalitarian and meritocratic (esp. texts 1, 5) is probably still correct.

3. At first glance, 7% does not seem to be a decisive figure. (The U.S. figure is quite similar.) But if you realize how many of them in later life occupy the really important, most powerful and influential positions in Britain and thus run the country, you must come to the conclusion that the author's claim is justified.

4. The author starts off by mentioning his return from a stay in the USA to a dramatic educational crisis in Great Britain. He then proceeds to state his unequivocal position in favour of the local comprehensive school for his children. He criticizes his class-conscious neighbours for preferring exclusive private schools. He deplores what he sees as a ruthless assault of the Government and the media on the comprehensive state schools. Though he admits that the situation in these schools is really bad, the author finds the official reaction to be inadequate and even ridiculous. In particular he points out the negtive results of the low pay rates offered to teachers in state schools. In the closing paragraphs he expresses his scorn for those British politicians who think the system they administer is not good enough for themselves.

**Additional questions**

1. Discuss the significance of the following phrases and sentences:
– ll. 9–12 (explain the use of quotation marks!);
– ll. 22–26: "avoided ... by the Volvo-load";
– ll. 73–76: "assisted places ... a famine".

2. The author compares British school-leavers unfavourably with Americans who at the same age are "bright-eyed at the prospects inherent in their youth". Discuss in the light of the other texts you have read (esp. 1, 4, advertisement).

3. Translate the following sections of the article: ll. 1–12, ll. 87–95 and ll. 106–111.

**Post-reading activity**

Classroom report: The importance of Britain's "public schools".
See Bibliography 2, 5, 7, 8, 9; also Skyline B (Klettbuch 51032), pp. 72–74.

# 7. Next term, we'll mash you (GK)

**Pre-reading activity**

1. Classroom report on the importance of Britain's "public schools". (Cf. post-reading activity, text 6; the term "preparatory school" should be introduced and explained.)

2. If you lived in England, would you prefer to go to a (state) comprehensive school or to a (private) public school/preparatory school? Give reasons.

3. Public schools and "their" prep schools are normally boarding schools. What possible advantages or disadvantages can you think of in connection with such boarding schools?

4. Do you think it is right for parents to spend such a lot of money on the private education of their children?

**Suggested answers**

1. This short story satirizes the aspirations and attitudes of a typically ambitious middle-class couple. The Manders are looking for a good, prestigious prep school for their son Charles. They

obviously want to keep up with the Joneses (i.e. the Wilcoxes in this case), and are willing to invest a fairly high amount of money into their son's education. Charles, who is to be a status symbol for his family, is treated like an object and not like a little boy with feelings and misgivings about his future.

2. Different answers possible:
– The main character in this story is Charles. Although he doesn't say anything and even his thoughts go unrecorded, he is the character around whom the whole story centres.
– The parents are the main characters. Although the story is supposed to be about a choice of school for the boy, the focus all the time is on the parents and their snobbish attitudes.

3. The typically English setting is evoked in the following passages:
– (ll. 5–9) trim, cows, white-fenced fields, highly-priced period houses, glassy sunlight, remote as a coloured photograph;
– (l. 22) Oxford;
– (ll. 28–31) tight-clipped hedges, crunch of gravel;
– (l. 38) playing-fields (typical of English schools);
– (ll. 45–48) red brick building, neat gardening;
– (ll. 60–61) great big grounds, London;
– (ll. 63–65) dappled dawns, gently shifting trees, black and white cows grazing ...;
– (ll. 65–66) Books, leather chairs, a table with magazines – Country Life, The Field, The Economist;
– (l. 74) City people;
– (l. 78) cricket match;
– (l. 95) cricket pavilion;
– (ll. 100–102) Finchley/Hampstead;
– (l. 119) Winchester;
– (ll. 167–168) cricket pavilion.

4. References to nature:
– "trim ... countryside" (l. 6);
– "The sunlight was glassy, remote as a coloured photograph" (ll. 8–9);
– "tight–clipped hedges" (l. 29);
– "Flowers, trapped in neat beds" (ll. 47–48);
– "great big grounds" (l. 60);
– "dappled lawns, gently shifting trees, black and white cows grazing" (ll. 63–64);
– "shivering trees and high racing clouds" (l. 203).
On the one hand, most of these descriptions imply or convey the impression of a neat elegance and pleasant exclusiveness; on the other hand, nature has been interfered/meddled with, everything is tailored to human needs (cf. trim, tight-clipped, trapped). This mixed image corresponds exactly with the themes of the story, i.e. its depiction of a society with fixed rules, standards, habits, etc. Mr and Mrs Manders' massive influence on their son's life, and their aim to make him fit into the exclusive, elegant upper class.
The "shivering trees" in the later part of the story suggest the boy's feelings (loneliness? alienation? fear?).

5. The headmaster and his wife are "like paired cards in Happy Families" (ll. 154–155), i.e. they are rather similar as to their outer appearance, their social behaviour and their character. Generally speaking, they are conservative people who are characterized as nice, friendly, clean and orderly. Everything is neat and attended to (cf. ll. 47–48, l. 53); they look after their school well. But unlike the Manders, they make no special effort to make an impression in clothes (ll. 105–110, 154–158) or in manner (ll. 93–98). This reflects the relaxed confidence of the upper classes.
Headmaster:
– (l. 22) Oxford chap;
– (ll. 154–168) conservative, clean, genial, not conceited or arrogant at all, honest, kind, tolerant educationalist, ("indulgent");
– (l. 234) nice chap.
His wife:
– (ll. 92–153) polite, friendly, sociable, self-confident, respectable, "not attractive, ... a bit homespun, but impressive all the same", strong voice (bossy?);
– (ll. 169–195) energetic woman with natural authority; obviously liked by the pupils.

6. Mr and Mrs Manders obviously belong to the middle (or upper-middle) class. They are obviously quite well off. They drive an expensive car with leather upholstery. They are willing to "buy the best" (cf. text 6 of this chapter) in education, and just about able to afford it. They speak more or less "normal" English with some colloquialisms and slang expressions. Examples: chap (l. 22), quid (l. 27), super (l. 108), bloody (l. 136), why it costs a bomb (l. 59), stuff (l. 139), I'll drop him a line (l. 241), It's pricey (l. 236). These are all fairly typical of middle-class speech as are such terms of endearment as "darling" (l. 13). Some (like "super") are considered more upper (or upper-middle) class. In the passages written as interior

monologue and in their behaviour typical middle-class attitudes are revealed:
- (ll. 19–24) a touch of snobbery, desire to consort with the right people;
- (ll. 39–42, 51–52) care with one's own appearance, desire to give a good impression;
- (ll. 53–61) interest in outer appearances, social occasions and in dressing up to create the right impression; upper-class ambitions; great interest in neighbours (the Wilcoxes);
- (ll. 69–79) money and social prestige very important, interested in useful contacts with influential people;
- (ll. 82–89) very careful with their son's outer appearance;
- (ll. 100–102) care to emphasize the "right" address (Hampstead borders on Finchley but is much more prestigious);
- (ll. 103–112) middle-class attitude of pricing and assessing other people; awareness of social pointers – quality and plainness in clothes rather than ostentatious fashions, the "right" accent;
- (ll.121–123) satirical side-swipe at Sally Wilcox;
- (ll. 135–139) awareness of social pointers;
- (ll. 236–238) middle-class attitude of worrying a lot about money and status;
- (ll. 244–245) attempt to instill their middle-class attitudes (social climbing) in the boy's mind.

7. Satire: practically all of the passages where the Manders reveal their social aspirations, snobbery etc. (see previous question); in addition ll. 169–176.
Mild forms of irony occur in the dialogue and in the interior monologue, i.e. examples of understatement, exaggeration and sarcasm, where the form of the words deviates only slightly from the feeling expressed: ll. 95, 100 (exaggeration); ll. 110–111, 122–123 (sarcasm); ll. 125–131; ll. 160–161; ll. 186–189; l. 235 (probably euphemism for dislike). The mother's final remarks also contain an example of situational irony. She may think she is sincere in asking the boy whether he would like to go to the school, but we know it is settled already.

**Additional questions**

*1. (In connection with SB question 2:) Charles does not say anything, even his thoughts go unrecorded. How and what do we learn about him nevertheless, and how do we learn it?*

*2. What does the choice of magazines (ll. 66–67) tell the reader about St. Edward's Preparatory School?*

*3. Try to explain why the room the boy is taken to is so shabby by comparison with the rest of the building and grounds.*

*4. The conditional sentence in lines 182–184 is not quite correct. What could/should Mrs Stokes have said? Try to explain her mistake.*

*5. Explain the boys' threat (ll. 218–219). Why should they behave like this?*

*6. (In connection with SB question 6:) Why are the Wilcoxes mentioned so often?*

*7. There is a change in the narrative style at the point (l. 169) where the headmaster's wife bears Charles away, which is maintained until he is returned to his parents (l. 229)–and reoccurs in the last paragraph (ll. 248–251). What is the effect of this change?*

*8. "His face is haggard with anticipation." What is the meaning and message of this final sentence?*

**Post-reading activity**

*Imagine the boy were less quiet and subservient than he seems in this story. Write a dialogue between him and his parents about what school he should go to.*

# 8. Accent and equality

**Pre-reading activities**

*1. What do we learn about attitudes towards language and accent in the story "Next term, we'll mash you"?*

*2. Talk about the picture on p. 187. What does it show?*
It shows a scene near the beginning of My Fair Lady, where Professor Higgins is fascinated by the flower girl Eliza Doolittle's cockney accent, and

Values in British and American Education

boasts to Colonel Pickering (left) that he could teach her to speak like a duchess. The story of both film musical and play is based on the Greek legend of Pygmalion, who fell in love with a statue he had created. In the play/film, Higgins sees the transformed Eliza as his creation, and falls in love with her. In the play she rejects him, but the film has been given a more conventional "happy ending". The book from which the following excerpt is taken deals with the need for people to acquire a "better" accent as the key to social betterment in Britain. The title relates more to the Shaw play (and film) rather than the Greek legend.

3. *Classroom report: Language and class in by G.B. Shaw's* Pygmalion/My Fair Lady. *See above.*

**Background Information**

Ll. 64–65: The quoted phrase comes from J. Feinberg's article, "The child's right to an open future", in W. Aiken and H. Lafolette (eds.), *Whose child? Children's rights, parental authority and state power*, Totowa, NJ: Rowman and Littlefield, 1980, pp. 124–153.

**Suggested answers**

1. The author accepts the gradual dying out of accent varieties in Britain, because he thinks that they would strengthen class-consciousness and perpetuate social inequality in his country. In such a development towards a standard accent he sees a good chance for Britain to become as "open and genuinely democratic" as the U.S.A. or Australia.

2. Honey attributes the relative classlessness of the U.S.A. and Australia to the fact that a relatively high percentage of Americans speak with a standard accent (General American) and that nearly everybody in Australia speaks with the same accent. (This theory could be questioned. Varieties of accents do exist both in Australia and in the U.S.A., but there is less or no stigma attached to them. A southern drawl, for example, might be laughed at by northerners, but a Texas oil baron would certainly see no reason to conform to their style of speech. There is some social stigma attached to "black English".)

3. Meaning of the argument: Society should become more tolerant and accept non-standard accents. Thus the pressure on a child to learn an extra language, a standard accent, would be diminished.

Author's opinion: John Honey considers this argument "simplistic". He even thinks it may be dangerous, and harmful to the children in question, because nobody can guarantee that social attitudes will really change.

Possible dissenting opinion: Honey may be right in fearing that children who do not learn the standard accent may go on being at a disadvantage. But trying to teach them all the "correct" accent merely perpetuates the situation, so that regional accents will never gain acceptance. But in fact they are gaining more recognition (e.g. on the BBC) and people should encourage this development.

4. John Honey's attack on his "professorial colleague" seems quite justified, if what he says is true. The professor is certainly guilty of hypocrisy if he supports a 14-year-old black girl in her belief that her strong Cockney accent will not cause any problems for her, whereas for himself and his children he has, of course, chosen social acceptance through acquiring a "good" accent. It is an example of "do as I say, don't as I do".

But: the professor's hypocrisy does not necessarily make his advice wrong.

5. "Open future" means that a child should later be able to choose from a variety of alternatives, that the gateway towards various opportunities should not be closed. The precondition for such a prospect is, he claims, the child's ability to speak a standard accent. Given the relatively great importance attached to class and language in Britain, it seems almost inevitable that the child with only one local accent at his or her disposal is doomed to a restricted kind of life.

6. Summary:
John Honey starts off by saying that he does not object to the eventual disappearance of accent varieties in Britain, because they are barriers on the way towards an equal, more open and truly democratic country like the U.S.A. or Australia. In the second section (ll. 17–30) he refutes the argument that society should change and accept the child with its individual (regional) accent as naive and even irresponsible towards the young generation, as nobody can guarantee that society will really change. The author then proceeds to illustrate the overriding importance of a standard

accent by dealing with concrete examples and by quoting some authorities. As a conclusion he repeats his claim that a variety of non-standard accents is to blame for social inequality. (ca. 120 words)

7. Translation (ll. 17–30): Ein simplistisches (zu sehr vereinfachendes) Argument besagt, daß wir, anstatt vom einzelnen Kind zu verlangen, sich der Gesellschaft anzupassen, vielmehr die Gesellschaft dahingehend ändern sollten, sich auf die Eigenheiten des Kindes einzustellen. Jene, die dieses Argument dazu benutzen, Kindern den Zugang zu jeglichem Bewußtsein darüber zu verbauen, welche Folgen es hat, mit einem ganz bestimmten Akzent und nicht mit einem anderen zu sprechen, erweisen ihnen eindeutig einen schlechten Dienst (einen eindeutigen Bärendienst), wenn sie nicht auch garantieren können, daß sich die gesellschaftlichen Einstellungen rechtzeitig geändert haben werden, damit jene Generation von Kindern davon profitieren kann. Leider ist solch eine Garantie unmöglich, und sei es nur aus dem einfachen Grund, wie ich wiederholt betont habe, daß es bei der Frage des Akzents um ein vielschichtigeres Bündel an Einschätzungen/Urteilen geht als bloß um gesellschaftlichen Snobismus.

Lines 45–70:
Mein professoraler Kollege ermunterte sie ebenso nachdrücklich, sich von niemandem sagen zu lassen, daß die Fähigkeit, nur mit diesem einen Akzent zu sprechen, irgendwie von Nachteil sein könnte. Obwohl ich keine Gelegenheit erhielt, dies zu sagen, konnte ich mir doch viele Situationen vorstellen, in denen dieser starke lokale Akzent ihre Chancen im Leben schmälern würde, (z.B.) sicherlich dann, wenn sie die Grenzen ihrer Gemeinde und ihrer unmittelbaren Nachbarschaft verließe. Es war schon ironisch, daß sie den Rat von einem Professor bekam, der selbst von einem lokalen Londoner Akzent zur Hochsprache gewechselt war, ohne die er seine Professur höchstwahrscheinlich nicht bekommen hätte. Mehr noch, er hatte sich für einen Wohngegend und für seine Kinder für Schulen entschieden, die sicherstellten, daß auch sie nicht mit einer Sprache durchs Leben gehen mußten, die beizubehalten er diesen jungen Teenager ermutigte.

Was hier wirklich zur Debatte steht, ist das Recht eines Kindes auf eine "offene Zukunft". Indem wir dieses Mädchen davon abbringen, ihr Sprachrepertoire durch das Einbeziehen einer allgemein akzeptierten Standardsprache zu erweitern, bestimmen wir von vornherein ihre Lebenschancen bei der Wahl ihres Arbeitsplatzes, in ihren gesellschaftlichen Beziehungen und allgemein in ihrem Lebensstil. ("she will be able to enjoy" ist in der deutschen Fassung implizit.)

### Additional question

*Terry Wogan (the talk show host referred to in lines 79–80) speaks with an Irish accent. Try to explain why such an accent is acceptable if Cockney isn't.*

### Post-reading activities

*1. Classroom reports:*
– *Language and class in Shaw's Pygmalion* – if not dealt with as a pre-reading activity.
– *Bilingual education in the U.S.A.*
   Cf. chapter 10, text 10.

*2. Discussion of Honey's arguments in the light of these classroom reports.*

## 9. Listening Comprehension: A working-class girl in a grammar school

### Methodisch-didaktische Hinweise

N.B. Es handelt sich um eine Neuaufnahme des Interviewtextes.
Eine Einleitung, Worterklärungen und Fragen zum Globalverständnis sind im Schülerbuch, S. 188 abgedruckt.

### Pre-listening activities

*1. Quotation from text 8: "If you were a good fairy, hovering over the cradle of an English child of today, the most prized gift you could bestow on it would be an impeccable accent." (ll. 73–76)*

*Values in British and American Education*

*Explain this statement and say whether it applies to any extent in your own country.*

2. *What accent (or dialect) do you speak at home? Is it the same as the way you speak in public/at school?*

3. *Consider the title of the recording. What does it seem to imply?* (A grammar school is not a "public school", but like the German "Gymnasium", to some extent, its pupils are seldom working-class children.) *Try to think of some problems the girl in question might have faced.*

**Transcript**

Implicitly and explicitly we were inculcated with our role in the 'art of conversation' which encouraged us not only to be correct (as not doubt working-class boys would be encouraged in the grammar school) but also polite and deferential (an attribute not necessarily encouraged among boys). My grammar school education reveals a *class* and a *gender ideology* at work on my language.

I managed to conform and meet the linguistic requirements of the school, but they could only be used within the school. I had to abandon them when I left the schol gates and had to change my language for home. Such 'bilingualism' is not without its disadvantages and can work to make one feel inadequate and unconfident in all language use. Mistakes at school could be an offence, but so too could mistakes at home. I was an constant terror of being exposed as a 'freak'. My way of dealing with this threat was to over-react. In my home environment I made a concerted effort to appear as 'one of the girls' and to do this I felt obliged to be louder than anyone else, to swear more, just to prove I wasn't different and hadnt been corrupted by the grammar school.

It was like leading a double life, for neither side would have recognised me in the other context. I was straddling two very different worlds and felt considerably threatened by the fact that I didn't belong to either. I had a constant sense of being different, which I interpreted as inferiority. I was always aware of the possibility of making a mistake and being exposed as fraudulent. I could not relax in either setting. I had a sense of inferiority within school because I didn't come from such a 'good' background as most of the other pupils. I was always uneasy when people began to parade their status symbols and discuss their father's occupations and where they lived. At school I felt ashamed of my background and attempted to conceal it. My Dad was a manual worker and we were pretty poor and I didn't want my classmates to know this. Nor did I want them to know that I lived in a 'rough' area, in a house that didn't have a bathroom.

At the same time I didn't want my friends in my neighbourhood to know that I was considered clever at school. (It is not of course unusual for some working-class kids who have received scholarships to be diagnosed in this way. One 'clever' working-class student vindicates the whole system and attests to the myth of equality of opportunity. However, it places enormous demands on such students.) In order not to be dismissed by my out-of-school friends I pretended that school was unimportant; I gave the impression that I didn't care about it. This of course demanded many subterfuges on my part. Life was a juggling process. Homework, for example, was difficult for me as I did not want my friends to know that I did it (I could not have preserved the belief that I didn't care about school if I indicated that I conscientiously did my homework). Because I didn't want my friends thinking I was a 'swot' (and withdrawing their friendship as a result) I tried to get all my homework finished before they came to call for me.

With my girlfriends the problems associated with school success were class ones and so that I could retain their friendship I disguised my attitude to school. But there are gender as well as class dimensions to this problem for it wasn't just with my girlfriends that I felt obliged to hide my school achievements. The problem of being seen as clever was particularly acute when it came to having boyfriends. I thought that being regarded as intelligent would make me less attractive to boys. I was already careful, therefore, to make light of my grammar school education and to refrain from mentioning how many O-levels I was doing. Again there was the fear of making a mistake for, to me, it seemed that it would be a mistake to be seen as being more clever than a boy.

The pressures on me were conflicting and varied. For quite a while I tried to negotiate two worlds, but the time came when such negotiation was no longer possible. The two worlds proved to be incompatible. The two sets of values ordained different futures and teh point came where I had to decide which future would be mine. Eventually the pull of the school was stonger for it held out the promise of social mobility through higher education. Once I decided to stay on at school after the statutory leaving age my fate was sealed. I could no longer pretend that school was unimportant or irrelevant. It was clear to my friends at home that I had marked myself as 'different' and from this point our paths were to diverge. They entered the world of paid work and they left me behind; I could not disguise myself as one of them any more.

From "A working-class girl in a grammar school" by Irene Payne in *Learning to lose* by Dale Spender and Elizabeth Sarah, eds., London: The Women's Press Ltd. Reprinted by permission.

## Suggested answers

I.1. Like the boys at her grammar school, Irene was taught to be linguistically "correct", but as a girl she was encouraged to be "polite and deferential" as well.

2. Irene was caught between two different worlds, i.e. her grammar school and her (working-class) home. In her attempt to adapt to both these environments, she had to change again and again. She lived in constant fear of making mistakes and over-reacted to that challenge.

II.1. Irene was leading a double life, and didn't know any longer where she really belonged. She lived in constant fear of making mistakes and of being branded as dishonest. At school she felt uneasy and dveloped a kind of inferiority complex because of her poor working-class background.

2. With her out-of-school friends she did everything to avoid the impression that she was clever at school, that she worked hard and conscientiously. In order not to lose their friendship she pretended that school was unimportant.

3. With boyfriends she was particularly careful to avoid the impression of being clever or intelligent, because she thought that that would make her less attractive to them. Therefore she intentionally made light of her grammar school education and didn't mention her achievements at all.

III. I think she should stay at school after her O-levels, because
– she obviously has got the talent/potential to do so;
– she should make the best of her potential;
– she will be able to climb her social ladder and overcome her working-class background;
– she will then be able to use her education to improve society in some way, to break down the social barriers that have caused her so much trouble;
– she should stop being influenced by her friends' sexist prejudice;
– her "friends" will soon leave her anyway.

I think she should go back "to her own world", because
– that is where she really belongs;
– she wouldn't then have to live in an identity crisis anymore;
– she wouldn't have to disguise anymore.

Irene's decision:
For some time Irene tried to muddle through, but in the end she decided to stay on at school, because the prospect of "social mobility through higher education" was stronger than the feeling of being "one of them". She was fully aware of the consequences of her decision which meant that she marked herself as "different".

## Post-reading activities

1. Discuss Irene's remarks: "One 'clever' working-class student vindicates the whole system and attests to the myth of equality of opportunity. However, it places enormous demands on such students."

2. Comment on the perspective expressed in the sentence "They entered the world of paid work and they left me behind."

# 10. Education and economic prosperity

## Pre-reading activity

*Quotation from question 6 c):*
"*Education is not for the sake of the student but for the sake of the state!*" Discuss.

This quotation should be presented on the blackboard or overhead projector, and the discussion can take the form of a brainstorming, in which certain important key words and phrases are noted either by the teacher or a chosen student. The source (Mori Arinori, Japanese Minister of Education, 1885–1889) should not be revealed until the end of the discussion.

**Suggested answers**

1. The British attitude towards education was for a long time "anti-utilitarian and anti-industrial" (l. 43), i.e. subjects with any practical value were despised. In other words, education was not a training for any particular purpose and there was no "central or national idea" (l. 2) behind it.

2. According to the author, the British ruling class and their public schools are to blame for the way British education developed: the aristocratic class stood in the way of technical and scientific progress, they adhered to their anti-utilitarian and anti-industrial prejudice and refused "to recognize that their privileged world is doomed".

3. Drastic consequences: Modern subjects like science and technology were long neglected, the importance of industry was underestimated. This outdated and "foolish" (l. 44) attitude contributed to Britain's industrial decline.

4. To some extent Macmillan's classics tutor was right. It is of course important for peple to "be able to detect when a man is talking rot" i.e. to distinguish between good arguments and bad ones, between important and unimportant matters. But the opinion that "that is the main if not the sole purpose of education" seems to be exaggerated. And it is doubtful if even he himself really meant that "Nothing that you will learn on the course of studies will be the slightest use to you in after life." In our times nobody would accept such an "idealistic" or naive notion of education.
Purpose of education today:
a) Development of one's personality:
– training of mind and body;
– teaching right from wrong (values!), character training;
– teaching of manners and social integration.
b) Acquisition of skills:
– basic skills (3 Rs: reading, writing, arithmetic);
– specialized skills needed in particular jobs and professions.

5. The Education Reform Act of 1988 centralized the English and Welsh education system by introducing a national curriculum and more powers and responsibility for central government. The Butler Act of 1944 had made it largely a local responsibility.

6. a) Points:
– science subjects are important to prepare children for our technical world;
– competition with other states (e.g. Japan) requires a high level of scientific education;
– but languages more important than ever (interdependent world, international exchange, tourism);
– human qualities (living together in peace, respect for others, responsibility, etc.) absolutely vital for mankind to survive in an ever more vulnerable world.

b) Points:
– competitive world: informed, intelligent, well-trained, flexible, responsible people are needed;
– therefore skills and human qualities must be taught at schools to prepare young people for their future roles in society/in the economic world;
– question of input/output: the more you invest in education (quality and length), the more you are likely to get out of it;
– it is self-evident that the quality of education is an important factor, but length is not necessarily decisive.

c) Points:
– Japanese culture even today stresses social responsibility rather than individual freedom;
– in the 19th century with the development of the national states this statement may have been understandable;
– but in our democratized, liberal world individual liberties, chances and capabilities must be given the first priority;
– an individual, humanistic approach to education will also benefit the state, because fully respected citizens are more highly motivated and will contribute more towards the common good than subservient subjects.

**Additional questions**

1. Discuss whether the following "useful" subjects should be taught at school: cooking, typewriting, computer skills, driving, dancing.

2. In the U.S.A. there is a scheme in which businesses "adopt" schools and give them financial support. What do you think of this idea?

# Test: The Pledge of Allegiance in public schools

Since public school children first recited the Pledge of Allegiance in 1892, whether they should be required to do so has been a continuing issue. In 1940, the United States Supreme Court ruled that the state could require all children to salute the flag. The court reversed itself in 1943 and held that the flag salute required by state law violated the religious beliefs of Jehovah's Witnesses, and, on that basis, compelling all students to salute the flag is unconstitutional. That decision has been upheld to date. No one, including teachers and students, may be compelled to recite the Pledge or punished in any fashion for refusing to do so.

Requiring school children to recite the Pledge, therefore, is a violation of fundamental constitutional rights and freedoms. Totalitarian countries impose political orthodoxy upon their citizens by mandating displays of allegiance; the United States does not, since the Constitution prohibits such mandates.

Recital of the Pledge may be opposed for other reasons as well. For most children, the ritual is meaningless, done without thought. As such, it does not foster love of country or patriotism. Children under 7 or 8 years of age have no clear idea of what the Pledge is. Teachers know how unintelligible the Pledge is for children and collect and chuckle over children's misrepresentations: "To the Publix for which is stands," "One nation invisible," "with liberty and jelly for all."

For children under the age of 6, the flag belongs to a class of objects like stars or things that are red and white. Some even think that the flag is alive. Around age 7 or 8, children know that the flag has something to do with a country, but the concept that a flag represents a country doesn't develop until 11 or 12.

Because the Pledge holds little meaning, reciting it is more an act of indoctrination than patriotism. Ritual acts of indoctrination do not promote patriotism, but they have the opposite effect. The consequences of indoctrination are unwillingness to accept social conflict, obedient orientation to authority, and failure to understand the meaning of democratic principles. In fact, frequent participation in patriotic rituals has been associated with lower scores on knowledge of civics and less support for democratic values.

Yet the school has long been seen as vital for the political socialization of children. Through rituals such as recitation of the Pledge, children begin to recognize and develop respect for national symbols. Even with the absence of any meaning, these rituals can orient children toward positive attitudes about country and lead to development of high levels of trust and liking for political leaders. Through imitation and identification with parents, teachers, and other school leaders, children learn and internalize political attitudes. Young children may be uncertain about the meaning of the Pledge or the flag, but they realize that the adults around them value both highly.

Exposure to recitation of the Pledge, when children are young and in school, is seen as a never-to-be-repeated opportunity to instill love of country. Especially on the affective level, recitation of the Pledge with a group of peers is an effective experience in political socialization.

The political orientation developed through imitation and identification can be followed with instruction as children mature. By age 8 or 9, the concepts behind the Pledge – citizenship, democracy, government, and politics – could be part of the curriculum.

To pledge or not to pledge? This is not the question. Under the U.S. Constitution, students are guaranteed the right to recite or not to recite the Pledge in public schools. Rather, the question is how to turn the ritual into a significant, meaningful act for those who wish to participate. Daily recitation too easily becomes indoctrination. Limiting the Pledge to special occasions, national holidays, and school assemblies might help children to sense that the flag, as well as the Pledge, holds special meaning for the nation. Children acquire this sense of special meaning gradually through stories, dramatizations, discussions about appropriate uses and care of the flag, and practice in handling it. They begin to feel pride both in their own accomplishments and in the flag.

Political socialization that goes beyond rituals and indoctrination involves much more than recitation of the Pledge. The school's role in political socialization is complex; one must consider attitudes, knowledge, and dvelopmental stages. Even very young children can be actively involved in the school community with rule setting, obeying rules, or seeking ways to democratically change rules that do not work. Older children can actually take part in the political life of the community, state, and nation.

Article by Carol Seefeldt in *Childhood Education,* September 1989.

**Annotation:**

**The Pledge of Allegiance to the Flag**  "I pledge allegiance to the Flag of the United States of America, and to the Republic for which it stands, one Nation under God, indivisible, with liberty and justice for all."
The original pledge was published in the Sept. 8, 1892, issue of *The Youth's Companion* in Boston. The phrase "under God" was added to the pledge on June 14, 1954.

**I. Language**

1. Find suitable substitutes for the words/expressions in italics within the given context. Do not change the sentence structure.
– l. 4: "the United States Supreme Court *ruled* ..."
– ll. 10-11: "That decision has been upheld *to date.*"
– ll. 16-17: "Totalitarian countries *impose* political orthodoxy *upon* their citizens ..."
– ll. 23-24: "it does not *foster* love of country ..."
– l. 71: "as children *mature.*"
– ll. 89–90: "in their own *accomplishments* ..."

2. Explain the following phrases. Do not use the words in italics. You may use a different structure.
– l. 59: "learn and *internalize* political attitudes."
– l. 67: "with a group of *peers* ..."

3. Find the corresponding abstract nouns (not the "*ing*-forms"):
– to refuse (l. 13)
– obedient (l. 43)
– vital (l. 49)
– uncertain (l. 60)
– significant (l. 79)

4. Name the "*ing*-forms" in lines 3 and 14 and explain their grammatical functions.

5. What kind of word is "developed" (l. 69)? What is its grammatical function?

6. "To pledge or not to pledge? This is not the question." (ll. 75–76) Name the stylistic device used here and explain its function?

**II. Comprehension**

Answer the following questions in complete sentences.
1. Why did the Supreme Court reverse itself in 1943 as to the question of the Pledge of Allegiance?

2. Sum up the reasons for and against the recital of the Pledge of Allegiance which are mentioned in the article.

3. Compare children's misrepresentations of the Pledge (ll. 29-30) with the real text and say in what way they are funny.

4. Can you tell from this article whether the author is more for or against the Pledge of Allegiance? Give reasons.

**III. Comment/Composition**

Write about 200 words on one of the following topics:
1. The Pledge of Allegiance in public schools should be abolished altogether/Such a Pledge should be introduced in our country.

2. The main purpose of schools is not the teaching of facts and figures, but the development of "good" citizens. Discuss.

3. Patriotism is old-fashioned and even dangerous.

# Bibliography

1. Bloom, Alan. *The Closing of the American Mind: How higher education has failed democracy and impoverished the souls of today's students*. Penguin Books, 1987 (sehr anspruchsvoll, anregend, für die Hand des Lehrers).
2. Critchfield, Richard. *Among the British: An Outsider's View*. London: Hamish Hamilton 1990.
3. Honey, John. *Does Accent Matter? The Pygmalion Factor*. London: Faber and Faber 1989.
4. Iacocca, Lee. *Talking Straight*. New York: Bantam Books 1988.
5. Jacobs, Eric and Worcester, Robert. *We British, Britain under the MORIscope*. London: Weidenfeld and Nicolson 1990.
6. Perspectives 1: *The American Dream*. Klettbuch 51361.
7. Perspectives 4: *Education in Britain and America*. Klettbuch 51364.
8. Randle, John. *British Life and Institutions*. Klettbuch 51344.
9. Spann, Ekkehard. *Abiturwissen, Landeskunde Great Britain/United States of America*. Klettbuch 929509.
10. Stevenson, D. K. *American Life and Institutions*. Klettbuch 5136.
11. Terkel, Studs. *American Dreams: Lost and Found*. London: Paladin Books 1980.
12. Terkel, Studs. *The Great Divide, Second Thoughts on the American Dream*. New York: Avon Books 1988.

# 9 The Struggle for Democracy

## Structure of the chapter

| | Great Britain | U.S.A. | |
|---|---|---|---|
| Historical development: working-class and women's rights, suffrage | 1. The call to Freedom<br>216 words<br>poem excerpt | 8. Equality before the law<br>374 words<br>fictional courtroom speech (novel excerpt) | Historical development: equal rights before the law (esp. blacks and women) |
| | 2. A working man's share<br>415 words<br>fictional speech (novel excerpt) | 9. A maxim for free society<br>393 words<br>political speech | |
| | 3. Two great movements<br>300 words<br>excerpt from social history | 10. The jury system perverted<br>796 words<br>excerpt from autobiographical narrative | |
| | 4. Listening Comprehension: Black Friday<br>3 min. 37 sec.<br>autobiography excerpt | 12. The Seneca Falls Declaration of Sentiments<br>503 words<br>declaration | 11. Is jury selection unconstitutional?<br>341 words<br>newspaper article |
| Present-day issues | 5. Put the rules of the game in writing<br>657 words<br>open letter (pamphlet) | | Present-day issues |
| | 6. A Scottish Parliament<br>782 words<br>newspaper article | 7. A way to rescue British freedoms<br>755 words<br>pamphlet excerpt | 13. Listening Comprehension: A claim to a share of America<br>10 min. 12 sec.<br>party-political speech |
| | | | 14. Congress should pass the flag amendment<br>423 words<br>newspaper commentary |

*The Struggle for Democracy*     195

## Suggestions for reports/papers/talks

Percy Bysshe Shelley: his life and works – after text 1

Lord Castlereagh and his political role – after text 1

Riots and strikes in the American Labor movement 1886–1894: a comparison with the Peterloo incident – after text 1

A study of recent election posters – after text 2

The suffragette movement – after text 4

Britain's unwritten "Constitution" – before text 5

A summary of Scottish history – before/after text 6

The novel (or the film) *To Kill a Mockingbird* – before/after text 8

The U.S. Constitution and the problem of slavery and racial discrimination – after text 9

Mark Twain: his life and works – after text 10

**Vocabulary**

*Thematischer Grund- und Aufbauwortschatz Englisch*, Klettbuch 51955, pp. 124–138, 145–146

*Words in Context, Thematischer Oberstufenwortschatz*, Klettbuch 51961, pp. 4–16, 58–61, 66–71

# 1. The call to Freedom

**Background information**

The peaceful meeting referred to in the introduction was broken up by the Manchester Yeomanry on the orders of the Manchester authorities, who feared a general uprising. The Yeomanry consisted largely of merchants, farmers and small tradesmen.
These classes thought they had the most to fear from concessions to the working classes.

Shelley wrote "The Mask of Anarchy" when he was in Italy in 1819–20, but it was not published until 1832, since it was regarded as too revolutionary at the time of writing. The complete poem consists of 91 stanzas. His wrath was targeted in particular at Lord Castlereagh whom he held responsible for this outrage. The second stanza leaves no room for doubt:

I met Murder on the way –
He had a mask like Castlereagh –
Very smooth he looked, yet grim;
Seven blood-hounds followed him:

Among these blood-hounds are Fraud, Hypocrisy and Anarchy – the latter in the guise of "God and Law and King". Then the "Men of England" are exhorted to –

"Rise like Lions after slumber
In unvanquishable number –
Shake your chains to earth like dew
Which in sleep had fallen on you –
Ye are many – they are few."

– a stanza which is repeated at the end of the poem, after the lines discussing the nature of Freedom and Slavery.

Shelley's state of mind at the time of writing is described by his wife, Mary Shelley, in a note she wrote for its first publication in 1832, ten years after he had been drowned in a boating accident in Italy:

"Though Shelley's first eager desire to excite his countrymen to resist openly the oppression existent during 'the good old times' had faded with early youth, still his warmest sympathies were for the people. He was a republican, and loved a democracy. He looked on all human beings as inheriting an equal right to possess the dearest privileges of our nature; the necessaries of life when fairly earned by a labour, and intellectual instruction. His hatred of any despotism that looked upon the people as not to be consulted, or protected from want and ignorance, was intense. He was residing near Leghorn, at Villa Valsovano, writing *The Cenci*, when the news of the Manchester Massacre reached us; it roused in him violent emotions of indignation and compassion. The great truth that the many, if accordant and resolute, could control the few, as was shown some years after, made him long to teach his injured countrymen how to resist. Inspired by these feelings, he wrote the *Mask of Anarchy* (...) The poem was written for the people, and is therefore in a more popular tone than usual: portions strike as abrupt and unpolished. (...) The most touching passage is that which describes the blessed effects of liberty; it might make a patriot of any man whose heart was not wholly closed against his humbler fellow-creatures."

**Pre-reading activities**

*1. Discuss the picture on page 192.*
The banners demand "Universal Suffrage" and "Universal Civil and Religious Liberty" (or "Liberties"?)."

*2. Read the first four words of Shelley's poem, and try to imagine how the people in the picture would have answered the question.*

**Suggested answers**

1. For the working man freedom means: bread, a happy family, a happy home. It means much the same thing to the "trampled multitude" (fire, clothes, food), which presumably includes the workers.
To the rich freedom is a "check" on their absolute powers over their victims.

2. The abstract notions associated with freedom are "Justice", "Wisdom" and "Peace". The poet uses anaphora, the repetition of the same word group "Thou art" at the beginning of three successive stanzas in order to drive his message home.

3. Regular four-line stanzas (with occasional five line exceptions) in iambic tetrameter, rhyming aabb; heavy use of special "poetic" language: unnatural word order (cf. ll 1–3), archaic pronouns and verb forms (thou art/dost/shield'st, thee, etc.). Most modern poems use ordinary everyday language and are generally much freeer and less regular in the use of rhythm. (Shelley and the other Romantic poets were often quite revolutionary as regards subject-matter and the feelings expressed in their poems, but generally held on to the poetic conventions of the classical past.)

4. England must have been a country where the majority of people were badly housed, poorly fed and without basic civil rights. The ruling classes, synonymous with the rich, oppressed these people; the laws could be manipulated. The Church had decisive influence on the intellectual climate of the time, and tried to influence people against any movements towards greater freedom. People were especially made to suffer by being sent to endless wars.

5. The poet sees all the difficulties and obstacles in the way of freedom but he is convinced that freedom will triumph eventually (cf. ll. 5–8, 36–37).

6. What is freedom? If oppressed people could answer this question, tyrants would be driven away as if they had never existed. Freedom is not, as some imposters say, a meaningless idea that will soon disappear. But it means different things to different people.
To the working man and the masses of people it means material safety, emotional security and a life in which the most basic human needs are catered for. (If England were a really free country, people would not be starving as they are now.) To the rich, freedom for the general public means a restriction on their absolute powers over their victims, the poor.
Freedom brings with it a number of important advantages to humanity; three are mentioned here. The first is justice – since freedom makes people equal, and makes it impossible for the rich to manipulate the law, as often happens in England at present. The second is wisdom – since free people will not be susceptible to the lies of official religion. The third is peace – since only tyrants cause wars and send thousands to their deaths (often in cause of suppressing freedom, as in Gaul).
But no matter how much English blood has been shed in the struggle for freedom, such setbacks will not stop its advance and final victory.

**Post-reading activities**

The following may take the form of classroom reports:

*1. Go to the library and find out more about Percy Bysshe Shelley.*

*2. Find out more about Lord Castlereagh and his political role.*

*3. The Haymarket Riot (1886), the Homestead Strike (1892) and the Pullman Strike (1894) are three landmarks in the history of the American labor movement. Find out more about these events and the issues at stake and compare them with the Peterloo Massacre.*

# 2. A working man's share / 3. Two great movements (GK)

## Background information

George Eliot's real name was Mary Ann Evans. She is regarded as one of the greatest of English novelists. Her novels include *The Mill on the Floss*, *Adam Bede*, *Silas Marner*, *Felix Holt the Radical*, *Middlemarch* and *Daniel Deronda*. She also wrote a number of philosophical and critical works and translated philosophical works from the German. The main topic of the novel *Felix Holt* is the contrast between corrupt politicians who only serve their self-interest, and the idealistic fighters for freedom and social justice. The backdrop are the parliamentary elections of the year 1832 in which the working class did not yet have the right to vote. Felix Holt is fervent militant of the working-class cause.

For details of the political background see the following excerpt: "Two Great Movements".

The camp meetings referred to in the poster (p. 195) were quasi-religious gatherings which had spread from United States frontier to Europe in first half of the 19th century.

## Pre-reading activities

*Think of recent strikes in your country and write down the demands that were at stake. What conclusions do you draw from your findings as to the present situation of the working people?*

## Suggested answers

1. He thinks that it is just an instrument in the hands of the ruling classes to uphold their position of power in the country. By giving the vote to some of the middle classes, they will be bribed into abandoning any political struggle for wider suffrage.

2. Religion, to him, is another instrument in the hands of the rich to keep down the masses and gain advantages for themselves. The masses are told that they have to wait for heaven and the after-life where all their sorrows will be over.

3. The speaker wants universal suffrage, annual (i.e. in this context: regular) parliaments, the secret vote and electoral districts in order to put into practice one fundamental principle of parliamentary democracy: one man, one vote. This differs from present-day parliamentary democracy in one important respect: his aspirations for "universal" suffrage are restricted to men.

4. It is an effective political speech. The speaker takes sides in an unequivocal manner and in matters which affect both the daily lives of the poor and their standing as citizens of their country. He uses the "them and us" dichotomy in order to arouse his audience's emotions. He never really identifies who the "they" in effect are, thus enabling the individual spectators to form their own image of the oppressors' attack.

The anaphoric use of "We must" is used to drive the urgency of his message home. The enumeration of the political rights that are needed is accentuated by the repetition of "and": "... we must have universal suffrage, and annual parliaments, and the vote by ballot, and electoral districts." (ll. 44–47).

5. The excerpt entitled "Two great movements" gives a factual account of the political struggle which forms the background of the novel *Felix Holt*. It contains a comprehensive list of the political demands of the Chartist Movement, which are identical with and complement the ones put forward in the speech extract from *Felix Holt*: universal manhood suffrage, annual parliaments, voting by ballot, equal constituencies, no property qualifications for Members of Parliament, payment of the Members of Parliament.

The speech extract fulfills the definition of the form of discourse called persuasion; his aim is obviously to persuade people into taking appropriate action. (This kind of discourse can also be called appellative.) It is, of course, imbedded in a narrative, the novel *Felix Holt*. "Two great movements" provides an example of exposition; the reader is given information on a specific field of interest.

## Poster, page 195

This poster is an emotional appeal to the working-class people of the Stockport area. It presents a vivid description of what working-class life is like. Adjectives play an important role: "horrifying work", "trifling wages", "the niggardly hand of capital". "Hand" is used metaphorically twice: "the hand of oppression" and "the niggardly hand of capital".

The urgency of their complaints is underlined by the anaphoric structure of the second paragraph ("We have, ..., we have ..., we have..."), which also bears witness to the futility of their efforts.
Hymns should uplift the spirits of the people present and give them a sense of solidarity and community.
This poster provides a real-life example of the kind of political agitation presented fictionally by George Eliot and described in a more abstract way by John Randle.

### Additional questions (text 3)

1. *Name the grammatical forms "enfranchised" (l. 5) and "convinced" (l. 11), and explain how they are used.*

2. a) *This passage contains several examples of the passive voice. Find them, and explain why this form was chosen.* (Ll. 1–3, 9–10, 16–17, 19–20, 21, 22, 23, 41–42.)
b) *Which of these ideas could have been easily expressed in the active voice?* (Ll. 1–3; 9–10.)
c) *Find at least one active sentence which might also be expressed in the passive voice. Explain any difference in meaning of emphasis.* (Ll. 6–7, 24–25, 28–29, 35–36, 37–38.)

3. *Find all the -ing forms (also in the Chartist poster, p. 195) and explain their use.*

### Post-reading activity

*Analyse election-campaign posters in your own country with reference to their lay-out, message and combination of verbal and pictorial elements. Report your findings to your class.*

## 4. Listening Comprehension: Black Friday (GK)

### Methodisch-didaktische Hinweise

Eine Einleitung, Worterklärungen und Fragen zum Globalverständnis sind im SB, S. 197 abgedruckt. Nachfolgend werden weitere Fragen angeboten.

### Background information

Sylvia Pankhurst (1882–1960) was the daughter of Emmeline Pankhurst (1858–1928), who in 1903 founded the Women's Social and Political Union, the most radical of all the suffragette movements. Emmeline Pankhurst was sentenced to imprisonment eight times. In 1918 she joined the Conservative Party.
Lord Asquith (Herbert Henry, 1st Earl of Asquith, 1852–1928) is referred to here as having vetoed a Bill to extend the vote to women. Asquith served as Prime Minister for the Liberals from 1908 to 1916. The Bill he vetoed (i.e. refused to refer to the House of Lords) was one of six that passed second readings in the House of Commons between 1886 and 1911 but failed to proceed any further.
As early as 1792, Mary Wollstonecraft had demanded equal rights for women (in her *Vindication of The Rights of Women*), but she was way ahead of her time. Agitation for women's suffrage can be said to have started in the 1850s, with an article by Harriet Taylor in the *Westminster Review*. In connection with the First Reform Bill, her husband John Stuart Hill (an MP at the time) brought in the first motion for women's suffrage, but it was defeated by 196 votes to 73. Some minor political rights were, however, won for women in the later decades of the century: e.g. the right of women votepayers to vote for and be members of School Boards, and the right to vote in local government elections.
The National Union of Women's Suffrage Societies was founded in 1897, and the Pankhursts' more radical movement in 1903. Their methods included heckling politicians' speeches, breaking windows, etc. in order to be arrested and thus draw attention to their cause, chaining themselves to the railings in Downing Street, and hunger strikes in prison.
But for all their efforts, the most decisive event in gaining support for the idea of equal suffrage rights for women (finally granted in 1918) was the part played by women in World War I (see Info Box p. 197).
The first woman to be elected to the British Parliament was Constance Markievicz, but as an Irish Nationalist standing for Sinn Féin in 1918, she refused to take her seat (see Ch. 4). The first woman to take a seat in the British Parliament was Lady Astor, elected in 1919.

*The Struggle for Democracy*

## Pre-listening activities

1. *Discuss the picture on page 196.*
The drawing shows a young woman who is wearing an academic gown being kept prisoner in a stockaded cage together with a convicted criminal and a mentally ill person.
According to the law, criminals and mentally ill people are not allowed to vote. The same applies to women – so the obvious question is: are women put on the same level as either or both of the other two classes of people? The young woman impatiently holds out the padlock waiting for the key to be handed over. She is clearly not of the opinion that she should be denied the right to vote. It must be noted, too that this is not an ordinary working-class woman but someone who has already made an enormous step forward to social recognition. At the time when this drawing was made, it was highly unusual for a woman to enter an academic career.

2. *What do people do – even today – when they feel strongly about something but cannot directly influence politics?*

3. *Think of recent scenes of violent demonstrations which have been shown on TV and report what you have seen.*

## Text

I saw Ada Wright knocked down a dozen times in succession. A tall man with a silk hat fought to protect her as she lay on the ground, but a group of policemen thrust him away, seized her again, hurled her into the crowd and felled her again as she turned. Later I saw her lying against the wall of the House of Lords, with a group of anxious women kneeling round her. Two girls with linked arms were being dragged about by two uniformed policemen. One of a group of officers in plain clothes ran up and kicked one of the girls, whilst the others laughed and jeered at her. Again and again we saw the small deputations struggling through the crowd with their little purple bannerettes: "Asquith has vetoed our Bill." The police snatched the flags, tore them to shreds, and smashed the sticks, struck the women with fists and knees, knocked them down, some even kicked them, then dragged them up, carried them a few paces and flung them into the crowd of sightseers. For six hours this continued. From time to time we returned to the Caxton Hall, where doctors and nurses were attending to women who had been hurt. We saw women go out and return exhausted, with black eyes, bleeding noses, bruises, sprains and dislocations. The cry went round: "Be careful; they are dragging women down the side streets!" We knew this always meant greater ill-usage. I saw Cecilia Haig go out with the rest; a tall, strongly built, reserved woman, comfortably situated, who in ordinary circumstances might have gone through life without ever receiving an insult, and died in December 1911, after a painful illness arising from her injuries. Henria Williams, already suffering from a weak heart, did not recover from the treatment she received that night in the Square, and died on 1 January ...

H. N. Brailsford and Dr Jessie Murray collected evidence from witnesses and sufferers, who testified to deliberate acts of cruelty, such as twisting and wrenching of arms, wrists, and thumbs; gripping the throat and forcing back the head; pinching the arms; striking the face with fists, sticks, helmets; throwing women down and kicking them; rubbing a woman's face against the railings; pinching the breasts; squeezing the ribs. A girl under arrest was marched to the police station with her skirts over her head. An old woman of seventy was knocked down by a blow in the face, receiving a black eye and a wound on the back of the head.

From *The Suffragette Movement*, by Sylvia Pankhurst, London 1931; reprinted from the 1977 Longman edition, pp. 343–4

## Suggested answers (Listening for the gist)

The incident takes place in front of the Houses of Parliament, obviously in connection with a demonstration demanding votes for woman. Acts of vicious violence are perpetrated indiscriminately by police officers, both uniformed and plain-clothes policeman.
They kick and manhandle women and prove their cynical callousness by laughing and jeering at them.
Some details:
A woman is knocked to the ground a dozen times and a man that wants to help her is thrust aside. Two girls with linked arms are dragged about by two police officers and one of a group of plain-clothes policemen runs up an kicks one of the girls while the others laugh and jeer at her.
The deputation of women is seen struggling its way through the crowd, carrying a bannerette

with the inscription: "Asquith has vetoed our Bill."
The bannerette is snatched and torn to shreds by the police.
Some women are knocked to the ground, picked up, carried a few paces and then flung into the crowd of sightseers.
This lasts for six hours.
Many women receive black eyes, bruises, disclocations and sprains.
Two women do not recover from the injuries and die some time later.
Two journalists testify to unspeakable violence committed by the police, which was even made worse by indecent behaviour on the part of individual policemen: one girl was marched to the police station with her skirts over her head, other women had their breasts pinched and were abused verbally; many other women suffered from acts of cruelty such as twisting and wrenching arms, wrists and thumbs; an old lady had her face rubbed against the railing of a fence.

**Additional questions**

1. *What does the "bannerette" tell us about the immediate reason for the demonstration?*

2. *Try to explain the behaviour of the police. (Consider that men at the time were brought up to be particularly respectful towards women!)*

3. *Sylvia Pankhurst tells us something about the kind of women who took part in the demonstration. What point is she making?*

4. *Look at the table "The struggle for suffrage", p. 197. How long did it take until the suffragette achieved their aims?*

**Post-listening activities**

1. *Group work: Give a short overview of the movement for women's suffrage. (Bibliography: 2, 3, 4, 8.)*

2. *Establish a semantic field that can be used to describe scenes of street violence.*

## 5. Put the rules of the game in writing (GK)

### Background information

Although Great Britain is often said to have no written constitution, there is in fact a "written" constitution in that all the Acts of Parliament form what might be referred to as the British constitution.

In principle, Lord Bolingbroke's dictum (1733) is still valid today: "By constitution, we mean, whenever we speak with propriety and exactness, that assemblage of laws, institutions and customs, derived from certain fixed principles of reason, directed to certain fixed objects of public good, that compose the general system, according to which the community has agreed."

In other words: The English constitution includes both fundamental principles and rights and the existing arrangement of governmental laws, customs and institutions. Parliament is the supreme legislative body. Its three elements are the Queen, the House of Lords and the elected House of Commons. Within the framework of this arrangement the government is "the Crown in Parliament". An Act of Parliament, therefore, is the supreme law of the land as there are no legal restraints imposed by a written constitution. It is worth pointing out that the highest-ranking members of the judiciary are also members of the House of Lords ("Law lords").

The American idea of a constitution is completely different. A constitution is no part of government at all but it is a written document distinct from and superior to all the operations of government. It is, in the words of Thomas Paine (1791) "a thing antecedent to a government; and a government is only the creature of a constitution." Consequently, a constitution could never be an act of the legislature but by the people themselves, hence the first words of the preamble to the American Constitution: "We the people...". A logical consequence is the strong position of the judiciary with the Supreme Court at its apex as final arbiter in all matters arising under the Constitution. In fact, there is the view, albeit a controversial one, in the United States that holds that "the Constitution is what the judges say it is." This has prompted the American historian Henry Steele Commager to state that "judicial review has been a drag upon democracy." Indeed, there has even been talk in the United States of an "usurpation of power" by the Supreme Court, after all a non-elected body.

Arthur Young suggested in 1792 rather haughtily that the American Constitution was like "a pudding made by recipe" and the Americans had become convinced that the English had no longer any consitution at all.

Lines 44–57: The author is probably referring to the following developments under Margaret Thatcher's government:
- the introduction of the poll tax (instead of property-based rates);
- the abolition of Greater London Council (was Labour-dominated);
- the weakening of the National Health Service;
- the banning of the book *Spycatcher* on grounds that it contravened the Official Secrets Act (even after the book was published elsewhere);
- the banning of union membership at the GCHQ (Government Communication Headquaters) in Cheltenham;
- the prosecution of civil servant Clive Ponting under the Official Secrets Act for revealing government deception concerning the sinking of the *Belgrano* in the Falklands War;
- the suppression of the TV documentary *Death on the Rock* on the Gibraltar affair (the shooting of three IRA activists by SAS officers in March 1989);
- the ban on IRA or Sinn Féin representatives speaking or being interviewed on TV.

**Pre-reading activities**

*1. The rules of the game and fair play: Take some sports disciplines of your choice and show where the analogy to society in general and politics in particular may lie.*

*2. Classroom talk: Britain's unwritten "Constitution". (See fact file p. 308; also bibliography: 11, 14, 15, 19.)*

**Suggested answers**

1. Mrs Thatcher is of the opinion that constitutional reform is not needed at all as the country and its citizens are served well by the constitutional arrangements as they are.
She does not see the need, indeed the point, of having a written constitution. She points out that a written constitution is in itself no safeguard against encroachment on the people's rights by the state, as the interpretation and practice of constitutional guarantees are more important than their being laid down expressly in a written document. In support of this argument she goes on to say that a number of states that have written constitutions still oppress their people.

2. It is the aspect of judicial review which appeals most to the members of Charter 88. This means the right of citizens to have legislative measures or government actions declared unconstitutional by the courts and therefore unenforceable, i.e. the citizens do not have to obey them.

3. She has not consulted with other parties or set up committees of inquiry on questions concerning
- the powers and financial basis of local government;
- the structure of public welfare and finances;
- the revision of the Official Secrets Acts;
- the freedom of expression of the media and their right to investigate the Government.

By acting this way she has, in Bernard Crick's opinion, tried to bring in constitutional change by the backdoor and to replace the old informal constitutional system by a rational market economy.

4. She has diminished the role of Parliament in the decision-making process and strengthened that of the Government in general and the Prime Minister in particular. She tried to make people believe that the Government is the best guarantor of their constitutional rights, but her methods have proved counterproductive. Nearly everyone, according to Crick, now sees the dangers that lie in that new constitutional arrangement.

5. It is exquisitely polite with touches of humour and irony. Examples:
- "or what you and I, I'm sure, ordinarily call waffle" (l. 31);
- "what we often called – did we not – 'the rules of the game'" (l. 46);
- "not all in a rush after 1688, that's 1066 stuff" (l. 59).

Possible reason: It is also part of the "rules of the game" to do things in the correct style, so that the opponent is never offended and given a reason not to pursue the argument.

6. Britain:
- unitary state;
- constitutional monarchy;

- parliamentary democracy (Prime Minister and cabinet ministers are Members of Parliament);
- bicameral system; only Lower House (House of Commons) members are elected;
- constitutional principle of Her Majesty's Loyal Opposition;
- Upper House (House of Lords): members are not elected but appointed for life, some seats are hereditary;
- Law Lords (members of House of Lords who act as a court of appeal).

USA:
- federal system;
- presidential democracy;
- strict separation of powers: President and cabinet members are not members of either the Senate or the House of Representatives;
- President and ministers (secretaries) are not answerable in the plenary sessions of the Congress for their actions;
- no constitutional principle of government-supporting parliamentary party and official opposition (voting across party lines is more frequent than in other parliamentary democracies);
- bicameral system: the Senate and the House of Representatives; members of both bodies are elected;
- complex system of "checks and balances" between the three branches of government;
- particulary strong judiciary; principle of "judicial review" has given the Supreme Court enormous policy-making clout.

7. (See *Politik Aktuell für den Unterricht*, 23 November 1990, 38/90.)
The German *Grundgesetz* fulfils (if only partially in some cases) a number of the Charter 88 demands:
- it is, of course, a "written constitution";
- it contains a "bill of rights";
- government is (in theory at least) accountable to parliament;
- it ensures a more or less fair electoral system = proportional representation based on party lists (but is the *5-Prozent-Klausel* really democratic?);
- it gives local government a probably sufficient degree of independence;
- the federal system is in itself a form of "devolution of power", and provides the equivalent of a "Scottish Assembly" in each of the *Länder;*
- the Judiciary and the *Bundestag* (cf. House of Commons) are not generally regarded as being in need of reform;
- it allows for judicial processes which can provide "redress for state abuse".

The one point not explicitly provided for is "freedom of information" (which is not quite the same thing as free speech or freedom of the press), and neither is there much public debate on the matter (demands for change tend to go in the opposite direction: *Datenschutz,* i.e. protection of privacy). The reason for the lack of concern may be that the tradition of state secrecy has not, in West Germany, gone to such extremes as in Britain. When abuse has been obvious, as in East Germany, demands for freedom of information have been successful: cf. the post-unification opening of the *Stasi* files.

Some current demands for constitutional change in Germany:
- the introduction of referendums (or plebiscites) as a modification of the present system of representative democracy; the addition of environmental protection as a general aim of the state;
- the modification (or elimination) of a basic right already in the constituion – namely the right to political asylum – on the grounds that it is too often abused.

Other points for discussion:
- Does the German Constitution give too much power to the political parties?
- Is the exclusion of women from the army in conflict with the general statement that men and women have equal rights?

**Additional questions**

*1. Put Margaret Thatcher's reply (ll. 7–23) into reported speech.*

*2. Find examples of metaphor in the letter (also in the quotes) and explain what they mean.*

**Post-reading activity**

*Rewrite this letter as a public speech and then present it to your class.*

# 6. A Scottish Parliament

## Background information

Area of Scotland: 77,080 sq km (i.e. slightly larger than Bavaria with 70,552 sq km)
Population of Scotland: 5.1 million (mid-1989 estimate; Bavaria: ca. 11 million)

Historically and culturally, Scotland is quite distinct from England. Its population – like that of Ireland – is mainly Celtic in origin. It was never conquered by the Romans. Ever since a united Scottish nation emerged in the 7th century A.D., relations with England have been strained. The Scottish monarchy was separate from the English until 1603, when James VI of Scotland acceded to the English throne as James I. Even then, the two countries remained politically separate until the Act of Union, 1707. And even after Union, Scotland retained many separate institutions, such as its legal and educational systems.

There are special arrangements for the conduct of Scottish affairs within the British system and separate Acts of Parliament are passed for Scotland where appropriate. There are 72 Scottish seats in the House of Commons, i.e. 11.1% of the seats with 8.9% of the population of the United Kingdom. Administrative tasks relating to a wide range of economic and social functions are the responsibility of the Secretary of State for Scotland, a member of the Cabinet, working through the Scottish Office, with its adminstrative headquarters in Edinburgh and an office in London. The principles and procedures of the Scottish legal system differ in many respects from those of England and Wales, stemming, in part, from the adoption of other European legal systems, based on Roman (statutory) law, during the sixteenth century.

The Church of Scotland, which became the established church in 1690, has complete freedom in all matters of doctrine, order and discipline. It is a Protestant church which is Presbyterian in form, being governed by a hierarchy of church courts, each of which includes lay people.

Most of the schools supported from public funds are provided by education authorities and are known as public schools.

The School Boards (Scotland) Act 1988 requires education authorities to establish school boards to play a part in the administration and management of the schools. The Self-Governing Schools etc. (Scotland) Act allows parents of children at public schools to opt for local self-management, following a ballot, and to receive funding directly from central government.

There are eight universities in Scotland: St Andrews, Glasgow, Aberdeen and Edinburgh being the most prestigious and oldest ones.

Ever since the 1920s there has been a strong Home Rule movement. In 1979, a proposal for an elected assembly for Scotland failed to gain the support of the required 40 per cent of the electorate to bring it into effect, even though a majority of those voting gave it their approval.

Ten years later (March 30, 1989) the first meeting of the Scottish Constitutional Convention was held. The full text of the declaration adopted at that meeting (partially quoted in Neal Ascherson's article, ll. 20–23, 100–104) is as follows:

"We, gathered as the Scottish Constitutional Convention, do hereby acknowledge the sovereign right of the Scottish people to determine the form of Government best suited to their needs, and do hereby declare and pledge that in all our actions and deliberations their interests shall be paramount.

We further declare and pledge that our actions and deliberations shall be directed to the following ends:

To agree a scheme for an Assembly or Parliament for Scotland; to mobilise Scottish opinion and ensure the approval of the Scottish people for that scheme; and to assert the right of the Scottish people to secure the implementation of that scheme."

In the list of participating parties (ll. 28–31) the "Democrats" are the Social and Liberal Democrats, and the SDP are the Social Democratic Party (i.e. those who broke away from the too-leftist Labour Party but refused to unite with the Liberals to form the Social and Liberal Democrats).

The form of Proportional Representation supported by the Democrats (and other small parties) and being contemplated by Labour (ll. 79–98) is not the German "list" system, but the "single transferable vote" system used in Ireland (north and south). This is a complicated system involving multi-seat constituencies which ensures that each successful candidate is elected on a personal vote. The campaign for a Scottish Parliament continues – as well as the more radical Scottish Nationalist

campaign for total independence. The emergence of several newly-independent nations in the aftermath of the collapse of communisme gave new life to the idea of some measure of independence for Scotland, and it was an issue in the 1992 general election. A public opinion poll organized by *The Scotsman* and ITN in January showed 50% favouring full independence, another 27% favouring a Scottish Parliament within the UK, and only 19% supporting the status quo. A later poll carried out by MORI reversed the proportions of those favouring full and partial independence. The actual results in Scotland (in an election in which the Conservatives retained their overall majority in Britain as a whole) were as follows:
Conservative 25.7% – 11 seats (+ 1)
Labour 39.0% – 49 seats (– 1)
Liberal Democrats 13.1% – 9 seats
SNP 21.5% – 3 seats.
This does not show any increase in the votes for the parties favouring independence or devolution (in fact, the Conservatives gained one seat), but it still shows a completely different pattern of voting from the rest of Britain, giving rise to further demands for change.
In the same general election, the Welsh nationalist party Plaid Cymru gained 8.8% of the Welsh vote, raising their representation in parliament from 3 to 4 seats.

### Methodisch-didaktischer Hinweis

Es empfiehlt sich, die Größenordnungen und kulturellen Unterschiede wie oben angeführt in einer Art brainstorming-Phase zu erarbeiten und sie als Ausgangsbasis für die Behandlung des folgenden Textes zu nehmen, wobei Bayern als Analogie herangezogen werden kann.

### Pre-reading activities

*1. What do you already know about Scotland and how it differs from the rest of the UK?*

*2. Classroom report: A summary of Scottish history.*
See Bibliography: 7.

### Suggested answers

1. The Scottish National Convention's primary aims are to work out a plan "for an Assembly or Parliament for Scotland", and to mobilize the public to that end.

2. Labour, the Democrats, the SDP, the Communists and, later on, the Greens, agreed to take part – unlike the Scottish Conservatives who roundly refused to do so. The Conservatives are, on principle, opposed to any form of devolution of power for Scotland. Surprisingly, the Scottish Nationalists also refused to participate, mainly on the grounds that the Convention, in their opinion, excluded the option of full independence.

3. – lack of legal standing (ll. 44–48);
– no chance of acceptance by Thatcher's government (ll. 49–55).

4. Changes include:
– cross-party cooperation;
– doubts about the fairness of the British "first-past-the-post" electoral system;
– the declaration of Scottish rights is in conflict with the basic British constitutional principle of the supremacy of (the Westminster) Parliament.

5. The author uses irony, sarcasm and hyperbole – or a combination of all three – to make his points. But he uses them in a complex way, and leavened by a tone of playful humour. Very often he seems to be mocking the convention itself, when he is really mocking possible English perceptions of it. Examples:
– the Convention is a "show" which is both "demure" and "subersive" (sarcasm/hyperbole);
– the foreign word *Prominenz* mocks its (self-) importance (playful sarcasm);
– he likens the Convention to "the clothes-moth, dry rot and the death-watch beetle", which pose "the most dangerous threat to British institutions" (hyperbole and – since the author does not see it so negatively but is mocking the way many English people might see it – ironic);
– the Convention assumes the dimensions of a "beast" with "subversive spines" (hyperbole/irony);
– he speaks of the "junk heritage which passes for British consitutional practice" (hyperbole); the "scandal of present Scottish government";
– he says that the janitor at No. 10 is expected to tell the bearers of the scheme "to get stuffed" (a gross colloquialism, implicitly hyperbolic).

The author obviously treats his subject more lightly than would normally be expected. Only very occasionally does he express a strong opinion directly (e.g. "the scandal of present Scottish government"; ll. 75–76).

6. The clearest parallel in modern European history is the movement for Irish independence at the turn of the century. The strongest demand was for "Home Rule" within the UK – until a polarization took place after the 1916 Rising (see Ch. 4) leading to full independence for the greater part of Ireland. Over the past two decades similar movements have got under way in various European countries. The following list is not exhaustive and can be completed by group work and in cooperation with political studies and history courses:
- Spain: Catalonia, the Basque province, Galicia, Andalusia
- France: Corsica, Brittany, Languedoc
- Italy: Lombardy, South Tyrol

Over the last three years, after the fall of the Berlin Wall and the collapse of what used to be the Communist Eastern Bloc, dramatic changes have taken place, and numerous newly independent states have emerged:
- Russia, Ukraine, the Baltic States, ...; in short: the disintegration of what used to be the Soviet Union;
- Croatia, Slovenia, Serbia, ...; the (violent) process of restructuring and reorientation in what used to be Yugoslavia is not yet over.

The only apparent exception to this general tendency towards fragmentation has been German reunification; but even this fits into the general picture of re-organization on national lines.

*Picture, p. 200:* The Welsh Nationalist Party *Plaid Cymru* is also a force to be reckoned with. It now has four MPs in the Westminster parliament (the SNP has three).

**Post-reading activity**

*Organize a debate or round-table discussion on the topic:*
*The nation state is a thing of the past.*

# 7. A way to rescue British freedoms

**Background information**

The European Convention on Human Rights: In 1950, members of the Council of Europe agreed to a European Convention for the Protection of Human Rights and Fundamental Freedoms, and to the establishment of a European Court of Human Rights. The European Convention on Human Rights has, over the years, developed a considerable body of case law on questions regulated in the convention; and the provisions of the convention are, in some European states (but not in the United Kingdom), automatically part of the constitutional or statutory law. Where this is not the case, the western European states have taken other measures to bring their internal law in line with the convention.

Lines 84–92: See note on text 5, ll. 44–57.

**Methodisch-didaktischer Hinweis**

Wenn gewünscht, kann die Reihenfolge der Texte so geändert werden, daß dieser Text direkt nach Text 5 behandelt wird. So könnte das Thema "Bill of Rights" zusammenhängender diskutiert werden.

**Pre-reading activites**

*Make a list of individual rights which you think are "inalienable", to use a famous phrase from the American Declaration of Independence. Then discuss how they can be best protected or enforced.*

**Suggested answers**

1. The growing acceptance and enforcement of the following ideas:
- democracy is more than just majority rule;
- liberty and minorities must be legally protected in the form of a written constitution which cannot easily be changed by Parliament;
- the need for a bill of rights which lays down the rights of individual citizens.

2. The United States is built on this very principle, and it is accepted by every member of the European Community and the great majority of other "mature" democracies, including India, Canada, and almost all other Commonwealth countries.

3. Britain still adheres to the constitutional principle of the unlimited sovereignty of Parliament, i.e. an Act of Parliament is inherently a part of the "unwritten constitution".

(Cf. text 5: Bernard Crick: "Put the rules of the game in writing", pp. 197–198.)

4. The author suggests that Britain simply enact a statute that guarantees that the principles of the European Convention, to which Britain is already committed by international treaty, are part of the law in Britain and enforceable by British judges in British courts. This would strengthen the role of British judges and, of course, limit the power of the politicians, who pass the laws at Westminster.

5. (Cf. : Crick, Dworkin, Ascherson.)
The discussion could centre on the apparent discrepancy between the way Margaret Thatcher is often seen, namely as a champion of individual freedom (free enterprise, no government interference in economic affairs, low taxes, personal responsibility, etc.) and the way she is seen by people like Dworkin, namely as an enemy of freedom (censorship, surveillance, etc.).

6. Both authors are strongly committed to the cause of a written constitution. But whereas Bernard Crick demands this in general terms, Ronald Dworkin makes a concrete suggestion as to how this might be achieved in Britain. As regards style and tone, Crick's letter is outwardly moderate and conciliatory, written as if its recipient were open to reasoned argument. Dworkin is more cutting in his attacks on the the politicians in general and Margaret Thatcher in particular: e.g. he says politicians "howl" (l. 38) whenever they think the judges limit their field of action. He says that the Tories have made "a shambles of liberty in recent years" (l. 35). He accuses Margaret Thatcher of "high-handedness" (l. 93) in these matters and implicitly accuses her of having brought about "freedom's decline" (l. 85), and he fears that the legacy of the Thatcher years will be "censorship and intimidation and surveillance and the curtailment of ancient liberties" (ll. 85–87) if the countries does not react swiftly and decisively. His criticism of the Labour Party is more muted (ll. 43–46).

## 8. Equality before the law (GK)

### Background information

*To Kill a Mockingbird* is Harper Lee's only published novel. She grew up in Alabama, and studied Law at the University of Alabama before taking up work in New York. Her novel undoubtedly contains autobiographical elements, making use of her memories of her southern childhood. The story is told from the child's point of view, namely that of Scout, daughter of the lawyer Atticus Finch. Her father has the function of explaining the sometimes absurd and uncomprehensible adult world to the children – also in the case of this trial: To their dismay of, the black man Tom Robinson was found guilty against the evidence. But Atticus Finch points out that the jury took a few hours to find a verdict and that there was one juror who initially was for an acquittal. "This," he says, "may be the shadow of a beginning".

*Trial by jury:* The selection and final composition of a jury has always been an especially controversial issue and American legal history is rich in landmark decisions in this field of which only the most important ones are given below:

– in the case *Norris v. Alabama* the Supreme Court ruled in 1934, that the fact that blacks had been absent from jury lists for 20 years was in itself proof of racial discrimination and therefore unconstitutional.
– in the case *Taylor v. Louisiana* the Supreme Court ruled in 1975 (!) that "If it was ever the case that women were unqualified to sit on juries or were so situated that none of them could be required to perform jury service, that time has long since passed."

In the Alabama of 1935, the year in which *To Kill a Mockingbird* is set, women were not allowed to sit on juries. And blacks (in spite of *Norris v. Alabama*) were still conspicuous by their absence. One of the main obstacles to the full implementation of the Sixth Amendment proved to be the fact that the Bill of Rights originally was binding only on the federal government in Washington and not on the individual states. Only in 1968, i.e. a hundred years after the ratification of the 14th Amendment, in the case *Duncan v. Louisiana*, did the Supreme Court rule that the "due process"-clause of the 14th Amendment was binding on the states in all those cases where a jury trial is mandatory in a federal court because, as the majority opinion reads, "we believe that trial by jury is fundamental to the American scheme of justice."

As to the jurors themselves, they were generally held in low esteem as the narrator in James Gould Cozzens' novel *The Just and the Unjust* remarks: "The truth was, it would never cross your mind to ask the opinion of any one of them on a matter of importance." Their task, however, has always been considered as a very responsible and difficult one, as Atticus Finch (in Harper Lee's *To Kill a Mockingbird*) observes: "Serving on a jury forces a man to make up his mind and declare himself about something. Men don't like to do that. Sometimes it's unpleasant." This responsibility extends beyond the level of individual responsibility and fairness to the level of the principle of democratic government. Judge Coates in *The Just and the Unjust* says: "The jury protects the court. It's a question how long any system of courts could last in a free country if judges found the verdicts. It doesn't matter how wise and experienced the judges may be. Resentment would build up every time the findings didn't go with current notions or prejudices. Pretty soon half the community would want to lynch the judge. There's no focal point with a jury; the jury is the public itself." (pp. 427–428)

Eleanor Roosevelt (1884–1962) – referred to obliquely in line 4 – was niece of President Theodore Roosevelt, and wife of President Franklin Delano Roosevelt. But she was also a political personality in her own right. In the 1920s she was active in several women's organizations. When her husband became President in 1933 (having recovered sufficiently from polio) she remained an active force, both as an adviser to her husband and various government agencies and by writing and speaking on social issues. She can be credited with many improvements in legislation to improve housing, education, health and the situation of minorities. After her husband's death in 1945 she was appointed a U.S. delegate to the U.N. where she took a particular interest in refugee affairs. She was instrumental in writing and passing the U.N. Declaration of Human Rights. She was again active in the 1960s as U.N. delegate, campaigner for the Democratic Party, and writer.

## Methodisch-didaktischer Hinweis

Dieser Text sollte im Zusammenhang mit dem folgenden Ausschnitt einer Rede Abraham Lincolns gelesen werden. In beiden Texten wird "equality" auf ähnliche Art definiert – mit dem Unterschied, daß Finch sich konkret auf das Spezifikum des Gerichtsprozesses und des "fair trail" bezieht. Dabei spricht einiges dafür, Text 9 zuerst zu behandeln. Texte 8, 10 und 11 erläutern dann verschiedene Aspekte des *jury system*.

Da es sich beim Auszug aus *To Kill a Mockingbird* um eine Rede handelt, empfiehlt es sich, den Text zunächst über das Gehör einzuführen (Cassette).

## Pre-reading activities

*1. Look at the picture on page 204. Describe the scene and answer the questions.*

(The judge is sitting in his elevated chair flanked by the American flag. The accused (the defendant) is standing upright in the dock. A witness (for the prosecution or for the defense) is sitting in front of the judge. The counsel for the defense (or defense attorney; here played by Gregory Peck as Atticus Finch) is talking to the defendant. The men on the left are the jury. This is an all-white, all-male jury.

In fact, as the novel specifies: "The jury sat to the left, under long windows. Sunburned, lanky, they seemed to be all farmers, but this was natural: townsfolk rarely sat on juries, they were either struck [i.e. not accepted as jurors] or excused. One or two of the jury looked vaguely like dressed-up Cunninghams [illiterate dirt-farmers of evil repute].")

*2. Classroom report on the novel (or the film)* To Kill a Mockingbird.

Novel by Harper Lee, 1960, available in paperback edition: Pan Books 1974. Film directed by Robert Mulligan, and starring Gregory Peck, 1962, available on CIC video.

## Suggested answers

1. – He starts off with a historical quotation which is known by a everyone and which certainly is undisputed.
– He gives it an unexpoected twist by claiming that it often is quoted out of context.
– He gives examples of where this quotation does not apply: intelligence, industriousness, clever-

ness (these examples are well chosen in that they only state the obvious).
- The mild dig at the "distaff side" of the Presidency (l. 4) that promotes such strange ideas about equality in the field of education will go down well with an all-male jury in a remote backwater town in Alabama (though it would today be quite unacceptable).
- His unexpected turn towards his definition of real equality makes people listen, and the examples are very graphic: pauper vs. Rockefeller, a stupid man vs. Einstein, an ignorant man vs. a college president.
- He then appeals to the self-esteem of the people who are listening to him, even going to the extent of naming this court in the same breath as the Surpeme Court of the United States.
- He insists that he is no idealist but that this is "a living, working reality". (Here he is probably pandering to the sympathies of the jurors, who are almost certainly no idealists.)
- He again takes up his main line of argument, that the humble people who sit on this jury are as important as the most eminent justices.
- He ends with an emotional appeal to their "sense of duty."

2. The comparisons in ll. 25–28 could be regarded as hyperbolic. (Though one could argue that they are meant literally: however different they are in wealth, intelligence, etc. in respect to legal rights they are in fact equal. Cf. text 9, ll. 21–26.)

3. Not just two definitions, but two different *kinds* of equality are referred to:
a) actual equality (i.e. identical characteristics etc.) in intelligence, ability, wealth;
b) equality (i.e. equal treatment) before the law.
One could find further examples of either kind:
a) identical appearance, moral values, etc.
b) equal rights in politics, employment, etc.

4. Some suggestions: unbiased, capable of reaching their own conclusion and standing up for it, no racial or religious or any other prejudices, a wide range of experience, material well-being that makes them immune to any attempts to influence them, no criminal record (the latter two rather controversial).

5. The enforceable rights of a human being are seen by both as the cornerstone of a liberal democracy. The enforcement can effectively be secured by the courts only. Atticus Finch takes advantage of the constitutionally guaranteed rights of a defendant (cf. Bill of Rights Amendments and 14th Amendment, fact file pp. 309–310) to try to get his client free. Dworkin wants to extend the scope of the courts to the scrutiny of laws and government practice – such as already exists in the USA and most other democratic countries.

# 9. A maxim for free society

### Background information

The United States Constitution originally took slavery into account without expressly mentioning it:
"Article One, Section Two, 3: Representatives and direct taxes shall be apportioned among the several States which may be included within this Union, according to their respective numbers, which shall be determined by adding to the whole number of free persons, including those bound to service for a term of years, and exluding Indians not taxed, three fifths of all other persons." (Invalidated after ratification of 13th Amendment which abolished slavery in 1865.)
"Article One, Section Nine, 1: The migration of such persons as any of the States now existing shall think proper to admit, shall not be prohibited by the Congress prior to the year one thousand eight hundred and eight, but a tax or duty may be imposed on such importation, not exceeding ten dollars for each person." (Direct relevance to Dred Scott case.)

*The Dred Scott case:*
In 1834, Dred Scott, a slave, was taken by his master to Rock Island, Illinois, a town in a "free" state, i.e. one in which slavery had been abolished. His master later took him to the Wisconsin Territory, where the Missouri Compromise of 1820 (see below), a federal law, had forbidden slavery. His master then brought Scott back to Missouri, a slave state. Scott, in a more or less contrived case, brought a suit against his master, claiming to be a free man because he had resided in areas which had banned slavery.

The Constitutional issues:
- Did Scott become free while living in a free state?
- Should Missouri have to recognize that freedom?
- Did the Supreme Court have the power or jurisdiction to this case?

The Decision announced in 1857:

The Supreme Court ruled by a 7 to 2 vote against Scott on all three issues.

Chief Justice Roger B. Taney wrote the majority opinion which became legal history. He said that Scott could not sue in a federal court, because he was not a citizen of the United States. He further wrote that no black person, slave or free, could positively be a citizen. "The question is simply this: Can a negro, whose ancestors were imported into this country, and sold as slaves, become a member of the political community formed and brought into existence by the Constitution of the United States ...? ... We think they are not ... included, and were not intended to be included, under the word 'citizens' in the Constitution ..."

Rather, Taney asserted that at the time the Constitution was written, blacks were "considered as a subordinate and inferior class of beings, who had been subjugated by the dominant race, and whether emancipated or not ... had no rights or privileges but such as those who held the power and the Government might choose to grant them." Blacks had "no rights a white man was bound to respect."

As to the question whether the State of Missouri had to respect Scott's status as a free man, Taney wrote that the ban on slavery in the Missouri Compromise was unconstitutional.

Under the Constitution's Fifth Amendment no one could deprive a person of his property without "due process of law" and "just compensation". But this was exactly what the Missouri Compromise amounted to because territories were open to all settlers, slaveholding or free. Once a territory became a state, it alone could decide whether or not to ban slavery. Therefore the Missouri Compromise was unconstitutional.

Missouri Compromise of 1820: The compromise proposed that Missouri be admitted as a slave state, and Maine as a free state. Thus the balance of power between slave states and free states was maintained. The compromise also called for slavery to be banned from the Louisiana Territory north of the parallel 36° 30'. The 13th Amendment (1865), which ended slavery, and the 14th Amendment (1868), which gave blacks citizenship, overturned the Dred Scott decision.

**Pre-reading activity**

*"All men are created equal." How do you understand this maxim? And how do you think it was originally meant?*

**Suggested answers**

1. Lincoln points out that the Declaration of Independence did not say that all men were equal in all respects, as in fact they visibly were not, but only in "certain inalienable rights, among which are life, liberty, and the pursuit of happiness." He then uses this point to refute the claim that blacks were excluded because at the time they were not seen as the equals of whites.

2. He rejects the idea that the authors of the Declaration meant to describe a present situation, or even to demand the immediate realization of each principle laid down. He says they meant to declare certain rights in principle, the enforcement of which might take time, and depend on circumstances.

3. Americans know that their society is far from being perfect but they have the Declaration of Independence, the Constitution and the Bill of Rights where, in ascending order of specification and concreteness, the rights of the individual are laid down. (cf. pp. 309–310)

4. Equality: equal, equal rights, equality of opportunity, to integrate, integration, egalitarian, egalitarianism, to level, leveller, levelling, unequal, inequality, discrimination, to discriminate against, discriminatory, to segregate, segregation, segregationist

5. Some ideas:
a) Full actual equality between the sexes/social classes/ethnic groups.
b) Even theoretical equality under law in many respects:
- restrictive legislation exluding women from certain jobs, the army, etc.;
- different pension laws for men and women;
- restrictive legislation imposing different conditions on women and men;
- the exclusion of people born in Germany from citizenship of that country, i.e. their classifica-

tion as foreigners because of their parents' nationality.

**Post-reading activity**

*Classroom report: The U.S. Constitution and the problem of slavery and racial discrimination.*
See Bibliography: 1, 3, 5, 6, 10, 12, 13.

**Illustration, page 206**

The poster describes the decision as "atrocious". It is one among other "outrages" against colored people under the Constitution of the United States. Note the archaic form of the time of day and the date. "2d instant" means the second day of this month. The form can still be found in the more formal kind of business correspondance, usually in the variations: 2nd inst./2nd ult. (=last month)/2nd. prox. (= next month).

# 10. The jury system perverted (GK)

**Background information**

Mark Twain was the pseudonym of Samuel Langhorne Clemens (1835–1910), America's greatest humorist. He was born in Montana, but grew up on the Mississippi. He was apprenticed to a printer and soon began editing various newspapers, and writing. He travelled all over the United States, living and working in New York, Washington, Cincinnati, New Orleans, and San Francisco, to name but a few. *Roughing It*, written in Nevada in the 1860s, is an early work, in which his portraits of people and incidents show much of the humour and insight of his later masterpieces *(Life on the Mississippi, Tom Sawyer* and *Huckleberry Finn)*, lacking only a coherent story to hold it together. In his Foreword to *Roughing It* Leonard Kriegel writes that if Twain "thought civilization desirable, he conceived of it largely in legal terms. The absence of law on the frontier meant for him the absence of standards of behavior – for Twain an appalling situation."

For information on the jury system, see text 8, background information.

**Pre-reading activities**

*1. Discuss the picture on page 209.*
Once again it is an all-male, all-white jury – as was still common in the 1950s. From the way they are dressed one might conclude that they are, with one exception – the juror with his hat on in the rear -, middle class. Though this might possibly be regarded as an "impartial jury" (in the terms of the Sixth Amendment) when all concerned (accused, victim or victims, witnesses) are white males, it is very doubtful if such a group could be impartial when the case involves women or ethnic minorities. (This is not an issue in the film, which has to do with one man's conscience, and how he will not be swayed by group pressure but finally persuades the others to agree on a "not guilty" verdict.)

*2. Classroom report on the film* Twelve Angry Men *(available on video: United Artists).*

*3. Think of any recent American court cases that have been in the news recently, and discuss the role of the jury:*
– How were the jurors selected?
– Were any jurors rejected, and if so, for what reason(s)?
– What was the verdict, and did it have anything to do with the composition of the jury?

**Suggested answers**

1. When Alfred the Great invented trial by jury one of the principles was that the jurors should be ignorant of everything relating to the crime and the defendant.
At his time of slow communication this was perfectly feasible but in Mark Twain's day and age anybody who doesn't know anything about a crime that has made banner headlines is either willfully ignorant or just plain stupid or both. The result is that juries are made up of people who simply do not meet the requirements of the Sixth Amendment to ensure a fair and impartial trial. In this excerpt he caustically describes the jurors as "desperadoes, beerhouse politicians, barkeepers, ranchmen who could not read" and "dull, stupid, human donkeys."

2. *Yes:* The following examples are elements of satire:
- "... all men capable of reading read about it. And of course all men not deaf and dumb talked about it." (ll. 41–43: sarcasm);
- "But of course such men (cf. l. 58–64) could not be trusted with the case. Ignoramuses alone could mete out unsullied justice." (ll. 69–71: sarcasm);
- his technique of denigration reaches its climax in the ascending order of obtuseness: "a murder which the very cattle in the corrals, the Indians in the sagebrush, and the stones in the streets were cognizant of!" (ll. 77–79: exaggeration);
- his rhetorical question as to the fairness of standing the principle of "equal chances" its head by preferring fools to intelligent people (ll. 93–95).

*No:* If this is the factual reality then "polemical" rather than "satirical" would be the word. He is just cramming a number of absurd facts into one short statement in order to drive his message home.

Because these are not, in Mark Twain's eyes, just weaknesses: they are the result of something which is principally wrong and should be adjusted to modern times. (Cf. text 11: "Is jury selection unconstitutional?")

3. Mark Twain:
- He concedes that the system was good a thousand years ago.
- But today (i.e. 19th century) the system ensures that only the worst can be jurors.
- If he could achieve his goal of adapting the system to modern times, then he would probably accept it as something valuable.
- He is very pessimistic about his chances realizing this: "every effort I make to save the country "misses fire"." (ll. 104–5)

Atticus Finch:
- To him the principle of trial by jury is one of the most important, if not the most important, asset of American democracy
- At least in the courtroom, he does not doubt as to the "living reality" of this principle.
- To him the members of the jury are all respectable people and he tries to win them over by expressly stating this fact. (This may, of course be flattery rather than his sincere opinion.)

Mark Twain will probably point out that the selection of the juries has no other results than those at his time. If Atticus Finch brings up the point, he might concede that an all-white, all-male jury is far from a representative cross section of society though, being a man of his time, he is unlikely to raise the matter himself. Mark Twain will probably say that Atticus Finch is far too idealistic and that the system will fail its task if people like Atticus and himself do not try to adapt it to modern times and as quickly as possible. After all, he might add, nothing much seems to have changed since when he wrote his book.

Atticus Finch might concede that things do not seem to have changed much on the face of it but that deep down there are signs of change that there was perhaps "the shadow of a beginning." He might point out the *Norris v. Alabama* case just pending or about to be decided or even ruled already. He might say that one has to talk to people in a way that makes them feel they are respected rather than despised in order to win them over. He might also argue that not the system in itself is wrong but the way people are brought up and they way they cling to their prejudices. He might finally point out that a "living, working reality" also means a permanent struggle for democracy.

(Before writing the fictional dialogue, the students should first decide which of the two is the "time traveller", i.e. whether the dialogue should take place in the 1860s or the 1930s.)

4. Übersetzung:
Die Männer, die die ersten 26 Friedhofskandidaten in Virginia City ermordeten, wurden nie bestraft. Und warum? Weil Alfred der Große als er das Geschworenengericht erfand und dabei wohl wußte, daß er es in bewunderungswürdiger Weise so gestaltet hatte, daß es für Gerechtigkeit in seinem Zeitalter sorgte, nicht ahnen konnte (sich der Tatsache nicht bewußt war), daß die allgemeinen Zustände im 19. Jahrhundert so gänzlich anders sein würden, daß das Geschworenensystem sich als das ausgeklügelste und unfehlbarste Mittel erweisen würde, das der menschliche Geist je erfinden könnte, um das Recht zu vereiteln. Alfred der Große hätte aus dem Grab auferstehen und das System ändern müssen, hätte er diesem Notstand begegnen wollen. Denn wie hätte er sich vorstellen können, daß wir Einfaltspinsel weiterhin sein Geschworenensystem benutzen würden, nachdem die Umstände es seiner Nützlichkeit beraubt hatten? Ebensowenig wie er sich vorstellen könnte, daß wir seine Kerzenuhr nach der Erfindung des Chronometers weiterhin benutzen würden.

## Additional questions

1. Find synonyms for the following words, and explain any difference in register or connotations:
slaughtering (l. 5); rough (l. 6); sorrowful (l. 35); idiotic (l. 41); esteemed (l. 58); standing (l. 62); biased (l. 65); unsullied (l. 71).

2. Pick out all the words (nouns and adjectives) Mark Twain uses to refer to people of low intelligence.

## Post-reading activity

Classroom report: Mark Twain: his life and works.

# 11. Is jury selection unconstitutional?

## Background information

For information on the constitutional history of jury selection, see text 8, background information.
Further reading:
Morton M. Hunt: *The Mugging*, Harmondsworth, Penguin, 1973. Covering the epic case of four young Puerto Ricans who are accused of mugging and murdering an elderly citizen, this is a gripping account of how the American jury system really works and how it runs counter to the ideals inscribed in the 6th Amendment.
Scott Turow: *One L: What they really teach you at Harvard Law School*, London: Sceptre edition, 1988. A highly readable account of how and to what goals lawyers are trained at the most prestigious of American law schools.

## Suggested answers

1. He did his research in order to find out whether the judicial practice was in line with the requirements of the 6th Amendment of the Bill of Rights which lays down the individual's fundamental "right to a speedy and public trial, by an impartial jury."

2. He found out, first, that the composition of most of the juries does not represent a cross-section of the community especially as far as the representation of ethnic minorities is concerned. He also found out that the system allows too many procedural maneuvres which sometimes drag out cases for years.

3. He points out that the working reality of the courts would be made more efficient. He does not fear the system being paralyzed by re-trials as laws could be passed preventing the change from having a retroactive effect. And besides, he regards it as more important to correct a serious deficiency in the system even if this causes some disruption.

4. Übersetzung:
Viele (Leute) befürchten, daß eine Änderung des Gesetzes mit der Begründung, die Bestimmungen (Forderungen) des sechsten Verfassungszusatzes seien in der Vergangenheit nicht erfüllt worden, zur Neuaufnahme von Tausenden von Verfahren führen würde, doch Willigan ist der Ansicht, daß es wichtiger ist, das Problem zu beheben. Die Gerichte müssen einen juristischen Weg finden, der es ermöglicht, daß ein solches Gesetz nur für zukünftige Fälle gilt und nicht auf vergangene Fälle angewendet wird. "Wenn man weiß, daß eine Schwäche existiert und sie nicht korrigiert (ausgleicht, behebt), wird das System in größere Schwierigkeiten kommen, als wenn man den Fehler behebt und dann abwartet, was passiert." Er gesteht jedoch zu, daß es zu Störungen während der Umstellung (des Übergangs) kommen könnte.

## Post-reading activities

1. Read the following criticism of the American system of justice expressed by former Supreme Court Chief Justice Warren Earl Burger:
When we look at the administration of justice in such enlightened countries as Holland, Denmark, Norway and Sweden, we find some interesting contrasts to the U.S. They have not found it necessary to establish a system which makes a criminalg trial so complex or drawn-out as it is in this country. They do not employ our system of twelve jurors. Generally, their trials are before three professional judges. They do not consider it

necessary to use a device like our Fifth Amendment under which an accused person may not be required to testify. They go swiftly and directly to the question of whether the accused is guilty.

*Which of the criticized features are part of your country's judicial system? Discuss their pros and cons.*

*2. Find out more about how jurors are selected in Germany.*

## 12. The Seneca Falls Declaration of Sentiments

### Background information

Many of the early feminists in the U.S.A. began as temperance or anti-slavery activists. A decisive moment came when women were barred from an 1840 world anti-slavery convention in London. Long concerned with discrimination against women, pioneer feminists Elizabeth Cady Stanton and Lucretia Coffin Mott called for a conference on women's rights in the summer of 1848. More than 100 men and women from the Northeast congregated at the Wesleyan Methodist Church in Seneca Falls, N.Y., and for two days (July 19–20) discussed the unequal status of women.

It is interesting to note that the last point that was included in the Declaration was the demand for women to be given "their sacred right to the elective franchise." This point was included solely at the insistence of Mrs Stanton, who overrode numerous objections that it was needlessly controversial including Quaker Lucretia Mott's complaint, "Why, Lizzie, thee will make us ridiculous." The Seneca Falls Convention formally launched the 72-year struggle for women's suffrage in the United States.

In 1860 Susan B. Anthony petitioned the New York legislature for women's property rights and the vote, with some success on the former but not the latter point. She also failed in her efforts to make the Fourteenth and Fifteenth Amendments apply to women as well as black men. Together with Elizabeth Cady Stanton, she organized the National Woman Suffrage Association in 1869, which campaigned both for a federal amendment and for voting rights in the individual states. Wyoming was the first state to grant female suffrage in 1869 (see table p. 211), but by the time of Mrs Anthony's death in 1906, only a few other states had followed: Utah, Colorado, Idaho. (For comparison: New Zealand and Australia were the only nations to have done so by this date; for the situation in Britain see text 4, background information.) The decisive federal amendment came in 1920, two years after British women had got the vote.

The wording of this Amendment is as follows: "The right of citizens to vote shall not be denied or abridged by the United States or any State on account of sex. Congress shall have power to enforce this article by appropriate legislation."

A new chapter in the struggle for equal rights for women began in the 1970s with the demand for an Equal Rights Amendment. The need for such an Amendment had been demonstrated by a number of cases brought to the Supreme Court by women demanding equal treatment with men, each of which was rejected on the grounds of long-standing custom. The first successful challenge to sex discrimination came in 1972, when a women challenged an Idaho law that gave preference to men over women as the administrators of estate, on the grounds that it contravened the Fourteenth Amendment (see fact file, p. 310).

The Equal Rights Amendment (whose wording – see picture p. 211 – follows that of the various voting rights amendments) was proposed by Congress in March 1972. In 1974, President Ford urged its ratification. By 1977, 35 states had done so. But by the end of the required time limit, it was still short of three states for full ratification and adoption as part of the Constitution.

Ironically, one of the Amendment's strongest opponents was a woman, Phyllis Schlafly, who claimed it would outlaw any special privileges for women, and should therefore be rejected.

### Methodisch-didaktischer Hinweis

Es empfiehlt sich, diesen Text nach der ersten Einführung parallel mit der *Declaration of Independence* zu lesen. Dieser Text steht auch in engem inhaltlichen Zusammenhang zu Text 6, Kapitel 11 (S. 250) und kann mit diesem Text im Sinne eines historisch-soziologischen Längsschnitt verglichen werden.

## Pre-reading activities

*1. "All men are created equal." Was this principle meant literally, i.e. restricted to adult males?*

*2. The "Declaration" we are going to read was written in 1848. Read the table on page 211 and find out what the situation was as regards voting rights at the time.*

*3. Read the first two paragraphs quickly, without trying to understand everything.* (Alternative: The teacher reads these two paragraphs aloud.) *Does anything sound particularly familiar to you?*

## Suggested answers

1. The authors feel that human history has deprived women of the place in society to which they are entitled by the laws of nature and the laws of God. They feel that it is time for women to assert these rights and to fight for them. They have written this particular declaration in order to lay claim to such rights as citizens of the United States.

2. They object to
 – the denial of the right to vote;
 – having to obey laws in whose formation they have had no say
 – having fewer formal rights than the "most ignorant and degraded men – both natives and foreigners";
 – married women being regarded as "civilly dead", i.e. they did not enjoy the right of citizens as they are granted by the Constitution and the Bill of Rights;
 – being deprived of property rights;
 – being regarded as legally incapable of responsibility for actions carried out in the presence of her husband;
 – marriage contracts which make women slaves of their husbands;
 – divorce laws and ensuing regulations which have been framed on the assumption of the supremacy of men.

3. They want to do away with this discrimination against women and the first step is to alert people's consciousness of this deplorable situation.

4. The style of this declaration is modelled on its famous predecessor – the Declaration of Independence. This can be seen in the word-by-word adaptations and in the overall structure of the document. The enumeration of the "history of repeated injuries and usurpations" (this passage being itself a quotation from the DoI) reminds the reader of the long list of grievances the colonists addressed to the King of Great Britain.

The anaphoric repetition of "He" is also taken from the DoI, "He" this time being "man", i.e. the male part of society. (In the DoI, "He" is the English King.)

They probably have chosen this form in order to give weight to their demands. They show that "men" in the DoI is obviously used in the sense of "adult males". (The generic uncountable "man" can be used to mean "mankind", "the human race"; but the countable forms "man/men" practically always refer to males.)

By invoking this historical precedent the signatories of this declaration want to make clear that they see themselves as an integral part of the American tradition, and as a section of society that has hitherto been deprived of the privileges conferred on male citizens by the constitutional framework of the United States.

## Question on picture, p. 211

– There might be constitutional arguments against it. The most important would be that the 14th Amendment (see p. 310) has settled the problem: "All persons born or naturalized in the United States, and subject to the jurisdiction thereof, are citizens of the United States and of the State wherein they reside. No State shall make or enforce any law which shall abridge the privileges or immunities of citizens of the United States; ...".
– There might also be reasons that belong to the realm of male prejudice towards women which are much more difficult to pinpoint.
– Some women may have feared the loss of the special treatment and privileges sometimes accorded to women on grounds of their "special role"/relative physical weakness, etc.

## Post-reading activities

*1. Classroom report on Elizabeth Cady Stanton and/or Susan B. Anthony.*
Sources: any American or British encyclopedia; also Bibliography: 3.

*2. Prepare a speech in favour of (or against) the Equal Rights Amendment and present it in class.*

# 13. Listening Comprehension: A claim to a share of America

## Methodisch-didaktische Hinweise

Es empfiehlt sich, den Redeausschnitt zunächst in seiner vollen Länge wiederzugeben, um den Eindruck der Authentizität auf die Schüler wirken zu lassen. Während des Abspielens sollen sich die Schüler bereits Notizen machen, da dies einer authentischen Situation gerechter wird. Diese Notizen können dann bei einem zweiten Durchgang, bei dem der Text segmentiert werden kann, vervollständigt werden.

## Background information

Mario Cuomo, Governor of New York State since 1983, delivered the so-called Keynote Address at the Democratic National Convention that nominated Walter Mondale in 1984. The purpose of the Keynote Address is to define in broad terms the party's aims and principles and to unite the various groups that exist within the party.

Cuomo's speech was enthusiastically received and made him a national figure overnight. As a consequence there was – and is – talk, even in 1992, that Cuomo might one day be the Democratic Party's nominee for the Presidency. But so far he has never made his intentions entirely clear to the American electorate.

Madison Avenue: name of an Avenue in New York City, centre of the advertising industry

## Transcript of the Speech

The difference between Democrats and Republicans has always been measured in courage and confidence. The Republicans, (Applause) the Republicans believe that the wagon train will not make it to the frontier unless some of the old, some of the young and some of the weak are left behind by the side of the trail. (Applause) The strong, the strong, they tell us, will inherit the land!

We Democrats believe in something else. We Democrats believe that we can make it all the way with the whole family intact. And we have more than once. (Applause) Ever since Franklin Roosevelt lifted himself from his wheelchair to lift this nation from its knees – wagon train after wagon train; to new frontiers of education, housing, peace, the whole family aboard; constantly reaching out to extend and enlarge that family; lifting them up into the wagon on the way; Blacks and Hispanics, and people of every ethnic group, and Native Americans; all those struggling to build their families and claim some small share of America – for nearly 50 years we carried them all to new levels of comfort and security and dignity, even affluence. And remember this: Some of us in this room today are here only because this nation had that kind of confidence. And it would be wrong to forget that. (Applause) So, here we are at this convention to remind ourselves where we come from and to claim the future for ourselves and four our children.

Today, our great Democratic Party, which has saved this nation from depression, from fascism, from racism, from corruption, is called upon to do it again – this time to save the nation from confusion and division, from the threat of eventual fiscal disaster and most of all from the fear of a nuclear holocaust. (Applause)

That's not going to be easy. Mo Udall is exactly right, it won't be easy. And in order to succeed, we must answer our opponent's polished and appealing rhetoric with a more telling reasonableness and rationality.

We must win this case on the merits.

We must get the American public to look past the glitter, beyond the showmanship – to the reality, the hard substance of things. And we'll do it not so much with speeches that sound good as with speeches that are good and sound.

Not so much with speeches that will bring people to their feet as with speeches that will bring people to their senses. We must make (Applause) we must make the American people hear our "tale of two cities."

We must convince them that we don't have to settle for two cities, that we can have one city, indivisible, shining for all of its people. Now ... (Applause) We will have no chance to do that if what comes out of this convention is a babel of arguing voices. If that's what's heard throughout the campaign, dissonant sounds from all sides, we will have no chance to tell our message.

To succeed we will have to surrender some small parts of our individual interests, to build a platform that we can all stand on, at once, and comfortably, proudly singing out (Applause). We need, we need a platform we can all agree to, so that we can sing out the truth for the nation to hear, in chorus, its logic so clear and commanding that no slick Madison Avenue commercial, no amount of geniality, no martial music will be able to muffle the sound of the truth.

We Democrats must unite, we Democrats must unite so that the entire nation can unite, because surely the Republicans won't bring this country together. Their policies divide the nation: into the lucky and the left-out, into the royalty and the rabble.

The Republicans are willing to treat that division as victory. They would cut this nation in half, into those temporarily better off and those worse off than before, and they would call that division recovery.

Now ... (Applause) We should not, we should not be embarrassed or dismayed or chagrined if the process of unifying is difficult, even wrenching at times.

Remember that, unlike any other party, we embrace men and women of every color, every creed, every orientation, every economic class. In our family are gathered everyone from the abject poor of Essex County in New York to the enlightened affluent of the gold coasts at both ends of the nation. And in between is the heart of our constituency, the middle class, the people not rich enough to be worry-free but not poor enough to be on welfare, (Applause) the middle class, those people who work for a living because they have to, not because some psychiatrist told them it was a convenient way to fill the interval between birth and eternity, (Applause), white collar and blue collar, young professionals, men and women in small business desperate for the capital and contracts that they need to prove their worth.

We speak for the minorities who have not yet entered the mainstream.

We speak for ethnics who want to add their culture to the magnificent mosaic that is America. We speak (Applause) we speak for womem who are indignant that this nation refuses to etch into its governmental commandments the simple rule "thou shalt not sin against equality", a rule so simple ... (Applause) I was going to say, and I perhaps dare not, but I will. It's a commandment so simple, it can be spelled in three letters. E.R.A. (Applause. Shouts of "E.R.A.")

We speak ... we speak for young people demanding an education and a future

We speak for senior citizens, we speak for senior citizens who are terrorized by the idea that their only security, their Social Security, is being threatened.

We speak for millions of reasoning people fighting to preserve our environment from greed and from stupidity. [...]

Now, we're proud of this diversity as Democrats, we're grateful for it. [...] But we, while we're proud of this diversity, we pay a price for it. The different people that we represent have different points of view and sometimes they compete and even debate and even argue. That's what our primaries were all about.

But now the primaries are over, and it is time when we pick our candidates and our platform here to lock arms and move into this campaign together. (Applause)

**Listening for the gist (suggested answers)**

1. The Republicans, he says, are a party that believes in the survival of the fittest. Only the strong will, according to them, inherit the land.

2. The Democrats, he says, believe that not only the strong will make it but all the members of the American family. And since Franklin D. Roosevelt they have helped those who were at a disadvantage (the Blacks, Hispanics and Native Americans) to become part of this American family. The Democrats have given them new levels of comfort, dignity and even affluence.

3. The Democratic Party has saved America from depression, from fascism, from racism and from corruption. Now the party must save America from division, from fiscal disaster and, above all, from a nuclear holocaust.

4. The Democrats must present the problems to the American people openly and honestly. The party must show unity and the various groupings within its framework must put the overall aim before their individual interests. Only if they can achieve this will victory be within realistic reach.

5. The members of the Democratic Party are a real cross-section of American society, geographically, socially and ethnically.

6. – Ethnic minorities want to enter the American mainstream.
   – Women fight for equal rights in general and the E.R.A. in particular.
   – The young want an education for the future.

- Senior citizens fear for security as the Social Security (system) seems to be under threat from the Republicans.
- Millions of people fear for the environment.

**Additional questions**

1. Explain the image of the "wagon train", and how Mario Cuomo uses it to emphasize differences in attitude between the two parties.

2. Pick out any other examples of striking imagery.

3. Comment on Mario Cuomo's style of oratory – how he deals with applause, how he varies the pace and the mood of his speech, etc.

4. Find an example where he departs (or seems to depart) from his script.

# 14. Congress should pass the flag amendment (GK)

**Background information**

Only in 1925, in the case *Gitlow v. New York* did the Supreme Court rule that the constitutional principle of "Congress shall make no law ... abridging the freedom of speech, or of the press" laid down in the First Amendment was "among the fundamental personal rights and 'liberties' protected by the due process clause of the 14th Amendment from impairment by the states." In 1943, the Supreme Court ruled, in the Flag Salute Case, that children cannot be forced against their will to take part in the daily Pledge of Allegiance ceremony in which the American flag plays an important part.

It should be noted here that Senator Dole's line of argument reflects the dissenting opinion in the Flag Salute Case as it was put forward by Justice Felix Frankfurter:

"Law is concerned with external behavior and not with the inner life of man ... One may have the right to practice one's religion and at the same time owe the duty of formal obedience to laws that run counter to one's belief."

Dole's use of the term "liberal" (l. 6) is a purely American one, a usage that runs counter to its older meaning. In recent years it has practically become a term of abuse hurled by right-wing "conservatives" at anyone suspected of wanting a greater role for the state in curbing abuses, ameliorating poverty, etc. In this particular case, however, it is not too inappropriate: The much-abused "liberals" want to retain freedom of expression, and protect it from being restricted by federal legislation.

**Pre-reading activities**

1. Do you think a flag is an important symbol of a nation?
Why? Why not?

2. Do you think Germans are emotional about their flag?

3. Why do you think the American flag is so important to Americans?

4. Classroom report: The Stars and Stripes – its history and significance.

**Suggested answers**

1. The American people, he says, strongly resent the fact that the American flag can be burned, defaced or ridiculed under the protection of the First Amendment. They feel that the American flag deserves no less than constitutional protection itself. The liberals, however, don't like that idea because it would itself be unconstitutional.

2. President Bush has come out in favor of a constitutional amendment. He chose the highly emotional scene of the Iwo Jima Memorial (cf. p. 129) to make his announcement. But he has also announced that he will not sign a federal statute that tries to protect the flag because this statute would itself be unconstitutional.

3. Senator Dole proposes the way of an amendment to the constitution. He says that the question in hand is not "free speech" but "conduct" and that the Constitution's sanctity would not be

impaired as its 26 previous amendments amply demonstrate.

4. Personal views. (Cf. majority and dissenting opinions in the Flag Salute Case and the majority opinion in *Gitlow v. New York* as quoted above as background information.)

5. He uses colloquialisms and short forms as in spoken language (ll. 10, 46, 47, etc.). He uses a variety of emotional terms to refer to the flag (ll. 4, 22, 59–60). Very frequently he uses the possessive pronouns "our" to stress that he feels close to the "American people" (ll. 11, 49), and "their, her" to stress the close relationship between owner and owned (l. 25). All that is meant to appeal to his readers' feelings.

That he is very good at polemics can be seen in the last paragraph. Here he lists all the "abominations" Congress and the federal states have been capable of (repeal of Prohibition: 21st Amendment ratified in 1933; imposition of the federal income tax: 16th Amendment, ratified in 1913) in order to drive home the message that an amendment in favour of the flag should be no problem at all.

6. Übersetzung:
Man sollte den Weg über die Verfassungsänderung einschlagen. (Der Weg, den man einschlagen sollte, ist der der Verfassungsänderung.) Ich weiß nicht, wovor unsere Gegner Angst haben: es geht (doch) nicht um den ersten Verfassungszusatz. (oder: es geht doch nicht um die im ersten Verfassungszusatz garantierten Rechte.) Es geht um Verhalten, nicht um Meinungsäußerung. Es geht darum, daß unsere Flagge vor Entweihung, nicht vor Meinungsäußerungen, geschützt wird. Und es geht auch nicht um die Unantastbarkeit der Verfassung, weil dieses große Dokument 26 mal durch Verfassungszusätze geändert wurde. Die Gründerväter wollten es so. Sie wollten ein lebendiges Dokument, das sich der Zeit anpassen konnte, wann immer die Menschen (das Volk) Alarm schlug(en).
Wenn wir die Verfassung ergänzen können, um die Prohibition zu widerrufen und eine bundesweite Einkommensteuer einzuführen, dann können wir sie ja wohl auch ergänzen, um das gute alte "Rot-Weiß-Blau" zu schützen.

**Cartoons, page 214**

Above: 1. An American flag is burning, i.e. someone has set it on fire. The Bill of Rights document is also burning, we can see the man who is setting it on fire.
2. The man burning the Bill of Rights is obviously reacting to the burning of the flag. This suggests that those who object to people being free to desecrate (e.g. burn) the American flag and therefore want to give the symbol special protection under the Constitution can only do so by restricting free speech and free expression, a basic right guaranteed in the Bill of Rights. This amounts to burning the Bill of Rights itself – an equal (or worse) crime than burning the flag.

Below: 1. A Main Street shop front, where a man is collecting signatures for a "flag amendment" or something similar. A strip joint where a dancer conceals her private parts with the American flag. The stripper ironically calls herself Old Gloria ("Old Glory", like "Stars and Stripes", is one of the names given to the American flag). A gun shop displaying the American flag in its shop window with an election billboard above. Another billboard asks people to drink "America's beer" with a flag underlining the slogan. A huge American flag is flying outside a second-hand car dealer's, and there is an ironic detail: A bank called "Flagg Savings and Loan" has the American flag as its symbol. (It should be remembered that the Savings and Loan scandal shook America and that it was a particularly embarrassing moment for President Bush because his son had allegedly been a party to shady dealings. It can also be seen as a pun: "to flag" meaning "to lose in strength").
2. All these trivial or ironic uses of the flag imply that "desecrating and defacing" the flag is quite commonplace – though those doing so (like the man from the strip joint) may not be aware of it.

**Post-reading activities**

*1. Conduct a group discussion on the possible limits of a citizen's rights in a democratic society. One could use Felix Frankfurter's opinion (see background information) as a point of departure.*

*2. (If not used as pre-reading activity) Classroom report: The Stars and Stripes – its history and significance. (Bibliography: 5.)*

# Test: Bill of Rights that's ours for the taking

During the revolutionary Eighties, Britain saw great social and economic changes, but our constitutional, political, and legal systems are the same in 1990 as before this social and economic revolution. Many of us doubted long before the Eighties whether the constitution offered our plural society sufficient safeguards against abuse of power by government and other authorities. The Eighties have transformed that doubt into a certainty that it does not. Even with the democratic input of universal suffrage, the constitutional settlement of 1689 is dangerously out of date.

Indeed, today's constitution lacks the checks and balances of the 1689 settlement. At least in those days Parliament could exercise its sovereign legislative power only if its two Houses were in agreement, and with the consent of the monarch. Now, whichever political party commands a majority in the Commons has the executive and legislative power of the state in its grasp: only the judges are independent, and by the terms of 1689 they have to obey the enacted will of Parliament.

The weakness of the constitution is the strength of the political party which controls Parliament and the executive.

Reform is needed if individual and minority rights and freedoms are to be secure: I therefore agree with others that a written constitution suited to today's society is necessary.

The rights of the individual, the rights of minorities, and equality of opportunity for all need the protection of a constitution which sets limits to the executive and legislative powers of the government. And however much the resistance of the two major parties with their vested interest in the present constitution will delay change, it will come.

For now, I opt for a Bill of Rights to be enacted in Parliament. Such a Bill of Rights would not be proof against change – Parliament can amend or repeal its Acts – but once enacted, it would, like Magna Carta and the Habeas Corpus Acts, be likely to remain, if only because of the opprobrium which would meet those who might try to repeal it. And once on the statute book, a Bill of Rights would govern administrative and governmental action, and would influence public opinion constantly and in a great variety of ways.

A model is to hand: the European Convention of Human Rights and Fundamental Freedoms, signed in 1950 and ratified in 1953 by some 16 European states, including the UK. The legal status of this convention is that of an international treaty binding upon the UK, but it is no part of British law unless Parliament chooses to incorporate it by Act of Parliament. It is a step which ought to be taken. [...] The UK has not done so, and justifies its omission on the ground that the convention's rights and freedoms are secure under the existing law. Experience has shown this to be far from the truth. The UK has a disturbing record of losing cases which aggrieved citizens have taken to the European Court of Human Rights. [...] If the convention were incorporated into our law, it would be enforced by our courts. This would be an enormous advantage to aggrieved persons seeking remedy. [...] Let us have the Act: let us call it what it ought to be, the Bill of Rights 1990.

ca. 552 words

Article by Lord Scarman in *The Times*, January 4, 1990

## I. Language

1. Explain the words/expressions in italics within the given context (you may change the sentence structure):
a) (ll. 7–8) *safeguards* against *abuse of* power
b) (ll. 11) *universal suffrage*
c) (ll. 40) I *opt* for a Bill Rights
d) (ll. 41–42) would not be *proof against*
e) (ll. 59–60) and *justifies* its omission
f) (ll. 63) *a disturbing* record
g) (ll. 68–69) aggrieved persons *seeking remedy*.

2. Grammar and Style
a) Explain these constructions and replace them by a subordinate clause:
(ll. 30–31) ... a written constitution suited to today's society ...
(ll. 69) ... persons seeking remedy.
b) Rewrite the passage in italics. Start with "if":
(ll. 56–58) ... but it is no part of British law *unless Parliament chooses to incorporate it* ...
c) Explain the use of the tense:
(ll. 59–60) The UK has not done so.
3. Translate from: l. 14 (Indeed, ...) – l. 39 (... will come.).

## II. Comprehension

1. What have the Eighties taught the British as far as their constitutional framework is concerned?
2. What would the immediate effect of a Bill of Rights be, according to the author?
3. What does the European Convention of Human Rights mean for those countries which have signed it? What are the British particularities in this case?

## III. Comment

Choose one of the two topics.
1. Say which view of democracy appeals more to you: democracy as a system of majority rule or a system in which the rights of the individual are inscribed in a Bill of Rights with a strong judiciary branch: In other words: do you prefer the British or the American way? Give reasons.
2. Do you think that Western-style democracy is a model for all countries all over the world? Give reasons.

# Bibliography

1. Blaustein, Albert P. *The United States Constitution, A Model in Natron Building*, reprinted in *The Bicentennial of the U.S. Constitution*. LEU-Materialien E 11, Stuttgart 1987.
2. Cox, Barry. *Civil Liberties in Britain*. Harmondsworth: Penguin 1975.
3. DiBacco, Thomas, Lorna C. Mason and Christian G. Appy. *History of the United States*. Boston: Houghton Mifflin 1991; Klettbuch 516153.
4. Hampton, Christopher, ed. *A Radical Reader, The Struggle for Change in England 1381-1914*. Harmondsworth: Penguin 1984.
5. *Information Please Almanac* (pp. 99–121, 613–665). Boston: Houghton Mifflin 1992; Klettbuch 516152.
6. Kammen, Michael. *A Machine that Would Go Of Itself, The Constitution in American Culture*. New York: Random House 1987.
7. Mackie, J.D. *A History of Scotland*. Harmondsworth: Penguin 1964.
8. Morgan, Edmund S. *Inventing the People – The Rise of Popular Sovereignty in England and America*. New York and London: W.W. Norton 1988.
9. Musman, Richard, ed. *United Kingdom? Untied Kingdom? The Story of Devolution*. Schöningh.
10. Myrdal, Gunnar. *An American Dilemma, The Negro Problem and Modern Democracy*. New York: Harper and Row 1944.
11. Orton, Eric, ed. *Mother of Parliaments*. Schöningh.
12. *Perspectives 2: The American South*. Klettbuch 51362.
13. *Perspectives 3: The Supreme Court*. Klettbuch 51363.
14. Randle, John. *British Life and Institution*. Klettbuch 51344.
15. Spann, Ekkehard. *Abiturwissen Landeskunde Great Britain/U.S.A.* (Chapters 1 and 2). Klettbuch 929509.
16. Stevenson, Douglas K. *American Life and Institutions*. Klettbuch 5136.
17. Thompson, E.P. *The Making of the English Working Class*. London 1966; Penguin edition available.
18. Turow, Scott. *One L: What they really teach you at Harvard Law School*. New York 1977; available in paperback: London: Sceptre Book 1988.
19. Wheare, K.C. *Modern Constitutions*. London: Oxford University Press 1960.

# 10  A Nation of Immigrants

## Structure of the chapter

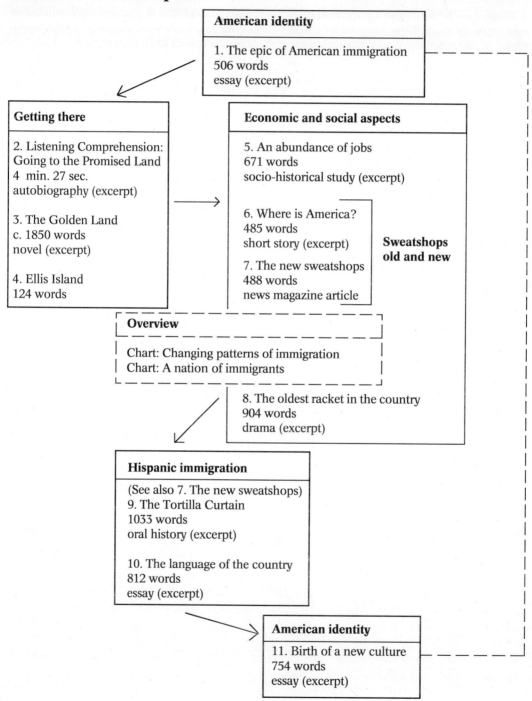

**Suggestions for reports/papers/talks**

Diversity and identity with regard to immigration in the USA – after text 1

Jewish immigrants to the USA in the 20th Century – after text 2

Book report on Henry Roth, *Call it Sleep* – after text 3

Examination of the family reunion depicted in "The Meeting" by Abraham Cahan (excerpt from *Yekl*) – after text 4

Report on one short story from *Native American Short Stories* or *Stories from the Black Experience* – after text 4

The emergence of industrial America – after text 5

The huddled masses – after text 5

Book report on Upton Sinclair, *The Jungle* – after text 6

Analysis of short story "The German Refugee" by Bernard Malamud – after text 6

The German-Americans – after text 6

American labour unions – after text 7

Book report on Arthur Miller, *A View from the Bridge* – after text 8

Analysis of Ch. 3 of Arthur Millers autobiography, *Timebends*, as background to *A View from the Bridge* and *Death of a Salesman* – after text 8

The situation at the Mexico-USA border – after text 9

The Hispanics in the USA – after text 9

Language and American identity – after text 10

The ethnic situation in Los Angeles – after text 10

*Topics related to the tests* (with bibliographical references):

The new Americans – after test 1 (Bibl. 7, pp. 334–341)

Chinatown and the Chinese Americans today – after test 2 (LC) (Bibl. 29, pp. 150–154)

Analysis of Amy Tan, "Waverly Jong: Rules of the Game" – after test 2 (Bibl. 12, pp. 51–65)

**Vocabulary**

*Thematisches Grund- und Aufbauwortschatz Englisch*, Klettbuch 51955, pp. 108–111; 115–117; 145–146; 263–265

*Words in Context*, Klettbuch 51961, pp. 14–22; 116–119

# 1. The epic of American immigration

### Background information

The passage is taken from the introduction to a lavishly illustrated book celebrating the USA as a country of immigrants on the occasion of the centenary of the Statue of Liberty.
Leslie Allen is a senior writer of the National Geographic Society. She has worked as a reporter, editor and freelance writer with a great interest in Latin America, where she lived for several years. She attended the Chinese University of Hong Kong for a year before graduating from Bryn Mawr with honors in English in 1975. Leslie Allen now lives in Washington, D. C.
Virtually as soon as the United States of America was born, Crèvecoeur posed the question of American identity: "What then is the American ...?" (ll. 43–44). He perceived that the country was peopled by diverse stocks from across the Atlantic. A very liberal immigration and naturalization policy, based on the assumption that the newcomers would merge with the host people (naturalization laws of 1790 and 1802), meant that many new citizens from various ethnic backgrounds left their imprint on American society. In 1790, the year of the first census, the English and their descendants constituted just under half of the American population. Their influence may have been great, but the English were not the parent stock of the American people as a whole. Native Indians, Blacks (20% of population in 1790) and the various immigrant groups prevented this. What did they have in common? What was it that

was peculiarly American? Crèvecoeur described the American as the new man who acted on new ideas, new principles and new opinions. The desire to live in a system that guaranteed liberty, opportunity, religious pluralism, democratic government and material advancement made the inhabitants into American citizens. "Clearly, the important thing about an American was what he believed in, not where his ancestors came from" (A. Mann, "From Immigration to Acculturation", in: L.S. Luedtke, *Making America*, p. 73).

Various metaphors have been employed to characterize this concept of variety within unity: the melting pot (coined by I. Zangwill in his play of the same name, 1909); the harmonious orchestra (Horace M. Kallen) consisting of a federation of national cultures; the ethnic mosaic; the salad bowl; the kaleidoscope and the multi-ethnic society. Some of these stress the idea of fusion, while others emphasize the independence of the individual components, i.e. cultural pluralism. The metaphors are rather static and fail to capture the dynamism of ongoing developments. Many Americans studying the history of immigration believe that over the generations since immigration there has been a continual process one could term mainstream conformity, which in turn has influenced mainstream culture.

## Methodisch-didaktische Hinweise

Das bestehende Selbstbild der USA als *country of immigrants* wird in diesem Eröffnungstext sehr umfassend ausgelegt: selbst die *Native Americans* und die als Sklaven hergebrachten *African-Americans* werden als Einwanderer gesehen, um dieses Konzept zu retten. Von daher kann auch gut die große ethnische Vielfalt betont werden und die eigentlich zeitlich vorgreifende Characterisierung der USA durch Melville als eine Welt im Kleinen hier angeführt werden.

Fragen aus dem Zusammenhang ethnischer Vielfalt und nationaler Identität sollen am Anfang und Ende des Kapitels den grundsätzlichen Rahmen für die Entfaltung der weiteren Aspekte des Themas abgeben.

## Pre-reading activities

*1. Try to conclude from the names of these people the countries their ancestors came from: Kennedy, Reagan, Cuomo, Kissinger, Dukakis, Bush.*
Ireland, Ireland, Italy, Germany, Greece, Great Britain
*Try to find more names.*

*2. Find out the origins of the following names of states of the USA: Georgia, Florida, Mississippi, Vermont, New York, Illinois.*
Georgia: named after King George II of England. Florida: was a Spanish possession; from "la fiesta florida" (the feast of flowers, i.e. Easter). Mississippi: Indian, "father of waters" (M. River). Vermont: French "vert mont" (green mountain). New York: in honour of the English Duke of York. Illinois: Indian word with French suffix: "tribe of superior men".

*3. Study a detailed map or an atlas index of the USA and try to find borrowed city names.*
E.g. Aberdeen (Idaho); Amsterdam (New York); Athens (Alabama, Georgia, Ohio, etc.); Bagdad (Arizona, Florida); Belfast (Maine); Berlin (Connecticut); Cairo (Georgia, Illinois); Cuba (New York); Damascus (Ohio, Virginia); Dresden (Ohio); Italy (Texas); Lebanon (Illinois, Virginia); Milano (Texas); Moscow (Idaho, Pennsylvania); Nederland (Colorado, Texas); Palestine (Illinois, Kentucky); Peru (Illinois, New York); Sparta (Wisconsin); St. Petersburg (Florida); Turkey (Texas); Venice (Illinois); Versailles (Indiana, Kentucky, Montana); Warsaw (Illinois, Kentucky, Montana, Virginia); Weimar (California)

*4. Is there anyone in your family who emigrated to the USA? If so, find out details and give a talk.*

## Suggested answers

1. The writer refers to the length of time in which immigration has been taking place in America. She also names the many nationalities and ethnic groups involved in this process and cites the number of immigrants for one decade of last century to indicate the extremely high percentage of foreign-born citizens in the American population of that time (10%). In evaluating this extraordinary historical development the writer employs an imposing comparison with ancient Rome. She glosses over the destruction of the Native Americans and the slavery of the Afro-Americans (note the euphemisms: "Africans, mostly in bondage" and "the dwindling Native American population", ll. 53 and 55). Neither does the reader learn anything about ensuing problems and conflicts

such as fears, racial tensions and illegal immigration.

2. This is a fairly uncommon perspective and only holds true if Native Americans and African-Americans are counted as immigrants, too. In a serious historical analysis the beginning of the process of immigration could be seen as the arrival of the first settlers. The perspective used here allows one to regard this as a continous process. It is, however, true that with the European settlers a sudden, often violent and fundamental change came over the continent, resulting in the destruction of the pre-Columbian culture. On a purely superficial level the statement is justified, as the Native Americans are descendants of peoples who moved into the Americas in prehistoric times.

3. The text is framed by quotations of two famous Americans. Though Melville's view is a deliberate overstatement, it nevertheless anticipates the present situation. It also graphically illustrates the ethnic diversity of the United States and its cosmopolitan, multi-racial character.
Thomas Paine's statement rightly rejects the idea of England as the parent country, attributing this role instead to Europe. Yet it is this view in turn which many use to justify their basically Eurocentric view of American culture, of which Native Americans and African-Americans seem to be only marginal members.

**Additional questions**

*1. Using key words and/or phrases, outline the progression of ideas in the text. (The next step would be to write a summary in your own words, using full sentences – see SB p. 181 Writing a summary).*
The USA a "world" (l. 1) – "... nothing to compare with it in diversity ..." (ll. 17–18). The first "Native Americans were themselves immigrants" (ll. 26–27) – "... the colonial settlers were ... immigrants as well" (ll. 34–35) – "They laid the cultural groundwork" (ll. 35–36) – "What then is the American ...? (ll. 43–44) – Varied motives for immigration of "non-Indian inhabitants" (ll. 60–61) – "Europe, and not England, is the parent country of America" (ll. 71–72).

*2. Why does the writer concentrate on the early stages of immigration in the introduction to her book?*
By focusing on the beginnings of immigration the author is able to stress the part played by immigrants from northern and central Europe, disregarding the cultural and social contribution made, particularly since the late 19th century, by people from other parts of Europe, from Asia and from the Spanish-speaking American countries. This slant also enables her to classify the American Indians as immigrants along with those people entering the country much later.

*3. What reasons for emigrating is the writer thinking of when she refers to "refugees, convicts, and adventurers"? Try to find other circumstances that make people leave their home countries.*
Refugees: escape from political and religious oppression. Convicts: sentenced to transportation. Adventurers: the desire to start something new, the quest for success.
Economic depression, famine, unfair social order, lack of material and social security, overpopulation, lack of agricultural land, stifling class systems etc.

*4. What is it that makes up "the American", i.e. what do all these diverse people have in common?*
It is their common goal "to make a new life" (l. 5). (Students could specify what this means, going beyond the text and referring to their answers to Question 3.) See also D. K. Stevenson, *American Life and Institutions* (Klettbuch 5136), pp. 14–16.

*5. Analyse the language and style of the passage.*
The writer employs a very elaborate style with dramatic, poetic language. The tone created by this is rather elevated.
– tendency to use superlatives and hyperbole ("not a nation, ... a world"; comparison with Roman Empire: "There had been nothing to compare with it"; US immigration "stands out")
– metaphorical, high-sounding phrases (to be borne on the first flood tide, to set sail, to arrive on its shores, midpoint, famine-stricken, the howl of ocean storms, ragged armadas, peasants sing brave hymns, ...)
– A note of patriotism is added to express the pride Americans take in this unusual chapter of American history and the singularity of their nation.

6. Find collocations for: *immigration, immigrant, to migrate, migration, migrant, migratory* and: *emigration, to emigrate, an emigrant*.
To restrict *immigration* by quota laws; German *immigrants*; They have *migrated* to the USA; *migratory* birds; many *migrants* in the city; There is a huge *migration* of Mexicans to the USA.
In the 1840s many *emigrated* from Germany to all parts of the world; mass *emigration* from Ireland after the Great Famine; Many famous *emigrants* left the Third Reich.

**Post-reading activities**

1. Write a short paper and/or give a talk on the following theme: Diversity and identity with respect to immigration in the USA.
See Bibliography 8, 17, 29, 37.
2. Make a list of American song titles (folk songs, pop songs ...) which deal with the theme of American identity. Pool your ideas in class and discuss predominant aspects of this theme in music.

## 2. Listening Comprehension: Going to the Promised Land (GK)

### Background information

Mary Antin was born in the small town of Polotzk, Russia, in 1881 and came to America when she was thirteen years old. She was educated in Boston schools and at Columbia University before starting her career as a writer. Her books are based on her own experiences as an immigrant and express a very positive attitude towards America and the life it offered. Her most widely read book is *The Promised Land* (1912), from which our excerpt is taken.
Polotzk was part of the "Pale of Settlement", the area in which Jews had been forced to live since 1804. The systematic persecution of the Jews increased in Mary Antin's childhood during the reign of Alexander III (1881–1894). As a result, almost two million Jews left Russia between 1881 and 1914.

### Methodisch-didaktische Hinweise

Eine Einleitung, Worterklärungen und Fragen zum Text sind im SB auf S. 217 abgedruckt. Das LHB enthält den Text und die Antworten auf die Fragen.
Nach dem recht theoretischen Einstieg (Text 1) soll eine authentische Stimme exemplarisch verdeutlichen, daß bei unterschiedlichen Einzelmotiven die Auswanderung nach Amerika häufig die einzige Lebenshoffnung darstellte und Amerika zum Symbol für die Erfüllung persönlicher Träume wurde. Trotz des lexikalisch schwierigen Textes eignen sich diese lebendigen, autobiographischen Erinnerungen gut zur Übung des Hörverstehens. In einer ersten Gesamtdarbietung steht das Verständnis der Haltung und Grundstimmung von Mary Antin und ihrem Vater zur Auswanderung und zu Amerika im Vordergrund. Zur Vermittlung des Detailverständnisses empfiehlt sich eine zweite Darbietung in zwei Abschnitten (1. Abschnitt ll. 1–24, 2. Abschnitt ll. 25–80).
Als interessante methodische Variante empfiehlt sich folgendes Verfahren:
– Man bietet zunächst nur den 2. Teil des Textes dar (ab "My father was carried away by the westward movement") und arbeitet die auffällige Amerikasehnsucht heraus, um dann die Frage nach möglichen Ursachen und Motiven zu stellen.
– Erst danach präsentiert man den Anfang des Textes mit der Beschreibung der Unterdrückung der Juden in russisch Polen.
Möchte man die etwas pathetisch klingende Hinwendung zu Amerika sofort kontrastieren, so kann unmittelbar auf diesen Hörverstehenstext Text 6 "Where is America?" eingesetzt werden.

### Text

It was a little before Passover that the cry of the hunted thrilled the Jewish world with the familiar fear. The wholesale expulsion of Jews from Moscow and its surrounding district at cruelly short notice was the name of this latest disaster. Where  5
would the doom strike next? The Jews who lived illegally without the Pale turned their possessions into cash and slept in their clothes, ready for immediate flight. Those who lived in the comparative security of the Pale trembled for their 10
brothers and sisters without, and opened wide their doors to afford the fugitives refuge. And

hundreds of fugitives, preceded by a wail of distress, flocked into the open district, bringing their trouble where trouble was never absent, mingling their tears with the tears that never dried ...
Passover was celebrated in tears that year. In the story of the Exodus we would have read a chapter of current history, only for us there was no deliverer and no promised land. But what said some of us at the end of the long service? Not "May we be next year in Jerusalem." but "Next year – in America!" So there was our promised land, and many faces were turned towards the West ...

My father was carried away by the westward movement, glad of his own deliverance, but sore at heart for us whom he left behind. It was the last chance for all of us. We were so far reduced in circumstances that he had to travel with borrowed money to a German port, whence he was forwarded to Boston, with a host of others, at the expense of an emigrant aid society.

I was about ten years old when my father emigrated. I was used to his going away from home, and "America" did not mean much more to me than "Kherson", or "Odessa" or any other names of distant places ...

I know the day when "America" as a world entirely unlike Polotzk lodged in my brain, to become the center of all my dreams and speculations. Well I know the day. I was in bed, sharing the measles with some of the other children. Mother brought us a thick letter from father, written just before boarding the ship. The letter was full of excitement. There was something in it besides the description of travel, something besides the pictures of crowds of people, of foreign cities, of a ship ready to put out to sea ... I heard something, as we read the letter together in the darkened room, that was more than the words seemed to say. There was an elation, a hint of triumph such as had never been in my father's letters before. I cannot tell how I knew it. I felt a stirring, a straining in my father's letter. It was there, even though my mother stumbled over strange words, even though she cried, as women will when somebody is going away. My father was inspired by a vision. He saw something – he promised us something. It was this "America." And "America" became my dream ... My father's letters warned us to prepare for the summons, and we lived in a quiver of expectation.

Not that my father had grown suddenly rich. He was so far from rich that he was going to borrow every cent of the money for our third-class passage; but he had a business in view which he could carry on all the better for having the family with him; and, besides, we were borrowing right and left anyway, and to no definite purpose. With the children, he argued, every year in Russia was a year lost. They should be spending the precious years in school, in learning English, in becoming Americans. United in America, there were ten chances of our getting to our feet again to one chance in our scattered, aimless state.

So at last I was going to America! Really, really going, at last! The boundaries burst. The arch of heaven soared. A million suns shone out for every star. The winds rushed in from outer space, roaring in my ears, "America! America!"

From *The Promised Land* by Mary Antin (Boston: Houghton Mifflin Company, 1912), pp. 140–142, 162.

**Suggested answers (Listening for the gist)**

1. The father's attitude is very ambivalent. On the one hand he is glad to escape the unbearable oppression in Russia and find freedom in America, while on the other he feels very sad about leaving his family behind. His letters express the optimistic anticipation of a happy family reunion and a better life in America ("elation", "a hint of triumph", "a promise"; he is "inspired by a vision"). His positive attitude is illustrated by the fact that he hopes they will become Americans soon, once they have learnt English.

2. They travelled by ship from a German port, the father going ahead of his family. Both the father and the family travelled on borrowed money, including a loan from an emigrant aid society. This shows their unfaltering determination.

3. First America did not mean anything to Mary; it was just another distant place like any other Russian town. But after some time America occupied the centre of her thoughts and aspirations: it was her great dream, the promised land, the new paradise.

**Listening for detail**
Part 1
*1. How does Mary Antin characterize the situation of the Jews in the Moscow area in the 1890s?*

*A Nation of Immigrants* 227

The situation was one of cruel oppression, poverty and hopelessness. Mary Antin refers to the Jews, who were forced to live in the Pale, as "the hunted". At the time in which this story is set, the Jews were to be expelled suddenly from Moscow and surrounding districts. Those living illegally outside the Pale were in grave danger. Terms such as "doom", "wail of distress", "fugitives", "trouble" and "tears" are used to describe the plight of the Jews.

*2. What parallels does Mary Antin see between the Jews' situation in Russia and the biblical exodus?*
Mary Antin sees many parallels between the fate of the Israelites in Egypt and that of the Jews in Russia. The Jews are oppressed like the Israelites. They are not allowed to move freely and are constantly plagued by fear and distress. Like the Israelites, those Jews outside the Pale are ready for flight at any time. Although they lack a deliverer like Moses, the Jews see America as the new Promised Land. The language of the last paragraph reveals that getting there is like a miracle for Mary Antin.

Part 2
*1. What details are given about the father's journey?*
Mary's father borrowed money for the journey to a German port, where he boarded a ship to Boston. The voyage was financed by an emigrant aid society.

*2. How is Mary able to remember precisely the moment when America came to mean the most important thing in her life?*
Mary was in bed with the measles when her father's letter arrived. The father's excitement infected Mary as well. Her enthusiasm for America and her "American Dream" was aroused.

*3. How do the tone and the mood of the first part differ from those of the second part?*
Both parts contain emotive language designed to create a stark contrast between the beginning and the end of the text. The tone is personal thoughout. Phrases such as "cry of the hunted", "wail of distress" and "tears that never dry" create a mood of despair, which then changes dramatically at the mention of the new "Promised Land". It becomes one of excitement and anticipation. In the second part, repetition, words like "elation", "triumph" and "dream", the imagery of the last paragraph and the use of exclamations all add to this effect. (See box on "Tone", SB p. 124.)

**Post-listening activities**
*1. Find out more about the biblical story of the exodus from the second book of the Old Testament (Exodus 1–19).*
In the biblical narrative the term "exodus" refers to the flight of the Israelites from Egypt, where they were slaves, under the leadership of Moses. On the eve of their departure God commanded them to eat a special meal including unleavened bread (bread without yeast) and mark their doors with a special sign (the blood of the lamb slaughtered for the feast). As the last of a series of plagues affecting the Egyptian oppressors, God brought death to the oldest child – and animal – of every Egyptian family, "passing over" those families whose houses were marked with the sign, i.e. the Israelites. The annual Passover feast is the celebration of this event. With the help of a further miracle the Israelites crossed the "Red" (probably "Reed") Sea and wandered through the desert for "40 years" (meaning a long time). Moses died before the Israelites reached the "Promised Land", then known as Canaan. Successively they settled east and west of the Jordan River (now parts of Jordan and Israel).

*2. Find out about the contribution of Jewish immigrants to American society in the twentieth century. Can you name any well-known Jewish Americans? Write a paper or give a talk on one such person.*
Peggy Guggenheim (art collector), Leonard Bernstein (conductor), Albert Einstein (physicist), Saul Bellow (writer), Arthur Miller (playwright), Woody Allen (filmmaker/filmstar), Bernard Malamud (writer). See Alistair Cooke, *America*, (Bibliography 5), pp. 274–286. See also Bibliography 14, 34.

# 3. The Golden Land

## Background information

Born in Austria-Hungary in 1906, Henry Roth emigrated to the USA as a child. His reputation as a writer is based on his novel *Call it Sleep*, which is his only major work. It remained largely unnoticed when it was published in 1934, but its rediscovery and republication in 1960 created a small literary sensation. The novel received widespread critical acclaim and aroused the interest of a broad public.

*Call it Sleep* describes the life of a small, sensitive Jewish boy named David Schearl. Life in New York is harsh for David, whose jealous father suspects that David is not his son. (For further details see the introduction to Harold U. Ribalow, *The History of Henry Roth and Call it Sleep*, New York, 1976.)

The passage reproduced in the SB presents the introductory part of the novel, entitled "Prologue". It is headed by a motto: "I pray thee ask no questions/ this is that Golden Land". Without referring to details of their origin, their former life or relationships, Henry Roth directly presents the family in their turbulent reunion on Ellis Island in 1907. In the opening episode we learn that Albert Schearl had already spent and worked some time in New York when his wife and son followed to join him in America. This pattern of immigration was quite frequent; it applies to the Antin family (Text 2) and it is reflected upon by the narrator when he ironically describes the national stereotypes in reunion scenes.

## Methodisch-didaktische Hinweise

Der recht lange und lexikalisch auch schwierige Text soll zunächst in der Form des *extensive reading* angegangen werden. Die Schüler sollen versuchen, die gesamte Passage mit den wenigen angegebenen Wörtern zu verstehen und zwar hinsichtlich der Ausgangssituation der Episode, der grundlegenden Personenkonstellation und der Handlungslinie (*basic situation, relationships of characters, action*). Entsprechende Verständnisfragen können zusammen mit den Aufgaben des SB gestellt werden.

Für die genauere Bearbeitung des Textes sollten die Schüler Passagen nennen, die sie aus ihrer Sicht für ergiebig, wichtig, interessant halten. Diese Passagen sollten dann lexikalisch und inhaltlich im Sinne des *intensive reading* erschlossen werden. Für die Aufgliederung in einzelne Textteile könnte die strukturelle Dreiteilung von Milieuschilderung und Beschreibung, direkter Narration der Handlung sowie szenischen Einschüben mit direkter Rede hilfreich sein. Möchte man die intensive Bearbeitung des Textes auf eine durchgehende lexikalische Detailerschließung gründen, könnten die Schüler in Gruppen- oder Partnerarbeit mit Hilfe von Wörterbüchern Annotationen erstellen und austauschen.

Eine methodische Variante: Im Sinne "schüleraktivierender Verfahren" (Bredella) kann die Erstbegegnung mit dem Text auch bewußt schrittweise gestaltet werden, um Sprünge, Lücken, Wendungen im Handlungsgang kreativ auszugestalten. Als Beispiel soll hier folgender Zugriff vorgeschlagen werden: der Text wird intensiv bis Zeile 126 oder auch 131 ("... said timidly"), also bis zu der erwarteten Begrüßungsszene gelesen; die Schüler werden gebeten, nicht weiterzulesen, sondern die Begrüßung und die erste Kontaktaufnahme selbst zu verfassen ("creative writing").

## Pre-reading activities

*1. Imagine the welcome Mary Antin's father (Text 2) gives to his family when they meet in America. Speculate on Mary's feelings when she steps onto American soil, when she sees the Statue of Liberty.*

*2. Answer the questions beside the picture on p. 220.*

Objects on the wall: for testing matching skills (playing cards and other cards) and general knowledge (flags). Insane barred from immigration 1882 (the literacy test of 1917 reinforced this barrier). Other groups barred 1882: convicts and people living on charity; the Chinese (for ten years). The man is fitting blocks into the right spaces (test of matching skills).

## Suggested answers

1. It "was a very curious meeting" (l. 126). They meet and stand silently apart for some minutes before saying anything to each other. Even when they do speak, there are no words of welcome. We are confronted with the hostility and the reproaches of the husband, which lead to uncer-

tainty and timidity on the part of the wife. It is especially striking that the father does not turn to his son at all in the first few minutes – and when he does, it is for rather a vicious attack. One would expect an enthusiastic welcome after the long separation: embraces, kisses, questions about one's health, the passage etc.

2. a) Step by step the reader learns that this family reunion has gone desperately wrong. The husband waited in Manhattan for his wife's arrival, assuming that as a third-class passenger she would soon be taken there. For financial reasons his wife and son had travelled as steerage passengers, who traditionally had to undergo long admission checks. The annoyed husband nevertheless made his way to Ellis Island, despite the negative information given by the shipping company. When they finally meet – just in time to catch the last boat to Manhattan – his wife does not recognize him at first sight. Then the father takes a dislike to the child's hat.

b) Although his wife apologizes and addresses him full of sympathy and affection, he remains offended and flies into a rage when provoked by the boy's cap, which betrays him as a recent immigrant. The father's comment in l. 215, "He's the cause of all this trouble anyway!", hints at a more deep-seated conflict.

c) The long period of separation has made them lead very different lives: the husband has become an American, a city man wanting to conceal his origins. The wife, however, has stayed a provincial woman despite her new city clothes. Perhaps the father is unable to form emotional ties to the son, who may be spoilt by the mother.

Later in the novel the reader learns that the father is embittered, having suspected all along that his wife never loved him and that the child is another man's son. Students might speculate as to why the author failed to reveal the husband's suspicion at the start.

3. The view of Liberty presented in ll. 185–191 is very ambivalent: Liberty's features are "charred with shadow, her depths exhausted"; her torch becomes "a black cross against flawless light". The perspective is that of "those on board who gazed" (ll. 184–185), i.e. the newly-arrived immigrants being transported to the "stench and throb of New York tenements" (ll. 3–4). Their newfound freedom contains an element of threat. Note the way in which the darkness of the figure is contrasted with the "brilliance" (l. 182) of the light. The scene evokes a feeling of awe in the mother and child (ll. 192–193).

It is useful to compare this part of the text with Emma Lazarus' poem "The New Colossus", part of which is quoted at the beginning of the chapter (SB p. 215). The whole poem is contained in Perspectives 1: *The American Dream* (Klettbuch 51361), pp. 10–11. It is inscribed on the pedestal of the statue.

4. The perspective throughout is the restricted point of view of the observer who gathers, and tries to interpret, a variety of impressions. His or her view is limited to what is seen and heard. A number of words and phrases such as "had evidently spent" (l. 51), "It might have been thought that ..." (l. 53), "perhaps he was merely too agitated" (l. 58) and "one guessed that" (ll. 67–68) emphasize the limited perspective. In ll. 99–101 the detached observer/narrator is projected into "the old peddler woman on the bench and the overalled men in the stern." This allows the reader to observe the behaviour of the family at close quarters. In ll. 239–241, when the tension reaches a peak, we see how the peddler and the overalled men react.

5. The restricted point of view allows the reader to choose his or her own interpretation of the scene. Note that the reactions of the peddler woman and the overalled men in ll. 239–241 differ, so that the reader is not manipulated by any one response. Following this incident, however, attention is focused solely on the woman's feelings as expressed in her behaviour. Hence most readers probably sympathize with the mother and child. Since no reason is given for the father's deep aversion toward them, it is hard for the reader to accept his refusal to give his family a warmer welcome once the initial misunderstandings have been cleared up, even though his annoyance at the frustrating circumstances (waiting all day in uncertainty, his wife's failure to recognize him, the provincial attire of his son and the son's crying) is understandable.

## Additional questions

1. *Collect the true historical and factual details of the text. Which element prevails: the historical details or the fictitious incident?*
Historical and factual background:
The steamer Peter Stuyvesant, Ellis Island, the Statue of Liberty; 1907 – greatest number of immigrants to the USA; only steerage passengers had to undergo long checks at Ellis Island; the Kaiserin Viktoria of the Hamburg-America Line; geographical detail; clothing of the time.
 Although many of the details in this passage are historically accurate, the writer's main interest lies in the characters and their story (historical fiction). Knowing that many details of Roth's life correspond to those of the story, we can also assume it is autobiographical fiction, though the passage itself does not reveal this.

2. *What are the wife's very first words in the novel? What feelings does she try to express in them?*
"And this is the Golden Land" (l. 131). Feelings: hope, disappointment, satisfaction, fear, disillusionment, uncertainty ... (open to discussion).

3. *Analyse and discuss the ethnic stereotypes described in ll. 103–115.*

4. *One of the greatest challenges for translators of literary works is to retain the emotional impact of the language. Ll. 18–35 of our text contain colourful description. Reread these lines aloud, as evocatively as possible. Then try to translate the following phrases in an accurate but colourful way:*
the full-bearded Russian; the scraggly-whiskered Jew; the wrinkled eyelids of the Danes; vivid costumes; speckled green-and-yellow aprons; silver-braided sheep-skin vest.
Vorschläge: der Russe mit dem Vollbart; der Jude mit dem wirren Backenbart; die faltigen Augenlider der Dänen; bunte/ grelle Trachten, grün-gelb gefleckte Schürzen; Schafsfelljacke oder -weste mit Silbertressen.

5. *Find synonyms for the words in italics:*
a) he paid only the *scantiest* attention to (l. 55)
b) *dull* clothes (l. 62)
c) *timid* look (l. 68)
d) *to gaze* (l. 69).
slightest
dark/boring/uninteresting/
shy/anxious/frightened
to stare

## Post-reading activities

1. *Look at the picture on p. 219 (SB) and answer the questions beside it.*
Possible interpretation: apprehension, exhaustion, fear, curiosity ... (women). American men: detached, slightly bemused (like the observer/narrator of the story? Like the "overalled men" of l. 92?)
Description of immigrant women: ll. 86–90.

2. *The text is ideally suited to presentation on stage, for the following reasons:*
– It contains few characters.
– It contains a lot of detail about the visual setting e.g. clothing.
– The dialogue is the main instrument for telling the story.
– Reactions of the characters are described in detail.
– Although open-ended, the scene has a unity of its own.
*In the following steps, rewrite this scene as the first scene of a play (Text 8, "The oldest racket in the country", will help you). Make notes on each step and discuss them in small groups. The logical conclusion – given time – would be for each group to present its scene to the class. How would the play then develop?*
*Title? Conclusion?*
*Steps:*
a) *Note essential elements of stage set.*
b) *Determine necessary characters. How are they dressed? Position at opening of play?*
c) *Extract dialogue from text.* d) *Write stage directions based on reactions of characters.*
e) *Combine 3 and 4. What about facial expressions, gestures, positioning, pauses, use of music and lights ...? Should the characters start speaking straight away? Add or change stage directions and dialogue if desired.*
f) *Write the script.*
g) *Try out the script. The difficulty here is how to represent the child and its crying. Using a doll and recorded crying would be one solution, but this could seem very artificial.*
h) *Performance!*
*If there is no time for a performance, the small groups could read out their completed scripts and discuss them with other groups. This exercise provides a good basis for discussing the difference between prose and drama.*

3. Write a book report on Henry Roth's Call it Sleep.
See Bibliography 27.

4. Compare the family reunion depicted in the text with Abraham Cahan, "The Meeting" (excerpt from the novel Yekl), in: Great Immigrant Stories, Klettbuch 57938, pp. 5–11 (paper or talk).

## 4. Ellis Island

### Background information

Joseph Bruchac, born in 1942 in Saratoga Springs (New York State), is of Slovak, English and Indian ancestry. His tribal affiliation is Abenaki. He is author, editor, publisher and activist on behalf of Native American writers. Bruchac has published many books, poems and short stories. Works: *Indian Mountain and Other Poems* (1971); *Entering Onondaga* (1978); *Iroquois Stories* (1984). One of his stories won a PEN Syndicated Fiction Award.

Being of ethnically mixed ancestry, Bruchac tries to reconcile the immigrant's experience with that of the Native American to answer the question of his personal identity. The gradual revelation that he was partly Indian, which had long been kept from him, coincided with the gradual emergence of a deep-felt identification with Native American culture. He grew to see himself as a mediator, a "translator" between two worlds, referring to himself not as "Indian" but as a "metis" (Lakota Indian word meaning "translator's son").

See Joseph Bruchac's autobiographical essay in Brian Swann and Arnold Krupat (eds.), *I Tell You Now*, University of Nebraska Press (Lincoln and London), pp. 197–203.

### Methodisch-didaktische Hinweise

Die Aufgaben verstehen sich als frei zu verwendende gedankliche Hilfen für ein flexibles Interpretationsgespräch. Dies kann initiiert werden in einem Erstgespräch mit der Frage nach der Haltung des *speaker* zur "Besiedlung" Amerikas durch die Einwanderer (*ambivalence, divided loyalty*). Sollte das Verständnis des an der Oberfläche Gesagten Schwierigkeiten bereiten, kann durch Gliederung der gedanklichen Struktur sowie durch Erläuterung und Verdeutlichung der syntaktischen Hauptlinien des Gedichtes eine Phase systematischer Texterarbeitung eingeschoben werden (3 parts: 1. Ellis Island and the Statue of Liberty and what they stand for; 2. The speaker's nostalgic visit to pay tribute to fulfilled dreams; 3. turning point – contrast: regretful mourning, for immigration meant invasion and destruction. Cf. Additional questions No. 2).

Die Analyse der Form und der formalen Elemente des Gedichts kann sich auf die wesentlichen Aspekte (vgl. Aufgabe 7) beschränken.

Ein "schüleraktivierender" Zugriff könte darin bestehen, daß entweder als Einstieg und Erstpräsentation oder als Schlußauftrag das Gedicht nur bis Zeile 18 oder 19 präsentiert wird mit der Aufgabe, einen antithetischen Schlußteil selbst zu verfassen.

### Pre-reading activities

1. Ellis Island and the Statue of Liberty have become symbols of national identity and have in recent years been the centre of national festivities. Which ethnic groups of the USA do not share the immigrant experience? How might they see these two symbols and the myth they created?

In an article in the *International Herald Tribune* of July 8, 1986, A. Fried warns against judging "the black experience" in terms of "the immigrant experience". Black people entered the country as slaves, involuntarily, and have long been the victims of racial oppression. Their fight for freedom has been part of the democratic process that has shaped the USA (see "Background information" on the listening comprehension in Ch. 11, "I have a dream", SB p. 249).

American Indians cannot be termed immigrants, since they originate from the country itself. Their minority status has a lot to do with the question of their right to live on the land they originally occupied.

Both African-Americans and Indians might say, with A. Fried, "When the statue, in its silent majestic eloquence, speaks for all the insulted and injured of America, then we will have cause to rejoice."

*2. Discuss the question posed in the caption to the picture on p. 223 (SB).*

See pie charts, SB p. 229. Examine trends after 1960. Most Asians enter the USA on the west coast, and most Hispanics via California. Hence a new immigration centre would have to be in the west. Los Angeles has been termed "the New Ellis Island". See the map of LA, with distribution of ethnic groups, on p. 12 of Perspectives 1: *The American Dream* (Klettbuch 51361).

**Suggested answers**

1. Although the speaker refers to himself directly only in the second stanza, we assume that he is a passenger on the tourist boat of the Circle Line passing Ellis Island on its way to Liberty Island.

2. The two islands were often seen by immigrants as a stark contrast, the "Isle of Tears" and the "Isle of Hope and Freedom". This contrast is reflected in the poem. Whereas it is the "red brick" of Ellis Island which stands out, Liberty Island is "green as dreams of forests and meadows." Whereas on Ellis Island people have to endure "long days of quarantine", Liberty Island is "waiting" for the immigrants to come. On Ellis Island, immigrants had to wait in line in the red brick buildings for various kinds of inspection. Though many were able to leave the same day, some, like the writer's grandparents, were kept in quarantine for long periods, and some were even sent back. Liberty Island, with its statue representing freedom, is, on the other hand, the embodiment of the "dreams" of the immigrants, dreams of an end to oppression and of owning their own land.

3. He comes because of "that part" of his blood which "loves that memory", namely, the memory of Liberty Island. People come to pay tribute to the "answerer of dreams".

4. With Slovak grandparents and Native American background (not specified further) the speaker is of mixed ancestry, which causes a conflict of identity. He is is torn between his gratitude to America for allowing the immigrant branch of his family to lead a free life on a farm and his regret that in this process the culture and lifestyle of his Native American forefathers was destroyed.
The sequence of thought at the end of the poem, giving the Indian elements greater prominence, seems to show that these prevail.

5. In the first stanza the speaker refers to the oppressed peoples of the "old Empires of Europe" (l. 6). They could not enjoy the fruits of a lifetime of hard work ("a thousand years" l. 12) because they were enslaved and exploited. They never owned what actually belonged to them (l. 13).
The forceful invasion of Indian land described in the third stanza led to private ownership of land by the once dispossessed whites. The concept of owning land is foreign to Indians; land belongs to the Earth, giving the Indians subsistence in a natural and seasonal way. The whites' greed and idea of ownership destroyed the way of life that was based on this concept.

6. The Statue of Liberty was dedicated in 1886. The speaker visits Liberty Island "nine decades" later (l. 16), i.e. in about 1976. He creates the impression that he composed the poem on location, or even on board the Circle Line ship. Poetry, however, is seldom composed in this way. The true significance of an event often emerges, for the poet, some time later, when it is "recollected in tranquillity" (William Wordsworth, Preface to the second edition of the *Lyrical Ballads*). Wordsworth's poem "I wandered lonely as a cloud" is a good example of this. Describing "a crowd ... of golden daffodils", the poet says:
"I gazed – and gazed – but little thought
What wealth the show to me had brought:

For oft, when on my couch I lie,
In vacant or in pensive mood,
They flash upon that inward eye
Which is the bliss of solitude; ..."
Hence we may assume that Bruchac wrote his poem at a later date, when the significance of his journey to Liberty Island became clear to him.

7. There is no regular rhythm in the poem, but the short lines have well-defined stresses. Where appropriate, the lines are longer, e.g. "waited the long days of quarantine" (l. 4).
The poem is structured not only by means of clearly defined thematic units, but also by repetition, e.g. "island" at the end of ll. 1 and 8, where a new thematic unit begins respectively. Cf. the repetition of "land(s)" in ll. 20, 22, 24.
The tone of the poem is nostalgic overall, with a sadder touch in the second half. This is influenced by the repetition already mentioned and by:

- concrete imagery indicating a broader meaning ("red brick of Ellis Island" l. 1; "sickness of Europe" ll. 5 and 6; "the tall woman" l. 9).
- poetic images: "as green as dreams of forests and meadows" ll. 9–10; "the answerer of dreams" ll. 18–19.
- poetic devices: alliteration ("waiting ... worked", l. 11); assonance ("green as dreams" ll. 9–10); personification (l. 9).

### Additional questions

1. Discuss the title and find alternatives.
"Ellis Island Revisited", "The Tall Woman", "An American Divided", "Two Souls"...
One may think that "Ellis Island" is a misnomer, as it does not reflect the conflict in question.

2. Write down the four basic statements (main clauses) which constitute the syntactic backbone of the poem. Examine the way in which the rest of poem is syntactically linked to them.
a) a Circle Line ship slips easily
b) I too come to this island
c) Yet only one part of my blood loves that memory
d) Another voice speaks of native lands
With the exception of c), all of these statements are enriched by further reflections. They are linked by adverbial phrases, relative clauses (some in elliptic form), participle constructions and adverbial sub-clauses. Whereas the first two parts are complex and highly hypotactical, the last part leads into two parallel statements about native lands.

### Post-reading activities

1. Read Claude McKay's poem "Outcast" (1953) and comment on this African-American's quest for identity, in: Frank Link (Hrsg.), Amerikanische Lyrik, zweisprachig, Reclam Stuttgart 1974.

2. Read one of the stories in Native American Short Stories (Klettbuch 57933) and give a report on it in class. The same exercise could be carried out using Stories from the Black Experience (Klettbuch 5793).

# 5. An abundance of jobs

### Background information

Alan M. Kraut is a professor of history at the American University in Washington, D.C., where he specializes in immigration and the ethnic history of the USA. His major work is *The Huddled Masses: The Immigrant in American Society 1880–1921* (1982), from which our text is taken.

### Methodisch-didaktische Hinweise

Dieser Text leitet innerhalb des Kapitels einen neuen Abschnitt ein (Texte 5–7), in dem die wirtschaftliche und soziale Situation der Einwanderer in den USA im Mittelpunkt steht.
Alan M. Krauts Text beschäftigt sich mit der wesentlichen Frage, wie es bei der Masseneinwanderung vor und nach der Jahrhunderwende nicht zum Kollaps des wirtschaftlichen und sozialen Systems kam und auf welche Weise die Neuankömmlinge integriert werden konnten, ohne daß es zu größeren sozialen Eruptionen kam. Die Antwort liegt in spezifisch amerikanischen Gegebenheiten, die möglicherweise – das wäre offen zu diskutieren – noch bis auf den heutigen Tag ihre Gültigkeit haben: die Größe des Landes, die wirtschaftlichen Ressourcen, die Größe der Volkswirtschaft, die anhaltende wirtschaftliche Expansion, die regionale und soziale Mobilität. So sagt Kraut für die Zeit um die Jahrhundertwende: "Rapid expansion of American industry kept foreign and American workers from actually colliding. Lateral and vertical promotion kept many native-born workers clear of newcomers" (ll. 88–92). Die Frage, wieviele Zuwanderer eine Volkswirtschaft und Gesellschaft auf humane Weise integrieren kann, stellt sich in zunehmendem Maße auch für Deutschland, was vielfache Aspekte für eine vergleichende Diskussion aufwerfen sollte. Bei diesen Gesprächen sollten vor allem genaue Fakten und Zahlen einbezogen werden, damit man nicht in unergiebige, ideologische Grundsatzdebatten zurückfällt.
An dieser Stelle bietet sich auch die Frage der Begrenzung der Einwanderung durch Gesetze an (siehe *fact file*, SB pp. 311–312).

**Pre-reading activities**

*1. Discuss the changing patterns and waves of immigration with reference to the charts on pp. 229–230 (SB). Compare in particular the periods 1900–1920 and 1980–1990. The fact file on pp. 311–312 will help clarify the background of the patterns discovered. Text 9, "The Tortilla Curtain", deals with recent immigration in more detail.*

Patterns that should emerge:
- 1820–1960: Predominantly European immigrants. The Immigration Act of 1965 put an abrupt end to this development. Note the high percentage of Irish and German immigrants, especially in the 19th century. From 1881–1920 more people came from southern, southeastern and eastern Europe.
- 1901–1989: Steady increase in immigration from the "Western Hemisphere", particularly Hispanics. These formed the largest group 1961–1980. Steady increase in the percentage of "Chicanos" (Mexican origin) among the Hispanics – now largest group. Decrease in immigration from Canada. Sharp rise in number of Asian immigrants after abolition of quota laws in 1965 and acceptance of Chinese immigrants.

Population statistics:
- In 1907 more than 1.3 million immigrants entered the USA.
- The decade 1900–1910 brought nearly 8.8 million immigrants representing more than 40 nations.
- US population 1900: 76 million.
- 1980–1990: about 9 million legal immigrants.
- Net immigration considerably higher because of illegal immigration.
- US population 1990: 249 million.
- The foreign-born population of the USA may at the moment exceed 15 million.

**Suggested answers**

1. The first paragraph introduces the topic by a topic sentence and two questions which are then answered in a general way: Immigrants soon found jobs in the USA after the Civil War because of rapid industrialization and a great demand for labour.
The second paragraph first deals with two contrasting views of the immigrants. The first idea concerns the legendary success of energetic immigrants, while the second focuses on the humiliating life of an exploited mass in sweatshops. The writer then ironically extends the second image to describe the media "creation" of the oppressed immigrant who becomes a political activist. The immigrants' fate in America cannot be stereotyped. Individual qualities, an abundance of opportunities and a demand for labour determined the immigrants' occupations and degree of success in America (third paragraph).
Fourth paragraph: The industrial cities of the North provided work, particularly for unskilled labourers, and the assistance of fellow-immigrants.
Fifth paragraph: high proportion of immigrant labour in all areas of industrial production, in some industries outnumbering native-born workers.
Sixth paragraph: the author concedes that in some industries native-born English and Irish workers were displaced by even cheaper Poles or Slavs, but he maintains that the concern of nativists was not always based on fact.
Conclusion: Immigrant workers did not displace American-born workers. The economy was expanding, due in part to immigrant labour. American-born workers were often promoted, making lower-paid jobs available to immigrants.

2. An abundance of immigrant workers certainly meant cheap labour and lower costs of production. Due to technological progress and the higher demand for goods, companies were able to invest and expand, which meant a greater and more finely differentiated work force. Hence on the whole there was not a displacement process but a regional and vertical shift. "Displaced" workers went west to new production sites or upwards into white-collar jobs.

3. Other pull factors include religious and social freedom, the availability of land and the desire to join relatives already in the USA. Push factors in past and present: famine, poverty, unemployment (e.g. Italy and Ireland); oppression, scarcity of land (e.g. Germany last century); the persecution of Jews (e.g. Germany, Russia).
- The USA today: immigrants come from Asia and other American countries, for both political and economic reasons.
- Germany: immigration from eastern Europe ("ethnic Germans"); asylum-seekers.
- Great Britain: immigrants from former Commonwealth countries.

– France: immigrants from former colonies.
– Israel: Jews from the former Soviet Union.

**Additional questions**

*1. In which industries was the proportion of immigrants highest? Study the text. Why is this so?*
Garment manufacturing, coal mining, slaughtering, meat packing, construction and confectionery. These industries were expanding rapidly, primarily due to population growth, and were at the same time labour-intensive. In addition, conditions were unpleasant, so that few native-born Americans were attracted to such industries.

*2. Find antonyms for the words in italics:*
a) an *abundance* of jobs *(l. 6)*
b) new *immigrants* *(ll. 6–7)*
c) *supply* and ...
d) *unskilled* labor *(l. 10)*
e) *white-collar* jobs *(l. 103)*
a) a lack; b) emigrants; native-born citizens c) demand (l. 50, l. 10); d) skilled; e) blue-collar

*3. Give collocations for words from the word family "to employ".*
Newcomers could quickly find employment (ll. 10–11); Immigrants were soon employed; 57.9% of all employees were foreign-born (ll. 68–69); At that time there was virtually no unemployment; unemployment rate; to be unemployed; Employers must provide good working conditions.

**Cartoon SB p. 225**

Wealthy gentlemen reject a poor newcomer, though they themselves were once poor immigrants. This is evident from their overpowering shadows. The cartoonist is criticizing the egotism and short memory of these well-fed and overdressed men. Yet what have they to fear from this poor creature? Their fears are unfounded.

Caption/title (suggestions) "Not today, thank you!"/"Full up!"/"Go back where you came from"/ "Short memory"/"Leaving old shadows behind". The original caption is "Looking Back".
There was a powerful and partly violent nativist movement, especially in California, after the Chinese were allowed to enter in great numbers in 1868. This movement led to mob violence, terrorism and, finally, to anti-Chinese legislation. In 1882 all Chinese immigration was suspended for 10 years. This law was renewed 10 years later. Eventually, in 1902, all Chinese immigration was banned. There was no basic change until the Immigration Act of 1965. See text of "Listening Comprehension" (pp. 252–253).

**Post-reading activities**

*1. One major factor in economic expansion is innovation and technological progress. List some developments, inventions and patents that made the USA the leading economic world power between the Civil War and 1900.*
Steel production by Bessemer process, railroad construction, laying down a standard gauge for the rails, oil drilling, electricity and dynamo, telegraph and telephone, the Singer sewing-machine. See Bibliography 7, 10, 22.

*2. Do you know any rags-to-riches success stories concerning immigrants?*
Carnegie (Bibliography 7), John Jacob Astor and Henry Villard (formerly Heinrich Hilgard). See Bibliography 38.

*3. Prepare a paper on one of the following topics and present it in class:*
*a) The emergence of industrial America*
See Bibliography 7.
*b) The huddled masses.*
See Bibliography 5, Ch. 9.

# 6. Where is America? (GK)

**Background information**

Anzia Yezierska (1881/1885?–1970) was born in Russian Poland and emigrated with her family to the USA in the 1890s. They settled in the "ghetto" of New York City's Lower East Side. She worked in sweatshops and laundries, leaving home at the age of seventeen. Anzia Yezierska attended night school to learn English and won a scholarship to become a domestic science teacher. She taught cooking from 1905 to 1913, during which time she also became an American citizen.
Encouraged by the noted philosopher John Dewey of Columbia University, Anzia Yezierska started writing. Her stories and novels deal realistically

with the lives of struggling immigrants living in the ghetto. She won instant fame with *Hungry Hearts*, a collection of ten short stories published in 1920. Hollywood turned *Hungry Hearts* into a movie, employing Yezierska as a script-writer.

Our text is a passage from "How I Found America", a widely anthologized story from *Hungry Hearts*. Anzia Yezierska was overcome with guilt for having become wealthy and well-known by writing about the poor. She found that education and success alienated her from her own people and that she was much happier when poor but one of them.

Although she wrote several more books, Anzia Yezierska's reputation declined after the Depression years. In the 1960s and 70s her achievements once more received recognition. Her protagonists being women, she was rediscovered by feminists. Social historians praised the authenticity of Yezierska's works. She died in poverty in Ontario, California.

## Methodisch-didaktische Hinweise

Der Text "Where is America?" steht schlaglichtartig für die harten Lebensumstände vieler Einwanderer der "ersten Generation". Im Unterschied zu ihren Arbeitskolleginnen reagiert die Protagonistin äußerst heftig auf die Bedingungen, da sie sich "ihr Amerika" ganz anders vorgestellt hatte.

Ein Rückgriff auf die Amerikasehnsucht von Mary Antin (Text 2 LC), eventuell als Einstieg, würde diesen stark gefühlten Widerspruch verdeutlichen. Daneben besteht ein enger inhaltlicher Zusammenhang mit dem folgenden Text, der die angesprochene Problematik in aktuellen Bezügen aufnimmt.

Die lebendige und sprachlich ganz eindrucksvolle Gestaltung der Erdrückung durch den harten amerikanischen Alltag sowie die tiefe Enttäuschung ist angesichts der Tatsache, daß Englisch die zweite Sprache der Autorin war, verblüffend – was allerdings für viele der hervorragenden amerikanischen Autoren polnisch/russisch/jüdischer Herkunft gilt (vgl. auch Mary Antin und Henry Roth in diesem Buch). Es wird empfohlen, eine intensive stilistische Analyse durchzuführen.

## Pre-reading activities

*1. Look at the picture on p. 227 of the SB. Discuss possible answers to the questions posed in the caption.*

Dark, congested environments and dangerous working conditions were part of the industrial scene in many factories even in the first half of this century. On-the-job accidents involving immigrants increased; they were often due to the language barrier.

– Sewing (woman on the right), ironing (man on the left).
– See "Background information" on text 7.

## Suggested answers

1. The speaker laments that she could not enjoy childhood (at home in Russian Poland) because she was forced to work. Now in her formative years she is denied a much-desired education, and the hard workday, requiring only her physical strength, stifles her emotional development as an adolescent. She feels alienated and frustrated, for she sees the prospect of a fulfilling adult life being destroyed by such daily drudgery.

2. Pleasant living conditions and surroundings, good education with intellectual challenges, a spiritually and emotionally fulfilling job and lifestyle.

3. Anzia is portrayed as being in a very excited and bewildered state of mind. All circumstances are seen through her sensitive eyes as she revolts against deadening conditions. Greatly astonished, she notes that her workmates bear these conditions with humour. The fact that the speaker's reaction is very subjective is underlined by the frequent use of first-person pronouns. Thus the speaker may seem egocentric. Yet the description of her exhaustion, of the filth and noise and the "vulgar jokes" presents an ugly picture of the sweatshop, helping to justify her reaction.

4. Physically hard work that leads to exhaustion and to spiritual and emotional numbness; the dirty, scruffy surroundings; the prison-like sweatshop; the deafening noise of the machines; the masses of uncouth workers on her way to work; the vulgar and "insensible" workmates

5. Concrete aspects that make her life unpleasant: getting up too late because of utter exhaustion; hurry, mother's warning; employer's punishment; rushed walk to work; unpleasant surroundings; sweatshop; noise; dirt; vulgar workmates
– Use of adjectives: deadweight sleep, utter exhaustion (ll. 4 and 5), iron hardness (l. 16), dilapidated building (l. 19), merciless grind (l.

23), galling grind (l. 48), crushing, deadening movements (l. 49)
- Verbs, participles, gerunds denoting hurried movement: e.g. to tumble (l. 9), I ate running (l. 11), choking each mouthful (ll. 12–13), pressing through ... throngs of workers (ll. 11–12), I felt a strangling in my throat (l. 14), raging around me (l. 22), to struggle (28), the munching of food (l. 43)
- Words denoting negative sounds: e.g. roar and the clatter (23), the grind of pounding machines (l. 24); loud, vulgar jokes (ll. 43 and 44)
- Harsh judgements through choice of words: sweatshop prison (l. 15); the day's torture (ll. 16 and 17); dirt and decay cried out from every crumbling brick (ll. 19–21)
- Agitated tone and forceful rhythm: e.g. I seized my bread and herring and tumbled down the stairs and out into the street (ll. 9–10); dirt and decay (ll. 19–20, alliteration); the roar and clatter, the clatter and roar (l. 23, chiasmus, onomatopoeia);

Half maddened, half deadened, I struggled to think, to feel, to remember – what am I – who am I – why was I here? (ll. 24–27, parallelism, interior rhyme, gradation); America – America – where was America? (l. 30, repetition, rhetorical question);

I didn't come to America to turn into a machine. I came to America to make from myself a person (ll. 58–60, contrast)

6. Whereas Anzia feels repulsed by everything to such a degree that she cannot have her tea and her lunch, Yetta makes a very down-to-earth impression. She senses that there is something wrong with her workmate and encourages her to eat something. Yetta also seems to have come to terms with her situation. In a very pragmatic, brief answer she expresses that without proper schooling one cannot expect anything better than this.

Anzia, however, revolts against this vicious circle by stating her right to a proper education.

**Additional questions**

*1. Find words or phrases synonymous to those in italics:*
a) I *felt for* the buttons (l. 2)
b) I *felt* a strangling in my throat (l. 14)
c) I struggled *to feel* – what am I (l. 25)
d) in my stifled heat *feelings* began to pulse (l. 38)
a) tried to find
b) noticed; sensed; perceived
c) determine; sense; perceive; recognize
d) emotions

*2. List some of the contrasts Anzia uses.*
- Must my youth die – unlived? (l. 41)
- Here only hands live and – hearts and brains die (ll. 50–51).
- I did not come to America to turn into a machine – I came to America to make from myself a person (ll. 58–60).
- Does America want only hands, only the strength of my body – not my heart, not my feelings, my thoughts? (ll. 60–62)
- "We ain't been to school like the American-born." – "What for did I come to America but to go to school." (ll. 64–67)

**Post-reading activities**

*1. Write a book report on Upton Sinclair,* The Jungle, *Penguin.*

*2. Write an analysis of the short story by Bernard Malamud, "The German Refugee", in:* Great Immigrant Stories, *Klettbuch 57938, pp. 18–33.*

*3. Write a paper or give a talk on the subject of German immigration to the USA.*
See Bibliography 29, 35, 38.

## 7. The new sweatshops

**Background information**

As the hiring of illegal immigrants was not seen as an offence until 1986 (1986 Immigration Act, see fact file, SB p. 312), sweatshops developed fast when masses of illegal immigrants entered the USA in the late 1970s and 1980s. Although it was, and still is, unlawful for illegal aliens to work in the USA, it was not unlawful for employers to hire them. Making use of an oversupply of labour, companies paid illegally low wages, especially for overtime work, did not grant any benefits, did not pay on time and violated protective laws and safety measures. They were in a position to do so because the illegal aliens did not have any rights; many were completely at the mercy of employers. The 1986 Immigration Act, which allowed for severe sanctions and penalties for the employment of illegal aliens, had some impact, but sweatshop conditions still persist because the overall number of immigrants is at a record high. As long as an immigrant will take any job to support a humble existence, some employers will exploit this situation. Employers, especially in the garment trade, maintain that cut-throat competition makes it imperative to lower costs by whatever means one can. "Some 3,000 of 7,000 apparel firms in New York, employing 50,000 workers, are sweatshops" (*Newsweek*, September 10, 1990). There are federal agencies trying to enforce protective laws by means of inspections and prosecutions, but as this *Newsweek* article clearly indicates, they are relatively unsuccessful.

## Suggested answers

1. See "Background information". Due to progressive labour laws and the power of the unions, sweatshops almost disappeared in the 1950s and 1960s but have since returned with the new wave of immigrants (ll. 24 ff.). Sweatshop workers, who are mostly unskilled, accept poor conditions for fear of being fired or even deported.

2. Being in America provides a livelihood for unskilled immigrant workers. Yet a poor command of English and the lack of support as a newcomer may mean that the loss of a job is equivalent to the loss of this basis. The phrase also refers to the unfounded fears of immigrant workers that their employers might notify the immigration authorities (INS) and have them deported.

3. See "Background information".

4. Garment manufacturing, the textile industry: the "rag trade" (ll. 33–34), and in almost all branches of manufacturing and labour-intensive work ("everything from plastics to flowers" l. 34). The introductory paragraph refers to dangerous occupations within construction firms (removing asbestos without proper safety measures). Working conditions on some farms take the form of modern slavery (ll. 45 ff).

5. + 6. There is a tone of irony, sometimes sarcasm, throughout the text. America is the land of opportunity primarily for those who break its laws to exploit immigrants, not for the immigrants themselves (ll. 62–69).
In the same manner the writer alludes to The New Colossus, the statue which welcomes all who "yearn to breathe free" (cf. l. 21), contrasting this with the work of immigrants in polluted conditions, breathing in asbestos fibres. This typically journalistic treatment can also be seen in the use of colourful imagery and an informal choice of words ("He was not naive enough to think" l. 1; "paved with gold – littered with asbestos" l. 2 and l. 4; "the growing muscle of unions" l. 25; "waves of immigrants lapped these shores" ll. 36–37; "manage a bust" l. 62).

Apart from these stylistic elements the arrangement of the material is quite typical of news magazine articles. It starts with a provocative human interest story which arouses both sympathy and indignation. The writer then tries to show that this is not an individual case but a general abuse to be found all over the country. He explains this and gives more striking examples. The agencies and private groups fighting the injustices are represented by quotes that reveal helplessness and resignation.

## Additional questions

*1. What is the writer's intention?*
From the journalistic treatment outlined above one can draw the conclusion that as well as exposing the facts about ongoing social injustice the writer wishes to arouse the reader, to make him or her see that traditional American ideals have become perverted (breathing free; land of opportunity). He may wish the reader to protest against this situation so that effective political and administrative measures can finally be taken to put an end to sweatshops.
Some students may argue that the tone of irony is a sign of resignation in view of the long persistence of sweatshops.

*2. Find a subtitle summarizing the immigrant workers' attitude.*
The original subtitle reads: "Desperate for jobs, workers tolerate the intolerable".

*3. Define "sweatshop".*
A "business that violates labor laws or health and safety codes" (ll. 40–41); "modern slavery" (l. 44); see "Background information". There is no legal definition.

*4. Are there sweatshops in Germany?*
There is certainly some illegal exploitation of foreigners, especially on farms, construction sites, and in private hire for odd jobs. But labour laws and company control are much stricter and tighter,

so that sweatshops in the American sense hardly exist. Nevertheless some German companies operate production plants in the Third World and in threshold countries, taking advantage of less stringent labour laws there.

5. Collect important vocabulary from the fields of jobs, works, success.
See "Vocabulary" at the beginning of this chapter.

### Post-reading activities
*Study the rise of the American labour unions and the development of labour laws.*
See Bibliography 10, pp. 413, 141, 566–568, 691, 692; Bibliography 9, pp. 355 ff; Bibliography 31, pp. 64–67.

## 8. The oldest racket in the country (GK)

### Background information
Arthur Miller, born in New York City in 1915, is one of the most important contemporary playwrights in the USA. *All My Sons* (1947) and *Death of a Salesman* (1949) brought him international success. Trying to find new subject matter, Miller "began to walk endlessly, often across Brooklyn Bridge. ... I knew that with *All My Sons* I had won a new freedom to create, and I would stand on the high point of the bridge's arch facing the wind from the ocean, trying to embrace a world larger than I had been able to conceive of until this time." (*Timebends*, p. 144).

In search of a story, Miller decided to lead the life of a Brooklyn longshoreman. In *Timebends* he describes "huddling" early in the morning with the other men, who were "mostly of Italian descent", "in doorways in rain and snow ... facing the piers, waiting for the hiring boss." With time Miller tuned in to the "Sicilian-English bravura" and was told the true story of a longshoreman who had reported two illegal immigrants to the Immigration Bureau. The two were brothers and relatives of his. They were even living in his house at the time. One of them had become engaged to the longshoreman's niece, and it was this he objected to. It took Miller some time to realize this was the story he had been looking for (*Timebends* p. 152). *A View from the Bridge* was first performed in 1955 and earned Miller a second Pulitzer Prize. It is written in two acts. Our passage is taken from the end of Act One.

### Summary of *A View of the Bridge*:
Forty-year-old Eddie Carbone, a simple longshoreman of Italian descent, lives in Brooklyn with his wife Beatrice and his young niece Catherine, who is an orphan. Marco and Rodolpho, two cousins of his wife, temporarily join the family after illegally migrating from Sicily. Catherine and Rodolpho fall in love, which arouses strong jealousy in Eddie. He tries to destroy their relationship and keep things as they have been. He accuses Rodolpho of being irresponsible, false and even homosexual to prevent their marriage. Full of contempt, Catherine turns away from Eddie. Raging with jealousy, Eddie informs the Bureau of Immigration about his two guests. Marco and Rodolpho are arrested but set free again on bail. Thus Rodolpho is able to marry Catherine and is permitted to stay. Marco cannot free himself from the Sicilian custom to seek blood in revenge of betrayal. He kills Eddie.

### Methodisch-didaktische Hinweise

Der Textauszug aus *A View from the Bridge* nimmt die zuvor angelegte Thematik der illegalen Einwanderung auf, verfolgt aber nicht deren wirtschaftlichen und sozialen Auswirkungen, sondern präsentiert in einer dramatisch dichten Szene tragische Verwicklungen, die sich aus dieser spezifischen Situation und einer bestimmten Personenkonstellation ergeben. Der besondere ethnische Hintergrund der Italo-Amerikaner wurde mit Bedacht gewählt und weist daher auch landeskundliche Aspekte auf (illegale Einwanderung vieler Italiener, die besondere Prägung familiärer und sozialer Beziehungen, eigene Mentalität). Im Vordergrund steht aber die Entstehung eines tragischen Konfliktes, der sich aus den Beziehungen der drei Protagonisten ergibt. Hinsichtlich des Kapitelthemas findet hier also thematisch eine Einengung auf individuelle Schicksale statt.

Als Einstieg wird vorgeschlagen, anhand der "Background information" und des Einführungstextes im Schülerbuch den Titel und die

Grundsituation des Schauspiels erklären zu lassen.

Da aus urheberrechtlichen Gründen keine Hörversion zur Verfügung gestellt werden konnte, sollte das mit entsprechenden Zugriffen wettgemacht werden. Anhand der ersten drei Fragen des Schülerbuchs kann in Gruppenarbeit ein szenisches Lesen und Darstellen vorbereitet werden. Dabei sollten die zum Teil recht komplexen Haltungen der Personen zueinander erarbeitet werden und die Sprechweisen, die Stimmungen, die Steigerung in dem Konflikt zwischen Eddie und Catherine auch anhand von Mimik, Gestik, Haltung und Bewegung für das Lesen und Darstellen festgelegt werden. Da Miller viele der genannten Zusammenhänge äußerst differenziert durch Regieanweisungen steuert, sollte im Rahmen der Gruppenarbeit dieser "dramaturgische" Text genau analysiert und beim szenischen Spiel oder Lesen umgesetzt werden. Die Gruppen spielen "ihre" Versionen vor; der Vergleich könnte idealerweise in eine offene Diskussion der Deutung und genaueren Analyse der Textpassage überleiten.

**Suggested answers**

1. Earlier in the play Rodolpho is introduced as a happy-go-lucky, pleasant, but somewhat naive young man who is fascinated by America. For a Sicilian his very blond hair is striking ("Danish invaders"). He is unmarried ("I have no money to be married") but has a lot of dreams ("When you have no wife you have dreams"). This picture of Rodolpho is supported by aspects of our passage, but due to the brevity of the excerpt the students' impression of Rodolpho's character may differ and should be discussed openly.

He seems to enjoy the new surroundings and looks forward to seeing the lights, the people, the theatres of Manhattan ("he's crazy for New York"). Everything is new to him, and he reacts with the wonder of a child. Yet he misses Italian sociability: there are no fountains in Brooklyn. He is willing to learn from Catherine, whose company he obviously enjoys. In spite of his naivety he senses Eddie's mistrust ("we only walk together in the streets", ll. 25f.). Nevertheless he wants to establish a good relationship with him ("Maybe you can come too", l. 40) and show Eddie that he has only the best intentions. On the whole Rodolpho seems to be hardly irritated by Eddie's behaviour. He seems to be in high spirits, optimistic and in a romantic mood when he goes off for his nightly walk by the river.

2. Seeing his warm relationship to Catherine endangered by Rodolpho, Eddie tries to estrange Catherine from him right from the start. He paints a very negative picture of Rodolpho: he is disrespectful, not having asked Eddie for permission to go out with Catherine; he is irresponsible, spending his first money on trendy clothes and records; "he is a hit-and run guy" (l. 115); all he has in his head is the glamour world of Broadway and a pleasant life in America. His is only polite and friendly to Catherine to win her love in order finally to get an American passport. According to Eddie he is all false and contriving; he is just practising the "oldest racket in the country" (ll. 135 f.).

3. The very sight of Catherine after her return makes him happy (l. 3). His first attempt to win her back is a yearning for intimacy, combined with a reproach ("*enveloping her with his eyes:* I bless you and you don't talk to me", ll. 48 f.). Eddie suffers when Catherine is absent and reproaches her for no longer being home with him automatically. His is obviously hit hard when Catherine admits that she likes Rodolpho ("He looks at her like a lost boy", l. 73). Eddie feels put out that Rodolpho's and Catherine's friendship excludes him ("it don't bother him if I mind" ll. 92–93). He places Catherine under emotional pressure ("Katie, youre gonna make me cry ..." ll. 109–110); "Katie, don't break my heart" l. 130). This behaviour is due to immense jealousy stemming from very possessive feelings toward her.

4. See "Background information".
All speculations are accepted and discussed within the given characterizations: Catherine and Rodolpho run away to marry – Eddie's reaction? Catherine begins to test and doubt Rodolpho's intentions – with what result? Eddie kills Rodolpho – in what plausible situation? Rodolpho attacks Eddie – implausible?

**Additional questions**

*1. Why is Rodolpho in a vulnerable position? Do you find it plausible that Rodolpho may have thought of the legal advantages of marrying Catherine?*
Rodolpho is Eddie's guest, and as an illegal alien he is more or less at Eddie's mercy and dependent

on his good will. This aspect must be considered in viewing Rodolpho. Rodolpho may have thought of the legal implications of marrying Catherine, but we are not led to believe this is his sole motivation.

*2. Analyse Catherine's reactions in the course of the argument with Eddie, paying special attention to the stage directions.*
First she is willing to react positively towards his reproaches to clear up misunderstandings (she hits him playfully on his arm, goes nearer to him to emphasize what she is saying, ll. 50, 64). It takes quite a lot of courage on Catherine's part to admit her love to Rodolpho openly, but in so doing she has wins a firm position from which to enter the ensuing verbal conflict (she holds her ground, ll. 68f.). She contradicts Eddie. She is first puzzled, then pained, finally becoming desperate and rushing away from Eddie when he insists on depicting Rodolpho as a cheat. In tears, she yells at Eddie to stop his false attack. It is quite clear that nothing will be as it was before. Eddie has lost Catherine. He is going to feel very hurt; his great jealousy is the cause of tragic events.

*3. Study Miller's use of language.*
Grammatically incorrect forms, incomplete sentences (leaving out words, especially connectives), statements made into questions by means of intonation – all this helps to create local colour and an authentic Italian-American background.

*4. Find out the syntactical structures in which Miller presents his stage directions.*
There are a few complete (short) sentences (e.g. l. 4, ll. 40–44). Past participles function as adjectives (e.g. "Catherine embarrassed", l. 8). Present participles functioning as elliptical progressive forms (present tense) stress slow, gradual movement and behaviour (e.g. "Eddie retreating"). There are elliptical sentences in the simple present to describe movement (Catherine turns to him, l. 82).

**Post-reading activities**

*1.* Try to find a summary and interpretation of the play in a reference book or theatre guide (English or German, e.g. Kindler). Present the main ideas in class, in English.

*2. Book report:* A View from the Bridge *(Penguin 18 15 71).*

*3. Paper:* Arthur Miller, Timebends – *Analysis of Chapter III of Miller's autobiography as background material for* A View from the Bridge *and* Death of a Salesman *(Arthur Miller,* Timebends, *Methuen or Minerva paperback editions).*

# 9. The Tortilla Curtain (GK)

**Background information**

Although the 1986 Immigration Act (see fact file p. 312) decreased the illegal influx of Mexicans, the border patrol still arrested 940,000 illegal immigrants along the Mexican border in 1988. It is estimated that a similarly high number enters illegally each year. Now many experts insist that tougher measures are needed to turn the 2,000-mile-long "Tortilla Curtain" into an effective barrier. Tougher fences and walls, fees and deportation all the way back to Mexico City are some of the proposals being discussed and tested.

A Tijuana research institute estimated that in 1986 and in 1987 1.75 mill. Mexican immigrants were working in the US illegally. During the Christmas season 700,000 to 800,000 undocumented workers returned to Mexico, only to re-enter the USA in February.

In urban areas on the border, illegal "commuting" poses many problems for the border patrol and for the economic and social life of the American cities.

**Methodisch-didaktische Hinweise**

Die Texte 9–11 greifen Entwicklungen der 80er Jahre auf, die vor allem durch die starke Einwanderung von "Hispanics" und "Asians" gekennzeichnet ist. Illegale Einwanderung und amerikanische Machtlosigkeit (Text 9 und Cartoon), der Kampf um eine echte multikulturelle Gesellschaft (Text 10: "bilingual education", "official language") sowie die Projektion einer neuen, veränderten amerikanischen Kultur und Identität (Text 11) kennzeichnen schlaglichtartig die gegenwärtige Situation von Amerika als Einwanderungsland.

## Pre-reading activities

*1. Examine the charts on pp 229–231 (SB) with special reference to recent changes in immigration to the USA and in the light of the following statistics:*

Immigrants Admitted from Top Ten Countries of Birth in 1988:
| | |
|---|---|
| All Countries | 643,025 |
| 1. Mexico | 95,039 |
| 2. Philippines | 50,697 |
| 3. Haiti | 34,806 |
| 4. Korea | 34,703 |
| 5. China, Mainland | 28,717 |
| 6. Dominican Republic | 27,189 |
| 7. India | 26,268 |
| 8. Vietnam | 25,789 |
| 9. Jamaica | 20,966 |
| 10. Cuba | 17,558 |

Breakdown of Hispanic population of the USA 1990 (US Bureau of Census):
| | |
|---|---|
| Mexican | 12.6 mill. |
| Puerto Rican | 2.3 mill. |
| Cuban | 1.1 mill. |
| Central and South American | 2.5 mill. |
| Other Hispanic | 1.6 mill. |

About 20 mill. (8%) of the US population are of Hispanic origin.

This activity could also serve as a post-reading activity.

*2. Answer the questions on the cartoon (p. 235) and the photo (p. 236).*
Cartoon:
The US border patrol at the Mexican border. According to the cartoonist the US border patrol is ridiculously ineffective and badly equipped. It is ludicrous to assume that the flimsy door, the butterfly net and the intimidating words will deter would-be immigrants.
Photo:
The sign indicates that it is not uncommon for people to cross the highway in this fashion. Economic pressures are the main reason for the continual migration of Hispanics into the USA.

*3. Study and describe the course of the Mexican-American border with the help of a detailed physical map (cities, rivers, deserts, mountain ranges, roads, railway lines).*

## Suggested answers

1. Die Szene war bizarrer als meine wildesten Träume. Als das erste frühe Morgenlicht die rauhe Wüstenluft erwärmte, tauchten Tausende von Mexikanern – Männer und Frauen, gekleidet in Polyester und Jeansstoff mit leichten Jacken und Baseballmützen – aus erbärmlichen Hütten auf, die die vorgelagerten Hügel von Ciudad Juárez bedecken. Sie machten sich daran, über den flachen Rio Grande zu drängen, hinüber zur texanischen Stadt El Paso.
Einige ließen sich auf den Schultern menschlicher Taxis über den hüfttiefen schlammigen Fluß tragen. Andere drängten sich in eine Flottille von Gummibooten. Männer mit hungrigen Augen füllten Eisenbahnbrücken; sie warteten bis ein einsamer Wagen der Grenzpolizei in einer Staubwolke vorbeigefahren war, ehe sie begannenn, ein massives Eisentor zu überklettern. Kleinere Gruppen von drei oder vier Menschen zwängten sich durch Löcher in dem 3,60 m hohen Drahtzaun, den man Tortilla Vorhang nennt. Dann sprinteten sie über die Autostraße. Während des ganzen Tages und der Nacht drangen hunderte von anderen Menschen in das Gelände von Güterbahnhöfen ein, in der Hoffnung, auf Züge aufspringen zu können, die nach Dallas, Albuquerque, Los Angeles, Denver oder Chicago – den märchenhaften Städten des Reichtums – fuhren.
Zwischen den fahrenden Massen und dem gelobten Land befindet sich eine Handvoll von Grenzpolizisten, bekleidet mit Cowboyhut und grüner Uniform. Ihre Polizeiwagen können allenfalls sechs bis acht Einwanderer einladen, um sie zu einer kleinen Polizeistation zu bringen, wo ihre Personalien aufgenommen und sie ein paar Stunden lang festgehalten werden. Wenn die Zellen voll sind, werden die Einwanderer nach Juárez zurücktransportiert. Innerhalb von Minuten überqueren sie wieder den Fluß.
Die Beamten der Grenzkontrolle des Bereichs El Paso, der das westliche Texas und New Mexico umfaßt, nahmen im Jahre 1986 312.892 illegale Einwanderer fest. Mindestens zweimal so viele kamen durch ...

Undercurrents, fast currents, a river bottom like quicksand and high water make crossing dangerous to those who are not excellent swimmers. Many have to find "human taxis" to carry them over or people who operate inflated rubber rafts.

A Nation of Immigrants 243

They have to select a time when the border patrol is busy elsewhere. They must beware of criminals. Women alone are in danger of being raped or killed.

2. Some of the Mexicans live in Juárez (Mexico) and "commute" illegally to El Paso (Texas, USA) to work there. When they are caught crossing the border, they are taken back to Juárez, but they try to cross again and again until they succeed. Rosa was once caught and sent back six times on the same day before she succeeded. She can rightly call this "a game", since arrest is not associated with any kind of serious sanction. When caught they are held for a few hours, driven back to Juárez and dropped near the bridge, where they can try again.

3. Mexicans are employed as housekeepers, maids, construction workers or farm helpers. They do the low-paid, unskilled and often hard work many Americans would not do under the same conditions.

4. An expert estimated that for every 100 employed illegally, 65 US workers are displaced or kept out of the job market (*Christian Science Monitor*, August 3, 1985). Thus many Americans leave the border area to find work elsewhere in the country. The effect on the border area itself is to be seen in heightened tension between Americans and Mexican communities. Despite their illegal status they strain the housing situation and social services in some cities.

5. Unrestricted immigration would create an explosive social situation, since 1–2 mill. people would probably enter per year. The character of the United States would change dramatically. Many maintain that border controls remain mandatory to keep out people like criminals and drug smugglers.

6. Oral history is written from the perspective of the people immediately affected. Instead of passing value judgements and giving general explanations it presents individual life stories, particularly everyday events. The task of generalization is left to the reader. Political decisions are dealt with from the receiving end. In our example the effects of attempting to close the Mexican-American border to illegal immigration are presented vividly. The advantage of oral history is that it avoids abstract statements which may be far removed from reality. The reader can identify with the situation being described. Yet this situation may not be representative, and unlike an expository essay, oral history fails to deal with the root causes and structure of the problem. An expository essay also presents arguments systematically.

**Additional questions**

*1. What does the title allude to?*
Tortillas are a Mexican food popular in the USA. The "Tortilla Curtain" is meant to remind one of the Iron Curtain, the barrier which divided Europe for many years of this century, forcefully preventing contact between east and west. It was erected by the East to keep their citizens in. The "Tortilla Curtain", however, was erected by the USA to keep Hispanics out. It neither sounds as frightening as the Iron Curtain (you can eat your way through), nor is it impenetrable.

Some readers will be reminded of a novel published by the renowned US author John Steinbeck (1902–1968) in 1935, entitled *Tortilla Flat*. In a humorous and sensitive way this novel deals with the lives of Californian *paisanos*, people of "a mixture of Spanish, Indian, Mexican and assorted Caucasion bloods" (Steinbeck). Tortilla Flat is the fictitious name of the town the story is set in.

*2. a) What are the deeper causes of the constant exodus of people from Mexico to the USA?*
*b) What constructive policies could the USA pursue to improve the situation?*
a) The basic cause for the constant exodus is the economic asymmetry between Mexico and the USA. Whereas Mexico possesses many characteristics of an underdeveloped Third World country, with poverty, unemployment, lack of social security, inflation and low economic productivity, the USA represents the First World of industry and opportunity.

b) Economic aid, investment of US money and know-how, and preferential economic relationships may in the long run decrease the great gap between the two countries, though there is no simple answer to this question. It also involves global economic policies.

**Post-reading activities**

*1. The situation at the Mexican-American border (paper or talk).*
See Bibliography 16 and 25.

2. Hispanics in the USA (paper or talk).
See Bibliography 13 and 25.

3. Read the text by Leonel I. Castillo entitled "The Never-Ending Stream" in Perspectives 10, Hispanic Americans (Klettbuch 5137), pp. 13–16. Using ideas from this text, write a short account, in the first person, of a young man or woman who leaves home in Mexico to cross the border into the USA and set up a new existence. Try to capture this person's feelings and reactions.

4. Read "Angelina Sandoval" (excerpt from Chicano by Richard Vasquez), in Great Immigrant Stories (Klettbuch 57938), pp. 34–43.

## 10. The language of the country

### Background information

In the 1980s some of the fifty American states passed resolutions making English their official language. An attempt to adopt an amendment to the Constitution making English the official language failed but may be repeated successfully in the future. The driving force behind this development is "U.S. English", a campaign founded and led by a former senator from California, S.I. Hayakawa, the author of our text, until his death in 1992. The text is part of his campaign, which includes efforts to restrict bilingual education programmes, eliminate non-English voting ballots and improve language proficiency at many levels. Some opponents see in these measures a backlash against America's latest immigrants, a means to keep them out. They refer to historical patterns in which people who were migrants themselves some time ago are most outspoken in restricting later waves of immigration (see cartoon, SB p. 225) and allude to the fact that S.I. Hayakawa is of Japanese origin and a third-generation Japanese-American. However, beyond any shallow American nativism the U.S.-English movement has found many serious and famous supporters (Saul Bellow, Bruno Bettelheim) who see American identity threatened if America becomes truly multilingual and multicultural.

*Ethnic Breakdown of Miami (Dade County):*
| | |
|---|---|
| Total | 1.9 mill. |
| Latinos | 42.7% |
| Anglos | 39.0% |
| Native Blacks | 16.3% |
| Others | 2.0% |

Among the Miami Hispanics (Latinos) the Cubans are by far the largest group. The Miami Cuban community has grown to nearly 700,000, about two-thirds of all Cuban Americans.

Contrary to the quotation by Maurice Ferre (see text ll. 26–36) – which of course serves Hayakawa's intentions well – current developments indicate an acculturation even in the extreme case of the Miami Cubans. Young professional Cuban-Americans of the second generation, having received a college education outside Miami, possess bilingual and bicultural skills that allow them to conduct business in English, to keep up relationships with people who do not speak Spanish and at the same time preserve their close ties within the Cuban communities.

### Pre-reading activities

*1. Comment on the multilingual voter notification card (SB p. 238). Note the caption. Why are there languages other than English? What would happen if it were in English only? Why is the question of "English-only" ballot sheets and voter registration cards a matter of principle to some people?*
One of the few preconditions for becoming an American citizen is a basic knowledge of English, enabling the immigrant to understand the basic processes of American democracy.

*2. Answer the questions below the photo on p. 237 (SB).*
The price; "shopping"; the street name and number; the postbox.

*3. Do you consider Germans/French, Italians etc. who do not speak their mother tongues still to be German, French, Italian?*

### Suggested answers

1. As a nation of immigrants the USA, lacking the common bonds of race, ethnic origin or religion shared by other countries, is united by a "love of

freedom and devotion to democratic principles" (ll. 6–7). Whereas these attitudes are abstract, it is the common language, English, which visibly and audibly expresses the unity they create. English is a common tool for expressing opinions and becoming informed. With its help, the diverse population of the USA feels like one people.

2. Hayakawa opposes bilingual education if it means teaching children school subjects in their own language rather than English (ll. 88–99), since it fails to achieve its objective of getting children "functioning quickly in English" (ll. 105–106). He maintains that bilingual teaching often fails to teach English efficiently and leaves the immigrant children dependent on their native languages, placing them at a disadvantage in college and professional life. Furthermore, Hayakawa points out that bilingual teaching also means the segregation of bilingual classes and English-speaking classes, thus creating cultural divisions.

Hayakawa's linguistic concepts are clearly based on the sociological concepts of the melting pot and acculturation as opposed to concepts of cultural pluralism. He comes quite close to the melting-pot metaphor when he admires the process in which "we have been able to forge a unified people from an incredibly diverse population" (ll. 17–19).

3. Some supporters of bilingual education are primarily concerned with the preservation of the cultural and ethnic identities of minority children (ll. 100–104). They are justified in doing so, since federal legislation in 1974 provided for instruction in the "cultural heritage" of such children. Hayakawa maintains that other advocates of bilingual education place emphasis on the child's ability to function appropriately in English (ll. 103–106).

4. "In some places, adopting English as the official language has no more significance than choosing a state bird or flower" (*Newsweek*, Feb. 20, 1989). But the campaigns changed public attitudes, and the amendments to the states' constitutions have the potential for creating future step-by-step provisions. Thus gradually ordinances can be introduced curbing foreign-language use on road signs, voter registration cards and in official communication by government employees. This has in fact already happened in some states.

Furthermore, the campaigns about "Official English" have shown that it is a purely symbolic issue. It is an attempt by mainstream America to protect its broad culture, of which English is seen as a core element.

**Additional questions**

*1. Analyse Hayakawa's sequence of arguments.*
a) The common language, English, is the most important factor in creating American identity and unity (ll. 1–19).
b) Striking examples to show that the status of English is endangered (ll. 20–44): English not part of citizenship; Spanish only in Miami; proposal of two legal languages for a multicultural America.
c) infeasibility of these proposals: India as deterrent (ll. 44–51)
d) criticism of government policy (ll. 52–61)
e) bilingual education as an example of this (ll. 62–115)
– Bilingual programs do not reach their proclaimed goals: immigrant children do not become proficient in English.
– They stay too long in bilingual classes.
Whereas Hayakawa's arguments on the status of the English language do not sound convincing (the examples are too selective and far from representative), his criticism of the abuses of bilingual education and his persistence in the main goal of bilingual education (better and faster proficiency in English) is presented effectively.

*2. Do you think that a multilingual USA would be in danger of social and political disintegration?*
(Examples: Canada, India, former USSR, former Yugoslavia)
All views founded on facts and sound arguments accepted.
One must differentiate between the USA and the other countries mentioned. Large numbers of immigrants to the USA came voluntarily; the USA is the embodiment of their hopes, a symbol of the fulfillment of aspirations. These people, it is said, want to share in a prosperous, democratic America while speaking languages other than English and preserving their cultural background. But is this aim enough to prevent disintegration?

*3. Construct a "word family" around the verb "to unify".*
unifying forces (l. 4)

unifying effects (l. 22)
unified people (l. 18)
to unify the various parts of Europe
German (re)unification

4. Find the noun from the following verbs in the text:
a) to recognize (l. 45)
b) to acquire
c) to advocate (l. 23)
d) to reside
e) to maintain (ll. 29, 101)
f) to depend on
g) to fail

a) recognition (ll. 23, 47)
b) acquisition (l. 68)
c) an advocate (l. 100)
d) residents (l. 35)
e) maintenance (l. 67)
f) dependency (l. 86)
g) failure (l. 113)

### Post reading activities

*Write a paper or give a talk on the theme of language and American identity.*
See Bibliography 4, 10 (pp. 38–40), 11.

## 11. Birth of a new culture?

### Background information

Henry Cisneros, a former mayor of San Antonio (Texas), is regarded as the leading figure of the political movement of the Spanish-speaking groups. In 1984 he was considered as a Democratic vice-presidential candidate, and in 1987 he headed a group of Hispanic leaders who presented the presidential candidates (Bush and Dukakis) with a National Hispanic Agenda.

In his essay, "The Demography of a Dream" (1988), he reacts to nativist fears – which were and still are widely held – that due to massive Hispanic and Asian immigration the USA would disintegrate and degenerate into a "Third World country". As Otis L. Graham (Stanford University) maintains, "For the first time in our history a majority of migrants speak just one language – Spanish – and most of them live in ethnic enclaves served by radio and television stations carrying the messages in Spanish. In such settings, the assimilative impulses of the national economy have a faint influence" (*New York Times*, July 1, 1986). With many Hispanics failing at high school (see *Newsweek*, August 10, 1991: "A Generation of Hispanics isn't Making the Grade"), and with the Mexicans, the Filipinos and many South-east Asian refugees not catching up economically, many believe that former patterns of Anglo-conformity will no longer apply and that the country will be threatened by separatism. They even see "a future in which American cities resemble Third World cities, with a vast gap between rich and poor and open political conflict between classes" (*New York Times*, July 1, 1986).

Cisneros utterly disagrees with this. He is sure that Hispanics will finally adopt American values and "will make the grade", and that with their assets they will give American society new impulses to move ahead, as immigrants have always done. The idea of the enrichment and the flexible development of American society due to the influx of immigrants from all ethnic backgrounds is almost as old as immigration itself. It was most clearly stated by Carl Schurz, who claimed that with constant immigration the USA would retain the vigour of a "young nation" and the faculty to renew itself from within (*True Americanism*, 1859): "Nations which have long subsisted exclusively on their own resources will gradually lose their original vigor, and die the death of decrepitude. But mankind (society) becomes young again by its different elements shaken together, by race crossing race and mind penetrating mind" (p. 77).

### Methodisch-didaktische Hinweise

Der Text knüpft einerseits an die Diskussion der neuen Einwanderungswelle der achtziger Jahre an (immigration charts, pp. 229, 230 und 231; Texte 10 und 11), rundet aber andererseits das ganze Kapitel ab, indem er die anfangs präsentierte Frage Crèvecoeur's, "Who then is the American?", nochmals stellt und neu beantwortet. Hispanische und asiatische Denkweisen und Haltungen gewinnen an Gewicht und legen multikulturelle Sichtweisen der amerikanischen Kultur, Gesellschaft und Identität nahe.

## Pre-reading activities

*1. Discuss the demographic trends revealed by the following figures (from the 1990s census) and their likely effects on American society:*

|              | Population 1990 | Increase since 1980 |
|--------------|-----------------|---------------------|
| Blacks       | 30 mill.        | + 13.2%             |
| Asians       | 7.3 mill.       | +107.8%             |
| Am. Indians  | 2 mill.         | + 37.9%             |
| Hispanics    | 22.4 mill.      | + 53.0%             |
| "Other race" | 9.8 mill.       | + 45.1%             |

*Compare these figures with Cisneros' predictions for the year 2000.*

## Suggested answers

1. The figures reveal that in many parts of California the non-Hispanic whites, the "Anglos", who see themselves as the national core of American culture and society, are a numerical minority. Furthermore, the trend indicates that soon this will be the case in many American cities and in the American "anchor states" (l. 24). A widely publicized projection of recent immigration trends claimed that by 2056 the whites ("Anglos") will be a "minority group" representing less than 50% of the American population. The change in the character of the USA can be circumscribed with the commonly-used phrase, the "browning of America", which means that Hispanic, Black and Asian cultural patterns will gain predominance over the Anglo-Saxon value system.

Hence in its ethnic mixture America really represents the "world" (cf. text 1), as the former European dominance comes to an end. In recognizing the specific values of the various cultures America is becoming truly multicultural. The centre of gravity within America is no longer the East; it has shifted to the Southwest and the South.

2. Cisneros does not see any danger of separatism or decline in the current development. On the contrary: he believes that the new immigrants prevent the "Classic, northern-hemispheric ... nation with an aging white population" (ll. 34–36) from stagnating, from becoming immobile, avoiding an economic and social crisis in a society whose age-structure is imbalanced.

In addition he believes that the rigid, WASP-dominated American culture will be softened by Hispanic and Asian attitudes. These stress warmth in interpersonal relations and keep up stronger family ties even beyond the nuclear family. At the same time he is sure that the Hispanic immigrants will adopt the American virtues they originally lack, namely a "strong sense of discipline, management of time, respect for deadlines, mastery over routine and results-orientation" (ll. 86–89). In Cisneros' view the clash of cultures will not lead to conflicts and separatism, but out of this cultural tension there will come "a richness, even a higher order of human development" (ll. 109–111).

3. Whereas WASPs would agree that they are success- and results-orientated and adopt a rational approach to life, they would certainly reject the assertion that mainstream American culture lacks "heart", familial closeness, compassion and solidarity. In addition many Anglo-Saxons would see Cisneros' optimism as to the Hispanics' dedication to American effectiveness very critically. Many Protestants would question the influence of Roman Catholicism as depicted here.

## Additional questions

*1. What is the function of the first two sentences within the structure of the text?*

These two sentences represent the basic thesis of the text. On the one hand it sounds like a reaction to an existing counter-thesis ("America is declining"), which is not discussed or mentioned in the text. On the other hand, the statement that America is changing forms the basis for the following progression of thought. First the writer cites factual, demographic changes before dealing with the impact of these on American society and culture. He sees changes that are positive throughout and result in a new and better American culture. The original title of the text, "Demography of a Dream", makes the reader see the positive meaning of the otherwise neutral word "change" from the very beginning.

*2. Why, according to Cisneros, will the new immigrants support basic American concepts and beliefs?*

Most Asians and Hispanics consciously selected America in order to start anew and to leave corrupt, ineffective and often oppressive systems behind. The love of personal freedom and the wish to advance are foremost in their minds. Hence they are very well equipped to adopt the American way of life. "The commitment they are making to the United States is total" (ll. 61–62). They, too, want to fulfil their American dream.

See Perspectives 1, *The American Dream* (Klettbuch 51361), p. 13.

*3. Study Cisneros' use of tenses in the first paragraphs of the text (ll. 1–43).*
For the factual predictions for the year 2000, future tense is used throughout ll. 2–16 (will be, will account for, will live).
In the last part of this passage Cisneros turns the situation round and argues on the basis of hypothetical conditions. Hence the structures are determined by the logic and grammar of *if-sentences*, Type II: "I would worry ... if the large immigrant ... populations were not here": Conditional I for main clause, past tense for if-clause.

**Post-reading activities**

*Write a paper or give a talk on the ethnic situation in Los Angeles.*
See Bibliography 36; Bibliography 23, illustration p. 12.

**Fact file: Cartoons**

1. p. 311: The Statue of Liberty is shown making a rather snobbish gesture of rejection. It is clear from the writing on the pedestal that immigrants – at least certain types of immigrants – are no longer welcome. This is just the opposite of the image embodied by the real Liberty ("the one we used to have"), whose pedestal bears the welcoming verses of "The New Colossus" (see p. 215 SB and Bibliography 23, pp. 10–11). The middle figure of the three at the base of the statue is clearly President Harry S. Truman. His question reveals his critical stance with regard to the McCarran-Walter Act of 1952 (see fact file), the year the cartoon was published. Truman vetoed the act, but Congress passed it nevertheless.

2. p. 312: Uncle Sam, who looks like a Mafia member himself, stands passively while the "rats" (socialism, anarchy, assassination, mafia ...) disembark "from the slums of Europe". Needless to say, this is a very negative picture of immigration. The cartoon was drawn shortly after 1901. In 1924, quota regulations virtually stopped immigration from southern Europe (Italy in particular). The figure appearing in the smoke of Uncle Sam's cigar is President William McKinlay, who was assassinated in 1901 by an anarchist of immigrant parentage.

# Test 1: Rich-heard Road-ree-guess: Becoming an American

**Einsatzort**

Der Klausurtext bezieht sich vorwiegend auf die Texte 9–11. Als gedanklicher Hintergrund ist die Erarbeitung des Textes 10, "The language of the country", unbedingt erforderlich. Daneben ist Rodriguez als ein Musterbeispiel für diejenigen *Hispanic immigrants* zu sehen, die eine starke Erfolgsorientierung aufweisen und sich daher bewußt einer Amerikanisierung unterziehen. Um dies richtig einschätzen zu können, sollte auch der Text 11, "Birth of a new culture?" zuvor bearbeitet worden sein.

**Note on the author**

For Richard Rodriguez, English is a second language. Born in 1944 in San Francisco, Rodriguez spoke Spanish at home. He still refers to English as his "public" language. Having attended Stanford University in California and Columbia University in New York, Rodriguez did graduate work in London and Berkeley. He now lives in San Francisco and is renowned as a writer and lecturer.

**Text**

Supporters of bilingual education today imply that students like me miss a great deal by not being taught in their family's language. What they seem not to recognize is that, as a socially disadvantaged child, I considered Spanish to be a private 5 language. What I needed to learn in school was that I had the right – and the obligation – to speak the public language of *los gringos*. (...)
Without question, it would have pleased me to hear my teachers address me in Spanish when I 10 entered the classroom. I would have felt much less afraid. I would have trusted them and responded with ease. But I would have delayed – for how long postponed? – having to learn the language of public society. I would have evaded – and for how 15 long could I have afforded to delay? – learning the

great lesson of school, that I had a public identity. Fortunately, my teachers were unsentimental about their responsibility. What they understood was that I needed to speak a public language. So their voices would search me out, asking me questions. Each time I'd hear them, I'd look up in surprise to see a nun's face frowning at me. I'd mumble, not really meaning to answer. The nun would persist, "Richard, stand up. Don't look at the floor. Speak up. Speak to the entire class, not just to me!" But I couldn't believe that the English language was mine to use. (In part, I did not want to believe it.) I continued to mumble. I resisted the teacher's demands. (Did I somehow suspect that once I learned public language my pleasing family life would be changed?) Silent, waiting for the bell to sound, I remained dazed, diffident, afraid.

Because I wrongly imagined that English was intrinsically a public language and Spanish an intrinsically private one, I easily noted the difference between classroom language and the language of home. At school, words were directed to a general audience of listeners. ("Boys and girls.") Words were meaningfully ordered. And the point was not self-expression alone but to make oneself understood by many others. The teacher quizzed: "Boys and girls, why do we use that word in this sentence? Could we think of a better word to use there? Would the sentence change its meaning if the words were differently arranged? And wasn't there a better way of saying much the same thing?" (I couldn't say, I wouldn't try to say.)

Three months. Five. Half a year passed. Unsmiling, ever watchful, my teachers noted my silence. They began to connect my behavior with the difficult progress my older sister and brother were making. Until one Saturday morning three nuns arrived at the house to talk to our parents. Stiffly, they sat on the blue living room sofa. From the doorway of another room, spying the visitors, I noted the incongruity – the clash of two worlds, the faces and voices of school intruding upon the familiar setting of home. I overheard one voice gently wondering, "Do your children speak only Spanish at home, Mrs. Rodriguez?" While another voice added, "That Richard especially seems so timid and shy."

That Rich-heard!

With great tact the visitors continued, "Is it possible for you and your husband to encourage your children to practice their English when they are home?" Of course, my parents complied. What would they not do for their children's well-being? And how could they have questioned the Church's authority which those women represented? In an instant, they agreed to give up the language (the sounds) that had revealed and accentuated our family's closeness. The moment after the visitors left, the change was observed. "*Ahora*, speak to us *en inglés*," my father and mother united to tell us. [...]

One Saturday morning I entered the kitchen where my parents were talking in Spanish. I did not realize that they were talking in Spanish however until, at the moment they saw me, I heard their voices change to speak English. Those *gringo* sounds they uttered startled me. Pushed me away. In that moment of trivial misunderstanding and profound insight, I felt my throat twisted by unsounded grief. I turned quickly and left the room. But I had no place to escape to with Spanish. (The spell was broken.) My brother and sisters were speaking English in another part of the house.

Again and again in the days following, increasingly angry, I was obliged to hear my mother and father: "Speak to us *en inglés*." (*Speak*.) Only then did I determine to learn classroom English. Weeks after, it happened: One day in school I raised my hand to volunteer an answer. I spoke out in a loud voice. And I did not think it remarkable when the entire class understood. That day, I moved very far from the disadvantaged child I had been only days earlier. The belief, the calming assurance that I belonged in public, had at last taken hold.

Shortly after, I stopped hearing the high and loud sounds of *los gringos*. A more and more confident speaker of English, I didn't trouble to listen to *how* strangers sounded, speaking to me. And there simply were too many English-speaking people in my day for me to hear American accents anymore. Conversations quickened. Listening to persons who sounded eccentrically pitched voices, I usually noted their sounds for an initial few seconds before I concentrated on *what* they were saying. Conversations became content-full. Transparent. Hearing someone's *tone* of voice – angry or questioning or sarcastic or happy or sad – I didn't distinguish it from the words it expressed. Sound and word were thus tightly wedded. At the end of a day, I was often bemused, always relieved, to realize how "silent," though crowded with words, my day in public had been. (This public silence measured and quickened the change in my life.)

At last, seven years old, I came to believe what had been technically true since my birth: I was an American citizen.

From *Hunger of Memory* by Richard Rodriguez (pp. 18–22). © 1982 by Richard Rodriguez. Reprinted by permission of David R. Godine, Boston, publisher.

**Annotations**

8 **public language**   the language spoken in public life (school, work, shopping, media, ...) as opposed to the "family language"
8 **gringo**   (derog.) English-speaking American
15 **evaded**   avoided
33 **diffident**   shy, not trusting own ability
110 **pitched**   set at a certain height

**I. Language**

1. Vocabulary
Each of the following exercises refers to the word or phrase in italics in its context:
a) 21: ... *their voices would search me out* ...
Explain. You may change the sentence structure.
b) 58–59: ... the familiar *setting* of home ...
Find a substitute; keep to the sentence structure.
c) 83: ... sounds they uttered *startled me.*
Explain. You may change the sentence structure.
d) 117: Sound and word were thus tightly *wedded*.
Find a substitute; keep to the sentence structure.

Give the corresponding noun for each of the following verbs:
e) 12–13: responded
f) 19–20: understood
g) 24–25: persist
h) 29: continued
i) 30: suspect

Give the corresponding adjectives for each of the following nouns:
j) 57: incongruity
k) 101: public
l) 15: society
m) 19: responsibility
n) 52: progress

2. Grammar and style
a) 23: to see a nun's face *frowning*
Explain the "ing-form".
b) 9–10: it would have pleased me *to hear my teachers address me*
114–116: *Hearing* someone's tone of voice, I ...
Explain both constructions.
c) 4–5: a *socially* disadvantaged child
34: I *wrongly* imagined
Explain the function of each adverb.

**II. Comprehension**

Answer the following questions in complete sentences. Keep to the information given in the text, but do not quote.
a) Explain the writer's attitude to the education of non-English-speaking children in America. How does he deal with the concept of "bilingual education"?
b) Why do Rodriguez' parents start speaking English at home? How does Rodriguez react?
c) Why was it a great step forward for Rodriguez to be able to speak out in class?
d) Rodriguez differentiates between being an American citizen "technically" (l. 124) and actually becoming one. Explain this difference with reference to the text.
e) Analyse the structure of this autobiographical essay. Try to distinguish between narrative and argumentative (or reflective) passages.

**III. Comment**

It may be possible to eat a Mexican meal, dance a Polish polka, sing in a Rumanian choir, preserve one's ethnicity however one wishes, but the one thing that all these must have in common is the use of the English language.
Explain and comment.

# Test 2: Listening Comprehension: The real Chinatown

**Methodisch-didaktische Hinweise**

Der thematische Zusammenhang mit den Texten 9–11 legt einen Einsatz nach der Bearbeitung der entsprechenden Texte vor allem aber der *charts* und *graphs* (S. 229–231) nahe. Hierbei sollte vor allem auf die Zahlen und Angaben hinsichtlich der "Asians" und "Chinese" eingegangen werden. Einen knappen Überblick über Geschichte und gegenwärtige Lage der "Chinese communities" in den USA gibt Thomas Sowell, Bibliography 29, S. 140–154.

Da dieses *radio feature* von der sprachlichen Schwierigkeit und dem Sprechtempo her nicht leicht verständlich ist, empfiehlt sich folgendes Vorgehen:
1. Ein- bis zweimaliges Vorspielen des ganzen Textes
2. Erneutes Vorspielen des 1. Teils (indirected listening)
3. Austeilen aller Aufgaben (1–5)
4. Bearbeitung der Aufgaben 1–3 für den 1. Teil
5. Vorspielen des 2. Teils ("directed listening")
6. Bearbeitung der Aufgaben 4 und 5 für den 2. Teil: "note-taking" erlaubt.

**Transcript**

For decades, New York City's Chinatown has been a big attraction for visitors to the area. This part of the city is often described as one of New York's more mysterious and exotic sections. Because most of its history has been invented by commercial tour operators, a group of residents known as the Chintown History Project has developed its own walking tour. Correspondent Andy Lanset reports:

"Of course, the landlords in the late 1800s tried to get every available dollar off their property, and they did this by building a second house in the backyard and, in part, they're responsible for the old mythology of there being hidden alleyways and secret doors and things in Chinatown..."

Charlie Chin's walking tour got started to set the record straight. For years, he says, tour-bus groups have been clogging Chinatown streets with visitors craning their necks to see the sights and hear history told by often ill-informed tour guides. Statements like "the Chinese brought ice cream to America", that "they're not interested in becoming U.S. citizens," and "all know how to speak English but prefer not to" are just a few of the fabrications he's heard.

"In monitoring some of the other tours that come through Chinatown, we've seen the incredible stereotypes, the out-and-out misleading information that's been given to people ... we're very concerned..."

The concern is a motivating factor to use the tour, for one, as a preventative measure in the fight against anti-Asian sentiment that has its roots in such misinformation and is far from disappearing. Just last month, anti-Asian flyers circulated in Brooklyn alleged that all Chinese-American businesses are laundering drug money and should be boycotted. Anti-Asian action like this in California, although more violent, brought many Chinese to New York in the 1870s.

As we walked through the heart of old Chinatown on Mott, Pell and Doyers Streets, Charlie Chin explained to his tour group that the nineteenth century Anti-Asian campaigns were instrumental in the passage of laws severely limiting Chinese immigration for a period of 60 years.

"The only people who were allowed to come over were either common laborers, who could only stay for a certain period of time, or professionals, which is one of the reasons why there still is a stereotype about a lot of Chinese in the country: that they are, alternately, either Chinese laundrymen or restauranteurs, or architects or research scholars and physicists, because there's this huge gap in the middle which has not been filled until very recently."

Some Chinese-Americans have suggested the Exclusion Act might more aptly have been titled the Extermination Act, since an 1989 Chinatown census reveals some 9,000 Chinese men but only 43 Chinese women resided here, figures that changed little until the end of World War II. It brought about what was called the Bachelor Society, an enclave that's very much alive today on Doyers Street.

"As we look around, you'll notice that there's an incredible number of barber shops all throughout this street. This is a tradition that has been kept since the 1870s. What would happen (is), of course, in the old days is that men who worked in laundries and restaurants would come in one day a week because they usually worked six days a week, and amongst the things they would have to do was have their queue rebraided, the front of their heads shaved, pick up their mail, find out the latest gossip, and that tradition has still pretty much held true on this old street ..."

From Doyers Street we went down some narrow blocks to the heart of old Chinatown, past restaurants and curio shops, to a storefront that played a significant role in modern Chinese history.

"We're on Mott Street now, some of these buildings as we look across the street, for instance this one over here that says 'Oriental Country Store' is 12 Mott Street. That was the office in 1905 of the

Young China Party under Dr. Sun Yat-sen. Dr. Sun Yat-sen spent an incredible amount of time overseas raising money for his revolution. He was so busy raising money overseas that he, in fact, was in Denver, Colorado, when the revolution began (and) read about it over breakfast in an American newspaper."

After his return to China in 1911, Sun Yat-sen was elected president of the first Chinese republic. But it was not until 1965 that a new chapter in New York's Chinatown history began. At that time restrictive U.S. immigration quotas were abolished and Chinatown boundaries soon moved south to City Hall and north into Soho.

"Up until very recently, Canal Street was the northern border of Chinatown, but today as we look up the street here on the other side of Canal on Mott we see that as far as the eye can see there are Chinese signs. So now this is now considered as part of Chinatown. Along with this is the investment, as I said, of overseas Chinese in new businesses and much larger businesses than they used to have ..."

Since 1965, 7,000 Chinese have emigrated to New York each year, raising the metropolitan area's Chinese population from 20,000 to well over 200,000. This growth has not only expanded old Chinatown but brought about the birth of new Chinatown in Brooklyn and Queens. Meanwhile, through their tours, Charlie Chin and the New York Chinatown History Project are shedding new light on the history of Chinatown and dispeling the myths that fuel prejudice. I'm Andy Lanset in New York.

From *On the Air. The English-speaking cassette magazine*. Summer Edition 1990, pp. 2–4. © Crossroads, Miami, Florida. Used by permission of Crossroads and On the Air.

## Annotations

1 **Chinatown**   a neighbourhood traditionally established by Chinese immigrants
11 **get every available dollar off**   make every bit of profit from
16–17 **set the record straight**   tell the true version of the story
18 **clogging**   blocking, making full
19 **craning their necks**   *here*: putting their heads out the window to see better. Extending their necks like cranes.
28 **out-and-out**   completely
32 **for one**   among other things
35 **flyers**   pieces of paper containing information; leaflets
37 **laundering drug money**   using illegally obtained money to conduct a legal business, thus hiding the true origin of the money. (This "cleans" the money.)
58 **Exclusion Act**   a law passed in 1882 which severely limited new Chinese immigration to the United States
64 **enclave (in a city)**   a group of people of common origin and/or with a common lifestyle.
74 **queue**   braid of hair at the back of the head, pigtail
77 **held true**   continued to be the practice
80 **curio shops**   short for "curiosity shops," shops displaying odds and ends
91 **over breakfast**   while having breakfast
99 **Soho**   in New York, the area of Manhattan south (So) of Houston (Ho) Street
100 **up until**   until
114 **Queens**   a borough of New York City, like Brooklyn
116 **shedding new light**   bringing new facts to public attention.

## Questions

1. What explanation does the Chinese guide give for the complex and dense pattern of buildings in New York City's Chinatown?

2. When did the Chinese first come to New York? Where did they come from and why did they move?

3. What fabrications and cliches were, and are, still spread about the Chinese?

4. What effects did the extreme restrictions of Chinese immigration have on the Chinese communities?

5. Which new developments have occurred since 1965?

## Post-listening activities

Write an analysis of Amy Tan's short story, "Waverly Jong: Rules of the Game", in Great Immigrant Stories (*Klettbuch 57938*), pp. 51–65.

# Bibliography

1. Allen, Leslie. *Liberty: the Statue and the American Dream*. New York, 1985.
2. Archdeacon, Thomas J. *Becoming American: an Ethnic History*. New York, 1983.
3. Brownstone, David M. *Island of Hope, Island of Tears: an Oral History of the Great Migration to America and the Passage Through Ellis Island*. New York, 1979.
4. Citrin, Jack. "Language, Politics and American Identity". *Dialogue* 1 (1991).
5. Cooke, Alistair. *America, a Personal History*. New York, 1984.
6. Daniels, Roger. *Coming to America*. New York, 1990.
7. DiBacco, Thomas/Mason, Lorna/Appy, Christian. *A History of the United States*. Boston: Houghton Mifflin Company, 1991 (Klettbuch 516153).
8. Dinnerstein, Leonard/Reimers, David. *Ethnic Americans: a History of Immigration and Assimilation*. New York, 1990.
9. Friebel, Isolde/Händel, Heinrich. *Britain – USA Now*. Frankfurt: Diesterweg, 1974.
10. Garraty, John A. *American History*. Orlando: Harcourt Brace Jovanovich, 1982.
11. Glazer, Sarah/Hayakawa, S.I. et al. "America's Official Language". In: *American Studies Newsletter* 22 (September 1990).
12. *Great Immigrant Stories*. Klettbuch 57938
13. "Hispanics in the United States". *American Studies Newsletter* 16 (September 1988).
14. Howe, Irving/Libo, Kenneth. *A Documentary History of Immigrant Jews in America 1880–1930*. New York, 1979.
15. Kessner, Thomas/Boyd Caroli, Betty. *Today's Immigrants*. Oxford/ New York: Oxford University Press, 1981.
16. "Life on the Line". In: *National Geographic* (June 1985).
17. Mann, Arthur. "From Immigration to Acculturation". In: L.S. Luedtke, ed. *Making America*. USIA Forum Series Washington, D.C., pp. 68–79.
18. Miller, Arthur. *Timebends*. London: Methuen, 1987.
19. Miller, Arthur. *A View from the Bridge*. Penguin.
20. Morrison, Joan/Fox Zavbusky, Charlotte. *American Mosaic: The Immigrant Experience in the Words of Those who Lived it*. New York, 1980.
21. *Native American Short Stories*. Klettbuch 57933.
22. *The 1992 Information Please Almanac*. Boston: Houghton Mifflin Company, 1992 (Klettbuch 516152).
23. Perspectives 1: *The American Dream*. Klettbuch 51361.
24. Perspectives 2: *The American South*. Klettbuch 51362.
25. Perspectives 10: *Hispanic Americans*. Klettbuch 5137.
26. Porter, Pedalino Rosalie. *Forked Tongue: The Politics of Education*. New York, 1990.
27. Ribalow, Harold U. "The History of Henry Roth and *Call It Sleep*". Introduction to Henry Roth. *Call It Sleep*. New York, 1976, pp. IX–X
28. Sinclair, Upton. *The Jungle*. Penguin.
29. Sowell, Thomas. *Ethnic America: A History*. New York, 1981.
30. Spann, Ekkehard. *Abiturwissen Landeskunde Great Britain/ United States of America*. Klettbuch 939509.
31. Stevenson, Douglas. *American Life and Institutions*. Klettbuch 5136.
32. *Stories from the Black Experience*. Klettbuch 5793.
33. Topical Texts: *The American Indian*. Klettbuch 50802.
34. Topical Texts: *Jewish Americans*. Klettbuch 50859.
35. Trommler, Frank/ McVeigh, Joseph. *America and the Germans: An Assessment of a Three-Hundred-Year History*. Philadelphia, 1985.
36. Ward, Leslie. "Immigrants Flock to Los Angeles". In: *American Studies Newsletter* 23 (January 1991).
37. Wilson, Clyde. "The Future of American Nationalism". *American Studies Newsletter* 25 (September 1991), pp. 24–28.
38. Wust, Klaus/Moos, Heinz. *Three Hundred Years of German Immigrants in North America*. Gräfelfing, 1983.

A number of videos concerning the USA as a multicultural society are available on loan from the USIS Video Library in Berlin. A catalogue can be obtained from: USIS Video Library, Hardenbergstr. 22–24, 1000 Berlin 12, Tel. 030/310001-13; Fax: 030/317945.

# 11 The American Dream in a Changing Society

## Structure of the chapter

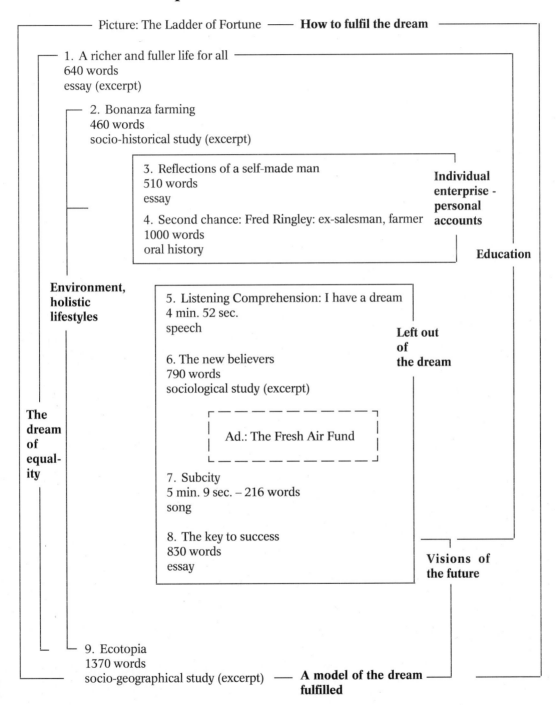

The American Dream in a Changing Society    255

## Suggestions for reports/papers/talks

Write informative notes on picture p. 241 for an exhibition in a museum – after discussion on picture

Summarize the content of the following three books (with reference to an encyclopaedia of literature): José Ortega y Gasset, *La rebelión de las masas*; Karl Jaspers, *Die geistige Situation der Zeit*; Aldous Huxley, *Brave New World* – after text 1

The significance of CAP (Common Agricultural Policy) for European farmers – after text 2

Agricultural problems in Europe and the local region – presentation outlining newspaper coverage over the past two weeks – after text 2

Talk: biographical details on four famous "self-made men" – after text 3

Paper or talk: the American Dream in Arthur Miller's *Death of a Salesman* – after text 4

Interview with fictional character(s) parallel to story of Ringleys – after text 4

Martin Luther King and the Civil Rights Movement – after text 5 (LC)

Interview with Mrs Ringley (theme: women and the American Dream) – after text 6

Fictitious account of Simone Baker's future life – after text 6

Summary of article, "Women in Business" – after text 6

Volunteer social welfare organizations in the USA – after advertisement p. 252

Review of songs dealing with subcity life – after text 7

Short essay (exercise in structured composition): What will schools look like in Germany in the year 2020? – after text 8

Debate: "The pursuit of happiness will leave the world in ruins" – after text 8

### Vocabulary

*Thematischer Grund- und Aufbauwortschatz Englisch*, Klettbuch 51955, pages as follows:
- Landwirtschaft: 12–15
- Stadt, Land: 21–23
- Ökologie: 23–25
- Charakter, Verhalten: 73–80
- Staat, Politik, Gesellschaft: 124–138
- Geschichte: 145–146
- Musik: 226–227
- Erziehung: 229–241

*Words in Context. Thematischer Oberstufenwortschatz*, Klettbuch 51961, esp. pp. 14–22, 56–61, 66–71, 78–83, 116–123, 148–162 and 180–183.

# Picture p. 241

### Background information

The practice of using visual images for didactic purposes is very old (cf. frescoes in ancient Jewish and Christian buildings, medieval art). The symbolic use of visual images can be compared to the use of metaphor in literature. The tree is a common symbol for the source of life or some desirable quality, e.g. the tree of life (Genesis 2–3 in the Bible), the tree of wisdom (Buddhism) and the tree of liberty (American War of Independence, French Revolution). Fruit is often used to symbolize the positive attributes gained as the result of a particular process, often a laborious one (in this case climbing a ladder) – cf. the "fruit" of the "Spirit" (again biblical, this time New Testament, e.g. Ephesians 5). The Greek myth of the labours of Hercules, who had to pluck golden apples from a tree, access to which could only be gained by way of many perils, uses similar symbolism.

Puritan beliefs form the ideological background to the illustration. The good (i.e. God-given) things in life were seen as rewards for possessing certain virtues – here the rungs of the ladder – which were not to be gained without effort. This belief underlies John Bunyan's *The Pilgrim's Progress*, an allegory in which the means of attaining such "rewards" was a path full of obstacles. The picture on p. 241 is a visual allegory. By the end of the nineteenth century, the Puritan belief in effort and divine "reward" had lost much of its religious flavour and become a secular philosophy – though in our picture the "favor of God" is still at the centre of all rewards.

This view of society is based on a dualistic moral framework with clear divisions between good and bad, right and wrong. At its core is the principle of cause and effect: if you adhere to a certain lifestyle, you will reap the corresponding rewards. Such a world view leaves no room for the effects of unavoidable circumstance or unjust social structures. Man is the master of his own destiny. The advertisement depicted on p. 169 illustrates what becomes of this way of thinking when taken to its logical, individualistic conclusion.

In 1835 Alexis de Tocqueville pointed to the quest for "fortune" as being an intrinsic element of the American Dream (see Fact File, SB p. 313).

"Policy" is a form of lottery. It is historically interesting that strikes and the stock-exchange are still never-ending sources of contention. After a period of acceptance of the stock exchange as a positive growth factor, Americans have once more come to doubt the moral value of being involved in it since the Wall Street scandals of the 1980s.

One could draw a parallel between this early American attempt to impart the values necessary for a fulfilled life and the current upsurge of interest in religion depicted in "Shopping for a church" (SB pp. 149–151). Many contemporary American parents who return to religion are motivated by "the realization that children need a place where they can learn solid values and make friends with peers who share them" (p. 150, ll. 21–23).

## Methodisch-didaktische Hinweise

Als *visual allegory* bietet das Bild genau so viele Sprech- und Schreibanlässe wie ein Text und stellt symbolisch einige Hauptelemente des *American Dream* dar. Deshalb empfiehlt es sich, das Bild als Einstieg in das Kapitel zu benutzen und es ausführlich zu behandeln. Das Bild bietet auch einen wichtigen Bezugspunkt für die Texte in diesem Kapitel und leistet Hilfe bei der Herstellung von Zusammenhängen zwischen ihnen. Zunächst dienen die Fragen in der Legende der Erschließung des sachlichen Inhalts ohne weiterführende Analyse. Nach deren Beantwortung bieten die "Additional questions" Anregungen für Wortschatzarbeit, Diskussion und kreative Übungen.

## Suggested answers (caption)

Some elements of interpretation:

1. The moral/ ethical dimension: dualistic moral perspective; composition and colour demonstrate the superiority of the lifestyle depicted in the foreground. The importance of education and family (bottom l.h. corner). Strikes and the stock exchange are not approved of. Morality and honesty are the supports for the virtues. Does the failure to gain success, riches, honour, influence etc. mean that one does not stand in the favour of God, or that one has not pursued the virtues named on the ladder?

2. The historical dimension: changing attitudes to the "vices". In the picture, the lottery, betting, swindling, gambling and dealing on the stock exchange are seen as ways of making material gain without effort. Strikes are seen as the refusal to work. The dualistic interpretation of behaviour does not allow for a more subtly differentiated view, e.g. that strikes could be a means of gaining greater social justice, or that dealing on the stock exchange could have a positive effect on the overall economy. The roots of dualism – in Puritanism (and its interpretation of Calvin); parallels to Victorian England. The part played by religion: has God been meant to sanction the American Dream?

The people at the foot of the ladder on the right are holding the tool typical of their trades: a sickle, a carpenter's iron square. To the left, the girl is holding a knitting frame, the boy school books, representing the expectations society has of them.

## Additional questions

1. Considering the qualities named on the ladder, what sort of person would he or she be who reaches the top (form adjectives from these qualities)?

2. If the fruits on the tree are the rewards for pursuing the virtues making up the rungs of the ladder, what "rewards" might those expect who pursue the vices in the background (form antonyms of the fruits)?

3. Thinking about success: how do you define it? What qualities does a person need in order to be successful in our day? Is there a difference between desirable and undesirable success? If

so, where do you draw the line? Discuss these questions in small groups.

4. Put yourself in the position of the artist. You have drawn the picture but not yet put in the words. What "virtues" would you place on the rungs of the ladder? What "fruits" would serve as rewards, what "vices" should be avoided? Or would you reject this scheme of cause and effect from the start? If so, what would you replace it with?

5. Imagine you have just discovered the picture in the attic of an old house, where it has been lying, covered in dust, for many years. You do not know who did it, or where and when it was drawn, or for whom it was intended. Look for clues in the picture. The identity of the artist may remain a mystery, but you might be able to pinpoint his place in history or say something about his world view.
Your find is to be exhibited in a museum in an English-speaking country outside the USA. Write the accompanying explanation for visitors to the museum.

6. Considering the purpose of this picture, why do you think it was more appropriate to do it as a lithograph and not as a painting?
Educational purpose, i.e. has to be reproduced.

# 1. A richer and fuller life for all

### Background information
James Truslow Adams' book *The Epic of America* appeared at a time when, especially in Europe, many books were published expressing scepticism about the future of mankind. Among these books are Ortega y Gasset's *La rebelión de las masas* (1930), Karl Jaspers's *Die geistige Situation der Zeit* (1932) and, of course, Aldous Huxley's *Brave New World* (1932). It is interesting that Adams' book is the only one written on an optimistic note – its author believes in mankind's potential for betterment. He draws his optimism from the fact that a democratic society like that of America was capable of building something like the American Library of Congress, an institution which to him embodies the finest elements of the American Dream. In fact, it was Adams who first coined the term "American Dream" (see Fact File, SB p. 313).
See the poster depicted on p. 45 of Perspectives 1: *The American Dream*, Klettbuch 51361. For Alvin Toffler's suggestions concerning a more just system of economic "rewards", see Perspectives 12: *The Caring Society?*, Klettbuch 51372, pp. 61–62. The text "The new sweatshops" (SB pp. 228–229) deals with the question of economic and social justice in the case of immigrant workers in the USA today. As a contrast, the listening comprehension in Ch. 10, "Going to the Promised Land" (SB p. 217) depicts the utopian vision of immigrants entering the USA at the turn of the century.

### Pre-reading activities
1. What do you know about the Great Depression in the USA? Pool your information in class.

2. Hollywood – dream factory. What dreams have been, and are, produced there?
See "Hollywood's view of society", SB pp. 126–128.

### Suggested answers
1. From rags to riches, from dishwasher to millionaire, material wealth, the promise of liberty and freedom of expression, freedom of religion, a classless society, the chance to be innovative etc. (see text of "Going to the Promised Land", Listening Comprehension in Ch. 10, A Nation of Immigrants); Fact File, SB p. 313.
In the text: summary in first sentence. A social order based on equal opportunity (ll. 10–15). In concrete terms: an economic base (ll. 44–45) involving a more equitable distribution of wealth (ll. 50–53); a set of values (l. 58) based on communal life (ll. 65–66); improvement of "communal spiritual and intellectual life" (l. 72).

2. Life should be fuller and richer for everyone; opportunity for each according to his or her ability and achievement; a social order without class barriers; every person should be recognized by others for what he or she is regardless of birth; not merely a dream of motor cars and high wages,

nor purely "individual selfishness, physical comfort, and cheap amusements" (ll. 86–87).

3. Personal: the dream of being able to grow to the fullest of one's potential; individuals must not live just for themselves and for the easily-gained pleasures of cheap entertainment and physical satisfaction.
Social: no repressive social order; communal life must rise to a higher level.
Material: wealth is a very important asset but should be more equitably distributed.
Intellectual: intellectual life must be distinctly higher than elsewhere; those who are on top must devote themselves to the good of the entire society; those at the bottom of the social scale must work hard to rise intellectually.

4. The tendency for individuals and classes to struggle against one another (ll. 75–79) and for individuals to live only for their own gain and cheap pleasure (ll. 86–87).

5. By the use of if-clauses denoting realistic possibility, James Truslow Adams implies that if his conditions are met, the fulfillment of the American Dream will be a logical consequence.

**Additional questions**

1. *Find examples of the present perfect in this text and explain its use.*

2. *Explain the form of the if-clauses in this text.*

**Post-reading activities**

*Summarize the content of the following three books (you may consult* Kindlers Literaturlexikon *or a similar work):*
– *José Ortega y Gasset,* La rebelión de las masas
– *Karl Jaspers,* Die geistige Situation der Zeit
– *Aldous Huxley,* Brave New World

# 2. Bonanza farming

### Background information

The tendencies described in the text can be traced back to the assumption that higher yields automatically mean higher income. Events of the 1980s in the USA, however, have shown this to be a mistake. Being an export-oriented activity, agriculture is at the mercy of global demand and the strength of the dollar. The mechanized nature of farming today means that farmers are forced to make large-scale investments (e.g. buying machinery), although their income may fluctuate greatly over the time needed for repayment. Bankruptcy is often the result. In the early eighties, exports dropped considerably after the imposition of a grain embargo on the USSR and because of the strength of the dollar. Yet grain production continued to rise, and the result was large surpluses. Prices dropped accordingly. Hundreds of thousands of farms disappeared from the landscape of the USA during that decade. These were developments that Moody could not foresee, but he accurately pictures the immediate social and economic consequences of the structural changes in agriculture in his day.

About 55 years after this text was written, the American novelist John Steinbeck wrote two significant novels focusing on the social effects of senseless exploitation of the land and those who work on it: *Of Mice and Men* (1937; Klettbuch 5785) and *The Grapes of Wrath* (1939). Though set in a slightly different historical context, these novels deal with similar issues to those raised by Moody in 1883.
See also *American Life and Institutions*, Klettbuch 5136, pp. 59–60.

### Pre-reading activities

1. *What do you associate with the term "bonanza"? Discuss in class.*

2. *Examine the statistics on p. 244. What tendencies in agriculture can you detect?*

3. *Describe the way in which rural life is depicted in Westerns.*

4. *Look at the picture on p. 244. Describe what you see, and answer the questions below it.*

Inventions: Cotton gin (1793), which revolutionized cotton picking – the output per picker rose from 50 pounds per hand-picking labourer to 1,000 pounds daily. Combine harvester, introduced before the end of the 19th century. Tractor. Milking machine.

Effects: More can be done with fewer people in a shorter period of time (see statistics p. 244). Labourers become more mobile as they search for employment. Machinery is expensive, and investments mean a financial risk which few can afford. The hirelings live in comparative poverty. Fewer farmers supply a greater number of people, with higher yields. The modern farmer is more like a businessman.

**Suggested answers**

1. The old farms, family homesteads, were rarely larger than one hundred acres, just enough to be managed by a single family. With the invention of machinery and the advent of the railroad the farms grew in size. Social structures changed dramatically: hired farm labourers under the eyes of overseers then did the work previously done by members of the family.

2. The owners of these farms do not invest emotionally in their farms. They are not interested in improving their estates beyond the bare minimum of what is necessary to be sure of good yields and profits. They are not interested in the fate of their labourers, whereas farms used to be home for a large number of people. Farmers now view farming like any other form of business activity. Pleasure is no longer sought on the farm itself, but somewhere else.

3. Farms no longer social units – division between work place and leisure due to sterility of farm environment. Communication between farms no longer easily established, i.e. loss of farming community. Social and economic gap between farm owners and hired workers. The latter have lost their social sphere completely and have no permanent home. Families suffer.

4. The agrarian ideal as pronounced by Thomas Jefferson, and the American Dream as defined by James Truslow Adams (equitable economic structures), have been betrayed by this development, in which crass economic interests take precedence over the commitment to improving communal life. Jefferson's view of those who work the land as "the most valuable citizens" clashes with the poverty and forced mobility of the hired workers.

5. The USA has become the bread-basket of the world, but intensive farming has affected vast areas, causing "natural" disasters, e.g. the creation of the Dust Bowl in the 1930s. Decades of overplowing and overplanting had broken the soil structure, which became powdery and fell prey to the dust storm; thousands of small farmers had to leave their farms and go west (cf. John Steinbeck, *The Grapes of Wrath*, which has also been made into a film).

Farming in places like California has placed enormous strain on the water supply, with potentially disastrous consequences. Many small and medium-sized farms in the Midwest, the American heartland, have disappeared over the last decade or so because of the overall economic situation, characterized mainly by high interest rates (see "If You Went Under, We'd Lose Money on You" and "One Family's Bankruptcy", *Skyline* Edition C, Klettbuch 51033, pp. 225–230). Farm labourers in California mostly come from Latin American countries, especially Mexico, adding considerably to the growing problem of illegal immigration into the western and southwestern states of the USA.

**Post-reading activities**

*1. Give a short outline of what CAP (Common Agricultural Policy) means to European farmers.*

*2. Collect newspaper clippings over a period of two weeks that deal with agricultural problems in Europe and your own country/region and present the main points to your class – in English.*

*3. Read (or re-read) the text on pp. 151–154, "The Amish answer". Compare Moody's attitude to that of the Amish.*

# 3. Reflections of a self-made man (GK)

## Background information

Ronald Reagan (President of the USA 1981 – 1989) was born in Tampico, Ill. in 1911. He was educated in a number of public schools in Illinois, one of them in Dixon, before he attended college in the same state. Before entering politics full-time he worked as a sports announcer, actor, television host and programme supervisor. He was President of the Screen Actors' Guild from 1947 to 1952 and 1959 to 1960, and Chairman of the Motion Picture Industry Council in 1949. During World War II he served with the Air Force. His rise to political power began when he became Governor of California in 1967.

*Success* is a magazine for people in business.

## Pre-reading activities

1. *When has a person "made it"? Make a list of possible personal achievements which in your view constitute "success".*

2. a) *Recall your thoughts concerning the poster on p. 241. Now compare it with the advertisement on p. 169.*
*How is success to be achieved in each case?*
b) *How does the following statement relate to your findings from part a) of this question?*
*It is "the ... American conviction that you can redesign your life and become anything you want to be – given a suitable incentive" ("Not just doing it for kicks", SB pp. 170–171, ll. 100–101).*

3. *What do you know about the career of Ronald Reagan, former President of the United States?* See "Background information".

4. *Look at the picture on p. 246 and answer the questions in the caption.*
The Amish still practise the old tradition of barnraising. A very impressive example of this is given in the movie *Witness*. The barn has to be raised between sun-up and sun-down without the help of motorised machinery. According to the traditional division of labour the women prepare the meals and look after the younger children.

## Suggested answers

1. The author suggests that "entrepreneur" is synonymous with America itself. People of entrepreneurial spirit came to America to settle the land; they built the cities, won the West and created the great institutions of the country. When the country was at war, it was such people who saved it. According to Reagan, entrepreneurs – now in the world of business – are still the people who guarantee the country a prosperous future.

2. Verbs like "build, create, win, succeed, drive" reflect the determination to overcome all odds, creating something better than before, in accordance with the American "vision" of making a new start.
Adjectives like "bright, clear, strong, safe, free" are of great intensity and emotion. They are associated with positive ideas and feelings.

3. Both "yet" and "despite" signalise the introduction of a thought which contrasts with preceding ideas. Having praised the entrepreneurs' role in building America, Reagan then emphasizes that the ordinary working people, too, play their part in this process. He sees this as proof of the American people's ability to out-perform anybody in the world. The word "yet", however, shows that Reagan differentiates clearly between entrepreneurs and other working people.
"Despite" indicates that something is different from what one could expect. "Despite our success, we are not a selfish people." In other words, success is generally seen to lead to selfishness. Reagan is keen to point out that this has never been the case in America. On the contrary, it is part of the American tradition to help friends and neighbours who are in need, he maintains.
These two paragraphs are an attempt to address possible criticism of the view that precedes them. Critics may have argued that entrepreneurs in the USA are selfish people and that the entrepreneurial spirit creates social divisions. By associating the entrepreneurial spirit with the "free spirit of voluntarism" (ll. 58 and 65), Reagan is suggesting that the promotion of the former in American society allows the latter to emerge.

4. His experience is meant to provide proof of his description of America. It is more than an ideal. Reagan wrote this statement during his time as President, and citing his own experience is meant to lend plausibility to his politics: he is stating his interest in the lives of all Americans, not just of those at the top of the business world.

*The American Dream in a Changing Society*

5. a) Reagan draws a picture of America which is highly positive, making the reader believe that everything is within everybody's reach if he or she only wishes to succeed. (Compare this with the poster on p. 241!)
b) –

**Additional questions**

1. a) What characteristics would make up the "entrepreneurial spirit" or "vision" as described by Reagan in ll. 7–15?
Initiative, courage, innovation
b) When Reagan speaks of "today's entrepreneurs" (ll. 15–38), he uses the term to mean business people only, such as the readers of the magazine Success. Comment on the difference between the two definitions of "entrepreneur/entrepreneurial" (ll. 7–15, ll. 15–38).
Defining entrepreneurs solely as business people means disregarding the initiative and courage of all other members of society. The real America is then virtually synonymous with its business world. Ll. 48–52 are an attempt to balance this view. (Students could discuss whether they find this attempt convincing.)
See also pp. 177–178 of *Skyline, Edition C*, Klettbuch 510331 (Teacher's Book), Additional Questions.

2. What are the implications of the statement that "wealth is not created in Washington, D.C. but in the marketplace of enterprise and ideas" (ll. 35–37)?

**Post-reading activities**

*The following are the names of some of the most famous American "self-made men": Thomas Alva Edison, Andrew Carnegie, John Pierpont Morgan, John Davison Rockefeller, Cornelius Vanderbilt, Samuel Goldwyn, George Mortimer Pullman. Gather biographical information on these men and present it to your class in a talk. Do you know of any well-known "self-made women"? Why is this traditionally a male phenomenon? Consider this in your talk and when you read further texts in this chapter.*
See Bibliography 2, 9, 14, 21, 22, 23.

## 4. Second chance – Fred Ringley, ex-salesman, farmer (GK)

**Background information**

In all his books Terkel studies ordinary people whose stories do not usually make it into print. These, however, are the real Americans. They are what America is made of. They confirm Richard Nixon's famous dictum that people, not government, have made America great.
The occupations of farmer and salesman are both deeply rooted in the American conscience (cf. Thomas Jefferson). The salesman is a powerful symbol of American restlessness and the strenuous effort of getting ahead. He has become a kind of a stock-figure of American literature (cf. among others Eugene O'Neill, *The Iceman Cometh*; Thornton Wilder, *The Eighth Day*; Sinclair Lewis, *Elmer Gantry*) with Arthur Miller's Willy Loman in *Death of a Salesman* being the most famous and tragic example – see Arthur Miller, *Death of a Salesman, Text and Study Aids*, Klettbuch 57763, pp. 105–127 and Wolfgang Stütz, "Geistes- und sozialgeschichtliche Anmerkungen zu *Death of a Salesman*", in: Eichler, Olbert, Stütz (Hrsg.),

*Arthur Miller, Death of a Salesman, Beiträge zur Behandlung des Dramas im Unterricht*, LEU, Materialien Englisch, E20, Stuttgart, 1989, pp. 9–18. See also *American Life and Institutions*, Klettbuch 5136, pp. 25–28.
For a discussion of the influence of television on American lifestyles see "They came, we saw, they conquered", SB pp. 128–130 and the cartoon on p. 129. A different view of American cities is presented in the text "What is American about America?", SB pp. 111–112. The text entitled "Lifestyles" (SB pp. 64–68) deals with the issue of occupations and the quality of life in a British setting.

**Pre-reading activities**

*Think of situations and reasons that would or could cause you to leave your home town. If you decided to leave when you had finished your education, what would you do? Where would you go? Discuss these questions in pairs.*

## Suggested answers

1. Fred was born and raised in Chicago, where he had been living until a year before the interview. He was what he describes as a typical middle-class family man of the suburbs trying incessantly to improve his social standing.

This is what he essentially means by being "caught up in the American Dream" (l. 32). He mentions all the outward trappings of the successful man: country-club membership, two cars, company car, expense account, all of which he eventually acquired. Yet instead of settling down to a contented life-style, he and his wife started worrying, drinking and smoking. They suddenly realized that despite having everything, they were "poor" (l. 46). So they decided to pull up stakes and try something new elsewhere. In traditional American fashion they went "West" (l. 65) – though geographically speaking they went south.

2. They own both a farm and a dairy bar, where they serve the local customers typical fast food products. However, they are not only in it for the business, trying to make as much profit as possible. They also feel needed by the locals, who come to their place in search of social contacts. Apart from the rural setting, which is obviously part of the American Dream, they have won a certain degree of personal independence. They are at the point of being able to decide when to open, when to close and when to go on vacation. This has been made possible by the decision to be among the "haves" (l. 89), investing sensibly and being willing to work hard to make their dream come true.

3. Fred Ringley proves that the American Dream is not synonymous with material wealth. The Ringleys' appreciation of the communal, social aspect of their work corresponds to Adams' urge to use wealth "in the interests of society" (text 1, l. 53). They have resisted the temptation to give in to "selfishness, physical comfort, and cheap amusements" (text 1, ll. 86–87). By instinctively turning to the country as the place in which to make his dream come true, Fred Ringley also proves Thomas Jefferson right. Jefferson pleaded strongly in favour of self-contained family farms, as the core communities of every successful society (cf. text 2 in this chapter).

4. Both Fred Ringley and his wife showed entrepreneurial spirit by not being content with their situation and by having the willpower to do something about it. The fact that they judiciously assessed the options and sensibly invested their money shows their clarity of vision and strong will. They showed initiative and courage by starting up all over again in activities which were completely new to them (farming and the restaurant business).

5. It is the American conviction that the individual can provide evidence as important as that contained in official documents (cf. Nixon's dictum, "Background information").
– It gives the reports the ring of authenticity.
– It might teach others what to do and what not to do, what to expect and what to be wary of.
– Readers take more notice of accounts stemming from people just like themselves.

## Additional questions

*Collect evidence to show that this was originally an oral account rather than a written text.*

## Post-reading activities

*1. Examine the cartoon on p. 247 and answer the questions in the caption.*
A treadmill, traditionally a toy for pet hamsters, is suspended between the pinnacles of two skyscrapers, symbols of American wealth and self-confidence. The American flag is flying atop one of the skyscrapers. A man is caught inside the treadmill. He is obviously a businessman, wearing a suit and a tie. He is desperately clinging to the bars of the cage, using the other bars as the rungs of a ladder. His face is torn in a grimace of strain and desperation. Despite his frantic efforts to climb higher, he remains where he is. In other words, once you are at the top it is futile to try to go higher. Yet the urge to do just that is irresistable. The treadmill is traditionally a symbol of never-ending drudgery, devoid of all job satisfaction. Even at the top it can be like this. Yet if you decide to change your situation fundamentally, the stakes are, literally, very high, as Fred Ringley himself experienced.

*2. Read Arthur Miller's* Death of a Salesman *and outline how the theme of the American Dream is dealt with in this play.*
See Bibliography 13, 16, 25.

*3. "I've reached a certain level of success... and what does it all mean?" This is not Fred Ringley* speaking, but David Robboy, from Portland, Oregon (SB p. 150, ll. 49–51, in "Shopping for a church"). In their early forties, David and his wife Deborah started reassessing their lives. Like Fred Ringley, they took a step in a new direction. What was this step? Can you think of any other possible ways of "changing direction" in life? The text "Ecotopia" (pp. 256–260) may give you some ideas.

See Bibliography 1, 3, 16.

4. Think up a similar story to that of Fred Ringley and his wife – you may invent the details. Make notes to give it a plausible structure. Then write down questions a reporter might ask your character(s) for a television documentary on people of entrepreneurial spirit. Working in pairs, practise interviews in which you take turns to be the interviewer and the interviewee. Present your interviews to the class. As a final step, write a short oral history of your partner's account.

## 5. Listening Comprehension: I have a dream

### Background information

Rev. Martin Luther King, Jr., black Protestant clergyman, spearheaded the Civil Rights Movement in the sixties until he was assassinated in 1968. Federal attempts to introduce desegregation in public transport, schools etc. (under President Kennedy) had been thwarted repeatedly by the governors of Southern States. They claimed the legal right of "interposition and nullification", which would enable any one state of the Union to oppose a Federal law it sees as violating the state's sovereign rights. In this way, the governors of Alabama and Mississippi in particular stopped blacks from voting and denied them equal opportunity. 1968 – the year of King's death – marked the centenary of the granting of citizenship to black Americans (14th Amendment – see SB p. 211). Yet as late as June, 1963, Governor George Wallace of Alabama could announce that segregation would continue there "today, tomorrow and forever". In Mississippi, voters had to prove they could read and give a "reasonable interpretation" of one section of the US Constitution. White registrars, as sole judges of what was and was not "reasonable", made sure whites passed the tests and blacks did not. Versions of this "Mississippi Plan" remained valid until they were overruled by the Voting Rights Act of 1965 (see SB p. 211).

The march of August 1963 was staged to put pressure on Congress to pass a new civil rights bill. In accordance with Martin Luther King's pleas for non-violence – he followed Ghandi closely in this regard (see "Gandhi's Salt March", SB pp. 40–42) – the march was peaceful, though on the same day four black children were killed when a bomb exploded in a church in Birmingham, Alabama, King's home town. The old Baptist hymn, "We shall overcome", was sung at the march and became the anthem of the civil rights movement. In 1964 Martin Luther King was awarded the Nobel Peace Prize. His subsequent drive to enforce voting rights for blacks in Alabama met with violent opposition on the part of state authorities, who then clashed with federal forces attempting to uphold these rights. This was the prelude to the Voting Rights Act. The number of registered black voters doubled within a year. A white backlash and violent riots followed. More radical and violent black leaders such as Malcolm X arose. Although many more black citizens are now gaining higher education and better jobs than in the sixties, appalling poverty, housing problems and unemployment among black people in the major cities of the USA today demonstrate that for these people at least, the American Dream is still a long way from coming true.

For more detailed information on racial struggles in the USA and on Martin Luther King see Perspectives 12: *The Caring Society?* (Teacher's Book), Klettbuch 513721, pp. 25–27 ("Background information" on the text, "The Dream and the Nightmare").

To illustrate his vision of the equality that is supposedly "self-evident" according to the Declaration of Independence, King uses a biblical metaphor. The prophecy of Isaiah 40:4–5 paints a picture of the coming of "the Lord" through a landscape in which all unevenness has been done away with. Like many Negro spirituals, King's speech fuses the "dream" with a religious faith which gains its models from Old Testament sto-

264  The American Dream in a Changing Society

ries and images of liberation. (For a similar use of Old Testament images see "Background information" on the text of the Welsh hymn in Ch. 7 Religious Life).

"My country, 'tis of thee..." was sung to the tune of "God save the Queen", the English national anthem. In underlining freedom as the prerequisite to America's becoming a "great nation", King is echoing the ideas of James Truslow Adams.

## Methodisch-didaktische Hinweise

Eine Einleitung, Worterklärung und Fragen zum Globalverständnis sind im Schülerbuch auf S. 249 abgedruckt.

Es empfiehlt sich, den Redeausschnitt in seiner ganzen Länge den Schülerinnen und Schülern vorzustellen. Da Martin Luther King eine sehr adressatenfreundliche Sprechgeschwindigkeit hat, dürften sie keine Schwierigkeiten haben, ihm zu folgen. Es ist denkbar, daß die Schülerinnen und Schüler sich während des Zuhörens Notizen machen.

## Transcript

I say to you today, my friends, ... though, even though we face the difficulties of today and tomorrow, I still have a dream. It is a dream deeply rooted in the American Dream. I have a dream
5 that one day this nation will rise up, live out the true meaning of its creed: "We hold these truths to be self-evident, that all men are created equal."
I have a dream that one day on the red hills of Georgia the sons of former slaves and the sons of
10 former slave-owners will be able to sit down together at the table of brotherhood. I have a dream that one day even the state of Mississippi, a state sweltering with the heat of injustice, sweltering with the heat of oppression, will be trans-
15 formed into an oasis of freedom and justice.
I have a dream that my four little children will one day live in a nation where they will not be judged by the color of their skin but by the content of their character.
20 I have a dream today – I have a dream that one day down in Alabama, with its vicious racists, with its governor having his lips dripping with the words of interposition and nullification, one day right down in Alabama little black boys and black girls
25 will be able to join hands with little white boys and white girls as sisters and brothers.

I have a dream today – I have a dream that one day every valley shall be exalted, every hill and mountain shall be made low. The rough places will be made plain, and the crooked places will be made 30 straight. And the glory of the Lord shall be revealed, and all flesh shall see it together. This is our hope. This is the faith that I go back to the South with.
With this faith we will be able to hew out of the 35 mountain of despair a stone of hope. With this faith we will be able to transform the jangling discords of our nation into a beautiful symphony of brotherhood. With this faith we will be able to work together, to pray together, to struggle to- 40 gether, to go to jail together, to stand up for freedom together, knowing that we will be free one day.
This will be the day – this will be the day when all of God's children will be able to sing with new 45 meaning,
My country, 'tis of thee,
Sweet land of liberty,
Of thee I sing.
Land where my fathers died, 50
Land of the pilgrim's pride,
From every mountainside,
Let freedom ring!
And if America is to be a great nation, this must become true. 55
When we allow freedom (to) ring – when we let it ring from every village and every hamlet, from every state and every city, we will be able to speed up that day when all of God's children, black men and white men, Jews and Gentiles, Protestants 60 and Catholics, will be able to join hands and sing in the words of the old Negro spiritual, "Free at last, free at last, great God Almighty, we are free at last!".

## Pre-listening activities

*1. Can you think of any other Negro spirituals dealing with the theme of freedom and release from oppression?*
Go down, Moses; Swing low, sweet chariot; All my trials, Lord; Wade in the water...

*2. What do you know about the American civil rights movement and Martin Luther King? Pool your information in class.*

**Suggested answers (Listening for the gist)**

1. Martin Luther King wants the United States to live up to the creed of "all men are created equal" as contained in the Declaration of Independence. His dream is one of racial equality, of ending oppression even in those states where it is worst, of living in a community of brotherhood where the words of the Negro spiritual become reality, "We're free at last!".
Note for the teacher: Here it would be useful to refer to two texts in Ch. 9 of the SB, "Equality before the law" (pp. 203–204) and "A maxim for free society" (pp. 205–206).

2. In the Negro spiritual "freedom" is liberation of the Israelites from Egyptian bondage. It is an image paralleling the Negroes' longing for freedom from slavery, freedom to live as equals among Whites, Jews, Gentiles, Protestants and Catholics. To Martin Luther King, freedom is freedom from oppression, humiliation and injustice; freedom means being accepted as equals among equals, that children of former slave owners and former slaves can live together peacefully and in mutual respect.

3. Georgia: a former slave state in the Old South (setting of the film *Gone with the Wind*).
Mississippi: a state characterized by injustice to black people – the denial of voting rights – also a former slave state. Alabama: "the words of interposition and nullification" (l. 23); segregation.

**Listening for detail**

*1. What does King consider to be a more just criterion for judging someone than skin colour?*
"the content of their character" (ll. 18–19)

*2. Which state in particular wishes to practise "interposition and nullification"?*
Alabama (ll. 20–26)

*3. From which arts or crafts does King draw his images for the hope he possesses?*
Sculpture or stonemasonry and music (ll. 35–39)

**Post-reading activities**

*Write a paper or give a talk on the Civil Rights Movement and Martin Luther King.*
See Bibliography 2, 10, 11, 17, 21, 23, 24.

# 6. The new believers (GK)

**Background information**

The title of the book from which this excerpt is taken reveals the author's view of the role played by women in the American Dream: they are in its "shadow". Indeed, the rags-to-riches legend, illustrated in Horatio Alger's story *Ragged Dick and Mark, the Match Boy* (New York: Collier Books, 1962; excerpt contained in Perspectives 1: *The American Dream*, pp. 34–38), is not often cited in a female form.
In the USA there are now more women than men graduating from college and even from high school. Yet women's wages still make up only 70–80% of men's wages on average (see statistics incorporated into the pre-reading activities). The Seneca Falls Declaration of Sentiments (SB p. 210) is an early example of women's protest against discrimination in the USA and marked the beginning of the organized women's movement. Yet it was not until 1920 that women were granted the franchise in all states (see "Voting rights: landmark dates", SB p. 211).

Asked his views on American society, in 1983, well-known futurologist Alvin Toffler termed women "unrecognized producers", i.e. people who "contribute value to the exchange economy" but are not rewarded for doing so. He calls for changes to this "archaic, unjust system" ("On Rewards and Welfare", in Perspectives 12: *The Caring Society?*, Klettbuch 51372, pp. 61–63). The plight of Simone Baker could be compared with that of the mother and daughters described in "Welfare Mother", also in *The Caring Society?*, pp. 28–30.

**Methodisch-didaktische Hinweise**

Die *pre-reading activities* bieten zwei verschiedene Einstiegsmöglichkeiten in diesen Text: zum einen über die eigene Erfahrung, zum anderen mit Hilfe der Statistiken, die die Situation der Frau in der amerikanischen Gesellschaft ein wenig verdeutlichen. Wichtig ist, daß der Einstieg nicht in eine allgemeine Diskussion über die Rolle der Frau in der westlichen Gesellschaft überhaupt mündet, sondern im Kontext der Überlegungen zum "American Dream" geschieht. Eine Verankerung in diesen Kontext kann mit Hilfe des Bildes am Kapiteleingang gewährleistet werden.

## Pre-reading activities

*1. Carry out a survey among your friends at school on their plans for the future. Evaluate your findings on a gender basis. Are there any significant differences between the expectations of boys and those of girls?*

*2. What do the following statistics tell us about the lives of women in the USA?*

– *Women as % of labour force (16 yrs and over):*
18% in 1900; 45% in 1990.
– *Women's wages (% of men's wages):*
Managerial level: 70%.
Service occupations: 72%.
Cleaning and labouring: 81%.
– *Median weekly earnings (late 1990):*
Managerial level: men $754, women $520
Sales occupations: men $502, women $299
– *% of mothers in the labour force:*

|  | 1955 | 1990 |
|---|---|---|
| a) with children under 6: | 18% | 58% |
| b) with children aged 6–17: | 38% | 75% |

*Statistics (percentages rounded off) from:* The 1992 Information Please Almanac. *Boston: Houghton Mifflin, 1992 (Klettbuch 516152), pp. 44, 46, 53, 54.*

*3. Interpret the following figures in terms of the differences in employment of white and black people (over 16 yrs of age) in the USA (1990):*

– *Managerial level:*
a) whites: 27% of white work force
b) blacks: 16% of black work force
– *Labourers:*
a) whites: 14% of white work force
b) blacks: 22% of black work force

*Source:* The 1992 Information Please Almanac, p. 54.

*4. Look at the picture on p. 241 of your book. What do you think the "rewards" of happiness, influence, success, etc. mean, in terms of her future, to the young girl in the bottom left-hand corner?*

## Suggested answers

1. Women in America used to mould their lives around those of other people. They saw it as their natural duty to keep house and attend to their husbands' and children's needs, making life as smooth as possible for them. Women adjusted their time-table to these priorities: dinner-time was when the husband returned home from work, and those women who did work outside the house saw to it that the working-hours did not interfere with their families' needs (ll. 81–92).

2. The new dream the author is talking about has all the attributes of male "success stories". Clothes, a briefcase and a privately-owned house or apartment are the visible signs of success.
A devoted husband and well-behaved children may be part of the dream (ll. 3–8). Above all, it incorporates the freedom of a woman to determine her own occupation, style and identity (ll. 93–98). The statement that women have "bought into" this image suggests that it was "sold" to them in some way. Certainly advertising (ll. 15–16) and the media in general have played a part, encasing the dream in an image of comfortable, secure middle-class suburban life (ll. 64–70), and the old dream of "rags-to-riches", exemplified by the stories of Horatio Alger, leads some women at the bottom end of the social scale to have unrealistic expectations. Yet it is primarily women themselves who shape the dream (ll. 93–95). The awareness of inequality, motivating force behind the American Dream from the start, leads women to want the same life as men have had for years (ll. 97–98).

3. They see themselves as smartly dressed, carrying briefcases (a sign of professional competence), going to work regularly and living in private houses or condos. Yet their outlook reaches beyond these things: they want to be centre of their own lives, work in men's jobs and earn the same kind of money for the same kind of work. Some go even further, trying to reconcile this new dream with elements of an older, more traditional version of the American Dream as described above.

4. The following points could be raised:
– Not just an American phenomenon but widespread in the whole Western world;
– Quantitative and qualitative increase in formal education has enabled women to live more independently;

- Technical progress has made housework less time consuming;
- Political awareness leads to the conviction that theory (equality) must finally be put into practice;
- Rejection of male privileges in working life;
- Rejection of fixed roles.

The question, "How have young women come to take on the American Dream as their own?" (ll. 73–74), implies that up to now this dream has not been theirs. Perhaps one could say that although the vision of an independent life for women is nothing specifically American, it parallels the American Dream by emphasizing individual initiative and equal opportunity.

**Additional questions**

*Explain the following terms in your own words: l. 32 vocational training; ll. 56–57 the quintessential image of the good life; ll. 76–78 women...did not perceive themselves as separate, independent entities.*

**Post-reading activities**

1. Turn again to the picture on p. 241. Considering Simone Baker's background, do you think it would be possible for her to reach the "fruit" on the tree in the way the picture prescribes? Discuss the question posed in ll. 14–17 of the text you have read.

2. Re-read the oral history of Fred Ringley (SB pp. 247–249). He speaks in the first person plural. Make up an interview with Fred's wife. You could work in pairs. Your questions could include the following points:
   - her expectations of the future when a teenager;
   - whether these expectations were fulfilled in her life in suburbia;
   - why she, like her husband, grew dissatisfied with life in suburbia;
   - whether her new life is the fulfillment of a dream;
   - how she copes with five children, work in the shop and work on the farm.

Conduct the interviews orally in front of the class. Those listening should take brief notes in order to compare the differing perspectives on Mrs Ringley's life and discuss them later.

3. Write a short account of Simone Baker's life as it might turn out.

4. Read the article entitled "Women in Business" in: *Special Perspectives:* The Economy and Business in Modern Society *(Klettbuch 51381),* pp. 13–14. Summarize the main points and present these to the class as a basis for discussion. You could compare this text with "Reflections of a self-made man" (SB pp. 245–246).

# Advertisement p. 252

The advertisement uses a cleverly contrived pun: to pull a rabbit out of the hat means doing something miraculous, i.e. it is magic. At the same time, "It's magic" is a colloquialism meaning that something is wonderful. So although it may not work wonders, it is wonderful just the same.

The composition: the picture divides the sentence, thus linking the two concepts of "magic" like a bridge and explaining visually what "it" in both parts is. Because only part of the sentence is positioned at the top of the poster, the reader is compelled to look at the picture in seeking the remaining words. Just as the picture is the link between the two thoughts, the rabbit in the picture bridges the gap between the two children. The white rabbit the children are cuddling is an animal which evokes positive emotions because it is fluffy and is the object of affection. By means of its mere presence it gives them a degree of the happiness they may lack in their home environment. The photo demonstrates that one does not need a miracle to make people happy; a little money is enough.

The intended play on words in the last lines (to make a donation/ to make a memory – note also the alliteration of "make" and "memory") adds a wider connotation to the concept of money, in the same way as the alliterative title of the organization (The Fresh Air Fund) associates money with something healthy and life-giving. Money, it is implied, can contribute to happiness, especially that of other people.

For background information on welfare in the USA, see *American Life and Institutions*, Klettbuch 5136, pp. 67–69, and Perspectives 12: *The Caring Society?*, Klettbuch 51372, p. 31.

## Activities

1. Find out about some other voluntary social welfare organizations in the USA – their aims, the way they operate, and the kind of people who support them.

2. Why do you think the president of the USA would want to encourage voluntary social welfare in the country? Discuss.
To keep alive the spirit of voluntarism that has prevailed through history as part of the American Dream; for purely humane reasons; and because the more voluntary social welfare networks are operating, the fewer social welfare programmes the government has to provide and finance.

3. Think of the sorts of things that would impress a child from the city on his or her first trip to the country. Try to put yourself in the position of one of the children in the photograph and write the account she or he would give a friend or parent after returning to the city.

4. Write a story about animals for children of this age. It would help you to look at English-language children's books first and to think about the main features of writing for children.

## 7. Subcity (GK)

### Background information

For information on Tracy Chapman see SB p. 175 and "Background information" on the song "Fast Car" (TB Ch. 8, Text 4).
In 1990 more than half of the US population was living in rapidly-growing cities of over 1 million inhabitants. Crime and gang violence are pressing problems in such cities. Black people and people of Hispanic origin are particularly hard-hit by poverty, as the following figures (from 1989) show:

Persons living below poverty level (as % of respective population group):

|  | white | black | Hispanic |
|---|---|---|---|
| Under 18 yrs | 14.8 | 43.7 | 36.2 |
| 18 – 21 yrs | 12.4 | 29.8 | 27.0 |
| Total | 10.0 | 30.7 | 26.2 |

(Source: *The 1992 Information Please Almanac*. Boston: Houghton Mifflin, 1992, p. 805)

The article on p. 174 of the SB, "It's a tragedy we cannot afford", deals with the social implications of the school dropout problem. For information on the history of American welfare see Perspectives 12, *The Caring Society?*, Klettbuch 51372, p. 31. In the same volume, see "Begging: To Give or Not to Give", pp. 22–25. See also the section on "Prosperity and Poverty" in *American Life and Institutions*, Klettbuch 5136, pp. 24–25.
Rape statistics illustrate the vulnerability of the underprivileged, e.g. unemployed black women: black women are significantly more likely to be raped than white women, and unemployed women (irrespective of race) are three times more likely to be raped than employed women. (Source: *1992 Almanac*, p. 824)

In an article in *The Guardian* (Feb. 16, 1990) Simon Tisdall cites the image of US inner cities as "a timebomb in the backyard of the American dream" and adds, "The puzzle is that hardly anybody seems to hear the clock ticking".

### Methodisch-didaktische Hinweise

Der Text auf S. 79–80 des Schülerbuchs, "Filed away in a cardboard box city" behandelt das Thema Armut in bezug auf Obdachlose in London und könnte – falls schon gelesen – zum Vergleich herangezogen werden. Es läßt sich ein Bezug zur Anzeige auf S. 252 (zum Leben benachteiligter Kinder in der Großstadt) herstellen, und in der ersten Frage zum Lied wird auf die Situation der jungen Simone Baker, die im vorhergehenden Text geschildert wird, eingegangen. Die Frage nach der Angemessenheit des auf dem Eingangsbild dargestellten Rezepts zur Erlangung des Glücks, die immer wieder im Laufe der Überlegungen zum "American Dream" gestellt wird, sollte auch hier zur Sprache kommen.
Eine mögliche Vorgehensweise ist, den Schülerinnen und Schülern nach der *pre-reading activity* das Lied vorzuspielen, ohne daß sie jedes Wort verstehen müssen (viele Konsonanten und Zeilenanfänge werden verschluckt, was das Verstehen erschwert). Die zweite Strophe des Lieds, "Here in subcity...", dient nach den darauffolgenden Strophen als Refrain. In ihm wird die vorletzte Zeile verschiedentlich gesungen – u.a. als: "Won't you please give...". Es ist hilfreich, vor dem Hören des Liedes darauf aufmerksam zu machen.

Daß diese Einheit sich optimal zum fächerübergreifenden Unterricht eignet (Musik), liegt auf der Hand.

**Pre-reading activities**

*What do you know about the history of protest songs in the USA – how they began, the main themes, some famous singers and songwriters, musical characteristics? Pool your information in class and consider how this movement fits into the theme of the American Dream.*

Woody Guthrie and the folk-singers of the sixties: Peter, Paul and Mary (Pete Seeger), Bob Dylan, Arlo Guthrie, Joan Baez... the Woodstock generation, protest against middle-class values, the Vietnam War... The acoustic guitar and the mouth-organ featured in early protest music; melodies were simple; songs often contained a refrain, and many were written in the form of ballads. Thus protest songs were linked to the tradition of folk and country music in the USA and used acoustic instruments.

The American Dream: many songs to do with freedom, protest against inequality...

**Suggested answers**

1. Simone Baker comes from an underprivileged background. She has been a drug addict since she was five. Her formal education is very poor, but she is trying to improve her situation and shake off drug addiction in order to do some vocational training and find regular work. Against all odds she still dreams the dream of middle-class respectability.

The woman in the song outlines her life-story: she used to be a hard working factory girl, then fell "through the cracks" (l. 17) of the social system. Contrary to what she had thought, the system was neither able nor willing to protect her and others like her, let alone help them. Simone Baker is still dreaming of climbing up the social ladder, whereas the speaker in the song has experienced a sheer drop to the bottom of society and even envisages "dying".

2. The "People" or "they" are those who deny the existence of "subcity". They still believe in the soundness of the system and think that those who are not as successful as they are have only themselves to blame. (Teacher's note: a reference to the picture on p. 241, with its dichotomy between virtues and vices, would be very apt here!) "They" are unwilling to accept that society has a role to play in protecting and helping people, that crime prevention is a social priority and that the problem must be tackled at its roots. In the refrain the singer indirectly addresses "Mr. President", indicating that "they" are also the political decision-makers. "I" or "We" are those who have experienced first-hand what it means to fall prey to the system, although they might have complied with its rules by working hard and trying to be law-abiding citizens. The singer underlines her adherence to American values and her belief in the system through the allusion to the motto found on American currency: "In God We Trust" ("Had my trust in God", l. 26).

They feel abandoned by those at the top, thus defining Ronald Reagan's protestations of solidarity (cf. Text 3) as hollow rhetoric.

3. "Sub" means, both literally and figuratively, "below, under". Thus "subcity" is the city that is to be found, literally, below the surface. This is very often the case, e.g. in subway tunnels, in subterranean passages and "under" bridges. It can, at the same time, mean a city which does not accord with the norms of the city "above" the surface.

Words with negative connotations, like "substandard, subhuman, subnormal, subversive", suggest themselves. "Subcity" also implies powerlessness.

4. By means of harsh irony in the form of a pun the singer shows that she feels President Reagan has never taken interest in her and her friends' plight. She stresses this by adding "honest", instead of the customary "kind" – to give him "kind regards" would be dishonest.

Passing on "regards" is a polite way of showing you care about someone. To disregard someone or something means not caring about that person or thing.

The metaphor of the "crack" implies that there is no absolute safety, that there is always the possibility of an accident, of something untoward. Yet this possibility is rather slight. Those who "fall through the cracks", in other words, are just very unfortunate, the exception rather than the rule. The system itself is still held to be watertight; no changes to it are necessary.

5. It is hard to say whether she has given herself up "completely". But she seems to be very desperate indeed. The fact that she "screamed herself awake" because she thought she "must be dying"

indicates that she still has the will to live. Anger and frustration are expressions of it; the singer is not passive. The survival instinct is evident. Yet the singer feels she has been given up by those in power (ll. 9–10).

fact (too much crime) differ radically. "They" say crime is a disgrace to those who commit it. Hard measures should be taken against criminals. The singer says crime is a disgrace to those who disregard people in the "subcity". "They" (government and big business) should be made responsible.

### Additional questions

*1. Find further examples of a play on words.*
relief (l. 8): means both welfare and release from some kind of burden
living (ll. 23–24): The basic verb is "to live", and to make a living is to earn money.

*2. Explain the irony of the line, "My sentiments exactly" (l. 12).*
A statement of complete agreement, yet the points of view and the conclusions drawn from the stated

### Post-reading activities

*1. Find more rock/pop songs that deal with "subcity" life and present the texts to your class. You can work in groups specializing in British or American songs respectively. Do you know any such songs from other English-speaking countries?*

*2. Write your own poem (or even a song!) dealing with the plight of an underprivileged group in the city.*

## 8. The key to success (GK)

### Background information

For texts on various aspects of the "minority mind-set" see Perspectives 12, *The Caring Society?*, Klettbuch 51372, especially pp. 41–43.
The placards in the photo on p. 250 show that education was one of the main concerns of the Civil Rights Movement. In fact, equal opportunities in education remained a constitutional issue throughout the history of the United States.
The case of Plessy v. Ferguson (1896) affirmed the "separate but equal" doctrine. The case of Brown v. Board of Education of Topeka (1954) then declared this doctrine unconstitutional on the grounds that segregated schools were "inherently unequal" (see Perspectives 3: *The Supreme Court*, Klettbuch 51363, pp. 17–19).
It is interesting to note that the black struggle for equal educational opportunities heavily emphasized the need for "liberal", i.e. academic, education in contrast to "vocational training" in order to achieve equality in status. Two black leaders represented these opposing viewpoints: W. E. B. Du Bois, a fervent supporter of liberal education, and Booker T. Washington, who advocated the need for vocational training. Cosby does not stipulate which direction he feels education should take in order to be the key to success for African-Americans. Yet it is "the real world of work" (ll. 98–99) that is the test.

### Suggested answers

1. The author introduces his reply by repeating the question and giving a brief resumé of past and present, with hope for the future. He then starts his actual reply by describing the minority mind-set, a frame of mind that characterizes widespread attitudes among African-Americans. It obstructs their path to success by leading them to believe racist presuppositions about themselves. They tend to blame others for their own failures and seem to choose the easy way out by adopting what the author calls a "victim's attitude" (l. 44). The author goes on to show that there have been African-Americans who succeeded by making an effort, thus boosting their self-confidence. He cites Paul Robeson and those African-Americans who have excelled in the world of sports.
The secret of their success is defined as the will never to settle for average. The new generation of African-Americans must learn that education is the key to success and that students must reach for the best. Like the people he cites, they dare not settle for second-best if they want to succeed in the real world of work. Provided this change of attitudes occurs, the author feels there is room for optimism concerning the prospects of African-Americans in the United States forty-five years from now.

2. It has made them feel weaker, with a lack of self-confidence and a feeling of powerlessness. The minority mind-set has become a self-fulfilling prophecy, stifling their ambitions. It has led to the adoption of the "victim's attitude" (l. 44).

3. They blame their own failures on racist attitudes of the whites. Cosby cites the case of a student who fails his exam and blames this on his professor's alleged racism, although he did not study hard enough for the exam in the first place. Generally speaking, "volunteer victims" are never at a loss for an excuse for their personal failures.

4. Born as the the son of a former slave in the late 1800s; college, graduation with honours and awards; named to an All-American team; law degree; star in Broadway and movie productions; international career as a concert baritone; tours the world in his fight for human rights.

5. By following the example set by African-American sporting stars, young people would learn how to take "control of their fate" (l. 83), working hard and never settling for second-best.

6. The universities open the door to a world of opportunities if students work hard and do not settle for a token degree. Education is also, in Bill Cosby's view, the key to the kind of self-confidence which allows them to be "in charge" (l. 104) of themselves and become good leaders.

7. The introduction sums up the circular structure: hope for the future, obstructions in the past and present. These are outlined step-by-step. In conclusion, Cosby returns to the starting point of hope, conditioned by the factors he has mentioned. The tenses reflect the structure below:

Frames: Future hope frames the whole article: "I hope". The word "minority" frames the third paragraph and forms a link with the second. "Fortunately" frames the story of Paul Robeson and introduces a new accent. The next section (ll. 80–104) is framed by phrases using the word "charge". Within this section, the word "But" marks a contrast. In the last paragraph, the repetition of the phrase "no longer" emphasizes the desire to break with the past, which is summed up in the question, "May I?" (ll. 110 and 34).

**Post-reading activities**

*1. According to D.L. Stevenson (American Life and Institutions, Klettbuch 5136, p. 51), education is "a fundamental part of the American Dream". Discuss this statement in relation to the views expressed by Cosby.*
See See Bibliography 1, 3, 9, 10, 11, 14, 17, 23.

*2. Look again at the advertisement on p. 169. Do you think the slogan would be applicable to African-American readers?*

*3. Design an advertisement for Ebony, remembering that it aims to increase the self-confidence and chances of success of its middle-class African-American readers. What visual image would you use? What slogan? What arguments? (Cosby's essay may help you). You may be able to work with the Art Department at your school.*
Suggested motifs (examples only): College graduates of mixed ethnic background; an African-American person exercising leadership in some form ... The slogan could be very similar to that of the advertisement on p. 169 (theme of equality).

| ll. 1–6 | Theme question. Hope; hindrances in past and present | future/ future perf./ pres.perf./ simple present |
| --- | --- | --- |
| ll. 7–21 | Situation up to now: negative past: minority, victim | pres. perfect |
| ll. 21–52 | Neg. effects of past on present | simple present |
| | Exceptions give hope for future: | |
| ll. 53–79 | 1. Paul Robeson | pres. perf./ simple past/ simple pres. (for hypothetical case)/ simple past/ pres. perf. |
| ll. 80–892 | 2. sporting heroes | simple present |
| ll. 90–104 | Today: students should learn from such success stories | simple present |
| ll. 105–113 | Future: hope repeated | future/ future perf. |

4. *Write a short essay in reply to the question, "What will schools look like in Germany in the year 2020?", expressing your hopes and reviewing developments in the past and present. Try to structure your writing in some way, not copying Cosby exactly but letting him give you clues. Use key words or phrases, framing devices etc. Be careful to use suitable tenses.*

# 9. Ecotopia

## Background information

For a brief overview of environmental issues in the USA see *American Life and Institutions*, Klettbuch 5136, p. 62. On p. 9 of the same work, author D. K. Stevenson names self-criticism as one aspect of the American Dream: the "debate about America is at the center of what it means to be an American ... Often the most patriotic Americans are also the most critical of their country". The interview with Fred Ringley (SB pp. 247–249) illustrates that the shift to a new lifestyle is often accompanied by a sharply critical attitude toward mainstream society.

Both "Ecotopia" and the story of the Ringleys illustrate modern-day attempts – the one fictitious, the other factual – to fulfill an ideal vision of a better life. The beginnings of America were also marked by such experiments, e.g. the Massachusetts Bay Colony, a self-governing, Puritan community set up in Salem and Boston in the seventeenth century. The missionary zeal of the colony ("We shall be as a city upon a hill, the eyes of all people are upon us" – see SB p. 264) could be likened to the model character of Ecotopia.

Massachusetts was also the site of Brook Farm, a nineteenth-century commune established by the "Transcendental Club", whose members included many renowned literary and intellectual figures. The ideals of that commune – simple lifestyle, shared labour, shared educational and social advantages, equal pay – strongly resemble the ideals expressed a century later by James Truslow Adams (Text 1, "A richer and fuller life for all"). A number of other texts in the SB deal with related issues. "An artificial climate" (pp. 138–139) describes, in conclusion, the social effects of the advent of air-conditioning to the southern USA (ll. 86–101). In "Students, get mad!" (pp. 176–178), Lee Iacocca urges young people to keep asking themselves "that big question ...: 'What kind of America do I really want?'" (ll. 112–114). This could be seen as the question behind the Ecotopia experiment.

## Methodisch-didaktische Hinweise

Es empfiehlt sich, diesen ungewöhnlichen Text durch Kartenstudium der USA und Vergleich mit der vom Autor entworfenen "Neuordnung" vorzubereiten. Bei dieser Tätigkeit können bereits Aspekte dessen berücksichtigt werden, was dann unter Frage 4 zur Gruppenaufgabe wird. Die Schüler müßten über genügend landeskundliche Vorkenntnisse verfügen, um topographische, klimatische, wirtschaftsgeographische, geschichtliche und sprachliche Vorstrukturierungen selbständig erarbeiten zu können (siehe auch *American Life and Institutions*, Klettbuch 5136, erstes Kapitel).

Aufgabe 6 eignet sich besonders für fächerübergreifenden Unterricht. Insbesondere kann hier auf die Kenntnisse aus dem Erdkundeunterricht zurückgegriffen werden, die die Schüler aus der Beschäftigung mit wirtschaftsgeographischen Problemstellungen gewonnen haben. Diese Kenntnisse können das Wissen über topographische und klimatische Verhältnisse sinnvoll ergänzen. Zusätzlich können auch Kenntnisse verwendet werden, die im Geschichtsunterricht gewonnen wurden und die sich mit den historischen Gegebenheiten, Affinitäten und Entwicklungen befassen.

## Pre-reading activities

*1. Look at the cartoon on p. 257 and answer the questions.*

Since it is placed at a roadside, the sign seems to indicate, for one thing, an aversion to motor traffic. This fits in with Oregon's image as an environmentally aware state.

Most road signs at a state border welcome those entering the state. People from Oregon, the cartoon also suggests, do not welcome newcomers – though with an area approximately the same as that of the pre-1990 Federal Republic of Germany and a population of only 2.84 million (1990), Oregon is very thinly populated.

2. *Introduction to the text – symbols:*
*Quebec:* the Bourbon lily: French heritage
*New England*: a Franklin stove (household woodburner stove invented by Benjamin Franklin, ca. 1740, and used widely in frontier, farming and urban homes)
*The Foundry:* smokestacks; industrialized area
*Dixie*: the battle flag of the Old (Confederate) South
*The Islands:* palm tree with dollar bills as "fertilizer" – Florida, the Bahamas etc. live from tourism
*Mexamerica:* a horseman's boot with Mexican-style spurs
*The Breadbasket:* sheaves of wheat
*Ecotopia:* a giant redwood
*The Empty Quarter:* mining equipment.

*Ecotopia:* a contraction of "ecology" and "utopia" – a place in which an ideal balance between human activity and the environment is maintained, and where an ideal way of living is possible.

3. *Look at the map on p. 259 and try to work out which cities might be the capitals of the nine nations.*
Answer according to Joel Garreau:
*Quebec*: Quebec. *New England*: Boston. *The Foundry*: Detroit. *Dixie*: Atlanta. *The Islands*: Miami. *The Breadbasket*: Kansas City. *Mexamerica*: Los Angeles. *Ecotopia*: San Francisco. *The Empty Quarter*: Denver.

**Suggested answers**

1. Similarities:
– Energy-saving (Ecotopia: solar power, combustion engine outlawed; Pacific N-W: alternative energy installations with tax credits, Department of Energy);
– Anti-pollution (Ecotopia: waste recycling, no pollution, incl. noise pollution, reduction of traffic, creeks flowing through city; Pacific N-W: ban on cans and one-way drink bottles, ban on storage of nuclear waste, security measures for thermal power stations);
– Emphasis on quality of life (Ecotopia: San Francisco split up into smaller units, small-scale technology, working week only 20 hours; Pacific N-W: Northern California divided into "bioregions", value of "non-pecuniary income" stressed, holistic approach to life).

Differences:
– Ecotopia has a woman president and new educational values stressing equality between men and women (the latter may also apply to the Pacific N-W, but it is not mentioned in the excerpt).
– Social life seems more regimented (promiscuity officially encouraged at certain times of the year, war games arranged as an outlet for aggression).
– It is generally accepted that human beings can communicate "meaningfully" with other forms of life (e.g. a tree), an assumption not common in reality, even in the Pacific N-W.
– Economic motives play a greater part in shaping lifestyles in the Pacific North-West.

2. The names that immediately spring to mind are those of James Truslow Adams, William Godwin Moody (based on the ideas of Thomas Jefferson) and Fred Ringley. They all stress the importance of the quality of life, though their themes differ. Adams emphasized the need for basic economic security but is of the conviction that the American Dream is more than just the accumulation of material wealth (see "Background information"). Moody's complaint that large-scale farming has destroyed the quality of life represented by the small farm, where people felt responsible not only for their immediate surroundings but for the country as such, is basically a plea for a holistic lifestyle. It is Fred Ringley who puts these ideas, as far as possible, into practice, leaving the rat-race of the city and a good job to live a more harmonious life in the country. There he and his family can fulfil their wish "to belong" and be part of a responsible neighbourhood (cf. Garreau ll. 140–152).
Ruth Sidel ("The new believers", SB pp. 250–251) can also be mentioned here, since the issue of equality between women and men is an important part of the Ecotopian ideal.

3. They fled a society built on the presupposition that unlimited growth is positive (ll. 2–4), where energy was gained from oil and nuclear power, the military and industry had priority, pollution and social injustice (racism, sexism) abounded and the quality of life was very poor (ll. 21–27). Problems, e.g. illness, were treated at the level of the symptoms but not the causes (ll. 100–118).

4. It is "typically American" to be willing to try something new, to try to fulfil a vision in a new

place, especially the vision of the ideal society. On the other hand, a self-critical attitude in terms of lifestyle could also be regarded as part of the American Dream (see "Background information").

5. Individual statements. Some factors: global and national economic structures (e.g. dependent on trade); the power of industry, e.g. the automobile industry; governments are hesitant to introduce strict environmental laws for fear of losing the support of industry and the consumer; consumers are creatures of habit and do not like to be restricted; modern forms of trade, business and marketing require complicated transport networks, e.g. air traffic, which are a source of pollution; society based on the theory that unlimited growth is positive; materialism of the Western world...

6. Cf. "Methodisch-didaktische Hinweise"

**Post-reading activities**

*1. Answer the questions below the poster on p. 258.*
The poster illustrates the precarious situation of the water supply in both words and pictures. There is only a thin protective layer of soil between the water and the mindless economic expansion (the object of amusement, e.g. figures on the far left) above. The creatures in green are preparing the "invasion plan" (see chart beside the water). Above ground, an elderly farming couple is hemmed in by industrial development. The two people are meant to resemble the couple in the famous painting "American Gothic" by Grant Wood (1930). The old, simple lifestyle of homestead farming is exposed to deadly risks.
The text is divided into two parts situated to the left and the right of the picture. On the left, the use of groundwater is described as it should be. On the right, pollutants are named. All of them are related to the activities described on the left and pictured in the centre. The word "unintentionally" reflects the apparent innocence of the figures in the picture. Yet the visual elements may seem rather confusing (e.g. the role of the green creatures), and the wording of the chart is too small in relation to the whole.

*2. Find out about the measures that are being taken in your area to secure the water supply.*

*3. Devise slogans that make people aware of the dangers to our water supply and of the necessity of taking individual steps. If possible, add pictorial elements of your own.*
*Work in groups.*

*4. Organize a debate on the following topic: "The pursuit of happiness will leave the world in ruins". You will need two teams of three people each, one team for and one against this statement. The first speaker introduces and defines the topic. The second speaker outlines the arguments, while the third sums up and refutes the arguments of the other team. The speakers alternate, i.e. Team A Speaker 1, Team B Speaker 1, Team A Speaker 2 etc. The two teams should sit at the front, facing the class. Each team should have time beforehand to prepare. There is a time limit of three minutes for each speaker. An adjudicator – possibly your teacher – allots points to each speaker for content and presentation, though the result is not revealed until the end, when it becomes clear which team has won.*

# Test: America II

So many of the false promises and blind alleys of America II arise not from any particular political persuasion, but from our posing. We imagine ourselves yeoman farmers, and create a suburbia that does not work. We imagine ourselves mountain men and mountain women in our mountain condos with computerized sensors in the fireplace, and then wonder why we do not feel fulfilled. We move into a condominium thinking we are leaving our troubles (along with the lawn mower) behind, and then the community association slaps a lien on our airspace because we have infringed on the tribal sensibility. We hire our own police to protect us, to create the illusion of safety, and put walls around our communities, then wonder why all those people are coming over the walls. Sooner or later, our posturing must be sorted out, decisions must be made.
America II is a transitional period, a crossroads, a choice among three directions. The first road is

the road behind us, the fading America of the smokestacks, giant metropolises, and seemingly unlimited economic expansion.

The second road is the road that much of America is now on.

It leads towards organized units that enforce social sameness, a commercialized nostalgia, a perversion of traditional democratic values and American hungers, towards walled enclaves, cults of disposable friends, overorganization, a kind of technological security that gives a false sense of protection while increasing our society's disruption. Down that road are private services for those who can afford them, and not much for those who cannot.

Down that road is that kind of world Orwell and Huxley warned us against, though it will be much more subtle and pervasive than they envisioned. The road to this particular future is lined with signs, futurists, and fortune-tellers telling us of the wonders and freedom of high tech and the value of escape. Home, they whisper as we pass, home is down this road, don't look back, don't question, don't worry. Home, down there, around that next corner, or maybe the corner after that. Down there is what you want, down there is home. All you have to do is wish. And pretend.

The third road, which looks vaguely like the second, leads to a quite different potential. Down this third road, which is poorly marked, are, indeed, dispersed cities and a new country, but within them is an intensified sense of responsibility, the realization that the farther the society disperses physically, the more we need human connections. Down this third road, instead of disposable cults, we form stronger and more lasting bonds of family and friendship; instead of walled enclaves, neighborhoods that reach out; instead of social and economic buffering, a recommitment to racial equality and the sharing of economic troubles. Down this road are communities, cities, and towns that approach some semblance of self-reliance, but in a way that assures a greater degree of equity; instead of a new countrified population that destroys the land it seeks to enjoy, a people who accept their stewardship of the land. At these destinations, which are not so much out there as they are within ourselves, we could find our place and touch each other. Down that road lies home. (562 words)

From: Richard Louv: *America II*. Harmondsworth: Penguin, 1985, pp. 302–304

**Annotations**

**America II** contemporary America as opposed to the America from the Founding Fathers to the present time
**4 yeoman farmer**   farmer who owns and works his land
**9 condo(minium)**   block of apartments, each of which is owned by the people who live in it
**12 lien**   a right over another's property to protect a debt charged on that property (Grundschuld)
**59 buffering**   support, protection from hardship
**62–63 semblance of**   likeness to
**66 stewardship**   caring, taking responsibility for

**I. Language**

1. Vocabulary
In the following you are to deal with the expressions in italics within the given context.
a. 4: ...create a *suburbia* that...
Explain; you may change the sentence structure.

b. 13: ...we have infringed on the *tribal sensibility*.
Explain; you may change the sentence structure.

c. 17–18: ...our posturing *must be sorted out*,...
Explain; you may change the sentence structure.

d. 22: ...and *seemingly* unlimited...
Find a suitable substitute; keep to the sentence structure.

e. 48: ...which looks *vaguely* like the second...
Find a suitable substitute; keep to the sentence structure.

f. 59–60: ...a *recommitment* to...
Explain; you may change the sentence structure.

2. Grammar and Style
a. 2–3: ...arise not from...but...
Explain why, in this case, there is no negative sentence with the auxiliary verb "to do".

b. 42–44: Home,...worry.
Explain the stylistic devices and their functions.

c. 62: ...towns that approach...
What kind of a relative clause is this? Could the relative pronoun be dropped? Give a reason.

**II. Translation**

Translate from l. 24: The second... to l. 42: ...escape.
(136 words)

## III. Comprehension

Answer the following questions in complete sentences. Keep to the information given in the text, but do not quote.
1. What are the contradictions of the contemporary American lifestyle?

2. Explain in your own words what the author means by "the fading America of the smokestacks, giant metropolises" (ll. 21–22).

3. What are the characteristics of life "down the third road"?

## IV. Comment

Comment on one of the following topics:
1. What different notions of the American Dream does the text deal with, and which is the one that appeals to you most?

2. "Americans move on to improve their condition: they quit their second home to ameliorate it still more; fortune awaits them everywhere, but not happiness." (Alexis de Tocqueville, *Democracy in America*, 1835). Does this still apply to contemporary America, or to people in the western world as a whole?

# Bibliography

1. Bloom, Allan. *The Closing of the American Mind*. New York: Simon and Schuster, 1987.
2. Di Bacco/Mason/Appy. *History of the United States*. Boston: Houghton Mifflin Company, 1991 (Klettbuch 516153).
3. Fussell, Paul. *BAD, or the dumbing of America*. New York: Summit Books, 1991.
4. Garreau, Joel. *The Nine Nations of America*. New York: Avon Books, 1981.
5. *Great American One-Act Plays*. Klettbuch 57821.
6. *Great American Short Stories*. Klettbuch 5771.
7. *Great Immigrant Stories*. Klettbuch 57938.
8. Herrick, Robert. *The Memoirs of an American Citizen*. New York: The Macmillan Company, 1905.
9. Hirsch, E.D., Jr. *Cultural Literacy. What Every American Should Know*. Boston: Houghton Mifflin Company, 1987.
10. Kozol, Jonathan. *Savage Inequalities. Children in America's Schools*. New York: Crown Publishers, Inc., 1991.
11. Lemann, Nicholas. *The Promised Land. The Great Black Migration and How It Changed America*. New York: Alfred A. Knopf, 1991.
12. Lewis, Sinclair. *Elmer Gantry*. 1927. London: Oxford University Press, 1983.
13. Miller, Arthur. *Death of a Salesman, Text and Study Aids*. Klettbuch 57763.
14. *The 1992 Information Please Almanac*. Boston: Houghton Mifflin Company, 1992 (Klettbuch 516152).
15. O'Neill, Eugene. *The Iceman Cometh*. New York: Random House Publishers, 1946.
16. Perspectives 1: *The American Dream – Past and Present*. Klettbuch 51361.
17. Perspectives 2: *The American South*. Klettbuch 51362.
18. Perspectives 3: *The Supreme Court*. Klettbuch 51363.
19. Perspectives 7: *Religion in America and Britain*. Klettbuch 51367.
20. Perspectives 12: *The Caring Society?* Klettbuch 51372.
21. Spann, Ekkehard. *Abiturwissen Landeskunde Great Britain / United States of America*. Klettbuch 929509.
22. Special Perspectives: *The Economy and Business in Modern Society*. Klettbuch 51381
23. Stevenson, D.K. *American Life and Institutions*. Klettbuch 5136.
24. *Stories from the Black Experience*. Klettbuch 5793.
25. Stütz, Wolfgang. "Geistes- und sozialgeschichtliche Anmerkungen zu *Death of a Salesman*", in: Echler/Olbert/Stütz, *Arthur Miller: Death of a Salesman. Beiträge zur Behandlung des Dramas im Unterricht*. LEU Materialien Englisch, E20. Stuttgart, 1989, pp. 9–18.
26. Wilder, Thornton. *The Eighth Day*. Harmondsworth: Penguin, 1967.

# 12. America and the World

## Structure of the chapter

| **U.S. role as world leader today** |
|---|
| Comic strip p. 261 |
| 1. A Second American Century?<br>c. 680 words<br>essay |

↓

| **Archetypes of U.S. foreign policy** |
|---|
| 2. Two archetypes in U.S. foreign policy<br>c. 540 words<br>scholarly article |
| 3. Let every nation know ...<br>c. 570 words<br>excerpts from speeches |

→

| **Historical development of U.S. foreign policy** |
|---|
| 4. The conscience of a president<br>c. 900 words<br>autobiographical excerpt |
| Cartoon p. 269 |
| 5. The Four Freedoms<br>c. 650 words<br>speech |
| 6. An investment in freedom and peace<br>c. 560 words<br>speech |
| 7. Rice for Sarkhan<br>c. 750 words<br>novel excerpt |
| Maps p. 273, 275 |
| 8. Listening comprehension:<br>The expulsion from Vietnam<br>3 min. 36 sec.<br>editorial |
| 9. Veteran<br>c. 1220 words<br>autobiographical excerpt |

←

| **Philosophical assumptions** |
|---|
| 10. The American liberal ideology<br>c. 1050 words<br>excerpt from scholarly work |
| Advertisement p. 281 |

## Suggestions for reports/papers/talks

The 1991 Gulf War: causes, course and consequences – after text 1

The Puritans in New England – after text 2

George Washington/Thomas Jefferson/James Monroe/Theodore Roosevelt/John F. Kennedy: their main political achievements (5 Referate) – after text 3

America's way into World War I – before/after text 4

Woodrow Wilson's 14-point plan for peace and the League of Nations – after text 4

The Great Depression and Roosevelt's New Deal – before/after text 5

The Pearl Harbor attack – after text 6

The Marshall Plan – after text 6

The Cold War – after text 6

U.S. involvement in Vietnam – after text 7

The Protest Movement against the Vietnam War – after text 8

Vietnam today – after text 8

The Vietnam Veterans' Memorial – after text 9

Any film or films dealing with the Vietnam War – after text 9

## Vocabulary

*Thematischer Grund- und Aufbauwortschatz Englisch*, Klettbuch 51955, pp. 124–146

*Words in Context, Thematischer Oberstufenwortschatz*, Klettbuch 51961, pp. 4–25

# Comic strip (Doonesbury)

## Background information

On January 16, 1991, a U.S.-led military alliance intervened (with U.N. approval) to drive the Iraqi invaders out of Kuwait, after their leader Saddam Hussein had rejected an ultimatum to conform with a U.N. Resolution and withdraw his troops. The war ended with the total defeat of Saddam's army after no more than six weeks.

In the optimistic mood generated by the war and its successful conclusion, (and also by the collapse of the Soviet Union as a rival power) President George Bush promised a "new world order" in which international law would be enforced in a way that had not been previously possible. Subsequent developments cast considerable doubt on such promises. But public opinion did force the Allies to take some action to protect the Kurds in the aftermath of the war. And the U.S. did feel obliged to repay the Arab countries for their co-operation in the Gulf War by putting pressure on Israel to solve the Palestinian problem. (Israel has not yet conformed with U.N. Resolutions 242 and 194 to withdraw from their occupied territories and allow Palestinian refugees to return to their lands.)

## Suggested answers

1. In the White House (Oval Office).

2. The thoughts in the first two frames are those of the President of the United States. His voice – or that of some representative – is speaking in the form of a recorded message on the White House answering machine in the remaining six frames. The caller could be any nation having problems with more powerful neighbours or with civil unrest.

3. It can only be referring to the Gulf War (Jan.–Feb. 1991) or its aftermath. (See date of publication and background information above.)

4. He is (gently) mocking U.S. pretensions to be the world's policeman, the "Top Cop". America's role as a superpower ready to intervene and solve all the world's problems is here exaggerated to the point of being absurd.

*America and the World*

# 1. A Second American Century? (GK)

**Background information**

At the time this article was written and published, a public debate was going on about America's proper role in the world. It was sparked off by two separate developments. One was the collapse of Communism, and with it the Soviet Union's role as a rival world power. The other was the invasion of Kuwait. In early August, 1991 Iraq's army, under the leadership of the country's dictator Saddam Hussein, occupied Kuwait in order to both gain control over its strategic position in the Persian Gulf and over its immensely rich oil resources. Thousands of foreigners were held hostage. The danger of an Iraqi invasion of Saudi Arabia was imminent. It was known that Saddam had (with help from Western nations as well as the USSR) managed to develop or acquire a very sophisticated range of armaments, and was close to having nuclear weapons.

The fact that the Soviet Union no longer supported Iraq meant that the U.S. could take a more energetic role than would otherwise have been the case. After Henry Grunwald's article was published, events speeded up. U.S. President George Bush managed to forge together a worldwide alliance against the dictator under the leadership of the United Nations. As all economic sanctions as well as diplomatic activities failed to force Saddam out, the allied forces defeated the Iraqi troops and restored the state of Kuwait.

Ll. 18–25: Henry R. Luce was publisher and editor-in chief of Time and Life magazines. He was husband of the noted writer, Congresswoman and U.S. Ambassador, Clare Booth Luce. Henry Luce's article "The American Century" argued against the "isolationism" predominant in the U.S.A. at the time (cf. ll. 76–86).

**Pre-reading activities**

1. Comic strip p. 261, as above.
2. Give your assessment of U.S. influence in the world. Use the chart below to distinguish between the various spheres. Will America's influence decline/grow/remain stable?

|  | low ⟶ high | | | | | U.S. influence will | | |
|---|---|---|---|---|---|---|---|---|
|  | 1 | 2 | 3 | 4 | 5 | decline | remain stable | grow |
| Political leadership |  |  |  |  |  |  |  |  |
| Military power |  |  |  |  |  |  |  |  |
| Economic power |  |  |  |  |  |  |  |  |
| Science and technology |  |  |  |  |  |  |  |  |
| Arts and culture |  |  |  |  |  |  |  |  |

(Der Fragebogen sollte von den Schülern anonym ausgefüllt werden und anschließend über OH-Folie die Ergebnisse zusammengestellt und ausgewertet werden. Dabei ergeben sich bereits zahlreiche Sprechanlässe, was bisweilen zu recht lebhaften Diskussionen führen kann.)

**Suggested answers**

1. The phrase means that the twentieth century has been dominated, shaped and moulded by the U.S., that the U.S. is the model nation for the rest of the world. It comes from an article by Henry Luce after the outbreak of World War II, arguing that America had an important role to play. Henry Grunwald's phrase raises the question whether such influence will extend into the next century.

2. a) The phrase has been frequently quoted, it has been used and heard again and again.
b) Whatever happens in the 90s, it won't affect the overall picture of a century dominated by the U.S.A.
c) America's Cold War policy of actively preventing any further expansion of Communism, (which) made it difficult for the Soviet Union to try to support revolutionary activities abroad.
d) The tendency to emphasize America's loss of power is growing.
e) The U.S. should adopt a defensive position (like pioneers in a wagon train in Indian Country), passively waiting for new challenges to come.

3. See background information. This question can be replaced by a classroom talk on the subject (see below).

4. Arguments against:
– social problems ... (ll. 1–8);
– the rise of the Soviet Union, of Communism (ll. 29–31);
– America's defeat in Vietnam (l. 32);
– the erosion of American power ... (ll. 68 ff.).
Arguments for calling this the "American Century":
– America's leading role in science and technology (ll. 36–43);
– the economic success of U.S. style capitalism (ll. 43–46);
– the defeat of the Nazis and of Communism, the revival of Europe and Japan, successful U.S. anti-communist containment policy (ll. 46–59);
– (not mentioned here) U.S. domination of popular culture (films, music, etc.).
Grunwald supports the latter view, and thinks the 21st century will, after all, be another "American Century".

**The posters, p. 263**

Joan of Arc: patriotic poster encouraging support of war effort; America's commitment in world affairs (here, in WW I) seen as its natural role ("Save Your Country").
America First Committee: pacifist, anti-war poster; favours a policy of isolationism, of keeping America out of international conflicts. Reason: involvement in war will destroy America's treasured principles such as freedom (represented by the shelling of the Statue of Liberty); probably a reference to war-time restrictions such as censorship and internment of foreign-born citizens. Message: one should put America (and its traditions) first before worrying about the situation in foreign countries.

**Additional questions**

1. *Look for examples of anaphora in the text, and discuss its effect.*

2. *What other rhetorical devices can you find? Discuss their effect.*

**Post-reading activities**

1. *Further on in the same essay Henry Grunwald writes:*
"But must America lead? Why not try for the good life without world responsibility? Why not, in Luce's words, settle for being a more powerful Switzerland? Partly because Switzerland has always been only Switzerland, while America, after playing its global and historic role, would suffer a permanent sense of loss and dislocation. But more important, the world has become too interdependent for the U.S. to create a prosperous, isolated enclave. While America's power to influence the world environment has declined, it has not disappeared by any means. But to wield such influence, the first task for the U.S. is to renew and rebuild itself, to restore its economic growth and productive capacity and replenish its wealth. The Second American Century must begin at home."
*Translate this passage into German.*
Suggested solution:
Aber muß Amerika unbedingt führen? Warum (wie Luce es ausdrückte) begnügen wir uns nicht damit, eine (Art) Schweiz zu sein, nur etwas mächtiger? Zum Teil deswegen, weil die Schweiz eben nur immer die Schweiz war, während Amerika, nachdem es seine weltgeschichtliche Rolle gespielt hat, unter einem permanenten Gefühl des Verlustes und der Entwurzelung leiden würde. Was aber noch wichtiger ist: die gegenseitige Abhängigkeit in der Welt hat viel zu sehr zuge-

nommen, als daß sich die Vereinigten Staaten eine blühende, isolierte Enklave schaffen könnten. Amerikas Macht, auf das Weltgeschehen Einfluß zu nehmen, ist zwar zurückgegangen, aber keineswegs verschwunden. Um jedoch solch einen Einfluß auszuüben, ist es die dringlichste Aufgabe der Vereinigten Staaten, sich selbst zu erneuern und wiederaufzubauen, sein Wirtschaftswachstum und seine produktive Macht wiederherzustellen und seinen Reichtum wiederzuerlangen. Das "zweite amerikanische Jahrhundert" muß zu Hause beginnen.

2. Discuss the above passage.
– Why, according to the author, is it not possible for the U.S. to return to an isolationist policy?
– Do you think there will be/should be a Second American Century?
– Does Germany have any world responsibility? Give reasons.

3. Classroom report: The 1991 Gulf War – causes, course and consequences.
See Bibliography 4.

## 2. Two archetypes in U.S. foreign policy

**Methodischer Hinweis**

Die Frage 1 kann als *first-reading activity* dienen.

**Suggested answers**

1. – America as an example to the nations (ll. 81–82); a "model of Christian charity", a "city upon a hill", i.e. they were to influence other peoples to imitate the goodness of American society (ll. 10–14, 66–68).
– America as the bringer of order through military might (ll. 82–83); God's elect people, God's avengers, bringing the forces of evil under control (ll. 42–43, 69–70).

2. "Model": The New Testament (Christ's words see annotations); John Winthrop preaching those words in his sermon of 1630 "A Model of Christian Charity".
"Bringer of order": The Old Testament (The Amalekites, "hellish fiends ... ruined fearfully"); Michael Wigglesworth compares the native Indians with the Amalekites in the 17th century.

3. From the very beginning it has been doubted
– whether the colonists were entitled to take the land, to build their colonies there; and whether America would be able to realize their high moral standards;
– whether America can really call itself superior to other peoples.

4. Examples of the first of these two archetypes will not be found in any actions taken by the U.S.A., but rather in various statements of America's "Manifest Destiny". Examples of the second archetype could include more aggressive statements such as President Reagan's denunciation of the "evil empire", but also:
– America's involvement in the two world wars;
– the War in Vietnam;
– McCarthy's Communist hunt;
– U.S. involvement in Central America;
– the Gulf War.

5. Personal opinions. Note that it could be argued that this is what America is already doing, i.e. pursuing its national self-interest, regardless of the high-sounding phrases used to justify its actions. Any intervention abroad can be seen as a way of securing its own sphere of influence, of making the world safe for Americans to do business in.

**Post-reading activity**

*Classroom report: The Puritans in New England.*
See Bibliography 1, 3, 4, 5, 7.

**Additional question**

*Paraphrase the three verses quoted in the text. (See p. 193.)*

# 3. Let every nation know ...

## Background information

President Monroe's message must be seen in the light of mainly the independence movement among the Latin American empires of Portugal and Spain as well as the Russian colonization of the Pacific Northwest (see fact files p. 314). Great Britain and the U.S. favoured the revolutionists of Latin America as they were looking forward to increasingly profitable trade with the newly independent republics. When, however, the European monarchies of Austria, Prussia and Russia began to talk of restoring the former Spanish and Portuguese colonies, the U.S. became deeply concerned. Thus the Monroe Doctrine was a direct warning to Russia and European powers to stay away from the affairs of all the nations in North, Central and South America. In the beginning it was a sign for the growing spirit of American strength and unity and eventually became a cornerstone of U.S. foreign policy.

## Methodisch-didaktischer Hinweis

Nach der Klärung der Begriffe kann Frage 1 als Auftrag für das *first reading* gestellt werden.

## Pre-reading activities

*1. The term "isolationism" has already turned up (text 1). Try to define it. Compare your definition with that found in various dictionaries.*

*2. What do you think is its opposite?*
Globalism, internationalism, interventionism; the latter term most commonly used.

## Suggested answers

1. Washington and Jefferson express isolationist attitudes; Roosevelt and Kennedy express internationalist positions. Monroe's "Message to Congress" has elements of both.

2. The main points of the Monroe Doctrine:
– The United States would not interfere in European affairs or in the affairs of American colonies already established.
– But the Western Hemisphere was no longer open to colonization by European powers.
– Any attempt by any European country to establish colonies in the New World or to gain political control of any American country would be viewed as an unfriendly act toward the United States.

3. The Roosevelt Corollary is an explicit redefinition and extension of the principles stated in the Monroe Doctrine. Roosevelt plainly says that he expects other nations to conduct themselves well, "to keep order and pay their obligations", and that "chronic wrongdoing" will force the U.S. to the "exercise of an international police power".
One could argue quite strongly that the term "corollary" is not justified: The Monroe Doctrine clearly promises non-intervention except in the case of another nation's intervention in North or South America, implicitly accepts the right of other American countries to run their own affairs (however badly), and even accepts the further existence of colonies. Roosevelt brings in totally new criteria for U.S. interference.
Term justified: Monroe Doctrine implicitly claims the American continent as a sphere of U.S. influence.

4. Washington – Jefferson: isolationist standpoint
Monroe: basically isolationist; foresaw America's international obligations and defined America's international role.
Roosevelt: America's willingness and readiness to international commitment and interference clearly stated.
Kennedy: a most powerful statement of U.S. willingness to play role of "world policeman" – in support of friends and in defense of liberty.

## Additional questions

*1. What rhetorical devices can you identify in these passages from speeches? Discuss their effect.*

*2. Then decide which passage you find most effective, giving reasons for your opinion.*

## Post-reading activities

*Classroom reports: George Washington/Thomas Jefferson/James Monroe/Theodore Roosevelt/John F. Kennedy: their main political achievements.*
See Bibliography 1, 3, 4, 5, 6, 9.

# 4. The conscience of a president (GK)

## Background information

For more than half of its course, World War I was a purely European affair, usually termed "the Great War". Its causes lay in a complex of historical rivalries, nationalism, balance-of-power politics, and armaments races. From the initial spark in Sarajevo it took only a few months to involve all the major European powers on the basis of various treaty obligations. Austria and Germany (the Central Powers) were on one side (in spite of treaty obligations, Italy refused to join them on the grounds that they were the aggressors against Serbia). On the other side were the Allies: France, Great Britain, Russia and Serbia, later joined by Italy.

The first two years resulted in stalemate, with the Central Powers dominant on the Continent, and the Allies supreme at sea. They drove German commerce from the oceans, conquered German colonies and kept the sea lanes to the U.S. open. Soon, however, the Germans' use of submarines was beginning to threaten their supremacy. Since submarines never rescued the crews and passengers of sunk ships, this began to turn American public opinion against them – especially after the sinking of the British liner *Lusitania* off the south coast of Ireland in 1915 with great loss of American lives.

President Wilson, however, tried to remain neutral and proposed peace talks in 1916 – which came to nothing because of both sides' confidence of victory and territorial gains. In the meantime, anti-German feeling was rising in the U.S.A., not just because of submarine warfare, but also because of a German diplomatic effort to involve Mexico against the U.S.A., should they intervene on the side of the Allies. On April 6, 1917, Congress voted to enter the war. Most Americans believed it would be a "war to end wars".

American intervention was decisive in winning the war for the Allies. President Wilson wanted a negotiated peace based on his famous "Fourteen Points", presented to Congress in January 1918. They included the freedom of the seas, reduction of armaments on all sides, self-determination of the various peoples, impartial adjustment of territorial claims, and the formation of an association of nations. But the eventual armistice was based on unconditional surrender, and the peace treaties were far more one-sided and punitive to Germany. Wilson compromised on several important points in order to get his main objective, a League of Nations, which was set up after the war. But the U.S.A. itself eventually abstained from the League of Nations, since the U.S. Senate refused to back Wilson. The U.S.A. emerged from the war considerably strengthened in industrial and economic power, but began to retreat again into its traditional isolationism.

## Pre-reading activities

1. Classroom-report: *America's way into World War I.*
See Bibliography 1, 2, 3, 4, 5, 8, 13, 14.

2. Entering the war was a crucial decision for President Wilson. Can you imagine what misgivings Wilson might have had in the hours of decision making?

## Suggested answers

1. Tired and exhausted but not weary; overworked but not overwrought; highly responsible with uncannily clear thoughts and reasoning; instinctive.

2. No illusions, fully aware of the whole range of consequences to the world, to his nation, to himself, to each individual involved in the war; people would go war mad.

3. He most feared that a war would promote intolerance and brutality, and that it would weaken American democracy.

4. – Wilson was a peace-loving isolationist. He didn't like giving up America's neutrality and plunging the whole world into the war.
– Wilson was sure about the outcome of the war, but he didn't like the idea of a dictated peace. He knew that the ideals of democratic government would get lost.
– The choice of evils: Staying out of war would mean a German victory, i.e. the destruction of democracy.

5. –

## Cartoon, p. 269

The cartoon shows a wedding ceremony in which Uncle Sam is being wed to Miss "Foreign Entanglements" (an allusion to George Washington's Farewell Address, p. 265. The wedding symbolizes America's farewell to the isolationist tradition, with Woodrow Wilson as the man who put the U.S.A. on a new political course as creator of a new world order (the League of Nations) in the wake of World War I. Wilson's role as peacemaker is symbolized by the paper entitled "Peace Proceedings" thrown carelessly on the ground.

The ceremony has reached the point where the celebrant asks anyone with any objections to speak out, but is cut off before the words "... or forever keep his peace". The man breaking through the window is from the Senate, carrying a document entitled "Constitutional Rights" in his hand. This expresses their criticism that Wilson's international diplomacy was contravening their democratic rights as representatives of the American people, and that membership of the League of Nations would endanger U.S. independence and sovereignty.

The cartoonist is against this new policy. This is shown by the powerful, effectful "interruption of the ceremony", Uncle Sam's deeply worried expression.

(The cartoon was published in the Chicago Tribune in 1918. Shortly after, the Treaty of Versailles failed to get the necessary two-thirds majority in the Senate, and the U.S.A. stayed out of the League of Nations.)

**Additional questions**

1. a) *Give the verbs of the following nouns: declaration (ll. 1, 12, etc.), provocation (l. 16), destruction (l. 44), tolerance (l. 79), assembly (l. 88);*
b) *– and the nouns of the following verbs: to avoid (l. 25), to devote (l. 44), to reconstruct (l. 49), to influence (l. 52), to struggle (l. 59), to consider (l. 62), to reinforce (l. 72), to maintain (l. 73), to refuse (l. 85), to conform (l. 85), to survive (l. 88), to exclaim (l. 93).*

**Post-reading activities**

1. *Classroom report: Wilson's peace-making efforts: his fourteen point plan for peace (January 1918) and the League of Nations.*
See Bibliography 1, 2, 3, 4, 5, 8, 13, 14.

2. a) *Write a short scene for a film script that shows Cobb's conversation with Woodrow Wilson.*
For the dialogue it is sufficient to rewrite the passages in direct speech. But more fanciful realizations of the scene should be accepted. The students should be reminded to include instructions for the actors.
b) *Act the scene.*

## 5. The Four Freedoms

**Background information**

By January 1941, when Roosevelt gave his "Four Freedoms" speech to Congress, the greater part of western Europe and many countries elsewhere in the world were under the control of aggressive dictators. First Poland, then Norway, Denmark, Holland and Belgium, had fallen to Nazi Germany. Britain had declared war on Germany after the first of these invasions, but were forced off the continent with the evacuation of Dunkirk and the surrender of France in mid-1940. Italy under Mussolini openly allied itself with Hitler's Germany. In the Far East, Germany's ally Japan advanced on French Indochina. Britain had successfully repulsed massive air attacks by the Luftwaffe (Battle of Britain), but remained under considerable pressure. British forces had fought off several Italian attacks on British colonies and protectorates in Africa and the Middle East. British shipping was forced out of the Mediterranian, and their sea-power in the North Atlantic was under constant threat from the German U-boats. So far, the U.S.A. had maintained its isolationist stance, but was being increasingly dropped into the conflict. British shipping was being protected by an armed convoy system set up in co-operation with the U.S.A. Relations with Japan were extremely strained, and trade was restricted to prevent the export of potential war materials.

After Roosevelt's speech, tensions rose even further with the increasing Japanese threat to U.S. trade routes, but fears of war were allayed by diplomatic moves to establish peace. This was the background of Japan's surprise attack on Pearl Harbour on Hawaii (see picture page 271), with which they hoped to knock out a weakened and unprepared U.S. battle fleet – but which in the long run only served to bring about their own downfall by finally bringing the U.S.A. into the war against them and the other Axis powers.

For biographical details of Franklin D. Roosevelt (1882–1945) see *Four Famous Presidents* by Alan Posener, Klettbuch 54822.

## Methodisch-didaktische Hinweise

Vor der Behandlung von "Roosevelt's Four Freedoms Address" ist es notwendig, den Rückfall Amerikas in seine isolationistische Haltung deutlich herauszustellen, um die Dimension des erneuten Kriegseintritts zu erhellen. Dies kann geschehen durch die Behandlung des vorangehenden Cartoons (siehe oben) und durch das Referat über Woodrow Wilson (siehe oben).

Da die authentische Aufnahme der Roosevelt-Rede auf der Begleitkassette vorhanden ist, soll dies für die erste Präsentation der Rede unbedingt genutzt werden. Der geschriebene Text soll erst danach eingesetzt werden, um die Fragen im Schülerbuch zu behandeln.

## Pre-reading/pre-listening activities

*1. Classroom report: The Great Depression and Roosevelt's New Deal.*
See Bibliography 1, 3, 4, 5, 9, 14.

*2. What was going on in the world in January 1941? What was America's role at the time?*

*3. In what way was the situation facing President Franklin D. Roosevelt similar to that facing Woodrow Wilson in 1917?*

## First-listening questions

*1. What problems does President Roosevelt see facing the U.S.A.?*

*2. This is often called his "Four Freedoms" speech. What are these "four freedoms"?*

## Suggested answers

1. His main aims are:
– to help the democracies regain and maintain a free world (ll. 50–51) by sending them war materials;
– to guarantee a future world four essential human "freedoms" (l. 74).

2. Outwardly Roosevelt was still trying everything to keep America out of any armed international conflict. He saw, however, and openly said that "the safety of our country and our democracy are overwhelmingly involved in events far beyond our borders" (ll. 23–26) and that "our policy should be devoted ... to meeting this foreign peril" (ll. 34–36).

3. a) The democratic nations of Europe, Asia, Africa and Australia are bravely defending their political freedom by military means.
b) an international law which is only advantageous to those who passed it.

4. The discussion will mainly focus on
– the break-up of the Soviet Empire, and the collapse of most Communist systems;
– the danger of new dictatorships emerging from the chaos;
– the problems of arms control in the new situation;
– the economic problems of third-world and ex-communist countries.

## Post-reading activities

*1. Classroom report: The Pearl Harbour attack.*
See Bibliography 2, 3, 4, 5, 9, 14.

*2. a) Before FDR no American President had run for a third term of office. FDR was re-elected three times. Try to find reasons for this.*
*b) The 22nd Amendment to the Constitution limits to two the number of terms a President may serve. Discuss the pros and cons.*

# 6. An investment in freedom and peace

## Background information

In 1944, Franklin D. Roosevelt was elected for a fourth term as President, but he died in April 1945, before the end of the war. His Vice-President Harry S. Truman (1884–1972) then became President, and led the U.S. through the final months of the war, Allied victory and the beginnings of the Cold War. He attended the Potsdam Conference in July 1945 after Germany's unconditional surrender, to decide on how that country should be treated. In effect, that conference divided Germany and Austria into Soviet and Western spheres of influence – though there was as yet no open rivalry between the wartime allies. In August, Truman authorized the use of the newly-developed atomic bombs on Hiroshima and Nagasaki. This was considered necessary to force Japan to surrender. It may also have provided a welcome opportunity to demonstrate U.S. military capabilities to Stalin. In the following two years, fears of a spread of Communist rule grew, trading to Truman's policy of containment.

In domestic politics, Truman was a "liberal". He supported (and partly succeeded in implementing) civil rights legislation, national health insurance, price controls, etc. He was elected for a second term in 1948, but did not stand for election in 1952.

## Information on map, p. 275

The exact date of the map is unknown, but it must have been published in the 1980s (Spain in NATO, New Zealand still in ANZUS, Soviet Union).

OAS: Created in 1948 by the members of the Pan-American Union (1910), the successor of the International American Conference, which was organized by the Latin American countries and the U.S. in the First International Conference of American States in 1889–90. The central body of the OAS has its headquarters in the Pan-American Union building in Washington D.C., on land given by the U.S.. The association's aims are the peaceful settling of disputes, the creation of a security system and the coordination of the work of other intra-American associations. In 1962, for example, the OAS members agreed on support for the US blockade of Cuba.

NATO: Stalin's effort to gain control of West Berlin provided evidence of threat of Soviet aggression. In April 1949 nine Western European countries joined the U.S., Canada and Iceland in the formation of the North Atlantic Treaty Organization. The member countries agreed that "... an armed attack against one or more of them in Europe or North America shall be considered an attack against them all ..." Besides they agreed on resisting such an attack by military action. The question whether the U.S. would be compelled to go to war to assist another country without an act of Congress was the very issue that had kept the U.S. from joining the League of Nations in 1919.

ANZUS (Australia, New Zealand, United States) Pact: Another treaty designed for mutual defense in the Pacific. It was signed in 1951. New Zealand left after a dispute concerning nuclear weapons in 1985.

## Suggested answers

1. The U.S. should offer help to those free nations in danger of being controlled by a totalitarian (in practice, this meant Communist) regime (ll. 25–28). Though change is legitimate, it should not be brought about by force, coercion or infiltration. Truman wanted to achieve this aim by offering those nations economic and financial aid. (ll. 31–33)

2. Financial aid to Greece and Turkey (and to any other free country desperately needing it) was held by Truman to be necessary:
– to guarantee "economic stability and orderly political processes" (ll. 33–34);
– to "give effect to the principles of the Charter of the United Nations" (ll. 42–43);
– to avoid a spreading of "confusion and disorder ... throughout the entire Middle East" (ll. 47–52);
– to "safeguard" the investment made in WW II, an "investment in world freedom and peace". (ll. 62–70);
– to destroy "misery and want", the fertile but "evil soil" that "nurtures the seeds of totalitarian regimes" (ll. 71–75).

In addition he claimed the U.S. could afford it since it amounted to only "a little more than one-

*America and the World*

tenth of one percent" of the money invested into WW II (ll. 65–68).

3. Lines 1–24: Truman describes the political situation in the world, i.e. the threat of Communism; he points out the most extreme alternatives (polarization).
Lines 25–34: he reminds Congress of America's duties, and outlines what needs to be done.
(These first two points follow the "problem-solution" pattern of argumentation.)
Lines 35–81: he supports his ideas with arguments showing what would happen without America's assistance.
Lines 82–85: he flatters his audience.
Rhetorical devices:
– allusions to some basic values of the Constitution (ll. 15–19);
– antithesis when contrasting the two extreme future developments (ll. 14–24);
– parallelisms, repetitions (ll. 25–34).

4. The map on page 275 shows that the U.S.A. had totally committed itself to the role of the leader of the Western World, i. e. to an internationalist foreign policy. The principles of this policy were the formation of alliances to contain, militarily as well as economically, the spread of Communism worldwide.
Note that Communism itself was seen as the threat: The map makes no distinction between those countries that had an aggressive capability or intention and those that did not, or between those that were members of a (hostile) military pact and those that were officially non-aligned. Nor does it recognize any danger or aggressive potential in numerous non-communist dictatorships and one-party systems here shown as part of the (presumably harmless) non-aligned nations (yellow). Saddam Hussein's Iraq being a case in point, one which should serve to demonstrate the dangers of such a one-eyed view of world affairs.

**Map, p. 273**

The percentage of GNP spent on foreign aid/development aid in 1987 was:
U.S.A. 0.2%
Great Britain 0.28%
(West) Germany 0.39% (in 1991: 0.35%)
Canada 0.46%
Norway 1.1%
The 1980 Brandt commission recommended a target figure of 0.7% of GNP.

**Post-reading activities**

*Classroom reports: The Marshall Plan/The Cold War.*
See Bibliography 2, 3, 4, 8, 13, 14.

# 7. Rice for Sarkhan (GK)

**Methodisch-didaktische Hinweise**

Der Text kann in häuslicher Arbeit gelesen werden, läßt sich allerdings im Unterricht ansprechend präsentieren. Dabei empfiehlt sich abschnittsweises Vorgehen (um das Lesetempo gleichzuschalten Vorlesen durch den Lehrer) mit Fragen zum jeweils weiteren Verlauf der Episode. Die Schüler sollen angeregt werden, Mutmaßungen anzustellen, kurzzeitig sich in die Rolle Krupitzyns zu versetzen. Vorschläge für Fragen nach der jeweiligen Zeile:
Line 15: *In what way could Krupitzyn have made use of the information about the grain ships?*
Line 44: *What do you think was the effect of this campaign? Guess what Krupitzyn's strategy was?*
Line 71: *Again try to explain Krupitzyn's plan.*
Line 78: *Why didn't the Americans protest?*
Line 87: *What trick did Krupitzyn employ to achieve this effect?*

**Suggested answers**

1. Information in text:
– the name Sarkhan/Sarkhanese;
– typhoons (l. 2);
– the destruction of the harvest results in immediate famine (ll. 4–5);
– foreign aid, food supply from abroad (ll. 10–15);
– food sold on the black market for high prices (ll. 17–18);
– rivalry between the U.S. and the Soviet Union to exert political influence;
– Communist party active in co-operation with Soviet Union (ll. 22–26, 76, 85).

All this suggests a south-east Asian (or east Asian) underdeveloped country with an agrarian, subsistance economy. It is politically unstable. Its need for foreign aid makes it susceptible to propaganda and political blackmail.

2. His intention is to make the native population believe that the Soviet Union is helping their country, that Russia and not America is a reliable partner, friend and ally.

His strategy is to make the best use of the secret information about the shipping of American rice to Sarkhan by making the American aid appear to be a Russian act of friendship.

The first step was to buy rice on the black market and to publicly and in a propagandist manner distribute it among the poorest in order to make the people aware of the help to come.

When putting on the forged "labels" he makes use of the fact that a) the Americans are not able to read the Sarkhanese inscriptions, b) the people of Sarkhan, like most people in the world, put more trust into the printed than into the spoken word.

3. America and Russia both tried hard to increase their influence in Third World countries. According to the Truman Doctrine (see text 5) America gave economic aid especially to countries most apt to succumb to the Communist ideology (cf. text 5, ll. 71–73). America's aim was to contain the spread of Communism.

4. According to COBUILD, propaganda is "information, frequently exaggerated or false information, which is spread by political groups in order to influence the public."
The episode is a typical example of propaganda
– because the people of Sarkhan were provided with false information,
– and because this was done in order to influence them politically.

5. One obvious change would be to demand that the diplomatic staff learn the language of the country they are being sent to or (better) give them special training in language and culture. The diplomatic service could also make more use of people who are already experts in foreign cultures.

6. Most foreign aid is given in order to provide emergency relief (e.g. food in the case of famines) or to build up sound economies and eventually narrow the gap between the rich and the poor nations. A discussion could centre in on the question whether such aid is given for purely altruistic reasons, or out of self-interest, i.e. to make the world a safer place for the already rich nations, to prevent wars, ecological damage, etc. which would eventually have global implications.

**Additional questions**

*1. From what point of view is the story told? How else could it have been told? Discuss the possible difference in effect.*

*2. One meaning of the title of the novel is given in the note on page 274. What is the other?*

**Post-reading activities**

*1. Write the "fiery speech" (l. 99) Louis Sears made a week later.*

*2. Classroom report: U.S. involvement in Vietnam.*
See Bibliography 2, 3, 4, 5, 10, 11, 14.

## 8. Listening Comprehension: The expulsion from Vietnam (GK)

**Methodisch-didaktische Hinweise**

Eine Einleitung, Worterklärungen und Fragen zum Globalverständnis sind im SB, S. 277–278 abgedruckt. Nachfolgend werden weitere Fragen zum Detailverständnis angeboten.

An dieser Stelle bietet es sich selbstverständlich an, das Thema Vietnamkrieg zu einer eigenen Unterrichtssequenz auszubauen. Der Hörtext läßt sich dabei sowohl als Einstieg, als auch am Schluß des Projekts zur Ergebnissicherung, einsetzen. Bei letzterem Einsatz sollten den Schülern die Fragen allerdings erst nach dem Anhören des Textes präsentiert werden.

**Background information**

U.S. involvement in Vietnam began with aid to the French colonial regime, and continued after partition (1955) in the form of a military advisory group set up in South Vietnam to help the regime there resist any incursions from Communist North Vietnam. When Viet Cong guerrillas began their campaign (1959) to reunite the country under Communist rule, more U.S. "advisors" were sent in. In 1965 U.S. planes began bombing North Vietnam, and the number of troops there rose to 200,000. Peace talks opened in Paris in 1968. In 1970 the scope of the war broadened when President Johnson authorized the bombing of Cambodia to cut off Viet Cong supply routes. Young men were being increasingly drafted to maintain the level of U.S. forces in Vietnam and Cambodia, and this – combined with a high number of American casualties – led to increased public opposition to the war. Many Americans were also coming to the conclusion that this was an unjust war, and news of a number of atrocities (e.g. My Lai) contributed to this impression. The Paris Peace Agreement of 1973 officially ended U.S. involvement in the war, though fighting went on on a smaller scale. In 1974 a Vietcong/North Vietnamese offensive drove South Vietnamese forces out of the Central Highlands, and Saigon itself fell in 1975. President Ford ordered U.S. ships to help evacuate refugees. An indirect result of the War was the coming to power in neighbouring Cambodia of Pol Pot's regime of terror, which was only ended by a Vietnamese invasion. U.S. casualties of the Vietnam War amounted to 46,520 dead and over 360,000 seriously injured. It was the first war the U.S.A. lost, and its effect on the national self-image was enormous.

**Text**

The war in Vietnam, like the war in Cambodia, has ended with a victory for the Communist-led revolutionary forces and a defeat for the upholders of the old ruling classes. That includes the
5 United States, which for 25 years – since the first aid to France in support of that country's effort to maintain its Indochina colony – has been upholding the old regimes.
The incredible thing, still, is the stubborn failure
10 of United States leaders to see what was going on, to see the hopelessness of their cause and to get out. A quarter of a century!
The American public and press must share the blame for this disaster of American foreign policy.
15 With rare and honorable exceptions, Americans went along bemused by the concept of American leadership of a "free world" struggle against Communism.
A succession of American presidents, secretaries of state, defense secretaries and generals told the 20 people over and over that America was winning. They distorted the evidence; they told outright lies. The facts were that the side America was supporting was losing.
Each American president since Eisenhower has 25 had the opportunity to move toward a political compromise in Vietnam. Each one lacked the courage to take a step which he feared might look like an American "defeat" or, as President Ford and Secretary Kissinger have been putting it, like 30 a failure to make good on a commitment.
In the end, this policy led to a much worse defeat and a much worse discrediting of America's international behavior than early withdrawal would have meant. 35
The fear of Communist takeovers, of a phony "domino theory" of collapsing "democracies", has been dominant in U.S. policy – even after the moves toward détente with the big Communist countries. 40
The misguided quarter century is now behind America, as President Ford said recently, although not in those words. Instead of losing face or encouraging Communism or losing confidence of the rest of the world, the United States probably 45 will gain in these respects from finally ending its military role in Asia.
The nation would have gained respect sooner if the government had acted on its own – 10, 15 or more years ago. Instead, action to end the 50 Indochina connection came only after the arousal of public opinion which drove one president out of public life, and led to the near-impeachment of another on charges of abuse of constitutional power. Even the ending was a foot-dragging busi- 55 ness with Ford, Kissinger and Ambassador Graham Martin holding the line in Saigon.
But public opinion finally did prevail; the machinery of democracy did work, though slowly. The country will be stronger, wiser and more effective 60 in world affairs we believe, as a result of ending this misadventure. The illusions of imperialism, of world leadership in terms of military power, of executive primacy in foreign affairs – those illusions, we hope and believe, are vanishing. 65

From The Des Moines Register, April 30, 1975. © 1975 The Des Moines Register; reprinted by permission.

## Suggested answers

1. – U.S. leaders, i.e. American presidents, secretaries of state, defense secretaries, generals, for failing to see the hopelessness of the situation, and for lying about it to the public;
– the American public, for being so easily deceived;
– the American press, for going along with this deception.

2. He expresses the hope that America will be stronger, wiser and more effective in world affairs and that the "illusions of a world leadership in terms of military power are vanishing".

## Listening for detail

*Listen for a second time and try to answer the following questions. Take notes while listening.*

1. *What do we learn about the beginning of the war?*
The U.S. helped France to maintain Vietnam as a colony.

2. *Which was the main reason for conducting the war?*
To prevent a Communist takeover in Vietnam.

3. *What reasons are mentioned for America's not getting out of the war sooner?*
– U.S. leaders were too stubborn to realize the hopelessness of their cause.
– A withdrawal was regarded as an American defeat, a failure of their foreign policy.
– The fear of losing face, of encouraging Communism, of losing confidence of the rest of the world.

4. *What made America move out in the end?*
The arousal of public opinion.

## Discussion

*"The side America was supporting was losing." Discuss whether (in the light of later events) this was really true.*
Obviously true in the narrow sense: the Vietcong much stronger, with considerable popular support in their anti-colonial struggle. But: events elsewhere have shown that Communist regimes are not economically viable, and left to themselves will have to adapt to reality. It could be argued that attacking such regimes from outside actually strengthens them: it is the most isolated and ostracized Communist regimes (Cuba, North Korea) that have proved longest-lasting.

## Post-listening activities

*Classroom reports:*
– The protest movement against the Vietnam War.
See Bibliography 3, 5, 10, 11, 14.
– Vietnam today.
Useful source: *National Geographic Magazine*, November 1989.

## Picture p. 278

The Vietnam Veterans Memorial is far less "heroic" in style than the Iwo Jima monument. As such, it may reflect the public mood of uncertainty and ambivalence towards the war. It was erected in 1982 as a belated tribute to those who died. (For a selection of contrasting attitudes to the War and to the monument, see the article "Honoring Vietnam Veterans – At Last" in *Time*, November 22, 1982; reprinted in *The Year in the USA – Holidays and Holy Days*, ed. Claus Haar, Klettbuch 51351.

# 9. Veteran (GK)

## Background information

U.S. policy in Vietnam was not supported unanimously by the American people in the early sixties, and with the escalation of the undeclared war, with ever more American soldiers being killed (1000 soldiers dying each month in 1968) Americans found the war meaningless and frustrating. Disagreement over the war issues, over the methods and the success of guerilla warfare, divided the nation. While the "hawks" continued supporting American involvement in Vietnam as a political means to contain Communism in Southeast Asia, the opponents, the "doves" saw it simply as a civil war among the Vietnamese people in which the U.S. had no business intervening. President Johnson was charged with sacrificing American lives, with killing innocent civilians and devastating the Vietnamese countryside (American planes discharged more than 4 million tons of bombs, mostly napalm and about 18 million tons of chemical defoliants – Agent Orange). By the end of the decade anti-war activists, mostly college students, managed to organize a nationwide peace movement which found support among all groups of society, from members of Congress to veterans to housewives. The year 1969 saw both the war's bloodiest fighting and the largest antiwar demonstrations (250,000 demonstrators in Washington). The war seemed more pointless every day. Despite Nixon's policy of "Vietnamization, i.e. the building up of Vietnamese forces for the defence of South Vietnam, while withdrawing American troops (which dropped from over 500,000 in 1968 to 480,000 in 1969, 235,000 in 1970, 160,000 in 1971), facts like intensified firepower (and still too many casualties), the bombing and the invasion of Cambodia, the My Lai massacre, further divided America and sparked new protests. Finally on October 24, 1972 National Security Adviser Henry Kissinger announced that "peace was at hand" and the final settlement to stop military action was signed on January 27, 1973. When after frequent violations of the cease fire by both North and South Vietnamese troops, President Ford asked Congress for more military aid to save South Vietnam from collapse, Congress refused. All this certainly wouldn't have been possible without the massive pressure exerted on U.S. politicians by the peace movement. April 30, 1975, the day Saigon fell into Communist hands, marks the end of the Vietnam War.

## Pre-reading activities

*1. Think about the following facts:*
– Over three million young Americans fought in Vietnam.
– The average soldier was about 19 years old.
– About 20,000 men deserted the military.
– 30,000 young men went to Canada and other countries to avoid the draft.
– Millions evaded the draft by going to college. (College students were exempt from the draft.)
*a) What do these facts tell you about the mood among young Americans during the Vietnam War?*
*b) What would you have done? Would you have voluntarily served in Vietnam (as did 10,000 women)? Give reasons.*
*c) Imagine a young soldier returning home from war disabled for the rest of his life. How do you think he would feel? How would he be treated?*
*d) What do you learn from the picture on p. 279? Answer the questions.*
It shows a demonstration of partly crippled Vietnam Veterans at a Republican Party Convention. The occasion is obviously the Convention that nominated President Richard Nixon and vice-presidential running-mate Spiro Agnew for re-election in 1972. Both groups, party delegates and veterans, are carrying American flags to show their patriotism. The veterans, however, are obviously angry about something, holding up clenched fists and probably shouting slogans, either demanding greater recognition for what they did in Vietnam, or protesting against having been sent to fight a senseless war.

*2. Comment on these graffiti left on latrine walls by GIs in Saigon:*
– "We'll bring peace to this land if we have to kill them all." General Custer
– "This is a war of the Unwilling
  Led by the Unqualified
  Dying for the Ungrateful."

## Suggested answers

1. Place: the floor of the National Convention hall.
Time: the 1972 Republican National Convention; Nixon's nomination for a second term of office.

2. a) He's a disabled Vietnam veteran. He served two terms in Vietnam, was awarded lots of war medals. He was wounded and paralyzed from the chest down. Ever since, he has been trying to defend the rights of all Vietnam veterans, and protesting against the War in Vietnam.
b) The political atmosphere seems to be tense. The tear gas and chain metal fence (l. 8) suggest that the political establishment feels endangered by the demonstrations going on, and so does the way the demonstrators were treated (ll. 9–11). The nation seems polarized into pro-and anti-war factions.

3. The most dramatic effects are achieved by contrasting his own situation, the treatment of all veterans, and the realities of the War with the elegant atmosphere of the convention, the ignorance of the people, the thoughtless cheers and chants (cf. ll. 1–19, 68–103, 143–155).

4. Any of the following adjectives to characterize the author: patriotic, proud, courageous, determined, persevering, stubborn, angry, idealistic, committed, politically aware, fond of publicity. The fact that he volunteered for a second tour of duty in Vietnam suggests that he may have once held different political views and has been forced by circumstances to revise his opinions.

5. The title first refers to the author himself, as he was born on that historic date (Independence Day; on July 4, 1776 the Declaration of Independence was adopted by the Continental Congress in Philadelphia). In this excerpt the author makes use of his birth date as a way of underlining his patriotic attitude and to make people feel embarrassed. There is also a sarcastic tone behind the title suggesting a loss of the values the American people fought for in the Revolutionary War.

6. The students should be reminded to take care when rendering direct speech in reported speech.

**Additional questions**

*Most of what Ron Kovic said at the convention is given in direct speech. Find the few examples of reported speech, and try to reconstruct his actual words.*

**Post-reading activities**

*1. a) Guess how Ron Kovic reacted to this experience.*
*b) Find the passage in the novel and finish reading the chapter. Report to your class.*
Second half of chapter 6; the student should also read the section left out after l. 142.

*2. Classroom reports:*
– *The Vietnam Veterans Memorial.*
  See notes on picture p. 278; also bibliography 3.
– *Any film or films dealing with the Vietnam War (Born on the Fourth of July, Coming Home, Platoon, etc.)*

# 10. The American Liberal Ideology

**Methodisch-didaktischer Hinweis**

Nach den *pre-reading activities* (unten) könnte der erste Teil des Textes (die ersten 23 oder auch 63 Zeilen) als Kopie oder auf Folie präsentiert werden; für das Wort *good* bzw. *goodness* soll eine Lücke gesetzt werden. Die Diskussion über das fehlende Wort wird den sehr dichten und auch langen Text entscheidend vorentlasten.

**Pre-reading activities**

*1. The word "liberal" has many different meanings, depending on the context. Write down one meaning that occurs to you. Give some examples of what it means to have a liberal attitude, as you have defined it.*
If Chapter 9 has been studied in class, students may bring up the later U.S. usage of the term "liberal", as used in the Senator Dole article, p. 213.

*2. Compare your notes with one another.*

*3. In what sense could the Americans be said to have a "liberal ideology"?*

**Suggested answers**

1. They imply that a good situation can easily be reinstated by removing "bad" individuals or groups from power – e.g. Hitler and the Nazis; that there will naturally be great opposition to such "bad" leaders; and that therefore much international diplomacy can be based on trust. The 1991 Gulf War provides illustrations of a number of the points mentioned here.

2. Since people are basically rational, they can be educated to see things the right way. If they are against the U.S.A. it must be because of some misunderstanding, and this can be cleared up. This is the basis of much of American foreign policy.

3. It comes from
– the belief that people are able to and did control their destiny (ll. 100–104);
– the feeling that U.S. achievements mainly come from each individual's efforts;
– from historical experience (ll. 87–117).
This optimistic philosophy means that all international problems can also be solved, that interna-

tional conflicts are only the result of some particular aberration (ll. 133–144).

4. At first sight the author's might seem to argue in favour of this "liberal" ideology. In fact his attitude is absolutely neutral, as can be seen from the way he presents even some obviously exaggerated and simplistic versions of the attitude he describes (e.g. ll. 22, 72–74). The use of quotation marks also serves to distance the author somewhat from the phenomenon being described.

5. After the disastrous experience of World War II a great deal of optimism was necessary to draft the Charter of the United Nations. The main ideas of it – to maintain peace, to provide security, to promote justice, to increase the general welfare, to establish and secure human rights world-wide – coincide with the main ideas of the American liberal ideology, especially in the notion that states will act collectively to deter aggression and that they must have a basic desire to see peace. Education, which is necessary to promote understanding among the peoples of the world, manifests itself in the UNESCO (United Nations Educational, Scientific, and Cultural Organisation).

### Advertisement, p. 281

The man is holding a copy of the American Declaration of Independence. The large caption seems to be suggesting that he can guarantee the success of the system of liberal democracy, should the Russians decide to "install" it in place of the totalitarian system they have just rejected. The small print of the text below, however, provides a nice example of bathos, or anti-climax (see p. 274). It is so extreme as to be quite funny. It turns out that they are merely advertising a copier system, "to ensure life, liberty and the pursuit of happiness in your office" – to deftly misquote the said document!

## Test: A profound change in thinking

The Marshall Plan after World War II was, of course, a dramatic departure from earlier American policy: a leap from the war-debt psychology to the psychology of foreign aid, from the vocabulary of the banker to that of the missionary, the humanitarian, and the social scientist. After World War I politicians had talked of reparations and "honest debtors," of interest rates and the capacity of countries to pay back what they had borrowed. Now, after World War II, they were talking about standards of living, they were comparing the health and prosperity and literacy of different nations, and they were examining the opportunities for personal freedom and the decency of political institutions everywhere. The Marshall Plan expressed a profound and sudden change in official American thinking and feeling about the relation between the New World and the Old: not only in the focus on recovery and prosperity rather than on principal and interest, but also in the call for initiative, collaboration, and planning by the benefiting countries. Its focus was not so much on individual nations as on Europe as a whole.

The Marshall Plan, because it was directed to former allies, was still a kind of war relief. If it succeeded, it would help once prosperous countries with high standards of living to put their houses back in order. But there was momentum in this enormous new enterprise of foreign aid. Like the gargantuan new undertakings in atomic research and in the exploration of space, foreign aid had a mass and a velocity which combined into a nearly irresistible accelerating force. When the American program moved from war relief to former allies whose language, religion, customs, and history were familiar and reached out to others who not only had not been allies but who were remote and hardly known, the United States had embarked on a boundless sea of hope. Except in the religious missions, the nation had no substantial precedent for a world-wide program of foreign aid. And however similar the missionary efforts may have been in spirit, they were dramatically different in scale. Whether offered as United Nations Relief and Rehabilitation, or under Point Four, or through the score of other programs, foreign aid now expressed faith that American wealth could raise the standard of living of people anywhere. A people with a higher, more nearly American standard of living, it was assumed, would be more apt to be democratic, and hence more apt to be peace-loving and friendly to the United States. Implied, also, was the complementary assumption that poverty, misery, and industrial backwardness would make any people less peaceful and less democratic, hence more prone to Communism, and therefore more inclined to join the enemies of the United States. This chain of reasoning, which implied some bold generalizations about history, was not always explicit. But, spoken or not, it lay beneath the quasi-religious faith in democracy, and expressed a traditional American confusion of the "ought" and the "is."

Some of the more obvious and more painful facts of foreign policy in the twentieth century should have given Americans pause. For as Russia had become more industrialized, and as she produced more goods for her people, she did not become more friendly to the United States. Russian industrialization was neither the product of democracy, nor did it prove to be a source for more democracy in the Soviet Union. As that country became stronger it did not become more peaceable. In the course of World War II the United States gave $11 billion of Lend-Lease aid to the Russians, but the government of Russia had never before been so hostile to the United States as in the years of the Cold War which followed. As the Soviet Union became stronger it became more bellicose, and in the little wars which it fostered and sponsored in Asia, it found allies in countries which had also been large beneficiaries of American foreign aid.

From Daniel J. Boorstin, *The Americans: The Democratic Experience*, New York: Random House 1974, pp. 577–578.

### I. Comprehension

1. Explain in your own words why the Marshall Plan expressed "a profound and sudden change in official American thinking and feeling".

2. Why does the author compare the Marshall Plan with atomic and space programs?

### II. Language

1. Paraphrase: "... foreign aid had a mass and a velocity which combined into a nearly irresistible accelerating force." (ll. 32–34)

2. Explain the use of "would" in ll. 27 and 56.

### III. Comment

1. Comment on the last paragraph, taking into account the collapse of the Soviet Empire.

2. Do you think that another "profound change in thinking" might help to overcome today's global problems? Explain.

# Bibliography

1. Boorstin, Daniel (ed.). *An American Primer.* New York: New American Library 1968.
2. DeConde, Alexander (ed.). *Encyclopedia of American Foreign Policy* (3 vols.). New York 1974.
3. DiBacco, Thomas, Lorna Mason, and Christian G. Appy. *History of the United States.* Boston 1991; Klettbuch 516153.
4. *Information Please Almanac* (pp. 99–121, 613–665, 974–975). Boston: Houghton Mifflin 1992; Klettbuch 516152.
5. Marker, Sherry. *Illustrated History of the United States.* London 1988.
6. Morrison, Samuel Eliot, Henry Steele Commager and William E. Leuchtenberg. *A Course History of the American Republic.* New York 1977.
7. Perspectives 1: *The American Dream.* Klettbuch 51361.
8. Perspectives 6: *The United States and Europe.* Klettbuch 51366.
9. Posener, Alan. *Four Famous Presidents.* Klettbuch 54822.
10. Pratt, John Clark. *Vietnam Voices.* New York: Penguin Books 1984.
11. Santoli, Al. *Everything We Had – An Oral History of the Vietnam War by Thirty-three American Soldiers Who Fought It.* New York: Ballantine Books 1982.
12. Schlesinger, Arthur M., Jr. *The Cycles of American History.* Boston, 1986.
13. Spann, Ekkehard. *Abiturwissen Landeskunde: Great Britain/U.S.A.* Stuttgart: Klett 1990; Klettbuch 929509.
14. Ver Steeg, Clarence and Richard Hofstaedter. *Great Issues in American History* (3 vols.). New York: Random House 1969.

# Übersicht über die Tonaufnahmen

*Selected Texts* (Klettnummer 510342), Symbol [S]

| Zeit | Seite (SB) | Text | Aussprache |
|---|---|---|---|
| 1'08" | 11 | Envoy | British |
| 11'23" | 26 | *A vision of Europe (Winston Churchill) | British |
| 7'18" | 40 | Gandhi's Salt March | Indian English |
| 2'53" | 74 | In retrospect: a letter to the editor (Ken Livingstone) | British |
| 2'08" | 86 | *The teddy bear's head (Wolfe Tones) | Irish English (song) |
| 5'33" | 99 | Civil rights in Derry | Irish English |
| 1'27" | 125 | At the Edinburgh Festival | Scottish English |
| 10'54" | 142 | True love | American |
| 5'13" | 158 | Private conscience and public duty | British |
| 2'42" | 167 | *Cwm Rhondda: a Welsh hymn (Pendgrus Male Choir) | Welsh (song) |
| 5'03" | 175 | *Fast car (Tracy Chapman) | American |
| 4'55" | 197 | Put the rules of the game in writing | British |
| 2'34" | 203 | Equality before the law | American |
| 1'00" | 223 | Ellis Island | American |
| 6'11" | 247 | Second chance – Fred Ringley, ex-salesman, farmer | American |
| 5'09" | 253 | *Subcity (Tracy Chapman) | American |
| 7'35" | 270 | *The Four Freedoms (Franklin D. Roosevelt) | American |
| 5'23" | 272 | *An investment in freedom and peace (Harry S. Truman) | American |

*Additional Texts for Listening Comprehension* (Klettnummer 510343), Symbol [L]

| Zeit | Kap. | Text | Aussprache |
|---|---|---|---|
| 6'46" | I,1 | Pomp and Circumstance | music |
| 3'32" | I,5 | Home thoughts | British |
| 2'22" | II,7 | An intensely religious society | British |
| 6'03" | III,2 | *Divided Britain (Frank Field, MP/Anthony Gibbs) | British |
| 5'14" | IV,3 | The English language in Ireland | British |
| 4'03" | V,4 | *Henry Moore – a sculptor speaks (Henry Moore) | British |
| 4'15" | VI,4 | Technology and culture | American |
| 4'15" | VII,9 | *The Prophet's Birthday in Bradford (Wright/A. Gibbs) | British |
| 5'35" | VIII,9 | A working–class girl in a grammar school | British |
| 3'37" | IX,4 | Black Friday | British |
| 10'12" | IX,13 | *A claim to a share of America (Mario Cuomo) | American |
| 4'27" | X,2 | Going to the Promised Land | American |
| 4'25" | X | *The real Chinatown (Andy Lanset/Charlie Chin) | American |
| 4'52" | XI,5 | I have a dream (Martin Luther King) | American |
| 3'36" | XII,8 | The expulsion from Vietnam | American |

* Originalaufnahme